Black Surrealist

Black Surrealist

The Legend of Ted Joans

Steven Belletto

BLOOMSBURY ACADEMIC
NEW YORK • LONDON • OXFORD • NEW DELHI • SYDNEY

BLOOMSBURY ACADEMIC
Bloomsbury Publishing Inc
1385 Broadway, New York, NY 10018, USA
50 Bedford Square, London, WC1B 3DP, UK
29 Earlsfort Terrace, Dublin 2, Ireland

BLOOMSBURY, BLOOMSBURY ACADEMIC and the Diana logo
are trademarks of Bloomsbury Publishing Plc

First published in the United States of America 2025

Cover design by Eleanor Rose
Cover images: Portrait of Joans as Mau Mau, circa 1955. Laurated Archive, courtesy of Laura
Corsiglia; background image detail from Joans et al., *The Seven Sons of Lautréamont*, courtesy
of Laura Corsiglia and Zürcher Gallery © Estate of Ted Joans.

Library of Congress Cataloging-in-Publication Data
Names: Belletto, Steven, author.
Title: Black surrealist : the legend of Ted Joans / Steven Belletto.
Description: New York, NY : Bloomsbury Academic, 2025. |
Includes bibliographical references and index.
Identifiers: LCCN 2024050976 (print) | LCCN 2024050977 (ebook) |
ISBN 9781501379543 (paperback) | ISBN 9781501379550 (hardback) |
ISBN 9781501379567 (epub) | ISBN 9781501379574 (ebook)
Subjects: LCSH: Joans, Ted. | African American poets–Biography. |
American poetry–African American authors–History and criticism. |
American poetry–20th century–History and criticism. | Beat poetry, American–History
and criticism. | Surrealism–United States. | Black Arts movement.
Classification: LCC PS3560.O2 Z55 2025 (print) | LCC PS3560.O2 (ebook) |
DDC 811/.54aB–dc23/eng/20250118
LC record available at https://lccn.loc.gov/2024050976
LC ebook record available at https://lccn.loc.gov/2024050977

ISBN: HB: 978-1-5013-7955-0
          PB: 978-1-5013-7954-3
          ePDF: 978-1-5013-7957-4
          eBook: 978-1-5013-7956-7

Typeset by Integra Software Services Pvt. Ltd.
Printed and bound in the United States of America

To find out more about our authors and books visit www.bloomsbury.com
and sign up for our newsletters.

cairo man
surly realist
dis member ship
jungle blackboards
cryptic script
stirring up
dead alive
tongues tired
tarred wool
manifesto folded
unclear arms
cracking open
ivory trunk
of brazil nuts
voodoo toenails
konker root
jockey cornsilk
purrs natch
contraband leader
scattering scat
sporadically all over
forever diaspora

"Ted Joans at the Café Bizarre"
Harryette Mullen

CONTENTS

ILLUSTRATIONS

PREFACE

he died a rich man   self-made   legend   one of a kind
he was the entire 20th century

    —STEVE DALACHINSKY

His Legend is a mustard seed compared to his real life.

    —AMIRI BARAKA

This book's title, *Black Surrealist*, is borrowed from a short autobiographical piece Ted Joans published in 1989 called "I, Black Surrealist." These two words, "Black" and "Surrealist," had for Joans extraordinarily deep and complex histories, and were just as complexly entwined with each other. Taken together, they begin to open up how he saw himself in the world: "First of all," he wrote, "I being a surrealist is as natural as I being Black."[1] In the pages to follow, I describe how Joans understood Surrealism via his Blackness, and how Surrealism became for him a "weapon" to survive—and thrive, through art—as an African American in the twentieth century. The subtitle, *The Legend of Ted Joans*, alludes to his Surrealist concept of a poem-life, in and through which he purposively cultivated positions on "truth" different from and often opposed to the kind of truth found in dictionaries or encyclopedias or official records predicated on what he derisively called "mere empiricism" (see also *Bird: The Legend of Charlie Parker*, the first book on Joans's friend and bop demigod). "You have nothing to fear from the poet but the truth," Joans declared in his most frequently reproduced poem, and perhaps the first thing readers of *Black Surrealist* should know is that his ideas of truth, in and out of art and life, were many-layered and poetic in aspect.

  Accordingly, the epigraphs above acknowledge the legendary proportions of Joans's poem-life. The first, an elegy written shortly after his passing by a friend, Steve Dalachinsky, insists that the notoriously impecunious Joans left the world a "rich man" not for the balance of his bank account, but for the exuberant abundance of his creative life, which was lived so widely and remarkably: he was "self made" for sure, inarguably "one of a kind"—and, for these and other reasons, a "legend."[2] How and why this word was attached to Joans is part of this book's subject, but clearly a poem like Dalachinsky's consciously participates in burnishing the legend of Ted Joans. To say he was "the entire 20th century" is either flagrant hyperbole or poetic truth (or both). Throughout this book, I certainly do try to show how Joans and his work intersect with an array of literary, cultural, and artistic currents of the global twentieth century—he was *there* at opportune moments in time and space, and seemed to have befriended everyone—so Dalachinsky's assertion may not be hyperbole at all.

The second epigraph is from Amiri Baraka, who had known Joans from back in the 1950s, during their bohemian days in Greenwich Village, when they would sometimes be confused for each other as Baraka had not yet abandoned his birth name, LeRoi Jones. This line was taken from a brief Foreword Baraka provided for the last major autobiography Joans completed, the still-unpublished "Collaged Autobiography," and given that project's persistent inaccessibility, I felt it fitting to repurpose Baraka's claim as entry in to this Preface.[3] Like his fellow poet Steve Dalachinsky, Baraka recognizes the legends that have accrued around Joans and his poem-life, proposing that his "real life" is even more stupendous than the stuff of capitalized Legend. There is an implication here that in the autobiography to follow, Joans will reveal his "real life" in such a way as to deflate or at least correct the legend, and readers will come out the other side duly impressed by this real life and all that was accomplished in it.

As far as I know, Baraka never actually read the manuscript of "Collaged Autobiography," but if he had, he would have seen that when Joans reconstructed his poem-life, his version of the real was Surreal to such an extent that the book doesn't exactly clarify "the facts." This, of course, is a challenge for any would-be biographer. My own approach has been to treat Joans's autobiographical statements as Surrealized representations of his poem-life, and so I rely on them for his impressions and judgments, but do my best to verify his historical facts before repeating them as such. The first part of *Black Surrealist* explains why I have taken this approach, and shows how it has led me down some circuitous, tricky-to-navigate roads. In a cartographic sense, remember, *legend* is the key to wayfinding.

Along several of those roads I have come to appreciate Ted Joans as a singularly important poet-artist of the twentieth century. To fully explain why requires the book itself, but it has to do with his originality and total commitment to liberation in multiple senses, his confrontational, often hilarious (though always carefully calibrated) undoing of established social and epistemological order—of how truth and the real are themselves (mis) understood. This undoing occurred in the face of obstacles very difficult to surmount: racism, institutionalized and more subtly expressed; colonialism and its legacies around the world; surprisingly unshakable notions of appropriate decorum, or appropriate art; the vastness of oceans and the Sahara Desert; the capitalist assumption that cultural currency requires hard currency; the underdevelopment of Africa; border control; the Cold

War security state; the mapping of the globe into First and Third Worlds characterized by clashing cosmologies and political economies; and what he called in one poem "anglo-saxon puritanical philosophy," among others. There was a certain flow in his life and art, a rhythmic aesthetic sensibility inspired by the jazz music he so worshipped, envisioned, again, through Surrealist prisms so that the course of his life, the fluidity of his art and of his perennial circulations, made him at home in various traditions he likewise remade his own, and at home in the world entire, a true global citizen-poet who swam in rivers of otherwise disparate and far-flung thought and imagination.

In terms of scope, *Black Surrealist* is interested primarily in Joans's writing, with some forays into his visual art, performance pieces, and short films along the way. Thus far, his reputation rests largely on this written work, although he was prolific in a range of other media, and had exhibited his painting, collage, and object-poems from the late 1940s on (in the last several years his visual and plastic arts have gained more of the recognition they deserve). In one sense, it is a false distinction to separate his creative production by genre or medium since Joans himself did not necessarily do this, and he delighted in turning genre inside out, inventing his own, or moving across media as inspiration and circumstances demanded. His visual and written work often go hand in hand as he liked to create collages to accompany his poems or make objects in which text and image interact. Along similar lines, it's a mistake to see his life, his poem-life, as categorically distinct from his more familiarly-articulated creative objects (poems, paintings, films, sculptures). As his friend Yuko Otomo put it to me, Joans felt that a poet's "cosmic mission" was to "*live life as a poem*—writing 'good poems' is actually secondary."[4] This position is for Joans fundamentally Surrealist, and has profound implications for how we understand his life, his representations of his life, and the wildly varied kinds of art he made over the decades.

The idiosyncrasies of Joans's cosmic mission, together with the vagaries of institutional and academic attention, have led to a pretty long distance between the originality and consequence of his literary and artistic achievement and his general recognition out in the world. In so many ways he was fugitive, impossible to pin down, even in his autobiographies. He was wayward, forever on the move physically, creatively, amorously, intellectually, spiritually—circulating the globe, cultivating networks of support in favored spots, leaving always art in his wake, sometimes in findable forms like poetry collections published by recognized houses in New York or London, sometimes in obscure ones like tiny pamphlets printed by a café in Amsterdam or by a US State Department Cultural Center in Yaoundé. Sometimes the wake was bespoke, one-off objects, or chalked drawings soon washed away; or photographs of ephemeral Happenings in Copenhagen; or rumors of a blockbuster reading in Dakar; or murals in a Parisian hotel now demolished; or suitcases packed with writing and artwork stashed and then left behind in the homes of friends around the world. His life and work demand engagement, but the minute you try to categorize him or fit him into a "movement" or "school" or cultural phenomenon, you will quickly discover that he resists such a move, that even writing about him can feel like too domesticating a gesture.

Still, here is *Black Surrealist*, another step toward a wider recognition of and reckoning with Ted Joans and what he has made. Where possible, I quote Joans on his life and art, on his understanding of important critical and aesthetic concepts. His written body of work is large, and in varying states of availability, and I draw on as much of it as I can, even if the source material is obscure, hard to obtain, or unpublished, because I want to give readers a sense of the range and variety of this work. Ideally, some of his out-of-print writing will be reissued, and some of his great unpublished work will find a willing publisher. I hope, too, that this book will help Ted Joans remain alive for future generations, and if those who best knew him and his work find *Black Surrealist* does him some measure of justice, I will be very happy.

———

Speaking of which. This book would not exist in this form, on this plane, without the generosity and support of those who were in the poem-life of Ted Joans. I owe special gratitude to artist Laura Corsiglia, Joans's partner for the last eleven years of his life. Laura understands Joans's work very deeply, on intuitive, emotional, and intellectual levels, and I am lucky to have had her thoughts throughout the process of researching and writing this book (even though she doesn't always agree with the finished product!). Laura's openness has allowed me to incorporate unpublished and unarchived material into this book, which has in turn enriched immeasurably its portrait of Joans and his work: à la vôtre!

One of the best things about writing this book was all the people I got to meet in Joans's ever-expanding circles of family and friends. My sincerest thanks and admiration go out to Joans's family for providing memories, contextual information, photographs and other material. Yvette Johnson was indispensable in helping me sketch out her father's life in Louisville, especially those years with her mother, Joan Locke, whose remembrances are a treasure. Like Yvette, another daughter, Daline Jones, has been consistently helpful and supportive over several years, and her mother, Joyce Hollinger, was so candid about her time with Joans in the 1950s. I also had a great time chatting with Daline's brother, Bob Jones, and hearing his perspectives. Representing the Scandinavian branch of Joans's family tree, another of his sons, Tor Jones, has been a true gentleman: forthcoming, encouraging, introspective. His mother, Grete Moljord, supplemented the descriptions of her time with Joans recorded in *Paris Tanger*, her wonderful Norwegian-language memoir. I was also very glad to speak with Russell Kerr, yet another of Joans's sons, who shared his thoughts, and details about his mother, Sheila Kerr. Joans's family is extraordinary, as are all the women in his life.

The list of people Joans counted as friends is dazzling, overwhelming, intimidating, and exciting all at the same time—so often I thought of Manthia Diawara's observation that "His friendship automatically legitimized you as a sophisticated person." To certain of these sophisticates I owe particular recognition for going far beyond and above what anyone ought to be expected to do, especially artist Yuko Otomo, for hosting me on MacDougal Street; publisher Michael Kellner, for opening his archives again and again; bookseller Harry Nudel, for taking me through his SoHo wonderland; writer and biographer Terence Blacker, for giving me great writing advice; and Sylvia Whitman, of the inimitable Shakespeare and Company in Paris, one of Joans's homes, for combing through her vast collections.

So many in and out of Joans's orbit helped this book along in ways great and small: Tara Allmen, Sarah Battle, Dominic Capeci, Ann Charters, Jean-Christophe Cloutier, Kenneth Cox, Doug Field, Frida Forsgren, Henry Louis Gates, Jr., Randi Gill-Sadler, Joan Halifax, Richard Robert Hansen, Juliette Harris, Jim Haynes, Hettie Jones, Marion Kalter, Robin D. G. Kelley, Liz Klar, Susanne Klengel, Thomas Klug, Sofia Kofodimos, Amor Kohli, Johan Kugelberg, Bob Lee, Mike LeMahieu, Heather Maisner, Zachary Manditch-Prottas, Maddie McGriff, Erik Mortenson, Reggin Nam, Camsey Noonan, Joanna Pawlik, Margaret Randall, Josephine Rydeng, Melissa Rzepczynski, Brett Sigurdson, Michael Taylor, Keri Walsh, Regina Weinreich, and Audra Wester.

A few more special acknowledgements are in order: to fellow Joans scholar and aficionado Kurt Hemmer, for helping me kick off this project by sharing material he had gathered for his "visual and aural collage," *Wow! Ted Joans Lives!*; and Lars Movin, whose book *Beat: på sporet af den amerikanske beatgeneration*, has an illuminating chapter on Joans, and who has been so helpful with Joans's Danish connections, including nailing down permissions for the Kaare p photograph of Joans performing at the Vingården in Copenhagen.

My (sur)real undying gratitude as well to Gwenolee Zürcher of Zürcher Gallery in New York and Paris, Joans's artworld champion, for looping me in to what is happening in that world, and for generously making available several high-resolution images for use in this book. Thanks to Gwenolee and Natalie Preston!

Lee Upton read nearly every word of this book—champagne for Lee!—and Josh Sanborn gave me his historian's eagle eye while he was not busy taking my money at poker. And my huge, galactic thanks to an all-around mensch and true expert on Surrealism, Jonathan Eburne, for reading this whole book, and taking the time to offer his brilliant, no-nonsense insights.

"Love Thy Librarian," said Joans, and without them this book would have been impossible. The largest institutional repository of Ted Joans material is the Ted Joans Papers at UC Berkeley's Bancroft Library, and I thank Susan McElrath, Iris Donovan, Dean Smith, Fedora Gertzman, and the rest of the staff there for all their assistance over the years. Beyond the Bancroft, manuscripts, correspondence, artwork, and other material is scattered far and wide, and I am humbled by all the assistance of numerous librarians at a range of institutions: Melissa Watterworth Batt (University of Connecticut), Trish Blair (University of Louisville), Kris Bronstad (University of Tennessee, Knoxville), Kelly Dunnagan (Louisville Public Libraries), Alison Fraser (University of Buffalo), Terese Heidenwolf (Lafayette College), Ben Jahre (Lafayette College), Dina Kellams (Indiana University), Thomas Lannon (Lafayette College), Rose Lock (University of Sussex), Ana Luhrs (Lafayette College), Meredith Mann (New York Public Library), Camille Moret (Loughborough University), Tim Noakes (Stanford University), Tom Owen (University of Louisville), Diane Ray (University of Iowa), Kathy Shoemaker (Emory University), Courtney Stine (University of Louisville), Valerie C. Stenner (University of Delaware), Katie Sutrina-Haney (Indiana State University), Charice M. Thompson (Howard University), Jonathan Trinque (University of Connecticut), Courtney Welu (Harry Ransom Center), and Natalie Woods (Western Branch Library). Sarah Beck at Lafayette College shot many of the high-resolution photos included in these pages.

This book would not of course be real without Bloomsbury and my editor Haaris Naqvi, who initially recognized merit in this project when it was little more than speculation. And my profound thanks to Hali Han at Bloomsbury, who has been an absolute pleasure to work with. Thanks also to Kate Greig and Geoff Reynolds for their meticulous editorial work. Some research for this book was made possible through a Mellon Summer Research grant awarded by Lafayette College, and I acknowledge that support gratefully.

To friends far and near: you are here in a million and one ways you may or may not know: the other TJ, Chimamanda, Carrie, Paul, Rob, expert in oaths, Jen, my informal and unpaid agent, all the Daves, Amitava, Colum, Petra, Teju, and Chris S., for debating with me about Joans. I'm pouring one out for my old friend Joe Shieber, in my disbelief that he's gone on too soon. Bummer, Maisie, Katie, all of whom were subjected to many an unsolicited meander about the ins and outs of this project—anyway, the book is for everybody, allyall, Joans would say, and I do mean *allyall*.

ABBREVIATIONS

"Aardvarkian"	Joans, "Aardvarkian Surreal Stroll Through Paris." TJP, box 14, folders 4–12.
Afrodisia	Joans, *Afrodisia.* New York: Hill and Wang, 1970.
ATJ	Joans, *All of Ted Joans and No More.* New York: Excelsior, 1961. New Revised Edition.
AW	Joans, *The Aardvark-Watcher/Der Erdferkel-forscher.* Berlin: Literarisches Colloquium, 1980.
BFP	Joans, *Black Flower Poems: Readings Jazz & Poetry.* Amsterdam: Amsterdamsch Litterair Café, n.d., but after 1972.
BM	Joans, *A Black Manifesto in Jazz Poetry and Prose.* London: Calder and Boyars, 1971.
"BMG"	Joans, "A Black Man's Guide to Africa." TJP, box 12, folders 10–16.
BPW	Joans, *Black Pow-Wow.* New York: Hill and Wang, 1969.
CHFP	Charles Henri Ford Papers, 1928–81, Harry Ransom Humanities Research Center, University of Texas at Austin.
"Collaged"	Joans, "Collaged Autobiography." Laurated Archive.
"Deeper"	Joans, "Deeper Are Allyall's Roots." Laurated Archive.
Dies	*Dies und Das: Ein Magazin von Aktuellem Surrealistischem Interesse* (Joans, editor). Berlin: 1984.
Double	Joans and Hart Leroy Bibbs, *Double Trouble.* Paris: Revue Noire Editions Bleu Outremer, 1992.
FBI	United States Federal Bureau of Investigation, Theodore Jones file. Assorted Documents dated 1968–72. Internal case file no. 157-10590.

FP	Joans and Joyce Mansour, *Flying Piranha*. New York: Bola Press, 1978.
FJP	Joans, *Funky Jazz Poems*. New York: Rhino Review, 1959.
FSG	Farrar, Straus and Giroux Records, New York Public Library, box 450, "Joans, Ted, General Correspondence, 1970s–80s" folder.
HBR	Hanuman Books Records, 1978–96, University of Michigan Library, Special Collections Research Center, Box 8, "Hanuman Books, Raymond Foye Files, Correspondence, Ted Joans" folder.
Hipsters	Joans, *The Hipsters*. New York: Corinth Books, 1961.
HS	Joans, *Honey Spoon*. Paris: Handshake Press, 1991.
"IBS"	Joans, "I, Black Surrealist." *Muzzled Ox* (special issue: Blues 10) (1989): 46–8.
"I Went"	Joans, "And I Went As Usual to the Desert." TJP, box 18, folder 16.
"I See"	Joans, "Je Me Vois (I See Myself)," *Contemporary Authors Autobiography* 25 (1996): 219–58.
"I, Too"	Joans, "I, Too, at the Beginning." TJP, box 14, folders 1–3.
"Jadis"	Joans, "Jadis si je me souviens bien," *Black Renaissance* (June 22, 2002): 91–4.
JHMP	J.H. Matthews Papers, Harry Ransom Humanities Research Center, University of Texas at Austin.
LHP	Langston Hughes Papers, Beinecke Rare Book and Manuscript Library, Yale University. JWJ MSS 26.
MBP	Joans, *Mehr Blitzliebe Poems*. Hamburg: Verlag Michael Kellner, 1982.
MFA	Michel Fabre Archives of African American Arts and Letters, 1910–2003, Rose Library, Emory University.
NDB	Joans, *New Duck Butter Poems*. Paris: Handshake Press, 1982.
Okapi	Joans, *Okapi Passion*. Oakland: Ishmael Reed Publishing, 1994.
ONDB	Joans, *Old and New Duck Butter Poems*. Paris: Handshake Press, 1980.

Our	Joans, *Our Thang*, drawings by Laura Corsiglia. Victoria: Ekstasis Editions, 2001.
"Outer"	Joans, "Niggers from Outer Space." TJP, box 17, folders 25–7.
PP1	Joans, *Poet Painter/Former Villager Now/World Traveller, Part I*, ed. Wendy Tronrud and Ammiel Alcalay. New York: CUNY Center for the Humanities, 2016.
PP2	Joans, *Poet Painter/Former Villager Now/World Traveller, Part II*.
"Razzle"	Joans, "Razzle Dazzle." TJP, box 15, folders 1–10.
RP	Franklin and Penelope Rosemont Papers, University of Michigan Libraries, Special Collections Research Center.
"Shut Mouth"	Joans, "Well Shut My Mouth Wide Open," TJP, box 19, folders 1–2.
"Spadework"	Joans, "Spadework: The Autobiography of a Hipster." Laurated Archive.
Spetrophilia	Joans, *Spetrophilia*. Amsterdam: Het Amsterdamsch Litterair Café, 1973.
Sure	Joans, *Sure, Really I Is*. Harpford, Sidmouth, Devon: TRANSFORMAcTION, 1982.
Tanger	Grete Moljord, *Paris Tanger*. Larvik: Forlagshuset i Vestfold, 2014.
"Teducated Mouth"	"The Teducated Mouth: John Barbato interviews Ted Joans": https://www.emptymirrorbooks.com/beat/teducatedmouth/
Teducation	Joans, *Teducation: Selected Poems*. Minneapolis: Coffee House Press, 1999.
TJP	Ted Joans Papers, 1941–2005. Bancroft Library, University of California, Berkeley. BANC MSS 99/244 z.
Vergriffen	Joans, *Vergriffen; oder: Blitzlieb Poems*. Kassel and Hamburg: Loose Blätter Presse, 1979.
Wow	Joans, *Wow*. Mukilteo, Washington: Quartermoon Press, 1999.

PART ONE

Poem-Life

Getting the facts straight is difficult for friendly biographers.
—TED JOANS, "COLLAGED AUTOBIOGRAPHY"

1

Life as Art

"Who am I?" asks André Breton in the opening line of *Nadja* (1928), a book that appeared the same year Ted Joans was born. Poised between fiction and memoir, dreams and waking states, *Nadja* offers a vision of the real beyond the real, proposing versions of truth severed from the literal, the factual.[1] Breton's answer to this question was *Nadja* itself, a book that would come to have a talismanic quality for Joans, and he echoed its opening line in his own autobiographical musings: "Who am I? I am Afro-American and my name is Ted Joans," a seemingly straightforward answer belied by other moments when he wondered "Who am I?"—and answered just "a peanut," "a grain of sand," "an animal who changes from a rhino to okapi."[2] Clearly with these last responses we have been shifted away from the "mere empiricism" teased in the first one into some other, non-literal orientation to the self.[3] In pondering what it might mean for "Ted Joans" to be a "grain of sand" or a peanut (or a "storage loft, spangled star, hammock, and back scratcher," as he states in another author bio), we are drawn into a Surreal realm of dreams, irrationality, pugnacious metaphor, outré juxtaposition—the realm we must enter to reckon with his life and work.[4] "WHO AM I?" Joans asks again in one of his Surreal novels. "To answer that is the purpose of this literary helicopter that you now, fortunately, hold in your hands. Hold on tight."[5]

What whirs around Joans are stories, marvelous tales that form a kind of Surreal legend that he purposively, carefully cultivated. There is the origin tale, that he was born on July 4, 1928, on a riverboat in Cairo, Illinois. There is the story that he became a well-known Beat poet in New York City, but then abruptly left the States to go live in Timbuktu, in a house he rented for five dollars a year. There is the story that he remade himself into a Black Power poet, only to return again to Surrealism. That he was a bop musician, painter, writer, filmmaker, and tireless traveler, a circulator and connector of people who knew everyone worth knowing, and whose life and work intersect in unexpected ways with otherwise only loosely-braided strands of twentieth-century artistic, literary, and political thought.

The story of Joans's childhood is hard to see through the mists of time, but reports of him in the press when he was still a teenager attest to his industry and precocity, and by his early twenties, he was famous in his home of Louisville, Kentucky, as a bop trumpeter, theater manager, and thrower of "fabulous" parties—he was also "Louisville's Salvador Dalí," as one admiring profile put it, for his growing body of Surrealist paintings. There is the story that, despite his local renown in Louisville (and a wife and two children there), he was constitutionally restless, felt he couldn't be contained by Kentucky, and so moved, alone, to New York City with the idea of launching his artistic career on a larger stage. As he had in Louisville, in Greenwich Village he became a minor celebrity, not necessarily for his paintings, but for what he called his "big surrealist costume parties," events which were really living art installations—"Happenings" staged, choreographed, before that term was coined.[6] At some point in New York he turned in earnest to an old love, poetry, which he had written from a young age, and this work caught fire just as the Beat Generation did, leading to what are some of the best-known stories about him: that he published quirky, fan-favorite books like *All of Ted Joans and No More* (1961) and *The Hipsters* (1961), that he held audiences spellbound as he performed his work in various bars, cafés, and coffeehouses in New York City's bohemian quarters, that he hired himself out in a notorious Rent-a-Beatnik business, and that he was accordingly reviled or lauded for so doing by those who thought he was either selling out, or was making a canny, ironic statement about the era's studied obsession with hipster authenticity.

At the height of his fame, he stunned everyone by leaving the United States entirely (and likewise leaving the second family he had started in New York, another wife and five more children). The reason for the move, he said, was to protest America's endemic racism. He opted instead for a peripatetic life of constant circulation in Africa and Europe, with only occasional forays back to the States. Given his personal history, this story goes, disavowing the States so dramatically made a perverse kind of sense, for American racism had expressed itself most brutally for Joans back in 1943, when his father was murdered by a white mob in Detroit. This story continues that Joans lived with the dark cloud of his father's murder for the rest of his days, and yet such an unimaginable blow also underscored to him the preciousness of relationships, and seeking out connections, links, became a dominant thread of his life. From his heroes André Breton and Langston Hughes—surrogate "February Fathers," in Joans's parlance—to the thousands of people he knew over the years, making friends was one of his specialties, and by the end of his life, he counted among his friends and collaborators true giants in the fields of literature, music, painting, politics, and philosophy.

It was, then, in his deliberate circulation around the globe and openness to chance encounters that his life came to represent an intersection of literary and cultural trends or movements: Surrealism crossing bop crossing the Beat Generation crossing Black Arts and Black Power crossing Abstract Expressionism crossing Négritude. He was friendly with figures as different as Paul Bowles and Stokely Carmichael, Joyce Mansour and Allen Ginsberg, Wifredo Lam and Archie Shepp. He met Aimé Césaire, Jean-Paul Sartre and Ella Fitzgerald; he had a portrait of himself signed by Malcolm X, Ornette Coleman, Albert Ayler, and others. In Greenwich Village, he once took Elizabeth Taylor and Eddie Fisher on a tour of a bohemian bar. In Tangier, he knocked around with "Africa's First Modern Artist," Fez-born Ahmed Yacoubi.[7] At the St. Regis in mid-town Manhattan, he did a photo shoot with Salvador Dalí himself—only to later renounce Dalí as a money-grubbing, phony Surrealist. When his buddy Charlie Parker died at only thirty-four, Joans's tribute was to originate the phrase "Bird Lives!" and chalk it around New York City. He published some forty books in his lifetime, many of which are now hard to find, and left vast archives of unpublished and little-seen work, including novels, autobiographies, poetry collections, Super 8 films, various kinds of painting, drawing, collage, frottage, sculpture, and a comprehensive guidebook to Africa that covers more than three dozen countries in those crucial postwar years of transition from colonial rule to independence.

In person he was charming and magnetic, a "talkative man," as he once put it, "whose conversations are a stream of steaming (like a tropical swamp?) anecdotes, free associated reminiscences, and out spoken reactions and opinions, most of which find their ways into poems."[8] As a lover, his reputation preceded him, and throughout his life he had various "femmoiselles"—a word he "invented for worthy liberated women"—who enriched his life, and vice versa.[9] He had ten children with four women on three continents (in the sixties in Gibraltar he had married again, this time a Norwegian woman with whom he had two more boys). While still back in New York he had opened the first Black-owned art gallery in the city, Galerie Fantastique. He exhibited his own visual work there and in such cultural capitals as Paris, Tangier, and Amsterdam. Once, in residence at the DAAD in West Berlin, another pioneer moment: he conceived and edited the first Surrealist journal out of Germany, which showcased a personal pantheon of Surreal artists, preponderantly female artists and artists of color. He believed deeply in collaboration, and even as it hobbled his prospects at major publishing houses, insisted on doing small books with other poets he admired, Jayne Cortez, Joyce Mansour, and Hart Leroy Bibbs, among them. He took collaboration to dizzying heights by turning the Surrealist game of *cadavre exquis* or exquisite corpse into *Long Distance*, a continuous drawing with more than 130 contributors created over nearly 30 years, a magnificent web of twentieth-century aesthetic currents that would become a centerpiece to a major exhibition at the Metropolitan Museum of Art—but only some eighteen years after his death.

A lifetime prior, the stories go, Joans had graduated with a degree in fine art from Indiana University in Bloomington, focusing on European art history, the history of modern arts, and avant-garde painting.[10] He became expert in many kinds of African art, and jazz, what he called *"the* Black classical music," lecturing all over Europe, Africa, and the United States, while always living on a shoestring.[11] "He was one of the least capitalistic human beings we'd ever met," recalled Yuko Otomo, a longtime friend; another friend, Michael Kellner, saw his life itself as an "anti-capitalist statement."[12] Despite a term as a visiting professor at UC Berkeley, generally he was ignored by academia, excluded from many retrospective Beat Generation conferences and gatherings in the 1980s and 1990s (his work appears in the first, hardcover edition of the field-defining *Portable Beat Reader*, but only his ghostly traces remain in the much more widely-circulated paperback edition). His singular contributions to the Black Arts Movement can be seen in his books *Black Pow-Wow* (1969), *Afrodisia* (1970), and *A Black Manifesto in Jazz Poetry and Prose* (1971)—but even these books cannot be fully explained by their connection to the Black Arts Movement, or any other movement. He had a special love for the Sahara Desert, and crossed it eighteen times, sometimes serving as a paid guide for other travelers.[13] He hated cold weather. He was a peerless performer of his own work, earning raves for his readings around the world: during Festac '77, the massive month-long celebration of African and Black art and culture in Lagos, he was mobbed after a reading by admirers demanding even more of his poetry. He had seven totem animals, the rhinoceros, okapi, tapir, aardvark, pangolin, echidna, and platypus, and combined their first letters into an alter ego, Dr. Rotapep, who starred in Sherlock Holmes-inspired mysteries—"I am at times," he claimed, "[a] detective fetish ... tattered deerstalker cap, bent magnifying glass, and several packets of gri-gris."[14] He loved jazz, it goes without saying, but also anvils, helicopters, garlic, making art from humble everyday objects, and regaling friends and fans with stories from a seemingly endless bag. His "holy trinity" was food, sex, and art—and he saw them as deeply, sensuously interconnected.[15] Once in Liberia, he was initiated in to a Poro secret society, and for much of his life was "inseparable" from his protective gri-gri, something mineral, something animal, something vegetable, "worn to perpetuate affinity with his ancestral spirits."[16] In 1999, Coffee House Press brought out his selected poems, *Teducation*, whose title refers to his particular way of being and learning in the world. "What does a Teducated moment feel like?" asked Robin D. G. Kelley. "A Teducation is sort of like, if Bird gets the Word—you think he's Meandering, but in reality he's running down some Anthropology and history and pure poetry … You don't have to agree with everything to get a Teducation, but you have to turn your mental chains into instruments of freedom."[17] In 2001, Joans was honored by the Before Columbus Foundation with an American Book Awards Lifetime Achievement Award. His final eleven years were marked by his romantic relationship with Canadian artist Laura Corsiglia, one of the great loves of his life, his muse and collaborator. Joans went "on to his ancestors," as he would put it, in the spring of 2003 at the too-young age of 74.[18] But like Bird Parker, he lives on—"is André Breton dead?" Joans asked, "Am I dead? How can a creative point of view ever die, when the very point of view changes with each creator?"[19]

———

Everybody knows that there are literary truths, poetic truths, that are unmoored from or only slackly-tethered to "facts" in the historical, encyclopedic sense, and that poetic truths can seem more profound, transcendent, and indeed human exactly because they don't necessarily concern themselves with facts—or, rather, because they remake facts in their own image. This is why we don't ask whether a poem is "fiction" or "non-fiction": the answer is yes, and we understand that its truths are something greater than the circumstantial biographical or historical facts that may have gone into making it. But what if a person thought of his life itself as a poem, as what Joans called a "poem-life"? Wouldn't this perspective inevitably change how a biographer might understand facts and truth within the context of that poem-life? As Janet Malcolm writes in a book that haunted me daily as I worked on this one: "Biography is the medium through which the remaining secrets of the famous dead are taken from them and dumped out in full view of the world. The biographer at work, indeed, is like the professional burglar, breaking into a house, rifling through certain drawers that he has good reason to think contain the jewelry and money, and triumphantly bearing his loot away."[20]

We risk the transgression because this loot is supposed to lead to the real story, the truth of a person's life, the low-down that can be reconstructed from letters and manuscripts and interviews. But what if, again, the subject of such an act considered his life a poem? Wouldn't this mean in turn that truth or facts or even "the real" itself might be better seen by literary lights than by historical, encyclopedic ones? Are the statements in the preceding biographical sketch true in a historical sense? In a literary one?

Joans had a famous dictum, "Jazz is my religion and Surrealism is my point of view," which announces that if we want to understand his life, his poem-life, we too must come to terms with Surrealism and its point of view. Varied and protean as it was, it is fair to say that Surrealism was about rejecting commonplace notions of truth or facts or even the real, and hardcore Surrealists conducted their very lives in full view of this rejection, refusing any meaningful distinction between life and art: they were one, inextricable, fused into a "poem-life."

From its earliest days, the term *Surrealism* has been subject to manifold, sometimes competing attempts to define it, a situation that has as much to do with the movement's fluidity as it does with the personalities involved, figures whose clashes led, eventually, to a splintering of Surrealism along political-ideological lines.[21] We don't need to wade too deeply into this prior factionalization except to note that André Breton was the charismatic intellectual center of the Surrealist group with whom Joans felt an early, deep affinity, and Breton laid out his version of Surrealism in his first *Manifesto of Surrealism* (1924). There he offered both a dictionary definition—"Psychic automatism in its pure state, by which one proposes to express ... the actual functioning of thought"—and an encyclopedic one: "Surrealism is based on the belief in the superior reality of certain forms of previously neglected associations, in the omnipotence of dream, in the disinterested play of thought."[22] It may of course seem somewhat paradoxical for a movement avowedly suspicious of fixed, encyclopedic kinds of truth to be accounted for in this way, and so it may accordingly be prudent to regard Breton's pithy statements with skepticism, and recognize that they can hardly be the final definitions of so capacious and variable a concept.

As I write this, Breton's "once and for all" definitions have reached their centenary, and so now have a hundred years of amplifications, clarifications, and repudiations attached to them—and indeed, after Breton's death in 1966, there was impassioned debate about whether Surrealism could survive without him at all. Survive it did, and it may be clarifying for our purposes to see Surrealism via a more recent explanation that has at least the benefit of hindsight. Here is a relatively straightforward definition from 2001 by Joans's friend Ron Sakolsky that I think can help us see why Joans called Surrealism his "point of view":

> The movement continues to elude all attempts to define it, but its basic aim has been constant from 1924 on: to assist the process by which the imaginary becomes real—or, as Franklin Rosemont puts it, "to realize poetry in everyday life." In other words, surrealists seek to create a truly free society in which the age-old contradictions between dream and action, reason and imagination, subjectivity and objectivity, have been resolved. Both collectively and individually surrealists have sought nothing less than a world turned upside down where life can be a wondrous festival fueled by the liberation of the passions, inspired laziness, and an absolute divergence from the tired and oppressive game of social injustice and self-degradation.[23]

The goal here, a world in which "the imaginary becomes real," demands that we stretch and expand our conventional understanding of "the real"—and the notion of a "goal." As Joans said, "My onward journey is neither dream goal nor reality goal, but the fusion of both. This resolution of opposites is the very essence of the surreal as announced in André Breton's manifestos."[24] Here he is thinking about statements such as this, from Breton's first manifesto: "I believe in a future resolution of ... dream and reality, which are seemingly so contradictory, into a kind of absolute reality, a *surreality*."[25] While such a resolution is rooted in the realm of the imaginary (as opposed to the province of reason), it can nonetheless have practical consequences and implications in its potential to liberate us from narrow, straitjacketed visions of "the real"—what Joans called "mere empiricism."[26]

Breton emphasized as much when he maintained that "the mere word 'freedom' is the only one that still excites me," and Joans often repeated this idea, noting, for instance, that "it is on freedom that surrealism is based, it is to the 'exaltation of freedom that surrealism has labored,' said André Breton wayback in the '40s at Yale."[27] Surrealism was and is a revolutionary movement and sensibility that, in working to make the imaginary real, destroys also those sacred cows—call them ideologies, customs, habits of being, "common sense"—that seem so immovably embedded in our very existence, but are really of course arbitrary, historically and socially contingent, and for those reasons fundamentally damaging.

How wondrous it might be to attempt a life of pure liberation, to reject outright the "oppressive game of social injustice and self-degradation," as Sakolsky puts it. For Joans, Surrealism was a tool—a "weapon" he pointedly leveled—for so doing. As he said, "Surrealism, you must not forget is, above all, a movement of revolt. It is not the result of intellectual caprice built on bushels of bullshit jivery. But rather of a tragic conflict between the powers of the spirit and the conditions of life."[28] The "powers of the spirit"—imagination—colliding with the "conditions of life": from this conflict emerges a repudiation of received wisdom about the "natural" order of things—ideas about, say, race or the inevitability of capitalism; or about what constitutes worthwhile art, or "knowledge" itself, or a life well lived. Joans was consistent in this point of view for most of his adult life, reflecting in 1987, when he was nearing sixty:

> my life is a spontaneous automatism, [that] however exciting and aesthetically rewarding, is not an end in itself. I am not "lost," but my life as the poem has no "destination" for it is a liberated onward journey. One surrenders to the poem's journey in order to discover le merveilleux ... Surrealism as a "goal" obtained is to be completely possessing mental freedom, hence it spurns all dogmatism, scientific or religious, and denies any principle threatening to limit the human potential.[29]

For a Black man who had spent much of his youth in segregated Kentucky, the "conditions of life" were all too often suffused with parochial racism that did nothing if not limit "human potential," and Surrealism was a means of

FIGURE 1.1 *Ted Joans, "Surrealism" drawing (undated). Note that in Joans's view, André Breton is the head of the Surrealist, (non)sacred cow. From TJP, carton 4, folder 15.*

survival in such a charged, venomous environment. Back in 1963, in a letter he wrote to André Breton—later published in Breton's Surrealist journal, *La Brèche*—Joans made his own manifesto-like declaration: "Without surrealism, I would not have been able to survive the abject vicissitudes and acts of racist violence that the white man in the United States has constantly imposed on me. Surrealism became the weapon that I chose to defend myself, and it has been and always will be my own way of life."[30] This is a usable sense of Surrealism that at once returns it to its revolutionary roots, and explains why it might have been revelatory for a young Black American curious about other ways of being in the world. Surrealism gave Joans permission to remake reality, to take, for example, the atmospheric oppressiveness of racism and deny it, to reject its seemingly inescapable pervasiveness and its power to define, categorize, and degrade.

As Joans elaborated elsewhere: "My point of view is surrealist, I therefore set out daily to live that poem that I have no control over ... I therefore am out to overthrow one's sense of the familiar/to sabotage your conventional habits/to put your real world on trial, thus causing your parents to be damn liars and hick fascists."[31] These are themes and preoccupations that run throughout much of Joans's poem-life, and his work: both are bluntly skeptical of "conventional habits" and continually put the "real world on trial," calling out disingenuousness, bad faith, the tyranny of rational thought, literal and figurative violence, facile aesthetics that are too easily digestible and thus too easily complicit in lies and everyday hick fascism.

And the politically-tinged language here is not incidental, for despite the popular (mis)perception of "surreal" as a rough synonym for anything strange or uncanny, the strain of Surrealism with which Joans most deeply engaged was fundamentally political in character, insofar as it was aligned with anti-colonialism, non-Western art forms, ideas, and epistemologies, and unwaveringly dedicated to liberation in both the abstract, existential sense, and in the real-world sense of liberating politically oppressed people around the globe. Thus with words like "sabotage" and "overthrow" and "trial," Joans was drawing a line back to earlier Surrealists of color who saw the movement as conducive to effecting "liberation" in its multiple senses.

As the great Martinican statesman and poet Aimé Césaire put it, prefiguring Joans's letter to Breton: "Surrealism provided me with what I had been confusedly searching for ... It was a weapon that exploded the French language. It shook up absolutely everything. This was very important because the traditional forms—burdensome, overused forms—were crushing me."[32] This sense of Surrealism informs Césaire's first poetry collection, *Les Armes miraculeuses* (1946), or *The Miraculous Weapons*.[33] His most famous poem, *Cahier d'un retour au pays natal* (1947), or *Notebook of a Return to the Native Land*, is also an anti-colonial political treatise that takes the dynamited fragments of the French language and uses them to excoriate the "conventions" of white supremacist French society. Likewise his political treatise, *Discours sur le colonialisme* (1955), or *Discourse on Colonialism*, is poetic in substance, lyrical and figurative in form. In an introduction to a recent English-language edition of *Discourse on Colonialism*, Joans's friend, the historian Robin D. G. Kelley, noted that "those passages which sing, that sound the war drums, that explode spontaneously, are the most powerful sections of the essay" (Kelley's introduction is, also not incidentally, dedicated to Joans and his partner Laura Corsiglia).[34]

Surrealism was also for Césaire and other Black radicals about a recognition of and return to Black cultures that were already infused with the spirit of Surrealism, even if this spirit hadn't been named as such. As Kelley puts it in *Freedom Dreams* (2002), figures like Césaire recognized that "a thorough understanding and an acceptance of the Marvelous existed in the lives of blacks and non-Western peoples—before Breton, before Rimbaud, before Lautréamont—in music, dance, speech, the plastic arts, and above all philosophy. We are, after all, talking about cultures that valued imagination, improvisation, and verbal agility, from storytelling, preaching, and singing to toasting and the dozens."[35] This recognition is crucial to understanding Joans's sense of Surrealism, for while it is certainly routed through Breton, Césaire and other self-identified practitioners, he also saw its spirit manifested everywhere in Black culture, and he often told a story about a favorite saying of his grandfather's to illustrate one of the "many surrealities traditionally prevailing in the African American culture." When "greeting an old friend who he had not seen in a long time," Joans's grandfather would exclaim, "Well, shut my mouth wide open, if aint slim Jim Jackson!"—and Joans asked: "How does one shut his mouth wide open? Can you the reader draw or paint a mouth shut wide open?"[36]

———

The notion that a Surrealist point of view could offer shape and substance to a person's life as well as his creative endeavors makes it decidedly tricky to sift out various orders of "the real" or "truth" operating within that life—which for a Surrealist is, of course, often the point. As Sylvia Plath's biographer Anne Stevenson wrote to Janet Malcolm, "Truth is, in its nature, multiple and contradictory, part of the flux of history, untrappable in language."[37] This is perhaps self-evident, and perhaps particularly the case when it comes to the lives of poets—and yet the fundamental suppositions of Surrealism put even more pressure on truth. Joans somewhat coyly announces in the line I borrowed as an epigraph for Part One of this book: "Getting the facts straight is difficult for friendly biographers." In his case, this difficulty stems from the idea that a Surrealist point of view interrogates "facts" as they are assembled by "conventional habits" or ways of knowing the past (and the present). Joans was particularly thoughtful and serious about interrogating how evidence, facts, are assembled as truth, and carefully constructed an image of himself and his poem-life as a kind of counter-assemblage to historical truth.

In one sense, this is hardly surprising, since writers and artists are natural self-mythologizers, and as Stevenson observes, truth is "multiple and contradictory." But Joans's approach differed in both substance and kind. In wrestling with how to render his life in this book, I have come to appreciate the extent to which he moved beyond simple mythmaking in a quest to actually *live* his poem-life, meaning that labels such as "fiction" or "autobiography" don't map neatly on to his ideas about and representations of himself. Joans's point of view demands that we approach his poem-life via his own idiosyncratic idea of truth, and recognize how it brushes up against—and sometimes inters—historical data. Crucially, this point of view sees the sort of "truth" locatable in archival records and primary sources like newspaper accounts as impoverished, and in fact materially linked to white supremacy and its erasure of both Black people and Black ways of knowing and forms of expression.

Consider, for example, that origin tale, as delivered in the "Ted Joans" entry in the *Dictionary of Literary Biography*: "He was born on a riverboat in Cairo, Illinois, on 4 July 1928, just after the annual street parade had ended."[38] This origin tale is repeated again and again in subsequent reference works and encyclopedias: "Theodore Jones (he later changed the spelling of his surname to distinguish himself) was auspiciously born on a riverboat on 4 July 1928 in Cairo, Illinois"; "His July 4, 1928, birth to parents who were Mississippi riverboat entertainers was auspicious in a number of ways."[39] What could be more fundamental a unit of information for friendly biographers than their subject's date of birth? And yet, despite how often it recurs as dictionary or encyclopedic truth, when this "fact" is confronted by the official archival record, it begins to look more complicated and fraught—or Surrealized.

Leaving aside for a moment the colorful detail of being born *on* a riverboat, with all its steam-puff associations with movement, music and a Mark Twain kind of Americana, Joans's date of birth, July 4, 1928, has irresistible symbolic texture. Obviously the concurrence with the American Independence Day underscores Joans's dedication to "liberation," and he was also fond of noting that 1928 was the year of Breton's *Nadja*, that lifelong touchstone, as well as the year Louis Armstrong recorded "West End Blues."[40] When referring to his birth, sometimes Joans would just present the facts, as in a résumé he prepared in the early 1980s: "Ted Joans was born July 4, 1928 in Cairo, Illinois, to a father who was Master of Ceremonies on the Mississippi River showboats and to a mother who encouraged his creativity."[41] Other times, he embroidered the tale: "Ted Joans was born on a riverboat in Cairo, Illinois, on 4 July 1928, just after the annual street parade had ended" (we can see where *Dictionary of Literary Biography* got its information)—or, more pithily, "Those cannon roared and I started kicking."[42] He often noted the irony of being born in a town with an African name that had long been infamous as a cauldron of racial tensions: there the stench of 1909 still lingered, when a mob of some 10,000 white citizens descended into Cairo's downtown square for the lynching of William James, a Black man accused of murder. "Yes Cairo," wrote Joans, "what a misnomer! This Cairo located at the most southern tip of Illinois, much farther south in dangerous racism than Mississippi."[43] Thus the date and place of Joans's birth, July 4 in Cairo, Illinois, could represent both the failed promises of American independence—freedom and justice, but not for all—and Joans's own unwavering dedication to independence and liberation in all its senses, a perversely perfect, propitious moment in time and space for him to come into the world.

But could it have been a little *too* perfect?

Acting from a sense of professional, academic responsibility, this friendly biographer felt duty-bound to verify Joans's birthday through official records, and turned up documents like his birth certificate and draft registration card—documents which, strangely (or not), challenge the origin tale. The birth certificate tells us that Theodore Jones was born, with the help of a midwife, on July 20, 1928 at 1112 Walnut Street, Cairo, Illinois. His parents were 17-year-old Theodore Jones from Ashport, Tennessee, and 21-year-old Zella Jones (née Pyles) from Arlington, Kentucky. His father's occupation is listed as "common labor" and his mother's as "housekeeping." Question #6 on the form asks simply: "Legitimate?" and the official has written in "yes." By the time he was required to register for the draft, 18-year-old Theodore Jones, Jr. was living at 710 Magazine Street in Louisville, Kentucky. Occupation: musician. Date of birth: July 20, 1928.

It appears, from these "official" documents, that just as he would later change his name from commonplace "Jones" to distinctive "Joans," at some point Joans also changed his birthday from unremarkable July 20 to auspicious July 4. In this way he was again echoing André Breton, who had also "adopted" a new birthday, February 18, 1896, rather than his "official" birth date, February 19—a less splashy change than Joans's, but a Surrealist precedent nonetheless.[44] More splashy, perhaps, was Breton's fondness for using 1713 as a numerical signature—this he did for multiple, complex reasons, because it resembled A.B. when written out, because the

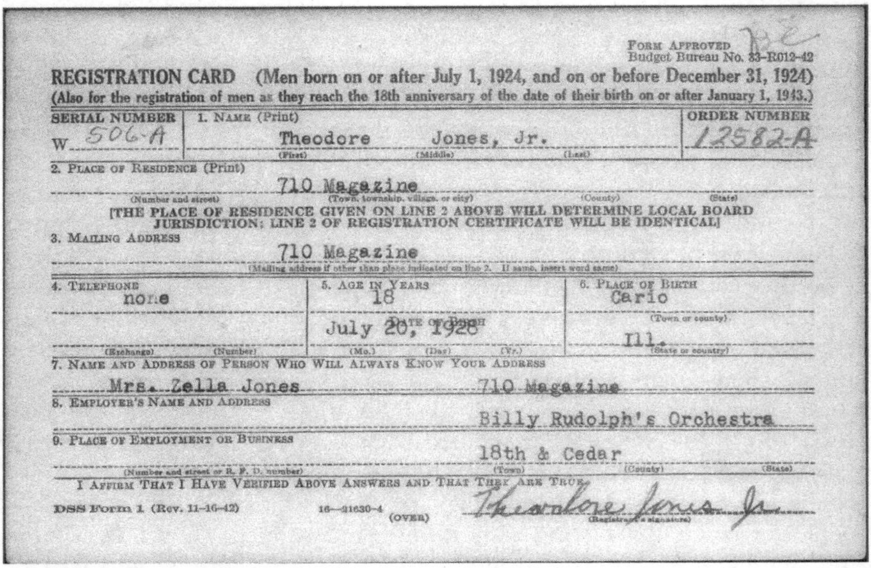

FIGURE 1.2 *Theodore Jones, Jr. draft registration card, 1946: "I affirm that I have verified above answers and that they are true."*

numbers had for him various occult meanings, and because other aesthetic associations were embedded in them: "Eternal youth," Breton wrote, "'1808 = 17': Birth of [Gérard de] Nerval. Publication of [Charles Fourier's] *The Social Destiny of Man; or Theory of the Four Movements*."[45] Beyond July 4, Joans's own adoption of the date-like 1714 as a numerical signature is similarly complex, as explained in the coming pages.

For Joans, both the name change and the new birthday were better reflections of how he thought about himself—the more unusual surname "Joans" was, he said, a "tribute" to Joan Locke, his first wife: "I started signing my paintings ted joan's, then ... made it plain Ted Joans."[46] This new name, he said, could perhaps symbolize a "self-controlled destiny of my own," as his father "was Theodore The First, and I was supposed to carry on by being named Theodore The Second, but hahaha I was too Yankee Doodle Dandy to stroll through life bearing such a silly-billy-goat title. So I became and I remain the self-made man with the lower-case letters."[47] The name change pushes back against what he was "supposed to" do, and in the course of explaining how "Joans" describes a "self-made man," he alludes also American Independence Day via another moniker he briefly adopts, the Revolutionary Era Yankee Doodle Dandy.

So here we are faced with another clash of truths—Joans's insistent truth that he was born on the Fourth of July, and the truth found in the official record, that he was born sixteen days later. Does this clash matter? What might it mean?

Joans, naturally, offers some possibilities. In "Je Me Vois (I See Myself)" his lengthiest autobiography in print (there are several lengthier unpublished ones), he lingers over an incident that occurred in an unspecified year, when he watched "the back of a Land Rover slip off a boat ramp and slowly sink into the Niger River shore waters."[48] This was a momentous event because the Land Rover was loaded with nomadic Joans's worldly possessions, notably:

> my original Cairo, Illinois, Alexander county birth certificate and also newspaper articles from the yesteryears Detroit riot in which Theodore Jones The First was mob murdered, which has yet to be avenged; nevertheless this serious matter has been told to specialists of traditional West African (wise women and men) sorcery who have cast the spell of physical misfortune upon the nefarious Caucasoid working-class men who are guilty.[49]

Lost in the river was the physical, archival evidence of the two most significant events of Joans's early life: his own birth, and the murder of his father. Whether or not a Land Rover literally sank in the Niger, Joans is working in the realm of metaphor here, telling us that official records and primary sources—his "original" birth certificate, and "newspaper articles" documenting his father's death—are insufficient and indeed irrelevant for understanding the truth of his poem-life. And, again not incidentally, the invocation of "traditional West African" sorcery also routes us back to Yoruba cosmology, for as Joans's friend Robert Farris Thompson explains—and Joans himself well knew—for the Yoruba, the goddesses who preside "over the river Niger, are famed for their 'witchcraft.' They are supreme in the arts of mystic retribution."[50]

Scholars who have written about Joans's handling of history in his creative work have noted, as Joanna Pawlik puts it, that his "practice used Surrealism to elaborate a particular historiographical mode, one that was nonlinear and non-teleological, and that harnessed temporal anachronism and spatial discontinuity to protest the uneven spread of political and cultural agency within modernity."[51] Certainly we see nonlinearity and "temporal anachronism" manifest in a variety of ways throughout his work. His collages, for example, purposively juxtapose and layer fragments from different time periods and geographies to emphasize imagistic, symbolic, or thematic continuities—echoes and associations across time and space—rather than notions of historical "progress" premised on chronological development in a Western, Enlightenment sense. When writing autobiography, Joans also used collage-like techniques, refusing to proceed chronologically, instead sketching vignettes and juxtaposing them via symbolic or aesthetic logics; these sketches may or may not be "true" from an empirical, archival perspective, but are nevertheless true poetically, as expressions of Joans's Surrealized point of view.

But beyond exploring nonlinearity and temporal disruption *in his representations*, what we are seeing when he changes his birthday to July 4 is a similar disruption of the real, a disruption of history itself—which of course like "the real" comes to us mediated through representations of various sorts. In this way, I see Joans's engagement with history—his own past, his family history, and deeper world history—as broadly comparable to the more recent work of cultural theorist Saidiya Hartman, whose theories and practice offer a productive way in to understanding Joans's poem-life. Contemplating archives related to transatlantic chattel slavery, Hartman builds on work of those who have theorized the violence embedded in these archives, concerned that she herself could be extending versions of this violence in engaging them. As she writes, "The archive is, in this case, a death sentence, a tomb, a display of the violated body, an inventory of property, a medical treatise on gonorrhea, a few lines about a whore's life, an asterisk in the grand narrative of history."[52]

How, then, to approach something called "the archive" tainted in this way? "If it is no longer sufficient to expose the scandal," Hartman asks, "then how might it be possible to generate a different set of descriptions from this archive? To imagine what could have been? To envision a free state from this order of statements?"[53] One possibility is a method she calls "critical fabulation," which draws on the archive but supplements its silences with imaginative reconstructions, amounting to "a critical reading of the archive that mimes the figurative dimensions of history":

> By playing with and rearranging the basic elements of the story, by re-presenting the sequence of events in divergent stories and from contested points of view, I have attempted to jeopardize the status of the event, to displace the received or authorized account, and to imagine what might have happened or might have been said or might have been done. By throwing into crisis "what happened when" and by exploiting the "transparency of sources" as fictions of history, I wanted to make visible the production of disposable lives (in the Atlantic slave trade and, as well, in the discipline of history), to describe "the resistance of the object," if only by first imagining it, and to listen for the mutters and oaths and cries of the commodity. By flattening the levels of narrative discourse and confusing narrator and speakers, I hoped to illuminate the contested character of history, narrative, event, and fact, to topple the hierarchy of discourse, and to engulf authorized speech in the clash of voices.[54]

Hartman's method of "critical fabulation" has become extremely influential in certain circles—the MoMA presented a collection gallery inspired by her work called "Critical Fabulations"—and though not the precise method Joans uses, it does share several affinities with his understanding of history, and how he handles the "facts" that might be seen as building blocks of historiography (or biography).[55] Hartman tells us that: "History pledges to be faithful to the limits of fact, evidence, and archive, even as those dead certainties are produced by terror. I wanted to write a romance that exceeded the fictions of history—the rumors, scandals, lies, invented evidence, fabricated confessions, volatile facts, impossible metaphors, chance events, and fantasies that constitute the archive and determine what can be said about the past."[56]

What Hartman calls "the fictions of history" Joans had also long recognized as constitutive of the Black experience and the availability of the Black past, as "facts" are for him similarly unstable: "Facts about Afroids," he observes, "especially those not well-known, are often merely gossip, bad-mouthing and mythmaking."[57] From such recognition of the highly-contingent nature of "facts" of ordinary Black life as they have been constituted by a white supremacist historical record, Joans would go on to play with and rearrange "the basic elements" of his own personal history—his date of birth, for example—not simply for the sake of pugnaciousness or glib iconoclasm, but to identify and refuse the way history has been made available via a knowledge regime, an archive, that he considers morally bankrupt, violent, and poisoned by its own fictions.[58]

Now, while Joans isn't necessarily talking about "the archive" as it is
constituted and imagined in relation to transatlantic chattel slavery, he
is certainly talking about records and repositories as they pertain to Black
life, which he sees as explicable only via the deeper histories of slavery
and colonial encounter on which Hartman is focused. In "Je Me Vois," his
autobiography quoted above, Joans writes, "I guess you the reader are hip
to the fact that any attempt to make a careful record of a Afroid family in
these United States is doomed to be cursory. Facts of Black family history
are scant, memories elliptical, and the most elementary dates difficult to
establish."[59] This is a recognition and acknowledgement of the sets of
issues Hartman would later name, and when Joans troubles the very idea
of a "careful record," he is challenging archival knowledge as the only
acceptable route to the truth, and will instead propose another model, a
kind of distorted mirror of what Hartman would come to do with "critical
fabulation."

Rather than beginning with scraps of archival fragments imbued in
violence, Joans often rejects such fragments outright so that he might
"envision," as Hartman puts it, "a free state from this order of statements."
This "free state" is for Joans filtered through the imaginative landscape
of Surrealism—which is why he follows up the statement "Facts of Black
family history are scant" with the assertion that he writes "spontaneously
and surreally automatic." But though the means differ, the larger ends are
broadly comparable to what Hartman is after, to "imagine what cannot
be verified, a realm of experience which is situated between two zones of
death—social and corporeal death—and to reckon with the precarious lives
which are visible only in the moment of their disappearance."[60] Joans, of
course, refuses to be disappeared.

2

Born Swinging

When Joans wrote about his life, he often took readers into the unverifiable realm of imagination, presenting facts unanchored from archival corroboration that are both true in the sense that they expose the fictions and limits of the archive, as in Hartman's observations, and because they speak to a greater, poetic or Surreal truth that is almost by definition at odds with the historical record: July 4 versus July 20. One of his favored metaphors for this sort of approach was "spadework," a word he used as the title of what would become a legendary, unpublished autobiography of the 1960s. *Spadework* is a play on the slang word for a Black person ("spade"), and the idea that one needed a "spade"—in the literal and slang senses—to truly "dig" both the past and present. "A spade is a sharp tool," Joans insisted. "Most people use it to dig with, in fact one can only dig deep with a spade (not a shovel which is kinda square). The spade is usually sharp and black ... If you really want to be dug, deeply, then you gotta get involved with a spade."[1] As with many of his favorite metaphors, the one behind spadework was seemingly simple but really layered with meaning and histories, so that for him it was hardly incidental that spades, in the sense of physical tools, are black, since Black people were brought to the Americas as implements: "Spades were ripped off and brought here as a living tool. They have been used as a tool ever since. Now-a-days spades dont stand for that shit."[2]

So it is through painstaking spadework that Joans encourages us to dig his early years. Although his childhood is particularly hard to excavate with the flimsier tools of official records or primary sources, he does turn up flashes and vignettes, out-of-context scenes that give a certain shape to this early life. In Joans's own "Black family history," facts are scant, and yet he emphasized how his younger years as Theodore Jones, Jr. laid the thematic, symbolic foundations for the coming poem-life of Ted Joans.

In elaborating his origin tale, he often dug even deeper than his date of birth, matter-of-factly claiming to remember, for instance, existing inside his father's scrotum:

It was a groove to be in there with all my brothers and sisters. We would all rap and laff and swim around each other and knew nothing of sleep. For in there all was wakeness, since there was no such thing as time. We often had to attach ourselves tightly to the sides of the in there walls to prevent being shot out into some mother-to-be. I held on a long 'time' (sic) before saying goodbye to my others and allowed myself to be shot out.[3]

As a Surreal version of "critical fabulation," this memory succeeds in couching Joans's genesis in an exuberant community not structured by time—indeed, the idea that there was "no such thing as time" seems a key condition of Joans's pre-history as a swinging spermatozoon. And thematically it confirms that conventional notions of time—"exact times" and "dates"—are of less use in understanding Joans's origins—and his poem-life—than trying to imagine a kind of dreamscape beyond time. As he writes, "I avoid chronological approaches in almost everything that I do. I dont talk chronologically and when I blew trumpet I did not blow a solo in a chronological musical manner. My poem-life is not (so far) actual chronologic."[4]

While the scene of Joans's pre-birth seems obviously unknowable on an empirical level, he rejects even this assumption, proposing this kind of "memory" as a specifically Black way of knowing. After describing the party in his father's scrotum, he anticipates his readers' skepticism or dismissal and addresses them directly: "this important pouch of wrinkled skin containing the testicles is where you and I, all of us came from. Try to git to that and remember. Allyall say yall can remember being 'inside' yall's mother, damn if that is all the far back you can remember ... your remembering apparatus is in trouble."[5] "Remembering," in this sense, isn't about recalling an event "as it actually happened" in historian Leopold van Ranke's old chestnut, but rather to "imagine what might have happened," as in Hartman's practice. Joans is interested in conjuring, via imagination, a scene outside of time and therefore rationality that nonetheless expresses a truth unlocatable in archives—in, say, his "original Cairo, Illinois, Alexander county birth certificate." This type of defiantly unverifiable but simultaneously true "memory" is a fitting origin of a poem-life, a place where "the imaginary becomes real," as Sakolsky says.

When Joans would write about his birth (or pre-birth) or his parents, he took pains to show how these events and people are connected to and reflective of a deeper Black past, suturing himself and his parents into communal experiences that embody Surreal truths. In the last book he published in his lifetime, *Our Thang* (2001), Joans asked the question: "Why Selected Poems as Autobiography?" By way of answer he drew attention to "the point ... at which the lived experience of *poésie* becomes transformed into cultural memory. Inevitably, there will be fewer and fewer

witnesses to contribute to—or in my case *contest*—the ideas about the past."
Again rejecting empirical corroboration in the form of "witnesses," Joans
imagines the "lived experience of *poésie*"—his poem-life—as a way to *create*
history, to embody a "cultural memory" that renders things like verification
moot.[6] According to such a view, it is perfectly sensible for poetry to *be*
"autobiography," so that, for instance, his poem "One Blue Note," which
recounts what he "knew" in his mother's womb, that "Jazz was a black
classical music / that is created each time one blew true," is as "true" as his
prose memories of partying in his father's scrotum.[7]

The idea that his father embodied a kind of Black "cultural memory"
runs through much of Joans's descriptions of him. Shifting into a vernacular,
in one piece Joans maintained that "Not a drop of 'white' blood" could be
found in his father's body: "He be tall in stature and spirit ... his height
was about 5 feet 8 inches, and him skin color was dark brown, but around
the butt he be coal black ... [he had] a long tireless tongue that he used to
get anything that he wanted and to get out of anything/place."[8] From this
emphasis on his father's physical Blackness and verbal dexterity ("Him Had
A Very Big Mouf!!"), Joans's spadework then turns up a deeper history that
reveals the connection between these two features: "Theodore's people were
stolen from Africa during the slavetrade. His entire village which was near
Ouidah in Dahomey was 'sold' to the ruling Dahomean king in 1714. They
were brought in seven boatloads to Virginia and there placed on the auction
block and dispersed in every direction but up ... Theodore's father was an
old story teller better known as a griot."[9]

Following Hartman, it may be easier to see how such a passage is true
in both the historical and Surreal senses: it's certainly the case that at some
point in the past, Joans's ancestors were enslaved and brought to the States
from Africa, but just as assuredly—and *because* of the conditions of this
enslavement—there are few available records of such movements (again:
"Facts of Black family history are scant"). In crafting his own cultural
memory, Joans confidently provides several "facts" to counter the lack
of "elementary dates" available to him: that his father's ancestral village
was "Ouidah in Dahomey"; that his ancestors were sold to the "ruling
Dahomean king in 1714"; that they were then "brought in seven boatloads
to Virginia." These facts signal Joans's Surrealized version of history, which
is not concerned with specific historical dates but the nature of historical
unrecoverability: while Ouidah names the infamous slave trading port in
what is now Benin, 1714 does not stand for the corresponding year in the
eighteenth century, but is rather his code for "Afro-American," as "1714"
resembles "A A" when written out.

As 1713 did for Breton, 1714 had for Joans many intricate meanings
nested in it: "1 is for real a one, 7 is the oath taking number, I again (you
already know) / 4 is for the fabulous four joined together [*sic*], thus making
without breaking / 1714 [written out like AA] AfroAmerican, you see thats

FIGURE 2.1 *Image of Joans reading from a sheaf of poems with the Surreal date "1714," for A.A. or "African American"; from back cover of* All of Ted Joans and No More *(1961).*

me."[10] The idea, then, is that in this telling, 1714 masquerades as a historical date, but is really and more importantly a way to index continuity with the Black past, despite a general lack of knowable dates attached to his family's encounters with the slave trade. (And note that in this history, Joans's ancestors were brought on "seven boatloads," not because Joans discovered this fact in some archived ledger, but because seven is a Surreal, "oath taking" number.)

And yet for Joans, Surrealized cultural memory is something that even the transatlantic slave trade cannot obliterate completely, as his father's "long tireless tongue" is a link to and evidence of the powers of the griot—a West African "story teller," poet, musician, genealogist and folk historian in one—whom Joans imagines preceding his father in an unbroken hereditary line. As he explains:

a griot is first of all a poet of rhythm and is au courant to all the happenings. He is the cat that "tells it like it is" and tells that truth outloud.

He is the man that walks down crowded streets talking or singing loud to himself (actually he's doing it for the people). There are thousands of griots today still functioning throughout Africa. Being a griot is a hereditary thing. Most of them were taught by their fathers and uncles whom were the greatest story tellers and it is they that have enormous quantity of traditional songs and melodies. In the good old days before slavery depleted the Western region of Africa, Theodore's father's father and uncles used to roam from village to town turning people on and off (some were putdown if wrong). These hip cats knew to the utmost details of alliances, hostilities, jivery, and conflicts.[11]

Although there were and are many kinds of griots across West Africa who are known by a number of names, Joans's description is basically accurate. In his comprehensive history, *Griots and Griottes: Masters of Words and Music* (1998), Thomas A. Hale explains the varying, multifaceted functions griots serve in different West African societies, and notes also a range of "ethno-specific terms for griots" in Wolof, Mande, Songhay, Bariba, Fula, Dogon, Hausa, and others; but for our purposes, it suffices to say that "griot" has emerged as a preferred term, and the one that Joans himself used.[12] Hale takes a deep dive into the historical origins of the griot, and details the assorted roles a griot may inhabit: "genealogist, historian, adviser, spokesperson, diplomat, mediator, interpreter and translator, musician, composer, teacher, exhorter, warrior, witness, praise-singer, and master or participant in a variety of ceremonies."[13] Even this list is "incomplete," Hale says, because griots under various names perform nuanced social and artistic functions in each region where they practice. Despite such multiplicity, Hale notes, the function of the griot "best known outside of Africa, thanks to *Roots*, is that of the genealogist."[14] Hale is referring to Alex Haley's book *Roots* (1976), which recounts how Haley traveled to The Gambia to consult a griot about his own family's history—the book was a sensation, touching off a genealogical craze in the States (later in this book, I'll explain how Joans responded to *Roots* in his own autobiographical book, "Deeper Are Allyall's Roots").

The griot as genealogist and historian is an aspect Joans is emphasizing when he characterizes them as poets, story tellers, and human archives. Given this combination, they exemplify an archival sensibility that is non-Western and primarily oral. A griot is for Joans history embodied, and "official" written records of corroboration are beside the point, as the griots themselves are the corroboration as they deliver truths otherwise invisible and certainly absent from other, white kinds of records. For Joans, this practice is no mere historical curiosity or distant cultural practice, but illustrative of what he himself is doing. After all, "being a griot is a hereditary thing," and there is a pointed collapse in his historical sketch, a purposive blurring between Joans's father, Joans's unknown and unnamed African ancestors, and Joans himself, the paradigmatic poet in his signature poem "The Truth," which is paraphrased in this sketch ("the man that walks down crowded streets talking or singing loud to himself"). Joans himself is, he reminds us just after this history lesson, a "griot surrealiste."[15]

Working in the tradition of truth-telling griots, Joans delivers his personal history as a great story, complete with mythic origins, symbolic heft, high drama, and a through-line that connects this story to the cultural importance of storytelling itself, back through an imagined (but real) lineage to Africa. In one autobiography, for instance, he vividly recounts being "about seven years old"—there's that magic number again!—and spread out "on the linoleum covered floor with one of the thick chinchilla rugs under me, studying the ancient map of Africa that my aunt Temple had brought to me from 'dem rich white folk' that she was a domestic four days a week ... I remember linoleum smell from those early times, when I was first 'discovering' the continent of Africa; in later years, my father taught me some of its history."[16]

This is a reversal of a famous passage in Joseph Conrad's *Heart of Darkness* (1899), in which a (white) adventurer, Charlie Marlow, describes poring over maps as a "little chap," and, drawn to the mysterious "blank spaces" of Africa, places seemingly without history, resolves to one day go there and explore.[17] Joans, by contrast, is drawn to Africa precisely because of its history, and his father teaches him about the names on the map, especially Timbuktu: he "pointed out the word Tombotu in a territory called Tonbuto that stretched along the Niger River ... My dad never made the journey to Timbuktu, or the continent of Africa, but I his only son did. But it was his coaching and inspiration that propelled me."[18] As a living link to the glorious Black past, a latter-day American griot, Theodore Sr. first drew Joans's attention to the fabled African city of Timbuktu (at least in this story), and as a grown man Joans himself becomes the fulfillment of an unspoken desire to return to their collective roots, walking the banks of the Niger River even as it swallowed his official records documenting a life in the States.

When Joans wrote about his mother, Zella, he tended likewise to associate her with a "heritage" that stretched back to Africa. Census records tell us that Zella's parents were Lemuel and Louise Pyles, that she was one of nine children, and that she grew up in Arlington, Kentucky, where her father was a laborer for the local flour mill, and that he owned his own property.[19] Joans is less concerned with these sorts of records than he is with, say, the meaning of cowrie shells, which he calls "objects of importance in my heritage," infused as they are with various kinds of power, and tangible links to a deeper past. Cowries are "very important in my family heirlooms," Joans tells us. "At this very moment my mother is wearing a cowrie shell attached to her grigri (juju amulet). Her forefathers and my father's forefathers wore the small ivory white shell."[20] As his father was figured as a hereditary link to an august griot lineage, so too is his mother marked by her gri-gri or juju linking her to African beliefs and epistemologies (Joans himself wore cowries, and they appear all over his visual work, from stylized drawings to actual shells incorporated into Surrealist objects).

———

Writing about his early childhood, Joans often paused over moments of Teducation such as learning about Africa from his father, or seeing in his mother's cowries reflections of a much deeper past, contemplating the meaning and effects of such moments. As a small child, he recalled, he "loved to read, write, do arithmetics and draw. I drew pictures every spare moment that I had. I drew on the backs of my school work and the walls of the outhouse. I studied very hard and my mother helped me at home. When I was a little older, I went with my dad every day after school and learned to work. I did all kinds of work, like chopping cotton, stripping tobacco, digging potatoes and later on I was taught to drive a team of tough mules."[21]

If his father introduced Joans to Timbuktu and African history, his tutelage also intersected with the kinds of work often relegated to Black laborers post-Reconstruction, placing Joans in a quintessential African American story: demonstrating aptitude in intellectual and creative endeavors but being stuck in the drudgery of manual labor, what he called "unskilled jive because that is all that they offer to young Afros."[22] In this way, in and out of school, Joans was learning what it meant to be Black in America.

Another formative educational moment came at the age of 5, when Joans's father gifted him "an old cornet he had found in a junkshop." He had scored the instrument at a discount because the valves were "petrified," as it had been "hanging on the wall since the Civil War came through Memphis."[23] This was hardly a horn to swing on, but that didn't stop Joans from trying his hand at "St. Louis Blues" the minute he got it. The gift led to Joans's very first participation in a band—and a lesson about self-presentation and racialized power dynamics.

Armed with his barely-functioning cornet, Joans was drafted into what he dryly called a "pickaninny band," the very premise of which was steeped in racist assumptions, that Black people, even small children, are natural performers, and this band's whole reason for being was to "entertain some whitefolks at a garden party." The children were coached by an officious deacon at Zella's church who rehearsed them over and over, threatening to "whip the living shit out of our black asses" if they embarrassed him in front of the white folk.

When at last the day of the garden party came, Joans's mother dressed him up in a starched white sailor suit with a stiff collar "like a razorblade," and the band was driven over to one of the toniest neighborhoods in Memphis (the Joneses had briefly moved there after Theodore Sr. quit the riverboat line). The lawn was thronged with a hundred white people, and Joans was amazed to see other Black musicians performing "Negro spirituals" and the like.

While Joans's band was waiting to go on, he witnessed an incident that would stay with him forever: a white man mocked and dressed down the deacon for trying to eat a watermelon that had been set aside for the kids. Little Teddy was both fascinated and mortified to see the deacon's "whole personality change" as he bowed and scraped before the white man of no consequence. "It was the very first time," Joans recalled, "I had ever seen a Black man Tom … I had never seen a Black man, especially a so-called 'dignified deacon' go down so low before a white man. It was my very first lesson of what really happens to avoid letting the shit hit the fan."[24]

In this realization that a white person may not see a Black person as he sees himself—in this case as a "dignified deacon"—forcing him to adjust his behavior or demeanor to conform to these white expectations, Joans joins a long line of Black authors recognizing what W. E. B. Du Bois called "double consciousness," a "sense of always looking at one's self through the eyes of others, of measuring one's soul by the tape of a world that looks on in amused contempt and pity."[25] Reckoning with this experience is pivotal to classic works of Black literature, from Ralph Ellison's *Invisible Man* (1952) to *The Autobiography of Malcolm X* (1965), and Joans insists that even as this moment revealed the phenomenon to him, he resolved then and there never to degrade himself: "I am very happy that I have never done a Tom bit for no man, be he white or black."[26]

Other glimpses Joans offered of his childhood are similarly freighted. Despite his love of reading, writing, and arithmetic, his early educational experience was segregated, and his elementary school was what he described as a one-room "shack" with rows for different grades. "I found out later," he wrote, "that the big brick school was for the whites and the old wooden one room shack for coloreds."[27] This was another lesson in atmospheric racism, and he resented the whole "system of segregation," indignant that it "blocked my full development."[28]

There was, though, a bright spot of sharing one room with kids in higher grades: Joans got to overhear what the teacher was saying to older students. In this way, he was in just the fifth grade when he caught his teacher reading from Langston Hughes's poetry collection *The Weary Blues* (1926), a transformative experience that would cause him to swell with his "first sense of racial pride and hopefulness."[29] Joans would later meet Hughes in New York City, and the elder poet would become a mentor and a friend, a model for writing a certain type of Black poetry. After hearing *The Weary Blues* for the first time, young Joans was inspired to try his hand at poetry, composing his own "Langston Hughes like poems." With these poems, he voiced the racial consciousness that had stirred unnamed when he had seen the deacon bow and scrape for the white man: "I wrote about how I couldn't go into the public libraries in the state of Kentucky. I wrote too about that one room shack school and overcrowding of students."[30]

The other great discovery—or recognition—of his youth was Surrealism. Like the racial consciousness that lay unarticulated within him until activated by Hughes, as far as Joans was concerned, a fundamentally Surreal point of view was a "natural" feature of Black culture: "The poetic spirit of the blues was my first taste of the Marvelous. The surreality of some of the blues lyrics haunted me healthily and aided in liberation of my inquisitive pre-teen imagination."[31] Why the blues? Joans alludes here to Paul Garon's *Blues and the Poetic Spirit* (1975; revised 1996), which offers a full answer:

> it is through poetry that revolt most enticingly penetrates the barrier of the prevailing morality; it is along this same sinuous path that the blues has developed as one of America's most stirring manifestations of poetic thought. To stem the tide of this revolt ... is to ignore the human capacity for fantasy ... Fantasy alone enables us to envision the real possibilities of human existence, no longer tied securely to the historical effluvia passed off as everyday life; fantasy remains our most pre-emptive critical faculty, for it alone tells us what *can be.* Here lies the revolutionary nature of the blues: through its fidelity to fantasy and desire, the blues generates an irreducible and, so to speak, *habit-forming* demand for freedom and what Rimbaud called "true life."[32]

We'll circle back to the ways a Surrealist "poetic spirit" is infused in the blues later in this book, but for now we can just note that Joans found in the blues a "naturally Black" Surrealist perspective, as he did in that saying of his grandfather's, "Well, shut my mouth wide open." These versions of "surreality," revolt, fantasy and desire, and a kind of truth that cannot really be otherwise represented, Joans sees as constitutive of everyday Black culture and therefore of his own early lived experience.

Beyond this sort of folk "surreality," Joans traced his connection to the more formal, European Surrealist movement to his favorite aunt, Temple, who worked as a domestic for a rich white family, and would rescue books and magazines from the trash and bring them to her inquisitive nephew. In addition to the maps of Africa Joans studied with his father, his aunt Temple also gave him magazines containing Surrealist paintings, and he "fell madly in love" with their "unusual imagery."[33] Another of the "Wasp-throw-aways" was David Gascoyne's book *A Short Survey of Surrealism* (1935), which became an early introduction to the movement's key players. "The most vital feature of surrealism," Gascoyne wrote, "is its exclusive interest in that point at which literature and art give place to real life, that point at which the imagination seeks to express itself in a more concrete form than words or plastic images."[34]

Although Joans felt alone in his youthful interest in Surrealism, still he continued to read Langston Hughes, whom the local Black community did appreciate, and when Hughes's poems would appear in the newspapers, Joans would cut them out and paste them by Surrealist clippings in his scrapbooks. "I embraced surrealism and the poetry of Langston Hughes wholeheartedly. These were 'ladders,' explosives, and a direct truth to help me get out of the filthy pit of enslavement in America."[35] While he couldn't precisely articulate it to himself at the time, young Joans was drawn to both Hughes and Surrealism for their revolutionary potential, for the way they opened up his small-town world and started to give him permission to see this world through new points of view.

3

The Mystery of
Theodore Jones, Sr.

While Joans was close with his mother—he was known as a "momma's boy" around Louisville—the hardest lesson of his childhood came via his father, and his eventual absence in Joans's life.[1] At some point in his very early childhood, Joans tells us, his father moved the family to Chicago, "where there was more money to be had and better schools for me."[2] While Theodore Sr. seemed to thrive in the big city, Zella hated it, and in Joans's telling, they would often argue because it was "a dirty drag to live in such a crowded, unfriendly and cold (too cold) world." Inevitably, Joans writes, "after a few years of unhappy slum living, cold weather and quarrels, my mom and dad did the great U.S. BIT … D I V O R C E ! !"[3] When his parents divorced, he says, "at the tender age of six … I was shuffled back 'n' forth between my mother, father, and grandmother via Greyhound bus and the howling (and rhythmical rattling) railways."[4] After this period of "back 'n' forth" movement that prefigured his later life of global circulation, Joans seems to have lost regular contact with his father, settling in Fort Wayne and Louisville with his mother and sister.

And then the second momentous event of Joans's early poem-life occurred: his father was killed during the infamous "race riot" in Detroit in 1943. Joans alluded to and described this event many times throughout his life, as in the passage from "Je Me Vois" quoted earlier, when he mentions "the yesteryears Detroit riot in which Theodore Jones The First was mob murdered."[5] Other times he specified there were "twentytwo 'workers' that lynched my father."[6] And at still others he reported soberly that "my father was mob murdered in Detroit during a so-called 'race riot.' I was fourteen years old living in Fort Wayne, Indiana with my mother. He was a factory worker returning from his job."[7]

Joans's most granular description of his father's death came in his autobiography "Spadework," in which he transports the reader to Detroit on Monday, June 21, 1943, describing his father "on the tram car [as] he rode on his way from his lathe repairman job, at a Ford factory":

> My father, on the Woodward street car saw the mob rush up from out of a tavern, then board the street car and with destructive hands drag the driver from the street car. Then [they] beat and kick[ed] him, then reboarded the street car and asked if there were anymore niggers on board. My dad stood up and said 'Yeah, Peckerwood-red-neck-bastard, I'm an American Negro!' The crazy mob was so shocked at my dad's announcement that they were silent for a few minutes. Then one of them, a young cracker, with a twenty caliber rifle ... fired point blank at my dad. His first bullet hit his stomach. My dad reached into his bib-overall backpocket and took out a small monkey wrench, then came toward the mob at the front of the car. Some of them ran outside but the young (now frightened) rifleboy fired again. This time dad was hit in the chest and fell to his knees. Rabbi D. Goldstein who witnessed the entire scene said that my father prayed to the Lord to give him just a little more strength to get close to the mob ... My father regained his strength. So with a bloody clenched fist and death in his eyes he lunged forward toward the youth with the rifle. The frightened boy tried to run, but the mob was so thick that he couldn't. By this time my dad was on him. He swung the monkey wrench with all his might, down upon the head of the rifleboy. He did it again and again. [Another member of the mob, Sam Johnson, a "big burly bare chested worker"] finally made it through the crowd. Then he shot my dad in the back five times and my dead dad fell over the body of the rifleboy. In his death throes he turned and gave a bloody grin to the mob.[8]

Later in this account, Joans explains that the witness, D. Goldstein, went straight to the "newspaper office, where he told the complete story of the murder to a reporter friend of his. The next morning the story sensationally made headlines in all the papers." Sam Johnson and the boy with the rifle both stood trial, but "never spent one hour in jail" because, the judge determined, they were decent "church-going white citizens" who had been merely caught up in an "awful outburst of mob violence."

The cinematic sweep here of course includes details that seem unlikely for Joans to have known—but then again, he names a particular witness, who then told the "complete story" directly to a newspaper reporter. It is therefore possible that Joans could have mined these facts from newspaper articles about his father's death, even as he has obviously framed such facts so that his father emerges as a heroic, noble figure who never lost his dignity even in the face of imminent death—as, in short, the opposite of the deacon who so shamefully crumbled before the white man in Memphis ten years prior.

When I first read this most intricate account in "Spadework," I couldn't help but wonder if the newspaper stories Joans mentions were the very same "newspaper articles from the yesteryears Detroit riot" lost in the Niger River along with his original birth certificate. The Detroit "race riots" are well documented, much covered in the press, subject to several state-sponsored studies in 1943 and 1944, and then later explored in professional histories.[9] Given the substantive available archive, I thought, the newspaper articles Joans mentions were recoverable, and I dove into contemporaneous accounts reporting what was happening almost in real time, sifted through national coverage, including an extensive photo spread in *Life* magazine, and studied minutely-researched histories such as *Layered Violence: The Detroit Rioters of 1943* (1991), by Dominic J. Capeci, Jr. and Martha Wilkerson. These documents afford anyone with an interest a much better sense of both the long-simmering racial tensions in Detroit that boiled over that summer, and of the backstories and circumstances of some principal actors in the violence to come.

But whenever I tried to find any reference to Theodore Jones in connection to the "Detroit riot," I was met with little success. After exhausting sources I could find in print, and puzzled at my inability to unearth the "sensational" newspaper stories Joans mentions, I spoke with Dominic Capeci, co-author of *Layered Violence,* an authoritative history of the events. Although Joans's father was not discussed in the book, I wondered if perhaps Capeci had seen references to him in the course of his research. Certainly the story Joans recounted about his father was plausible, Capeci thought, but after searching through his files, he could find no written record of it happening.

Theodore Jones's murder seemed to have slipped through historical cracks, and I was further perplexed when Joans's second eldest daughter, Yvette Johnson, told me that she had never heard about her grandfather's death from family members. She had grown up in Louisville, where her mother, Joans's first wife, Joan Locke, had been close with Joans's mother, Zella. But no one had ever mentioned to Yvette the story of her grandfather's death. She had seen references to Theodore Jones, Sr. being killed in Detroit—but only in things her father had written. It did not seem part of family history, as none of Yvette's numerous cousins (Joans's sister's children) had heard the story either.[10]

And yet as I continued to work on this book, I kept finding Joans, at various points in his life, insisting on his father's murder, and so guided as I was by an idea of history as "faithful to the limits of fact, evidence, and archive," my failure to recover archival evidence of Theodore Sr.'s murder continued to gnaw.[11] The archive was yielding very little, but it did turn up a death certificate for a Black male "John Doe," who died in Detroit on June 23, 1943, from a "cerebral hemorrhage following a fractured skull."

"The archive is," Saidiya Hartman writes, "in this case, a death sentence, a tomb, a display of the violated body." I speculated that perhaps this "official record" might be displaying the violated body of Joans's father without naming him, compounding historical violence both because he was invisible in the archive—there but not there—and because he was never afforded legal justice—or, as Joans puts it, was never "avenged."[12]

I posed this possibility to another historian of the Detroit riots, Thomas Klug, who reportedly had compiled detailed lists of those involved, including the fatalities. Perhaps, I thought, he had further information about this John Doe that might help me link him to Joans's father. Klug was indeed familiar with that record, but was quickly skeptical it was Joans's father: if, as Joans described, the killing had occurred on Woodward Avenue, an epicenter of the violence, it would have been headline news—but Klug confirmed my own research that there was not a single mention in any local paper of the scenario detailed in "Spadework."[13]

These papers do, however, recount events *like* the one in "Spadework." *The Chicago Bee* reported of the riot that "colored passengers were pulled off street cars," and the *Michigan Chronicle* that James Turner, "a motorman on the Woodward line, was dragged from his car at Eliot and Woodward by a mob of whites and severely beaten."[14] Such horrific scenes were in fact widely reported, and the July 5, 1943 issue of *Life* magazine featured a nine-page spread packed with unflinching, nearly pornographic photographs of the violence. These photographs display, for instance, a young Black man making "a dash across Woodward Avenue, Detroit, with a mob of whites in pursuit"; and another a "struggling" man being "hauled from a streetcar near downtown Detroit by four white men."[15]

On the one hand, as the first draft of history, such journalism confirms that people did experience circumstances very much like the one presented in "Spadework." But still, a tingle crept up the back of my neck as it dawned on me that such accounts could have served as source material for Joans, who may have been sketching in details of an event that he could not have known much about directly. The matching particulars in *Life* magazine seemed especially striking given what I knew of Joans's collage habits—that, for instance, he liked to play with this magazine, as when he created a collage of himself on the October 11, 1954 cover, with the headline "Conquest of Life Cannot Be Beat" (Figure 3.1).

And yet, even as I was unable to find "proof" of Joans's father's murder, I hardened in my view that the murder was compounded by the stunning failure of the criminal justice system, and by the profound omissions in the archive. Given the multiple tragedies sedimented in his father's death, I thought, Joans's efforts to name it, to reconstruct it in "Spadework" and elsewhere via his own kind of "critical fabulation," amounted to a correction of the historical record, and an intervention in "the archive" and its limits. In this spirit, I wanted to substantiate Joans's stories, to bring his father's death into the light to the extent possible, and coming up short in my own research, I tried a different tack. Still guided by—or stuck on, Joans might

FIGURE 3.1 *A collaged cover of* Life *magazine, in which Joans has become the cover story (ca. 1954). Laurated Archive.*

say—the general methods and assumptions of professional historiography, I engaged the services of a genealogist, Melissa Rzepczynski, to see if she had any new routes to corroborating Joans's story. Rzepczynski pursued her own lines of inquiry, and as immersed as I had been in Joans's own personal archive, I was surprised by what she ultimately found.

Like me, Rzepczynski was unable to locate any mention of Joans's father being killed in Detroit, but she did discover a document that seemed to upend Joans's account: Theodore Jones, Sr.'s obituary. According to this obituary, which ran in the *Fort Wayne Journal Gazette*, Joans's father died in Gary, Indiana in April, 1975. There is little doubt that this Theodore Jones was Joans's father, as it mentions a daughter, Joans's sister, Marie Price (who likely placed the obituary in her hometown paper), as well as a son, Theodore Jr., of "Timbuktu, Africa."

As with the clash between Joans's statements about his date of birth and his "original" birth certificate, here we are faced with a somewhat startling discrepancy between his own curated archive and a primary historical source. I have described my own experience trying to "confirm" Joans's account of

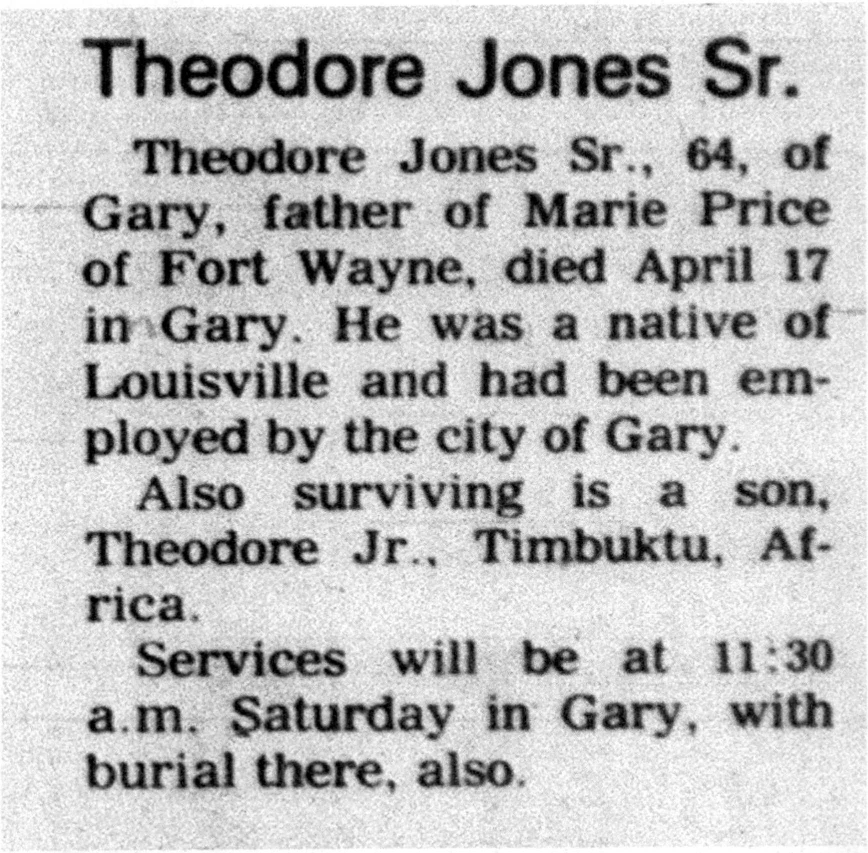

Theodore Jones Sr.

Theodore Jones Sr., 64, of Gary, father of Marie Price of Fort Wayne, died April 17 in Gary. He was a native of Louisville and had been employed by the city of Gary.

Also surviving is a son, Theodore Jr., Timbuktu, Africa.

Services will be at 11:30 a.m. Saturday in Gary, with burial there, also.

FIGURE 3.2 *Theodore Jones, Sr. Obituary.* Fort Wayne Journal Gazette *(April 24, 1975).*

his father's death because it may offer a small indication of what it has been like to sit with his accounts of his own life, to balance his adamant and detailed writings with what is, finally, locatable (or not) in the historical record. Creating such a tension or confusion between the imagined and the real is, for Joans, part of the point.

One disturbing dimension of this experience I hadn't anticipated was how a single document, this four-sentence clipping from a small-town newspaper, apparently negates the references Joans made to his father's death over many years, the detailed description of it in "Spadework," and those brief occasional writings scattered throughout his life, like this one, from the author bio on *Afrodisia*'s back cover: "he survived a precarious childhood (his father was pulled off a streetcar and killed by white workers in 1943 during the Detroit race riots)."

What did Hartman write? "History pledges to be faithful to the limits of fact, evidence, and archive, even as those dead certainties are produced by terror."[16] If "history" is produced in this way, a brief notice in the *Fort Wayne Journal Gazette* represents the power and authority of the archive, thereby obliterating Joans's poetic truth just in virtue of its existence. Is that, Joans asks, a kind of violence?

———

So "getting the facts straight is difficult for friendly biographers."
So Theodore Jones, Sr. was not, in fact, killed by white workers in Detroit in 1943.
But Theodore Jones, Sr. was, nevertheless, largely absent from Joans's childhood.

So in the symbolic economy of Joans's poem-life, his father was killed by white workers in Detroit in 1943, a dishearteningly American end of spectacular proportions that offers another kind of origin myth: the father whose terrible loss must be "avenged." Joans's poem, "Dead Serious," opens:

One day my dad
talked back to a white
a mob caught him
before he was out of sight
and I asked
mama if those sheet wearers
had come into town.[17]

The "mob" in this case is not in Detroit, but in an unnamed Southern town, and the details and imagery are more evocative of an all-too-familiar scene of white terror: "I remembered watching / them tying him to a tree," and then burning his father's body. The poem goes on to imagine an elaborate revenge scenario, as the speaker methodically gathers intelligence on all the "old sheet wearers of my town" (86), works out "a plan on paper," and then guns them all down with a sniper rifle, just before a white mob comes for him, too: "They came, two hundred strong, and with a / tank, they were no fools / I got at least thirty, before the tank's cannon got me / but I died happy ... cause now my dad had been avenged, by his son" (87). The story of a father who abandoned or drifted apart from his family is more difficult to frame in such epic terms, is perhaps paradoxically more painful to articulate and accept than a defiant, heroic death at the hands of ignorant hick fascists as in "Spadework," or a story about a Klan lynching being "avenged" by the son. I haven't seen Joans writing about his father's absence directly, except when he describes it, poetically, as a mob murder. This is telling in and of itself, and perhaps sheds light on why he subsequently crowned his literary mentors, Langston Hughes and André Breton, his "February Fathers" (fathers who, he says in another poem, never "met my mother").[18]

Certainly explaining his father's absence via Detroit in 1943 imbues it with a profound sense of historical—rather than only personal—tragedy, makes him an emblem of white supremacist violence that characterizes so much of the Black American experience. Like a birthday on July 4, the death of Theodore Jones, Sr. during "race riots" fuses the personal and the political, the private and the public, into a mythic tale replete with symbolism and appalling truths about endemic American racism, an encapsulation of Joans's "precarious childhood" and resonating with differing senses of that adjective, which means, the Oxford English Dictionary tells us, both "exposed to risk, hazardous, insecure, unstable" and "insecurely founded or reasoned, doubtful, dubious."

4

Famous in Louisville

The remainder of Joans's "precarious childhood" is similarly difficult to untangle or "verify." After shuffling "back 'n' forth between my mother, father, and grandmother via Greyhound bus and the howling (and rhythmical rattling) railways," Joans settled with his mother and sister in Fort Wayne and Louisville, where he most likely attended the Madison Street Colored Junior High School in the Russell neighborhood, and then later Central High School.[1] Madison had been built to merge two other schools for Black children in segregated Kentucky, and was later closed and turned into apartment buildings.[2] Ray Johnson, a jazz pianist whom Joans called "my protégé," had attended Madison and Central High at the time, and recalled playing in bands around town with Joans.[3]

As we know from the story about the garden party, Joans had been involved in music from a very young age, and was in a number of bands throughout his later teenage years in Louisville. In 1946, on that draft card mentioned earlier, he stated that he was living at 710 Magazine Street, and listed his occupation as a member of "Billy Rudolph's Orchestra"—a reference to a band called The Wild-Rooters. This was a bop band made up, as fellow member Sam Clark put it, of "teen age musicians": Joans, Clark, Andy Sack, Sonny Walker, and Zebe Sloan.[4] From 1945 to 1947, they played whatever gigs they could get around Louisville, from high school dances at the YMCA to night clubs to barbecue joints.

Although they eventually became a favorite band around town, there were a few bumps along the way when they were starting out. Back in 1945, just when bop was beginning to catch on, The Wild-Rooters played nightly at a Louisville venue called Kemp's Playhouse. The crowds loved the energy in the band's numbers, inspired by Charlie Parker and Dizzy Gillespie, but the more old-fashioned owner, Kemp, apparently didn't understand what all the fuss was about, and one night he reached his breaking point, and when the band was on intermission, he demanded they play "real music." But Joans insisted that they only knew bop, and finished out their set as planned. At the end of the night, he went to collect the band's money, and

Kemp was now apoplectic: "Do you guys expect to get paid for that Lapa Doo, Scootie Foo and Ooo Ya Coo?" he spat. Joans calmly reminded him that they had been contracted to provide music, they had done so, and now they expected to be paid. Kemp exploded, pulled a gun on Joans, and ran the band out of his club. That was their last gig there.[5]

Kemp's reaction to the Wild-Rooters' music suggests just how strange it could have seemed at the time, especially to the uninitiated. In his Wild-Rooters days—and then in another band he started around 1947, the Be-Boppers—Joans's trumpet playing was unabashedly inspired by trumpeter and bop innovator Dizzy Gillespie, on the forefront of this new music, and already revered in hip circles (but not, apparently, in whatever circles Kemp ran in). Because white America tended to associate bop with a kind of ineffable hipness, they also tended to miss its avant-garde complexity and conceptual density. At the time, Gillespie, like his collaborator Charlie Parker, was distinguishing himself by playing "extended improvisation in difficult keys," which had the effect, as Ben Sidran puts it, of separating "the serious musicians from the 'no talent guys.'"[6] For Kemp, the Rooters' music might have seemed nonsensical or unnecessarily baroque, but for Joans, it was the real-deal *because* it was so musically and intellectually dense, and so technically difficult. As the early jazz historian Marshall Stearns observed, this sort of technical difficulty and improvisational exuberance was connected also to a deliberate rejection of both commercialized swing music and white expectations of Black performers, which Gillespie and other bop musicians of the 1940s had "associated with 'Uncle Tomism.'"[7] Gillespie's style of bop rebuked both the white musical establishment and more commercialized forms of Black pop music, so it is unsurprising that young Joans would be drawn to his example.[8]

Joans was hardly alone in his devotion to Dizz, and in fact Gillespie's personal style and mannerisms became templates for a growing cohort of young hipsters in urban Black enclaves around the country. During his Wild-Rooters and Be-Boppers days, Joans self-consciously modeled not only his trumpet playing but also his personal style on Gillespie—as he said, "Dizzy had been my musical and mirth idol for many many decades ... when I blew trumpet wayback yonder in Kentucky and Indiana I attempted to imitate his approach to trumpet (I failed miserably) and even his physical appearance by growing a goatee, wearing a beret and I wore horn-rimmed glasses even though I only needed glasses for reading!"[9] Such "copycatism" was widespread enough that in 1946, *Downbeat* magazine worried that "the fad of copying Dizzy" could diminish real understanding of his innovative music, reducing him merely to an emblem of "the flauntingly unconventional, over-hip musician."[10] Whatever the risks, Joans was a true devotee, and several years later, in 1953, when he was taking extended vacations to New York City with an eye on moving there permanently, he learned that Gillespie was appearing at the Lyric Theater back in Louisville, and abruptly cut his trip short so he could fete him with an "elaborate dinner party."[11]

By 1948, the "fad" of imitating Gillespie's style was apparently newsworthy enough that even the non-music magazine *Ebony* reported on it.[12] In response to this story, 15-year-old Joan Locke of Louisville, Kentucky wrote a letter to *Ebony*'s editors proudly explaining that her boyfriend, "Ted 'Derbytown Dizz' Jones," was a dedicated "disciple of Dizz. He is the bop-cat of Louisville."[13] Joan included a photograph of her boyfriend for good measure, and *Ebony* ran it with her letter. Ted Jones—not yet Joans—was twenty years old, and this was the first time he would appear in a national magazine (see Figure 4.1 below).

Joans had met Joan Locke while playing a gig at Club La Conga in Louisville, probably sometime in 1948, and things developed quickly between them: by November 1949, she was pregnant. While Joans was twenty-one at the time, Joan was just sixteen. Her mother, who was deeply Christian and considered upper middle-class for that time in Black Louisville, was not happy when she discovered the pregnancy, and felt it would be best if the couple marry before the baby was born. The family began planning a big wedding in Louisville for March 1950. Ted and Joan Jones's first daughter, Sylvia, was born that July.[14]

The newly-married couple secured an apartment in Beecher Terrace, in Louisville's West End. Named for Henry Ward Beecher, brother of *Uncle Tom's Cabin* author Harriet Beecher Stowe, Beecher Terrace was a public housing complex for Black residents of the segregated city. In the 1940s, Beecher Terrace was a sought-after place to live for Louisville's Black

FIGURE 4.1 *Twenty-year-old Ted "Derbytown Dizz" Jones, sporting a Dizzy Gillespie outfit, pictured in* Ebony *(February 1949).*

FIGURE 4.2 *The big wedding of Ted Jones and Joan Locke (right), Louisville, Kentucky (March 1950).*

citizens—the community there was close-knit and vibrant, and the recently-built homes featured amenities unavailable in most poor and working-class residences across the city. This included bathrooms (at the time, many low-cost homes in and around Louisville still used outhouses), central heating, and refrigerators. Significantly for Joans, Beecher Terrace also boasted recreational spaces that became hubs of social activity, and he often played gigs there, raising his profile in the community. The complex fronted Walnut Street, the Black business district of Louisville, a lively, thriving neighborhood that some called the "Harlem of the South."[15]

During these years, Joans was becoming more and more well known around Louisville—between 1951 and 1953, when he decamped permanently for New York City, he appeared in the pages of Louisville's Black daily, the *Defender*, no fewer than 35 times. Often this coverage was in the context of Brazzle Tobin's "Scouting Derbytown," a column focusing on the Louisville music scene. Reading through the *Defender's* rather extensive coverage of Joans in those years is to see various aspects of his legend already forming, and one can discern a kind of transformative arc, from "Ted Jones" as a local bop trumpeter to a respectable theater manager to a Surrealist painter—and then to a *bohemian*-Surrealist painter—and then, finally, to "Ted Joans," the ex-Louisvillian bohemian Surrealist painter who pulled up stakes for New York City, and was, as Tobin wrote, "compiling in New York what he could not obtain here in Louisville … a pagan empire."[16]

This coverage is remarkable for how self-consciously it can acknowledge the many stories that were already swirling around the 23-year-old still known as Ted Jones. In one column from the fall of 1951, for example, Tobin writes:

> Many a story has been told of how (former trumpeter) Ted Jones overnight gave up his music to become an employee of the Palace Theatre. Some say that he pawned his horn and couldn't raise the money to redeem it, others insist that he gave up in despair because he didn't have the ability. While recently discussing the advantages, disadvantages of trying to please the public with Ted at the "Top Hat" I asked him why and how he really made his exit from the music business.
>
> Here is his story. Ted had grown tired of the constant rigorous routine of playing eight hours nitely and rehearsing four hours daily and was in search of another medium of livelihood. In the meantime he was engaged to Joan Locke. He knew that as long as he had his trumpet around the house that he might be tempted to accept jobs later. This led him to take his horn to the foot of Fourth and River and toss it into the Ohio. His last playing job was with the Louis Dabney band at the "Casino Club" in '49.[17]

Even at this early point in his life, familiar themes emerge: stories whir around Joans containing high drama, uncertainty and intrigue, the makings of a legend—but there is also, on Tobin's part, a desire to bring these stories under control, to cut through to what "really" happened. Reading this particular story I thought again of Janet Malcolm's wry reflection on "archival material," her observation that "newspaper stories that were originally written ... to excite and divert and be forgotten the next week— now take their place among serious sources of information and fact, and are treated as if they themselves were not simply raising the question of what happened and who is good and who is bad."[18] In the way the tale of the trumpet is framed, Tobin seems to allegorize the tension Malcolm names, noting those rumors whirring around Joans—"some say" this, "others insist" that—and wanting to get the straight dope, but then ultimately delivering what may or may not be definitely true: "Here is his story."

The "story" of tossing the horn into the river became a well-worn piece of Joans's legend, and by the next year it was already surfacing in another *Defender* article as a symbol of how he had transformed—not from musician to theater manager, as in Tobin's column, but from musician to Surrealist painter. "When Ted Jones, a former musician decided to become a surrealist painter, he tossed his horn in the river so he would be able to keep his mind on his brushes. By 'drowning' his trumpet, Ted said he was able to collect a bet from a couple of musician friends, who told him he would not get music out of his system."[19]

The image of "drowning" the trumpet remains, but its meaning has shifted from a symbol of Joans's familial commitment to a symbol of his artistic commitment—this is the version he would refine in "Spadework," where the scene has moved from Louisville to Bloomington, and he tosses his trumpet into the river not because his engagement to Joan Locke necessitates a steadier income, but because "Joan"—here called "Joan Lochstein"—has broken it off, and he is devastated:

> I'd never play again. I'd never touch a horn, in fact I told them [his friends] I was gonna throw my trumpet in the river … In the center of the bridge, I took the horn halfway out the leather case and kissed it. I said goodbye to it, took the mouthpiece out of the side pocket, then zipped up the bag. Then said "Well fellows here goes my musical career and now I have only my paintings to love." Then I … tossed it into the river. It made a loud splash.[20]

In all versions of the story, as Brazzle Tobin intuited, what's most important is that it's a *story*, a dramatic, and dramatically symbolic, break from a former self, a metaphor for an unrecoverable past, the trumpet lost in some river just as those official documents of his childhood would later be lost in the Niger.

His horn safely resting at the bottom of one river or another, Joans settled into the role of theater manager, husband, father, and breadwinner—and hub of Louisville's music scene. There were numerous theaters along Walnut Street, including the National, the Palace, and the Lyric. Once Joans sought steady work in earnest, he took a variety of jobs at these places, serving as what he called a "backstage flunkey" at the National, and then working his way up the ladder. In time, he became assistant manager of the National and manager of the Palace.[21] Aside from the money, theater work appealed to him because the stages of the Walnut Street theaters hosted, in his words, "giants of modern Black music blowing daily."[22] His jobs there gave him access to these musicians, and as a young man he got to know an incredible array of musical "giants," from Dexter Gordon, Art Blakey, Gene Ammons, Maurice "Shorty" McConnell, Billy Eckstine (who had a very young Miles Davis in his orchestra), Fats Navarro, Gerald Valentine—and yes, even Dizzy Gillespie himself. "What an education," Joans exclaimed.[23]

Joans's interest in and knowledge of "modern Black music" put him in good stead with the performers who came through Walnut Street, and the apartment in Beecher Terrace became a favorite post-gig destination. Joan took her homemaking duties seriously, and when her husband would come back from work with gaggles of musicians in tow, she would have spreads of food and cold drinks waiting for them. These gatherings became so frequent that Joans once suggested moving the refrigerator into the living room for easier access—an odd request, thought Joan, since they had a beautiful kitchen where the refrigerator obviously belonged. Never one for the obvious or typical, Joans really felt the refrigerator ought to be

FIGURE 4.3 *Ted Joans clasping hands with Dizzy Gillespie, probably 1953. Laurated Archive.*

moved, and, remarkably, Joan recalled this difference of opinion as their only major disagreement.[24] The couple fell into domestic routines, with Joans using envelopes to sort their money to be allocated to rent, utilities, groceries, and the like. Despite his artistic sensibilities, he was in those years a conscientious provider—and even once gave Joan 100 brand-new dollar bills as an anniversary present.[25] In September 1952, they had another daughter, Yvette.

In time, the apartment in Beecher Terrace would also host strange, unconventional parties that prefigured the increasingly sophisticated events Joans would stage in New York City and beyond. In March 1951, the couple held a "Surrealist party," and Joans's twenty-third birthday party that July merited a brief mention in Tobin's "Scouting Derbytown" column for the weird fact that "at Palace Theatre employee Ted Jones' recent birthday party, a pie with candles was used instead of the usual cake."[26]

By the next year, Joans's birthday party had moved far beyond substituting pies for cakes to feature hints of those later, Greenwich Village party-events.

Georgetta Chambers, who wrote a society column for the *Defender* about the "younger generation," reported on the party with some wonder:

> We were fortunate enough to get a bid to one of TED JONES' fabulous parties last Friday night ... Must admit it was different from any party we've attended previously. TED delighted the guests by reading four of his surrealist poems and explaining his works of art which were on display. His decorations were most unique. Names of people who have influenced his life were extended from the ceiling on ribbons hung in diagonal angles giving a modern art effect.
>
> Everyone sat on the floor to partake of the luscious hors d'oeuvres and loaves of French bread, both black and white, which we broke off in immense chunks.
>
> The event which was TED'S birthday turned hilarious when our artist-host brought out three birthday cakes, which were provided because he feels that often guests are slighted with a 'measley [*sic*] paper-thin slice.'"[27]

No longer known primarily as a "Palace Theatre employee," Joans is now a local Surrealist artist and poet, and the legend grows: his parties are "fabulous," "most unique," "different from any party we've attended previously" (and, at other times in the *Defender*, Joans himself was referred to as "the fabulous Ted Jones").[28] As would be the case in his more well-known and much more elaborate events in Greenwich Village, his twenty-fourth birthday party was also a performance and advertisement for Joans's creative endeavors—even the "black and white" loaves of French bread foreshadow the way he would pointedly play with black and white imagery in his subsequent New York events, an integrationist statement for a mixed-race crowd that would draw the attention of the national press.

As suggested by the reference to Joans's "works of art" on display, concurrent with his throwing of increasingly elaborate Surrealist parties, he was also turning with more dedication to Surrealist painting. While managing the Palace, he would come home round about midnight and paint in the kitchen while pregnant Joan and tiny Sylvia slept in the next room—he worked "simply for art sake," but did have an "ambition" to make his paintings pay.[29] He labored on this painting assiduously, and exhibited his work around Louisville. In June 1951, one "Surrealist Art Exhibit" at the Western Branch Library, where Joans showed his paintings along with fellow musicians Billy Rudolph, Kenny Owens and others, drew "throngs of spectators."[30] Although it seems only a few of these spectators actually purchased his work—he characterized income from his art at the time as "negligible"—he continued to show new pieces, and by the summer of 1952 was on his eighth exhibit at the Western Branch, and had produced over 150 pieces.[31]

Among these artworks was a series he named "Scouting Derbytown" in tribute to Brazzle Tobin's *Defender* column, which consisted, as Tobin reported, of "Surrealist art portraits of local notables."[32] Joans did portraits of such "local notables" as WGRC disc jockey William "Tobe" Howard, former manager of the Wild-Rooters and by then a prominent DJ whose "soul sound" program was a fixture in the homes in Joans's neighborhood, as well as of the Louisville jazz pianist and bandleader Lionel Hampton.[33] He also did "surrealist and abstract studies" of Frances Parrish, wife of University of Louisville sociology professor Charles Parrish, a woman whom Joans was apparently "hung up on" for a time—he would also immortalize (and Surrealize) her in his later poem "The Enigma of Frances Parrish of Paris France."[34] He painted portraits of Salvador Dalí, Abraham Lincoln, and the Mona Lisa. (Unfortunately, Joans's Surrealist paintings from the Louisville years have been lost—or, if any are still extant, they must be in private collections, and as of this writing I have not seen them.)

Despite his notoriety, Joans's work was not necessarily accessible to the average Louisvillian. "To ordinary viewers," remarked one observer, Joans's Lincoln portrait "looks like a wash room scene," so distorted that "the revered Emancipator would not know himself."[35] For Joans, the confusion of Lincoln's portrait with a "wash room scene" was precisely the point, for he had intended the piece to represent Lincoln "shitting," a critique of his image as the "revered Emancipator."[36] As he said later, Lincoln "didn't declare war on the south (his birth place) to abolish slavery but he declared war to keep the union togather [sic]. His position was the same as Dwight Ike's in the Little Rock rumble with Orval Faubus" (when, in September 1957, Arkansas governor Orval Faubus had prevented nine Black students from integrating Little Rock Central High School as was federally mandated, President Dwight Eisenhower federalized the National Guard to force the issue, but Joans felt this act was more politically expedient than morally expansive).[37] Likewise Joans's take on the Mona Lisa, what he described as "a Mona Lisa with her face upside down," baffled the regulars at Dave's Bar at 13th and Magazine Streets, where it was included among a long-term, ever-rotating exhibit of his work. Those regulars would look up at a painting like his Mona Lisa, Joans said gleefully, "and think they're drunk."[38]

Although Joans's work could be bewildering for some viewers, the art world was beginning to take notice, and for his efforts he was being consistently lauded in the *Defender* as a "fabulous" hometown artist. By mid-1952, he was becoming known even beyond Louisville, as he was profiled by *Glare* magazine. The author of the feature, Kay Flemming, was suitably impressed by Joans's energy and abilities, crowning him "Louisville's Salvador Dali." His paintings, she assured her readers, were "undoubtedly the works of genius."[39] "Art is like a religion," Joans told Flemming, "inspiring, exalting, undying and always capturing the heart of its creator." Despite still holding down his job as a theater manager and tirelessly networking on the Black music scene, Joans had also become, at least in Flemming's eyes, "the most promising painter of surrealism in Louisville."[40]

EXPONENT OF MODERN ART, Ted Jones, holds one of his pic-
tures at the exhibit of Louisville amateur artists at Western branch
Library, 10th and Chestnut sts.—Defender photo.

FIGURE 4.4 *Twenty-two-year-old "Ted Jones" with his Surrealist portrait of
Salvador Dalí; in 1954, he would present this portrait to Dalí himself in New York
City. From* Louisville Defender *(June 9, 1951), 3.*

His growing interest in and dedication to painting went hand in hand
with his desire to visit New York City, which he rightly viewed as home to
the best and brightest of American and expatriate artists. In 1951, when
he had saved the funds to do so, he began taking two-week expeditions to
New York City, where he first explored Harlem and then Greenwich Village.
He was drawn of course to the creative energy of the big city—on his first
trip there, he met Jackson Pollock at a bar—and decided that in order to
really thrive creatively, he needed to live in New York, and did move there
permanently in the fall of 1953. It was thanks in no small part to his trips
out to Greenwich Village that Joans came to be seen around Louisville as a
"local surrealist artist" who was bringing a bit of bohemian New York back
home. A few months before his "fabulous" twenty-fourth birthday party,
for instance, he threw another bash that, at least as far as the *Defender* was
concerned, had "all the aspects of New York's famed Greenwich Village."[41]
The paper dedicated an entire story to this party, reporting that "people in all

of the arts attend and during the evening entertain with their own particular specialty whether it is reciting an original poem or ballet dancing." Again, what would come to be classic themes of Joans's poem-life emerged: "One of the highlights of the evening is Mr. Jones' unforgettable 'Trip Around the World,' when foods or beverages of various countries are served. At each point on the imaginary globe, famous people who have made notable contributions in the field of art are mentioned."[42]

As he began to plot his departure from Louisville, Joans would even leverage his Surreal bohemian parties to finance his trips out to New York. In May 1952, he threw a "pre-vacation" party where friends and well-wishers showered him "with everything-needed-for-a-trip."[43] Coverage in Georgetta Chambers's society column helped raise the profile of Joans and his parties, so it was little wonder that a month later, while on that New York excursion partly financed by party-goers, Joans dutifully reported back to her that Greenwich Village certainly was "the place for him."[44] Further aspects of the legend were brewing: Joans was simply too big a personality, too big

TED JONES, local theatre manager, more widely known for his Surrealistic art, is shown beside the "Lady," a recent painting. Jones will leave in the near future for New York, where he and his wife will make their home.

FIGURE 4.5 *Joans with his painting, "Lady," a couple of months before his move to Greenwich Village, August, 1953. Note the bohemian artist's get-up. From* Louisville Defender *(August 13, 1953), 8.*

a talent to be contained by Louisville, and by August 1953, a momentous move, seemingly inevitable, was on the horizon: "After throwing another in the series of his wild parties Palace Theatre manager Ted Jones made all the preparations for his trip to N.Y. where he expects to set up permanent residence."[45]

———

These were also the years when Joans was supposed to have been in college at Indiana University at Bloomington. As he put it on one résumé: "1946–1951, Indiana University at Jeffersonville, Indiana and Bloomington, Indiana. B.A. Fine Art. Emphasis on European art history, the history of modern arts, and avant-garde painting."[46] Another résumé smoothed these facts out into a story: "Immersed in music, painting and poetry during his formative years, thus a firm foundation was laid for his later pursuits, leading to a Bachelors Degree in Fine Arts from Indiana University in 1951."[47] On virtually every thumbnail biography of Joans, there is a variation on: "studied Fine Arts at Indiana University" (*Black Manifesto*) or "received a B.A. in Fine Arts from Indiana University in 1951" (*Black Pow-Wow*) or earned a "B.A. in Fine Arts from Indiana University" (*Our Thang*). Such statements were hardened into archival truth in the *Dictionary of Literary Biography*: "Joans remained settled long enough to receive a Bachelor of Fine Arts degree from Indiana University in 1951."[48]

At the time, this aspect of the Joans legend wasn't quite crystalized: one profile, from the summer of 1952, noted in the same breath that while "Ted went to Indiana university," he "has never had any formal art training. He is a student of art, however—reading all the books he can get his hands on and often sitting in on lectures at the University of Louisville."[49] A connection to the University of Louisville turns up in an earlier newspaper story, which paraphrases Joans as saying he had been "a student at the Art Center School"—a reference to the University of Louisville Art Center, which is now their School of Art.[50] In a biographical note in *All of Ted Joans and No More*, he kept it vague: "I came to the Village scene after doing the school bit in Indiana, Kentucky, and Illinois" (94).

For its part, Indiana University Bloomington has no record of Joans having attended. As Dina Kellams, the Director of University Archives, put it to me after extensive searching into these archives: "you have official word from the IU Registrar that they have no record of him at IUB."[51] Given the additional mention of "Indiana University at Jeffersonville" on that résumé quoted above, Kellams and I wondered if there would have been classes available to Joans in Jeffersonville, which is just across the river from Louisville (Bloomington is about 100 miles away). Sure enough, from 1941 on IU did have an Extension Division, and in fact their first student was a Black woman from Louisville seeking educational opportunities outside the segregated city.[52] This was all promising, and Kellams was able to search records from the Extension Division between 1946 and 1953 since, as it turned out, actual class rosters are still retained. And yet she found no mention of Joans ever being officially enrolled there, either.[53]

Once again, the truth of Joans's poem-life runs into the "official word," and once again, Joans talks back to this word in the particular ways he framed his education in Bloomington. The opening scene of "I, Too, at the Beginning" (1986), Joans's unpublished, book-length memoir of his Greenwich Village years, describes his graduation day in Bloomington—but naturally in the story Joans has been "officially ejected" from the graduation ceremony itself:

> At Indiana U., observing from a window (whilst the others who were also officially ejected from the cap and gown graduation commencement, on the grounds of being "psychosexual nemesis" played tarot cards) I watched the indemnificational exercise ritual with dry eyes, as the classmates filed up to get a rolled piece of paper and a handshake. Our forfeiture for being the "seven scourge" at I.U. was this exclusion of confinement. We, the Dada Seven, didn't mind, because we were committed to being unaccommodating to all official demands and customs, after we had passed our exams.[54]

In this telling, Joans and a handful of friends were barred from the graduation "exercise" for some manner of unspecified shocking behavior, apparently sexual in nature. The resulting lack of evidence of having graduated, the "rolled piece of paper and a handshake," was of no matter, for Joans had the knowledge, had passed his exams with no time for "official demands and customs" (in "Spadework," Joans wrote that "just before graduation came ... I did something that I dont think any other AfroAmerican had ever done ... and that was ... I Q U I T! Yep, I just up and split").[55] As with those other "official" documents from the early part of his life, formal university documents and rituals are irrelevant—and he would later create his own "diploma" of sorts, his Birdland "membership card," which lists as his address "Fine Art Library Painting Section / Indiana U. Bloomington" (see Figure 14.1).

Given their proximity to Beecher Terrace, it's almost certain that Joans did attend or sit in on classes at both Indiana University's Extension Division in Jeffersonville, and at the University of Louisville, and if he was never officially enrolled, it would explain the lack of any paper trail at either institution. He could have attended classes in Bloomington as well, but it would have been more of a hike from Louisville. In "Spadework," Joans mentions "studying for a BA in painting" and working "hard under men like" Justus Bier, a German-born art historian who taught at the University of Louisville between 1937 and 1960.[56] Bier was a familiar figure in the Louisville art world, having founded the Allen R. Hite Institute of Art and Design at the university, and serving for years as Arts editor for the Louisville *Courier-Journal*, for which he wrote a regular arts column. In that column, back in 1947, Bier had reported on a major Surrealist and Abstract exhibit he had seen in Chicago, which ran under the title "Surrealist Exhibition In Chicago Proves Exciting," likely introducing many Kentuckians to Surrealism.[57]

At the time Joans was living in Louisville, Bier taught, in addition to his regular courses, at the University of Louisville's Division of Adult Education, so that in the fall of 1952, for example, he offered "Studies in 20th Century Art."[58] It seems likely to me, given the references in the *Defender* to Joans "often sitting in on lectures at the University of Louisville," that he audited Bier's regular classes or the ones offered through the Division of Adult Education.[59] In any case, in one of his *Courier-Journal* arts columns from 1951, Bier did mention Joans as being part of an exhibit called "Louisville's Own Contemporary Painters" then being shown at the Western Branch Library.[60] (In what may be a telling historical correspondence, in 1955, the *Defender* ran a story about Gregory Ridley, the first Black person to get a Master's degree in Studio Painting from the University of Louisville, and Ridley remarked, apparently unprompted, "I am not a surrealist"—perhaps a nod to the more famous son of Louisville's art scene.[61])

In the Ted Joans Papers at Berkeley, there is a surviving typescript of a "surreal play" signed "by ted joans 1949 U of L," and Joans has handwritten in: "presented at the Belknap Playhouse [located at the University of Louisville] by Art Center students."[62] This play, titled "Dont Fucketh With Me"—a warning, perhaps, to any future friendly biographer burgling this period of his life—concerns a theme of much of his work, interracial desire, and uses allegorical figures such as Mr. and Mrs. Blackass and Mr. and Mrs. Whiteass, as well as animals like Rhinoceros, Giraffe, and Tiger to explore this theme.

The climax of the play is a rhinoceros coming on stage to address the audience directly about the taboo (and, in some states, illegality) of interracial coupling:

> these two people that you have banned from your worlds are only doing that which is marvelous, beautiful in fact anything that is beautiful is marvelous ... I mean to say that these people are free of everyday fears and frustrations that all of you possess, tis they that are letting their subconscious minds lead them into the true world of the marvelous, that surreal world where one exist[s] in between the state of being half in dream and half awake.[63]

If this sounds manifesto-like, it's because Joans borrowed some language from Breton's first *Manifesto of Surrealism*: "anything marvelous is beautiful, in fact only the marvelous is beautiful."[64] So he was thinking in strident terms when he conceived this play, seeking to enlighten his audience (at the University of Louisville?) just as he sought to enlighten guests at his Surrealist parties in Beecher Terrace.

The title of the play confirms this sense of stridency, as it refers to Joans's own personal "motto" at the time: "I have a flag, a personal flag. It does not fly in the wind but in my imagination. It has a big black rhinoceros on it, the background is red, and just below the rhinoceros is a white strip of heraldic ribbon that has my motto on it, it reads: DONT FUCKETH WITH ME!!"[65] Just as the rhinoceros in the play was cautioning against "conventional-ridden minds," Joans's personal motto was directed at anyone who tried to pigeonhole him, judge him, or restrict him based on any kind of demographic marker.

That this play and Joans's "personal flag" prominently feature the rhinoceros shows also how he was attached to his totem animal from a relatively young age. Joans loved the rhinoceros for its connection to Africa, its stalwart incapability of ever being domesticated, its obvious dangerousness, and for the phallic symbolism of its horn (in his poem "Sanctified Rhino," he catalogued the adventures of the title creature, his alter ego: "So the rhino who balled the virgin / on the twelve o'clock saturday bright / blew his horn, for she was reborn").[66] The rhinoceros was also, as Joans said of himself, "an endangered species."[67]

"[T]his is the age of the rhinoceros," Joans announced in "Spadework," elaborating that he had:

> thought a lot / an awful lot about my animal / an African as well as Asian animal / the rhinoceros and many of the new folks in my life either think that I'm insane or putting on a publicity bit / but they are all wrong / I like them because I <u>like them</u>. I have dug the rhinoceros for a longtime ... and the many other hipper animals. The horse which is the symbol of the whiteman/and the eagle/have had it! They are finished / the rhinoceros is in the power now/and the only thing that I think the whitemen (of evildoing) can do is get out.[68]

This hip animal would be Joans's totem and emblem throughout his life, and the line drawing in the flag (Figure 4.6) would be transformed in the rhino-shaped rubber stamp he would use in later years, in the rhino doodles that often accompanied his signature on books, and in his frequent use of rhinos and rhino motifs in his visual art from the late 1940s up until his death (for an image of his 1957 painting, *Land of the Rhinoceri*, see Figure 13.3). In 1959, when the Beat Generation was capturing the public imagination for better or worse, Brazzle Tobin in the *Defender* recalled Joans's sermons on the rhinoceros as homegrown ancestors of the Beat phenomenon: "The extensive poetry reading displayed by the Beatniks from coast to coast isn't new here. Ted Jones, currently living the life of a Bohemian in New York's Greenwich Village, conducted such sessions here as far back as '39 ['49]. His eccentric lectures were directed at 'The Hippopotamus' and 'The Rhinoceros.'"[69]

FIGURE 4.6 *Joans's "personal flag." From TJP, box 16, folder 45.*

Despite his relative success and fame in Louisville, the lure of New York City was just too strong, and after several trips there between 1951 and 1953, in the summer of 1953, Joans began making preparations in earnest to move there, and he did so that October. Of course his wife Joan and their two daughters were a major complication in Joans's plan to live the bohemian life in Greenwich Village, and the move was hardly a clean break, as he returned to Louisville for a time in 1954 to straighten out his "domestic affairs."[70] Despite the split, Joan herself would survive—and thrive—in Louisville, raising Sylvia and Yvette there as a beloved member of the community.

But for Ted Joans, the taste of New York had proven that Kentucky was simply too provincial for his ambitions, in spite of—or maybe because of— his family there. As Joan put it later, "Louisville was not ready for him, and he felt constrained."[71] If liberation was the great theme of his poem-life, then there seemed no better place to explore liberation in its many potential forms than New York City, home to the twinned poles of Joans's imagination, Harlem, "the world's largest modern Black metropolis," as he called it, and Greenwich Village, the very epicenter of the avant-garde, the place where he went to live as a bohemian, and to make his fortune as the first "'may-be-modern master-painter' of the Afroid species."[72]

PART TWO

Biting the Big Apple

5

The Most Celebrated
Actress in the World

Elizabeth Taylor wanted a taste of bohemia. It was 1959, she was arguably the most famous actress in the world, and so was used to getting what she wanted. The popular press at the time was filled with stories about hard-drinking "modern painters" and tousled-haired poets who were thumbing their noses at convention and almost single-handedly shifting the terms of what counted as art or culture. A Beatnik craze was gripping America, and these fascinating creatures were headquartered, so far as the media could tell, in Greenwich Village and the Lower East Side of New York City. Taylor wanted a tour, and dragged along her new husband, Eddie Fisher. Her point person for the expedition was Seymour Krim, a hip Jewish writer and editor of the racy *Nugget* magazine, an operator with connections all over the New York arts scene. When Taylor's people reached out to Krim, he knew just the person to introduce Taylor and Fisher to the "real" bohemia: Ted Joans, poet, painter, bon vivant, raconteur, Village celebrity.

Krim brought Taylor and Fisher to Joans's Astor Place studio to introduce them to "how a 'beatnik' lived," as Joans joked, keeping "beatnik" in scare quotes, as always.[1] The couple was accompanied by Academy Award-winning director Joseph L. Mankiewicz (who would go on to direct Taylor in *Cleopatra*), and Taylor's old friend, Paddy Chayefsky, one of the most successful screenwriters of the era, who tagged along with his wife to gather research for a teleplay he was planning called "The Angel-Headed Hipster"—maybe, he thought, Joans could even star in it.[2]

As always, Joans was an affable host, and welcomed the entourage to his suitably shabby studio, a one-time commercial loft furnished with rugs and ancient overstuffed chairs scrounged from the streets on garbage days, or else sourced from thrift shops uptown. He showed off his huge "jazz action" paintings filled with "frenzied brush strokes" of "surrealist automaticism," and cajoled them to buy one—or several. An irresistible attraction in the studio was Joans's double bed, which he had raised eight feet off the floor and made accessible by ladder, another creative space where he had entertained countless "laymates" over the years.[3] Taylor was apparently fascinated, and Joans claimed that she even "climbed up into my eight foot bed while her husband and the others read excerpts of my poetry below us."[4]

Certainly the domain Joans had carved out on Astor Place was a universe apart from Elizabeth Taylor's rarefied air, and yet he was able to connect with her as he was able to connect with so many people of different worlds. She confessed to liking his poetry, and either purchased a copy of his booklet *Funky Jazz Poems* (1959) or Joans gifted her one.[5] While she seemed "honored" for the glimpse into Joans's world, Fisher was assertively bored, "obnoxious and rude," as Joans put it, mocking the studio's arty squalor. Still, after the tour, Joans offered to take everyone to a real bohemian watering hole, the Cedar Tavern, a favorite haunt of his and a "true unspoiled artist's bar and restaurant."[6]

The Cedar, located on the corner of 8th Street and University Place, was a bar frequented by now-iconic painters like Jackson Pollock and Willem de Kooning, a place where, on any given night, patrons could have rubbed elbows not only with those painters, but with Frank O'Hara, LeRoi Jones, Allen Ginsberg, Jack Kerouac, and others, writers who were tearing down what poetry, "literature" itself, was supposed to do or be. Joans described the Cedar as "a nondescript place with a long bar, booths on the side and in the middle, two toilets, a large wall clock always set ten minutes ahead, a sink between the two toilets, and bohemian nonstop avant garde ambience."[7] The sink between the bathrooms turned out to have special significance in Beat lore since one night Kerouac, drunk out of his mind and bloated with beer, couldn't take it any more and let loose into the sink. Painter Helen Frankenthaler caught a glimpse of Kerouac, was horrified, and reported the behavior to the surly bartender, who bounced Kerouac and promptly hung a sign behind the bar: "No Beatnicks [*sic*] Allowed."[8] Ginsberg's boyfriend, poet Peter Orlovsky, looked on in bemusement, remarking, "There comes a time when everybody must take a piss in the sink."[9] The Cedar was the scene of a thousand stories like this, a true artists' refuge, with cheap food and drink, and free-flowing conversation.

For its unparalleled ambience, the Cedar was the natural spot to indulge Taylor in her desire to go adventuring in bohemia, an impulse Joans would later satirize in his book *The Hipsters* (1961), a comic, Surrealist burlesque of the Village scene so fascinating to "outsiders" like Taylor. In that book Joans imagined an "annual international six day hipster convention at the Evergreen Cedar Tree Tavern"—the name is a lighthearted mash-up of the Cedar Tavern and the underground literary magazine *Evergreen Review*—and the fact that any writer or artist on the Lower East Side would have immediately gotten the joke speaks to the Cedar's preeminence in artistic circles.[10]

Despite the Cedar being only a block or so from Joans's Astor Place studio, he wasn't about to pass up the opportunity to ride in Elizabeth Taylor's limousine, and the entourage glided over to the bar in style. Joans burst into the crowded, smoky bar, leading mink-clad Taylor to a back booth where he ordered tavern staples for the group: bad spaghetti, garlic bread, and thin red wine. Such a motley crew inevitably drew stares from the regulars—it seemed to poet Margaret Randall that Taylor and Fisher "were looking for the painters they'd read about in the mass media and who had sparked their curiosity. We returned their curious gaze with our own."[11] Joans, though, was always comfortable around celebrity, was not necessarily above courting celebrity when it suited him, but the other regulars were either star-struck or perhaps indifferent, as only the Abstract Expressionist painter Franz Kline, who by this time had already become an old pal of Joans's, had the temerity to amble over and say hello.

After soaking up the atmosphere over spaghetti, Fisher had his fill of grungy bohemia and was itching to leave. Krim joked that maybe Joans should pick up the check. Finally Fisher threw some bills on the table and stood, a sure sign the jaunt was over. Everyone shook hands cordially, and Joans, forever strapped for cash, had the limo drop him over at Café Bizarre, where he kicked off one of the marathon poetry reading sessions that were a main source of income in the late 1950s.[12] In one poem he would read at places like the Bizarre, Joans alluded to this strange and exciting night with one of the world's most glamorous stars, insisting "I am a man I am a man I have held the / hand of Elizabeth Taylor ... SO dig me American don't call me BOY!!!"[13]

Joans's brief encounter with Elizabeth Taylor and Eddie Fisher suggests the degree to which he had become *the* hipster to know in New York in the late 1950s. In less than a decade, he had gone from being locally famous in Louisville to locally famous in New York City—and of course New York was a much bigger pond, so his celebrity there sometimes translated to coverage in national magazines such as *Time*. Joans's friend Robert "Bob" Reisner, jazz historian and proprietor of the famed weekend jazz club, The Open Door, once observed that "in Greenwich Village you can't walk a block with him [Joans] but that you have to stop while he receives the big hello. If he was walking with Eisenhower, the beats in the Village would say 'Who's that guy with Ted?'"[14]

6

Inside the Magnetic Fields

But how exactly did Joans remake himself, in the span of ten years, from the virtuoso of Walnut Street and Beecher Terrace, "Louisville's Salvador Dali," to a figure more famous than Eisenhower to those hipsters, Beats, and avant-garde painters in New York, the very epicenter of world-changing artistic and literary activity? The answer is many-layered, but has to do in no small part with Joans's boundless energy and undeniable charm, what Gerald Nicosia calls his "irresistible magnetism," and ability to make friends while always keeping himself open to surprising or unexpected connections.[1]

There's a concept in Surrealism called *le hasard objectif* or Objective Chance that helps explain how Joans thought of those unexpected encounters that so often shaped his poem-life. Franklin and Penelope Rosemont, founders of the Chicago Surrealist Group and Joans's friends from the 1960s on, saw him in an "alchemical light as a wandering international instigator of surrealist chance encounters"—a perfect, incandescent description of him.[2] Objective Chance, as Penelope Rosemont later explained, "identifies unforeseen encounters that coincide amazingly with one's own desire."[3] Reflecting on Joans specifically, Rosemont thought that his attunement to Objective Chance was one of the crucial characteristics of his poem-life, which, by definition, had to be open to its operation. "Even the simplest occurrences of objective chance," says Rosemont, "offer an electrifying insight into 'how life works' ... Incidences of objective chance, and the 'enchanted situations' they tend to create, seem to have the strongest effect on people who are, as it is said, 'tuned in to the same wave-length.' Indeed, sometimes it appears that poets are alone in recognizing these encounters for what they are, and in trying to follow through on them, to see where they lead."[4]

For Joans's later-in-life "spiritual wife," Laura Corsiglia, Objective Chance works "like magnets," so "when your mind and heart seize on certain things, they have a tendency to show up and manifest and run into each other, and that when you are alert and looking out for these marvelous occurrences you both notice and propagate them."[5]

New York in the 1950s was unbelievably rich in the magnetic fields that might attract like-minded artists to one another. "The chance encounter of beautiful people," Joans said, "or a beautiful situation, or a beautiful image, is a whole surreal experience."[6] As he circulated in the bars, coffeehouses, gallery exhibitions, poetry readings, parties and similar spaces and events, he was open to those chance encounters that might nourish his varied creative interests, from Surrealism to bop to painting to poetry to sex.

As he said of his New York years, the tempo of "bohemian life was full of change, exchanging and discovery ... I was amongst the very best at that time."[7] A sense of "discovery" was paramount in Joans's poem-life, and from a Surrealist point of view, chance encounters encourage exploration and discovery in all kinds of guises. As one observer of Surrealism put it, Objective Chance names "the whole of those phenomena which manifest the invasion of daily life by the marvelous," and Joans saw his "daily life" in New York City, his poem-life, as meaningful both when he was touched by the marvelous and when he induced awakenings of the marvelous in others.[8]

7

Home to Harlem

Whenever Joans paused to recall his grand arrival in New York City, he would, somewhat uncharacteristically, fix it to a specific date, saying that on July 20, 1951, he stepped off the bus at the 34th Street Greyhound Terminal in mid-town Manhattan, armed with two suitcases and big ambitions: the birth of a new life.[1] Of course this was not true in the encyclopedic sense, but in the poetic one, as he was writing himself into another kind of origin story, the wide-eyed small-town boy coming to make good in the big city. "I knew I had the necessary 'teeth,'" he said, "all that I needed was the opportunity to sharpen them then I would 'bite' the Big Apple with gusto."[2]

If he was conflicted about leaving Joan and the girls in Kentucky, he didn't let on, instead characterizing the people "back home" as more provincial than the larger-than-life New Yorkers hurrying past him on the sidewalks. Walking in awe the few blocks from the bus terminal to the William Sloane House YMCA, where he had booked a cheap bed, Joans remembered feeling "smaller than I had ever felt. Everything seemed to be bigger than I was, even the throngs of passing people seemed larger than people back home."[3] And yet, true to the hero's transformative trajectory, on that very first walk he resolved to "stand out and be different than all of this crowd of people," to be "as strong and taller than all the others."[4]

Back in Louisville, as he was throwing parties to raise funds for his move, he had also carefully mapped out the various streets and neighborhoods in New York, and settled on the Sloane House YMCA as his home base because it seemed to be centrally located. But those best laid plans quickly went awry. Once the largest residential YMCA in the world, unbeknownst to Joans, Sloane House was also an infamous queer space and cruising spot dubbed the "French Embassy" in mid-century gay circles.[5] At the Sloane House, after taking his first high-rise elevator ride to an upper floor, Joans was immediately propositioned by a towel-clad man who followed him down the hallway. Desperate to clean up after his big cross-country bus ride, Joans waved the man off and found his way to the showers, where another naked man promptly gave him an even more blunt offer: "For a buck," he said, "I'll do anything at all."[6] A startled Joans attempted to go about the business of showering, but when the man put a hand on him, Joans elbowed him in the face—"if someone touches me," he wrote later, "he or she is violating my human right—they are disrespecting my existence."[7]

These lines come from Joans describing the incident as "my welcome to New York City" in the opening pages of "I, Too, at the Beginning" (1986), an unpublished autobiography of his years in the city.[8] In the context of that manuscript, the Sloane House represents both Joans's introduction to New York and its many heterodox or underground spaces, and also an opportunity for him to assert his resolute heterosexuality, such that he's obliged to physically fend off a queer come-on as his first act in the city. In fact, his set piece about the Sloane House is filled with slurs used to describe its queer residents, and is a way for Joans to set the stage for New York City to emerge as his own heterosexual erotic playground. As we will see in the coming pages, there was a tension throughout the 1950s and 1960s between Joans the family man, the husband and father, and Joans the sexually liberated, avowedly hetero artist who threw around terms like "laymates" and "chicklets" and would boast in magazine profiles about "the many women who think they have a claim on me."[9] The casual dismissal of queerness was part of this hypermasculine posture, even as once established in New York he would befriend many out-queer writers and artists, a change from Kentucky and Indiana where, he said, "nothing was that blatant."[10] In those years, for all his other forward-thinking positions on art, race, sexuality, and global politics, he could still write in terms of sexual binaries, for as he announces in "Spadework": "I shall never be a fag nor queer, because women are my prime reason."[11] He echoes this sort of language when describing the Sloane House in "I, Too, at the Beginning" (and in an interview conducted in 1982, around the time "I, Too" was drafted), but the older he got, the more he softened his language.[12]

In the last autobiography he wrote, "Collaged Autobiography," he still insisted on a capacious heterosexuality as central to his identity, romanticizing his "yesteryear laymates"—but not, in contrast, pathologizing homosexuality:

I was always interested in women and enjoyed being around old women and young girls, from eight to eighty, blind, cripple or crazy. I dug them all, and so far they have deeply dug me. Each Fourth of July I receive gifts and cards from friends throughout the world. Most of those birthday gift recognitions come forth from females. Of course some of them are yesteryear laymates, one night dates and countless international playmates. I never had physical interest in homosexuality. Many of my close friends and acquaintances are gay. They respect my heterosexuality as I respect their homosexuality.[13]

In general, I find Joans's 1950s-era framing of homosexuality in keeping with the constitutionally homophobic culture of the time, even as he befriended a number of queer-identified people in New York, Tangier, Paris and elsewhere. That said, as will become clear in the following chapters, a crucial point to remember is that the continual insistence on his own sexual prowess was also very much racialized insofar as Black sexuality, and Black male sexuality in particular, was dangerous to flaunt and burdened by a centuries-old mythos of Black male hypersexuality. However much it might have relied on deindividuating those "countless" laymates when advertising his uncompromising, robust heterosexuality, particularly with white women, Joans was also laying claim to his own bodily autonomy in an environment where interracial coupling, especially between Black men and white women, was perilous, violence-inducing, and in many places illegal.

For all these reasons, the encounter at the Sloane House provides another possible origin point for Ted Joans, the performatively virile world traveler who would come to be famously comfortable in his own skin, connecting with any person in any cultural situation or foreign-seeming space. The idea would be that, in retrospect, Joans portrayed his younger self as socialized enough in the mores of a homophobic culture to be put off by the overtures in the Sloane House, and so that younger self scrambled out of there after only one night, decamping instead to the Harlem branch of the YMCA up on 135th Street.

With the move from the Sloane House, Harlem became the first place in New York Joans experienced for any length of time. Both a neighborhood and the symbolic heart of Black literary, musical, and cultural achievement, Harlem would have held a certain mystique for any artistically-minded Black person in the 1950s—as Joans said of his arrival there: "This was my first time in Harlem physically, but I had always been in Harlem mentally."[14]

For Ralph Ellison, writing in 1948, just a few years before Joans arrived, Harlem was an enigmatic, alluring space of "extreme contrasts," at once "a ruin" filled with "crimes, casual violence, crumbling buildings with littered area-ways" and also a dreamy "setting of transcendence."[15] Fittingly for Joans, Ellison leans on decidedly Surrealist terms to describe this duality: the material sordidness seemed "indistinguishable from the distorted images that appear in dreams," and yet only in Harlem was it

> possible for talented youths to leap through the development of decades in a brief twenty years ... Here the grandchildren of those who possessed no written literature examine their lives through the eyes of Freud and Marx, Kierkegaard and Kafka, Malraux and Sartre. It explains the nature of a world so fluid and shifting that often within the mind the real and unreal merge, and the marvelous beckons from behind the same sordid reality that denies existence. Hence the most surreal fantasies are acted out upon the streets of Harlem.[16]

Ellison's evocative descriptions of Harlem perhaps suggest its appeal to Joans beyond the neighborhood's obvious status as a center of Black life and culture: if it could be a fluid, dreamlike place of extremes that merged the real with the unreal, a stage of "surreal fantasies" and an environment where "talented youths" could flourish with astonishing speed, then it in fact was the perfect place for Joans to try out new versions of himself beyond what he had been doing in Louisville, to take the next steps in his Teducation.

8

The World of Langston Hughes

Beyond the sort of duality Ellison identifies, for Joans Harlem had always been filtered through the writing of Langston Hughes, and in moving there, he said he was "following in Langston Hughes' Harlem Footsteps."[1] "I had read his works," Joans recalled, "before I ever came to Harlem. When I did come I followed in his footsteps by staying at the Harlem 135th Street YMCA and visited almost daily (during cold days) the Schomburg Library down the street from the Y ... [where] I studied Black American history and discovered Black American artists who were never included in the art books that were available back home."[2]

Coming from segregated Kentucky, Harlem was for Joans "the world's largest modern Black metropolis," offering opportunity for "transcendence" at every turn, and educational possibilities galore, not only in formal scholastic institutions like the Schomburg, but in social spaces like The Savoy Ballroom, a massive dance hall on Lenox Avenue between 140th and 141st Streets that had hosted the best jazz musicians in the world since 1926, the heyday of the Harlem Renaissance, and continued to do so until it closed in 1958.[3] Or Lewis Michaux's African National Memorial Bookstore on 7th Avenue, one of the few bookstores in the country devoted to Black literature, culture and history (and from which Joans's father had ordered books to be shipped back to the Midwest). Or nearby Small's Paradise, the famed Black-owned nightclub dating to 1925. Joans had stepped into a concentrated wealth of Black culture just waiting to be tapped.[4]

The Apollo Theater on 125th Street held a special place for him, as an even grander version of the theaters he worked in on Walnut Street back in Louisville. Joans said he had spent "a great deal of time ... getting my Harlem education," watching live acts and taking in films like *Thief of Bagdad* (1940) and *Sahara* (1943), which featured Black actor Rex Ingram, one of his favorites—perhaps because Ingram was born near Cairo, Illinois to a father who worked on Mississippi riverboats, just like Joans. He gravitated in particular to the Black films the Apollo would showcase, including the 1920s work of Oscar Micheaux, whose *Within Our Gates* (1920) is the earliest Black-directed film to survive; or *The Bronze Buckaroo*, a 1939 Western aimed at Black audiences.[5]

Such places were crucial to his Teducation: "I got 'hipper-than-thou' during my stay in Harlem. My street education up there was taking 'classes' day and night in the jukebox joints, jazz clubs, poolhalls, barber shops, Michaux's bookshop, Siefert's Afrika House and hanging out on corners with the hipsters."[6] The places Joans names are the very kinds of ordinary, everyday spots in Harlem that Langston Hughes mythologizes in his first collection, *The Weary Blues* (1926), which opens with poems such as "To a Black Dancer in 'The Little Savoy,'" and "Lenox Avenue: Midnight." In the collection's title poem, "The Weary Blues," Hughes describes "a Negro play / Down on Lenox Avenue the other night / By the pale dull pallor of an old gas light," and it is scenes (and rhythms) like this Joans would likewise celebrate in poems like "Passed On Blues," which valorizes "the world of Langston Hughes": "the sonata of Harlem / the concerto to shoulder bones / pinto beans / hamhocks In the Dark."[7]

For Joans, frequenting those everyday spaces was like walking around in a Hughes poem or story come to life. "Passed on Blues" describes Harlem as populated by people with "the Jess B. Semple hip sneer" (2), a reference to Hughes's best-known fictional creation, Jesse B. Semple, a character who animated the columns Hughes wrote for the *Chicago Defender* in the 1940s. Semple was, as fifties critic Arthur Davis summarized it, "an uneducated Harlem man-about-town who speaks a delightful brand of English and who, from his stool at Paddy's Bar, comments both wisely and hilariously on many things."[8]

The very first time he walked the streets of Harlem, Joans saw versions of Semple everywhere. At 125th and Lenox Avenue:

there were fifty or sixty of Langston Hughes' Jess[e] B. Semple characters. Their physical stance, clothing, laughter and unique gesticulations were just as Harlem Street hip as their original rhythms in their Afroid English. I felt like I was in an institution's library or an outdoor human experimental laboratory. I knew that I must "enroll" in this university of Harlem streets to learn how to survive … I knew that I would have to pay some Harlem dues to obtain the high holy bestowment of becoming "His Hipness."[9]

This is Joans's poem-life in action, a blending or overlaying of the fictional with the real: his first introduction to Harlem was filtered through recollections of a fictional character seemingly come to life on every street corner, blurring lines between Hughes's fictions and Joans's first-hand experiences. Imagining that he was somehow materialized in a vast living library or "experimental laboratory," the real-life corollaries to a place like the Schomburg Library, he was becoming a wiser version of himself. In the

coming years, after Joans had befriended Hughes personally, he had even
written to him: "I too am Jess Simple," noting the coincidence that both he
and Semple had been married to women named Joyce (he's referring here
to the Joyce he had met in New York, whom we'll come to in a moment).[10]

Joans later declared that Hughes's work "gave all Black people something
to be proud of … a natural truth of our unique heritage. I can honestly say
that it was in the poetry of Langston Hughes that I first got really hip to the
who and *what* and *why* of my own *raison d'etre*."[11] In addition to Hughes's
poems celebrating Black life like "Lenox Avenue: Midnight" or "The Weary
Blues," Joans was particularly influenced by what he called Hughes's "hand
grenade" poems, which he defined as "poems that you write to blow up
and get rid of things that block the human desire … for example, racism,
sexism, and another thing that's really heavy on women, is ageism."[12] Later,
in the 1960s, Joans explained that "revolutionary poetry" amounted to
"The correct word / at the correct time / calculated to explode / inside of the
target's brain."[13] For Hughes's "hand grenade" poems, Joans singled out as
an example "Merry-Go-Round," a poem from the collection *Shakespeare in
Harlem* (1942):[14]

> Where is the Jim Crow section
> On this merry-go-round,
> Mister, cause I want to ride?
> Down South where I come from
> White and colored
> Can't sit side by side.
> Down South on the train
> There's a Jim Crow car.
> On the bus we're put in the back—
> But there ain't no back
> To a merry-go-round!
> Where's the horse
> For a kid that's black?[15]

This is the sort of deceptively simple poem that could be read aloud to
audiences and that makes a clear, poignant point about the absurdity of
segregation. It appealed to Joans as something that could be lobbed into
polite (white) society to blow up conventional thinking, and he would write
countless of his own hand grenade poems over the years, including, to take
an early example, "Uh Huh" (1954). That poem is a dialogue between two
speakers:

> There it is
> yep uh huh
> that's it

there's no doubt about it
uh huh

And so on, and readers don't know what the object of discussion is until
the final line:

right before the eyes
a truth
uh huh
reality
Well I be damn
here uh huh now this is it Uh Huh uh huhuh huh uh
huh uh huh THE COLORED WAITING ROOM[16]

This is a good example of Joans's version of a hand grenade poem insofar
as its meaning explodes in the final line (in the retrospective collection
Teducation, "Uh Huh" was included in the first section, "Hand Grenade").
Throughout the majority of the poem, from the opening to the penultimate
line, readers are treated to what seems to be inarticulate people speaking in
slang and ambiguous filler phrases like "uh huh." But that final line reveals
that the speakers are reacting to the real, material facts of segregation, a
revelation which then recontextualizes the previous conversation as a kind of
stunned shared disbelief. Joans returned to hand grenade poems throughout
his life, but first developed them, as I'll explain in more detail later, as he
read to largely white audiences in Greenwich Village coffeehouses, intending
to "blow up" their worlds in direct ways.

The operations of Objective Chance led to Langston Hughes himself
happening to hear Joans read his poetry one night in Café Rafio on Bleecker
Street. When Joans recognized him, he was instantly apprehensive in the
presence of his longtime hero, and started frantically shuffling through
his material, which he had prepared for the "tourists and beatniks" who
frequented Café Rafio, but not for someone of Hughes's stature. He wanted
to find something suitable for Hughes's refined ear, and Hughes could
apparently see Joans's nervousness, approached the stage, and urged Joans
not to change the program on his account.[17] Joans appreciated the knowing,
practical advice and went on with his reading, if a bit shaky with Hughes
looking on.

Joans remembered Hughes coming up to him after the reading and
saying: "You sure do get those words up off the paper. Boy, you can read
your poems!"

Then, glancing around at that crowd, Hughes continued: "You gotta lotta
nerve telling all these White folks how square they are, ain't you scared?"
He then looked at Joans "with that certain look that Black folks can convey

to each other when in the midst of Whites, and [they] both exploded with laughter."[18]

After initially bonding over blowing up a white audience's world, Hughes invited Joans to hear him read to a largely Black audience up in Harlem, and the two remained friendly until Hughes's death in 1967—in 1963, Joans had even considered naming one of his sons "Lars Langston Joans."[19] Naming a child after a mentor and friend is no small thing, and underscores the extent to which Hughes was an ongoing influence in Joans's creative life. Joans did title his autobiography, "I, Too, at the Beginning," as a nod to the "Epilogue" to *The Weary Blues*, in which Hughes writes: "I, too, sing America. / I am the darker brother."[20] Over the years, Joans would variously refer to Hughes as "the, I do mean THE, poet of Afroamerica," as his "mentor and guide," and even as one of his two "February fathers" or "spiritual fathers" (along with André Breton).[21]

As Joans knew from a young age, Hughes wrote about the Black experience in a way that felt familiar and relatable, in contrast to most poets working in a white European tradition—"he wasn't talking about Zeus and Arcadia," as Joans put it.[22] The two kept up a correspondence even after Joans had left the States and was living part-time in Timbuktu. Hughes would go on to write a generous review of *The Hipsters*, solicit Joans's poetry for anthologies, and send him books, clippings, and the occasional cash infusion. In July 1966, some nine months before Hughes's death, Joans organized what would be Hughes's last major reading in Europe, a celebration at the famed Paris bookstore Shakespeare and Company, where Hughes insisted Joans play trumpet as he read work from *Ask Your Mama: 12 Moods for Jazz* (1961), an echo of the first time Joans had ever heard him read in Harlem, naturally to jazz accompaniment.[23]

9

Babs Gonzales and the Origin of "The .38"

One memorable oral poem that had its genesis in Joans's Harlem experiences was called "The .38," a tense, unflinching piece in which the speaker overhears a neighbor verbally and physically abusing his wife before ultimately shooting her with the titular .38 caliber handgun. Written in 1953, the poem begins with the declarative phrase "I hear," and repeats it fifty-four times as the speaker moves from overhearing the initial abusive argument ("I hear him push and shove her around the overcrowded room / I hear his wife scream and beg for mercy") to hearing him shoot his wife, until the husband finally comes to the speaker's door and shoots him, the last line narrating the fraction of a second before his death: "I hear it [the bullet] singe my skin as it enters my head the .38 and I hear death saying 'hello, I'm here.'"[1] The poem became by the later 1950s one of the more popular he would read aloud in Village coffeehouses, but the particular circumstances from which it arose show how intimately it was connected with Joans's own Harlem experience.

The origin of "The .38" came after Joans moved himself out of the Harlem branch of the YMCA at 135th Street and over to a rooming house recommended by musician, writer, international gadfly, and one of his "foremost hip professors of the streets," Babs Gonzales.[2] For Joans, Gonzales was the "greatest hipster of the Bebop epoch," a Black composer and jazz musician who had been dubbed "king of the 'Bop Poets.'"[3] Though only nine years Joans's senior, Gonzales had packed in lots of life experience, having worked for Errol Flynn out in Hollywood, avoided being inducted into the army by turning up to his physical in drag and painted toenails, and with his first band, Three Bips and a Bop, had a hit song with "Oop-Pop-a-Da," among many other adventures. In fact, the broad outlines of Joans's and Gonzales's lives overlapped in some ways, as Gonzales would circulate through the New York scene, but then live for long stretches in

Europe. Gonzales spoke French and even planned to open a club in Paris called Le Maison du Idiots (the grammatical incorrectness was part of the joke). The Parisian club didn't pan out, but in 1958, he did open one in Harlem called The Insane Asylum. As Joans would as well, by the early 1950s, Gonzales was known as a kind of hip ambassador, having written a "Bop Dictionary" that he would take around to shows and sell for fifty cents a piece.[4] Jack Kerouac had singled out Gonzales as one of the original hipsters who had inspired his vision of the Beat Generation, describing a scene in 1948 when he saw Charlie Parker "strolling down Eighth Avenue in a black turtleneck sweater with Babs Gonzales and a beautiful girl."[5] Like Joans, then, Gonzales seemed to know everyone. In a brief preface to Gonzales's second autobiography, *Movin' on Down the Line* (1975), Maurice Kulas marveled that Gonzales "has met people on three continents, from all walks of life. From Kings, artists, executives, socialites to whores, pimps and dope peddlers."[6] Gonzales had even roomed briefly with Charlie Parker, as Joans did in later years (I'll discuss Joans's relationship with Parker in detail later).[7]

Joans deeply admired Gonzales, and credited him with being one of his early New York teachers, who hipped him to the nightlife in Harlem and other parts of the city: "Babs was patient with my questions, and it was his teaching that inspired my own Teducation. Babs was one of those unsung heroes of Jazz and American humor."[8] Gonzales thought that a room at the YMCA was too restrictive for a young artist such as Joans, assuring him that if he moved into a place of his own, he could indulge in more freedoms, could listen to music as loud as he wanted, entertain women, and "smoke reefer with impunity"—these were reasons enough for Joans to pull up stakes and move.[9] Joans went about turning the tiny room Gonzales recommended into an idyllic bohemian pad, equipping it with just a lone piece of furniture, a bed, but stocking it with an old Remington typewriter and orange crates and wine cases to serve as book shelves and record holders. There he was able to write some, paint, do drawings and collages, and blare "the great sounds of the classic Black music."[10]

Complications arose when Joans got involved with a "Mrs. Johnson," the wife of the police officer who ran the rooming house on the side (and, in a Surrealist universe, perhaps a relative of "Sam Johnson," the villainous Detroit worker featured in "Spadework"). Knowing that she was married to a police officer, Joans did his best to restrict their relationship to niceties exchanged in the hall, but Mrs. Johnson had other ideas, and became more and more forward until one evening she turned up at his door with a bottle of Thunderbird and a couple of wine glasses.

As Joans had it, Mrs. Johnson claimed she just wanted to innocently toast "you and me in intellectual friendship and may it last forever," but of course he knew she was planning "something groovy." Since there was no furniture in the room but the bed, they inevitably wound up sitting there, one thing led to another, and she reached down to unzip his fly. After their love-making session, Mrs. Johnson's husband was due home any minute, so he rushed her back to her own place—a scenario that had all the makings of a classic blues song.

A little shaken that they had cut it so close, later that same night, Joans overheard the couple in a shouting match, and though he couldn't make out everything perfectly, he did hear one phrase distinctly: "The .38." Mrs. Johnson had once shown Joans the .38 in her husband's underwear drawer, and it was a gun "that could speak any language that confronted it, it was a badassed snub nosed special gun that policemen and some Harlem tuff guys escorted around." Joans then heard Mrs. Johnson's husband "downstairs knocking the hell out of his wife" ("The .38" opens "I hear the man downstairs slapping the hell out of his stupid wife again").[11] After a terrible fight, she screamed and ran out of the building. Joans remained petrified in his room, convinced that the husband would easily be able to read his "guilty face," and he imagined in elaborate, grim detail the man kicking open his door and killing him with the .38.[12]

In the poem "The .38," Joans takes these events and reimagines them. Rather than running out of the building, the wife runs to the speaker's door, is then dragged away and shot by the husband, who then somewhat inexplicably returns to kill the speaker as well. Although in the poem the husband is overheard saying "I warned you and now it's too late" (*ATJ*, 75), there is no real discernable relationship between the speaker and the couple. In fact, much of the poem's power comes from the speaker vividly overhearing a man brutalizing and killing his wife, their only apparent connection to him the thin walls they share, and so he has to envision what he cannot see directly. When the woman runs to the speaker's door ("I hear her banging on my door / I hear him bang her head on my door" [74]), the sense is that she is doing so out of wild desperation, and he is simply too afraid to involve himself in other people's business. In this way, the poem reads at first like a chilling report of the random violence that can characterize the urban experience.

And yet there are some strange details, as for instance when the speaker refers, on three occasions, to the wife's "beautiful body" (*ATJ*, 74, 75). While this phrase can be read as a sympathetic lament for the woman being abused and then murdered, placing the origin of the story in an assignation with the married Mrs. Johnson means we might see the poem's speaker rhapsodizing about her "beautiful body" because he has intimately known it. This background would also explain why the wife rushes to the speaker's door rather than outside the building, and why the husband subsequently storms up to the speaker's room and kills him; this isn't an instance of random urban violence, but revenge for being cuckolded. "The .38," real-life and poetic license blurred into a poem-life, is in this case a morality tale, and Joans noted that when reading the piece, he sometimes subtitled it "for Xtians": "Thou Shalt NOT Commit (or admit) A d u l t e r y and Get Caught!"[13]

Such a backstory also helps explain the collages Joans made to accompany the poem in *All of Ted Joans and No More*: a door handle, an assignation, a .38, an advertisement for Smith & Wesson guns, a coffin, and a frightened Black man up against a wall in a defensive posture with a noir shadow cast behind him. With the backstory in mind, the poem reads like Joans's guilt come alive—or at least like an expression of his relief at not getting caught. As he said, "I paid dues to write that poem .38," and it was "read and reread in the coffee houses and poetry sessions and became quite popular, and if I may say so it still is, perhaps it too will survive to fly like Poe's Raven or one of Bessie Smith's great 'warning' blues."[14]

10

Greenwich Village,
Experiment in Democracy

Despite the riches—and occasional terror—of Harlem, Joans was drawn to the bohemian energy of Greenwich Village, and after making frequent trips down from Harlem, he eventually established himself there. He lived in a number of locations in the Village, a small studio above Café Rienzi at 107 MacDougal Street, a cold water flat on Barrow Street, a studio on Astor Place across from the popular jazz club the Five Spot—and for a time even in a converted linen closet at 40 Bedford Street.[1] Joans forged countless friendships in and around the Village, from Ricky Brightfield, who would become a giant in the Choose Your Own Adventure young adult series, to Arthur Frommer, who was soon to launch his "Europe on 5 Dollars a Day" empire. Byron Le Gip, Tuli Kupferberg and Sylvia Topp, Diane di Prima, Gregory Corso, Allen Ginsberg, Jack Kerouac, LeRoi and Hettie Jones, Seymour Krim, Ray Bremser, Charlie Parker, Fred McDarrah, Arthur "Weegee" Fellig—these are just some of the people he met in Greenwich Village. As mentioned earlier, while on "vacation" from Louisville, he ran into Jackson Pollock, and later became friendly with other artists such as Franz Kline, Claes Oldenburg, and Willem de Kooning.

It was apparently that early encounter with Pollock that had convinced Joans to settle in the Village. He had been walking by the San Remo—like the Cedar patronized by writers and artists—and spotted Pollock drinking at the bar (he had recognized Pollock's photograph from *Life* magazine). When Joans breathlessly told Pollock that he was himself a painter and planning to head to Europe to further his training, Pollock scoffed and told him the best education he could hope for was in those very streets.

"If you want to learn to paint the hairs up someone's nose or their asshole," he said, "then go on over to Europe, they'll teach you all that and more. But you will still not be, what you call 'an artist.' Naw, it is best for

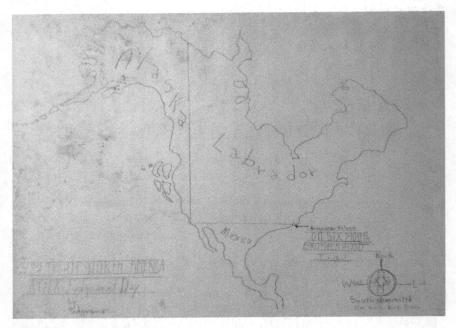

FIGURE 10.1 *Joans's Surrealist "Map of North America After Judgement Day"* (ca. 1955), his update to the famed Surrealist world map, "Le Monde au temps des surréalistes" or "The World in the Time of the Surrealists" (1929), which has a similarly large Alaska and Labrador, but not Canada or the United States of America. Note that in Joans's version, the United States has vanished except for Greenwich Village ("On Six Month Brotherhood Trial"), and "South" has been "eliminated" as a cardinal direction (at this time, Alaska had not yet been admitted as a state; Labrador had just joined Canada in 1949 as part of Newfoundland, but by specifying "Labrador" on this map, Joans is evoking historically Inuit, Innu, and Mi'kmaq lands). Laurated Archive.

you to get down to painting right here, right now; for some of the wonderful things are happening in painting, sculpture, and music, right here in this very city, <u>even</u> in the Village!"[2]

That was good enough for Joans, and he resolved to make his life in the neighborhood.

Although long home to artists and bohemians who were more progressive than middle class America, Greenwich Village also had the all-too-familiar instances of racism that Joans was forced to navigate, and his early years there were partly characterized by this tension. On the one hand, he found the Village "the most livable and inspiring place in the city" and "an experiment in democracy," but on the other, he found "racism was just as violent in Greenwich Village as it was anywhere else in Up-south U.S.A."[3] While "hip people never hassled black people," other residents did, and soon after he moved there, other Villagers like painter Bob Hamilton and local character Lil' Ernie, whom Joans described as a "very hip Black Marxist Villager," warned Joans against venturing down predominantly Italian American streets like Sullivan, Thompson, and Carmine.[4] "On these streets after sun down or broad daylight weekend especially Sundays," Joans realized, "a spade could be bopped by a Wop."[5]

Still, another early guide to the Village's streets was Gregory Corso, an Italian American born in Greenwich Village. Short, dark-haired, and willing to fight at the drop of a hat, Corso had as a child been essentially orphaned and left to his own devices on the streets of New York. In and out of foster homes, juvenile detention, and finally jail, Corso was street-wise and tough— but also a remarkable autodidact who adored Percy Shelley and would go on to become a leading poet of the Beat Generation.[6] Two years younger than Joans, Corso was an indispensable guide to the Village streets, and cautioned Joans about his plan to move out of the MacDougal Street studio and into a building on Bedford that he had heard about from a friend from Louisville, the dancer Anthony Bass.[7] The building was filled with artistic types, and was cheap, but it was in the heart of Little Italy which, Corso told him, was territory of a local mafia based on nearby Carmine Street. Ronald Sukenick remembered that at the time, "the Italians were very insular. Tribal. Hoods loafing around storefront social clubs directing dead deadly looks at Bohemian interlopers, especially if they seemed to be gay or, in their view, worse, were like Ted Joans, Black."[8] Given such circumstances, Corso thought as long as Joans steered clear of Carmine Street itself, he would probably be all right, but he advised him not to bring any white women into the neighborhood, and to spend his money "in the local shops where the elder Italians owners will later speak well of you."[9]

It turned out that the Bedford Street building didn't have any available apartments, but Joans liked the vibe, and the landlady, May Perazzo, let him stay in the kitchen until something opened up. Although Perazzo was fond of Joans, a snag with a previous tenant meant that the bigger place Joans had hoped to rent in the building was unavailable, and he asked if he could live in a linen closet they had passed in the hall. Perazzo was confused as the room wasn't fit for habitation. But Joans persisted, saying that the snugness appealed to his artistic sensibility, and he negotiated a rock-bottom monthly rent for the 8' × 4' space. There was room enough for an old mattress, a record player, and a tin box in which he kept "nuts, raisins, all-bran, peanut butter, bread, cookies," and other non-perishables (peanut butter was one of his lifelong staples, economical, nutritious, easy to transport and store without refrigeration, and references to it turn up throughout his work).[10] The bathroom was down in the basement, but the space was low maintenance, affordable, and private enough for Joans to entertain women in contorted love-making sessions. His friends called the place "la cabine téléphonique"—the phone booth.[11] For Joans, it was weirdly ideal, and it was there, he said, "that I became more surreal-in-mind and life than ever. It was a changing point in my life."[12] He kept the telephone booth for some two years—likely the period when he was going back and forth from Louisville with some regularity—and found it a "good beginning" to his Village era.[13]

Money was scare, and although he had redoubled his efforts at painting once settled in the Village, his art wasn't bringing in enough to live on, and he was forced to take various odd jobs to make ends meet. An important one was as a file clerk at UNESCO, where he was tasked with going through magazines and clipping out articles or other items concerning Africa. "I met my first foreigners' daily there," he said, "and took advantage of learning some common sentences in foreign languages."[14] The drudgery of clipping things from magazines was tempered both by the bonus of learning scraps of foreign languages, and also by the magical fact that he was being paid to immerse himself in Africa and its representations in contemporary media and academic books. From the moment he had studied that map of Africa as a young boy, he had been fascinated by the continent, and this interest had only grown as he aged, so as tedious as the UNESCO job could be, it also deepened his interest in and knowledge of Africa in the years before he would live there. As he said, the job "prepared me for Africa before ever setting foot on the Mother continent, although it had changed considerably by the time I arrived. But I did get my first African political enlightenment while working at the UNESCO."[15]

This day job at UNESCO certainly did prepare Joans, and informed some of his creative work. There is, for example, a poem in *Afrodisia* called "Shave & a Haircut & a Circumcision" that has its roots in the clippings he had made for his UNESCO job. This piece is arranged as a block of prose—a prose-poem, in the context of a poetry collection—and describes in an ethnographic manner how boys in Timbuktu are circumcised by barbers:

> The barber of Timbuctoo not only shaves and cuts the hair of his clients, he also circumsizes them. The aspect of the barbers is terrifying. Their faces are painted white with black on the forehead and cheeks. Some of them also make black circles around their eyes. They wear large yellow turbans and old robes that are decorated with grigri, objects trouvés and other charms. Each carries a leather bag with his equipment in it.[16]

Joans had come across this excerpt at UNESCO, and typed up a copy for his own use, along with passages from J. Olumide Lucas's *The Religion of the Yorubas* (1948), which explained that "Dada is the god of new born babies," tickling Joans's irreverent sensibility (in his poem "My Trip," Joans would later note that "Nigerian love babies with curly hair are called DADA no relation to ole Tristan [Tzara] who the Roumanian Embassy in Athens denied knowing").[17] Joans typed the "Shave & a Haircut & a Circumcision" excerpt just as it would later appear in *Afrodisia*, and attributed it to "Reggin Nam, Sudanese Rituals."[18] Unlike the other two sources on the surviving sheet of paper, no such work exists—in fact, "Reggin Nam" was one of Joans's alter egos; in a 1967 short story, Reggin Nam is described as "an Afroamerican nomadic hipster, who hitched and hiked in Africa each winter to avoid the cold weather of Europe and America."[19] Read the name backwards.

The excerpt Joans appropriated for *Afrodisia* actually comes from Horace Miner's *The Primitive City of Timbuctoo* (1953). Miner writes: "The aspect of the barbers is terrifying. Their faces are painted white with black on the forehead and cheeks and around the eyes. They wear large yellow turbans and tattered robes and are covered with charms. Each carries a pouch for his equipment."[20] Joans quotes this language almost verbatim, making only minor adjustments such as changing "charms" to "grigri, objets trouvés and other charms"—and then eighteen years later he published it as a prose-poem in *Afrodisia*. In the context of that collection, the inclusion of this piece is a way to celebrate the "primitive" ritual being described, but also a way to subtly mock Miner's repulsed fascination with the "local customs," all of a piece with Joans's lifelong effort to "demystify" Africa.

The UNESCO job was paying the bills, but at the same time Joans was becoming increasingly involved in the city's creative and intellectual scenes so that he really was burning the candle at both ends. "I was participating in my new Village bohemian activities so much," he recalled, "painting or visiting museums and galleries during the entire days and going to wild or intellectual parties that last all night, so much so, that I begin to neglect my good salaried UNESCO job."[21] The situation finally came to a head when Joans's boss called him into his office and forced him to make a choice, "Do you want to be a well-paid UNESCO worker, or do you want to be a leading bohemian figure [?] ... I respected his wise confrontation and told him that it was best for my life desire of surreality to relinquish any form of institutional employment. It was the first job that I had upon arrival in New York and it was the last 'good job' that I would ever have."[22] As André Breton put it, "There is no use being alive if one must work. The event from which each of us is entitled to expect the revelation of his own life's meaning ... *is not earned by work.*"[23]

Joans simply wasn't suited to "institutional employment," his "own life's meaning" was located elsewhere, and quit his job at UNESCO, choosing instead to scrape funds together through more creative means. In his New York years he did occasionally have other "straight" jobs for brief periods, trying to marry his creative or cultural interests with his need to support himself. A notable example was his stint running an African restaurant called Bwana's Table, which was renamed the less colonial Port Afrique.[24] Although the place did marginally better after an African diplomat patronized it,

Joans felt that at the time in New York, there was little interest in African food and culture, even at Port Afrique. "People were laughing at me when I wore African clothes," he said, "when I talked about Africa. I couldn't get a black woman to wear African dresses. I had to use white girls in African clothes as waitresses."[25] This sense was confirmed when *Ebony* conducted a survey of its readers regarding topics they wanted to see covered in the magazine's pages: Africa came in last.[26] The restaurant wasn't catching on, and the general lack of interest in Africa really began to bother Joans, and he dreamt up ways to Africanize New York—and to make a little money while doing so.

11

The Mau Mau Take Manhattan

Quitting the job at UNESCO allowed Joans to devote more time to his creative pursuits, including painting and developing what he would call his "big surrealist costume parties."[1] Although he had hoped to make his name as a painter, he actually started to become well known around New York for these parties, which were at once ways for him to generate cash *and* artistic explorations very much like the "Happenings" that would become vogue at the end of the 1950s—as he said, these events were "not only creative but commercial."[2]

An early Surreal costume party Joans held was called "Manhattan Mau Mau." Together with Charlie Parker, painter Harvey Cropper, fashion designer Byron Le Gip, and photographer Weegee, who documented the event, Joans daubed guests in face and body paint, "undressed half of the two hundred sixty-five girls present, and sold Dada slogans to the public."[3] The walls of Joans's studio were adorned with Surrealist drawings, including his trademark rhinoceros, fliers celebrating the "geniuses" André Breton and Sigmund Freud, and notices simply proclaiming: "DADA." Joans presided over the proceedings like a Master of Ceremonies, dressed in a white suit that he had painted with Surrealist portraits and signed boldly on the jacket. With half his face painted a glaring white, he mounted a stool and performed poetry for the guests. Charlie Parker went around stripped to the waist, face painted with elaborate white "Mau Mau" markings.

Joans's principal collaborator for this party was Byron Le Gip, a young West Indian in a beret and a shocking earring who led an hour-long "Somnambulist Conga Line." Le Gip would go on to have a long career in the Village as a fashion designer, but in the mid-1950s he and Joans would often organize parties together, with Le Gip beating on conga drums for hours on end while Joans chanted or recited poetry. Joans said he relied on Le Gip to get his "soirées organized correctly and it was he and I that made bread from those so called square tourists that invaded the Village scene."[4] "Manhattan Mau Mau" raged on all night, and at dawn the hold-outs trudged off to a "psychological breakfast," where they discussed Surrealist poetry with Joans and were served "sweat from a psychoanalyst's couch."[5]

The "Manhattan Mau Mau" event caught the imagination of people in the Village, and was covered by the Black interest magazine *Our World*, which noted that:

> The old Greek god Bacchus, who threw some of the wildest parties in history, had nothing on Ted Jones' Surrealist Open House in Greenwich Village, New York. His studio apartment looked like Dante's Inferno as Villagers, weirdly made-up and costumed, went in for a night of revelry … The host gave out with an irrational outburst on surrealism, defining it as a 'state of the spirit.' Guests left 'race hates' at home.[6]

This last point suggests the main reason why *Our World* was interested in the party, because it was, by design, unabashedly interracial—reporting on yet another of Le Gip and Joans's parties in September 1955, *Our World* observed that it was dedicated to "love across the color line": "Many Negro, white, Village hangers-on, are 'hungry' for love affairs with other race."[7]

Such a statement would have been scandalous to large swaths of the country, which was very much in the throes of ongoing reckonings with race and racism, the legacies of slavery, and the far-reaching consequences of Jim Crow. The landmark *Brown vs. Board of Education* decision, which ruled segregation in public schools unconstitutional, had just been handed down in May 1954. The following summer, a Black boy, 14-year-old Emmett Till, would be tortured and killed for allegedly whistling at a white woman in Money, Mississippi, galvanizing the Civil Rights Movement anew. Despite the relative permissiveness of Greenwich Village, it was still a brave—and political—act to host a party where Black and white people were freely mixing and enjoying themselves in Joans's Surrealist world. In this context, Joans's hypermasculine flaunting of his sexuality—in his poetry, autobiographies, statements to the press and general public persona—was also about confronting the lurid spectaularization of Black male sexuality head-on, and taking control of that narrative, at least for himself.

Indeed, aside from any money he earned, for Joans the defiant mixing of races was a large part of the point, a social and political statement underscored by the name of the party itself: "Manhattan Mau Mau." Joans had become fascinated with the Mau Mau, the popular term for the Kenya Land and Freedom Army (KLFA), a Black-led group that fought against British colonial rule in Kenya from 1952 to 1960. From about 1952 to 1957, images and stories about Mau Mau circulated widely through American culture, as for instance in Robert Ruark's novel about the Mau Mau, *Something of Value* (1955), which was made into a film of the same name starring Rock Hudson and Sidney Poitier (1957); or in *Simba* (1955), a British film about the Mau Mau whose movie poster featured a cartoonish

African "savage" wielding a machete-like panga and a skull impaled on a staff (Joans hung *Simba* posters at some of his Mau Mau parties, and his costumes seem to play off the film's imagery).

As cultural historian Joel Foreman explains, there were two broad ways the "Mau Mau signifier" circulated in American culture at this time: "One, manifesting racist fears and resistance, signified a resurgence of deplorable African savagery; the other, the desire for equal treatment and freedom from colonial authority, signified an emancipatory political movement grounded in legitimate grievances."[8] In other words, those disposed toward white supremacy and the maintenance of colonial power structures tended to see in "Mau Mau" evidence of African "savagery," and newspaper and magazine reports so inclined tended to focus on the Mau Mau as terrorists, emphasizing images of "assassination, primitive oath takings, and blood rituals." As Joans himself noted, at the time "there was a considerable amount of popular interest in the media about the Mau Mau, all negative and of course anti-African."[9] For him, in contrast, Mau Mau represented the promise of and hope for the collapse of white supremacist colonial rule, and the coming of a postcolonial, Black-led Africa.

With this in mind, we might be able to better appreciate how loaded it was to name an event "Manhattan Mau Mau" and then invite people of all races to party and drop their inhibitions. In Joans's ironic embodiment of racist Hollywood images of "deplorable African savagery," he reclaims what he called "Mau Mau ritual" for Surrealist, integrationist ends. This was a rebuke of white supremacist conventions of social order exemplified by British colonial rule in Kenya—or Jim Crow laws in the States. Joans's Mau Mau events flouted such conventions as flagrantly and flamboyantly as possible, as at a later "Mau Mau Festival" he helped organize at the Pantomime Theater in Greenwich Village, during which a white woman, Sykes Sheppard, was crowned "Queen of the Mau Mau" and awarded seven golden apples from "Kenyatucky."[10] Of course such a deliberately provocative approach carried risks: Charlie Parker had gigs canceled after a photograph of him in white face paint as a "Cool Mau Mau" appeared in *One World.*[11]

Joans used the term "Mau Mau" frequently from this time on, and although its meaning may seem fixed to the Mau Mau fighters in Kenya, as an acknowledgement of solidarity with the global freedom struggle, he also developed a more expansive sense of the term (that said, in 1971, before an admiring audience in Nairobi, Joans would read poetry dedicated to Mau Mau leader Dedan Kimathi, whom he praised as "a freedom liberating-force"—see, for example, "No Mo Space For Toms"—and his "A Black Man's Guide to Africa" would recommend Kenyan museums showcasing "some of the weapons our Mau Mau brothers used during their struggle for liberation").[12] In general, he saw the spirit of Mau Mau as "brother" to the spirit of Surrealism insofar as both movements were about tearing down an

FIGURE 11.1 *Joans as Mau Mau, ca. 1955. Laurated Archive.*

established order or sabotaging "conventional habits"—this is why, in *All of Ted Joans and No More*, he defined Mau Mau as "Any Negro."[13]

In an unpublished "Mau Mau Manifesto," Joans conceived of Mau Mau as a kind of specifically Black Surrealist point of view, insisting that like Surrealism Mau Mau contained an "illogical sensibility," an interest in the subconscious mind, and a rejection of national borders—but from a Black perspective. He wrote:

Mau Mau is the inevitable ... mau mauism [*sic*] by its insistence on illogical sensibility, is a brother to Surrealism and also related to Dadaism but is more serious in its aesthetic attitude than the current "pop art." ... Mau Mauism is indebted to the Afro-American "ways and means" more than negritude. Mau Mauism is completely opposed to nationalism in any form, thus the Mau Mau poets can write or speak in any tongue.

Mau Mauism is dangerous to those that oppose it ... Mau Mauism is very concerned with the secrets of the self, which is buried in every creative soul. Thus it is wise for one to discover his truth with a "spade." A spade is what one must dig with. One must use a good and sharp spade to dig deep. To get to, and to carry out into everyday life that all important sub-conscious mind, one must be able to Dig! The sub-conscious is the truth. A truth most of the time too crude and potent for the square-shy and conventional ridden lives to bear ... The all important sub-conscious can be reached with a spade and a mau mau [sic] spade at that, to dig deep.[14]

From this viewpoint, "Mau Mau" is not *merely* an expression of solidarity with global Black people—although certainly it is this—it is also an attitude leading to an appreciation of Surrealist truths. As Joans imagines it, Mau Mau is a particularly Black route to Surrealism, "indebted" as it is to Black "ways and means." At one of his Mau Mau events he hung a cardboard version of what appears to be a Kota reliquary statue marked with the Swahili legend "Mau Mau na Surrealist hodari sana," or "Mau Mau are expert Surrealists." This reorientation of the "Mau Mau signifier" is a deliberate realignment of it with a Surrealist commitment to liberation, a move that prefigures how, in the 1960s, Joans would locate Surrealist themes and ideas in various kinds of African cultural and aesthetic expression.

A few years after "Manhattan Mau Mau," in October 1959, the police in Greenwich Village were cracking down on the cafés on and around MacDougal Street, and they also raided bohemian or "Beatnik" parties, looking to make examples of people they took to be trouble makers. A minor scandal erupted around the Village when the police raided one such party and made a big show of arresting Ronald "Mau Mau" Jackson, a figure *The Village Voice* called "one of the more flamboyant coffee-shop Mau Maus."[15] While *The Village Voice* implied that Jackson's arrest was an arbitrary show of force against bohemians, the more mainstream press characterized Jackson as a menace, noting that he was arrested on a gun charge and for marijuana possession at a "beatnik party."[16]

Joans paid tribute to "Mau Mau" Jackson in a collage piece that eventually became part of his book *The Hipsters*. Using an image taken from a nineteenth-century history of white explorers in Africa, this piece depicts a long line of tribesmen in central Africa carrying an explorer's gear; but Joans has changed the context, making the image about a return to New York. The title is: "The Ronnie Manhattan Mau Mau Return from Mexico."[17] In this image, Joans identifies a continuity between the white supremacist regulatory practices of Europeans in Africa and the local New York police arresting Black people—but he flips the script so that the image becomes one of triumphant return. The collage superimposes an image of the gastrointestinal system from an anatomy textbook over the first figure in the line, and in *The Hipsters*, Joans jokingly urges readers to "Notice that their leader has plenty of guts."

12

Salvador Dalí at the St. Regis

Joans's "big surrealist costume parties" brought him early notoriety in New York, and he doubled down on his image as a Surrealist when he staged a photo shoot with certainly the most popularly-known Surrealist painter in the world, Salvador Dalí. In 1954, Joans made a pilgrimage up from Greenwich Village to the St. Regis Hotel in mid-town Manhattan, where Dalí had spent his winters in residence since 1934. Both Dalí and Joans were known for making spectacles of otherwise small events—store window displays, birthday parties—and Joans had arranged for *Ebony* magazine to send a photographer along to document the meeting. This was a real coup for Joans, and not wanting to waste the opportunity, he was ready with the portrait of Dalí he had painted back in Louisville.

At the meeting Joans and Dalí greeted each other with a "French embrace" and Dalí tried looking through a "Surrealist eye" that Joans wore on a chain around his neck. Joans presented the portrait, and even played some bop on a piano, while Dalí listened attentively.

The photo spread and accompanying story wound up appearing not in *Ebony*, but in *Hue*, another Black interest magazine owned by Johnson publications. Perhaps as a testament to his own growing celebrity—at least for Black readers—the story in *Hue* actually focused on Joans, not Dalí, who at that point was one of the most recognizable artists in the world, even to those who didn't really follow art. In fact, the title of the article, "Mad Genius," refers not to Dalí but to Joans, noting that he is a "worshipper of the rhinoceros and ... perhaps the most authentic of all the bohemian residents of New York's Greenwich Village."[1]

After the lead photo showing Joans meeting Dalí (Figure 12.1), the balance are focused on Joans, showing him "serious, eloquent as he lectures on rhinoceros"; at a party, "surrounded by worshipping women"; engaged in a "typical madcap prank" of hanging himself up in a coat; and posing with a goatee shaved off half the side of his face. Under a section heading

FIGURE 12.1 *Joans presents Salvador Dalí with a portrait. From* Hue *2.3 (January 1955), 37. Photograph by Moneta Sleet Jr. Credit: Johnson Publishing Company Archive.*

"Self-Acclaimed Genius Flees Country to Avoid Women," *Hue* informed its readers: "A true surrealist believing in 'freedom of emotional and physical expression,' unpredictable Ted Joans spends most of his time impressing others with his genius. Soon after he shocked Louisville, Ky., by quitting a promising musical career, he took a job as a theater porter, zoomed up to manager in two months. Then before taking up art, he was a successful disc jockey and stage comedian. At his parties he lectures on existentialism, the rhinoceros and the beauty of giving. Recently he accepted a UNESCO music teaching job in Liberia to escape, he says, 'the many women who think they have a claim on me'" (back in Louisville, Brazzle Tobin had also reported that Joans was toying with taking an "Art teaching job in Liberia. His examination papers are already in. His fate rests on whether his grades, and required physical examination are passable").[2]

Profiles such as this, together with all the stories about his parties, contributed to the making of the Joans legend, as the Louisville-famous Ted Jones was becoming New York-famous Ted Joans within just a couple of years of having moved there. This story also represents a kind of last gasp of Joans's devotion to Dalí-inspired Surrealism, for it was not too long after their meeting that he rejected Dalí as being too commercialized and therefore not a "true" Surrealist (he also felt Dalí had "stolen" the rhinoceros from him—by 1955, as Ian Gibson writes, "Dalí made sure that he obtained the maximum publicity for his rhinomania").[3] Joans finally renounced Dalí with as much force as Breton had back in the 1930s, when he put Dalí on trial and "expelled" him from Surrealism. In 1984, when Joans edited his one-shot Surrealist journal, *Dies und Das,* he included a 1974 interview in which Dalí announced his disdain for Black art and jazz. Joans's cutting introduction explained that Dalí "ceased being a surrealist when he became enamoured of Adolf Hitler, converted to Catholicism and totally immersed in commercialism."[4] This indictment was capped off by Joans wishing that Dalí would die "soon." When Dalí did finally die, in 1989, Joans told Franklin and Penelope Rosemont, his Surrealist friends in Chicago, that he had been at an "African Embassy party" when he heard the news, and had "automatic replied: GOOD!"[5]

13

Meeting Joyce and the Galerie Fantastique

However much the grandiose claim in *Hue* that Joans was "fleeing" the States to escape women did indeed resonate with his leaving Joan and Sylvia and Yvette back in Louisville, he remained in New York another six years, partly because of a woman he met at the Café Rienzi in Greenwich Village. This café was a special place for him at the time. Opened in June 1952 by a "group of artists whose idea it was to have a European style café here in America," as their menu announced, Café Rienzi was immensely popular among the artistic set, and as Joans recalled, "young bohemians flocked" there because other neighborhood mainstays like Café Reggio, with its dark old world charm and strong espresso, was the province of those local Italians who took a hard line against "unconventional clientele."[1] Café Rienzi featured reasonably priced food and coffee, tables for chess and checkers, and a rotating display of artwork for sale, usually sourced from local Village artists—Joans in fact had his first New York "One Man exhibition" in the light-filled front room there.[2]

Over the course of the 1950s, Café Rienzi became another go-to gathering place for artists and writers of the ever-expanding counterculture. When, for example, a wide-eyed LeRoi Jones had first come to the Village, he sought out the café in particular: "the old Rienzi, with its gestures in the direction of Continental sophistication, had turned me on. I thought everyone in those places was a writer or painter or something heavy."[3] Ted Joans claimed he had been the third customer ever when the Rienzi opened, and he was later granted "special priorities due to my charismatic, magnetizing, Rienzi-advertising and daily support. I had my own special reserved table by the window. If someone else sat down there and they did not know Ted Joans, then the waiter or waitress would ask them to change to another table."[4] As he would in his later years at the Café Le Rouquet in Paris, Joans ensconced himself at his table at the front of the café, making drawings, writing poetry, and holding forth to friends or curious "tourists."

FIGURE 13.1 *Twenty-six-year-old Ted Joans at Café Rienzi with an unknown woman, 1954. The beret and glasses were typical accessories at this time. Laurated Archive.*

Objective Chance worked its magic once again in the spring of 1955, when a sudden rainstorm drove a young woman to duck inside the Rienzi. Joans was at his reserved table, drawing a series of rhinoceroses, and looked up to see a "young thin attractive Waspy woman," slightly wet but not worse for the wear. Joans recalled this woman sitting down at his table and asking him "unhip questions" like "Is that supposed to be some sort of symbol?" and "Who taught you how to draw like that?"[5] Annoyed that she was evidently unaware that "the Rienzi regulars were hip to me not wanting to be disturbed when I was drawing," Joans tried to give her the cold shoulder. But the woman persisted, assuring him that she wasn't like any of the countless college girls who "do their weekend bohemia" in the Village. As a matter of fact, she said, she might like to buy one of his paintings. This was the password, and Joans perked up considerably.[6]

The young woman was named Joyce Wrobleski, and she would go on to be Joans's most significant romantic partner in the second half of the 1950s, during which time they lived together and had five children. She was from a conservative Catholic family in Michigan, and had fled her unhappy home life the instant she turned 18. She arrived in New York with no concrete plans except making it on her own in the big city, and on her own terms. By the time she had met Joans, Joyce was living with a roommate on Riverside Drive and working as a receptionist at an import/export company down near Wall Street. Although she wasn't particularly bohemian in inclination, she enjoyed strolling around in Greenwich Village because the shops and restaurants were inexpensive, and there always seemed to be something interesting going on.

The day she met Joans, Joyce had been walking down MacDougal Street when that spring rain burst hit, and she jumped into the nearest coffee shop, which happened to be Café Rienzi. For her part, Joyce couldn't quite recall if she had approached Joans as he remembered, but she was drawn to his "self-assurance," his "ego," and the fact that he was clearly a "popular artist" in the Village.[7] After that first chance encounter, Joyce was smitten, and immediately dumped her boyfriend to pursue things with Joans.

Joyce fell hard, and before she knew it, she had moved out of her Riverside Drive apartment and into Joans's Astor Place studio. In just a few months she was pregnant with their first daughter, Daline (whose name was a last vestige of Joans's admiration for Dalí), who was born about a year after they first met, in April 1956. The couple would go on to have four more children together: twins Ted Jr. ("Teddy") and Teresa (born April 1957), Jeannemarie (born February 1959), and Robert (born July 1961). Although Joans referred to Joyce as his "wife," the couple never legally married. They did go so far as to secure a marriage license, and were planning a trip to the Justice of the Peace, but Joyce backed out at the last minute because her Catholic upbringing still haunted her. Marriage was a sacrament, and she felt it was a mortal sin to get married outside the church (Joans may have also still been technically married to Joan Locke). But still Joyce's attraction to Joans was magnetic, and she vowed to stay with him despite the lack of legal sanction. As she told me, "He was the first love of my life."[8]

After living briefly in the Astor Place studio, Joans and Joyce moved together to a shabby place on Cooper Square, which was too cramped for the two of them, let alone a future baby. Once Joyce was pregnant with Daline, she insisted that they look for larger accommodations, and so Joans's family and creative lives became even more entwined as they moved again, this time into a storefront apartment at 108 St. Mark's Place, which afforded the family more room to grow, and Joans the space to open an art gallery he dubbed Galerie Fantastique.[9]

Joans refurbished the storefront to convert it into a gallery, and he and Joyce and the newborn Daline lived in the back. Rent was just $35 a month.[10] Behind the gallery space was a bedroom, kitchen, and a small water closet with a toilet. There was also a tiny room for Daline's crib (and soon enough the cribs for the twins). It was an improvement over the Cooper Square place, but only marginally: Joyce had to climb out the rear window just to

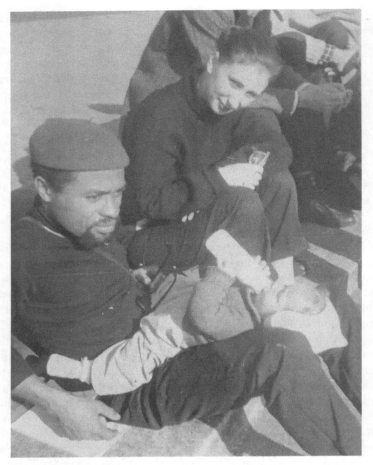

FIGURE 13.2 *Joans and Joyce with baby Daline, New York City, 1956.*

hang laundry on the line, and there were mice running around most of the time.

The Galerie Fantastique itself represented an important moment for Joans as it was what he called the "very first Black owned fine arts gallery on St. Mark's Place," through which he was able to showcase the work of "many young whites as well as Black painters, photographers and sculptors."[11] It was also an ideal space to promote his own work, and he thought of his very first solo exhibit there as an "attack on some of the Tenth Street racists," the gallery owners and artists he felt were shutting him out of the scene. The show was titled NEW NEW because the two words "upside down spelt Mau Mau."[12]

Although much of Joans's Surrealist painting of the mid-1950s is either lost or in hiding, one piece that did survive is a magnificent, dreamlike study of innumerable rhinoceroses dominating a barren plain, a kind of phantom Africa. This painting, *Land of the Rhinoceri* (1957), uses a subdued, neutral palette of sage, khaki, rust and browns to depict different species of rhinoceros engaging in various activities in an arid, sand-colored expanse (see Figure 13.3). While echoes of Dalí's signatures appear, as a shape melting over an undulating rock outcropping in the central foreground (a Picasso-like face is hidden in those rocks immediately to the right of this shape), in its obsessive variation on the rhinoceros, *Land of the Rhinoceri* seems to assert Joans's claims to the animal, as he sets his finely-wrought, anatomically-sensitive figures in an impossible dreamscape.[13]

By the time Galerie Fantastique opened, Joans seemed to have largely turned away from his Dalí-inspired work of the type pictured in *Land of the Rhinoceri* or the *Hue* profile, and toward what he called his "jazz action" paintings. Dalí's work was highly technical and precise, but Joans was becoming fascinated with the "automatic spontaneity" in Abstract Expressionism and thought that it was a better route to creating canvases that might "actually 'swing' like the jazz music I adored."[14]

In this new work, he wanted to capture the rhythmic physicality of his own body movements.[15] Now he was influenced by "Picasso's gestures when he was photographed painting with light," and by the French Abstract Expressionist painter Georges Mathieu, whose theories of "lyrical abstraction" emphasized speed of execution and what Joans took to be an absolute commitment to spontaneity.[16] He had also become close with Franz Kline because they lived down the street from each other. As Joans said of Kline: "I loved him, copied him, drank with him and laughed at the absurdities of the world with him."[17] Joans considered Kline "one of the greatest artist[s] that the USA has produced," and was intrigued by his huge black-and-white canvases, a color scheme which Joans felt was thematic: "Kline meant a lot to me due to his black and white subject matter. He really used black more often than he did white. He was concerned with black. Being from the Pennsylvania coal mining scene he knew of many blacks ... But it was not the color of morbidity or sadness. No, it was a color of strength and life. It was the black of jazz."[18]

Joans's new "jazz action" paintings were influenced by Kline, though he specified that he was open to using "bright colors" as opposed to only black and white. The important thing was that the paintings captured spontaneity on the canvas, and in this way were what he called "automatically Surreal."[19] From January 16 to 29, 1959, the Phoenix Gallery held a solo exhibition of Joans's "jazz action" painting (see Figure 13.5), priced between 25 and 300 dollars. *Arts* magazine reported that "The abstractions are generally centrally fixed, like one loud blare, with lines crossing furiously at a point of concentration and thinning out toward the canvas edges."[20] The first jazz

FIGURE 13.3 *Ted Joans, Land of the Rhinoceri (1957). Oil on Masonite. 31 13/16 × 56 11/16 inches. Virginia Museum of Fine Arts, Arthur and Margaret Glasgow Endowment, 2021.593.*

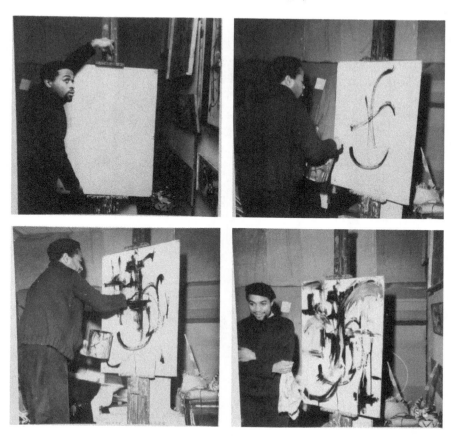

FIGURE 13.4 *Ted Joans making one of his "jazz action" paintings. New York City, December, 1957. Laurated Archive.*

action painting he sold was titled "DeKooling Blues," a tribute to Willem de Kooning, another painter he had met at the Cedar (Kline and de Kooning had both once recommended Joans for a John Hay Whitney Fellowship, but he "didn't get shit").[21]

Galerie Fantastique was a perfect place for Joans to showcase his work. He touted the gallery as "specializing in Dadaism, Surrealism, Primitivism, Fantastic and Children's works."[22] The idea was to promote his work, and to encourage camaraderie among underrepresented artists he admired by providing them wall space—operating the gallery as a money-making business was always beside the point. As Joyce put it, Galerie Fantastique was a place for Joans to "show off his work and have conversations with other artists."[23] And as a sort of artist's community center, the gallery became known around town. In a profile piece in *The Village Voice*, for

FIGURE 13.5 *Advertisement for an exhibit of Joans's "jazz action" paintings at the Phoenix Gallery, a co-operative gallery of which he was an original member. From January, 1959. TJP, carton 3, folder 49.*

example, John Wilcock noted one local bohemian's droll catalogue of all the cheap things to do in town: "Ted Joans of the Galerie Fantastique has Dixieland parties ... every Friday night, I believe; I've never been there, but I hear they're pretty good. A dollar—and take your own booze."[24] When LeRoi Jones passed through Galerie Fantastique, he recalled seeing the work of "Reggin Nam," which everybody knew was really Joans's work (Jones found it "Gross ... but fascinating").[25]

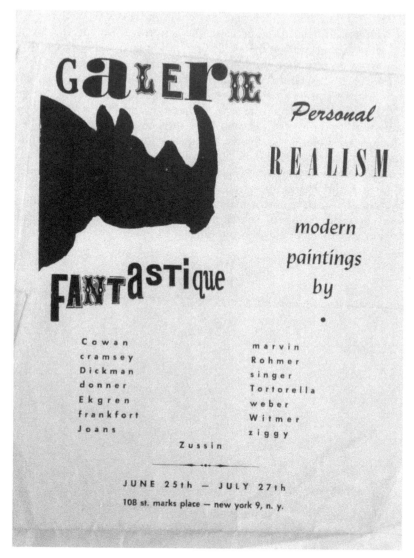

FIGURE 13.6 *Promotional flier for Galerie Fantastique. TJP, carton 3, folder 49.*

The Galerie Fantastique stayed open for around a year, but once the twins were born, Joyce again insisted that they move to better digs, and took it upon herself to locate a proper home for their growing family. What they could afford was out on Staten Island, a rental on Olympia Boulevard next to the Miller Field airbase—the very end of the bus line. It wasn't much, but at least it was "a real house with bedrooms and bathrooms."[26]

As far as Joans was concerned, Staten Island may as well have been Outer Mongolia for its distance from the action in Manhattan, but Joyce was adamant about putting their kids first and moved anyway, over Joans's objections—a pattern that would repeat itself again in the mid-1960s, with his Norwegian wife, Grete Moljord. At the time, Joyce didn't have a real sense of Joans's stature in the art or poetry worlds—that he was a rising "star." She saw him just as the love of her life and father to three small children, with two more of his own back in Kentucky, to whom he would occasionally send clothes and care packages. Joyce thought they should all live together on Staten Island, which would provide the stability the kids needed. But Joans retained his Astor Place studio, and in fact tended to spend most nights there, in order to paint, he said, and remain connected to the scene. This arrangement inevitably put a strain on their relationship, and over the next couple of years, the pressure would build to a breaking point—but still Joans couldn't bring himself to uproot completely from the Village.

14

Bird Lives!

The pull of the magnetic fields in the Village was simply too great for Joans to resist, as he seemed daily to meet fascinating people, creative geniuses, and marvelous potential lovers. There he befriended a veritable Who's Who of twentieth-century tastemakers: writers, artists, musicians, actors, and others who, with hindsight, would be recognized as among the most significant cultural producers of the postwar era. He had to be in the center of the action, at least for the time being.

In the days before the Beat Generation exploded with the obscenity trial surrounding Allen Ginsberg's *Howl and Other Poems* and the publication of Jack Kerouac's *On the Road* in 1957, one important friendship Joans cultivated was with Charlie "Yardbird" Parker, probably the greatest alto jazz saxophonist of the twentieth century, and in many people's view the spiritual and artistic godfather to the Beats. As Ralph Ellison put it, "for the postwar jazznik, Parker was Bird, a suffering, psychically wounded, law-breaking, life affirming hero"—a sense that Ellison thought Ted Joans himself had captured very well in a "wild surrealist poem."[1]

"Bird was," Joans wrote, "the personification of many things for poets and hipsters of the Beat G ... Bird was a bringer of beautiful music, an alto saxophone poetry. Spontaneous poetry, the essential of that poetry was to share it by living it, not in disrespect of self and others, but in complete active state of embracing the marvelous. Live like a Bird solo, which is an audio cyclical surreality."[2] Joans and many others saw Parker as a quintessence of Black genius, a titanic figure who lived his own truth without conforming to societal standards, the very embodiment and symbol of avant-garde experimentation.

Born in Kansas City in 1920, Charlie Parker came to New York City in 1939, and a decade later was successful enough that a jazz club, Birdland, was named after him—throughout the 1940s and early 1950s, he played Birdland regularly, right up until the last days of his life, when he did back-to-back gigs there on March 4 and 5, 1955.[3] Parker's close association with

bop and its rapid development meant that his music became the soundtrack
of the Beat Generation and Parker himself an emblem of liberated Black
aesthetic innovation in the 1940s and 1950s.

As Scott DeVeaux explains, "bebop emerged against the background of
the Swing Era, a time in which jazz-oriented white dance bands flooded the
marketplace and Benny Goodman was crowned King of Swing."[4] Given this
background, bop has variously been understood as a non-commercial, avant-
garde, and Black form of artistic expression.[5] In this view, bop was born as
a reaction to the kind of big band jazz that had ascended in popularity
during the swing era, and according to legend, in 1942, a group of musicians
got together at Minton's Playhouse in Harlem and invented a new form of
jazz: trumpeter Dizzy Gillespie, pianist Thelonius Monk, guitarist Charlie
Christian, drummer Kenny Clarke, and saxophonist Charlie Parker. In his
book *Blues People* (1963), LeRoi Jones sketches this legend, but then quotes
Thelonius Monk saying that "histories and articles put what happened [at
Minton's] over the course of ten years into one year. They put people all
together in one time and one place."[6]

However impossible it may be to pin down the precise place and date a
new musical genre was birthed, it is the case that bop was widely seen as
a thrillingly complex and dazzlingly innovative form of artistic expression
often directly associated with Harlem and its "underground." In the preface
to his long poem *Montage of a Dream Deferred* (1951), Langston Hughes
explained that some of the formal techniques he was using in his "poem on
contemporary Harlem" were analogous to what one found in bop, as both
were "marked by conflicting changes, sudden nuances, sharp and impudent
interjections, broken rhythms, and ... punctuated by the riffs, runs, breaks,
and disc-tortions of the music of a community in transition."[7] In one of
those Jesse B. Semple stories that Joans loved, Hughes has Semple theorize
the origins of bop like this: "Every time a cop hits a Negro with his billy

FIGURE 14.1 *Joans's Birdland "membership" card, ca. early 1950s. Laurated
Archive.*

club, that old club says, 'BOP! BOP ... BE-BOP! ... MOP! ... BOO! ... '
That's where Be-Bop comes from, beaten right out of some Negro's head
into those horns and saxophones and the piano keys that play it."[8] For
Joans as for many others, bop was, as he put it, "a Black revolutionary
musical direction for Black musicians to create for the people and to be
supported by the people for it was a modern Black music of the Black
people."[9]

Joans's observation that bop was "revolutionary" points to the reasons
why Charlie Parker was so influential to him and others—it was not merely
because of his musical innovations but also because he represented a social
attitude that emphasized individual expression at the expense of conforming
to the expectations of (white) society. In *Black Talk* (1971), jazz musician
and writer Ben Sidran explained Parker's importance in the context of the
rise of Black consciousness, and reaches back to the Reconstruction Era to
explain this history:

> Whereas mainstream America had told the emancipated Negro, "It is
> important *how* you play the game," the Negro, particularly after the
> failure of Reconstruction, had begun to speculate that it was perhaps
> more important whether or not one chose to play the game at all ...
> Parker's generation, having intuitively recognized that the ground rules
> were stacked against them, was the first to declare the "game" not worth
> playing and so became the first to articulate isolationism in a socially
> aggressive manner.[10]

For Joans and others in his generation, Parker's life and music represented a
refusal to play the game, an insistence on creating art on one's own terms, an
attitude broadly aligned with what Sidran calls a "hip ethic." As he explains:
"At the root of the hip ethic is an almost arrogant assertion of individuality,
a fight for personal integrity in the face of growing urban depersonalization
and the rejection of the stifling inhibitions of Western society."[11] Joans
thought of Sidran's *Black Talk* as the "definitive book on the formulation of
the music nicknamed 'Jazz,'" and even declared the book "as important to
me as the Surrealist Manifestoes," so it's safe to say that Sidran's analyses
resonated with him.[12]

Although Joans had actually first heard Parker play back in Louisville
when his sister took him to a "skating rink for Black people," they hadn't
met personally until Joans had come to New York.[13] One of his first
orders of business was to seek out Parker, and when he learned that his
musical idol was performing at Birdland, he put on his best clothes for the
"sacred musical moment of my life" and went to see the show.[14] Given
that he always described jazz as his religion, it's no surprise that Joans
characterized hearing Parker's set at Birdland as a transfiguring, holy
experience:

It was a spiritual reassurance that all was possible, that is, IF you were hip to the Why/When/How/Where/What and Who. That *who* depended upon the knowledge of yourself, and your actions, *indoors*, and *outdoors*. The phrases that spewed from his lava hip lip horn of plenty actually preached to me. I listened to every righteous riff, the short signifying statements ... and the long ornithological flights ... I was in paradise, a musical paradise to be sitting in Birdland listening to Charlie Parker in person.[15]

Spiritual. Righteous. Preached. Paradise. It's no overstatement to say that Joans always insisted on the religious dimensions of truly great jazz, and in the transcendent power of Parker himself.

Things only got better that night. After the set, Joans was in disbelief to see Parker himself ambling right over to the bar for a drink. Joans worked up the nerve to approach.

"Mister Parker," he said. "I want to thank you, not only for tonight's music but for all the music that I have on recordings of yours. Thank you, sir!"

Parker wasn't put off by his gushing fan as Joans had feared, and the two fell into a brief conversation, with Joans explaining that he was a jazz aficionado and painter looking to make it in the city. Joans even got to shake Parker's hand, which he saw as "an unknown universal treasure."[16] In *Bird: The Legend of Charlie Parker*, a collection of reminiscences he edited, Robert Reisner observed that "To the hipster Bird was their private possession ... they treasured their little brushes with him," a remark certainly borne out by Joans's awed recollections here and elsewhere.[17] In this way, Joans was akin to those countless people who came into Parker's orbit at various moments in his life, nearly all of whom spoke about him in reverent, if not mythic tones.

During the time they knew each other, Joans said, Parker was "suffering from poverty, and I was 'the impecunious poet.'"[18] From Parker's entwined money troubles and addiction issues arose what has become a well known story about Joans and him, that they "lived together," as Joans said, in his cold water flat on Barrow Street.[19] This story Joans told many times, always emphasizing that he and Parker were both broke and freezing for lack of heat in the building. One day, another tenant, Ahmad Basheer, whom Joans called "a saintly hip philosopher," found Parker fallen down or passed out drunk in the gutter in front of #4 Barrow.[20] Basheer recalled rushing to Parker's aid, and enlisting the help of three others to wrestle him upstairs, where Parker slept it off. By that point, Parker was suffering from ulcers and the advanced cirrhosis of the liver that would ultimately kill him—which is why Basheer could claim Parker "stayed on as a guest in my one room for the rest of his life."[21] As Joans recalled it, Basheer wound up getting "put out" of his room, and so both he and Parker found themselves staying in Joans's room next door.[22]

Curiously, Basheer didn't mention Joans in his contribution to *Bird: The Legend of Charlie Parker*, but Joans's own remembrance transformed the stories into history: "I slept with Charlie Parker, nothing sexual, just that on Barrow Street, we all lived together, Bird, Basheer, and myself, with very little steam heat. We slept together to keep warm a little. We only got steam four hours a day, from six to ten."[23] Later Joans said that he had given Parker the key to "my #4 Barrow Street (one room cold water) flat," and in subsequent retellings would vary the length of time Parker stayed there, from "a few nights" to "off and on for several weeks."[24] Joans remembered both sleeping in the same "imitation double bed" with Basheer and Parker, and rotating use of the bed, with Parker reminding them that he didn't roll in until 3:00 or 4:00 in the morning, so "you cats should get up and let me sleep."[25]

Whatever the exact circumstances and length of time, the story of Joans "living" with Parker was picked up in Russell Ross's biography of Parker, *Bird Lives!* (1973), which informs readers that Joans, Parker, and Basheer "shared a flat" for "several weeks," the lack of heat driving them to "sleep in the same bed, under a pile of overcoats and sweaters."[26]

In reviewing Ross's book, Joans took the opportunity to confirm and correct the historical record:

Yes, just as Russell reported, Bird, Basheer and I did share a top floor room at 4 Barrow Street, a rundown flophouse … We had two rooms for a while, then when bread got too thin we all shacked up in my front room. Yes, just as Russell stated, Bird did stay there off and on for several weeks, and he would often shout down the stairwell (not airwell) … "what the fuck, you jiveass cocksuckers think we are up here, three black Eskimos?" And we three did sleep in the same narrow double bed, out of necessity, and to keep warm.[27]

As in all his retellings of these events, Joans stresses the adverse conditions, and the fact that he and Parker were both suffering, presumably for their shared commitment to art. As he once said, "The hipsters knew that America extracts great prices from its mythical figures, therefore the heavy dues Bird paid."[28] In his destitution, Parker becomes a "mythical figure"—and perhaps a little of this mythos rubs off on Joans as he amends and elaborates the record, emphasizing their mutually distressed circumstances.

Joans took up the theme of freezing with Charlie Parker in one of the many poems he wrote about him, "Ice Freezes Red." Named after a 1947 Fats Navarro tune, "Ice Freezes Red" was inspired by an incident that occurred early one morning sometime during the winter of 1954–5.[29] Joans,

FIGURE 14.2 *Joans and Charlie Parker (center) in face paint preparing for one of Joans's Surrealist parties, New York City, 1954. Joans is wearing one of his signature pieces from those years, an eye pendant given to him by a favorite girlfriend, Sally Gilbert, whom he nicknamed Sali in homage to Dalí. Laurated Archive.*

Basheer, and Parker were hanging out in front of an all-night diner on Sheridan Square, bitterly cold but too "proud" to head back up to the room at Barrow Street, whose heat was turned off anyway, and they all tried to warm up by standing over the steel grates where "some subway heat oozed up from the I.R.T. line below."[30] They stood talking and laughing into the early hours of the morning, "too broke to go inside the J&R all-night diner for even a cup of coffee," hoping that someone they knew would come by and invite them over to warm up at a party. At some point in the dark, cold night, a car full of "loud white men" pulled up, yelled racial slurs at them, and sped away.[31]

"Ice Freezes Red" tells this story, first thrusting readers into the icy night—the words "cold" and "cold night" are repeated numerous times, overwhelming the poem as it overwhelmed Joans, Parker, and Basheer huddled on the street corner.

That cold night
When we all hated to say good night
that night when all had frozen
that cold night
when we continued our conversations
just to keep from going to that cold cold room
called home
The cold night when everybody was gone (*ATJ*, 58)

The poem provides sharp, sensory details from that night (in addition to feeling the cold, we smell breath "reeking of onions" [58] and hear the "strange / flapping noise, that only the trouser cuffs can make" [59]), which invites us into the intimate scene where the bodies of the three men are being assailed by winter cold. It builds to the moment when the loud white men pull up and shout their racial slur before speeding off, and the poem ends with Joans, Parker, and Basheer shuffling back to the Barrow Street apartment, "Because we were no longer cold—not now, / We had been heated up, by hate" (60).

The "hate" here has two registers, the racist hate of the white men in the car, and the hate that has been aroused in "we"—the three Black men subjected to the slur while merely trying to survive in the cold. Like many of Joans's poems, "Ice Freezes Red" adds another layer of meaning in its final lines, which encourages a rereading. In the first half, the men are not named or otherwise marked except as human bodies vulnerable to the cold ("We stood trembling and shuffling our bodies" [58]). But then halfway through the poem, one of the men remarks, "I've always said that <u>winter</u> ... / was 'strictly for whites' only," thus marking the men as non-white as they share a laugh over the comment (59). When toward the end of the poem they are identified by a slur, one sees more clearly that being out in the cold in the middle of the night was a condition of their Blackness. In reminiscing about that incident, Joans realized with "a tremor of terror that we, the few Blacks dedicated to Fine Arts were Black explorers and settlers in a hostile, wild and sometimes physically dangerous asphalt concrete jungle."[32] The poem implies a correspondence between the men's Blackness and their freezing circumstances, so the notion of "cold" takes on figurative as well as literal resonances.

After testifying to the epithet hurled at them from the car, Joans deflates the power of the slur by finally naming himself and his companions:

We stood ... silent for want of something to do
Then we three, me Ted Joans, Basheer Ahmad the Moslem,
and him, the bird, Charlie Parker,
[...]

headed for Barrow Street to that cold place called home. (59–60;
    unbracketed ellipses in original).

This act of naming takes over the racial slur but does not erase it, and as
the men trudge back to Barrow Street, the freezing temperatures become a
physical instantiation of the cold reception of Black people in America, the
"cold place called home."

When "Ice Freezes Red" appeared in *All of Ted Joans and No More*,
it was accompanied by a collage that offers another illustration of the
constellations of issues at play in the poem. Four images surround the number
"1714," which as we know from Part One of this book is Joans's numerical
signature and code for African American: an image of a mother and child
from an indeterminate African tribe, arranged so they are standing on a log-
like arm Joans has drawn on to an illustration from a medical textbook, an
operation on a penis. Above this is an illustration of a pointing machine, a
device for measuring the dimensions of a person or object in order to sculpt
it, in this case a white girl holding a cat, and finally surmounting all this is

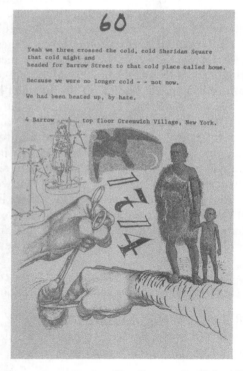

FIGURE 14.3 *Collage accompanying "Ice Freezes Red" in* All of Ted Joans and
No More.

an image of a flying bird. Here we have Blackness through the eyes of the white colonial gaze (the ethnographic illustration of the African mother and daughter); a scene of literal emasculation, which is an echo of the encounter with the white men in the car as depicted in the poem; and what is often behind such slurs and fear, an idealized image of white femininity and innocence, which must be reproduced exactly and preserved, as if in marble. 1714 is the hub of these spokes, and above it all is the soaring figure of Bird, who will ultimately break free.

Years later, after he had left the United States, fed up with the sort of experiences described in this poem, Joans starred in *Jazz and Poetry* (1964), a short film by Dutch filmmaker Louis van Gasteren, which featured him reading "Ice Freezes Red." He "blew" the poem, as he put it, to the accompaniment of a Dutch jazz quartet in the Amsterdam nightclub Scheherazade, a performance captured in the second half of *Jazz and Poetry* (in the film he also reads "The Truth" and "Hallelujah, I Love Jazz So"—elsewhere titled "Jazz Is My Religion").

As the film shows him reading the poem onstage at Scheherazade, van Gasteren intercuts the live reading with the shadows of three chatting men thrown onto a brick wall, and scenes of Joans himself acting out the poem, blowing into his hands on a street corner and stamping his feet against the cold. As he performs the climactic scene of the poem, the film has shots of a speeding car filled with white men, who careen by as Joans reads the devastating racial slur yelled from the open window. The dramatization makes for quite an affecting experience, and *Jazz and Poetry* is well worth seeking out.

In the film, Joans prefaces his reading of "Ice Freezes Red" by informing his Dutch audience that the poem is about a real-life incident that had happened to him in "New Amsterdam." He explained further that now, in 1964, he wintered in Africa and summered in Europe, fleeing the latter when it got too cold. "I don't dig cold weather," he said. "Nor do I dig bigotry. Bigotry and cold weather run hand in hand as far as I'm concerned."[33] Such a sentiment, that the cold weather somehow indexed the cold-heartedness of bigotry, became associated with Joans to such an extent that when Tuli Kupferberg wrote about all the hip characters in New York in his poem "Greenwich Village of My Dreams," he referred to "Charlie Parker & Ted Joans talking / in Sheridan Sq Park & its cold man!"[34]

There are two corollary poems to "Ice Freezes Red": "Last Night in Newark" and "They Forget Too Fast." In "Last Night in Newark," Joans is again with three people ("we black men three and sister soul in back")—not freezing but in the "humid Newark summer." The scene is very similar to "Ice Freezes Red": "out of nowhere white they came" / "but before they could say 'boy' / they were greeted with a barrage of black poetry / from LeRoi." The situation recalls "Ice Freezes Red," but does so in the context of the Black Arts Movement, so LeRoi Jones can conjure Black word magic that repels white ire and prevents a scene like the one depicted in the earlier poem.[35]

The other companion piece, "They Forget Too Fast," was written on March 15, 1962 in Timbuktu, for the seventh anniversary of Parker's death. In that poem, Joans recalls Barrow Street "WHERE WE SHARED: POT / PAINT / POEMS / MUSIC," and Sheridan Square, site of the incident recounted in "Ice Freezes Red."[36] As if to counter the long-ago racial slur, Joans imagines a "STATUE OF CHARLIE PARKER TEN FEET TALL THREE TONS / OF CONCRETE" that even in his fantasy is overrun with actual birds "WITH OVERSTUFFED GUTS" who shit all over Parker's likeness, obscuring his genius and legacy.[37]

Another example of the world catching up with Joans came in 1999, when Parker's hometown of Kansas City really did dedicate a statue of him, by artist Robert Graham. This statue, naturally, is called "Bird Lives," a fact that pleased Joans to no end. In an art piece he created in May 1999, he drew an outline of Parker hunched over his saxophone, a version of an image he had used way back when, in the painting *Bird Lives!* (1958), around which he wrote a letter to Parker, reading in part: "Kansas City has at last unveiled a tribute, a statue of you on that statue is my graffiti that is now world known—BIRD LIVES."[38]

Joans and Charlie Parker remained friends until 1955, when Parker died from hard drinking and heroin abuse at only 34. Joans saw Parker's addictive personality as a cautionary tale—once he witnessed Parker negotiating with one of his dealers in the Barrow Street apartment, and, pausing to sample some cocaine, Parker looked up and said, "Dig, Ted, you must not ever do drugs. I am telling you that you don't need the kick. After all, my man, you are high on life." Joans insisted that he always kept Parker's advice close to his heart, in his later years claiming that "I still refrain from any kind of heavy-drugs, including cigarettes, whisky and heroin" and would, when he learned that friends had taken up cocaine, admonish them forthrightly: "you do NOT need to sniff such shit."[39]

The incident with the cocaine occurred in the last few months of Parker's life, when he was frequenting the Barrow Street apartment. He died on March 12, 1955, in the rooms Baroness Pannonica de Koenigswarter kept at the Stanhope Hotel on 5th Avenue in New York City. Known to her friends as Nica, the Baroness was fabulously wealthy, born into the Rothschild family, and was also an outspoken jazz aficionado and patron who haunted the music clubs around the city. When news broke that Parker had died in her room, it was a scandal; the *New York Daily Herald*, for instance, proclaimed "Bop King Dies in Heiress's Flat."[40]

Parker had dropped in on the Baroness on his way to a gig in Boston, but looked and felt so unwell that he remained in her apartment for the next couple of days on doctor's orders. After rest and frequent check-ins from the doctor, by that Saturday night, March 12, Parker seemed to be feeling better, and was watching Tommy and Jimmy Dorsey's television program, *Stage Show*, with the Baroness and her daughter. When a team of jugglers came on, tossing bricks to one another with expert precision, the Baroness recalled Parker's delight: "Bird was laughing uproariously, but then he began to choke," and he passed soon thereafter.[41] In that ordinary and unglamorous way, the world lost one of its true musical geniuses.

However banal, the details of Parker's death help explain Joans's otherwise cryptic poem "Birdeath," which retells these events somewhat elliptically. The poem initially appeared in *Funky Jazz Poems* (dedicated "to Bahsheer" [*sic*]), and then as the very first poem in *All of Ted Joans and No More*, suggesting its importance to Joans. It opens:

995 way up on 5th Ave
995 Stanhope on many upper floors
he sat and dug TD on TV
TD on TV thus dug he
at 995 5th Avenue
in March
like 55
Stanhope
at 81
street I repeat
he sat and dug TD on TV
death came with the juggler
at 995 way up
on many upper floors (*ATJ*, 1)

The poem's action is fixed at a specific time and place, made notorious by the newspaper accounts of Parker's death. There is a tension in the poem between proximity and remoteness, so Parker is both far away in exclusive Stanhope Hotel, "way up on 5th Ave" from the perspective of a struggling artist down in Greenwich Village, but also seemingly close, as readers witness an intimate moment of Parker digging "TD on TV." That "TD" stands for Tommy Dorsey, one of the hosts of the television show Parker was watching when he died, and the use of initials suggests also an insider familiarity of speaker and subject that turns that moment into a mantra of sorts, as the speaker repeats that the television brought death to Parker: "I repeat / he sat and dug TD on TV"; "I repeat / death came by TV"; "I repeat / TV brought death to the Bird" (1).

At first, the poem seems to merely be retelling the lurid and slightly absurd circumstance of Parker's death. Certainly it does this, but there is also a larger symbolic meaning to the television being connected to Parker's death, as Joans felt Parker's particular genius simply couldn't be captured by television. "Did Bird ever appear on television?" he once wondered. "Were their TV cameras that fast, to catch Bird's flow of quicksilver sounds and his cursing his exploiters out on his alto saxophone? I doubt it! Bird was not slated to become a regular anywhere, for he too lived automatic."[42] For Joans, television, the increasingly dominant technology of information and entertainment in the 1950s, was simply insufficient when it came to Bird's soaring flights—and so it was perversely fitting that "TV brought death" to him (and later, when Joans developed his Happenings in Europe, he used a "TV Man" figure as a symbol of the corrosive effects of contemporary techno-culture, as explained in Part Three of this book).

In Joans's private mythology, 995 5th Avenue also had special significance because it was across the street from the Metropolitan Museum of Art, where he and Parker had once visited and marveled at a vessel or cup made by Renaissance artist Benvenuto Cellini. He recalled admiring the "Cellini vessel," which both he and Parker "wanted to liberate for our personal drinking purposes ... [Parker said,] 'Now dig this fabulous cup to sip slowly from, alone or in a crowd, sipping the very best of beverages. Shit man, the drinking from this Cellini alone would be intoxicating.'" In fact, the Cellini vessel was a kind of ghostly object haunting the poem "Birdeath" and linking Parker to Joans. The poem was written, he said, in the Met

> while standing before that treasure. The poem says nothing about the vessel, but in reality it ["Birdeath"] is "955 5th Avenue Blues." It tells of the Bird coming to the Baronesses [sic] pad, digging TV, the Tommy Dorsey Show, a juggler comes on, causing Bird to start laughing, which perhaps ruptured some weak artery inside of his decaying body and thus later death itself driving those Swing Low Sweet Chariots all the way from Afrika.[43]

The "Cellini vessel" in question is now catalogued as a nineteenth-century copy of a late Mannerist gold cup, but was attributed to Cellini when Joans wrote the poem. He made a sly nod to how the object linked him to Parker in the collages he created to accompany "Birdeath" in *All of Ted Joans and No More*. There are images of a singing bird in a heart-shaped cut-out, as well as a bird-like creature with a human face—an old illustration of the mythical harpy—both obvious references to Parker's nickname. But the fabulous cup Joans and Parker bonded over also features a sculpture of a harpy, a bird with a human face, so that same image in *All of Ted Joans* is a secret connection back to that day in the Met, a furtive testament to Joans's relationship with Parker, there for any reader to see but freighted also with a private meaning only Joans would have known about once Parker passed.[44]

Ironically, the most famous story about Joans and Parker occurred after Parker's death, when Joans's spontaneous response was to scrawl "Bird Lives!" across New York City. This phrase was later used by Ross Russell for the title of his biography of Parker, and became so associated with

FIGURE 14.4 *Detail from what Joans called the "Cellini vessel" showing a harpy or other bird-like creature with a human face; Joans echoes this form in his illustrations of "Birdeath" in* All of Ted Joans and No More.

FIGURE 14.5 *A repurposed image of a harpy used to illustrate the elegy on Charlie Parker's death, "Birdeath," in* All of Ted Joans and No More *(1), both a nod to Parker's nickname, Bird, and secret link to the "Cellini vessel" that Joans and Parker had admired together at the Metropolitan Museum of Art.*

Joans that his *New York Times* obituary headline was "Ted Joans, 74, Jazzy Beat Poet Known for 'Bird Lives' Graffiti."[45] When the graffiti proliferated around New York City, Joans didn't take public credit for it right away—he later claimed that he had discussed it in his entry for Reisner's collection, *Bird*, but that Reisner had cut it over fears the NYPD would arrest Joans for vandalism.[46] In the book, Reisner himself was purposely vague about the graffiti's origins, saying only that "For days and weeks afterwards [after Parker's death], on sidewalks and fences I saw the crude legend written in chalk or crayon, BIRD LIVES."[47]

In later years, Joans would tell and retell the story. When he heard news of Parker's death, he immediately put on some of Bird's records, then arranged for three "hipster" friends to meet him at the table he had specially reserved for him at Café Rienzi. The four converged there: Joans, Donald Brand, Joel Axelrod, and Julian Josephson, and Joans explained what he had been planning. They were to begin in the Village, then fan out "in four directions by subway in Queens, Bronx, Brooklyn, and Harlem," scrawling "Bird Lives!" with chalk and bits of charcoal Joans had provided.[48] He warned them they could face a $50 vandalism fine if caught, but that it was worth the risk for a "public tribute to a great human being who had created a music that we patterned our lives to."[49]

When Russell described these events in his biography of Parker, he specified that the foursome had spray paint, something which Joans took pains to correct: "We had white chalk and a few sticks of charcoal and not 'pressurized canisters of paint' as Ross Russell erroneously reported."[50] Literary critic Amor Kohli sees this detail as crucially important for the "meaning" of Bird Lives, which he reads as performance art in line with a "jazz aesthetic." As Kohli writes, "key to understanding Joans' participation in a jazz aesthetic is in its privileging of process over product," noting that "Jazz's ephemeral quality provides it with a meaningful sense of vitality."[51] For Kohli, it is important that Joans stressed it was "not spray paint" he used, because chalk and charcoal are changeable, subject to "external factors: rain, snow, wind, etc. Graffiti written with chalk will blur and run."[52] It is in this dynamic mixture that Kohli sees the deeper aesthetic work of "Bird Lives!": it pays homage to Parker in its very form, representing on a literal level that he is "free," while also echoing the intangible, dynamic and ephemeral quality of bop itself. This sense of "Bird Lives!" as an ongoing project that is never "finished" or "final" also extends to the ways the phrase was again repurposed and extended upon Joans's own death, when Laura Corsiglia encouraged friends and admirers to chalk "Ted Joans Lives!" around Vancouver and other cities throughout the world, and in the use of "Ted Joans Lives!" for a title of a short "visual and aural collage" made by Kurt Hemmer and Tom Knoff in 2010.[53]

15

The Coming of the
Beat Generation

Just as Charlie Parker represented new energies in music, and Franz Kline and Willem de Kooning new energies in painting, by the mid-1950s, a new energy in literature was about to break across the country—and just as Joans knew Parker and Kline and de Kooning, he also befriended the lead figures of this new literary movement, Jack Kerouac, Allen Ginsberg, and Gregory Corso, among others. The so-called Beat Generation had its origins back in 1943, when some Columbia University undergraduates started hanging around an older writer who was deeply interested in various kinds of "undergrounds" that were far from normative culture. These undergraduates were Kerouac, Ginsberg, and Lucien Carr, and their elder mentor was William S. Burroughs. Kerouac, Ginsberg, and Burroughs would go on to become the core three writers of what Kerouac dubbed the "Beat Generation," inspiring both a rebellious social attitude among America's youth, and a constellation of restless innovations in literary expression. The Beats shared Joans's general skepticism toward what Ginsberg called Modern Bourgeois Culture, as well as his interest in tossing out conventional academic wisdom about the way to "truth," and to a life well lived.[1] Six years younger than Kerouac and two years younger than Ginsberg, Joans was still back in Louisville when those two had first met at Columbia, but in the mid-1950s, he got to know them around the Village, and as he began to write more of his own poetry, he joined the wave of Beat poets drawing crowds in the bohemian coffeehouses around town.

For this young, postwar generation, bop was the soundtrack. Kerouac wrote: "as to the actual existence of a Beat Generation, chances are it was really just an idea in our minds—We'd stay up 24 hours drinking cup after cup of black coffee, playing record after record of Wardell Gray, Lester Young, Dexter Gordon, Willie Jackson, Lennie Tristano and all the rest, talking madly about that holy new feeling out there in the streets."[2]

This "holy new feeling" was articulated in different ways by the major works of Beat literature, notably Kerouac's novel *On the Road* (1957) and Allen Ginsberg's poem "Howl" (1956), both of which stress the Beat connection to the kind of hot jazz Joans loved. In "Howl," Ginsberg catalogues the "best minds" of his generation, which he pictures "contemplating jazz" and "seeking jazz."[3] In *On the Road*, Kerouac's antihero, Dean Moriarty, is constantly entranced and energized by bop, and narrator Sal Paradise names specific records like Dexter Gordon and Wardell Gray's *The Hunt*, which, he says, had Gordon and Gray "blowing their tops before a screaming audience that gave the record fantastic frenzied volume."[4] In another magnetic connection, it was Dexter Gordon who would later crown Joans "the last of the great hipsters."[5]

When Kerouac would write about bop, he always emphasized its energy and spontaneity, what Sal Paradise in *On the Road* calls "the surprise of a new simple variation of a chorus" (201). Inspired in part by bop improvisation, Kerouac would develop a composition method he called Spontaneous Prose, an example of which is his 1953 novel *The Subterraneans*, written in just three days. That book's narrator (and Kerouac's alter ego), Leo Percepied, is a writer devoted to innovation and experimentation—and to jazz clubs, his frequent haunts throughout the novel. One memorable scene has him listening to and communing with none other than Charlie Parker as he played a gig at The Open Door. (Although the real-life events in *The Subterraneans* took place in New York City, Kerouac changed the location to San Francisco to avoid libel suits; in the published novel, The Open Door was renamed the Red Drum.)

In *The Subterraneans*, Percepied rhapsodizes:

> up on the stand Bird Parker with solemn eyes who'd been busted fairly recently and had now returned to a kind of bop dead Frisco but had just discovered or been told about the Red Drum, the great new generation gang wailing and gathering there, so here he was on the stand, examining them with his eyes as he blew his now-settled-down-into-regulated-design "crazy" notes—the booming drums, the high ceiling.[6]

Kerouac places Parker—"the kindest jazz musician there could be while being and therefore naturally the greatest"—at the very center of a new Beat "generation" (14). The spontaneous style of *The Subterraneans*, which introduces motifs and riffs on them without following a predetermined plot or scheme, is an example of one way a "jazz aesthetic" was imported into writing by Kerouac and other Beat writers, including Joans. Kerouac frequently insisted on the connection between Spontaneous Prose and bop, as in his famous piece "Essentials of Spontaneous Prose," which explains his "procedure": "sketching language is undisturbed flow from the mind of personal secret idea-words, *blowing* (as per jazz musician) on subject of image."[7]

Recognizing the connections among bop aesthetics and Beat aesthetics helps us see why Joans thought he was well within his rights to claim he was present at the "beginning" of the Beat Generation, as he often insisted. Even though Kerouac and Ginsberg formed their "Libertine Circle" while Joans was still in Kentucky, and he didn't meet Kerouac or Ginsberg until the mid-1950s, he had been a bop hipster, "Derbytown Dizz," since the late 1940s. And, crucially, as far as Joans was concerned, he was circulating around New York's hip spots—jazz clubs, coffeehouses, artist and writer bars like the Cedar—in the years before the "Beat Generation" became the object of media fascination and derision in 1958 and 1959.

Thus it is not quite correct to assume, as some observers have, that Joans merely rode on the Beats' coattails in order to promote himself. He was already long on the scene in New York, and while he certainly did exploit the media's obsession with the Beats to his advantage, he also saw some broad affinities between his Surrealist point of view and what the Beats were doing, and so his poetry of the later 1950s can be seen as an extension of his earlier sensibilities. As he declared, "I'm a surrealist operating in beat waters with suitcases filled with the marvelous for those of the Beat Generation that dig it!"[8] In fact, he always insisted that "I didn't argue my way in to the Beat scene, for I was already on the scene, afterall [sic] Greenwich Village was my beat, and I was one of those known black bohemians. Therefore when [in the late 1950s] newspapers, magazines, and other mass media would do a Beat bit concerning Greenwich Village, I was the chosen one, not by choice but by sheer reputation and availability."[9]

Joans further locates the origins of the Beat Generation specifically in attitudes and sensibilities of urban hipsters who dug bop but were also interested in modern poetry and visual art, thus writing himself into a "small minority" who birthed the Beat phenomenon:

> The young people who became what Time-Life pronounced "the beat generation" grew up with contemporary jazz ... At the beginning there was only a small minority interested in poetry, jazz, and contemporary painting. But the hipsters spread the contagious words about what was really happening that had positive values. Some of the poets often "preached" their poems, or attempted to "blow" the poem as though they were playing a sax or trumpet. All these poets were on Bird or Prez [tenor saxophonist Lester Young].[10]

During the latter 1950s, Joans turned his creative efforts to writing, and would "blow" his poems to rapt audiences all over New York City, joining in the Beat spirit of Kerouac, who announced that he wanted "to be considered a jazz poet blowing a long blues in an afternoon."[11]

The main venues for Joans's poetry were the coffeehouses that were cropping up around Greenwich Village in the early to mid 1950s, and in these spaces he developed his "Beat" poetry. As he said, "I do accept the label of being one of the Beat poets, who read evangelical-like to those fortunate squares, and to East coast hipsters my 'beat' poems."[12] When in later years Joans would maintain that he was "at the beginning" of the Beat Generation, he always located this beginning in his readings in Village coffeehouses:

I wailed & wailed
In coffee shops wayback when
Especially on lucrative weekends
I read to tourists and squares
I wanted to change and transform
The minds of conventional Americans.[13]

16

Coffeehouse Connection

By 1958, Joans had a lot going on: he had two kids back in Kentucky from his marriage to Joan; Joyce was out on Staten Island with their three kids, and was pregnant with a fourth, Jeannemarie; he maintained his studio on Astor Place, and was using it as a headquarters for his parties and paintings. He still exhibited visual art when he could, but as the Beat phenomenon swept the country, he realized he could make more money reading poetry to the crowds who descended on the Village to see genuine, authentic Beats in their natural habitats. It was always somewhat of a game, but Joans felt that his dues paid did make him a true Beat, so he leaned in to his image as the quintessential coffeehouse poet. As he said, "After struggling with painting during the day and reading my poems in various coffee houses each night I made a decision to 'divorce' painting and devote fulltime to my lucrative natural 'mistress' poetry. She and I have never parted, we are one."[1]

Although today the word "coffeehouse" might conjure an image of a thousand identical Starbucks piping in the same pre-approved music and selling the same carefully curated merchandise, in New York City in the 1950s, small independent coffeehouses had their own distinctive identities, were places where young people crowded around tables to talk and smoke for hours, or to hear up-and-coming poets and musicians perform. By the latter part of the decade, Village coffeehouses were ground zero for commercially-visible versions of "the underground," as bohemian types gathered at their favorite haunts, and savvy owners actively promoted their establishments as epicenters of hip culture.

Of course poets have been lingering in coffeehouses and cafés for centuries, but it was really with the coming of the Beat Generation that the right kind of poet could find it "lucrative" to read to audiences in coffeehouses in and around identifiably "countercultural" neighborhoods like Greenwich Village. This had to do with the fact that so-called bohemians elicited a particular kind of fascination from normative culture, and those living typical middle-class lives were by turns repulsed and captivated by

Beat bohemia, and many grew increasingly hungry for interaction with real-life non-conformists. This hunger reached a height from 1958 to 1960, after the publication of *On the Road* and *Howl and Other Poems*. These works lamented a dominant culture that marginalized—or, according to "Howl," "bashed open [the] skulls"—of non-conformists.[2] Ironically, this society responded by commercializing the Beat phenomenon, confusing Beat writers with the made-up image of the Beatnik, the bearded, bongo-playing layabout who appeared in countless popular depictions of bohemia, from "Beatsploitation" novels such as *Like, Crazy Man* (1960) (whose cover featured an image of Joans reading in a coffeehouse), to films such as *Bucket of Blood* (1959) to the television show *The Many Loves of Doby Gillis*, co-starring the most lovable of the fake Beatniks, Maynard G. Krebs.

In Greenwich Village, coffeehouses were understood by tourists and skeptical journalists alike to be the places to discover Beat bohemia, and in the summer of 1959, at the height of the "Beatnik" craze, CBS News dispatched 24-year-old Charles Kuralt to MacDougal Street to investigate the goings-on. In his report, Kuralt told viewers that Village coffeehouses were operating outside the confines of normal or respectable society, explaining that such places were at war with mainstream culture: "The poets in the Greenwich Village coffeehouses have won their battle against the lawgivers, the cops, and the squares. The coffeehouses, like the Gaslight here on MacDougal Street, are still operating without what might be called their poetic license, and the poets, the Beat and conventional alike, are still filling the night with smoky, blank verse."[3]

Kuralt was right to zero-in on the Gaslight, as it was a nerve center of what Joans called the "true underground"—a place where poets would read their real work to a mix of fellow poets and tourists.[4] Joans felt there was a hierarchy of coffeehouses, from the legitimate "authentic" places like the Gaslight frequented by local writers and artists, to "tourist traps" that were designed mainly to extract money from naïve out-of-towners. Ever savvy, Joans read across this range, establishing himself as the preeminent coffeehouse poet of the era, eventually making enough money to support his family by skillfully playing to what those crowds thought they wanted to hear out of a genuine "Beat Generation" poet, and never letting these largely white audiences forget that he was one of the very few Black poets reading on the scene.

This is how Joans characterized his time reading in Village coffeehouses:

At first we read only to the "hip group" usually found at the time in the coffee shops. But after tremendous Beat Generation publicity that swept the nation, we fled to our studios and "secret uncommercial" coffee houses. It was fun reading for kicks, but trying to take care [of] a family was "something else." So I returned to the more popular and highly commercial coffee shops. There I was confronted with the public

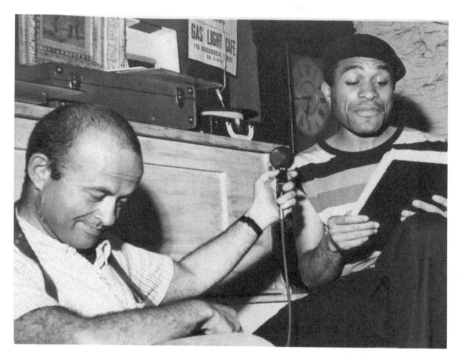

FIGURE 16.1 *Ted Joans at the Gaslight Café, New York City, probably 1959. Laurated Archive.*

en masse. Tourists, weekend beatniks, creepniks, teenage hoodlums and too, the college crowd. I had to read shorter poems, use a microphone and communicate.[5]

By the "'secret uncommercial' coffee houses," Joans meant places like the Seven Arts Coffee Gallery, which was actually in mid-town Manhattan at Ninth Avenue and 43rd Streets, an establishment he recalled as a "strictly poets-for-poetry sake place" where one would read mainly to fellow poets.[6] But the "popular and highly commercial" places were another animal altogether, and for Joans as for some other poets associated with the Beat movement, in the latter 1950s there was often a balancing act between wanting to create meaningful art and giving those "tourists" and "weekend Beatniks" what they wanted so as to get paid.

Joans's solution was to perform the role of a Beat poet, enthralling audiences with dramatic readings of his swinging, colloquial poetry on a range of pressing topics, from taboo ones like sex and how to have more of it, to controversial ones like racism and how not to reproduce it. And although there was a pragmatic or perhaps even cynical side to Joans playing to square crowds in exchange for money, he also did see himself as doing consequential work, taking the opportunity to educate and enlighten the crowds whose attention he held. As he wrote in April 1959:

I AM
AWFULLY SORRY
YOU DONT LIKE
   MY
   EXTREMELY
   WONDERFUL
   MARVELOUS

   POETRY
NEVERTHELESS/IT IS
SUCH HONEST AND
                    SINCERE

CRITICISM
      WHICH
            CONSTITUTES
THE VERY ESSENCE
      OF OUR
                    DEMOCRATIC
WAY OF LIFE[7]

At the height of the coffeehouse poetry craze, Joans was said to pull in an incredible $300–400 per night as he read his work at one place, passed around a collection hat for tips, then rushed off to the next venue to do it all over again.[8] "I would begin the weekend evening of Café Bizarre on West Third Street," he recalled, "which was a big garage-like coffee house where half-clad waitresses waited on the throngs of tourists and weekend beatniks. After reading there I'd run to Café Wha on MacDougal Street, in the basement, where a West Indian master congo drummer held forth, Victor. Then I'd go on to the real Beat poetry café, the Gaslight."[9] His exhausting circuit wasn't limited to these places, as he also appeared at Café Veriglio, Limelight, Peacock, Cino, Manzini, The Bitter End, Continental, Borgia, and Café Rafio (where Langston Hughes had seen him read).[10] It was these performances that sustained his family in the latter 1950s, and that allowed him to build a reputation as "one of the few beats to make a living reading in coffee shops," as one syndicated 1960 column put it.[11] Eventually Joans's coffeehouse performances led to the publication of his first major book of poetry, *All of Ted Joans and No More*, and his brief appearance in Stewart Wilensky's documentary, *Village Sunday* (1960), where he is shown reading from his poem "The Sermon" in Café Bizarre.[12]

17

Poet-In-Residence at Café Bizarre

In fact, the way Joans became a popular and paradigmatic Beat poet "blowing" his work in coffeehouses can be thrown into high relief by pausing over the curious establishment that was Café Bizarre, located at 106 W. 3rd St. (and later razed to make room for an NYU Law School dorm). The Bizarre was founded in 1957 by Rick Allmen, a self-described "restaurateur, poet, philosopher, double entry bookkeeper, connoisseur … kooky playwright" known also around town for his movie star good looks.[1] Allmen would go on to write the salacious sex novel, *Stanley: The Don Juan of Second Avenue* (1974), dedicated to "all those generations, past, present and future, who grew up and will grow up in sexual ignorance."[2]

Although Joans would sometimes call it a "tourist trap," Allmen had conceived Café Bizarre as a provocatively transgressive space that he once characterized as "experimental theatre."[3] A sign above the door read: "Bizarre encompasses another world not unlike the Arabian nights."[4] And the place attracted legitimate talent from the start: on opening night, patrons were treated to performances by Village folk fixture David von Ronk, "the Mayor of MacDougal Street," and Odetta, the "Voice of the Civil Rights Movement."[5] Allmen did his best to cultivate his café's bohemian vibe, and the space became known for its weird décor and inventive menu as much as for its artistic offerings: there was a panoply of ever-changing murals on the walls and an assortment of apparently random objects hung from the ceilings—wagon wheels, fishing nets, shark jaws and, most famously, an enormous grotesque head with bugged-out eyes and a stringy hipster goatee (visible above Joans in the photo of him reading; see Figure 17.1). Though the city habitually thwarted Allmen's attempts to secure a liquor license (as they did to most of the Village coffeehouses in those years), customers could hang out all night sipping coffee, noshing on "Kooky Kombination" plates, or indulging in ice cream sundaes with names like Schizophrenic Sunday and the Suffering Bastard. With such playful odes to abnormality, Café Bizarre drew both bohemian Villagers and curious tourists, and became known for its permissive, irreverent atmosphere where a healthy dose of humor was always injected into the proceedings.

A canny businessman, Allmen was explicit about associating his place with the Beats, a move immediately apparent in a 1959 LP he released, *Café Bizarre Presents Assorted Madness*. Subtitled "Beat Generation Poetry, Beat Erotica by the Beat and the Unbeat," this record purported to define or embody a Beat ethos, but also did so ironically, in tension with what square America thought about the Beats. The more Joans read in the Bizarre and elsewhere, the more he traded on the public's fascination with Beats and hipsters, while never quite conforming to their expectations. He quickly became one of the marquee poets at Café Bizarre, where he described himself as "poet-in-residence."[6] At one point, he was reading at the Bizarre almost nightly from 7:00 p.m. to 2:00 a.m., and was such a fixture there that Allmen had even printed up postcards featuring the photograph of Joans reading in the café that had appeared in *Holiday* magazine.[7]

Although he drew consistent, appreciative crowds, Joans's irreverent poetry meant that it was probably inevitable he would sometimes run into trouble. Once at the Bizarre he was reading a version of a poem published as "Confession mais Jamais sur dimanche" (or "Confession— but never on Sunday"), which he described as "influenced by the unhip Catholic confessional ritual" and "arrogantly confessing to America, the Fatherland."[8] That evening a half-dozen Catholic dock workers happened to be in the audience at Bizarre, and after Joans's set, they let him know he would have to "answer" for his insults. The burly men waited outside the Bizarre to give Joans a beating, but when some of the kitchen staff (large ex-football players) heard about what was happening, they armed themselves with knives and cleavers and escorted Joans out through the gauntlet of dock workers and over to his next gig at the Gaslight. The dock workers were menacing enough that the Gaslight's owner, rough-and-tumble John Mitchell, grabbed a rifle in case they continued to press the issue. Never one for physical confrontation, Joans was rattled, but undeterred from earning his money for the rest of the night.

The occasional run-in with insulted dock workers notwithstanding, Joans was an inordinately popular figure on the coffeehouse circuit, largely for the way he managed to inhabit that fuzzy space between "commercial" Beat poet and "authentic" artist. By 1960, *The Village Voice* mockingly called Joans "the messiah of tourist kicks" and "the poet laureate of commercial exhibitionism," but he understood that in an environment charged by Beat mania, categories like "authentic" and "commercial" were unstable and fluid, and so best left in scare quotes.[9]

Such an attitude is evident in one of Joans's best-known poems, "The Sermon," which he read and refined in Village coffeehouses.[10] "The Sermon" is both a paradigmatic, "authentic" Beat poem, and the perfect example of the sort of saleable poetry tourists or weekenders imagined they wanted to hear,

FIGURE 17.1 *Joans in a beret and all black, reading in Café Bizarre in 1959. Another photo from this same night was used to accompany Jack Kerouac's essay "The Roaming Beatniks" in the October 1959 issue of* Holiday *magazine. Photo by Burt Glinn.*

and he would usually "blow" it accompanied by the now-standard call-and response jazz tune "Moanin," composed by Bobby Timmons and recorded at the time by Art Blakey and the Jazz Messengers.[11] The poem proclaims a kind of Beat insider knowledge while purporting to also communicate this knowledge to eager audience members, all while maintaining a cool ironic detachment.

Despite any ironies, it's also true that with poems like "The Sermon," Joans always had deeper goals in mind, nothing less than the resolutely unironic goal of inducing a "moral revolution in the United States."[12] As he put it in later years: "I would often read 'The Sermon' three times a night on weekends in the many public coffee houses that featured Beat Generation poetry ... Reading in the crowded coffee houses to the wannabe—Beats, the tourists, and those poetic women (who wanted to absorb what it meant to be hipper-than-thou) was almost a religious quest."[13] Joans could claim

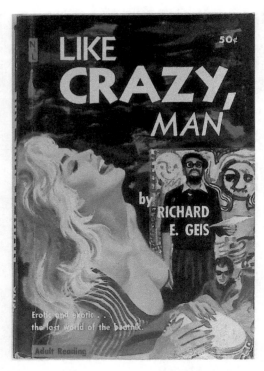

FIGURE 17.2 *Cover of Richard E. Geis's "Beatsploitation" novel,* Like, Crazy Man *(1960), part of which was inspired by the* Holiday *magazine image of Joans reading at Café Bizarre. The adult novel cashes in on the notion that Beat women were sexually promiscuous.*

a higher purpose with "The Sermon" because he saw it as a vessel for delivering people usable knowledge, "to change and transform America by getting the wise (hip) words of poetry to the worthy women of this potentially great country." Joans enlisted a hip aesthetic in the name of social reform, to "save" his audiences and readers from what he considered the worst elements of Modern Bourgeois Culture, chief among them racism.

Although many Village social spaces were certainly more welcoming to non-white patrons than most other such spaces at the time, it was also the case that they remained predominantly white, and that the poets and performers tended to be white as well (with the obvious exception of jazz clubs, which in places like New York still attracted white audiences). As a Black poet, Joans used his visible difference to his advantage to both occupy a position of "authentic" hipness as indexed by his very Blackness, and to demand anti-racist thought and action from his captive listeners. When reading in the coffeehouses, Joans was of course "hip to the fact that many of those tourists had never had an Afro-American wail against their united way of openly stated racism. I used humor, but that humor was very black, not the *humour noir* that ... André Breton had sought in the European literati ... [but a] Harlem influenced *humour noir*" that stimulated "their minds into an order where they too could be saved, by an introspective activity which would result in being hip."[14] In other words, for Joans at this time, to be hip wasn't to talk or dress a certain way, but to engage in "introspective activity" and reject aspects of American society and culture he found particularly pernicious—not just racism, but sexual repression, materialism, unoriginality, a lack of curiosity, and a general absence of open-mindedness and generosity. As he put it in the poem "Je Suis un Homme," "I am just a rightsized hipster who is out to destroy bigotry and old styled ignorance" (*ATJ*, 2).

"The Sermon" opens:

So you want to be hip little girls?
you want to learn to swing?
and you want to be able to dig and take in everything
Yes dig everything as poet Ginsberg said?[15]

Right away Joans directly addresses and perhaps confronts his audience, enticing them with his supposedly insider knowledge, which he legitimates via a reference to Allen Ginsberg, the most famous of the Beat poets ("The Sermon" explicitly insists "you must own a copy of Howl— / you must have a copy of Jack (on the road) / Kerouac on your shelf" [*ATJ*, 33]).

But given that "The Sermon" first percolated in those bohemian coffeehouses, we know that Joans isn't speaking to a readership of *abstract* "little girls," but rather to the particular young women who frequented places like the Bizarre—that is, specifically white girls, usually middle class, yearning for some contact with "hip" culture. For Joans, being hip, being able to "swing," was a Black thing, and so his first piece of advice is to check any and all bigotry at the door:

Now dig me pretty babies, I'd like first of all for you
to get rid of that umbilical cord that your drag-
ass prejudiced parents have around your neck,
You don't need them to lay their antique anglo-
saxon puritanical philosophy on you now (32)

By insisting on a contrast between those who want to be "hip little girls" and their parents, Joans echoes the general cultural sense that the Beat Generation was a white youth movement, and that the girls' parents would accordingly embody a retrograde attitude demanding to be rebelled against.

This is why he names the specifically "anglo-saxon" origins of the parents' "antique" and "puritanical philosophy."

That this philosophy is characterized by racial prejudice is made explicit elsewhere in the poem with the exhortation: "If you want to be hip ... you must help <u>free</u> our people behind the Cotton / curtain" (33)—that is, those Black people living in the Jim Crow South. The deft use of the plural possessive adjective, "our," encourages the white girls to imagine oppressed Black people in the South as their people, not as belonging to a group of "others." More subtle are the moments in "The Sermon" when Joans contrasts the elder generation's "antique anglo-saxon puritantical philosophy" with his advice for becoming a "beautiful nonsquare angel": "<u>sleep</u> with everybody! but don't make it / with no body but Santa Claus, J.C.—/ and other bearded cats you dig" (32). Coming from a Black poet speaking to a predominantly white audience, the "everybody" here signals interracial sex still generally taboo at the time but often practiced by Joans, celebrated in his performative parties, and positively depicted throughout his poetry (and while "J.C." implies Jesus Christ thanks to its juxtaposition to Santa Claus, it really means the messiah John Coltrane—incidentally, the Church of St. John Coltrane has been going strong in San Francisco for more than fifty years).[16]

Sometimes in "The Sermon" Joans adopts the voice of the cool elder friend or sibling ("<u>you must</u> / <u>not</u> <u>sit</u> around and <u>wait</u> for that mytho- / logical <u>Right Guy</u> to come along" [34]), focalizing this advice through other key Beat texts: "<u>No</u> / pretty baby, you should read Gregory / Corso's poem <u>Marriage</u> before ever doing / that bit" (34). "Marriage," by Joans's pal Corso, remains one of the more well-known Beat poems for the ways it skewers social expectations surrounding conventional courtship and marriage with comic scenes of meeting the parents ("back straightened, hair finally combed, strangled by a tie"), cheesy honeymoons in Niagara Falls, and then eventual life in a Connecticut suburb with lawnmowers, golf clubs, and Community Chest.[17] Joans name checks Corso and "Marriage"— and "Howl" and *On the Road*—to reverse what might be considered cultural authority, not "parents," but the pantheon of younger writers who challenge conventional mores regarding marriage, sex, and racial attitudes. Ultimately, "The Sermon" became one of Joans best-loved coffeehouse poems for its ironic humor, swinging rhythm, and hip advice that both was and wasn't sermonizing.

18

Funky Jazz Poems

Given the draw of coffeehouse poems like "The Sermon," Joans figured he could monetize this work in other ways, and began thinking more seriously about publishing his writing. He recalled that after one particularly successful reading, with people "applauding and whooping it up because of my unpublished poetry," he had remarked to Allen Ginsberg that he was going to hunt down a mimeograph machine to have "copies of my popular poems printed to sell to the people."

But Ginsberg thought some publisher would be interested. "Dig that applause?" he said. "Those people like your poetry, and there in their midst is someone who will ask to publish you."[1]

An offer did come when Sheldon "Shel" Deretchin approached Joans with a proposal to publish his work. Deretchin was a Village resident and publisher of a science fiction magazine when the genre was just tipping into literary respectability (Deretchin had the distinction of being enrolled in the first-ever college level course on science fiction back in 1954).[2] Joans liked to pun on Deretchin's name, calling him "Mr. New Deretchin or Old Erection Press," a play on the real press New Directions, and its own pun on "Nude Erections."[3] Given that his main interests at the time were in science fiction, Deretchin may seem a strange figure to publish Joans's work, but he was apparently enthusiastic enough about the poetry itself that he wanted to bring it to a wider audience—Joans appreciated the interest, calling Deretchin a "NYU law student hip enough to publish my first book of poems."[4]

Deretchin printed Joans's first book—what Joans called a "booklet"—titled *Funky Jazz Poems*, about 20 pages that showcase some of his coffeehouse poetry. As is apparent from the cover (Figure 18.1), the title is somewhat confusingly presented, with the words "Jazz Poems" reading vertically to the left of Joans's portrait, and the word "funky" (in quotation marks), to the right. I have also seen copies in which Joans has handwritten in "Beat" across the top of the cover. In other writing, Joans referred to the booklet as "Funky Jazz poems," and on a list of published books he made in connection to his West Berlin fellowship in the early 1980s, he listed it as "Funky Jazz (Beat Poems)," which may create further confusion about the existence of another, separate book titled "Beat Poems" that is sometimes included in secondary bibliographies with the date 1957.[5] Because Joans referred to the booklet in the above way, I use the title *Funky Jazz Poems*, and because he called this work his first booklet of poems, and placed it chronologically first on the list just mentioned, I don't think another distinct book with the title "Beat Poems" exists.

Funky Jazz Poems included well-liked poetry such as "The Sermon," "Jazz is My Religion," "The Truth," and "Birdeath," among others, and featured Joans's signature, Max Ernst-inspired collages to accompany the poems.[6] Somewhat ephemeral and fugitive even at the time, the physical publication of Joans's first poetry booklet set the tone for much of his later work insofar as it was produced outside the big, commercial publishing industry, a product of an alternative, underground, do-it-yourself publishing spirit encapsulated by the "mimeographic revolution," when the relative availability of mimeograph machines led to an explosion of literary publications inexpensively printed and assembled on people's kitchen tables. In those days, it was probably the case that Joans didn't have access to big publishing houses anyway, but a commitment to alternative distribution venues was also an ideological one, and even over the course of his whole literary career, he only published a few books with larger, established houses, while the vast majority of his books and booklets were put out by smaller, avowedly non-mainstream publishing ventures. In the case of *Funky Jazz Poems*, the exact print run is unknown to me, but the booklet was largely distributed around the time it was published, predominantly in New York City, and copies are now exceedingly rare and difficult to find.

The earliest distribution happened on foot, when Joans gifted a copy to a lesbian friend, Felicia, because they had been through "a lot of things together," and then handed out more copies to other people in the Village: his friend Bob Hamilton, and Mimi Margaux, a dancer and bohemian beauty whose photograph had appeared with Joans's in *Holiday* magazine, as illustrations to Kerouac's essay "The Roaming Beatniks." Echoing the caption under Margaux's photo in *Holiday*, "If Mona Lisa were alive and with it today, she might achieve this particular degree of inscrutability," Joans called her the "Mona Lisa of the Beat Generation."[7] The fourth copy went to Mary, Joans's favorite waitress at the Bizarre.[8]

Funky Jazz Poems featured an introduction by Bob Reisner, the jazz aficionado and ornithologist extraordinaire whom Joans had first met in Marshall Stearns's course on jazz history at the New School. Reisner had impressed Joans with his knowledge and appreciation of Charlie Parker, so much so that Joans would go on to enroll in Reisner's own course in jazz history at Brooklyn College.[9] Reisner was by that time known in all the hip

FIGURE 18.1 *Cover for Joans's first booklet of poems,* Funky Jazz Poems, *with an author photograph by Fred McDarrah. Across the top of this copy is written in Joans's hand "Poems for Soul Brothers and Sisters Like," with a former owner's name written across the bottom. I have seen other copies with the word "Beat" written boldly across the top in Joans's hand. This is almost certainly the same work that appears in some bibliographies as "Beat Poems" (1957); in "Spadework," Joans refers to* Funky Jazz Poems *as "my first published booklet of poems" (36).*

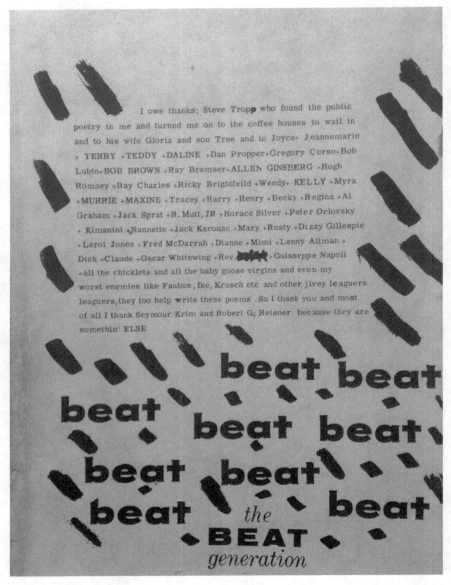

FIGURE 18.2 *Back cover of* Funky Jazz Poems, *acknowledgements that read like a Who's Who on the Village bohemian scene in the late 1950s. As suggested by the lower half of the page, in this case, Joans wasn't shy about linking the book to the Beat Generation.*

circles as the proprietor of The Open Door, and after Parker's death, he put together the tribute mentioned earlier, *Bird: The Legend of Charlie Parker*.

Reisner's introduction to *Funky Jazz Poems* served as a hip credential, and in it he tells a story of his first encounter with Joans, illustrating the latter's hustling entrepreneurial spirit. According to Reisner, the two had first met back in 1953 when Joans had turned up at a jazz club Reisner had been managing with the tattered copies of some of Reisner's articles of jazz criticism. "Maestro," said Joans theatrically, "I have come bare-foot from Kentucky to meet the author of these fabulous articles."[10] Reisner was of course suitably impressed and waived the cover, only to later discover that Joans had "used this plot to gain admission to higher and higher places."

19

All of Ted Joans and No More

Joans's first major book of poetry, *All of Ted Joans and No More*, appeared in 1961, reprinting the poems in *Funky Jazz Poems*, along with many others. It was published by Martin Geisler, owner of Paperbook Gallery, a popular bookstore with four locations in Greenwich Village. Believing that "the potential market for paperbacks has reached the point where it more or less involves the whole population," Geisler established Excelsior Press to capitalize on the growing popularity of inexpensive paperbacks, and had already had some success with *Views of a Near-Sighted Cannoneer* (1961), a collection of cultural criticism by Joans's friend Seymour Krim, the one who had hooked him up with Elizabeth Taylor (the poem "Soul Brother Seymour" in *All of Ted Joans* is about Krim: "You the near sighted cannoneer / grabbing Hipness by the balls / and having no squarenik fear / of taking some of the rough & tumble falls" [31]).[1]

Geisler published *All of Ted Joans and No More* in a run of 500 copies in July 1961, priced it at 75 cents, and sold it largely through Paperbook Gallery. It quickly sold out, so Geisler wanted to do a second run of 2000 copies and up the price to one dollar. For the revised edition, Joans asked to make some corrections and enhance the poems with "collage drawings." He did so, but unbeknownst to him, the book was printed with all his handwritten revisions intact (see Figure 19.2). It seems an editor at Excelsior, Eugene Braun-Munk, thought the handwritten corrections were "*beautiful* in its abstract-surreal presentation," and so had it printed exactly as submitted, handwritten notes and all.[2] This became the "new revised second edition" of *All of Ted Joans and No More*, printed in September 1961. The new edition sold briskly as well—Joans noted that "the weekend tourists and 'wannabe beatniks'" kept buying the book, and the money he made helped finance his travels abroad.[3]

The cover of *All of Ted Joans and No More* was deliberately provocative in the way his interracial parties had been provocative: it displayed the nude body of a white woman on a Black man's book of poetry, a clear reproach

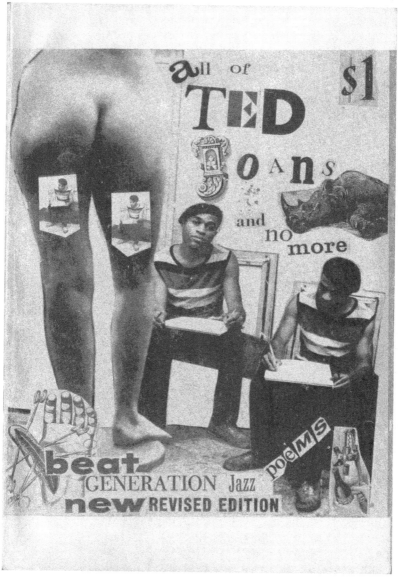

FIGURE 19.1 *Cover of the* New Revised Edition *of* All of Ted Joans and No More, *published in September 1961 and priced at one dollar. Joans has added the image of the rhinoceros, the portrait of himself on the woman's thighs, and the collages at the bottom around the subtitle.*

to the normative racial status quo. In "Spadework," Joans recounts an (imagined) radio interview, in which the host can't seem to get over the fact that "you, a colored man included a white woman on the cover of your book," insisting that "things like that just isn't done" (85, 87). Joans, bored with this line of questioning and eager to get into a discussion of the poems themselves, replies, "because this chick's a symbol, an American truth, a naked truth. I only love truth when it is naked, dig?" (85).

The most obvious difference between the first and second editions of *All of Ted Joans and No More* is the use of multicolored paper, the addition of the collages, and the retention of the hand corrections. In viewing the editions side by side, the first one seems comparatively "straight" in terms of the physical presentation and layout, and in the absence of illustrations, while the second edition has a much wilder, Surreal feel, insofar as it is often difficult to pin down the "definitive" or "final" version of the poems. In this way, Joans's retained handwritten corrections become thematic, lending the second edition an air of being always in progress.

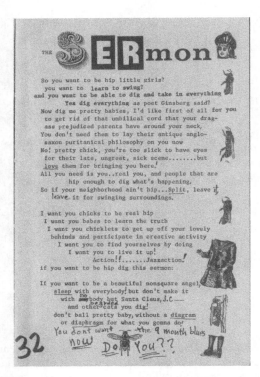

FIGURE 19.2 *The first part of "The Sermon" as it appeared in the New Revised Edition of* All of Ted Joans and No More, *which included Joans's collages, and retained his handwritten corrections.*

The New Revised Edition also includes more poems, and a glossary of various slang terms that Joans invented to describe people in the Village ("Bronx Bagel Baby," "Jivey Leaguer," "Creepnik," "Deadnik," "A-Trainer," etc.). Such terms are used without explanation in the poems, and the glossary lets readers in on Joans's private vocabulary, alluding to and updating works like Cab Calloway's *Cat-ologue: A Hepster's Dictionary* (1938) or Babs Gonzales's pamphlet, "Boptionary," which Joans owned. In Joans's glossary, we learn that "Bronx Bagel Babies" are "young teenage girls (mostly white girls) who visit the village for kicks or a fling with anyone different," which again sheds light on his target audience in a poem like "The Sermon." He would go on to revisit the nuances of these and other categories in his other important book of his New York years, *The Hipsters*, which is discussed in detail in the coming pages.

The New Revised Edition included a brief afterword by Joans, titled "Last Words and Turn You On" (dated September 1961) that offers some biographical highlights from his time in the Village:

> I came to the Village scene after doing the school bit in Indiana, Kentucky and Illinois, came here to paint and I did, and still do, I have exhibitions almost annually on Ten St. with the avant-garde, used to throw big surrealist costume balls and gigantic birthday parties, got married and saw the birth of four masterpieces that ex-wife and I created, Daline, Teddy, Terry and Jeannemarie, after four years, divorce, blues, beat bread, then split for Europe ... I'm splitting and letting America perish in its own vicious puke or letting America find and live that Moral Revolution that I hoped would happen. (94)

Ending as it does with Joans about to take his leave from the United States, these "Last Words" have the ring of retrospective finality, and the emphasis on "Moral Revolution" is one way to understand the artistic or ethical aims of *All of Ted Joans and No More*. As we saw in "The Sermon," by "moral" Joans does not of course mean the "antique anglo-saxon puritantical philosophy" of Modern Bourgeois Culture, but something like its opposite, a progressive, "revolutionary" stance that embraces anti-racism, free love, and liberated survival inside the framework of a capitalist society without fully embracing the ideological norms of capitalism.

This position is laid out most explicitly in the poem "It Is Time for a Moral Revolution in America," in which Joans's Surrealist point of view skewers the contemporary moral or political order by reimagining what might count as "political." The list poem ticks off numerous facets of this moral revolution, which range from the abstract (It is Time "for the religious and racial bigots of America to retire" [52]) to the political ("for Patrice Lumumba to return to this world and / kick the shit out of Uncle Thomas Bunch the shoe- / shine boy of the U.N." [55]). Taken together, these

FIGURE 19.3 *Back cover of the first edition of* All of Ted Joans and No More, *published July 1961; note Joans's painting of Charlie Parker,* Bird Lives! *(1958), positioned behind him.*

FIGURE 19.4 *Collaged back cover of the New Revised Edition of* All of Ted Joans and No More.

suggestions do not necessarily present a coherent political philosophy, but rather a Surrealist rebuke of the norms and cultural logics governing society.

Other Surrealist poems in *All of Ted Joans and No More* evince sly commitments to anti-racism in a global context. "Pygmy Stay Away From My Door," for example, seems at first blush to deploy the term "pygmy" as a kind of Surrealist image that intrudes into the quotidian. But "pygmy" is also a trope imported from a caricatured, white colonial view of Africa, which would suggest that the repeated title phrase, "Pygmy Stay Away From My Door," is about keeping such racialized caricatures at bay.[4] If this is the case, then lines like "the swinging swahili had snored" and "the blacks have raised a flag" continue the Black Surrealist tradition of irreverent political critique (23).[5] During the Mau Mau uprising, the British repressed the movement, in part, by hanging over a thousand Black "convicts"—that is, swinging Swahili speakers because the Black people had raised a flag.

Another poem in the collection, "To Africa I Went," picks up on this idea with a speaker who travels to Africa to find it quite different from what is depicted in the white Western imagination:

So this is Africa of savage folk
where people will put you in a pot
the only pot they offered me
was to smoke and cannibalism was a British joke. (36)

Like "Pygmy," this poem evokes the old Hollywood B movies Joans watched as a kid, with their images of British explorers in pith helmets being captured and cooked in huge cauldrons by grunting natives. This is the sort of "comic" imagery that does real harm in the way it reduces a whole continent to menacing "savage folk." After he traveled to and lived in Africa, Joans would become increasingly interested in crafting counter-narratives to this sort of white supremacist representation, from his poetry in *Afrodisia* to his detailed travel guide, "A Black Man's Guide to Africa."

In keeping with his understanding of Surrealism, then, there is certainly political content to the range of poems in *All of Ted Joans and No More.* Given that "It Is Time" yearns for the president of the United States to "write a thesis on jazz" while exhorting the "U.S. Congress to pass a bill authorizing the giant erection of two huge representational statues of Jackson Pollack [*sic*] and C. Parker" (52), it makes sense likewise to recognize the "jazz poems" in the book as not only celebrating the genre and its great artists (which they do) but also advocating for a particular sensibility and attitude that is freer, more open to abstraction and spontaneity, and therefore less ossified when it comes to conventional social or political norms.

In later years, Joans was careful to distinguish between "jazz and poetry," which is "simply to read a poem with jazz accompaniment," and "jazzpoetry," which, while "done often with jazz accompaniment ... [is] not just a poet reading with the musical background, the poet must be able to swing the word (not sing) and creatively read the poem in the same spirit as a jazz musician taking a solo."[6] This was his ideal of "jazzpoetry," and shows why works of this type are not really understandable outside their performative contexts, since for poems like "Birdeath," "Lester Young," "Miles Delight," "Hallelujah, I Love Jazz So," and "I Love A Big Bird," the performance *is* the point, and would be "creatively" different each time (for an example of Joans performing "Jazz Must Be a Woman" with Jimmy Garrison on bass, recorded in 1961, listen to the record *Europa Jazz* #50 [1981], which also features live tracks by Ella Fitzgerald, Ray Charles, and Dizzy Gillespie).

In the most well known of the jazz poems, "Hallelujah, I Love Jazz So" (elsewhere titled "Jazz Is My Religion"), Joans announces: "Jazz is / my religion its all American all the way like good / God Almighty coca cola and the cowboy Jazz is here to / stay" (48). Aside from insisting on what he sees as jazz's transcendent and ineffable qualities, this poem also reminds us that jazz is at once a distinctly American art form and a distinctly Black one: "Jazz is my religion, and its color is often / black and blue" (48). The allusion is to "(What Did I Do to Be So) Black & Blue," a Fats Waller tune popularized by Louis Armstrong, and containing the line: "My only sin is in my skin / What did I do to be so black and blue?" So resonant was this song that Ralph Ellison has his nameless narrator listening to and quoting it in the Prologue and Epilogue to his masterpiece *Invisible Man*, so it definitely had legs in the African American literary tradition, which Joans well knew. Thus while "Hallelujah, I Love Jazz So" has a celebratory, exuberant tone, it also foregrounds the way jazz was developed by Black artists in a generally oppressive and discriminatory environment: "Jazz is my religion it wasn't for me to choose, / 'cause they created it for a damn good reason / as a weapon to battle our blues" (48)—in this way, jazz seems the inevitable soundtrack of both Black joy and Black suffering.

In fact, when the cover of *All of Ted Joans and No More* announced that the book's contents were "beat generation jazz poems," it was signaling the way Joans wanted to bring his resolutely Black perspective to bear on the much publicized Beat phenomenon. The book's preface emphasizes his position as a Black poet on the largely white, Beat coffeehouse scene: "when Joans reads or as he says 'blows a poem' he puts all of his 'soul brother' emotions into each poem, what the audience is watching is not a well-rehearsed performer, but a proud and witty Negro who knows what he is reading about." This preface doesn't let readers forget that even in his "Beat poems," Joans sees the Beat Generation through his "proud and witty" Black perspective.

20

If You Should See a Man ...

Probably the most well-known and reproduced piece in *All of Ted Joans and No More* is a short poem titled "Voice in the Crowd," later re-titled "The Truth." This poem became one of Joans's lifelong signatures, an affirmation of the power of poetry that he would use as the lead poem in collections spanning several decades, including *Black Pow-Wow* (1969), *Mehr Blitzliebe Poems* (1982), and *Double Trouble* (1992), and as the final poem in his retrospective collection *Teducation* (1999). He tended to open and close his readings with "The Truth," and claimed it was the "only poem I've memorized."[1]

Over the years, the poem was printed with slightly different line breaks, spacing, and capitalizations across these volumes, but in *All of Ted Joans and No More* it looks like this:

> If you should see / a man / walking
>   down a crowded street / talking aloud / to himself
>   don't run / in the opposite direction
>   but run toward him / for he is a <u>poet</u>!
>
>   You have nothing to fear / from the poet
>   but the truth.[2]

There's a clue as to the general "you" Joans has in mind here in another poem in the collection, "The Jivey Leaguer." In the glossary in *All of Ted Joans*, we learn that a Jivey Leaguer is a "white male that is obnoxious, and yet more schooled than the common thug, and a bit more restrained than a Juvenile Delinquent" (93); in the poem dedicated to him, Joans declares further: "Jivey Leaguer you are afraid of the modern poet" (90). Thus while the "you" of "Voice in the Crowd" / "The Truth" shouldn't be taken to be restricted to a Jivey Leaguer, the latter poem points us to the sort of person Joans is addressing: white, square, interested in conformity and afraid of many things besides a "modern poet," from "growing a beard" to "undiluted democracy" to "jazz unless it is watered down" (90).

Another context for this poem is the flowering of the Beat Generation, which produced the kind of "modern poet" that so terrified bourgeois Jivey Leaguers. We know, in fact, that Joans had Beat poets specifically in mind as models for the declaiming poet because "Voice in the Crowd" / "The Truth" first appeared in *Funky Jazz Poems* under yet another title, "This Place Really Swings." In that booklet, the poem looked liked this:

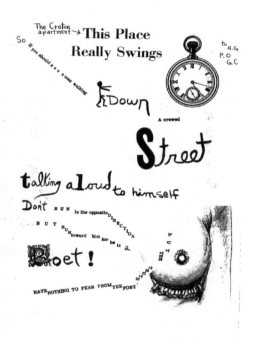

FIGURE 20.1 *"This Place Really Swings," later re-titled "The Truth," as it first appeared in* Funky Jazz Poems. *The "place" in the title refers to the Croton Street Apartments, where Allen Ginsberg lived at the time; the dedication "to A.G. P.O. G.C." refers to Ginsberg, Peter Orlovsky, and Gregory Corso.*

There are two crucial features of this version that link it to the Beats: the notation "The Croton apartment" and the dedication to "A.G. P.O. G.C." The initials stand for Allen Ginsberg, his boyfriend and poet Peter Orlovsky, and Gregory Corso.[3]

The Croton was an apartment building at 170 E. 2nd Street in the East Village where Ginsberg and Orlovsky lived from August 1958 to March 1961, and it became a Beat hub as visitors crashed there and other poets, including Bob Kaufman, took apartments there.[4] As Albert Saijo recalled of the building after driving cross-country from San Francisco with Kerouac and fellow poet Lew Welch in November 1959, there were "tenement houses on both sides of the street with tiny businesses tucked into the bottom of the buildings a step down from street level ... The staircase and hallways of the building had a cavernous feel."[5] Joans clearly wanted to associate the "place" in "This Place Really Swings" with this magnetic apartment building and Ginsberg's home base, a move that by extension associates "the poet" in the poem with Beat poets specifically.

And yet despite this initial association, in subsequent reprintings of "This Place Really Swings," Joans would drop this insider reference as he changed the title from "Voice in the Crowd" to "The Truth."[6] As attested by its prominent inclusion in a range of Joans's books, this version of "The Truth" had manifold afterlives. In 1968, he even published a slim volume that was just the poem translated from English into 36 other languages, from Amharic and Armenian to Bambara, Fulani, Hausa, Hebrew, Ibo, Swahili, and Vietnamese, "by friends of ted joans all over the world."[7] In 1978 in Tunis, Joans wrote "a parody on my own poem, The Truth" called "Hat Shoe?" that offers another kind of translation, the language of puns "outside of syntax": "Now hat shoe has seen / her hand / talking hound around / without a leash / outside of syntax."[8] The following year in Paris, Joans revisited and reworked "The Truth" once again in "Poet Key," a poem that amplifies the image of a lone poet to imagine instead a community of like-minded poets telling the truth to those "prisoners" living in everyday, ordinary society:

> Yes we walk   talk to ourselves
> Not because   we are alone   for
> This place is crowded   with prisoners
> Some are lifers   most are insane
> Yet amongst the "crazy ones"
> There is a   poet   or two: see he!   hear her?
> Yes we walk   talk to ourselves
> So there is hope   here   if they
> Who do not know how   to be cool
> Would listen   to our loud whispers
> Could be inspired   by her poem sigh
> Then within   a tiny time   prison
> Would be   completely destroyed with
> An all together poet-key   in harmony[9]

Although "Poet Key" underscores the universality Joans eventually attached to the image of the poet depicted in "The Truth," the initial dedication of "This Place Really Swings" and mention of the Croton points to a kind of shadow history lurking behind the poem. The wild-eyed, archetypal poet of "The Truth" began life as a specifically Beat poet connected to the Croton in the late 1950s, a figure who was talking back to a Modern Bourgeois Culture afraid of anything too different.[10]

And while there is no "J.K." in the original dedication to "This Place Really Swings" / "The Truth," Joans likely also had Jack Kerouac in mind as well, since he later anointed Kerouac the "hippest of the Croton Apartment poets."[11] Joans had respect for Kerouac as both a jazz aficionado and stylist whose *On the Road* "was the revolt in America's conventional tightassed publication world."[12] Widely held to be the "Bible of the Beat Generation," *On the Road* described the adventures of writer Sal Paradise and his friend Dean Moriarty as they crisscross the United States on a series of road trips. Dean exposes Sal to another America beyond the homogenized, white-bread suburbs, and inspired countless young people to question the normative culture of their parents' generation.

What Joans liked about *On the Road* was its freewheeling style, but he actually found the accounts of hitchhiking and escaping the claustrophobia of white middle America to pale in comparison to the experiences of Black Americans, who couldn't opt in or out of white society as Sal sometimes seems to do. Joans was also convinced that the "source" for *On the Road* was Langston Hughes's 1935 short story, "On the Road," thus locating the book's "real" origins in the Black American experience.[13]

As Joans said of *On the Road*:

> I found the prose fresh, but the experiences were deja vu and deja done for me, a Black American.
>
> My uncles who hoboed back and forth, up and down America, would put the book to shame, if they would have written their episodic life ... Perhaps if I would have been a young White guy with a three-meal-a-day background and no risky adventures, then I would have been excited about *On the Road*.[14]

Despite this critique of Kerouac's most famous work, Joans was quite fond of him personally, and in fact saw him variously as "white and black" or "neither white nor black"—as, in any case, outside the racial binaries that could seem so fixed in the 1950s. "Jack Kerouac was not only a writer," Joans said, "but also a poem, and that part of Jack is what interested me."[15]

It may have been Gregory Corso who brought Kerouac to one of Joans's parties, either at his 22 Astor Place studio, or at photographer Hugh Bell's studio on West Third Street, where Joans was sometimes permitted to host events in exchange for granting Bell the right to make and sell photographs of the proceedings.[16] In Joans's telling, the first night they met, Kerouac burst into the party drunk, not an uncommon state to find him in, and looked Joans up and down as a glimmer of recognition broke across his face:

"You're the cat," he said, "that digs the rhinoceros, aren't you?"[17]

Joans said he was, Kerouac introduced himself as Jack, and Joans didn't learn until later that the "wild, dancing, boozing and straight-ahead hipster" was the writer everyone around town seemed to be talking about.

The two men became friendly, bonding because, as Joans said, Kerouac was "the first white poet that I met that was hip to Bird."[18] Not only was Kerouac hip to Bird, but he knew all the little jazz spots in Harlem from his time in New York in the 1940s, and he would bring Joans to these places when they would get together.[19]

One story Joans told a few times happened when he and Kerouac had gone to the Five Spot Café to hear Horace Silver play. The Five Spot was another fabled establishment where Joans himself had recorded some statements then included in Seymour Krim's anthology, *The Beats* (1960), among them a comment on the Five Spot itself, that it was "avant-garde in jazz and atmosphere."[20] As they had bonded over Charlie Parker, so too did Joans and Kerouac bond over their mutual appreciation of Silver's virtuosity on the piano, and Kerouac once remarked that he wished he could stage a "play-off" between Silver and the white musician Dave Brubeck, piano to piano in a boxing ring. Despite the fact that Brubeck was far more celebrated in the national press, Joans and Kerouac were both "hip that Silver would destroy Brubeck in the first few chords."[21] That night, Kerouac was eager to hear Silver play, but was light on cash, and so at his urging they stopped back at Joans's studio to borrow against his "rent money stash."[22] With the money secured, Kerouac popped into Astor Liquors on the corner of Lafayette and Astor Place to buy a bottle of Thunderbird, and then the pair swayed the block or so over to the Five Spot, passing the bottle back and forth so they could get good and buzzed on the cheap.

Once inside, they settled into a small table near the band, and dug Silver as he went through his repertoire, from his early hits like "The Preacher" and "Doodlin" to "Come on Home" and "Room 608." During an intermission, Kerouac suggested they write poems and draw portraits of each other. He said, according to Joans, that he would "write a holy poem for you and you can do Horace Silver Doodlin of my Kerouac Whacky noodle same time, okay?"[23]

They played a "surrealist game" on a Five Spot publicity poster, Kerouac muttering, "A for Africa, and a black beacon eye in the middle brain, wise and diamond hard eye, bat winged angel berethead of big hear all ears."[24] For all these cryptic musings, Kerouac produced what Joans thought was a rather insipid drawing—he remembered Horace Silver stopping by their table during the intermission and being unimpressed—but Kerouac also composed a pithy Surreal poem to accompany his drawing:

These my Dravidian
    keeners
Thus my Holy Twat

My prick is
        an Empire Building
One Hundred Miles High[25]

Joans, for an answer, produced a "semi-academic portrait of Kerouac," and a poem that amounted to some of the highest praise he could give a white guy: "I know a man who is white and black. And his name is, Jack—the Kerouac."[26]

After the intermission, when, appropriately, Silver was playing "Creeping In," a woman crept over, touched Kerouac on the shoulder, and asked him if he was the famous author Jack Kerouac. He shushed the woman, and Joans tried to brush her off.

"He'll be right back," Joans said. "He had to pee, gone to the toilet, sit and be quiet!"

Drunk and undaunted, the woman (and her two friends) pulled up chairs from a table nearby. "You're Kerouac, aren't you?" she pressed, loudly complaining about "Beatnik going-ons."

Finally, an aggravated Kerouac turned to her and said, "Be quiet, can't you respect this sacred session of sounds for the soul? That is handsome angel Horace Silver and his holy band!"

The woman rather indignantly tossed some crumpled bills on the table, thinking the two broke-looking artistic types would never refuse a round of drinks. At this point Joans was fed up and suggested she go to the more tourist-friendly McSorley's Ale House down the street.

"Who are you?" the woman demanded.

"That's Ted Joans!" cried Kerouac. "You have to be careful, Corso informs white women that Ted will fuck them at the drop of their drawers!"[27]

This shut the woman up for the time being, and she sank back into her chair, "drunk, chain smoking, and talking too loud" with her friends.[28] Eventually as Joans and Kerouac continued to ignore her and refuse her offers to buy more rounds, she knocked over all the glasses on the table in a rage and was thrown out. It turned out the woman was Diana Barrymore, daughter of famed actor John Barrymore.[29]

———

Throughout his life, Joans would occasionally advertise his connections to Kerouac, as in his poetry collection *Mehr Blitzliebe Poems* (1982), which reproduces in full (and in facsimile) a letter Kerouac wrote to Joans on February 13, 1963. Kerouac is enthusiastic:

I always loved you because you were so much like me, i.e., openhearted + crazy-souled + honest—Don't accuse me of not having written to you, what could I do in 1959 with 3,000 friends but keep silent. I wish I were with you but I've scrounged with the Yaqui Indians in West Coast Mexico ... Anyway, Joans, make Africa, as I'm going to have to make my own area, Arctic Canada, soon, to find out my soul—your soul is my soul.[30]

This letter certainly does attest to the affection between the two men—and Joans seemed justly proud of it, as it was not only reproduced in *Mehr Blitzliebe Poems* but also on the back cover of *Our Thang* (2001), a late collection of Joans's poetry and drawings by Laura Corsiglia.

21

The Notorious
Rent-a-Beatnik Business

Beyond his friendships with Kerouac, Ginsberg, Corso, and others, one of Joans's more well-known—and notorious—connections to the Beat Generation was his involvement in the so-called "Rent-a-Beatnik" business in late 1959 into 1960. This brief episode has been much written about as one of the more colorful features of the Beatnik Era, and has stuck to Joans's legacy in part because it illustrates the degree to which he could game the cultural mood to his advantage. If Joans capitalized on the interest in the Beat Generation by transforming himself into a paradigmatic Beat poet and reading poems like "The Sermon" on the Village coffeehouse circuit, the Rent-a-Beatnik scheme pushed this role to absurd ends as he would get paid for turning up at parties and embodying some square figment of the Beat archetype.

The Rent-a-Beatnik business was conceived by Fred McDarrah, a *Village Voice* photographer who became known for documenting the Beats and other literary and artistic types in and around the Village during the 1950s and after. In November 1959, housewife Joyce Barken from the tony enclave of Scarsdale called *The Village Voice* to inquire about hiring poets to read at a Beatnik-themed party she was planning, and McDarrah had happened to answer the phone.[1] He thought the woman was joking at first, but when it developed that she was perfectly serious, he sensed a money-making opportunity and told her that were she paying, he certainly could scrounge up some Beatniks.[2]

After this call, Joans had been walking with his children outside the *Village Voice* offices on Greenwich Avenue when McDarrah approached him about a new venture: some rich person was willing to pay $150 to have genuine "Beatniks" appear at a party and amplify the sort of authentic Beat poet performance Joans was already doing nightly. Joans was in.

McDarrah wanted him to round up some more people to attend; as Joans remembered:

> I offered three guys and four girls 5 dollars an hour each, plus transportation via bus-subway. I myself received 50 dollars for reading and running the "beatnik" party. The hosts were rich business exec type. The house was a ranch style with every imaginable comfort. Wine, cheeses of all nations were in abundance. The rich squares had a ball and so did the poor beatniks. We only worked for one hour, but stayed on to partake in the foodstuffs. After that first joke that paid off, McDarrah received more and more requests for Beat poets with beatniks.[3]

In Joans's view, these parties were mutually beneficial in the sense that the poor "Beat poets" and Beatniks—note the distinction he makes above—got good meals and decent pay, while the "rich squares" got to feel like they were in close contact with authentic bohemians—without having to leave the comfort of their suburban living rooms.

The first event was such a success that McDarrah took out what would become an infamous ad in *The Village Voice*: "Rent Genuine Beatniks: Badly Groomed but Brilliant." It was an ironic ad, but people took it seriously. As McDarrah recalled, he charged $40 per night, plus $5 a person, and "Props like bongo drums, guitars, or candle-topped Chianti bottles cost extra."[4] The response to the ad soon became "overwhelming," as McDarrah put it, and he developed a stable of poets and Beatniks for rent including Tuli Kupferberg (who would later go on to co-found *The Fugs*), Mimi Margaux (whom McDarrah had identified as "extremely well-informed on beat activities"), and Ronald Van Ehmesen ("more of a religious poet ... no visible source of income).[5] As Joans said:

> This agency of course was a joke that became a commercial success ... and for me it was a social-aesthetic-triumph because I got into the homes of the squares and laid my poetic bit right in their laps. I was much braver than the cats that preach from a pulpit, or on radio, T.V., stage etc. I brought my messages in person into their very homes. It was white America that I was preaching to and Fred McDarrah booked me into white homes.[6]

Joans certainly recognized that he was playing a role, that he was conforming to and reproducing what these wealthy white people imagined a Beat poet to be. "They want a stereotype they can *control*," he said at the time.[7] But he also admitted that appearing at the Rent-a-Beatnik parties had boosted his profile as he was quoted in connection to it, in among other places, *Time* magazine, the *New York Times*, and Leonard Lyons's syndicated gossip column, "The Lyons Den." Joans always insisted that his presence in white wealthy spheres extended the sort of outreach he was doing in the Village coffeehouses, and Lyons had even quoted him saying "Man, we'll try the new states, Hawaii and Alaska—where they've never seen a Beat."[8]

In retrospect Joans liked to characterize the people at these parties as "lost souls that had needed poetry":

It was a new kind of hip-missionary work for me to do, especially I as a Black pontificating about how to change and help transform America, a brave thing to do in those years, especially courageous in the white square's home which were miles and miles away from Harlem and Greenwich Village. But I did, and I am glad that I had the opportunity to tell America to its face in its own private dwelling place, plus I got paid.[9]

As he did with his coffeehouse poetry, Joans was able to see his performance as a "stereotypical" Beat as part of a larger push toward "moral revolution": he was a Black bohemian poet speaking his truth to these party-goers, however dumbly they had chosen to costume themselves. As he deadpanned to *Time* magazine (still firmly embodying his "Beat" persona): "I told them [the people who 'rented' him for Beatnik parties] what the beats are really like. Everybody thinks the beats always smoke pot, smell horrible, and all that jazz. I take a bath every day, man."[10] To speak the truth, he would read work like "The Sermon," which made quite an impression on the human interest reporter for the local Long Island paper: "Bearded Ted Joans snaps it out in his 'Funky Jazz Poems,' climaxed by his 'Sermon to a Young Chick'—tender and exciting advice to a beat-minded girl in a square world."[11] Given Joans's history of proto-Happenings around New York City, it's not that hard to see his involvement in the Rent-a-Beatnik business, as Laura Corsiglia does, as a kind of "guerilla theater cultural seminar."[12]

Another, less obvious way the Rent-a-Beatnik business made Joans more publicly visible, at least from his point of view, was that McDarrah was eager to help elevate Joans's celebrity in order to keep the business humming. In 1960, Elias Wilentz, co-owner of the 8th Street Bookshop, edited *The Beat Scene*, still one of the best anthologies of Beat writing around, and what Joans called "the first superbly distributed done and mass distributed hip book on the Beats."[13] The book was loaded with McDarrah's photographs, and featured a 15-page spread on Joans—much more space than was given to any other writer, including Kerouac and Ginsberg. *The Beat Scene* contained only one of Joans's poems—"Let's Play Something," which would also appear in *All of Ted Joans and No More*—but had nine photographs of him in various guises. There was Joans in a beret, looking serious as he reads his poetry; one of him in an ankle-length raccoon fur coat and full beard, posing next to his paintings in his studio; one of Joans the family man, arrayed on the grass in Washington Square Park with Joyce and their four children. There is also one of Joans overseeing what is captioned as his "biannual birthday party in his Astor Place studio"—and in fact there are five more pages of photos of this party (held on July 25, 1959), which document the crowded rooms of people of various backgrounds, from Village hipsters to the square weekenders Joans would captivate at the coffeehouses, all dancing and drinking in a space where the walls bore hand-scrawled notes declaring "le sang des poetes" and posters welcoming "girls of the beat generation."[14]

The ratio of photographs to poetry in *The Beat Scene* underscores the extent to which Joans could be viewed as more of a personality than a writer or artist, the hipster par excellence and man about town who seemed the very embodiment of the bohemian lifestyle. As he wrote in the lone poem in the volume: "Let's play something. Let's play anything. Let's play bohemian, and wear odd clothes, and grow a beard or a ponytail, live in the Village for 200.00 a month for one small pad and stroll through Washington Square Park with a guitar and a chick looking sad" (104). *The Beat Scene* offers the impression that Joans was both "playing" at *and* living the bohemian life— so much so that in fact "play" and real life, performance and authenticity, become blurred. When confronted with a photo of shirtless Joans in a beret, posing before an enormous mock-up of a *Life* magazine cover, one is never quite sure if the pose is serious or shtick, both or neither.

Such ambiguity is of course part of the appeal, but the spread in *The Beat Scene* reified Joans's legend while giving shorter shrift to his painting and poetry. In fact, Joans felt that Rent-a-Beatnik was ultimately to blame for the extent and nature of the anthology's coverage: "The spread on me was overdone, but I know why it was done, because McDarrah wanted to do all he could to make my image known so that he could continue his Beat Bizness; Rent-A-Beatnik!"[15] Whatever McDarrah's particular motivations with respect to Joans, he did broadly consider Rent-a-Beatnik and *The Beat Scene* mutually sustaining; as he said, "I didn't want to get into the Beatnik rental business at all, but rather to promote my forthcoming book, *The Beat Scene*."[16]

The sense of Joans as not a "real poet" or merely hamming it up for the publicity was in fact reinforced by the lengthy passage that opened the Ted Joans section of *The Beat Scene*. The passage appeared in quotation marks, as though it had been written or spoken by Joans:

Whenever I meet some old buddies from Indiana University its [*sic*] the same old questions they ask—why aren't you painting, what's all this clowning publicity for, since when are you a poet? Well, I'm not really a poet except for Allen Ginsberg who grabbed me one November day in nineteen fifty eight and said he was bored stiff with reading in the coffee shop and why didn't I do it because I was great ... now I'm making more money than I ever made from my painting. At least now I have enough coming in steady to keep the family on Staten Island well off ... As for all the showoff stunts well hell that's just part of the job and making a living.[17]

This statement certainly appears to undercut any claims Joans might have had to being a "serious" writer—and that ensuing poem, "Let's Play Something," is a breezy affair you can imagine appealing to coffeehouse audiences. The subsequent photos of Joans's parties and various get-ups only confirm his apparent penchant for "clowning publicity" and "showoff stunts," casting them in a lighthearted but perhaps cynical light, as necessary evils to survive.

But Joans later disavowed this statement totally, in fact claiming that he didn't write it at all: "It was also Fred McDarrah that conjured or vomited up that jive blurb at the beginning of the part of his book on me. I never said that, and if I had it would be a lie."[18] Whether or not he made this statement to McDarrah in 1959, the fact that Joans later cast doubt about its origins suggests the degree to which he wanted to be understood as a legitimate poet and not merely an ironic coffeehouse performer out to make a cynical buck. In fact, he was both these things at different moments, was able to become the hip coffeehouse wailer or "authentic" stereotypical Beat at rich people's parties—all while also creating art on his own terms.

The notorious Rent-a-Beatnik business apparently fell apart after a US Treasury agent cornered Joans at the Conrad Shop on MacDougal Street, a favorite bohemian jewelry store, and started questioning him about how much he made in the enterprise, and how much he paid in taxes. "The latter question was too much," Joans recalled. "For Fred and I had paid not one cent of tax nor did we keep any kind of records of our unorthodox business. It was not really a business it was more of a entertaining phenomena. Yet the treasury agent was serious and meant business with a capital B."[19] Joans was spooked, wormed out of the situation by giving the agent a phony address, and telling him that McDarrah had gone off to Italy, probably for good. He didn't see the agent again, but the encounter spelled the "end of the Rent-a-Beat bit."

A fact often eclipsed by the surprisingly well-publicized Rent-a-Beatnik business was that Joans was also by 1959 in the very center of other artistic networks and creative exchanges. Attuned as he was at the time to the power of publicity, he organized what would become a pair of readings at the Artist's Studio in February 1959. This event produced one of the most famous photographs of Jack Kerouac, standing on a ladder and reading with his arms outstretched. Shot by McDarrah, this photograph was featured on the cover of *The Beat Scene*—although Joans is cropped out on this cover, in the original photograph, he is visible to Kerouac's right (the left of the photo) smiling and thoroughly enjoying himself beneath a "No Smoking" sign he had pinned up.

For that reading, Joans had invited Barbara Moraff, Edward Marshall, Frank Lauria, Dan Propper, Jack Micheline, Ray Bremser, Sandy Bethune, Carl Yeargens, Marc Schleifer, Seymour Krim, and LeRoi Jones—who in turn invited Kerouac, Allen Ginsberg, Gregory Corso, and Frank O'Hara to appear as well. Joans called it a "heavy poetry event," and certainly it was: these were all known writers on the scene at the time, many of whom would go on to be recognized as among the more significant voices of the Beat Generation and postwar letters more generally.[20] It was a "Jazz at the Philharmonic kind of scene," Joans said, in which "each poet would come forward, sit or stand to 'blow his solo' poem or short prose bit. Each poet did his Beat or non-Beat best for the other poets."[21] The sense that these writers were "blowing" for one another was key, for Joans took this to be a serious, non-commercialized event, in contrast to his frenetic readings at coffeehouses, largely for curious out-of-towners in desperate need of his preaching. Of course the fact that the event was subsequently commercialized via *The Beat Scene* is simply the story of the Beat Generation, and how it was all but impossible to disentangle artistic production from media coverage and the reach of capitalism.

22

The Hipsters

Trading on his involvement with the Beats, Joans's other major book of his New York years was *The Hipsters*, a parting shot before he decamped to Europe and Africa. The book is unique in the pantheon of Beat literature as it was made up of collages accompanied by Joans's humorous captions, a genre he called "collage-prose."[1] It was published by Corinth, a small press started by booksellers Ted and Elias Wilentz in 1959. Their bookstore, 8th Street Bookshop, founded back in 1947, had become by the late 1950s a hang-out spot for writers—Ted Wilentz's later wife, Joan, remembered the store as "being the equivalent of a singles bar in the 50s," a status that helps explain the access the Wilentzes had to put *The Beat Scene* together (a book Corinth itself ultimately published).[2]

Ted Wilentz recalled that both he and his brother were "interested in publishing, so we jumped in. For a while we thought we might make Corinth into a fully-fledged business, but that fantasy dwindled as time went on."[3] But during its years of operation (1959–73), Corinth Books did publish a number of Beat and other avant-garde writers, from Kerouac, Ginsberg, and Gary Snyder, often in association with LeRoi Jones's Totem Press. These Totem/Corinth titles included Kerouac's *The Scripture of the Golden Eternity* (1960), Gary Snyder's *Myths & Texts* (1960), and Philip Whalen's *Like I Say* (1960). Corinth was, then, an ideal home for *The Hipsters*—and further cemented Joans's association with the Beats. He signed a contract for *The Hipsters* in June 1961, agreeing to be paid $150 for it, $75 up front and $75 upon publication, and then 10 percent of net receipts of sales thereafter.[4] This was hardly enough to live on, of course, but every little bit helped, and because *The Hipsters* was a Corinth title, it further boosted Joans's profile in New York.

The Hipsters resists summary because it doesn't have a plot—at least in a conventional sense—and much of the humor comes from the visual puns in the collages, and the interaction of those collages with Joans's captions. Those familiar with the collages of the German Surrealist artist Max Ernst would immediately recognize their influence on *The Hipsters*—and, for that

FIGURE 22.1 *Ted Joans with friend Nicolai Welsh on the cover of* The Hipsters *(1961). Joans and Welsh are propped up against the wall with no other means of support than their own hands clasped on each other's knees.*

matter, on *All of Ted Joans and No More*. Like *The Hipsters* after it, a work such as Ernst's *Les Malheurs des Immortels* (1922) contains collages with descriptive captions. Always keeping an eye on the dissonant and the absurd, Ernst held a distorted mirror on "the real" by rearranging and recontextualizing source material from the most ordinary of places. As David Gascoyne put it in *A Short Survey of Surrealism*, Joans's early bible on the subject, the illustrations from *Les Malheurs des Immortels* were "formed of inconsequential fragments cut from Victorian magazines, treatises on anatomy, botany, mechanics, etc., [and] give a most vivid impression of reality."[5] Joans also sourced his illustrations from Victorian accounts of African exploration, anatomy books, and the like—but, as I will explain in the coming pages, his choice of source material was hardly "inconsequential," and in fact is integral to understanding what he is doing in *The Hipsters*.

In terms of abiding themes, the book is "about" the Greenwich Village scene right around 1960, and has its truly hip denizens fleeing New York City as it becomes increasingly gentrified and hostile to bohemians and non-conformists. Joans saw the book as a "warning of what could (and it did) happen within one decade, if the hipsters did not help hip the unhip."[6] *The Hipsters* is about how the dream of a democratic bohemian society centered in the Village was being eroded by those "unhip" people with other, antithetical values (money and social conformity chief among them). And just as a poem like "The Sermon" purports to let the unhip in on hipness, or the Rent-a-Beatnik business claimed to deliver an authentic Beat to rich people in the suburbs, the joke of *The Hipsters* is that it *seems* to offer a kind of ethnographic access to hipness, but in fact thwarts that very impulse at every turn.[7] Built from droll and ironic collage illustrations loaded with visual puns and acerbic commentary, *The Hipsters* sketches a collision of cultures, using as its "Dramatis Personae" a host of character types Joans had named in *All of Ted Joans and No More*, including The Cool Hipster, The Jivey Leaguer, The Creepnik, The Folknik, The Hipstressnik, and The Hipper-Than-Thounik, providing comic vignettes of these characters at work and play in the Village.

The book is divided into five sections: The Scene; Dramatis Personae; Act 1: That Day; Act 2: That Night, or Nite Scene; and Act 3: The Flight. The book concludes with a Surrealist essay titled "L'Envoi." In the first part, Joans sets the scene (and plays on the sense of "scene" used in a book like *The Beat Scene*) emphasizing that he is discussing Greenwich Village in a particular moment in time. The book opens with a collage of a nineteenth-century village in the Egyptian countryside, a concentrated warren of thatched roofs surrounded by an angled pole fence. Some villagers are transporting firewood or thatching through the fence, and Joans has superimposed an image of a dinosaur-sized lobster just outside the village walls—in "L'Envoi," he writes that in Greenwich Village "the fuzz are all over at every exit and entrance watching me and you, ubiquitous as a giant lobster that Davey Jones has released from his locker."[8] Thus the Surreal image of the giant lobster in the book's opening collage signals the menace of authority, policing and regulation, lurking just outside the walls of the village, despite which the caption is bright and optimistic: "Here is Greenwich Village, New York, the home of the hipster, hipnick, beat, beatnik, flip, flipnik, etc., where several thousand top people of all races, creeds and colors work, play and live in sometimes peace and sometimes harmony and all try to enjoy the lofty fruit of U.S. d e m o c r a c y." But the giant lobster portends the destruction of this multiracial peace and harmony, as illustrated in the rest of the book.

As Joans is setting the scene, he makes references to real-life events that symbolized this destruction for him and many others. For instance, under a collage of a massive birdcage set high above humble thatched huts, there is the caption: "The Jivey Leaguers built Washington Square Village, a huge new bird cage for the very rich. They have their own flag, own constitution and their own private fuzz." Washington Square Village was (and is) a massive, 2000-unit apartment complex that formed a "superblock" at Bleecker and Mercer Streets. Owned by nearby New York University, the imposing complex opened in December 1957, permanently changing the character of Greenwich Village, much to the dismay of long-term residents. Even the *New York Times* saw the construction of Washington Square Village as symbolizing the passing of an era—in a piece wistfully titled "Bohemian Flair Fades in the Village," Ira Henry Freeman lamented that these new expensive, air-conditioned apartments would drive out bohemian types, noting that the new residents would see nary a "batik scarf on the wall or a candle in an empty wine bottle."[9] For all the comic Surreality of the book, then, Joans was explicitly placing his characters in a particular moment in the Village's history.

One new character type profiled in *The Hipsters*, but not seen in *All of Ted Joans*, was the "Folknik," a nod to the influx of folk singers into the Village that had picked up steam by 1961—when, to take a famous example, Bob Dylan arrived there from Minnesota. Dylan would later recall sitting on a barstool in the Kettle of Fish on MacDougal Street and watching "heavy people going by, David Amram bundled up, Gregory Corso, Ted Joans."[10] But in the context of *The Hipsters*, the Folkniks represent a demographic that was spectacularly crushed under the weight of state-sanctioned surveillance symbolized by that giant lobster.

This is how the Folkniks are described: "FOLKNIKS carry musical instruments and long loose flowing hair as they sit on the steps of the hip folklore music shop or every Sunday gather at the Washington Square circle. (Notice the sad three meals-a-day look and the folknik who has been fingered out by Commissioner of Parks Newbold Morris for playing in the Square that Sunday he banned folknik singing)."

FIGURE 22.2 *Ted Joans in Washington Square Park, decked in a safari suit, ready to lead an expedition deep into the wilds of Greenwich Village. Laurated Archive.*

The reference there is to an incident in March 1961, when New York City Parks Commissioner Newbold Morris cracked down on "minstrels of unsavory appearance" who were playing in Washington Square Park.[11] These minstrels were what Joans called "Folkniks," and Morris's order banning them from the park was met with widespread outrage—less than two weeks after the ban, on April 9, 1961, folk singers rioted in Washington Square Park, battling police for over two hours.[12] Ten people were arrested. The banning of folk singers and the subsequent confrontation was, like the monstrous Washington Square Village, widely held to be symbolic of the increasing gentrification of Greenwich Village, the backdrop of all the action in *The Hipsters*.

This book's "plot," such as it is, has outsiders coming on to the Village scene, both tourists (Touristniks) who "point and stare at the natives," and "foreign emissaries" on a "Rockerfeller [*sic*] Brothers grant to study hipsterism and the dilemma of modern man" (see Figure 22.3). Joans detects the strong whiff of colonialism as the "natives" are held up to scrutiny by foreigners, only to eventually be displaced by those foreigners. The running joke of *The Hipsters* is the play on the word "village" to refer to both Greenwich Village and the primitive African village in the colonial imagination. This is why the Greenwich Village "natives" are often illustrated by Victorian-era drawings depicting various peoples of Africa in their own villages; earlier in the 1950s, Joans would dress up in a khaki suit and pith helmet to lead "Greenwich Village Safari" tours from Washington Square Park (see Figure 22.2).

The material for the collages in *The Hipsters* comes from a mix of nineteenth-century publications. The source illustration for the "Touristniks," to take just one example, is C. G. Bush's "On the Mountains," which first appeared in *Appleton's Journal* in 1870. The line drawing features well-to-do, Victorian-era white people, the man dressed in a three-piece suit and a boater hat, the woman in a bonnet and carrying a parasol, looking out over a summit; in *The Hipsters*, the object of their gaze becomes the residents of Greenwich Village, and Joans has superimposed on another nineteenth-century image of what are probably enslaved people leaning out of a window in bemusement at the Touristniks' fascination.

But despite the range of material Joans drew on for his collages, most of the source images in *The Hipsters* come from just one book: James W. Buel's *Heroes of the Dark Continent* (1890), a weighty tome containing over 500 illustrations of Africa—or, more accurately, of Africa seen through colonial eyes. The "heroes" of the book are European explorers, colonial administrators, military men and the like who, as the book's lengthy subtitle announces, went adventuring in Africa, "discovering" exotic peoples and having "thrilling" experiences—the precursors to the "foreigners" coming into Greenwich Village to "point and stare at the natives," as Joans put it.

Heroes of the Dark Continent reads like a compendium of and apologia for European involvement in Africa, which culminated in the Scramble for Africa, a period roughly from the 1880s to the First World War when European powers were carving up the African continent for their own empires. As we know from his work at UNESCO and his elaborate Mau Mau events, Joans had of course been long fascinated and disturbed by the history of colonial Africa, seeing his own lived experiences with racism and segregation in the States reflected in the experiences of Black people living under colonial rule in Africa, a connection that became a major theme of his poem-life in subsequent years.

This interest only redoubled when Joans moved from New York to Europe and Timbuktu and spent much of the 1960s and 1970s traveling around the continent of Africa, becoming in the mid-1960s and after increasingly invested in the politics of decolonization, and the entwined aesthetic developments of Négritude and the Black Arts Movement. Sourcing images from *Heroes of the Dark Continent* was thus a way for Joans to suggest that what was happening in Greenwich Village was an echo of what happened and was happening in colonial Africa, with Black people in both cases having to be "wise, aware, shrewd"—a more global sense of "hip"—in order to survive. In drawing this connection, Joans is not of course implying that colonialism in Africa and the gentrification of Greenwich Village amount to the same thing or are moral equivalents, but he is rather affirming a global Black experience by noting, satirically, some parallels between the two circumstances: that privileged white people are "exploring" elsewhere; that "natives" are subject to the (white) Western impulse to categorize, label, and map; and that people of means often express a need to claim literal ownership of places they consider "exotic"—all with the effect of Black people the world over having the most "injustices inflicted" upon them. In *The Hipsters*, after a "group of hipsters" flee Greenwich Village, they end up "lost in the middle west and swallowed up by the Mississippi never to be heard from again"—an event illustrated by two facing collages, both of course sourced from *Heroes of the Dark Continent*.[13]

FIGURE 22.3 *From* The Hipsters *(1961). The caption reads: "From the four corners of the earth arrive four foreign emissaries all bearing some kind of nutty bit to turn everyone on. They're on a Rockerfeller Brothers grant to study hipsterism and the dilemma of modern man."*

The Hipsters works through Surrealist juxtapositions like this, playing with echoes and associations, so that, in another example, a collage illustrating "four foreign emissaries" is based on an engraving from *Heroes of the Dark Continent* depicting Sir Samuel White Baker, a British explorer and one-time Governor-General in the Nile Basin (see Figure 22.3). In *Heroes*, Baker is flanked by his chief engineer, Edwin Higginbottom; the Egyptian officer Lieutenant Colonel Abd El-Kader, one of Baker's aides-de-camp; and one Lieutenant Baker.[14] Thus those "four foreign emissaries" who have arrived in Greenwich Village "to study hipsterism and the dilemma of modern man" contain also the ghostly imprints of real-life historical figures deeply entangled in the colonial enterprise in Africa (even as this particular engraving depicted the men at a time when they were ostensibly in Egypt to eradicate the slave trade). It's an open question as to how many details of this history Joans knew or had in mind when he appropriated this image, but it is clear that it represents white, Victorian-era explorers involving themselves in Africa, and this is the basic sense readers are meant to register when paging through *The Hipsters*.

Joans's Surrealist touch, which immediately has the effect of puncturing the dignified and self-important aspect of the original portraits, is to superimpose huge images of walnuts over the crotches of the three white men (but not Abd El-Kader), a comic, literal signifier of the "nuts"—fortitude, audacity, or arrogance, depending on your point of view—one needs to presume to travel to a foreign place and then confidently administer it.

One particularly rich and humorous collage draws together deeper colonial histories and some contemporary racial politics undergirding figurations of "hip" (see Figure 22.4). As anyone would know who took Joans's advice in "The Sermon," which urges aspiring hipsters to "know thyself / by reading Norman Mailer's White Negro" (*ATJ*, 33), the reference here is to Mailer's instantly-controversial essay, "The White Negro." First appearing in *Dissent* in 1957, the essay became one of the more well-known analyses of the hipster phenomenon, but the most pertinent part to understanding what Joans is doing in *The Hipsters* is Mailer's claim that "the source of Hip is the Negro." Mailer writes:

> Knowing in the cells of his existence that life was war, nothing but war, the Negro (all exceptions admitted) could rarely afford the sophisticated inhibitions of civilization, and so he kept for his survival the art of the primitive ... So there was a new breed of adventurers, urban adventurers who drifted out at night looking for action with a black man's code to fit their facts. The hipster had absorbed the existentialist synapses of the Negro, and for practical purposes could be considered a white Negro.[15]

This is the idea that Joans echoes when he says in his essay "Black-Flower" that "the Afroamerican is and has always been the true hipster."[16] In fact,

A white Negro is insolently received by some square maumaus who
misunderstood his treatises on hipster theory. (Notice the com-
pletely integrated horse dashing to greet him.)

FIGURE 22.4 *Page from* The Hipsters *spoofing Norman Mailer's essay "The White
Negro."*

"Black-Flower" also echoes Mailer's language of "survival," and in *The
Hipsters*, the image of "adventurers" coming into a place like Greenwich
Village with an eye toward getting hip by adopting the posture and language
of Black hipsters is of course its own kind of colonization.[17] Mailer insists
that "civilization" is coded white while "primitive" and "native" are coded
Black, and thus to be a so-called "White Negro" is to reject white-coded
civilization and embrace Black-coded "art of the primitive."

Such a formulation may seem ripe for criticism and counter-attack,
and Mailer was hardly without detractors—perhaps most famously James
Baldwin—and Joans's "white negro" collage certainly joins in the fray.[18] It
is an especially rich example of how Joans playfully deploys categories like
"civilization" and "primitive" throughout *The Hipsters*, presenting them as
seemingly stable ideas but then undercutting and ironizing those ideas. The
source engraving from *Heroes of the Dark Continent* depicts a village of the

Gogo or Wagogo people in what is now central Tanzania. The pith-helmeted white man in the center is none other than Henry Morton Stanley, one of the most celebrated "explorers" of Africa (of "Dr. Livingston, I Presume?" fame), and the caption encapsulates how *Heroes* is framed from a white, Western point of view. It reads: "Impertinent Curiosity of the Wagogo" (216). While the Wagogo are held up as objects of curiosity to white readers of *Heroes* (just as the varieties of "hipsters" are held up as objects of curiosity to white readers of *The Hipsters*), the Wagogo are not permitted to be curious about the foreigner arrived in their midst—hence such curiosity is deemed "impertinent."

The Wagogo were in fact notorious for their hostility to outsiders. As Stanley himself wrote of them in his memoirs—unironically titled *In Darkest Africa* (1890)—"No natives know so well how to aggrieve and be unpleasant to travelers. One would think there was a school somewhere in Ugogo to teach low cunning and vicious malice to the chiefs, who are masters in foxy-craft."[19] This sort of historical "knowledge" is again the ghostly imprint behind Joans's collage, which has Stanley transfigured into "a white Negro" and arrived in a "primitive" land to survey and chart and extract. In Joans's version, he is met not impertinently but "insolently" by those who "misunderstood his treatises on hipster theory." This last phrase is key, and points to the parts of "The White Negro" Joans liked: for all Mailer's controversial or problematic assertions, Joans did agree with his fundamental claim that "the source of Hip is the Negro," a fact obvious to Joans and any other Black artist or musician at the time.

In *The Hipsters*, Joans's use of the illustration "Impertinent Curiosity of the Wagogo" reverses the gaze assumed in *Heroes of the Dark Continent*, for in Joans's hands it is the Stanley figure who looks awkward and strangely posed, hemmed in not only by the Wagogo, but by the additions Joans has included in the collage, an aardvark—one of his totem animals—a giant toad, the skull of a warthog. Together with the insolent Wagogo, these African animals frame the white figure, emphasizing that *he* is one who doesn't fit the scene, that he is the interloper, the exotic stranger. About to nudge the white figure is a zebra, the only being in the image apparently receptive to his presence, and the parenthetical joke, that the zebra is really a "completely integrated horse," marks it as not only a visual pun, but a corollary to the idea of a "white Negro," which similarly attempts to integrate and reconcile two opposing existentialist realities in one body.

———

In considering the arc of Joans's poem-life, *The Hipsters* was a fitting farewell to the Village scene, and it was well received. Langston Hughes wrote that the book was "the <u>definitive</u> volume of hipsterology."[20] Perhaps owing to their friendship, Hughes was in fact effusive about *The Hipsters*, asserting that "Contemporary American satire has not, to my knowledge, produced anything better than this Ted Joans commentary. THE HIPSTERS is fun—and thought provoking, too. It would be Required Reading on my list for all students of our time." Joans's other "February Father," André Breton, was similarly enthusiastic about the book, calling it "truly surrealist and full of 'humor noire.'"[21]

If, for Joans, the book was a "warning" of what could happen "if the hipsters did not help hip the unhip," by 1961, his fears were coming true, not only as evidenced by the new "elite" buildings going up in Greenwich Village, or by the hard line city authorities were taking with various bohemian elements, but more importantly by a general shift in the cultural position of the "hipsters," which was being increasingly diluted and commercialized. The "Jivey Leaguers" were winning, Joans thought, taking their tepid version of "non-potent hipsterism to the White Power Establishment on Madison Avenue ... Causing millions of unhip adults and twice as many youngsters, to worship electricity and its machinery as music."[22] Joans is naming the roots of the latter-day "hipster" phenomenon, when the word came to connote white appropriation of Black culture, and a general investment in specific types of consumer goods to advertise refined, non-mainstream style and taste.[23]

———

He wasn't alone in feeling that the Village's true countercultural residents— hipsters, Beats, avant-garde artists, or jazz musicians—were being absorbed and watered down by the very bourgeois culture that had previously alienated them. In fact, in January 1961, Joans had even participated in a symbolic "funeral for the Beat Generation" held at filmmaker Robert Cordier's apartment at 85 Christopher Street, the idea being to memorialize an underground scene that was now transforming into something different. In attendance were many well-known Beat and Beat-adjacent personalities, including Joans's buddies Seymour Krim, Tuli Kupferberg, Sylvia Topp, Ted Wilentz, as well as Shel Silverstein, James Baldwin, and Norman Mailer. Like Joans, those gathered at the "funeral" were there to acknowledge and mourn the shifting cultural winds.

But for Joans, one of the few Black people associated with the Beat scene, the Beat Generation was seeming more and more irrelevant to what he was doing as a Black artist. He related to something James Baldwin had reportedly said at the funeral for the Beat Generation: "I shall continue to write my creations whether there is or is not a Beat Generation." He even recalled Baldwin saying "I feel that Ted like any Black artist will continue to paint his pictures, like he did before there was this so-called Beat Generation—Black people don't need [it]."[24] Historian Sean Wilentz—whose father Elias and uncle Ted had run the 8th Street Bookshop and published *The Hipsters*—sees the funeral as emblematic of how "the Beat phenomenon was running out of steam," and notes that it took place just after Bob Dylan's arrival in Greenwich Village, signaling the passing of the countercultural torch to a new generation. As Wilentz writes, "most of the writers had gathered to bury what was left of a movement that they believed had been thoroughly co-opted by the commercial mainstream. What had begun as an iconoclastic literary style (whether one approved of it or not) had become, the detractors said, just another fad, a subject fit for television comedies."[25] To emphasize the point, later that night, some of the guests even bore a coffin in a "funeral march" around the streets of the Village, an act very much in keeping with the sort theatrical events Joans had been spearheading throughout the fifties.[26] As he later told Justin Desmangles, "The whole thing was getting so commercial, we decided to bury it! … We had a proper funeral with a casket, with the words Beat Generation painted on it and carried it in a procession through [Greenwich] Village. Afterwards there was a wake and we all paid our respects."[27] In this way, then, *The Hipsters* was indicative of a wider sense that the unhip had won out over the hip, and though Joans had managed to profit from the "mainstreaming" of the Beat phenomenon through his coffeehouse readings and Rent-a-Beatnik gigs, New York City was holding less and less appeal to him as he turned his sights on Europe—and, ultimately, Africa.

23

André Breton and the Seeds of Self-Exile

While the Village was undergoing its own cultural shifts, Joans was also finding it increasingly difficult to balance his creative and home lives. During the height of his success as a coffeehouse poet, when he kept a whirlwind schedule of readings, attending art openings, and generally making himself available on the scene, Joyce and their children were still living out their domestic routine on Staten Island. The home provided stability for the children, even as Joans insisted he had brought a little Village bohemia to the outer borough: "There we lived in an Upper bohemia lifestyle with our four young masterpieces of humanity. We entertained successful people of the arts, and those young supporters of the arts who had money to do just that. Our home was a weekly salon. The walls of our humble, yet sophisticated house, was adorned with contemporary paintings, signed posters, African art and photographs."[1]

FIGURE 23.1 *Joyce in all black, bohemian cat eyes, and dark lipstick, April 1958. Poupée (doll) was Joans's pet name for Joyce, connected in his mind to artist Hans Bellmer's famed doll, which he had photographed over the years in various states of assembly or contortion, notably in the book* La Poupée *(1936). Laurated Archive.*

Joyce remembered that time differently, that Joans more or less lived in his Astor Place studio and would show up to Staten Island once in a while to play with the kids.[2] Whatever the specifics of the domestic arrangement, it's clear that he and Joyce weren't really living together as a family—at least not as anything resembling a conventional nuclear family—and with her and the kids safely ensconced over the water, Joans was free to indulge more freely in his liaisons with other women back in the Village, women who sometimes stayed for days, weeks, or even months at the Astor Place studio.

"At one time," Joans crowed, invoking once again his magic Surreal number,

> I had seven young women lounging around my studio; there were university students, high school girls, and one runaway. I had a stack of disinfected double bed mattresses from Fifth Avenue apartments throw aways. My studio had one or two stringent rules: No guys allowed, unless I've checked him out in my Rienzi coffee house table-office, and the other rigid law was No Smoking. These chicks, chicklettes, and at times hens were wonderful to share my studio with. It was the only situation of its kind in America, or even the world.[3]

He would write love poetry to various of his "chicks" and "chicklettes"— and it hardly mattered if he didn't quite remember their names. "And my darling," went one from August 1959, "even though I forget your name and I called you baby ... we love at times cause we dig it."[4] Such behavior was hardly a secret around town—as Fred McDarrah's wife, Gloria, put it much later, "I couldn't imagine being married to him. He was Mr. Unfaithful."[5]

Joans's energetic extramarital activity of course took its toll on his relationship with Joyce—in "Spadework" he details charged encounters between Joyce and various of his girlfriends—and despite the idealized bohemian home life he had imagined would always be waiting for him on Staten Island, she grew increasingly frustrated with his conduct.[6] "When I would come home," Joans said, "often on a Monday after spending the entire weekend in Manhattan taking care of business, my joyful children would greet me at the front yard gate, but their mother would be an iceberg of silence."[7]

Joans had long been itching to see the world, and in March 1960, he applied for a passport with the intention of traveling to Europe in order, as he wrote on his application, "to study art history and obtain material for my book on new avant-garde painters and poets of this generation."[8] That summer, he and Joyce left for trip with the idea that it might be good for their strained relationship. Joans's sister and one of her teenaged daughters came to the Staten Island house to watch the kids, and Joans and Joyce sailed for Europe with some money he had saved from his coffeehouse readings, Rent-a-Beatnik appearances, odd jobs, and occasional painting sale. It was his first trip abroad, and the first step in a new life of nearly constant travel and movement that would characterize his next thirty years (and the trip was evidently news back in Louisville, as that summer the *Defender* reported that "Surrealist artist Ted Jones is currently touring European countries as a poet-painter in the modern vein").[9]

The couple traveled throughout the United Kingdom, Germany, France, Italy, and Scandinavia, experiences reflected in some poetry collected in *All of Ted Joans and No More*, including "Down and Out in Paradise" (tagged "1960 somewhere in Europe"), and the long poem, "Travelin'." This poetry shows Joans's excitement at finally being outside the United States, where he hoped, for one thing, that racial prejudice wouldn't be so pronounced: "I'm completely enthralled by what each country has / in store ah so I remain / down and out in paradise forever and forever more" (*ATJ*, 29). Although they were operating on a shoestring budget—Arthur Frommer had apparently tasked them with specific reconnaissance missions for his *Europe on 5 Dollars a Day* books—Joans and Joyce managed to bum around Europe for a month or two.

A marvelous highlight of the trip for Joans was running into his great literary hero, André Breton himself, then 64, on the rue Bonaparte in Paris. This initial encounter, Objective Chance working overtime, inaugurated a closer association with many of the French Surrealists whom Joans had long admired from across the Atlantic. He was bowled over by the run-in with his idol, and excitedly recorded the experience later that day:

> yes today 2-day! I met 1413. He was standing there on rue Bonaparte bless his heart a-standing in grey suit with grey shoes too but like a magnificent old lion—a rare maned lion—or a flesh rock of Gibraltar—he standing on rue Bonaparte near the Beaux Art awaiting for the Bus—I trust my French and I ask—which was a task—"Etês [*sic*] vous M. 1413?" he responded Oui we yes I am—I tell 'em how glad I am and that I love him since long time. I kiss him he kiss me we kiss and embrace each other—he my brother mon frère—It was a great day today for me because I met 1413.[10]

The number 1413 is a variation on 1713, which as we know was Breton's own numerical code for his name: he had "noticed that his own signature, when reduced to initials, resembled the number 1713."[11] Joans would later use "1713" quite frequently to refer to Breton, as in his poem "The Statue of 1713" (written March 5, 1967), which imagines a statue of Breton out in the desert borderlands of Mali and Algeria:

> The statue of André Breton
> stands at Tanezrouft Trail's end
> the pedestal on which it stands
> made of marvelous owl wings from Mali
> ...
> The author of *Nadja* is sculpted nude[12]

In Joans's telling, this marvelous statue causes "showers of electric sparks to fall," is "taller than forty-two giraffes' necks," and "leans toward the East ignoring the West" (*Teducation*, 220–21). Formally, "The Statue of 1713" also loudly echoes Breton's own poem about Lautréamont, "The Deadly Helping Hand":

> The statue of Lautréamont
> Out on the plains
> With its pedestal of quinine pills
> The author of the Poems is lying flat on his stomach[13]

Unsurprisingly, Joans often characterized that first chance meeting with Breton as a kind of fulcrum from his life in the States in the 1950s to his life in Europe and Africa in the 1960s and beyond. Later, he would embroider this story further, claiming that when he stopped Breton to pay him respect as the founder of Surrealism, Breton instantly recognized him from the letters and photos he had sent from the States.[14] From there, Joans writes in "I See Myself," Breton invited him to his famous home at 42 rue Fontaine, "the most fabulous dwelling place in modern literature and art," where Breton's wife, Elisa, was waiting, and could translate, as she spoke impeccable English and Joans was still at the time learning French.[15] Joans made no mention of visiting Breton's apartment in the notes he jotted down on the day of the meeting, and whether he was invited there after that first run-in at the bus stop on rue Bonaparte, certainly it was the case that this chance meeting began a friendship and correspondence with Breton that lasted until the latter's death six years later, in 1966.

If not immediately after that first meeting, Joans did indeed visit Breton's apartment on many occasions, as the photographs of them together attest. Breton introduced Joans to his circle of fellow Surrealists in Paris, and Joans would soon appear in Surrealist journals such as *La Brèche* (which published Joans's collage "X"—part homage to Malcolm X and an extract from his "Alphabet Surreal"—as well as excerpts from an admiring letter to Breton), and *L'Archibras* (which in 1968 ran a "Black Power"-themed issue featuring Joans's essay "Black Flower" and a photo of him with Stokely Carmichael).[16] It was in that letter to Breton published in *La Brèche* that Joans began by borrowing the opening line of *Nadja*, "Who am I?" and responding in kind: "Who am I? I am Afro-American and my name is Ted Joans. Without surrealism, I would not have been able to survive the abject vicissitudes and acts of racist violence that the white man in the United States has constantly imposed on me. Surrealism became the weapon that I chose to defend myself, and it has been and always will be my own way of life."[17]

Joans recalled meeting up with Breton at café La Promenade de Vénus, the famed gathering place for the Surrealists in Paris, and was invited

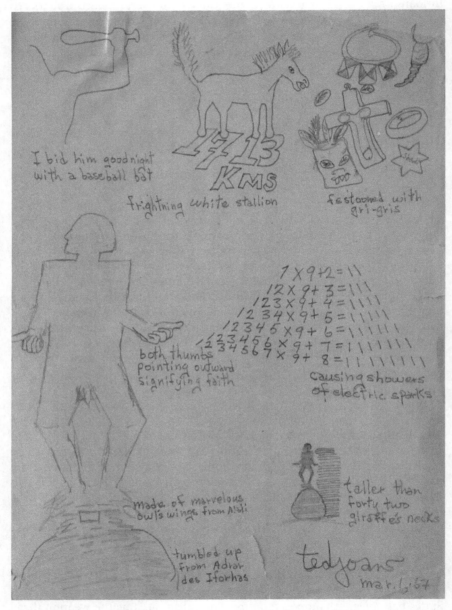

FIGURE 23.2 *Drawings Joans made on March 6, 1967 illustrating lines from "The Statue of 1713" such as "taller than forty-two giraffes' necks"; "both thumbs pointing outward signifying faith"; "causing showers of electric sparks," and so on. TJP, box 2, folder 44.*

to the Bretons' apartment for lengthy dinners and conversation. At once such dinner, Breton, who throughout his life had defiantly refused to learn English, nonetheless turned to Joans to recite a carefully memorized line: "The only cause worth serving is that of humankind's liberation." Joans toasted him with a glass of Cahors wine.[18]

More often repeated in accounts of Joans's connections to Surrealism is another remark Breton was said to have made, that Joans was "le seul surréaliste Afro-américain" or "the only Afro-American Surrealist," a distinction reproduced, for instance, in the omnibus *Dictionnaire Général du Surréalisme et de ses environs* (1982), which included the phrase in the Joans entry by the American scholar J. H. Matthews.[19] When Joans and Matthews were corresponding ahead of this entry, Joans took the time to explain Breton's statement more fully:

I'd like to hip you to what Breton meant, first of all I was the only U.S. spade cat that actually dug surrealism deep enough to come straight to the big cat himself: Breton. It was not my poetry that was of surrealist interest to Breton and the other international surrealists, it was me/ living "spontaneous automatic," as though I was a persistent jazz solo or "writing" poems with my night and day adventures. My "great" poems are those that are lived and experienced to the fullest.[20]

Throughout this poem-life of "spontaneous automatic" adventure, Joans would salute Breton in a variety of forms, from collages and drawings to poems, often pointing to that first meeting in Paris in 1960 as a foundational moment in his own "liberation," as in "Oh, André, you father of everything," a poem collected in *Spetrophilia* (1973):

Your point of view liberated us.
How can I thank you for the exquisite encounter
on rue Bonaparte in Paris (june 1960)
of a giant in grey and an Afroamerican sunbeam.
…
I ask myself did we who were fortunate enough
to have an exquisite encounter with you,
know who, how, what, why, where, and when of
Wet fishes cannot always swim.[21]

Despite the excitement and aesthetic nourishment Paris and other European cities were providing for Joans, Joyce was missing their children, and thought they should be heading back home. Joans wanted to stay, and finally put Joyce on a ship back to the States alone. She was disappointed that he wouldn't accompany her back to New York, although not necessarily surprised, and he remained in Europe on his own for another month or so.[22] This differing sense of how long to stay out on the road foreshadowed larger cracks that were forming in their relationship, and once Joyce sailed back to the States, Joans complained to Seymour Krim that she had "returned to the evil arms and advice of her mother—who doesn't dig me at all ... I've tried to conform but I'll never be able to do that '9 til 5 forever bit.'"[23]

Besides Joans being temperamentally unsuited to the "9 til 5 forever bit," another specific catalyst of his impending break-up with Joyce occurred in Paris in the form of another "exquisite encounter." Rushing to a café, Joans bumped into—and knocked over—Christine Gondre, a convulsively beautiful 21-year-old French woman who had struck Joans like a bolt. As his friend Michel Fabre put it, referring to the enigmatic figure who had so beguiled André Breton, when Joans saw Christine, "Nadja suddenly became reincarnated."[24] Joans was immediately taken by Christine and they plunged in together, first rushing around Paris, and then roving through Western Europe, experiences recorded in a continuation of his never-ending poem "Travelin'," which he was now calling "Travelin' (with Christine)."[25]

In Paris Joans had alighted for a time in August and September 1960 at the magnetic Beat Hotel, an otherwise nondescript rooming house that had gained fame for attracting writers such as Allen Ginsberg and William Burroughs.[26] Given his knack for finding centers of creative activity, it was probably inevitable that Joans would be pulled to the Beat Hotel at some point, and after they fell in together, Christine would join him there whenever she could.[27] As scholar Ted Morgan memorably described the hotel: "There were thirteen categories of hotels in Paris, and the hotel at 9 rue Git-le-Coeur was at the bottom of the list ... It was a dingy place, with peeling walls that had once been painted gray, and cracked, dirty windows, and sparsely furnished rooms, without carpets or telephones, lit by a single forty-watt bulb."[28]

The hotel was unassuming and cheap, perfect for Joans, plus its proprietor had a fondness for bohemian types, so the place became a draw for writers and artists looking for inexpensive lodging in Paris. Given that the hotel had no name, at some point after 1956, when Ginsberg and Peter Orlovsky moved in (with Gregory Corso not far behind), people started calling it the Beat Hotel. On and off from 1958 to 1963, William Burroughs lived there, and it was there that Burroughs's friend and collaborator Brion Gysin discovered the "cut-up method," which Burroughs would use in many later experimental works.[29] The place was, in short, a hotbed of creative activity, and Joans and his energy would have fit right in. "Things were happening in every room," Burroughs recalled. "People were writing, painting, talking and planning, and [proprietor] Madame Rachou presided in her little bar with the zinc counter."[30]

Like many others before him, Joans left his physical mark on the building, and subsequent visitors were treated to a drawing of a rhinoceros gouged into the plaster of one room. As photographer and one-time resident Harold Chapman described it, "Falling off the animal's back was a voluptuous large-thighed girl, naked, with her legs wide open. The drawing was titled and signed: 'The chick that fell off a rhino,' Ted Joans."[31] As was the case with other murals and remnants of its bohemian residents, the rhino mural was destroyed when the hotel was sold in 1963.

But Joans's memories of the Beat Hotel remained, and he wrote about his experiences there in his autobiography, "Spadework," from the early 1960s, and fictionalized them in his book, "Razzle Dazzle," from the early 1980s. In the latter book, a novel of sorts, Joans's alter ego, Theodor Green, stays at the Beat Hotel with a newfound French lover named Theodora Oregon— surely inspired by Christine Gondre, as "Oregon" is a near anagram of "Gondre." In "Razzle Dazzle," Joans describes the physical features of the hotel in vivid, highly realistic terms, from the "old wine and stale cigarette stench" of the lobby to the "small one-tap sink" in the corner of room 18, providing details down to the "grimy sink plug on a corroded copper chain" and "a grimier soapdish with bits and pieces."[32] "Razzle Dazzle" merges such realist descriptions of daily life with Surreal, dreamlike events impossible in the real, rational world. The scenes at the Beat Hotel are crisply realistic, and emphasize those aspects of the place that made it a "fleabag flophouse" (209)—that phrase itself alluding to a *Time* magazine piece calling the hotel "the *fleabag shrine* where passersby move out of the way for rats."[33]

But it was in his depictions of the many writers and artists in residence at the hotel where Joans demonstrated his connections to various literary movements streaming through Paris at the time—not only Breton and the Surrealists, but Gregory Corso and William Burroughs and other erstwhile Beat writers. "Razzle Dazzle" captures the Beat Hotel's bustling bar with its myriad personalities holding forth, with much of the action centered around Corso, who in Joans's telling lives up to his reputation as *enfant terrible* of the Beats. Theodor overhears Corso blustering:

"I am not only an American, I am a great American! I am almost nationalist about it," a young, bushy, black-haired guy was informing an emaciated older lady listener. "I love America like a madness, but I am afraid to return to America. I'm even afraid to go into the American Express ... "

"But Gregory, dear, I hear that you are writing a book about the American Express, so how can ..."

"Bullshit, I ain't writing about the American Express. It's the title of my book—that's all." (223–24)

The book in question was Corso's only novel, *The American Express*, published by Olympia Press in Paris in 1961. Although Joans had known Corso for almost ten years, by 1960 their relationship had soured, with Corso aghast at Joans's stint in the Rent-a-Beatnik business. That

August, Corso complained to Allen Ginsberg that he was fed up with Joans, who he felt had too easily breezed into Paris (and eventually Venice) and "changed everybody's impression about Beat. He showing off his clippings ... A big professional spade and beatnik sickening, and I'll never forgive him for selling his no soul to people for 50 dollars an hour."[34] In those days, Joans was wary of his perceived "enemies" in Paris, and called Corso a "crank," cautioning friends to "Beware of Corso!"[35] By 1980, he had relaxed his attitude toward Corso, writing a poem about him, "Along the Paris Corso," which lauds him as "an old golden poet" and fondly recalls the days of the bygone Beat Hotel, "our alma mater."[36] For his part, Corso liked to call Joans a Boy Scout for not smoking, and tease him about how tidy he kept his place: "You ain't no Beatnik! You're a Neatnik!"[37]

Despite Corso's naysaying, Christine must have been suitably impressed by whatever "professional" grandstanding Joans was engaged in, and they soon took off from the Beat Hotel on a two-week, whirlwind trip around Europe, much to the consternation of her father. This was the time Joans described in "Travelin' (with Christine)."[38] That poem breathlessly chronicles how they zoomed around from Amsterdam to Brussels, from Munich to Venice, and back to Paris, often sleeping outdoors and cadging meals when they could. Joans associates these new cities with Christine: "Amsterdam—is yours Christine," "Venice is yours Christine," and so on, and the sense is that his "enthrallment" with each new place is deeply entwined with sharing the experiences with Christine, whom he memorializes in aesthetic terms, describing her as "greater than Lenny da Vinci's Lisa chick."[39]

In fact, Joans and Christine wound up falling for each other so quickly that he proposed. Her parents were dismayed both by the speed they were moving and by Joans's apparent lack of income (likely they were unaware of Joyce had his various children back in the States). When Christine brought Joans home to Rouen to meet her parents, her father took Joans aside to determine his intentions. Michel Fabre describes this meeting as "like a caricature" of a foreigner's "encounter with traditional France."[40] Joans confirms such a sense in "Spadework," where the meeting reads as a kind of parody of the father-meets-his-daughter's-boyfriend scene familiar from American popular culture clichés (and likewise satirized in Corso's poem "Marriage").

According to "Spadework," Christine's father brought Joans into his study to give him the third degree:

"Mister Joans," he said. "How do you support yourself?"
"By selling a bit of writing and my paintings, sir."
"Oh, I see, you do not have an occupation," he continued. "You just
    live a mere bohemian existence, right?"

"Right and wrong, sir." I said.

"What do you mean mister Joans of 'right and wrong'?"

"I mean sir, that you are right when you say I live a bohemian life but you are wrong when you say I do not have an occupation."

"Bah, art is not an occupation and it never pays off to the young. You must wait until you are ancient before you will ever be successful."

"Oh well sir, I've done pretty good so far."

"Mister Joans you want to marry my daughter, huh?"

"Yep."

"Of course you know that we are opposed to such a ridiculous thing."

"Yep, I know sir."[41]

The interrogation continues in this fashion, with Joans parrying the father's bourgeois (though understandable) concerns. Finally they move from the subject of finances to religion, and Christine's father wants to know if Joans will convert to Catholicism in order to marry his daughter.

"No sir never."

"Are you an atheist?"

"No sir, just a surrealist animist."

This response, coupled with Joans's admission that he had "not one damn dollar" to his name, was too much for Christine's father, and he forbid Joans from ever seeing her again.[42]

Needless to say, such indignant opposition by Christine's father put pressure on their relationship, and was one of the catalysts for Joans finally returning to the States. According to "Spadework," Christine's father had arranged for Joans's travel documents to expire so he was forced to return to the States; he even supposedly paid for Joans's passage back, just to get rid of him.[43] US government records tell a different story, that, at the end of his financial rope, Joans had appealed to the American Embassy for repatriation assistance. According to Joans's Passport Record file, he told the embassy that while traveling by train back to Paris from Naples, his wallet containing $253 had been stolen and that he needed to request a subsistence and repatriation loan. Joans was loaned $328.97 for a trip back to the States, and was booked on the Queen Elizabeth to New York. He arrived back in the States on October 13, 1960, and repaid the loan in November 1961, just before leaving the States again, this time for good.[44]

Back in New York, Christine was never far from his mind, and his near-term plan was to raise enough funds to reunite with and marry her. Joyce immediately saw an appreciable change in him when he finally came to visit the kids on Staten Island. "It was not a joyful reunion," she recalled. She had already started working again, despite being pregnant with their fifth child, Robert, and Joans's insistence on staying in Europe while she made her way home alone had demonstrated what she perceived to be his fundamental lack of interest in family life. "We had five children together," she told me, "and that's no small thing—but in his life, it was a small thing. It was a blip."[45]

The last straw was when Joyce discovered some letters between Joans and Christine—in one of them a lovelorn Joans had declared to Christine: "you stole my heart."[46] If such professions weren't enough, Joans was now planning to meet up with Christine in Tangier just as soon as he could put together enough money for a return trip. Joyce had reached her limit, and called her mother to help pack her things. Though she was pregnant and mother to four young children, it was clear to her that the relationship with Joans had run its course, and she took the children to live in Michigan, where Robert would be born.

Joyce and the five children stayed in Michigan only another few years, then moved to Southern California, in no small part to escape the racism that the mixed-race children seemed to encounter everywhere in and around Detroit. It was 1965, and Joyce packed her Chevrolet with all her worldly possessions, from clothes to pots and pans, in with her five small children, and made the drive to San Bernardino because she knew the weather was nicer than in Michigan, and that racial attitudes might be more open. Somehow, miraculously, through sheer determination, she had arrived on a Wednesday, and by the following Monday had found a job, a place to live, and had all the kids in school.[47]

Growing up in California, Joans and Joyce's children didn't really have a personal sense of their father—they knew who he was, of course, Joyce never hid anything from them, but they had no relationship with him.[48] It wouldn't be until 1976 that one of them met their father again, when Teresa sought him out in Paris. As Robert told me, as a child, he just didn't know much about his father, and didn't see Joans himself until after Teresa had re-established contact. That was 1978, when Robert was 17. After that time, they kept in touch and would occasionally see each other, and despite Joans's general absence from Robert's early life, he now takes the expansive view that, in creating mixed-race children in such a difficult environment, his father was "sending a message" to the world that, fundamentally, all people are people—a simple message perhaps, but one the world is still learning.[49]

From Joans's perspective, after the European trip Joyce had absconded with his children, writing in "Spadework" that she had taken "my four fabulous masterpieces away" and that "I shall miss them and will not be able to see them grow … I cry for them one by one."[50] In *Afrodisia*, Joans echoes this language in a bitter poem addressed to Joyce, titled "Kidsnatchers":

white ones stole my babies
master pieces of humanity
white ones hide my babies
although they're black like me[51]

He extended the racialization of his split with Joyce and subsequent separation from his kids in *Black Pow-Wow*, which includes a poem titled "Why Else?" dedicated "to my first son Ted Nkrumah." In this poem's framing, Joans's Blackness is the real issue that "they" could not get over. The poem opens with the declaration that "I FELL IN LOVE WITH A VERY STRANGE GUY" (Teddy), only to have him snatched away:

BUT THEY   WOULDNT LET ME   LOVE HIM
IN AMERICA   BECAUSE HE WAS   MY SON
AND   JUST HAPPEN   TO   BE BORN
TOO   WHITE![52]

The way Joans read his separation from Joyce and the kids in terms of race reflected his general feelings about the United States at the time: that it was irredeemably racist, exploitative, and overly interested in restricting what he, personally, could do or be. For Joans, the dissolution of his relationship with Joyce—whom he categorizes in these later poems as "THEY," "white ones"—only put an exclamation point on his sense that the New York chapter of his life was coming to a close. In an open rebuke of Joyce, *All of Ted Joans and No More* was bookended by ecstatic mentions of Christine, as it was "dedicated to mon amour in France / Mlle. Christine Gondre"; and in the "Last Words" appending the volume, Joans announced that he was leaving the States and planning "to take my love to Morocco with me and live there" (94).

Joans would leave the States again in December 1961, this time for the next three decades, only occasionally returning to visit for brief periods. If he felt New York was now limiting him both personally and creatively, he had set his sights on connecting with his African roots and exploring the decolonizing continent. While he had made initial contact with André Breton after that chance meeting in Paris, he had come to view Europe as more of a stop-over point for his larger goal of living in Africa. "In spite of my consistent interest in Surrealism," he said, "I did not choose Paris or Europe as my <u>destination</u> when I made my strategic withdrawal from the U.S.A. to avoid further abject vicissitudes of such a racist society. <u>No, I did not follow</u> in [Richard] Wright's, [Chester] Himes' and [James] Baldwin's <u>Europebound</u> footsteps. Instead, I rode a slowboat back to ... AFRICA."[53]

In his guise as showman with a serious point to make, when Joans announced his move publicly, he maintained that he was abandoning the States in protest of the racial conditions there, telling *Jet* magazine:

This is a self-imposed exile. I'm disgusted and unhappy with America because of racial discrimination and the general attitude toward artists in this country. America does not support its art; it doesn't appreciate the arts. This country doesn't support jazz, the only native art form produced by the U.S. The American public still doesn't accept jazz because it is the Negro's music. The music of the Negro reflects America … I plan to stay away until America has its moral revolution. I'm not coming back until I can travel freely anywhere in the 50 states of my country—including Mississippi.[54]

He made a similar statement in the "Last Words" of *All of Ted Joans and No More*, insisting that he was exiting the States because "they will not let me live democratically … so I'm splitting and letting America perish in its own vicious puke" (94).

With pronouncements such as this, he was putting a finer political point on his departure from the States, prefiguring the work he would pursue over the next decades, which would draw on his Surrealist point of view to explore Africa, its relation to the rest of the world, and his own sense of self—along the way once again remaking the who, what, and why of "Ted Joans."

PART THREE

Africa and Beyond Africa

24

Tangier / Interzone

After departing New York, Joans hit the ground running in Africa and Europe, trying on the nomadic lifestyle he would lead over the next thirty or so years. Scarred from childhood stretches in the freezing winter temperatures of the Midwest, Joans came to hate cold weather, and was determined to reside in warmer places like Timbuktu or Tangier in winter months, and then move around Europe in the summers, setting up bases of operation in Paris and Amsterdam in particular.[1] Despite leaving behind in the States two ex-wives and six children—with Joyce pregnant with a seventh—Joans seemed to be only looking ahead, excited to investigate as much of independent Africa as possible with the idea that what he would find there might nourish him creatively. As he theatrically declared to Langston Hughes, he had "died in America December 14th and was reborn in Africa December 24th 1961."[2]

Speaking in the broadest of strokes: Africa was a dynamic continent in the early 1960s, especially for a Black American, because a wave of independence had begun after the Second World War, and one former colony after another was declaring (or battling for) independence, and working to establish governments by and for Black people. For Joans, Africa in the 1960s seemed a kind of magnetic utopia largely free from the "abject vicissitudes" of American racism. Of course the reality on the ground was far more complex and varied from region to region, but even so, "A Black Man's Guide to Africa" (1971), Joans's major statement on the continent and a product of his travel to some forty countries, retains a sheen of wistful excitement for a Black-run Africa that might remake world history for the better: "Come on!" he writes, "There is no racism in the independent countries of Africa, so leave that racist bag at home!"[3] For Joans, the fact and idea of independence itself, of political and existential liberation, was paramount, and Africa was its epicenter: the decolonization process had begun in the 1950s as the French pulled out of places like Morocco in 1956, and in 1957, when four former British colonies and territories were united under the name Ghana, a newly independent country led by Kwame

Nkrumah (Joans had named his first son, born the year Ghana became an independent nation, Ted Nkrumah). Other countries followed, with a spate in 1960 alone, including Nigeria, Mali, Senegal, Cameroon, Guinea, Togo, Congo, Benin, Somalia, Niger, and Gabon, all of which Joans visited over the course of the 1960s. He was determined to experience each and every one of the independent countries in Africa, and was ecstatic about the prospect of participating in a new era of Black self-governance.

———

When Joans had left Christine Gondre in Paris, they had assured each other they would meet up again in Casablanca, and then start a new life together in Tangier. Despite his high hopes for a fresh start with his "Funky French Valentine," Christine never did turn up in Casablanca after Joans sailed from the States in December 1961, and their relationship fizzled as quickly as it had ignited.[4] Joans went on to Morocco anyway, with the port city of Tangier in mind as his destination. This was an ideal place for him to establish an early base of operation in Africa as it was known for its bohemian art scene, cheap cost of living, and generally permissive atmosphere.

For these reasons, after the Second World War, Tangier had attracted literary exiles from the States, notably William Burroughs, who lived there off-and-on from the late 1950s as he wrote his underground masterpiece *Naked Lunch* (1959). Tangier's famed International Zone, a tax-free, cosmopolitan section of the city administered by various nations, was the inspiration for *Naked Lunch*'s Interzone, a nightmare version of that real-life Zone, as refracted through Burroughs's dark and absurdist sensibility. American literary lights like Tennessee Williams and Truman Capote also frequented Tangier during those years, as did lesser-known poets such as Harold Norse and Alan Ansen—in his memoirs, Norse told a story about being on the beach one morning with Joans and Tennessee Williams, and Joans losing his patience with what he perceived as another "little Beatnik girl" who was following "famous writers" to Tangier: "Cancha tell we're busy?" Norse recalled Joans snapping, "We can't be pestered all the time by groupies, see!"[5]

However Joans may have felt about in-groups and hangers-on in Tangier, certainly the glue holding the expatriate literary community together was Paul Bowles, an American writer and composer who had been living in the city since 1947. Known for his novel *The Sheltering Sky* (1949), a searing portrait of an American couple adrift in North Africa, Bowles had gone into voluntary exile in Tangier with his wife, Jane, and for years it was something of a rite of passage for Western writers to make pilgrimages to see the Bowleses, and a loose-knit community of expats developed around them. Bowles seemed granddaddy to the Beats and other countercultural types, and many agreed with Norman Mailer, who declared that "Paul Bowles opened the world of Hip. He let in the murder, the drugs, the incest, the death of the Square ... the call of the orgy, the end of civilization."[6] In 1964, the young writer John Hopkins put it a bit more mildly, observing that "Tangier is a magnet for wandering artists and writers. They all migrate to Paul's apartment" (Hopkins would later co-found the underground London paper *International Times*, where Joans's work would appear on occasion).[7]

The story of Tangier at this time—at least from a white, Western perspective—is that it was a place where anything goes, an antidote to Western hang-ups, an exotic dreamscape of freedom and renewal. Michelle Green, in her definitive work about Bowles and his circle in Tangier, frames the city's allure like this:

> To the expatriates who landed there after World War II, the International Zone of Tangier was an enigmatic, exotic and deliciously depraved version of Eden. A sun-bleached, sybaritic outpost set against the verdant hills of North Africa, it offered a free money market and a moral climate in which only murder and rape were forbidden. Fleeing an angst-ridden Western culture, European émigrés found a haven were homosexuality was accepted, drugs were readily available and eccentricity was a social asset.[8]

It was this sort of freedom that appealed to Bowles and the writers and artists who arrived after him—as Green puts it, "Newcomers saw Tangier as an existentialist Utopia—a place where everyone could seize a part of the same bizarre dream."[9] Of course such a view depends on a healthy dose of exoticism, and Joans wasn't immune from exoticizing or romanticizing Africa, especially when he first arrived there. But unlike Bowles and other white expatriates, Joans's Blackness meant that he felt an ineffable, at times strongly spiritual connection to Africa, and understood his movement through the continent in the context of this Blackness, and so was more attuned to the operations of Orientalism than many of his white counterparts (a perspective evident, for example, in "The Rhinoceros Story," a collage book he made soon after arriving in the city, and discussed in the coming pages).

For Joans, the scene in Tangier bristled with life and inspiration, was what he called "an international creative one of artists, writers, poets, actors, playwrights, wealthy drifters, old & young remittance men & women, night clubs, jazz clubs, sinister smugglers & hustlers' clubs."[10] Freedom, cheap living, the promise of a like-minded artistic community, and just enough sordidness to keep things interesting—these are the aspects of the city that had attracted Joans. But even from his earliest days there, he envisioned the city not as a terminus, a "dream at the end of the world," as Green's book about Bowles's Tangier calls it, but a starting point, a launching pad to the rest of Africa. Nevertheless, by 1964 Joans was so woven into the bohemian expatriate scene that when *Esquire* magazine ran a story on Tangier, he was featured in one of the photographs, chatting with fellow expat John Mitchell (former owner of the Gaslight). William Burroughs wrote the captions, but the proper spelling of Joans's name didn't quite make it in, as he was identified as "Ted Jones of Timbuctoo, Norway and Tangier, poet, world traveler."[11]

Paul Bowles got the spelling right when in January 1962, he reported to Allen Ginsberg that an eccentric painter-poet had blown into the city with a trail of Beatnik fame behind him: "A guy named Ted Joans has taken the apartment next to Ahmed's and set up housekeeping. He claims to be on his way to Tombouctou, but will keep the place here while he's gone. Ahmed delighted, as he has an enormous collection of jazz records."[12]

In less than a month after being "reborn" in Africa, Joans had managed to find the heart of the Tangier literary and artistic community flourishing around the Bowleses. The "Ahmed" in Bowles's letter is Ahmed Yacoubi, an artist and storyteller whom many people considered the most important painter in Morocco, and who would become a close friend and collaborator of Joans's. Born the same year as Joans, Yacoubi was originally from Fez, where the Bowleses had met him back in 1947. Impressed with the young artist's work, the Bowleses became patrons of sorts, encouraging Yacoubi in his art, buying him supplies, and even arranging for galleries to show his work. Yacoubi's paintings and drawings had a Surrealist quality to them, and although he was illiterate, he came from a tradition of oral storytelling, and once he moved to Tangier, he entranced the expatriate community with his tales, which were often irresistibly hallucinatory, walking that enchanted fine line between the absurd and the macabre. And Joans immediately saw what Yacoubi was doing in his painting, recognizing an instinctively Surrealist point of view and indifference to Western aesthetic norms; as he said, Yacoubi "painted dreams money could buy. They were primitively done pure magic" (the allusion here is to Hans Richter's 1947 film, *Dreams That Money Can Buy*).[13]

Such a sensibility appealed as well to William Burroughs, who recognized a kindred spirit in Yacoubi, and became another champion of him and his work. In the fall of 1961, just a few months before Joans arrived in Tangier, Bowles had arranged for an English translation of one of Yacoubi's stories, "The Night Before Thinking," to be published in the *Evergreen Review*. Burroughs provided "comments" on the story, which underscored that it had come to Yacoubi "under the influence of majoun a form of hashish jam" popular in Tangier.[14] Yacoubi would eventually introduce Joans to majoun, and Joans later built his short book, *Honey Spoon* (1991), around majoun, dedicating it to Yacoubi, "Africa's First Modern Artist."[15]

After landing in Tangier, Joans quickly befriended both Bowles and Yacoubi. He admired Bowles as a wise elder, and related to Yacoubi as an outsider artist, arguing that his work had "the power of the primitive, the

FIGURE 24.1 *Joans and his wife Grete Moljord with Ahmed Yacoubi and an unknown woman in Tangier, 1962. Joans once recalled: "I used to do little fantasy things like out of movies. I'd wear a white cotton suit, black shirts, a red tie and a fez. I'd come along the middle part of Tangiers, the Moroccan police or the Moroccan hustlers would say, 'See that man, he's a rich man'" ("Teducated Mouth").*

strong inner force found in self-taught geniuses as Le Douanier Rousseau, Bill Traylor, and Adolf Wölfli."[16] After Joans moved into Yacoubi's building, Yacoubi became his "best friend in Tangier," and the pair developed a synergy as the more reticent Yacoubi would seem content to listen as Joans held forth on a thousand different topics, and yet was ready to step in to teach Joans the nuances Tangier living.[17] As Joans said, Yacoubi "hipped me to the How, Who, Where, Why and When-Whats of Tangier ... He instructed me in the ways of dealing with Arab merchants and shopkeepers. He also taught me the smattering of Moroccan Arabic I speak. Whenever wherever I speak, in my limited few phrases, who listens tells me 'I'm from Fez.'"[18] For all this Teducation, Joans bestowed on Yacoubi the honorific title "North African Babs Gonzales," linking him to his other important teacher back in New York.[19] As far as Joans was concerned, Yacoubi was a true "Soul Brother," and "one of the few men that I have met that waves his flag in the same colorful high sky that I have flown my battered rag for so long. He too is an insane madman of marvelous living."[20]

25

"The Rhinoceros Story"

Joans's arrival in Tangier inaugurated an extraordinarily creative period during which he often worked on longer writing projects such as his autobiography, "Spadework," while also turning out poetry, short stories, and articles—and this is not to mention numerous drawings, paintings, and collages he also produced, sometimes with the express aim of selling them to make ends meet.

One piece Joans created early on in Tangier bridged writing and visual art, and was called "The Rhinoceros Story." His technique was to cut words and phrases from various source documents, and then rearrange them to comic effect, while also ironically commenting on global race relations. Given this method, "The Rhinoceros Story" was in the same broad genre as his latest book, *The Hipsters*—but a key difference is that there are almost no images in "The Rhinoceros Story." If it is a "collage-novel," it is a collage of words. The book does open with an image of a rhinoceros that, as Joans noted, was "an ancient artist's idea of Durer's famous rhinoceros engraving, which was merely a figment of Albrecht Durer's imagining after reading a description in a letter to him from Portugal."[1] Three other images of rhinoceroses punctuate the text, including one on the last page that serves as a kind of signature, appearing as it does under the phrase "Sincerely yours!"[2] Other than this, there are only a few other images scattered throughout the book, and it is instead based on text from sources that allowed Joans to imply a continuity between the "Chronic Racial Bias" (56) he was witnessing in Morocco and what he knew of such bias back in the States.

Joans said that "The Rhinoceros Story" was inspired by William Burroughs and Brion Gysin's cut-up method, the process of which Burroughs explained like this: "Take a page or more or less of your own writing or from any writer living and or dead ... Cut into sections with scissors or switch blade as preferred and rearrange sections. Looking away. Now write out result."[3] Burroughs's idea was to change the relationship between the author's intention and the resultant text, and while Joans was a bit more prescriptive in how he arranged his cut-up words and phrases, the idea of deforming and recontextualizing the original meaning of these words and phrases appealed to him, and "The Rhinoceros Story" is one of his more extended uses of the cut-up technique.

Like *The Hipsters*, which repurposed images from *Heroes of the Dark Continent* for much of its source material, in "Rhinoceros Story," Joans relied on a historical account of European colonial involvement in Morocco—material which he later identified as "Moroccan historical documents proving that the former Spanish Sahara was once part of the Royal Moroccan Empire"—for many of the book's "background" pages.[4] While this document appears to be a rather dry history of the region, Joans covers up portions of the text, or orients it such that certain phrases jump out at the reader: "to wipe out all resistance in the country" (23); "the Moroccan's profound hatred of the French" (29); "to settle and put an end to differences which had arisen between France and Morocco" (47). Over these pages, Joans pasted words and phrases from more contemporary material sourced from both Morocco and the United States—snippets of news items, advertisements, and magazine articles that spotlight those disturbing phrases in the source texts. For example, the cut-up phrases "Miss. Jim Crow Wall Falling" and "My Black Magic: And You Mix With the Best" are juxtaposed over the page with the line about "differences which had arisen between France and Morocco," suggesting a continuity between colonial relations/ tensions and the contemporary Jim Crow South in the States (47).

In its extensive use of clippings, "The Rhinoceros Story" is also reminiscent of what Joans's friend Tuli Kupferberg was doing back in New York with his magazine *Yeah* (1961–5), which was made up almost entirely of clippings of magazines and newspapers and arranged to highlight the absurdity of contemporary social mores on topics such as racism or gender norms or the widespread fascination with guns and violence (Joans had done the cover art for *Yeah* #1 [December 1961], what he called "a provocative drawing of a Black slave woman being forced into a sexual [position]").[5] As Kupferberg noted in 1962, "As the editor of a satirical magazine, one of my tasks is to survey the daily press for items suitable for reprinting. The task of selection becomes harder and harder and I am often tempted to simply reprint the entire issue of the New York Times as the greatest satirical journal being published today."[6] In "The Rhinoceros Story," Joans is working in much the same spirit, pulling choice words and phrases from both historical sources and print media that when collaged together point to the contemporary persistence of colonial logics evident in the "underlying" pages about Moroccan history.

An example of how this works is a page dominated by an excerpt from a *Life* magazine "Story of the Week" for December 8, 1961—the week before Joans left the States for good. This story relayed an incident in which an ambassador from Chad, Malick Sow, was refused service in a Jim Crow diner while on a diplomatic trip to the States. Sow's experience was, dispiritingly, a common one among post-independence African diplomats traveling in the Southern States around Washington, DC, a fact that emphasized the cruel absurdity of segregation, and exposed America as backward-looking in the context of a global culture moving generally toward racial equality, not away from it. But when *Life* interviewed Mrs. Leroy Merritt, co-owner of the diner that had refused Sow service, she was both unapologetic and totally un-self-aware, shrugging off the criticism that had come her way, casually using the nastiest of racial slurs and saying "I couldn't tell he was an ambassador. We serve them if they don't get noisy but only out of the goodness of our hearts. I said, 'There's no table service here.' We've got our life savings in this place, and the main part of our trade is southern truck drivers."[7]

Life prominently displayed this quotation (including the use of the slur) from Merritt on the first page of this "Story of the Week," and Joans cut it out in full, pasting it over a page from the history of colonial Morocco, and further framing it with the cut-up phrases "Why U.S." and "LOST MONEY?" concluding the page with "Money's all right, if you care for that sort of thing" (61). The result is an acerbic critique of Merritt's justification, that she discriminates against Black people so as not to upset her "southern truck driver" clientele, an example of moral cowardice in the name of economic gain that Joans knew to be characteristic of both Jim Crow and the wider project of colonialism. If an idea holds "The Rhinoceros Story" together it is this, and Joans makes similar points throughout with darkly comic juxtapositions of contemporary cut-up phrases set against the backdrop of Moroccan colonial history, underscoring a through-line from his experiences in the States and what he was still witnessing in Tangier, where there was, for example, an obvious Arab servant under-class in the orbit of the city's wealthy expatriate residents.

"The Rhinoceros Story" also had a curious afterlife since soon after it was completed, the book went out of Joans's possession and he didn't see it again for decades. As he told it, the sequence of events went like this: one day he was playing trumpet with jazz pianist Race Newton at a venue in Tangier called the Fat Black Pussy Cat. This establishment had been opened by none other than John Mitchell, the founder of the Gaslight Café in Greenwich Village—the very same man who had defended Joans when he had been threatened by dockworkers back in his Beat poetry days. By the early 1960s, Mitchell had also left New York for Tangier, and opened an outpost of the Fat Black Pussy Cat (the original had been—and still is—in Greenwich Village). Joans used to hang out at the Tangier Pussy Cat, and would occasionally play music and host poetry events there. The day in question Joans and Race Newton were jamming before a small crowd that happened to include Paul Bowles and William Burroughs, who were carrying on a subdued conversation while Joans and Newton played.[8]

After the set—which was punctuated by sounds of Mitchell on the street outside pummeling a Spanish man who had insulted him—Joans went over to introduce himself to Burroughs in what would be their first meeting. Joans mentioned that he had just finished a project inspired by the cut-up method, and invited Burroughs over to his apartment the next day to take a look at "The Rhinoceros Story." Burroughs accepted the invitation, and after lunch took enough interest in the piece that he asked to bring it back to his place for closer examination. Joans agreed, flattered that the celebrated elder writer was intrigued by his work.

But not long after Burroughs borrowed "The Rhinoceros Story," Joans left Tangier for another trip, and lost track of the book amid his wanderings. In fact, it wasn't until the early 1990s that he had heard about a "rhinoceros book" in a collection connected to Burroughs housed at New York University's Fales Library. Joans wondered if this could be the same book he had created so many years ago in Tangier, and the next time he was in New York he made an appointment with the Special Collections department at NYU to view the item in person. When he presented himself at the appointed time, Joans, already skeptical of "the archive" as a project and imaginary, felt that the library staff was surprised and perhaps a bit suspicious to see a Black man turn up in the rarefied air of university archives. Perhaps, he thought, they had "grown to fear Afroamerican males, due to the unholy (often unhip) African Americans of the hippy variety that had taken over Washington Square Park" (which was a stone's throw from the library).[9]

These apprehensions notwithstanding, he was ultimately permitted to view the object, and sure enough it turned out to be the very "Rhinoceros Story" he had lent Burroughs in Tangier in 1962. He proceeded to argue that the book was rightfully his property and that NYU should relinquish it to him on the spot, but the library staff didn't budge. They did, however, agree to make a copy for him, which now resides in the Ted Joans Papers at Berkeley, while the original manuscript of "The Rhinoceros Story" remains to this day in the Fales Manuscript Collection at NYU.[10] For Joans, the fate of "The Rhinoceros Story" seemed to echo its content about "Chronic Racial Bias" in Tangier and the States insofar as three decades after its indictment of Jim Crow segregation and colonialist white supremacy, he was still met with yet another incarnation of institutional bias when he tried to access his own work that had somehow found its way, without his permission, into a repository that restricted its availability.[11]

26

Timbuktu Ted

Although Tangier proved generative for Joans creatively, and he had made many friends there, Bowles, Burroughs, and Yacoubi among them, almost right away he made good on his idea of using the city as a base from which to explore the rest of Africa. He did maintain an apartment in Tangier for the next few years, but he didn't stay put for very long. The remote city of Timbuktu, Mali, held an almost magical attraction for him, and soon after establishing his apartment in Tangier, he set off south, down to Marrakesh and then to the edge of the Sahara Desert, the perils of which he would have to brave to reach Timbuktu, a place he knew intuitively would become a spiritual home for him.

When Joans was thirteen, he was fascinated to come upon Laura C. Boulton's *National Geographic Magazine* article, "Timbuktu and Beyond."[1] In that sweeping essay, Boulton describes traveling all over West Africa searching for the origins of American jazz music, and in the process chronicles the many "colorful" tribes in the region. "Timbuktu and Beyond" was richly detailed and lavishly illustrated with photographs—and, unsurprisingly, framed by the white Western point of view that Timbuktu was inaccessible and quasi-mystical. The article opens "Timbuktu always had been to me a name of mystery and romance," and then dutifully quotes from Alfred Lord Tennyson's famous poem "Timbuctoo" (1829), which conjures a fantastic, though wholly imaginary, version of the city's splendors.[2] In the course of the article, Boulton does dispel some Victorian-era myths about Timbuktu, but ironically understands its contemporary importance in terms of modern-day colonialism, announcing: "Desert City of Romantic Savor & Salt Emerges into World Life Again as Trading Post of France's Vast African Empire."[3]

In 1941, when Boulton's article was published, Timbuktu was indeed still part of "France's Vast African Empire," but when Joans first arrived twenty-two years later, Mali was two years into independence, and so he viewed the city through the lens of a newly independent state that would soon reassert its prominence on the world stage. Even so, the Western image of Timbuktu as a place of "mystery and romance" was powerful, nearly irresistible, and Joans was acutely aware of the imaginative baggage the city carried. It was, he wrote, "the most mythologized, fabled, and joked-about city in the entire world. To most English speaking people it is a synonym for extreme remoteness and its (historical) inaccessibility."[4] Joans was drawn to Timbuktu partly because of this history, and he wanted to get to know the place for himself, to wipe away the centuries of fables and myths, which more often than not were rooted in racist ideas about "primitive" Africa.

As he wrote in his poem "Spare the Flies But Kill The Lies":

Timbuctu? they snigger in London
"Father told me there is no such place"
Timbuctoo had universities and commerce
"Mother said, Africans are the uncivilised race"
Timbuktu is older than Paris or London
...
It's just bloody imperialist lies
that they continue telling you[5]

To combat such "bloody imperialist lies," Joans always turned to the Black history of the city and its region. He was captivated by the notion that, as he put it, Timbuktu had once been "a big commercial center and seat of powerful empires. It was the intellectual center of ancient Africa. There were important universities here. Africans came from all over to study and learn trades in Timbuktu ... Timbuktu was more important in ancient times than New York City is today in modern times!"[6] By the mid-1960s, when the Black Power and Black Arts Movements began to flourish, Black writers and intellectuals became increasingly strident in their calls to reject colonial, white supremacist images of Africa. In 1965, novelist John O. Killens asked "Who will uninvent the Negro? ... Who will re-create the ancient glory that was Timbuktu and Kush and Ghana and Songhay? It is important for us to know that our history on this earth did not begin with slavery's scars."[7] Joans would certainly strive to answer Killens's challenge, joining in the effort to "uninvent" white Western ideas about "the Negro" and recovering Timbuktu as a seat of Black Power and history. He had resolved, as he vowed to fellow Surrealist Charles Henri Ford, to "PUT TIMBUCTU on the world HIP map."[8]

Joans dreamt of founding an "International Black Art Center" in the city, to "restore Timbuktu as a great center of learning and Black Culture."[9] He wanted to dedicate the center to the memory of Langston Hughes and the Martinique-born poet, Étienne Léro (whom he called the "very first Black Surrealist"), but like some of Joans's most ambitious ideas, this one never came to fruition, partly because he couldn't raise the funds to do so.[10] Even a few years before he died, Joans still lamented the fact he had never secured a "grant of funds" sizeable enough to "construct the poured concrete building of traditional Malian-Voltaic" architecture in Timbuktu to house what he was then calling the "AAAAA (AfroAmericanAncestralArtAssociations) ... not only ... a living museum of African artifacts," but also a center for "various instructors, learned professors, and sorcerers."[11] Though that dream remained unrealized, at the very least he could have a shirt made: "U of Timbuktu," his real alma mater.

Yet if Timbuktu was on the one hand the center of Joans's Surrealist world, it was on the other a place for him to retreat and recharge, and he tended to winter there alone, enjoying a kind of meditative solitude. As he wrote in 1967: "I get a lot of writing, painting and trumpet practice done here. It is peaceful and uncrowded. Here in Timbuktu I *really* listen to the recordings and, for the first time in my life, I read and remember all that I read ... I come here alone and each winter I live here alone. I have had my own spiritual revolution, surrealist visions and aesthetic experiences here, all by my damn self."[12] In his work, Joans was always after a "moral revolution," and his own "spiritual revolution" would come by reconnecting with himself in Timbuktu, node of global African culture and a link to a deep African past. Joans consistently called Timbuktu his favorite place in all of Africa, noting in later years that: "I have arrived at Timbucktu so many ways by air, camel, crowded truck, back of a bike, pirogue, and on foot ... and each time I get the same thrill that it's always the 'first time.' You know what I mean, it's like falling in love for the hundred [sic] time with some one else each time, you dig? I love the city, its people, its history, its natural way of life, and most of all its great future."[13] This love is why, by 2000, he had crossed the Sahara eighteen times.[14]

Upon first coming in to Timbuktu after traveling south from Tangier, Joans marveled at the energy in the relatively compact, low-slung town. Popularly believed to be made of mud, the city's buildings intrigued Joans, and he investigated further, soon discovering that the "materials that go into what most houses of Timbuktu are made of is: clay, sand, straw, some dirt, even at times dung, and all mixed (by hand and feet) with water."[15] Such a statement was typical of how Joans wanted to be precise about Timbuktu, even down to its very name: "It is said," he noted, "that the Tuaregs called the watering place (which they used occasionally) after the first slave that remained at the spot, a black woman, Buktu. The place of Buktu in Tamachek is 'tin-Buktu."[16]

The granular detail here is not incidental, as for Joans it served to "uninvent" the image of Timbuktu that had been fabricated in poems like Tennyson's. And if Timbuktu was a physical space where he could retreat and recharge, it also offered the intellectual conditions for seeing the world as it was, freed from the taint of white philosophies. In an unpublished manuscript called "Aardvark's Paw at Timbuktu," Joans noted that "Philosophy assumes to regulate the disparity between what things are and what we think they are. But at Timbuktu, I dream that my lofty Saharan assumptions pronounce philosophy as simply a point of view."[17] He elaborated:

> In Europe today, as has always been European tradition to restrict themselves in a habit of thought that they (including publishers!) now almost "naturally reject" any valid information not so misrepresented as to fit their already 'established' point of view. Thus, for most English speaking people, Timbuktu remains a myth, and to publish a good book of prose on Timbuktu is anathema. Who knows better than the active poets that yall are losing the ability to consider taking anything into your consciousness save through the deforming prejudice of your intellect? Aardvark's Paw at Timbuktu can smash this sort of prejudice, just as [Alex Haley's] Roots did for Black diaspora birthrights.[18]

This is a fundamentally Surrealist position—that the intellect, in the "European tradition," is coded white and overly invested in rationality—and living in Timbuktu helped Joans see outside and around the "deforming prejudice" of this kind of intellect. In short, Timbuktu, as a physical, spiritual, intellectual, and aesthetic space made the universalizing tendencies of the European tradition even more visible, and encouraged him to explore other kinds of "valid" knowledge production.

In Timbuktu Joans rented a traditionally constructed home—what he called a "Sudanic house"—for a pittance of between five and twenty-five dollars a year.[19] Sometimes he claimed the house was the same one that Robin Maugham, nephew of Somerset, had lived in while writing his diaristic report on human trafficking, *The Slaves of Timbuktu* (1961).[20] There was a four-inch thick front door that could not close completely due to constant waves of sand, and so he would hire locals to keep an eye on the place when he wasn't around.[21] The house had no electricity or running water, and he quipped that in Timbuktu, "water doesn't 'run,' but walks to your house, on the steady head of a water carrier."[22] Typical of many homes in Timbuktu, there was an inner courtyard where Joans took to sunbathing in the nude, totally undisturbed by the outside world. He had an old bathtub that he would fill with water carried in and heated by the sun.[23] He could then bathe outdoors without being bothered, or lounge around nude, one of his favorite activities, or read and write for hours, courting those "surrealist visions and aesthetic experiences."[24]

As Joans returned again and again to Timbuktu, the stories go, eventually he built up a small "staff" of seven (!) local women who ran his little household. There was, he said, the "water maid," who didn't run but walked to Joans's door with a two-gallon bucket of water on her head three times a day; a "market maid" who shopped for fruit and vegetables, helping him with his "home menu" of "fabulous black surrealist soulfood dishes," including sweet potatoes, okra, grain rice, black-eyed peas, and ground nuts—in all their local varieties.[25] There was a "fish market maid" who walked daily to Kabara, a fishing village on the Niger River about 8 kilometers south of Timbuktu, where she sourced the freshest of fish for Joans; a "washing maid" who did all his laundry; a "bread maid," who baked fresh bread every morning in the town's public ovens; and a "house maid," who cleaned the place so methodically that Joans called her "Mademoiselle Neatnik."[26] He insisted that these women were strictly household help and not love interests, and joked that if he did bring a woman to Timbuktu, she might conclude that he had various wives installed around the world.[27]

The seventh woman was a "favorite companion and language teacher Reggin Nam, she who controls the house, pays the staff, rents camels for me, collects my mail, keeps me informed, and at times photographs me—naked."[28] "Reggin Nam" is of course the name Joans had once used as a teasing pseudonym, the signature he had put on some work he exhibited back at the Galerie Fantastique in New York. The true identity of the Malian "Reggin Nam" remains unknown, at least to me, but the author photo on paperback version of *Afrodisia* does show Joans stark naked, sitting erect, forming a kind of totemic triangle with his body—a photograph attributed to Regginam, Telebit, Mali. "The photo of me on the back of this book," Joans wrote, "wearing three grigris of which signifys [*sic*] that I do believe that all religions are personal, as personal as a bowel movement, thus you, your mother, sister & brother & father should keep your religion & god worship to yourselves—and please do NOT attempt to cloth me with it."[29]

So remote as to be almost imaginary, and for this reason the very center of Joans's Surrealist world map, Timbuktu was an ideal place for him to think, create, and flee Europe's cold winters. Although the solitude was for him regenerative, throughout his life he was also constantly encouraging other Black people to travel to the city. In 1968, he told *Muhammad Speaks*, the official newspaper of the Nation of Islam, that "Timbuktu is now a center of Islam; it is also a center of ancient Black culture. I think Black people should visit the old cities of Africa like Timbuktu, Gao, Kano and others in the same spirit that whites visit Athens, Rome or Paris. Because of the distortions Europeans have forced in the view of Timbuktu's history only about 100 tourists come to Timbuktu in a year."[30] While keenly interested in Timbuktu's Islamic history—and no doubt emphasizing it here to appeal to readers of *Muhammad Speaks*—Joans was also attuned to the fact that, as he put it elsewhere, "In spite of Timbuctoo's long Islamic history there is still a great deal of animism here," warning that "especially the first night at Timbuctu when one isn't hip to the cold djinii, an evil white spirit that settles here nightly ... There is a whole lotsa chini-bibi going on today at Timbuctoo, so be careful when the sun sets."[31]

27

Grete Moljord

Although he would return countless times to Timbuktu throughout his poem-life, Joans's initial foray there was relatively brief, and after securing his Sudanic house, he looped back up to Tangier, where he would have another chance encounter that would again change the course of his life. It was now February 1962, and Joans swaggered back onto the Tangier scene, regaling everyone with tales of far-flung Timbuktu and his adventures crossing the vastness of the Sahara. "The Sahara is NOT a desert totally of SAND," he would tell anyone who would listen. "That is all a white man's myth and shoved on one generation to the other via films and jive books. The ergs (sand covered land) are not as plentiful as the regs (rocky covered land) and the hammada (stony hard soil often dried river beds etc). Just do not forget, 'the Sahara is an ocean of LAND, not an ocean of sand.'"[1]

These were the sorts of lessons, both practical and ideological, that he liked to lay on people, and one night shortly after arriving back in Tangier, he burst into an expatriate party where everyone was talking and drinking in a thick haze of kif smoke—Joans had dubbed these kinds of expats "Kennedy's Kif Korps."[2] As he was circulating through the room, chatting with friends and acquaintances, detailing his trip to Timbuktu and the nuances of desert travel, he noticed someone he didn't recognize, a good-looking blonde sitting on the floor, serenely smoking and talking with a friend.

This was Grete Moljord, a striking 22-year-old Norwegian who was visiting Tangier from Paris, where she had been recently supporting herself with modeling work. Curious about the world, Grete had traveled to Tangier with an American friend, Peggy, and they bummed around the city on the cheap, sharing tiny rooms, experimenting with hash, and soaking up the atmosphere. Grete had heard about the Beat writers, and knew that some were said to frequent Tangier. Beyond the more established figures like Paul Bowles or the enigmatic William Burroughs, another name seemed to be floating around the Socco Chico in those days: Ted Joans, a Black poet-painter from America, who crashed part-time in Tangier but was always off in Timbuktu or otherwise foraging around the continent. Grete wasn't particularly interested at first, but Peggy knew of Joans's poetry and had wondered when he might blow back in town.

Now Joans was standing over these two young women, smiling broadly, gregarious, magnetic, wanting to know what they were up to in Tangier. Joans found Grete "beautiful and seemingly shy," and was impressed by the bohemian vibe of both her and Peggy, whose zany energy called to mind the "two Marx sisters."[3] After chatting well into the night, Joans suggested that Grete join him for dinner the following evening. She accepted, somehow drawn to this charismatic man with apparently boundless vitality.[4]

In her memoir of these years, Moljord recalled turning up at Joans's small apartment, where he pulled out all the stops, playing his Thelonius Monk records and detailing their intricacies, showing off artifacts he had brought back from Timbuktu, and making an elaborate vegetarian dinner. She was enamored, suddenly feeling as though Joans were a missing puzzle piece in her life.[5] Two days later they were picking out the names of their future children—and in a mere six months they were married with a baby on the way. It was typical of the way Joans could fall hard and fast for "worthy" women he admired.

Joans characterized his first meeting with Grete differently, that he had magnanimously offered to let both Grete and Peggy stay at his place after learning they were broke—and his place wasn't a small apartment, either, but a palatial "two storey villa, in the beach-harbour section" of town that he had dubbed Villa Bebop. In Joans's version of events, it was a month before he and Grete got together romantically, not a day or two—something he attributed to respecting her shyness.[6] Years later, I passed Joans's account of the "Villa Bebop" along to Grete and she found it to be "pure fiction."[7]

In her telling, Grete was so sure about Joans that she almost immediately moved out of the room she shared with Peggy and into his place (the small apartment, not the Villa Bebop). Joans had lots of friends in Tangier, and was eager to introduce this gorgeous model around as his new woman— once together, they were hardly seen apart.[8] They enjoyed a few weeks in Tangier as a newly-minted couple, but ever restless, Joans was itching to get on the move again, and wanted to show Grete his favorite spots up in Spain. After slipping out of North Africa, they stayed over in Granada, were unimpressed by the Alhambra, and then made their way to Madrid, where he was excited to take Grete through the Prado, which he considered the "greatest museum in the world," rivaled only by the Met in New York and the Kunsthistorisches in Vienna. Grete was an ideal travel companion, he thought, with a "spirit of iron ... my motor and my guide."[9]

By mid-May they were back in Paris, visiting the poet-activist Jean-Jacques Lebel (whose translations had introduced many French speakers to Beat writers), as well as the Black American expatriate painter Bob Thompson, a friend of Joans's from Louisville and New York. They also attended an exhibition by Max Ernst and met Ernst himself, along with poet Jacques Prévert.[10] These were just a few of the many artists and writers whose friendship Joans cultivated in Paris and other places.

After a short stay in Paris, Grete went to visit her family in Norway while Joans remained in the city. Although she was ecstatic about her new relationship, Grete's family did not share her enthusiasm once they discovered her new boyfriend was Black. Her sister in particular was aghast when she saw the snapshots of Joans and Grete in Tangier. Grete was shocked by her family's provincial reactions, since in bohemian Paris and Tangier she and her friends had always spoken of Ethiopians or Nigerians or simply Africans, but never felt it necessary to mention the color of a person's skin in a derogatory sense. She was disheartened by her sister's views, but ultimately undeterred, as confident as she was in her love for Joans.[11] He faced Grete's family when he came up to Norway for a visit, during which time they learned of her pregnancy. Brushing aside Grete's sister's concerns about how dark the baby might be, Grete and Joans were overjoyed, with Joans delighting in the notion that "a little you / me" was on the way.[12]

The couple decided to make their home in Tangier, and Joans headed down to Morocco with Grete following soon thereafter. The plan was to get married at once in Gibraltar. Grete, for one, didn't have particularly romantic views of marriage, but figured that if they were going to be living together and having a baby, they ought to make it official. They flew from Tangier to Gibraltar, and were married in a simple ceremony on August 10, 1962, some six months after they had first met. Joans wore a white cotton suit and Grete a dark blue nylon dress; Ahmed Yacoubi, up from Tangier, served as their witness.[13] Joans felt the "wonderful Norwegian that I married is the best thing that has happened to me here in Africa. I know it's strange—but so am I. I love her very much and hope to have more babies."[14]

———

Back in Tangier, Joans and Grete settled into their new life together. They would stroll arm in arm along the beach and Joans would read and write and draw in the shade while Grete splashed in the surf. He memorialized one such moment in the poem "My Beauty Wades," which describes Grete wading "into African water / that kisses Europe's / southernmost shores," while Joans, "a nonswimming poet," looks on, musing about her "pregnancy / which she fertilized / in this wet warm water."[15] It was as though the very waters of Africa were suffusing their unborn child with magical energy.

In Tangier they lived simply, subsisting on salads and vegetarian stews cooked over a paraffin stove otherwise used for winter heat, and entertaining a steady stream of friends and acquaintances. Although Joans was long accustomed to the stir that an interracial couple could cause, even in bohemian enclaves, Grete felt at times like an object of scrutiny as they were held up as a model of a "modern" interracial couple.[16] With the baby on the way, they managed to find a slightly larger apartment near the water, two rooms separated by a kitchen and bathroom in the middle. Joans sourced second-hand furtniture from the local flea markets and installed a desk and chair in one room so he could type late into the night without disturbing Grete and the eventual baby in the other.[17] He worked as much as he could.

28

"Spadework: The Autobiography of a Hipster"

With the baby on the way, the general lack of money was more urgent than usual, and despite his happiness with Grete, Joans was becoming increasingly desperate on that front. He would stay up until all hours writing articles that he hoped to sell to American magazines, but money never seemed to materialize. He was constantly reading, writing, and making small paintings for sale, but wasn't generating enough to support his new family. He redoubled his efforts on a big book he hoped to sell, an autobiography he called "Spadework: The Autobiography of a Hipster."

By the time he had left New York, the unfinished "Spadework" was already known to the hip intelligentsia because he had been promoting it and dropping hints that a major new work was brewing. In the "Last Words" appended to the second edition of *All of Ted Joans and No More*, for instance, he teases "I am still working on SPADEWORK, an autobiography of my life in Greenwich Village and I hope it will not be banned in America" (94). Corresponding from Tangier in February 1963, he dispatched an open letter to underground publisher John Wilcock announcing that "Spadework will be sent to Normal [*sic*] Mailer perhaps for an introduction. [Burroughs] is too busy zooming around the world scene to write the intro and Paul Bowles perhaps will do the preface" (Bowles did indeed agree to write a preface).[1] Touting the idea that his autobiography would carry the approval of Mailer, Bowles or Burroughs was advance publicity for "Spadework," and he was eager to have it published—but on his own terms. As it turned out, though, he didn't have to worry about negotiating with publishers, because "Spadework" was rejected outright by a string of editors, who found it both libelous and too formally experimental—even by 1983, when James Miller wrote a short entry on Joans for the *Dictionary of Literary Biography*, he could still count "Spadework" among the "promised titles" as yet unpublished.[2]

Although he had probably started "Spadework" sometime in 1959, Joans only turned to it in earnest in Tangier while Grete was pregnant, and he had a completed typescript by the end of 1962, working on some of the final pages as the Cuban Missile Crisis was unfolding over thirteen days in October, an experience written into the book: "This evening I sit here waiting like the rest of the world wondering what will be the outcome of the Kennedy Cuba blockade and I dig Monk playing in his unique style for it will be the same for colored peoples of the world when it is over anyway so when two whitemen such as these start growling threatening each other one should dig Thelonius Monk jazz pianist extraordinaire" (82).

The breathless sentence and swerve away from a world-historical event created by "whitemen" to a focus on Black creative excellence are both typical of the form and sensibility of "Spadework," which plays with the ethics of attention as it questions what sorts of phenomena, ideas, people and artworks tend to merit "serious" consideration, and which do not.

The book is very much a product of a crucial transitional period in Joans's life, after he had made the huge move from the States and was looking to live an itinerate life—while also now negotiating his domestic situation with Grete and the impeding baby. Despite his successes in New York, Joans had not had a blockbuster, reputation- and money-making book like *Howl and Other Poems* or *On the Road*, and he really felt "Spadework" could be that book for him. Hence the sweeping, grandiose claims that place him on the forefront of generational change as he imagines a national— and international—white readership that will be chastened and enlightened while fellow readers of color will marvel at the genius of their own native son:

I am the Rimbaud Negro that he left in Ethiopia, I am the black petal from Baudelaire's Fleur de Mal, I am the hip black raven of Edgar Allen [*sic*] Poe[,] I am the divorced husband of Breton's Nadja and I am the guilty conscience of many many many many ofay (US) men that swam in the dirty creek poorass cornpone rapers of my early aunts grandmothers sisters and various other women folk / Oh how you will deny this truth and when I continue this here note book of true nonTV confessions you'll be sick of truth and embrace lies and the false front that you have always kept in reserve for just such emergencies. (14)

Naturally, despite its subtitle, Joans's "book of true nonTV confessions" is far from a straightforward autobiography, and it mutates into many forms, moving between pages of associative "psychic automatic" prose-poetry to finely-detailed, realist scenes of his exploits in New York, to linguistic experiments reminiscent of Burroughs's cut-up method, to performatively-vulgar descriptions of particular sex acts with various partners and lovers. There are riffs on Western art history, contemporary "literary" writing, and African aesthetics mixed in with glimpses from Joans's childhood and colorful stories about hanging out with people such as Franz Kline and Jack Kerouac and Charlie Parker—in short, the makings of a legend.

"Spadework" remains unpublished, but there is a surviving typescript of 105 pages with handwritten corrections. It seems as though Joans would often use a new blank page as a limiting factor, as there are many vignettes, memories, philosophical speculations, or descriptions that are contained to a single page, collaged against a fresh scene or thought on the next page. As one might expect, "Spadework" purposively blurs fact and fiction, frustrating readers looking for definitive, verifiable answers from Joans's life. In one of the book's many self-reflexive passages, Joans exclaims: "WOW WHAT TROUBLE YOU CAUSE ME SPADEWORK! Grete like her predecessors is very interested in reading you before I finish you and that I'd never do. They all want to know my factual as well as fictional life before I have it exposed before the public. How would they know what was true and the real, or what was surreal and wishful imagination of ted joans" (47).

Such moments reveal Joans's commitment to his Surrealist point of view, for even his putative "autobiography of a hipster" refuses to yield a stable truth of the type found in conventional histories or reportage, even for someone as close to Joans as his own wife. Instead, he was creating "a published truth, to turn 'em on" (103), a Surrealist vision of "living the marvelous life," a poem-life which recognizes no hard-and-fast distinction between "factual" or "fictional."

"I am the sole director of this fantastic surrealist epic," Joans declared, "my life which is Spadework" (35). His real life, and his often "fantastic" representations of it, are merged as "spadework," and to read the book is to follow Joans's idiosyncratic associations and marvelous connections that overwrite historical truth with a Surrealized version—a poetic kind of sense, a poetic truth. Beyond any prospective commercial viability, personally

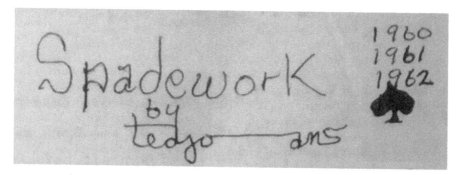

FIGURE 28.1 *Handwritten title header on the surviving typescript of "Spadework."* *Laurated Archive.*

he felt "Spadework" was a crucial step in the "direction of freedom" and was "like mental housecleaning" (101)—and the typescript reads like a testament to Joans's experiments with writerly freedom, a space where he can say whatever he wants without self-censoring, where he has given himself permission to "go all the way" (42).

While he says multiple times throughout "Spadework" that he refuses to revise it or otherwise compromise his artistic vision, at the same time, he was keenly interested in publishing it, not only for financial reasons, but for the recognition it might prompt. In his reflections on whether his uncompromised vision might actually be published, Joans placed "Spadework" in the same vein as other contemporary, avant-garde writing that was pushing boundaries in terms of both conventional form and acceptable content. An obvious point of comparison was Burroughs's The Naked Lunch, which had been published by Olympia Press in Paris in 1959, and then in the States by Grove in 1962 (when the definitive article was dropped from the title). Naked Lunch's pugnaciously nonlinear structure and graphic sexual content caused a sensation in the States, and in "Spadework" Joans noted that he had "just read in Newsweek that Burroughs' Naked Lunch is hailed (as what it is) a great masterpiece of truth" (103). In fact, the Newsweek piece was framed by praise lavished on Naked Lunch by the likes of Norman Mailer and Mary McCarthy, reluctantly admitting that given such plaudits, one must read it "with one eye on posterity."[3]

Joans was composing "Spadework" with his own eye on posterity: "Sometimes I wonder," he writes, "if it shall be published and acclaimed as a good piece of literature? Allen Ginsberg, Gregory Corso, Lawrence Ferlinghetti, Jackerouac [sic], Ray Bremser, William Burroughs etc etc have all had their surrealbeatbits pushed into public domain. Why then O why cant I?" (42). Such plaintive moments suggest that, however much he claimed not to care about what anyone thought of "Spadework," at the same time he did also long for the book to be recognized by establishment organs such as Newsweek, which would ironically accord him a kind of countercultural legitimacy—and an indisputable place among the pantheon of avant-garde writers named above.

When the typescript of "Spadework" was completed, Joans hopefully mailed it off to the original publisher of Naked Lunch, Olympia Press, whose owner, Maurice Girodias, had made his name publishing both erotic fiction and potentially shocking or scandalous literary works no American publisher would touch, not only Naked Lunch and Gregory Corso's The American Express (1961), but such now-classic works as Vladimir Nabokov's Lolita (1955). Given this history, Olympia seemed to Joans a natural home for "Spadework," and he was excited for its reception.

And yet the manuscript languished there, even as assistant editor Gerald Williams insisted that it "certainly had more merit than many of the other books Olympia was publishing at the time."[4] Williams suspected that

Girodias's resistance had to do with a fight Joans had had with one of the publisher's close author-friends, but could never be sure. In any case, at one point Joans caught up with Williams in Amsterdam and demanded that Olympia move on the manuscript and pay him an advance of $700, money needed to support his new family.[5] Williams knew that given those undisclosed personal antipathies, Girodias was unlikely to publish "Spadework" at all, let alone pay that great a figure for a lewd, highly-experimental and probably libelous work. Still, Williams suggested that perhaps Joans could retype the shabby, ragged manuscript as a gesture of good faith.

"Ya, I know it's barely legible and all that," Joans reportedly said to Williams. "But you know, man, I saw Burroughs' *Naked Lunch* before it was retyped and, wow, it looked worse than mine ... But I'm not going to retype it, because you know, if I do, I'm going to start making changes and that would eventually destroy it. I do not even want to reread it!"[6] Williams's caricatured rendition of Joans's speech aside, here again was a paradox fundamental to virtually all his efforts to get published: though in undeniably dire financial straits, he refused to adjust his artistic vision to suit the norms and expectations of the publishing industry—even a boutique, sometime-salacious and sometime-avant-garde publisher like Olympia.

In September 1963, Williams wrote to Joans officially passing on "Spadework," saying that the decision had come "direct from the big cheese" himself (Girodias).[7] Williams did seem somewhat puzzled by Girodias's decision, telling Joans "you'll get it published somewhere else and make Olympia look like some kind of new asshole." Joans, of course, was defiant, even inserting a rejoinder to Olympia's rejection of "Spadework" into a new section of the book itself, punning on the press's name:

> Olumpia (eggroll) press said that spadework was a disgrace to common avant-garde decency. He [an editor there] said it was illegible and there was no value in it at all. GREAT!! I seriously really dont give a blackass turd, what you, WHITEMAN say or even think about SPADEWORK. Shit paleface fool, you and your fathers, sons and brothers (Uncle Sams and Toms too) have done every god damn thing to me and other coloreds of the USA that could be done. So I am not begging you to publish SPADEWORK, HO, HELL NAW! I am <u>demanding</u> that you do it![8]

Olympia's reaction notwithstanding, Joans felt that with "Spadework" he was continuing the "moral revolution" that he had promised in *All of Ted Joans and No More*. In the closing pages of the book, he asserted:

> Through surrealist truths (points of views) négritude, and of course jazz I hope I can influence the cultural life of our times it is my answer to your white wrong wrongs (slavery and race hatred). I have vigorously

worked for the liberation of myself from the whiteman and thus I have worked simultaneously for the white man's liberation from emotional and moral bondage which is dangerous for the soul (98).

As explained in more detail later in this book, Joans recognized the manifold connections among Surrealism and Négritude, a movement that was at bottom about reorienting Black aesthetic production away from Western, European models and categories. One can read the "surrealist truths" of "Spadework" as a repudiation of Western ideas about genre (autobiography versus fiction; poetry versus prose), and as a challenge to rational ideas about epistemology and historical "fact" (concerns, broadly speaking, that both Surrealism and Négritude share). If Joans had worked to liberate himself from the knots of "race hatred" by moving to Africa, he was also staking out an aesthetic manifesto that purposively rejected white Western aesthetic standards. Thus when he wonders if "Spadework" will be "acclaimed as a good piece of literature" (42), the adjective "good" is highly charged, associated as it is with establishment tastemakers such as *Newsweek* that would surely fail to recognize the various liberatory goals Joans was working toward, despite their hesitant recognition of a book like *Naked Lunch*.

———

When even a supposedly forward-looking house such as Olympia had passed, it dampened Joans's hopes that "Spadework" would be published at all, let alone "acclaimed." But after Olympia's rejection, he tried again with City Lights Books, Lawrence Ferlinghetti's famed Beat publishing house in San Francisco. Ferlinghetti was familiar with Joans's work from at least the early part of 1963, when Jack Kerouac had sent him a copy of Joans's seven-page tour de force poem, "Afrique Accidentale," which Joans had planned to include in "Spadework." That poem announced Joans's bona fides as chronicler and interpreter of the new Africa, detailing what it was like to be "the only Afroamerican spade" traveling through remote parts of the decolonizing continent on the cheap.[9] Ferlinghetti found "Afrique Accidentale" "great," and wanted to include the poem in the first issue of his new literary review *City Lights Journal* (1963). He wrote to Joans suggesting a few minor adjustments (the poem builds to the speaker's arrival in Timbuktu, which Ferlinghetti felt "let him down").[10] Joans was so excited about being published by City Lights that he made the uncharacteristic concession of giving Ferlinghetti permission to "edit it or chopout what you feel aint makin the true poetic bit all-the-way do what thou pleases."[11]

"Afrique Accidentale," written in Timbuktu in April 1962, helped establish Joans's image as a hip global wanderer and student of all things

African—at least in the minds of those inclined to read *City Lights Journal*.[12] The title is a play on "Afrique-Occidental Française," or French West Africa, a term for the eight French colonial territories that had existed from the late nineteenth century until 1958. Joans liked to refer to the region as "Afrique Accidentelle Française," and so the title "Afrique Accidentale" replaces the old "Occidental" with the Surrealist "Accidental," emphasizing once again how he was open to meaningful chance encounters in a landscape no longer defined by colonial maps.[13]

In *City Lights Journal*, "Afrique Accidentale" was accompanied by a photograph of Joans on the road to Timbuktu, in shorts and sandals, sunglasses pushed up on his forehead and a rucksack on his back, stepping forward, but looking over his shoulder to the camera (Figure 28.2). Joans sometimes used copies of this photograph as a kind of postcard-sized calling card with the caption "tedjoans enroute to Timbuctoo 1962" printed on the front. The particular photo in Figure 28.2 was given to Joans's friend, Moroccan-born French actor, director, and critic Robert Benayoun, who later included the image in his book, *Le Rire des Surréalistes* (1988), to illustrate his discussion of Joans.[14] And Joans himself returned to this image throughout his life. Forty years after the photograph was taken, in 2002, he repurposed some Trader Joe's brown paper shopping bags for a series of ink drawings featuring this image, variously surrounded by rhinoceroses, scenes of Timbuktu, and Tamasheq writing.[15]

The poem "Afrique Accidentale" itself exudes the energy of dusty roads and crowded buses, and reads like a roving camera that captures everything in its purview. Written in a breezy, wryly humorous tone, the poem catalogues the various accidents or chance encounters one experiences while traveling throughout Africa, mixing more realist descriptions with dreamlike Surrealist images: "Now to close my eyes for a peaceful night of sleep / I count African rhinos, not American sheep."[16] The speaker is Joans or an alter ego very close to Joans, who declares: "I have traveled a long long way on the Beat bread I made" (77), a reference to the funds Joans himself had raised reading in Greenwich Village coffeehouses and performing in the Rent-a-Beatnik business.

Beyond the tactile descriptions of life on the road, the poem also evinces a sly awareness of the Cold War politics playing out in decolonizing Africa, so the speaker observes "Russians, Chinese Reds, and some Poles / Karl Marx sent 'em here, sun bakes their souls air-conditioned U.S. Embassy / my white country being real nice to me" (73). This reference shows Joans's sensitivity to the way neocolonialism was creeping through the supposedly independent states of Africa, as communist and Western countries alike were vying for both economic footholds as well as softer cultural influences—hence the US embassy's willingness to be "nice" to Joans, since "showing off" African Americans abroad was one way to counter charges of domestic racism and embarrassing situations like an American diner refusing an African

FIGURE 28.2 *Ted Joans en route to Timbuktu, 1962. This particular photograph was given to "mon ami" Robert Benayoun; Joans's personal copy, which he came to call his "Black Power postcard," was signed by Malcolm X, Aimé Césaire, Ornette Coleman, and others.*

diplomat service, an incident Joans had skewered in "The Rhinoceros Story." Throughout the 1970s and 1980s, Joans would take advantage of the US State Department's interest in showcasing African Americans abroad by performing his work in American cultural centers across Africa, Europe, and beyond (an experience I discuss in more depth later). But even in this poem about his earliest trips in Africa, Joans registers the operations of neocolonialism, something that he would become increasingly attuned to over the course of the 1960s as he grew more and more interested in Black Power and Pan-Africanism.

After Ferlinghetti published "Afrique Accidentale," he and Joans kept up a friendly correspondence, and Ferlinghetti even visited Joans and Grete when traveling through Morocco, reading some poems at Joans's big art show in June 1963.[17] With "Spadework" rejected by Olympia, Joans was hopeful Ferlinghetti would be interested, and was newly optimistic that it would see print.[18]

Ferlinghetti was looking forward to reading the much talked-about manuscript, but found himself almost immediately disappointed. "It is full of libel," he told Joans, "and other suable matters which would cause any publisher to drop it or insist the real names be in some way changed or disguised."[19] Despite the earlier blessing he gave Ferlinghetti to do what he pleased with "Afrique Accidentale," Joans bristled at the suggestion that any part of "Spadework" be changed, and told Ferlinghetti he could excerpt parts as is in *City Lights Journal*, but remained inflexible when it came to edits: "I could change the names to avoid hassles but I wouldn't feel right about it."[20] And in "Spadework" itself, Joans was resolute about allowing the book to be published only if he retained complete creative control over it:

> But no, this time I shall not compromise as I did on the Hipsters (they cut me to ribbons). The h o n e s t Hipsters is somethin else/ and I would have been proud of it/ Who knows what will happen to SPADEWORK! I shall not let you rape this, alter this, change this, exclude this, or perhaps even publish this! So editors of wellknown publishers, this Afroamerican author knows what he wants and is going to git it! (42)

Aside from the potential "suable matters" of people's real names being used in the manuscript, after a more careful read, Ferlinghetti concluded that the writing itself and overall structure simply didn't work for him. He told Joans:

> One of my main objections to your writing, to be specific, is that just when I am beginning to get interested in some scene you are graphically and (colorfully) (quote) relating you suddenly switch and take off on some other subject(s) in what you evidently think is great surrealist technique but which I find distracting more often than not, losing the interest of the reader ... if you really told your story straight through from the beginning, as you start to do, it would be an important book, even though it still would be loaded with Surrealist Shit.[21]

This was a typical reaction to "Spadework" and related autobiographies that Joans wrote over the years: his basic technique was to jump around in time and "collage" scenes next to each other that may be related imagistically or symbolically but that do not proceed "straight through from the beginning" as Ferlinghetti wished they would.

Despite Ferlinghetti's disapproval, the collage-like structure of "Spadework" makes sense for a person whose poem-life was "not (so far) actual chronologic."[22] To revisit some language explored at length in the first part of this book: "I avoid chronological approaches in almost everything I do. I dont talk chronologically and when I blew trumpet I did not blow a solo in a chronological musical manner."[23] As discussed in Part One, Joans connected his own personal experience to a larger story about Black life in the United States: "any attempt to make a careful record of an Afroid family in these United States is doomed to be cursory. Facts of Black family history are scant, memories elliptical, and the most elementary dates difficult to establish. I ... therefore [write] spontaneously and surreally automatic."[24] With such a perspective on history in mind, we can see how Joans felt the "collaged" nature of "Spadework" was both an aesthetic and ideological non-negotiable. The style and organization of "Spadework" were not *extraneous* to Joans's life story, but *inextricable from it*, and he was unwilling to budge to please City Lights or any other publisher. As he insisted in a later book, explaining his constant use of flashbacks—which he calls "flashblacks"—"for the hip reader, the flashblack in its most highly developed form, is a boppish deft, dramatic device that should move the reader like an Art Blakey drum roll, thus enlarging and illuminating the 'plot' to this jazz concerto, bringing a tremendous degree of free excitement."[25] Ferlinghetti seemed stuck on the "plot" of Joans's story as it progressed through time, while "Spadework" attempts to enact the "free excitement" of echoes and associations, unexpected meanings and symbolism in juxtapositions, a "surreally automatic" sense of being poised between dream and waking life, between unconscious and conscious experiences. Joans would publish "Spadework" only as he envisioned it, "that is with collages and creative typography," a demand that publishers, Ferlinghetti included, were unwilling to meet.[26] City Lights rejected the book.

Joans tried to get "Spadework" and other versions of his autobiography published for years, but to no avail. In 1972, he sent an "autobiographical" manuscript to Mary Ellen Wang at Hill & Wang, who had published his poetry collections *Black Pow-Wow* and *Afrodisia* in 1969 and 1970, respectively. This manuscript he called "part TWO of Spadework (covering my arrival into New York 1951 up to 1972)" and gave it the title of "I, Black Surrealist" or "Well, Shut My Mouth Wide Open" (works with these names do survive and are different documents). He described this text as "dealing with the poets, painters, writers, and of course women of this/that time of my life," and it is likely a version of the typescript "I, Too, at the Beginning," an autobiography that covers Joans's New York years, and now housed at the Ted Joans Papers at Berkeley.[27]

Despite the hope Joans placed in his autobiographies, subsequent editors tended to agree with Ferlinghetti's assessment that their structures were too opaque to readers. Even as late as 1982, Lawrence Hill, Joans's former publisher, passed on "I, Black Surrealist." What Hill told Joans was an echo of what Ferlinghetti had said seventeen years prior, "it is filled with fascinating but all too brief insights into your life and the poets and jazz people you knew ... The problem is that you [*sic*] ms does not center around or focus on a single theme. It is more like a series of sketches for two or three books—one your autobiography and the other on jazz poets and surrealism."[28]

Ultimately, neither "Spadework" nor "I, Black Surrealist" were published, but their typescripts sit at Berkeley and in the Laurated Archive just waiting for an intrepid publisher to bring them back to life.

29

Babyshow

As Joans was finishing "Spadework" and trying to get it published, the rest of his poem-life continued on, indifferent to his perennial financial woes. By January 1963, Grete was almost nine months pregnant and she and Joans began to make preparations for the baby. They decided that he should be born on Gibraltar because Grete felt the hospitals would be better there and she could be assured the staff would speak English. They arrived on Gibraltar at the end of January with only enough money to stay at a hostel while they awaited the due date, January 28th. When it came, they went to their appointment at the imposing white hospital clinging to a cliff side, and sheepishly inquired as to how much the birth was going to cost them. A sympathetic doctor arranged to charge them as little as possible, but informed them that Grete wasn't ready to go into labor just yet, and they were sent back to the hostel.[1] The days dragged on as they waited for the baby to come, wandering Gibraltar and trying to spend as little money as possible. Finally Grete went into labor on February 10, and their son, Tor Lumumba, was born. Joans insisted on naming his son Lumumba "in memory of the great Congo martyr and to really <u>show</u> the entire world that Lumumba 'Lives'" (had the baby been born a girl, Joans wanted to name her Nadja, after, he said, the "Nadja that I know within my heart that is allusive, tantalizing and marvelous").[2]

Tor Lumumba was a healthy 9-pound boy, and his parents were overjoyed, with Joans excitedly telling friends, "the baby is British, American and Norwegian and called a Gibraltarean!"[3] But they soon discovered it would take many days to secure proper travel documents for him, time that they simply could not afford to stay on Gibraltar. At a loss for what to do, they finally decided to smuggle Tor back into Morocco by swaddling him against Grete's chest and concealing him under a voluminous coat. Grete held her breath as they inched through passport control into Morocco, praying that Tor wouldn't make any noise as officials examined her documents. Miraculously, Tor didn't make a peep, and they successfully spirited him over the border and back to their apartment in Tangier.[4]

The new family was the toast of the town, as everybody wanted to come by and see the baby. Sensing an opportunity, Joans revived his old New York City party acumen and threw not a baby shower, but a "Babyshow" when Tor was just a couple of weeks old. Price of admission was a gift. Yacoubi bought Tor a tiny infant's djellaba, and Eugenia Bankhead—sister of actress Tallulah—gifted him a blue plastic bathtub.[5] Some local Peace Corps volunteers brought peanut butter and brown sugar and toilet paper.[6] Yacoubi and Alan Ansen, the "human-encyclopedia-dictionary poet," read some poetry, and Joans read an aerogram from Kerouac congratulating him on the baby.[7] It was a successful debut for Tor, and a precursor to a larger art show Joans had been planning for months.

———

Held at the Casino Municipal de Tanger, Joans's "Exhibition and Sale of the New Afro-American Surrealist Paintings" ran from June 13–18, 1963.[8] This was a major solo exhibition that allowed Joans to showcase his latest visual work on the African continent, and he dedicated it to Langston Hughes (who sent his regrets that he couldn't attend, telling Joans he was "most flattered to have a WHOLE exhibit dedicated to me!").[9] Given that Joans had been running into trouble publishing "Spadework" and selling articles, the exhibition in Tangier was also an opportunity to straighten out his finances, as he confessed to Hughes, "I am gambling on this exhibit to pull me out of the financial rut."[10] The paintings ranged from erotic pieces to critiques of capitalism (work lambasting what Joans called the "Godollar"), to paintings inspired by colors and patterns he had seen while staying with the Bambara and Bobo on his travels.[11] His frustrations with his financial situation bubbled up in the anti-capitalist pieces, and he explained that in them he was "destroying the religious feeling for money that many people have become addicted to. I hope to attack every country's money that I visit. [My paintings] are the vanguard of that attack."[12] His poetry showed equal disgust; this is from "Bread": "Money is your mother/money is your father/money [/] is your entire family/all your living and dead relatives [/] mean money/money is your god/money is your god/money is your [/] god."[13]

About 60 people turned up to the opening, including the American consul and some of Joans's wealthier Tangier acquaintances. Ferlinghetti happened to be visiting at the time, and he agreed to read poetry with Ansen. Yacoubi recited some work in Arabic.[14] The irony that he was attempting to generate money with work attacking capitalism was of course not lost on Joans, and he and Grete tried to tip the scales in their favor by spiking the orange juice in the punchbowl with a generous amount of vodka.[15] Lubricating the gallery goers in this way certainly didn't hurt, and Joans eventually sold twelve paintings.[16]

Grete was pleased that some money was coming in, but realized too late that Joans had been planning all along to resume their travels if he earned enough from the show. She was surprised, and slightly alarmed, that Joans wanted to pack up their Tangier apartment and head back up through Spain and on to Paris. She had just felt settled in their life in Tangier, and besides they had an infant to consider—but Joans's yearning to circulate was insatiable, and he was undeterred.

"This will be a life in suitcases," he informed Grete, and she relented.[17]

They sold their second-hand furniture, Joans stashed his books, paintings, and African "ritual art" with friends in Tangier, and once again they were on the move. They traveled through Spain, then Paris, and Grete went up to Norway so her family could meet the baby while Joans went to Copenhagen and Amsterdam, where he had booked gigs performing poetry in coffeehouses and jazz clubs. They lived this nomadic life for the next year and a half, moving from city to city as Joans chased work, hounded publishers about "Spadework," and created what he called his "mail-a-painting bit." After Tor was born, he claimed to have exactly ten dollars to his name, but over fifty oil paintings and hundreds of drawings that he was eager to monetize. He blasted out form letters to friends around the world, inviting them to buy his work to help support a destitute artist and his family. "My bit," he said, "is that I send everyone a note stating that I am mailing them an oil from Africa that I feel that they would like to own and if they dig it they can mail me twenty dollars to me in care of the American Expr."[18]

Joans's efforts did bring in trickles of money, enough for the family to get to Greece for the winter, and they landed in Athens in the fall of 1963. There was a small underground literary scene in the city, a key force of which was writer and publisher Leonidas Christakis, who heralded Joans's arrival in his magazine Το άλλο στην τέχνη or A Different Kind of Art: "he has come to Athens to bring a 'Happening,' to wake up the dull intellectuals, and to disturb the noncreators. To make something exciting 'Happen.'"[19] Despite such grandiose claims on Christakis's part, from Grete's point of view, it was never clear why Joans had insisted on Athens in the first place, as he had only vaguely talked of "opportunities" there, and of how the climate might be good for his asthma.[20] As it turned out, opportunities were not exactly abundant in Athens, and Joans felt that even he could not make "something exciting" happen there: "Man this scene is DEAD. Ain't nothing happening and ain't nothing going to happen and ain't nothing really happened since the days of the Acropolis."[21] Joans acknowledged Christakis as a "swinger of isolated talent" whose magazine "sometimes shakes up the local dead heads," but in general felt that the underground scene was a poor facsimile of what he and his friends had been doing in New York in the 1950s.[22]

Even still, he had high hopes that "Spadework" might finally be published in Athens. In fact, after reading the manuscript aloud to a local publisher—very likely Leonidas Christakis—a deal was struck to publish the book. Things got so far as typesetting and even running some test sheets in red and black ink, but the plan ultimately fell apart.[23] Apparently Joans's friends Alan Ansen and Charles Henri Ford, both of whom were living in Athens at the time, tried to rescue the project, but to no avail (a couple of years later, Ford would honor Joans with a collaged portrait of him with the working title, *The Ace of Spades is Me—Ted Joans*, part of Ford's *Poem Posters* series).[24]

By the end of the year, not only was Joans unable to fund the printing of "Spadework," but he was struggling even to support Grete and Tor, and so was forced to revive the "mail-a-painting" scheme once again, appealing to everyone he could with a form letter:

Dear Friend:

Please help me and if possible do it at once. I am stranded in Athens with my family without any money to eat and sleep. If you can help me in this emergency please do so. I shall send to you a painting or some newpoems. Please send it to the American express Constitution Square Athens Greece. I thank you very much.[25]

He had even convinced *Jet* magazine to run the following notice in their "New York Beat" section: "Artist Ted Joans, once a colorful Greenwich Village beatnik poet, writes in despair from Greece that he is stranded, broke and in need of assistance," noting further that "Messages and contributions could reach him at the American Express office on Constitution Square."[26]

Joans was hanging around Constitution Square when news came that John F. Kennedy had been shot in Dallas. A tavern owner on the Square had suggested Joans write a memorial poem to Kennedy, and while he scratched out some lines, the owner announced he was planning to hang a sign in the window, "No Texans Allowed." Joans just shook his head, insisting it was hateful and nonsensical to post such a sign, especially as Texan Lyndon Johnson had just been sworn in as the new US president.[27] The poem became "J.F.K. Blues," a relatively straightforward dirge focalized through Joans's particular preoccupations: "Because of him [Kennedy] American spades dug deeper into their fight ... against Southern segregation & Northern discrimination"; "Because of him for the first time in U.S. history jazz was played in the White House."[28] In Joans's memorialization, Kennedy was a white man on the right side of history, an opinion that would shift by the later 1960s when he went through his Black Power period and soured on white people in general.

Still broke in Athens, Joans and Grete spent Christmas with Alan Ansen, who wintered there in a book and art-filled home, often hosting literary soirees. At Ansen's place Tor was at least able to enjoy a properly decorated Christmas tree, a bright spot in an otherwise gloomy winter during which a rare snow settled over the city. "It is raccoon coat weather or heavy mink," Joans wrote, "So forget all that phoney publicity about 'sunny all year round Greece.' That's a lot of B.S., dig me man, it's cold here."[29] Back at their shabby hotel room, the heat was too feeble to do much and Tor developed a sore throat and fever. An exasperated Grete felt it was impossible to care for her child in such conditions and gave her husband an ultimatum: either he had to secure a sufficiently heated apartment with a proper kitchen and bathroom, or she would take Tor back to Norway. Joans was dismayed and felt undermined, as though Grete didn't believe in him and his abilities—but she was laser focused on Tor's health, and went in secret to the Norwegian embassy to see about arranging funds for her to travel back to Norway with her son. Joans was outraged, but Grete stuck to her ultimatum, and in January 1964, with Tor finally well enough to travel, she made good on her promise and returned to her homeland.[30] Joans was dejected, but determined to redouble his money-making efforts and join them when he had the funds to do so.

The scene in Athens remained dead, the weather was freezing, but he made one more significant connection there before moving on. Sheila Kerr was a young, intrepid woman from the Isle of Arran, off the west coast of Scotland, just about 50 miles from Glasgow. In the 1960s, Arran was still largely rural, with its main industries being farming and tourism, and Sheila started a horse trekking business there that she would go on to run for forty years. The business operated in summer months, leaving winter open for travel, and when the globe-trotting Sheila met Joans in Athens, she was on her way to India or some other far-flung locale—as Joans recalled of her, "After reading Jack Kerouac's On the Road, Allen Ginsberg's Howl, and the weekly newspaper The Village Voice, she had hit the wide world looking to discover herself." She and Joans ran into each other while things were deteriorating with Grete, either just before or just after she took Tor back to Norway, and Joans found Sheila "attractive in a lean young Katherine Hepburn way. She had a great boney face full of wisdom and eyes of a severe judge."[31] Eager to get out of cold dead Athens, Joans suggested to Sheila that she revise her travel plans and come with him to North Africa. She was independent, strong-willed, and much more worldly than the traditional culture back on the Isle of Arran might indicate—in other words, she was up for the adventure, and she and Joans were off again.[32]

By March they had made their way through Sicily and on to North Africa. Passing through Tunisia, Joans borrowed a trumpet so he could play the old Dizzy Gillespie tune "Night in Tunisia" in Tunisia, but found the country "not swinging—weather bad—people sad," and pressed on to Algiers, Algeria. "Great people, Happenings!" he wrote to Charles Henri Ford. "Algeria a new country run by youth[,] controlled by youth and youthful in its future outlook."[33] It was not Joans's first time in Algeria, and he was so proud to see the country pulling itself out of the devastation wrought by its bloody war of liberation from France (1954–62). His first visit had been shortly after Algeria had gained its hard-won independence, and he had witnessed first-hand "scars of war ... very much in evidence, bullet holes, ruined buildings (... destroyed by the departing colonists), and signs warning one against land mines. It was not a country that was ready for tourism then."[34] In less than two years, Joans was heartened to find both the country's infrastructure and the mood of its people much improved.

But on the personal front, his life was complicated again when Sheila learned she was pregnant—their baby boy, Russell, would be born in October 1964. Sheila harbored no illusions about Joans's abilities or intentions to stay with her long-term, and it seemed that just as soon as they were together, Joans had drifted back up again to Copenhagen, where he found a new "Danish chicklet" while simultaneously trying to patch things up with Grete in Norway.[35] Sheila raised Russell with no real involvement from Joans, telling Russell when he was old enough that his father was an "extraordinary" person, an artist who was temperamentally unsuited to a regular 9 to 5 existence. Accordingly, Russell only met his father a handful of times, but recalled attending the Edinburgh Festival when he was five and seeing his father performing. Joans introduced Russell from the stage, and even had a spotlight put on him. Later Joans took Russell on a trip to Norway to meet his brothers Tor and Lars, but his involvement was minimal beyond that.[36] His poem, "S O N day Poem," from 1971, does memorialize his time with Russell, emphasizing his blended background:

His eyebrows are his
yet arched like his mother
Harlem is his natural look
although Scotland is stuck
on his polite tongue like tape
His energy endless and
interest insatiable all true
However that makes my son
so wonderful to see
He is a new
Better version
Of me![37]

30

Happenings in Copenhagen

After the trip with Sheila, Joans landed in Copenhagen, where he set up semi-regular gigs performing his poetry and hosting Happenings, during which he could make and sell art. Although his poem-life was driven by writing and making art, still he needed money to survive, and Copenhagen turned out to be a good place to monetize his talents. In the mid-1960s, there was in fact a small but active Black expatriate enclave there, and the city boasted a music scene that, as one observer puts it, "rose to become the jazz capital of the world besides New York."[1] As fellow Black expatriate writer Cecil Brown said: "Jazz, of course, refers to the music, but in Copenhagen, at that time in the 60s, it was more than the music"—and Brown goes on to cite as an example of Copenhagen's jazzy vibes the presence of Ted Joans himself, "the jazz poet" who would turn up at the Drop Inn, a bar frequented by Black expats, to "read his jazz poetry."[2] For Brown, Copenhagen was "an alternative to Paris" where one could encounter a stimulating mix of "war resisters, draft dodgers, and seekers of solace from brutish American racism," Joans among them.[3] (Joans would in fact appear as a hardly-disguised character in Brown's first novel, which I'll touch on more later.) So despite a sometimes white-bread reputation, Joans felt Copenhagen was a city where his talents would be appreciated and properly remunerated—after all, it had a "beatnik group like Paris, Berlin and Amsterdam."[4] And Copenhagen was within easy reach of Grete and Tor in Norway, as he still hoped, despite having a child with another woman, to mend their relationship and live together as a family, if he could earn a little more money.

In addition to the "jazz and poetry" readings Joans held around the city, in Copenhagen he also found a creative outlet in the various Happenings he hosted in bars, cafés, and other venues. For Joans, these Happenings certainly did have a commercial function—as he charged admission and sold various art objects at them—but they were also very consciously an extension of the Happenings developed in New York when he was on the art scene there in the late 1950s.

The term "Happening" refers to a kind of performance piece that takes place in and makes use of a particular environment (a loft, bar, gymnasium, etc.) and features the artist and others moving through this environment and interacting with various materials, often found objects. American artist Allan Kaprow coined the term, but noted that it had soon taken on a life of its own as people assumed a "Happening" denoted simply a spontaneous event:

> The name "Happening" is unfortunate. It was not intended to stand for an art form, originally. It was merely a neutral word that was part of a title of one of my projected ideas in 1958–59 ... But then it was taken up by other artists and the press to the point where now all over the world it is used in conversation by people unaware of me, and who do not know what a Happening is. Used in an offhand fashion, the word suggests something rather spontaneous that "just happens to happen."[5]

In his later explanations of Happenings, Kaprow took pains to underscore that while they certainly do make use of chance elements (such as random objects sourced from the streets, or the spontaneous interactions of the participants), there is a general plan or "script" for them, even as they are ideally performed only once. Borrowing from the language of painting, Kaprow defined a Happening as *"a collage of events in certain spans of time and in certain spaces"* whose "form emerge[s] from what the materials can do."[6] "In this way," Kaprow continued, "a whole body of nonintellectualized, nonculturized experience is opened to the artist and he is free to use his mind anew in connecting things he did not consider before."[7] Insofar as Happenings are attuned to chance operations and exploit the unexpected assemblage of disparate materials to yield a "nonintellectualized, nonculturized experience," they are very much in keeping with the spirit of Surrealism, and its practice of collage and juxtaposition, so it is easy to see why Joans was attracted to the form.[8]

In his own explanation of a "Happy Hip Happening" he staged in Copenhagen in October 1964, Joans in fact drew a direct line back to Kaprow, an old New York acquaintance, telling his audience, "Allan Kaprow, a well-known New York artist and professor started the present day 'happening' scene. It was he that decided to act out his ideas with objects, people and paint. Kaprow was the first in the avant-garde of those exciting 50s to apply the word 'happening.' I knew Kaprow and I witnessed some of those early happenings."[9]

The Happenings Joans mentioned were held at places like the Hansa and Judson galleries in New York, and he was almost certainly present at some of them—he knew many key players associated with these early Happenings, including painter Bob Thompson, who appeared in Kaprow's

18 Happenings in 6 Parts in October 1959. Joans was also friendly with important innovators of the form like Claes Oldenburg (he attended early Happenings involving Oldenburg's famed Ray Gun) and Red Grooms (who was, with Joans, a founding member of the Phoenix Gallery).[10] Characteristically, Joans also tied the phrase "Happening" to Black culture, noting that "What's happenin' man?" is a "common greeting phrase often heard in the Harlems of the United States and amongst Hipsters of the world ... This word 'happening' has now been applied to the new avant-garde activities, when ever the creative artist (or artists) perform their work before the public."[11] No matter their particular genealogy, Happenings were new routes for Joans to explore his Surrealist point of view—as Jean-Jacques Lebel put it, "The Happening tries to loosen the labyrinthine knot of the Real; it is, above all, a deliverance from the tangled thicket of the knots of culture."[12]

In Copenhagen, Joans staged Happenings in which he and other participants would interact with found objects, often to the accompaniment of jazz music. Figure 30.1 is a photograph of a 1965 Happening Joans held at the Vingården, at the time one of the top venues for jazz in Copenhagen, and one can see the assemblage of apparently random objects, advertisements, fabrics, and photographs of babies. As Kaprow explained:

The use of debris, waste products, or very impermanent substances like toilet paper or bread, has, of course, a clear range of allusions with obvious sociological implications, the simplest being the artist's positive involvement, on the one hand with an everyday world, and on the other with a group of objects which, being expendable, might suggest that corresponding lack of status which is supposed to be the fate of anything creative today.[13]

Erik Andersen, who played drums during at least three of Joans's Happenings at the Vingården in 1964–5, recalled how Joans would dramatically strip his clothes off down to the briefs and hat shown in Figure 30.1. Other moments included stuffing a bunch of grapes down the front of those briefs and joking about the perception of size; or having a bikini-clad volunteer, Nina Hagen, lay prone on a table in order to decorate her body with fruit and other objects, a reference to Meret Oppenheim's *Cannibal Feast* installation held on the opening night of the Surrealist EROS exhibition in Paris in 1959.[14]

While Andersen does not detail any potential symbolic significance of these objects, it is likely that many held specific meanings for Joans, and the use of something like a banana—visible in other photographs from these Vingården Happenings—wasn't incidental. In fact, in a 1967 piece detailing the "theory and practice" of Happenings, Joans's friend and "French high priest of Happenings," Jean-Jacques Lebel, insisted on the importance of bananas to the art form: "To be banana—to be high, switched on, beat, way out. According to the Haitian painter Jacques Gabriel, this term is also used by voodooists. To participate wholly in a Happening, one must be banana flambé."[15] Certainly Joans would have known about this sense of the banana, and clearly he was evoking the spirit of Kaprow's New York Happenings, working with assemblages of "debris" or otherwise expendable objects. He also engaged in a favorite technique of those earlier Happenings: flinging paint or other liquids on people or objects. Arne Bendorff, a pianist who with Andersen had sometimes accompanied Joans at the Vingården, recalled one Happening in which he dumped ketchup all over a female participant, probably again Nina Hagen, who had draped herself on the piano.[16]

We can better see how Joans conceived of Happenings by pausing over a script he had written for one titled "A Message from Timbuctu" (ca. 1964–5):

15 minutes loud African drumming
the hipster attired in white dinner jacket, black tie, and no trousers
    enters
a large map of Africa is painted before the spectators
a pair of black trousers are given to him as he tears them to shreds
when he finishes several girls dressed in bright colored robes and
    faces painted half black with burnt cork go through the audience
    collecting money and giving gifts
gifts are little packages of sand
a large cardboard wearing figure walks across turning around slowly
    enabling the spectators a chance to read the letters that are painted
    on all sides of the box that he is wearing TI / M B / UC / TU
double breasted hipstress walks across backward then as the hipster
    and hipstress move a bed (or camping cot) back and forth across
the cot is filled with various kinds of fruits, vegetables and jars of
    peanut butter
they sit on the floor and use the cot as though it was a table
they eat and make peanut butter sandwiches for the spectators
which are distributed to spectators by the girls in colored robes and
    halfblk faces
Food poem is read and hipster joins girl in bed
they are both wrapped slowly in stripes of colored paper by girls
then the entire bed is covered in white muslin
the girls reappear with cans of black waterbase paint
they toss splatters of black paint onto the muslin covered couple
the couple moves in very sexy gestures under the muslin
man wearing TV set on his head and a long tube tied under him
    chases girls away from muslin covered couple. then he takes
    a can of red waterbase paint splashes the couple. Couple lays
    motionless. Man with TV head set leaves.

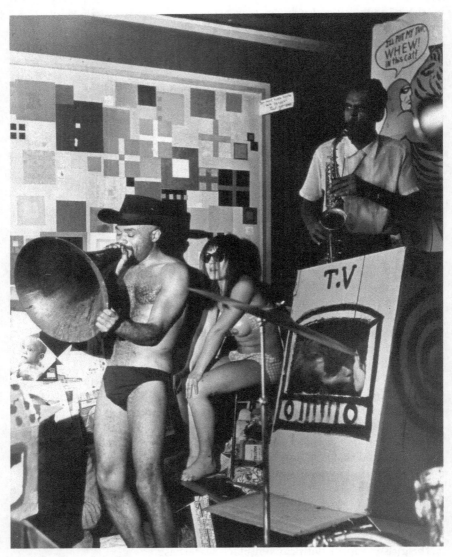

FIGURE 30.1 *A Ted Joans Happening at the Vingården in Copenhagen, June 13, 1965. Photograph by Kaare p and used with his permission.*

Music and the couple rises slowly togather [*sic*] heads covered with
   muslin
they walk close to the spectators
the poem 125 ways to Sex is read
they embrace in a long kiss under the muslin
Timbuctu box wearer appears again turning slowly throwing black
   candy to the audience
he ties a large red piece of cloth around the muslin couple leads them
   away
Drums begin to play / fertility figure appears, he dances waving
   colored cloth
girls join him in the dance wearing bathing suits and all black faces
   or sun glasses
two men in TV head pieces walk back and forth across with split
   open box that reads Ti Mb Uc Tu opposite side is shown on last
   trip across Fu Ck Yo U!
girls hold taut the splattered muslin cloth/fetish figure probes it with
   blk phallus while he dances/hipstress appears wearing pool/ he
   plunges into it with phallus[17]

In terms of its relationship to other Happenings, the first thing one might note is how "A Message from Timbuctu" alludes to and borrows from other work. The "man wearing TV set on his head," for example, reprises a figure from Jean-Jacques Lebel's *For Exorcising the Spirit of Catastrophe* (October 1962). Like "A Message from Timbuctu," *For Exorcising* begins with Black music (non-specific jazz rather than non-specific African drumming) and features Lebel as a man with a TV set on his head who "hallucinates in electronic language, waving yin-yang code flags. (Political propaganda in electronic code)."[18] In Paris, Joans participated in Happenings with Lebel, and had explained to his Danish audiences that "the 'happening' was exported to Europe in the person of Jean-Jacques Lebel," informing them that Lebel's "exciting happenings in many European countries … are more Surrealist (as my own) than his American contemporaries."[19] If in *For Exorcising* Lebel was using the TV Man character as commentary on how the medium of television is implicated in the dissemination of "political propaganda," then it makes sense that Joans would borrow the figure for "A Message from Timbuctu," as his "man wearing a TV set" interrupts a hip couple engaged in "very sexy gestures," violently flinging red paint on them.

Over the course of "A Message from Timbuctu," the TV Man gets displaced as an object of devotion by a "fertility figure," a fetish object presumably African in origin. Thus the technologized values of the West, in which a person's head is literally replaced by a television, are eclipsed by the non-technologized or "natural" values represented by the fertility figure, who embodies the free coupling of the participants acting out intercourse under the gauzy muslin.

I'm using the term "fetish" here purposively because one thing Allan Kaprow insisted was that Happenings can have "a kind of primitive or 'magical' tendency through the creation of images which have the feeling of fetishes."[20] For Joans, the fetish was a vital—in multiple senses of that word—example of non-Western (i.e., non-white) Black African knowledge (on the other hand, as Michel Fabre reports, he was tickled to "learn that, during the 1931 Exposition Coloniale, the Paris surrealists had opened an anticolonialist exhibit displaying European 'tribal fetishes' like Bibles, crucifixes, and stereotyped images of blacks of the kind found on Banania cocoa boxes").[21] Joans frequently associated himself with fetishes, writing, for instance, that:

> As a fetish figure, there is no escape from me, except one. To cause a fetish to "leave you alone," to make a malevolent spirit be a restful, reasoning and disseminate joy and good fortune the reader should: find some animal dung (not domestic) and eat it. Sprinkle freely with fine sifted sand, red cayenne pepper, and wrap tightly in a dried bananaleaf. Eat undomesticated animal excrement and you shall be at peace with me. I can guarantee you that I will not "bother you" and I will "leave you alone."[22]

In the case of "A Message from Timbuctu," gifts handed out to audience members, "little packages of sand," are fetishes of Blackness, of both the Sahara and of Joans, who functions in the Happening as a "fetish figure" himself. As he later wrote, "perhaps I'm only a grain of sand, but even so I am a fetish … If you have ever had a grain of sand stick to your body, foot, face, or fingers, then I can enter your all."[23] In such a fetishistic sense, Joans is everywhere and nowhere at once, inconspicuous, perhaps, but difficult to get rid of, and generative for those with the right mindset: "I am merely a disintegrated tiny rock, and heavily populate the beaches and deserts of the world. All children adore me and play with me … I too like the hipster of minerals I am, have my own bag, sandbag."[24] (A poem in *Afrodisia*, "Sand," explores the idea of how a world can be found in something so tiny as a grain of sand: "I am Just a grain of sand / one fourth of Africa / and spread out / all over this / sandy world" [56]—recall again the lines I quoted at the opening of this book: "Who am I? … a grain of sand"). In "Message," Joans's "little packages of sand" counteract how television has been accorded a magical, fetishistic quality in Western culture, which has led to a flattening of the libidinal energy expressed by the "sexy" couple.

As Lebel tells us of Happenings, "The random element, the non-respect of taboos, the broadening of awareness—these constitute an indictment of the falsehoods of civilization and of the rules for living which it lays down everywhere."[25] "A Message from Timbuctu" puts a finer point on the "falsehoods of civilization" by denouncing "civilization" when it is only visible as white and Western, and opposing such a view with what he might call the "truths of Africa." The Happening opens with a hipster literally shredding trousers, a constraining Western garment, symbolically jettisoning the covering of sexuality they represent. White women with faces "painted half black," then thread their way through the audience, collecting money in exchange for those "little packages of sand," which are linked to a figure with a costume lettered TIMBUCTU moving through the space; here Africa is eclipsing the West. Blackness itself is literalized by the black paint soon flung on the scantily-clad couples who begin to act out the "very sexy gestures" under the muslin as the TV Man exits the scene. Africa is associated with unrestrained, "natural" libidinal energy, and Joans's poem "125 Ways to Sex" is read—the list poem covers everything from "ofay sex / maumau sex" to "NAACP sex / White Citizen Council sex" to "avant-garde sex."[26] It is, in other words, a joyous affirmation of all kinds of sex without restriction, something that, in the context of "A Message from Timbuctu," is associated with a broadly African sensibility, an idea underscored in the final movement, when the lettering on the Timbuctu Man's body is transformed into "Fu Ck Yo U!" as a "fetish figure" uses a black phallus to probe the girls under the paint-splattered muslin.[27]

While certainly strange, provocative, and a heady mix of "food, sex, and art," the Happenings held in Copenhagen and Paris were also enterprising ventures for Joans.[28] Lest his audiences think that "avant-garde" signaled merely an art-for-art's-sake aesthetic purity, Joans was sure to clarify for them that "The early happenings [in New York in the 1950s] were not only creative, but commercial. This happening that you shall witness this evening shall be just that COMMERICAL!"[29] Just as the "little packages of sand" were exchanged for money during the performance of "A Message from Timbuctu," in another Happening in Paris, "The Nice Coloured Man," the titular character in fact dispatches white girls "into the audience [to] get him some money," which he pockets as they begin reading from newspapers. This is an act that reverses white exploitation of Blackness in real time, as Joans extracted money from a predominantly white audience as part of his anti-racist performance.[30] As he told that crowd of 200 in Copenhagen: "All the creations that you witness are for sale and will be sold at every price that you can imagine. The money from this happening will be applied to the 'Timbuctu Safari Fund.' Your contribution is highly appreciated."[31]

Another example of artwork Joans made and sold during performances at the Vingården was a series of watercolors inspired by the Danish jazz pianist Leo Mathisen, and one of his signature songs, "Take It Easy Boy,

Boy" (1940). That song was released just as the Nazis occupied Denmark and banned singing in English. Still a fixture in the Copenhagen clubs, Mathisen would scat the song so as to make the lyrics unintelligible, and it became a sort of resistance anthem for Danes living under Nazi occupation. When Joans heard this story, he liked it so much that one evening at the Vingården, as the band behind him played "Take It Easy Boy, Boy," he began painting abstracted figures inspired by the song and the defiant spirit it represented. These pieces, watercolors accented with crayon and chalk, were in yellows, greens, and reds, abstracted figures that convey a sense of movement, and that were when finished available for people in the audience to purchase.[32]

———

Given that, as a genre, Happenings are attuned to the creative possibilities of their environment, it's also worth mentioning briefly how during his time in Copenhagen, Joans tried to turn the whole city into an art installation. One night he and some accomplices spent hours chalking what he had characterized as the "largest nude in history of man," from City Hall to the Vingården, envisioning the drawing as part of the Happening writ large.[33] The drawing apparently ran for over 2 kilometers through the streets of Copenhagen, and when the police caught wind of what was going on, they dispatched squad cars to investigate. But Joans and his crew had already vanished in the early morning hours, and the confounded police were left washing away the seemingly endless lines as best they could.

As he did in many places he stayed, Joans left a mark on Copenhagen that far outlasted the transitory chalk lines in the streets. Earlier I alluded to Joans's appearance in one of Cecil Brown's books; this was his 1969 satirical novel, *The Life and Loves of Mr. Jiveass Nigger*. In that book, set largely in and around the Black expatriate scene in Copenhagen in the mid-1960s, readers encounter Ned Green, author of a poetry book called "*All of Ned and No More*," ensconced in a bar (the real-life Drop Inn), "pontificating to a small group of people who had surrounded him."[34] Green is described as "like a rocket out of its resting pad, out of the beat-poetry era; beat was very important to his poetry ... [when reading he] succeeded in making his voice sound like an ax riffing, then like a trumpet blaring" (49). Beyond the obvious allusion to *All of Ted Joans and No More*, Brown's Green also shares some strong biographical similarities with Joans, and is depicted as a "lady's man" who had fathered children all over the world (50). Grete Moljord even makes a cameo appearance in *Jiveass* as the "beautiful Norwegian girl" who accompanies Green around Copenhagen.

Brown's novel satirizes many aspects of the Black experience in Europe at the time, and the Green character represents shifting tastes from the Beat era to the Black Arts and Black Power era, a shift that broadly describes

Joans's own creative arc from the beginning of the 1960s to its end. At one point, Green explains to the novel's protagonist, George, that he had just come from a poetry reading with Langston Hughes: "Ned went on about the poetry reading, about how black it was" (51). Brown skewers the ways Green trades on his Blackness as though he is merely playing it up to seem more culturally relevant—or perhaps to sell more books. One scene has a fascinated Danish woman at the Drop Inn point to Green's "African skullcap"—of the type Joans himself favored at the time, as seen, for instance, on the cover portrait of *Black Pow-Wow* (see Figure 35.1)— and asks: "Why do you guys wear those funny little hats?" Green explodes: "Why do Danish men wear the shit on their heads that they do, you don't call *that* funny, do you? ... as soon as a black man starts wearing something that's representative of his culture, his blackness, you want to know ... 'why d'you wear those funny little hats?'" (51). In Brown's hands, the Green figure may come off as a little bit too performative and a little bit too opportunistic, but the point Green makes here about normative (white) culture does ring true, that what constitutes "funny" headgear of course depends on the way in which one has been acculturated, an observation that Joans would explore in much more depth by counterpointing white, Western imaginaries to Black African ones in books like *Black Pow-Wow* and *Afrodisia*. Joans, for his part, found *Jiveass* to be a worthy satire that he spoke of in the same breath as his own *The Hipsters*.[35] Decades later, Brown would call Joans "the best of the Beat poets."[36]

———

Beyond Copenhagen, throughout 1964–5, Joans was also shuttling around Northern Europe, particularly Amsterdam, and up to Norway to see Grete and Tor.[37] Although their relationship had grown somewhat strained, during one such visit in the summer of 1964, Grete became pregnant again, and would give birth to her second son with Joans, Lars Kimani, on March 19, 1965. As with his other children, Joans was thrilled, delighting in Lars's blended background: "He is white like a Viking at sea / He is blonde as a Norwegian can be / He has a Caucasian mouth, a Negro / nose and smiles like the sun at me."[38] Despite—or because of—the birth of their second child together, Grete had resolved to stay in Norway, where she was entitled to state aid.[39] Joans couldn't bear to live in Norway, which strained the marriage further, to the point of breaking, though he refused to sign divorce papers as Grete had asked.[40]

In fact, Joans continued to try to earn money in an attempt to keep his family with Grete together. In addition to his in-person Happenings and jazz poetry readings, he even appeared on Danish and Norwegian television, where he conducted what he called "Jazz happenings."[41] One poem he began reading at these appearances was "Pubik Pak," a send-up of advertising and consumerism that was "a big hit poem" for him, as it satirized the very culture of capitalism that so bedeviled him.[42]

A prose-poem in the voice of an archetypal snake oil salesman, "Pubik Pak" touts all the wonders of the miraculous titular product that will change any person's life:

> Good evening PUBIK PAK listeners! How is the family? and especially your mother since she too has switched to PUBIK PAK? PUBIK PAK! PUBIK PAK that all-american product! PUBIK PAK displayed in store windows and on counters all over the world! PUBIK PAK the safe, the provened, the most dependable and sought out household article of its kind![43]

One can imagine Joans performing this piece in an appropriately comic, fast-talking manner, addressing his audiences as though they are the targeted consumers for "Pubik Pak." The irony, of course, is that such audiences were indeed the targeted consumers of Joans's poetry, including "Pubik Pak," which he presented in these contexts to generate cash.

So the paradox embedded in the poem is that it's a critique of consumerism that packages itself as an object of consumption (as Joans put it in a later poem, "I continue eating watermelons on TV for a fee").[44] In "Pubik Pak" itself, we never learn precisely what the titular product is—the implication, of course, is that it is some sort of prophylactic—and so "Pubik Pak" signifies both the wondrous, unnamed product in the poem *and* the poem itself, a collapse that puts a different spin on the speaker's increasingly ridiculous claims: "the answer to the world's problems is PUBIK PAK! the world health organization of the united nations distributes PUBIK PAK to the poor! ... remember if you want to be popular with the girls, and with the boys you had better get hip with PUBIK PAK! ... PUBIK PAK is the answer to your personal problems! PUBIK PAK is always there to safeguard you and your loved ones! PUBIK PAK enriches your ego!" (139).[45]

Amusing as it is, there is a real disgust with materialism and consumerism underlying "Pubik Pak," a disgust that became hardened in Joans's mind as he increasingly began to blame his money problems on white people, and on a structurally-racist European culture that prevented him from earning enough to support Grete and their boys. Back in Copenhagen in January 1966, Joans unloaded in a letter to Langston Hughes: "I'm growing to hate white people of Europe," he declared, and went on to explain that he remained estranged from his family because he could not earn enough to support them:

> Europe offers me and my children no great today or tomorrow. Europe exploits her visitors if they stay too long—and wish to grow. Europe has

economics slanted away from my talents ... Europe will recognize, organize and supervise one's artistic endeavors—but will not allow an American to make big money. One is free in Europe—completely free—if one has money. Nobody cares about an American without money.[46]

This theme continued apace in other letters he fired off to Hughes, in which he complained about being "fed up" with these "damn Europeans" and their "parental attitude of supremacy."[47] The object of Joans's ire in this particular case was Dr. Rosey Pool, a Dutch academic and translator, who had invited him to contribute to her anthology, *Beyond the Blues: New Poems by American Negroes* (1962), and apparently hadn't forwarded Joans "the big bread that I work harder than hell for"—"big bread" was for Joans always around the corner, and though it often seemed tantalizingly close, he could never quite seem to catch up with it.[48]

31

On the Black Arts
Movement and Négritude

Although that annoying need for money loomed around the edges of his poem-life, it was hardly the only thing causing Joans to think in new ways about how the structures and values of the white world seemed to be shutting him out. It goes without saying that themes of race and racism had long played a central role in his work, but by the mid-1960s, he began to think more about and experiment with a specifically "Black aesthetic" that coincided with the use of this term by the writers, artists, and musicians who came to form the Black Arts Movement.

LeRoi Jones, Joans's friend from their Greenwich Village days, is widely acknowledged as the founder or catalyst of the Black Arts Movement, which took place roughly between 1965 and 1975. After Malcolm X was assassinated in New York City on February 21, 1965, LeRoi Jones had a crisis of consciousness, and felt compelled to leave his Jewish wife, Hettie, and their two children in Greenwich Village. He moved up to Harlem, where he established the Black Arts Repertory Theatre School with the intention of promoting a Black aesthetic by and for Black people. Jones wanted to foreground the power of the imagination as a "practical vector from the soul," and declared that "Revolutionary Theatre" would "destroy" white Americans "and whatever they believe is real."[1] The watchwords here, "imagination" and the "real," had of course been special preoccupations of Ted Joans's long before 1965, and he had often explored them in his work via Surrealism. But LeRoi Jones was calling for a materially and recognizably Black imagination that would not merely counter a white imagination but side-step it completely, a goal that was both an aesthetic choice and political act.

One of the most important theorists of the Black Arts Movement was Larry Neal, who worked closely with Jones at the short-lived Black Arts Repertory Theatre School. He described the movement like this:

Black Art is the aesthetic and spiritual sister of the Black Power concept. As such, it envisions an art that speaks directly to the needs and aspirations of Black America. In order to perform this task, the Black Arts Movement proposes a radical reordering of the western cultural aesthetic. It proposes a separate symbolism, mythology, critique, and iconology. The Black Arts and the Black Power concepts both relate broadly to the Afro-American's desire for self-determination and nationhood.[2]

For Neal, LeRoi Jones and others who came to be associated with the Black Arts Movement, the ideal art to strive for was decidedly not "protest literature" since that still assumed a white supremacy to be militated against, the notion that, as poet Ethridge Knight put it, "change will be forthcoming once the masters are aware of the protestor's 'grievance.'"[3] What Jones and Neal were after, by contrast, was a blanket dismissal of white culture in favor of embracing Black culture and a Black aesthetic. Neal goes on to write:

When we speak of a "Black aesthetic" several things are meant. First, we assume that there is already in existence the basis for such an aesthetic. Essentially, it consists of an African American cultural tradition. But this aesthetic is finally, by implication, broader than that tradition. It encompasses most of the useable elements of Third World culture. The motive behind the Black aesthetic is the destruction of the white thing, the destruction of white ideas, and white ways of looking at the world. The new aesthetic is mostly predicated on an Ethics which asks the question: whose vision of the world is finally more meaningful, ours or the white oppressors? What is truth?[4]

For Joans, "the truth" had always been what was spoken by the poet, but with the coming of the Black Arts Movement, the poet's Blackness became central to how that truth was framed—not for white audiences, but for fellow Black people in the United States and around the world.

With the Black Arts Movement, there developed an invigorated critical mass of Black writers, artists, thinkers, and musicians exploring how culture could become a weapon in the fight for Black Power, which Stokely Carmichael and Charles V. Hamilton had defined as, fundamentally, "a call for black people in this country to unite, to recognize their heritage, to build a sense of community."[5] In such a context, "the truth" was Black and seen as an antidote to the violence, lies, and destruction of the "white thing." As Joans put it in 1968, "Black Power is the best thing that has happened to the United States since the birth of jazz. It is a black truth, like jazz."[6]

Although the Black Arts Movement grew from Harlem and then other urban centers in the United States, its practitioners always stressed the continuities among Black America and the Black Third World, which had been decolonizing in the 1950s and 1960s; as Larry Neal said, "the most meaningful statements about the nature of Western society must come from the Third World of which Black America is a part."[7] In this way, there are multiple links and affinities between the Black Arts Movement and a precursor movement, Négritude, a term most often associated with Aimé Césaire, who had, like Joans, found in Surrealism tools to articulate both his own sense of Blackness, and the complex layers and ironies of colonialism. Ideologically, Négritude was broadly aligned with the Black Arts Movement, but its roots in Surrealism made it particularly appealing to Joans, who cultivated those roots in his late 1960s books like *Afrodisia* and *Black Pow-Wow*.

As Clayton Eshleman and Annette Smith explain, the term "Négritude" was coined by Césaire and his friends Léon-Gontran Damas and Léopold Sédar Senghor in Paris in the mid-1930s, when they were editing *L'Etudiant noir* or *The Black Student*: "A neologism, it is made up (perhaps on the model of the South American *negrismo*) by latinizing the derogatory word for a black ('négre') and adding a suffix for abstract nouns (latitude, solitude, exactitude, etc.). It signified a response to the centuries-old problem of the alienated position of the blacks in history, and implicitly called upon blacks to reject assimilation and cultivate consciousness of their own racial qualities and heritage."[8]

In these two basic impulses, to identify the "alienated position of the blacks in history" and to "reject assimilation and cultivate consciousness of their own racial qualities and heritage," Négritude was an ancestor of the Black Arts Movement, which is partly why Larry Neal argued for seeing Black America in a global context, as part of the "Third World."

We can see the way Joans picked up strands of both these movements in his poem "Afrodisia," which announced its debt to Négritude with a dedication to Aimé Césaire, whom he had elsewhere lauded as a "well-known Black surrealist."[9] "Afrodisia" is Joans's own neologism, a punning cousin to both Black Power and Négritude that he deploys like this in the poem:

WHEN THEY FORM THEIR WHITE MOBS TO MURDER
   ME OR SHOOT ME
FROM GREAT DISTANCE WITH THEIR GUN
IT'S OUR AFRODISIA THEY HOPE TO KILL
…
ITS AFRODISIA ABOUT WHAT THEY SECRETLY CHAT
ITS AFRODISIA THAT THEY FEAR/HATE/ADORE/
   (DIG OR DON'T DIG)
DISTANTLY OR UPTIGHT CLOSE BY
ITS AFRODISIA THAT NATURAL POWER
THAT IS POSSESSED BY BLACK YOU AND BLACK I[10]

Here "Afrodisia" is the erotically charged version of Black Power that was essentially and distinctly African in origin, something Joans saw Négritude as likewise stressing. In Césaire's *Notebook of a Return to the Native Land*, the poem in which the term Négritude first appeared, Césaire purposively erases distinctions among the first-person speaker and a collective Black past, declaring, for instance, "My memory is encircled with blood. My memory has a belt of corpses!"[11] André Breton singled out this quality of the poem, observing that behind its "floral design there is the wretchedness of a colonized people ... Behind all of this, only a few generations back, there is slavery and here the wound reopens, yawning with the entire width of a lost Africa, with ancestral memories of abominable tortures, with the awareness of a monstrous and forever irreparable denial of justice inflicted upon an entire collectivity."[12] "Afrodisia" is also informed by "ancestral memories," and in it Joans adopts a similar technique of collapsing the first person with the third person—when asked if his poem-life was a "personal poem," Joans responded "Yes, yes, but it's a collective poem," a seemingly paradoxical or antinomic statement crucial for understanding his idea of "Afrodisia."[13]

Joans elaborated an explanation of "Afrodisia" as a concept in "First Papers on Ancestral Creations," an article he published in *Black World* in 1970, the same year *Afrodisia* appeared:

> Black is the embodiment of all colors. Blackness absorbs the colors of all animals, minerals and vegetables. This strong force called "Black" is the spiritual power that emanates from Africa. This blackness that gives strength, rhythm and spiritual meaning to many things in the rest of the world is what I call "Afrodisia." This Black Power is the basis of jazz and popular modern music. This same Black strength is the spirit of all modern art, figurative and non-figurative. This same "Afrodisia" is the liberating force found in the speech, manners and philosophy of the youth.[14]

If Afrodisia is a kind of "Black Power," it is one firmly rooted in Africa and made visible—if not fully "knowable"—by attending to its most widely-circulated features: strength, rhythm, spiritual meaning, and "naturalness," perhaps *the* signal characteristic of Africa Joans insisted on throughout his writing of this period (see, for example, his essay "Natural Africa" [1971]).[15] But just as the poem "Afrodisia" figures the concept as being opposed to whiteness insofar as it appears to threaten whiteness and white supremacy, "First Papers on Ancestral Creations" goes on to propose a theory of Black creation underwritten by Afrodisia that assumes a kind of ontology unintelligible to a white, Western point of view.

The basic thesis of "First Papers" is that African arts are primarily and essentially communal and ritual in purpose, are spiritual objects through which a contemporary creator may channel the Afrodisia of his ancestors.

Emphasizing the idea of rhythm, Joans argues that "Black rhythm is found in all African cultures ... [and] is spiritually controlled by ancestors" (69). Offering an example of a wood carving, he explains that the "basis of this creation is spiritual communication that prompts an animist to action. All of this is made possible to function only by the ancestors. This is, therefore, ritual art" (69). This "basis" for Black art is fundamentally—and, Joans thought, catastrophically—misunderstood by a white Western perspective, which wants to both fit such Black creations into white aesthetic categories, and to possess these objects by acquiring them with money, thereby removing them from the "sacred soil" of Africa (70). Such impulses drain the object of any real life or power: "When these Black art creations are collected by non-animists and placed in museums or private collections, they cease to function. The spirits abandon these bits and pieces, thus leaving the new owner with 'just a highly 'artistic' carving' from Africa" (70).[16] Not only does locking these objects up in museums or private collections destroy their primary "function," but if treated carelessly, such objects can in fact be dangerous, can become real, material instantiations of Black Power: "All Black creations should be respected and feared, or left alone. He that tampers with these bits and pieces of Black creations shall suffer at the hands of the revenging spirits. This may sound like 'mumbo-jumbo' to white-eyed readers, but it's just that arrogant point of view that will destroy Western civilization (sic)" (70; "(sic)" in original). "Afrodisia" can thus be seen as a kind of fusion of Black Arts and Négritude, emphasizing as it does the "Black Power" inherent in Black art that can only be understood through a spiritual, non-rational, and non-verifiable connection to the African past.

———

Another illustration of Joans manifesting the swirling conjunctions of Black Arts and Négritude is his 1990 artwork, Old Cuntry (Figure 31.1). Joans thought of work such as Old Cuntry in a tradition of "syncretic creative activity, more or less in the category of religion, but definitely in the category of survival" (this is Laura Corsiglia's gloss).[17] There is urgency in this view, and to understand Old Cuntry as a syncretic object that functions spiritually, as a means of survival in the world, one would first note that it was created on wood, which Joans saw as a particularly African or Black medium: "wood is the material most often used by artists and craftsmen of Black Africa. Wood is a living material, and in Africa south of the Sahara, what is done in wood derives magical power. The smooth surface wood that I play-work upon ... was once a trunk or branch of a tree whose roots drew nourishment from the earth."[18] The collaged title of this piece, Old Cuntry, routes us to this attitude toward wood in the Old Country of the African continent, but invokes it via the eroticized notion of Afrodisia: "cuntry," not "country" (I discuss his related poem, "Cuntinent," in the coming pages). And as we can also see, Joans does not merely use the wood as a blank canvas to cover, but rather interacts with it, so the anatomical stamp surmounts a line drawing that attends to the knot still visible in this machined board (one observes this technique as well in his "Jazz Drawings" on wood boards from the mid-1970s).[19] Likewise the red triangle framing the collaged title, *Old Cuntry*, meets the six black triangles at the precise spot on the board where a grain runs its full length. This right side of the piece displays a plastic container with clippings of Joans's hair anchoring the six black triangles topped with a cowrie shell nailed to the board, adding up to magic number seven.

Joans used his own hair with some frequency in his work, a material which, as Joanna Pawlik puts it, "he found to retain its bodily intimacy even when cut and stuck on paper, but he also saw hair as a way of referencing other non-Western cultural practices that utilize human hair or believe it to be invested with certain spiritual or magical powers."[20] In the same year he produced *Old Cuntry*, Joans explained that "there are good and evil spirits still very much alive and highly active in many pieces of African sculpture," and Corsiglia later told me that in his role as a "fetish maker," Joans would sometimes describe himself as a "sorcerer," so it makes good sense to see this piece as a spiritual object, a totemic artwork that alludes to African aesthetic practice and in such allusion can be read as both fetish and autobiography.[21]

But if *Old Cuntry* is to be understood as an extension of Joans, literally and aesthetically, it also has Surrealist antecedents, in light of it being also a poème-objet or object-poem, "a composition which," André Breton explained, "combines the resources of poetry and plastic art, and thus speculates on the capacity of these two elements to excite each other mutually."[22] A few years before he made *Old Cuntry*, Joans reflected on why and how he might create what he called an "objet-surréaliste," which could begin with found objects: "I hope to subvert the practical and conventional existence of this 'thing' by adding other 'bits' and 'pieces' of this and thats, since aesthetic value is of strictly secondary importance and the creative adventure toward poésie is the major matter. Constructed or discovered, the surrealist object is a solidified dream and therefore subject to interpretation."[23] A work like *Old Cuntry* is a spiritual object, object-poem, and objet-surréaliste, and there is no contradiction in this simultaneity, since the outcome, if not the goal, of both Surrealism and traditional African worldviews in which spirits may animate objects is a challenge to what Joans called "the prosaic world of reason." In its use of assemblage and collage, *Old Cuntry* thus displays also Joans's Surrealist interests and techniques, a productive marriage of this point of view with the Old Country point of view he was explicating in "First Papers"—viewpoints that were, broadly speaking, not necessarily dissimilar in the first place.

As Joans's insistence on the spiritual or supernatural dimension of African ritual art may suggest, it is important to note that in addition to visual pieces like *Old Cuntry*, in his written work in *Afrodisia* and other books, we find self-conscious invocations of his ancestors in the form of the

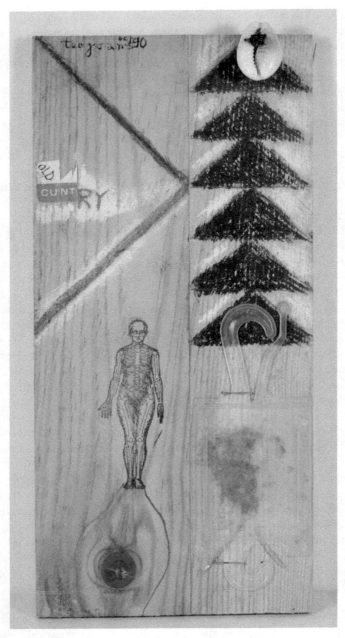

FIGURE 31.1 *Ted Joans,* Old Cuntry *(1990). Pencil, ink, wax crayon, cowrie shell, plastic, staples, artist's hair on wood panel. Collection of Author. In 2023, the Musée Cantonal des Beaux-Arts in Lausanne, Switzerland, purchased four pieces from the same series as* Old Cuntry.

"black magic" that had likewise been conjured by LeRoi Jones and others during the Black Arts Movement. In terms of language use in particular, one way to understand how Joans saw his own black magic working is to look at German scholar Janheinz Jahn's widely-read book *Muntu: The New African Culture*, whose English-language edition appeared in 1961. In "First Papers," Joans cited Jahn as one of the "few white men" who "have dared to face Black facts and honestly bare them," and *Muntu* helps us understand how Joans thought of his own work as in line with the ancestral creations he was encountering during his travels in Africa.

"All magic is word magic," Jahn writes, "incantation and exorcism, blessing and curse. Through Nommo, the word, man establishes his mastery over things."[24] In illustrating this idea, Jahn in fact quotes from Césaire's *Notebook*, in which the speaker declares: "I would find again the secret of the great communications, of the great conflagrations. I would speak storm. I would speak river. I would speak tornado."[25]

Jahn goes on to explain:

According to African philosophy man has, by the force of his word, dominion over things, he can change them, make them work for him, and command them. But to command things with words is to practise "magic." And to practise word magic is to write poetry—that holds not only for Africa. Thus African philosophy ascribes to the word a significance which it has also in many other cultures, but there in poetry only. That is why African poetry is never a game, never *l'art pour l'art*, never irresponsible.[26]

Joans echoes this thinking pretty explicitly in "First Papers" when he likewise insists that in Africa, "They do not create an 'Art' just for 'Art's Sake'" (68), and that "It is alright to say that he [an African artist/creator] is a possessor of specific magic" (71). Jahn concludes: "The word of the poet has not only called the 'things,' it has *produced* them, it is Nommo, word seed."[27] This sense of the word *producing* things, not merely *describing* them, is key to understanding what Joans is doing in his late 1960s poetry.

In *Black Pow-Wow*, for example, Joans evokes Nommo in "This Poem Is":

this poem is
          black as magic in Africa
this poem is
          read across counties, interstates plus international lines
this poem is
          dangerous to the violent and a threat to evil's overt actions
     ...
this poem is

     organizing the mass sons of soul with incendiary truths
this poem is
     promoting pride of Africa's future and great past
this poem is
     inciting us to self defense[28]

This is a conception of poetry as "magic," as capable of doing things in the world; as Jahn writes: "the word produces, commands and conjures."[29] Routed through Joans's sense of both Black Arts and Négritude as evoking some essential, "natural" African ideas about the power of the word, poetry becomes "dangerous" in its ability to organize, incite, overthrow. Likewise in "Poem Why," in *A Black Manifesto*, he writes that a poem "is a sharp bolt of / lightening [*sic*] that frees man" and that "The poet's poem power prowls / through the nasty neon streets / demystifying death."[30] However reductive it may be to speak about a universally "African" idea of language, the notion of a Black poem being "black as magic in Africa" was quite powerful to Joans and many other Black American writers in the latter 1960s, and essential to keep in mind when reading his work of the period.

———

Joans also had some more material connections to Négritude via the *Présence Africaine* literary review, and the bookshop it had spawned, located on the rue des Écoles in Paris. The *Présence Africaine* literary review was (and is) an enormously influential cultural and political magazine that Léopold Sédar Senghor called "the primary instrument of the Négritude movement."[31] Upon launching *Présence Africaine* in 1947, Senegalese writer Alioune Diop declared it was open to "all contributors of good will (White, Yellow or Black), who might be able to help define African originality and to hasten its introduction into the modern world."[32] This was a somewhat radical proposition at the time, but in the heady intellectual atmosphere of postwar Paris, the review flourished and *Présence Africaine* grew to become one of the most significant anti-racist and anti-colonialist publishing houses in the world, producing not only the review but also books by African poets, novelists, and intellectuals. By the mid-1950s, *Présence Africaine* was easily the most well-known Pan-Africanist review, a "hub for black intellectuals in the diaspora," and a natural place for the writers and thinkers associated with Négritude to publish their work.[33]

Joans avidly read *Présence Africaine*—and would later publish in its pages—and so was inevitably drawn to the Présence Africaine bookshop, which he called the "sole soul place in Paris ... an important black cultural center."[34] As he did at other cultural touchstones like George Whitman's Shakespeare and Company, also in Paris, or Bernard Stone's Turret Bookshop in London, Joans liked to hang around the Présence Africaine bookshop, connecting with people, sourcing books, and exchanging ideas. At one point, he even installed an "anti-book-thief fetish" at Présence Africaine, boasting that it was so powerful a mere ten paperbacks were stolen over the course of a whole year.[35] Of course, when possible, he also frequented the Présence Africaine branch in Dakar, where on any given day he might find himself debating the Martinican novelist Joseph Zobel about who, exactly, constituted an "Afroamerican."[36]

32

Meeting Malcolm X

It was under the auspices of *Présence Africaine* that Alioune Diop invited Malcolm X to speak in Paris, an invitation which led to Joans meeting both Malcolm and Aimé Césaire. On November 23, 1964, a year and a day after John F. Kennedy was killed in Dallas—and almost three months to the day before Malcolm himself would be killed in Harlem—he spoke to overflow crowds at the Salle de la Mutualité, Joans among them. Because he was in Paris on Diop's invitation, the topic of Malcolm's talk was "African Revolution and Its Effects on the Afro-American Struggle." He had just finished an eighteen-month trip through Africa, including Egypt, Nigeria, Ghana, Liberia, Guinea, and Kenya, meeting with post-independence leaders like Gamal Abdel Nasser (Egypt), Sékou Touré (Guinea) and Jomo Kenyatta (Kenya), and in his talk he stressed the connections among African Americans and Africa:

> It is true that for many years those of us of African ancestry in the West were reluctant to identify with Africa, but this was [the result of] an image projected by our enemies. This enemy created a negative image of Africa as a jungle, a place full of wild animals, etc. The image was made hateful to us. They knew that once we were made to hate our own origin, we would hate ourselves. And all people of African ancestry throughout the world would hate Africa and hate themselves. They did it so shrewdly and so successfully that they created those of us in the West who hated ourselves—our nose, our lips, our skin, our hair.[1]

This sort of critique was likewise at the heart of the Black Arts and Black Power movements, and its appeal to Joans is obvious, as he had been making similar points for years, from his Mau Mau events to early poetry like "To Africa I Went," which mocked the "image" Malcolm is criticizing here, the "Africa of savage folk / where people will put you in a pot."[2] Emphasizing the solidarity between African Americans and Africa also became of particular importance for Joans throughout the 1960s, and

Malcolm galvanized him that night, as he galvanized so many others who heard him speak.

In Paris, Joans marveled at Malcolm's rhetorical abilities and stage presence, calling him a "magnetic voice brother" in whom he recognized a "Black positive power that I had heard in the music of Charlie Parker, Thelonius Monk, Dizzy Gillespie and other Bop revolutionaries."[3] He was further buoyed that Malcolm had broken from the Nation of Islam; as Malcolm had insisted that night, he was speaking in a "non-religious" capacity, not as a minister, but as a political leader of the Organization of Afro-American Unity (which he had consciously modeled on the Organization of African Unity).[4] Joans had never particularly cared for the Nation of Islam, with its prescriptions for "proper" moral conduct and even respectable dress, so this Malcolm—the "new" Malcolm—was much more to his taste.[5]

At some point that night, Joans had the opportunity to meet Malcolm, and produced his "en route to Timbuktu" photograph and asked Malcolm to autograph it. Once Malcolm had signed the photograph—under "boogie woogie queens gaze," as Joans put it in his poem "Gri-Gris"—it became a kind of talisman for Joans, one of his "sacred treasures," and that night he had Aimé Césaire autograph it as well, and then would go on to present the photograph to other artists and "revolutionaries" at opportune moments, so their signatures could share the same physical space as Malcolm's and Césaire's.[6] Eventually Joans would add eight more names: Ornette Coleman (in October 1965); Albert Ayler (November 1966); Stokely Carmichael (July 1967); LeRoi Jones (July 1968); Archie Shepp (October 1969), Cecil Taylor (May 1987), Max Roach (1996), and James Baldwin (unknown year).[7] This particular photograph of Joans en route to Timbuktu thus became a way for him to link together otherwise far-flung revolutionaries—in literature, philosophy, music, and politics—under his own sign, an image of him looking back while stepping forward to a spiritual and intellectual center of Africa. As a pantheon of some of the finest Black minds in the world, the photograph is comparable to the ways Joans would draw together seemingly disparate figures in books like *Afrodisia* and *Black Pow-Wow* to create a personalized canon of the "black aesthetic."

Three months after his encounter with Malcolm, Joans was in Guelmim, Morocco, a dusty, red-clay town on the northern edge of the Sahara, when he got word of Malcolm's assassination. It was perversely symbolic that a "white Englishman pushed a French-Moroccan newspaper" at him announcing the news.[8] In a memorial poem, "True Blues for a Dues Payer," written on February 23, 1965, Joans recorded his disbelief: "I stood facing East with wet eyes & trembling hands under / quiet Maghreb bright night sky I didn't cry but inside / I said goodbye to my soothsayer His Hipness Malcolm X / a true dues payer!" This poem was later included in the commemorative volume, *For Malcolm: Poems on the Life and the Death of*

Malcolm X (1967), with the quoted lines ending the piece. ("True Blues for a Dues Payer" was also published in *Black Pow-Wow*, but Joans changed the final line to the more straightforward: "I said goodbye to you whom / I confess / I loved Malcolm X."[9])

In the aftermath of Malcolm's assassination, Joans also published other memorials to him, notably "Black February Blood" in *Présence Africaine*. If "True Blues for a Dues Payer" recorded Joans's immediate, personal reaction to learning about the death, "Black February Blood" takes more of a bird's eye approach, linking Malcolm's murder to Congolese leader Patrice Lumumba, who "was murdered / and made a martyr / in the month / of February" and Abudakar Tafawa Balewa, the first prime minster of independent Nigeria, who was assassinated during a coup (but actually in January 1966).[10] The poem goes on to connect these three murdered leaders with Kwame Nkrumah, the president of Ghana who was overthrown in a coup d'état in February 1966:

> and still yet I can not forget
> that not one
> > CHINESE RED
> > RUSSIAN RED
> > or even CUBAN RED
> did anything militantly
> to honor
> these BLACK February dead

This conclusion calls out those in the communist world who claimed interest in promoting racial solidarity as a bulwark against Western hegemony, accusing them of hypocrisy, of failing to recognize and honor Black leaders, a position that was broadly in keeping with a thinker like Aimé Césaire, who tended to be skeptical of both America/Europe *and* the Soviet sphere.[11] Although it may be difficult to see this in hindsight, from a "mainstream"— that is, white—American perspective, it was a controversial act simply to memorialize Malcolm, let alone link him to other "martyred" African leaders, as there was a prevailing sense that since he had preached violence, Malcolm had gotten what he deserved, a perverse come-uppance for his instantly-repeated remark after Kennedy's assassination: "the chickens [were] coming home to roost."[12]

On the other hand, for many a Black person, particularly left-leaning activists who were broadly frustrated with Martin Luther King, Jr.'s non-violent approach, Malcolm's death was the rocket engine of the Black Arts and Black Power Movements. LeRoi Jones's aforementioned move to Harlem and founding of the Black Arts Repertory Theatre School was only the most visible instance of this, and Malcolm's example certainly did inspire Joans to become more explicitly political in his writing, which became more and more aligned with a Black Arts/Black Power ethos in the second half of the 1960s, culminating in *A Black Manifesto in Jazz Poetry and Prose* (1971). This book was dedicated to both Charlie Parker and Malcolm X—"two men," Joans said, "who aided in the change and transformation of the human condition."[13] In this period, Joans also published two of his most well-known books, *Black Pow-Wow: Jazz Poems* (1969) and *Afrodisia* (1970), both of which were published in the States by a relatively large house, Hill & Wang, as part of its "American Century" poetry series.

   Afrodisia is Joans's major poetic statement about his views of Africa, and is divided into two parts, the first containing poems about or otherwise inspired by his travels through Africa, while the second part features erotica whose function he saw as helping Black people "have a total revolution to liberate themselves," the liberation of one's sexuality being central to this goal.[14] *Black Pow-Wow* is generally more strident in tone than *Afrodisia*, and is a product, in part, of a trip Joans took back to the States in 1968 to attend Black Power conferences and interact with those on the Black Arts scene. A distillation of Joans's Black Arts/Black Power period is *A Black Manifesto in Jazz Poetry and Prose*, which opens with a raw, militant Black Power manifesto inspired by political figures such as Malcolm X and Stokely Carmichael (whom Joans had dubbed the "the Apollinaire" of the Black Panthers) and, going back further, Surrealist poet Étienne Léro and his "explosive Black journal," *Légitime Défense*.[15]

   In addition to these three books, there are two other significant works Joans wrote in the latter 1960s and early 1970s, but that were never published in their entirety: a novel provocatively titled "Niggers from Outer Space," and a comprehensive guidebook to Africa pitched to Black Americans, "A Black Man's Guide to Africa." Begun in Copenhagen in 1964 and finished on a trip to Harlem in 1968, "Outer Space" was what Joans called a "surrealized ... Black Power Dream" that imagined black aliens from outer space who literally turn white people Black through forced copulation.[16] Insofar as it ends in a utopic vision of a Black-run America in which things like capitalism and racial discord have dissolved away, "Outer Space" can be read as a classic Black Arts Movement text. "A Black Man's Guide to Africa" was a project Joans had been working on intermittently since his move to Tangier, and had different incarnations by the later 1960s, when he began focusing on it in earnest. By that time, he was envisioning the book as a way to introduce Black Americans to Africa, and to "help demystify the lies and false pictures of this great continent."[17] In this way, the book is both travel guide and ideological intervention, a specific, concrete enactment of the "black unity" espoused in both the US-based Black Arts Movement, and the more explicitly transnational Négritude movement, which interrogated Blackness in the context of French colonialism and its legacies. As both a document of a particular historical moment and as a crystallization of several of Joans's preoccupations throughout the 1960s, "A Black Man's Guide to Africa" remains one of his more significant unpublished works.

3 3

Black Cultural Guerilla

One way Joans described his presence in Europe in the 1960s was as a kind of sentinel keeping watch for developments in the Black Arts. Calling himself a "Black cultural guerilla," Joans claimed that he "finally did go to Europe to <u>colonize their minds</u>, to attempt to transform and change the young people of Europe by surrealist and jazz ways and means."[1] In one of his memoirs, "Well Shut My Mouth Wide Open," Joans reflected on his role as a "Black cultural guerilla," and took the martial metaphor several steps further by imagining a reverse colonization of white Europe by a "surrealist onslaught of Blackness."[2] Such Blackness was visible, Joans thought, in the "Black arts of music and dancing," which were popular among the youth of Europe.[3] From this foothold, Joans fantasized that incarnations of Blackness would take over Europe, renewing a continent he often referred to as a cemetery, an eventuality both inexorable and morally justified: "Shit, brother and sister Black Amerika, allyall knows that we done paid and still are paying enuff dues, to own the land, so I advocate the colonizing of the Euro tribal grounds."[4]

Beyond just music and dance, in Joans's dream of a Black-colonized Europe, white ways of knowing would be rejected wholesale, capitalism would become irrelevant, and the "whole of the Euro tribal systems especially clock time and inhuman schedules will be for Black colonizers to undo in London."[5] With the help of vanguards like "General Sorcerer Dexter Gordon" and "Field Marshall Ted Curson" (74), the old Anglo-Saxon and Celtic notion of "civilization"—which had for centuries been passed off as the only real or legitimate notion of civilization—would be displaced by Black visions of civilization and culture. "Blackness alone will scare them into total submission, especially since they'll perhaps welcome the liberation of change, transformaction, and dream that we shall bring" (72). In this view, Joans's circulation through Africa to Europe and back again was not only necessitated by his financial demands, but was an opportunity also for infiltration and observation, crucial acts of a coming global revolution. Echoing LeRoi Jones's famous declaration that "we are black magicians, black arts / we make in the black labs of the heart," Joans likewise declared: "We must conjure and conquer with Black arts, that magic cannot be stopped."[6]

Joans explored the idea of Black colonization of white countries in a more literal sense in his "Black Power Dream" novel, the defiantly-titled "Niggers from Outer Space." He had conceived the project in Copenhagen in 1964, and the title was pugnaciously political insofar as it adopted the most vicious of racial slurs and reimagined its meaning. Joans was inspired by comedian and activist Dick Gregory, who had published his *Nigger: An Autobiography* in September 1964. Joans was impressed by the audacity of the title, marveling that "We have taken the very Word from the racist and make it work for US instead of against us."[7] Like Gregory's autobiography, "Outer Space" (and its title) can be profitably understood in the broad context of the entwined Black Arts and Black Power movements. The plot has black aliens coming from outer space and surreptitiously raping white people (as well as animals), acts which turn white people's skin black. Unsurprisingly, as more and more white people are turned black, a national crisis erupts that is political, cultural, and existential all at once. The shaken US president addresses a panicked nation, dropping all pretenses to racial bonhomie: "My fellow white Americans ... The white power structure of this country which controls the white power structure of other lands is faced today by an awesome black thing that seeks to destroy our white way of life."[8] The tide cannot be turned back, however, and as millions of white people are inseminated with Blackness, eventually the remaining white population segregates themselves on the West Coast, away from a newly-formed government by and for Black people.

Literary critic William L. Van Deburg has identified a strain of Black Arts fiction depicting a "new post-revolutionary world ... [in which] the air was clean and the water pure. Hunger existed only in history books ... Money was abolished and war removed from the national vocabulary ... White America's once-dominant school of acculturation had been placed in permanent recess."[9] Joans's "dream" in "Outer Space" is certainly in keeping with this strain, as the book culminates in a utopic vision achieved after the space aliens have turned enough white people Black:

> The population merged into one creative force, guided by the spirit of total COMMITMENT TO BLACK UNITY. They knew that at last they had gained true Black Power through segregated living ... There were no slums, no poverty, and no more ignorance. There was not one unfed human being. Everything was really swinging ... They called it the Blackland of Black Magic ... The civilization was a black civilization. The power base was black. The important people were the black people. (36–41)

In this way, "Outer Space" is a wish fulfillment that grew from the Black Arts moment, a fictional version of Black Power's real-life calls for the segregation of the races and the establishment of a Black-centered society. But it also harkens back to global Black cultures as they existed prior to colonialism and the slave trade, which Aimé Césaire, for one, had described in ways reminiscent of Joans's "Blackland of Black Magic": "Their customs were pleasing, built on unity, kindness, respect for age. / No coercion, only mutual assistance, the joy of living, a free acceptance of discipline. / Order— Earnestness—Poetry and Freedom."[10]

Although the novel's premise of "Black Power through segregated living" may seem straightforward enough, it's worth pausing over a few details to understand some specific points of connection with Black Arts/Black Power thinking. The first thing to note is that in "Outer Space," "Blackness" is not linked simply to the color of a person's skin, but is rather something ineffable that "real" Black people recognize and share. Because of this, white people who had their skin turned black by the space aliens are depicted as "white-blacks," integrated into the newly-organized Black society, but always only aspirationally Black. Fixated on the physical, the surface of things, the "white-blacks" strive to become what they consider more Black, curling their hair and undergoing "plastic surgery to widen their lips and noses" (37). This situation is Joans's response to Black Power statements like the one he had heard Malcolm X make in Paris, that white culture had made Black people hate themselves, hate "our nose, our lips, our skin, our hair."[11] As Stokely Carmichael would put it in 1966: "A broad nose, a thick lip and nappy hair is us and we are going to call that beautiful whether they like it or not."[12] Despite their efforts, the "white-blacks" in the novel "never did learn to think black due to the bare fact that they were not black inside. Their soul was still a white thing and not a black soul. They never could achieve that higher place of spirituality … Contact with blackness did not make them black people" (37). Joans's vision in "Outer Space" is thus broadly in keeping with the foundational assumption of Black Power, that Black is Beautiful, while also insisting that Blackness is something beyond merely the physical.

The other thing to note about "Outer Space" is its use of "black humor bits" (35) to skewer prevailing white attitudes about Blackness. One of the more devastating ways Joans does this is by describing how Blackness is an existential plague for white people. As the US government hires "experts"— all purposively associated with white, Western ways of knowing—"noted dermatologists, skin specialists, space scientists, and biologists" (22), "the best money could buy, all devoted in trying to solve BLACK PLAGUE" (21). These experts finally conclude, ironically, that "The harm that is done [to white people turned black] is not physical harm, unless one considers being black a physical harm" (22). Thus while there is of course nothing scientifically or objectively harmful about being Black, social attitudes are so ideologically powerful that they pass for scientific knowledge: "Most of them [white people turned black] could not speak coherently or didn't want to. Being turned black was too much for their minds to bear. Some had gone completely insane" (23). In such darkly humorous dimensions, "Outer Space" is comparable to Melvin Van Peebles's film *Watermelon Man* (1970), starring Godfrey Cambridge, like Dick Gregory a well-known Black comic of the era. Cambridge plays a typical middle-class white man who mysteriously turns Black, leading to a series of encounters both comic and sardonically telling about simmering racist attitudes just below the surface of a supposedly integrated society (back when he was a struggling writer-actor-director in Paris, Van Peebles would sometimes team up with Joans to sing together in front of café terraces, and then pass a beret around for donations).[13]

FIGURE 33.1 *Joans as the "Ace of Spades," detail from the countercultural newspaper* Other Scenes *(1968).*

Joans likewise skewers the moral panic among white America as it concerned African Americans' growing interest in their African roots. At one of the emergency meetings of Congress depicted in "Outer Space," a Southern Senator insists that those Black Americans who "STUDY ABOUT BLACK FOLKLORE OF AFRICA AND ... HAVE LEARNT ALL BLACK MAGIC TRICKS AND TRADE ... ARE NOTHING MORE THAN MODERN WITCHDOCTORS/ AND IT IS THEY THAT HAVE BROUGHT THIS TERRIBLE BLACK MALADY ON THIS GLORIOUS WHITE NATION" (23). Such thinking leads to investigations of "Black Power militant groups," who stand accused of inviting the space aliens to earth (33). One Senator proposes a law forbidding Black Americans from traveling to Africa at all because, he thinks, such movement must somehow be connected to the "Black Plague" brought by these aliens (30). The running joke of "Outer Space" is that the aliens are metaphors for a re-evaluation and reorientation of Blackness that certainly was inaugurated by the Black Arts Movement and "Black Power militant groups," as well Black Americans' renewed interest in and travel through Africa and its newly independent states. As far as Joans was concerned, "Outer Space" was "prose of the griots," a Black book in a Black tradition of telling it like it is.

Joans did try to publish "Outer Space" when it was completed, even as he insisted it should not be revised. The book "shall not be 'worked over,'" he informed publisher Arthur Wang, "I am not a dentist or doctor. I am merely a poet who has decided to write something long for a larger audience than my poetry."[14] Although like "Spadework," the full manuscript of "Outer Space" never was published, Joans also reached out to Grove Press, where Gilbert Sorrentino rejected it as just "not for Grove Press."[15]

An excerpt did appear in *Other Scenes*, John Wilcock's "newspaper of art and revolution" out of New York. This excerpt was published in the December 1968 issue, alongside articles denouncing the draft and the war in Vietnam, essays on sex, Bob Dylan, and lists of domestic and international political prisoners. In this context, "Outer Space" can be seen as of a piece with a generally revolutionary or countercultural ethos of the late 1960s (if not one, in the case of *Other Scenes*, aimed exclusively at Black audiences). Joans's collages adorn the text, and he is pictured in the middle as the Ace of Spades, imagery carried over from *All of Ted Joans and No More*, and the cheeky iconography of "Spadework" (Figure 33.1).

34

A Black Man's Guide to Africa

The proposition in "Outer Space" that the extraterrestrials appeared as a result of African Americans traveling to Africa is a wry reference to both the kind of transnational Black solidarity articulated by Malcolm X in Paris (and at the heart of much Black Arts thinking), and to the fact that Joans himself was then circulating through Africa with increasing frequency. After his domestic life with Grete began to fall apart, Joans was often out on his own and nearly impossible to pin down, in the winter months invariably in Timbuktu, on his way to Timbuktu, or otherwise working his way around the African continent. Finally Grete had decided that she needed to stay in Norway with her two boys, and wanted to end their marriage, but still Joans didn't agree. He held out on signing divorce papers, still believing that it might work between them. But ultimately the couple was divorced in 1969, ending Joans's great romance of the 1960s.[1]

In his poetry, Joans would emphasize both the prosaic realities of traveling in remote regions like the Sahara (the difficulty of securing gasoline, the way sand would worm its way in to everything) and his contact with putatively "authentic" aspects of various African societies. "I have gained entrance into secret societies in Africa," he wrote in *Afrodisia*, "sorcerers/marabouts/ and magicians turned me on They who decorated me with grigris I still call myself Ted only because you wouldn't understand who I really am now."[2]

He elaborated on such contact with "secret societies" in "First Papers on Ancestral Creations," that piece he published in *Black World* aiming to explain an African aesthetic sensibility to Black Americans:

In Liberia, in the Northern sector where I was taken to a sacred grove to be initiated into a Poro Society ("a" because there are many Poro societies), a judge of me was a (masked) fetisher. He was infested with grigris and jingling bells and pieces of metal … I cannot reveal to you either in writing, or in any form, what really went on during my initiation into the Poro Society. I have sworn to my ancestors to hold fast these secrets. African animists beliefs permeate Black creations which are the basis of Black culture.[3]

Such statements are of course by their very nature impossible to "verify" in an encyclopedic sense—and this fact is part of their power for Joans. In their reference to closed rituals and fleeting moments of cultural connection, Joans's claims about being initiated into "secret societies in Africa" evoke an abstract, aesthetic sense of "black magic" proposed by LeRoi Jones and others associated with the Black Arts Movement, but also literalizes it, implying that Joans had access to the real, unmediated, non-commercialized, non-Westernized "Africa," the well-spring of Blackness from which so many African American writers and artists of the era drew inspiration, and sought out when making pilgrimages to the continent. As he once put it in a third-person statement of his career highlights, "A member of a Northern Liberian Poro Society, Mr. Joans has sworn to hold fast its secrets. He has participated in many other tribal rituals in various parts of Africa and is inseparable from his gris-gris, worn to perpetuate affinity with his ancestral spirits."[4] In this telling, Joans has succeeded in accessing what is generally off-limits to outsiders, a "secret" connection to the "ancestors" that has changed his very being, but about which he can only be non-specific.

What he could articulate with granular specificity was precisely how an American, a Black American in particular, could travel to Africa and access the fullest experience possible. Joans was bothered that while on his journeys through Africa, he tended to see white travelers on the road, not Black ones, and this became the motivation to again take up work on his guidebook, this time addressing it to Black Americans specifically. In November 1970, as he made his way from Fort-Lamy (now N'Djamena) in Chad to the Central African Republic, he worked on an article based on his observations called "Africa Is the Richest Continent."[5] This piece became "Natural Africa," published in *Black World* magazine, and in it he lamented:

I question every Black in the United States who is not planning to visit Africa ... It really bugs me that I have never met a Black sister with a rucksack on her back, clad in well-worn bluejeans, and riding on the top of a transsaharan truck. I have seen just too many white ones doing just that ... I hope that they will start coming and fast. I hope that they will stop chanting, "I'm Black and I'm proud," and start chanting, "I'm *back* and I'm proud!" Come on over for a visit.[6]

Although from at least 1962 Joans had already begun gathering notes on his travels with the idea of doing a book he would call "A Hipster's Guide to Africa," it was only after his split with Grete, and the newfound freedom that entailed, that he really threw himself into the project, envisioning it now as a guide pitched to Black Americans.[7] In the latter 1960s he was able to travel over almost all of Africa, trying out hotels and restaurants, and seeking out the richest experiences, the most authentic places to buy art and handicrafts. He put all this knowledge into "A Black Man's Guide to Africa," a monumental volume covering a startling diversity of African countries exhausting simply to list: Kenya, Mali, Republic of Ivory Coast, Popular Republic of Congo, Algeria, Gabon, Ghana, Uganda, Sierra Leone, Somalia (The Somali Democratic Republic), Democratic Republic of Congo, Malawi, Republic of Zambia, Republic of Togo, The Gambia, The Republic of Guinea, Mauritius, The Islamic Republic of Mauritania, Tunisia, Libya, Equatorial Guinea, Chad, Malagasy Republic, Senegal, Republic of Burundi, Ethiopia, United Republic of Tanzania, Central African Republic, Egypt, Republic of Liberia, Morocco, The Cameroon Federal Republic, The Republic of Niger, Republic of Upper Volta, Republic of Dahomey, Republic of Nigeria, The Democratic Republic of Sudan, and Republic of Rwanda. The book is an immense accomplishment, a capacious and idiosyncratic document of a particular time and place, something broadly akin to Michel Leiris's equally monumental *L'Afrique fantôme* or *Phantom Africa* (1934), part travelogue, part ethnography, part memoir by a leading Surrealist thinker, and later friend of Joans's. While Leiris was not writing a travel guide, as in "A Black Man's Guide to Africa" he makes no pretense to scientific detachment but rather explores his wholly subjective impressions of traveling through the continent. The book's authority in fact comes from Leiris's willingness to probe his increasing discomfort with the very basis of his nearly two-year travels through sub-Saharan Africa, from Dakar to Djibouti: he was serving as a "secretary-archivist" for a colonial "anthropological expedition" funded by the French government.[8] *Phantom Africa* is now considered a classic of twentieth-century French letters, and in my view, "A Black Man's Guide to Africa" is a comparable achievement.

The first thing readers would likely notice about "A Black Man's Guide to Africa" is the writing style, which adopts a sometimes over-the-top Black vernacular as a means of connecting with Joans's intended African American audience, a strategy explicable by the Black Arts/Black Power atmosphere in which he was writing. Given that language itself was so charged in the political and aesthetic environment of the latter 1960s, the push to "preserve the black idiom" felt absolutely vital to the continuing existence of both a "Black aesthetic" and Black culture writ large.[9] Joans consciously drew on this idiom to make the otherwise daunting or remote possibility of traveling to and navigating Africa more accessible to Black Americans who may not have even ventured outside the United States at all. As he explained to Hoyt Fuller, editor of *Black World*, "A Black Man's Guide" "will be my most important book[.] it will also be the first complete prose bit for me no poem no politics and yet unusual in all its guidebook-surrealist aspects. Four letter words, Black language, glorification, etc shall abound. It should sell and I feel it will."[10]

The then-current interest in a particular kind of Black aesthetic helps clarify both why Joans thought "Black Man's Guide" would sell well, and

why he adopts "four letter words, Black language" throughout. Although he
suggested to Fuller that "no politics" were to be found in the guide, of course
it is a political act both to write a guide to Africa for African Americans (as
is satirized in "Outer Space"), and to use an unabashedly Black idiom in so
doing.

Consider, for example, Joans's explanation of how to obtain a passport:

> HERE IS SOME OFFICIAL BULLSHIT that one has to take into
> consideration. First of all: PASSPORT! ... When you fall by the office
> to cop your passport, be sure and have something to show that you are
> a U.S. citizen. Yeah, I know it's a big drag, but brother you have to go
> through the motions, if you wanta git a passport ... Sometimes obtaining
> a passport aint no sweat, but if you are unlucky and run into a cracker ...
> man you got troubles! (5)

Here the bureaucracy of (white) American civilization is figured as a
necessary evil for mobility, freedom, the promised land of Africa, and the
use of slang and slurs serves to bind Joans and his readers together in an
oppositional relationship to the official state, united in their shared goal of
getting out of this state.

Beyond its style, "A Black Man's Guide" is very much a Black Power
document, not only for the way it assumes and celebrates the wonder and
diversity of African art and culture but also for the way it explicitly argues
for solidarity between African Americans and Africans. This connection
is materialized in the monetary contributions potential African American
tourists would make to the economies of developing, recently-independent
African nations. As Joans writes, "I am hip to the struggle against
colonialism, neo-imperialism, and all the other imported sicknesses that
Africa is suffering from," and notes that one small way to combat such ills
is to transfer wealth from the United States to Africa via tourist dollars (6).
He therefore insists throughout that his readers should prepare to spend as
much money as possible on the continent, something he frames as a moral
obligation:

> When I travel around in Africa, the Euro-youth people that I meet are
> suffering from a malady of PINCHING PENNYS, FREE-LOADERS and
> SHORT CUTTERS. These unfortunates got their sickness from trying to
> do Africa-On-Five-Dollars-A-Day. So they got their first case of tropical
> diarrhea from eating vegetables and fruits that had been washed in some
> badass polluted water ... These travelers are always searching for the
> most cheapest place to dine. They dont think about their health, all that
> they are thinking about is SAVING MONEY! Why did they come to
> Africa in the first place, if not to spend some of them dollars? Africa is
> a continent of millions of poor people, but proud people, and un-selfish

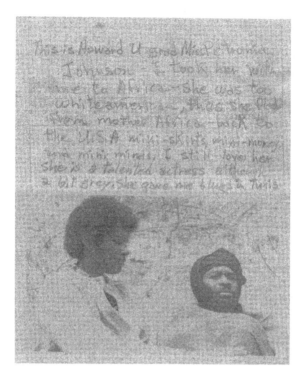

FIGURE 34.1 *Ted Joans and short-lived companion Petronia Johnson traveling through Africa, probably in late 1968. This photograph was printed on the back cover of* Shuffle Boil *4 (summer/fall 2003).*

people, thus many of the young Euro travelers make it a THING to free load off the poor people whom have befriended them. I call these vicious furthermuckers, new-colonialists. They come not to give or share, but to TAKE. (6)

Here again, Joans cautions his imagined Black readership against adopting the same extractive attitude he saw in so many white visitors to Africa. "Afroamericans should visit Africa as tourists," he writes later, "and should also aid Africa by investments, teaching, doing research work, aid in the struggle against disease and ignorance, plus start projects that would restore some of the African institutions" that had been decimated by colonialism (47). To be authentically "Black," Joans was saying to his readers, they must avoid the sort of freeloading he saw white Europeans doing, and instead recognize African people as brethren, and contribute materially by spending those American dollars. African American tourism in Africa was about both enriching Americans culturally, spiritually, aesthetically, and a means to start, if just as a trickle, a global redistribution of wealth to benefit Africans.

As "A Black Man's Guide" tells it, Black Americans stood to gain a priceless education by visiting the continent. In addition to practical travel advice, Joans wanted to Teducate in the sense of undoing images of Africa perpetuated by centuries of white, Eurocentric narratives about the continent and its people. As a usable guide to hotels and restaurants, the book cannot be untangled from this Teducation, for as announced on the very first page: "This guide book to Africa is your own personal guide to all the exciting places on the continent. It was done to encourage tourists to visit Africa, and to help demystify the lies and false pictures of this great continent."[11] Even when the book is at its most practical, still it is suffused with a political consciousness that directs readers to Black-owned airlines or hotels, or to experiences that Joans considered most indicative of a "real" or "authentic" Africa—often in pointed contrast to what most Western tourism companies tended to offer. He had said that he wanted the book to be useful to people like his mother and her friends, so that they could experience the continent beyond what he called the "Koca-Kola country of African tourism," Kenya and its game parks, which he felt were over-promoted by US-based tour operators.[12]

Joans's general skepticism of Kenya stemmed from the country's saturation in British colonialism, which was in turn responsible for East Africa being seen in the West as a stand-in for all of Africa, and for what he called the "Swahili craze" afflicting many Black Americans in the 1960s and 1970s:

> the reason for the Swahili craze is obvious. I saw all those old movies where any African who was allowed to speak beyond those "ugs" and "ungawas," well, he spoke Swahili, such as "bwana" or "mkubwa." Why? Well, the reason starts in Britain, Britain colonized Kenya, and built a British city called Nairobi. Then they cranked out so-called "African" movies like Hollywood. And one of the results, for a good example, is that there are more Afro-Americans and Europeans knowing about the Masai and the Watutsi than the Bambara or the Dogon.[13]

The recommendations and observations in "A Black Man's Guide" are therefore oriented around education and demystifying the "lies and false pictures" of Africa, so despite its packaging as a usable travel resource, Joans also saw it as doing similar work as his other Black Power-era fiction and poetry (including "Outer Space," *Afrodisia*, *Black Pow-Wow* and *Black Manifesto in Jazz Poetry and Prose*). On the topic of advising readers where to locate authentic African art Joans was especially passionate. In the chapter on Senegal, for example, he stresses the masses of "joke-art" available for sale in Dakar—what he considers inauthentic tchotchkes made for the tourist trade and not representative of legitimate Senegalese aesthetic practice: "I hope that all my Afroamerican brothers and sisters NEVER BUY any of this junk. I have seen hundreds of Euros loaded down with this joke-art. That is great to pull a hype on Euros. But it is really serious business when black brothers and sisters fall for this jive, when there is still authentic African creations of value to be had" (104).

Buying "joke-art" was "serious business" as far as Joans was concerned because it meant falling for and literally buying in to a "false picture" of Africa—it's fine for white Europeans to be duped into thinking they own an example of real African art, but it's a grievous sin for Black Americans, and his guidebook was designed to prevent such missteps.

As I hope is clear from this brief tour, "A Black Man's Guide to Africa" is a rich and multi-layered snapshot of a pivotal, transitional decade in African history, and the excitement Joans feels in traveling through Black-run, independent countries is palpable. "Ghana made fantastic progress in a very short time," he observes, "and as one strolls through the streets of Accra one can see what happened. The colonialists called Ghana 'the gold coast' when they should have been hip enough to know that it was really the 'soul coast' for independence" (75).

Unhappily, like "Spadework," "A Black Man's Guide to Africa" was never published, but a completed typescript dated 1971 is housed in the Ted Joans Papers at Berkeley, along with notes and source material (travel brochures and the like).[14] Joans did have a contract to publish "A Black Man's Guide" with Grossman Publishers in New York, and was scheduled to deliver the manuscript in August 1970.[15] He was paid a handsome $3,000 advance for the book, but owing to a complicated dispute with Grossman, it never actually went into production.[16]

One source of the dispute was the contract itself, which was issued to both Joans and a woman he had met in Africa while at work on the book, Joan Halifax. This new Joan was an American anthropology student in her mid-twenties, and once Joans's relationship with Grete was truly over, he got together with Halifax, and they traveled and lived together for a year or so, sharing a car and a storage unit in Dakar—in fact, Joans even began to call her his "wife." While the couple was never legally married, Joans had long-held ideas about other ways to validate a "marriage," writing approvingly, for example, about strolling with a lover up the steps of the Tour Saint-Jacques in Paris: "do this simple action 7 times within 7 weeks or 7 months, you can assure yourselves that surreally you are married."[17] It was in this sort of sense that he and Joan Halifax were married.[18] A brilliant person, Halifax was keenly interested in the Civil Rights struggle, and found Joans both magnetic and a "demanding teacher."[19] During their time together, Halifax helped Joans on the various projects he was finalizing in the late 1960s, working with him to select material for *Afrodisia* and *A Black Manifesto in Jazz Poetry and Prose*.[20] While Joans wrote all of "A Black Man's Guide," the plan was for Halifax to supply photographs to accompany the prose, which explained why Grossman had issued a joint contract—to "Ted Joans and Joan Halifax Joans," as it stated. The couple had a somewhat acrimonious falling out as Joans was completing these projects: he wrote a poem to her called "Later!" that implores her to "Spare me the parting passion play ... Your term at this university is over!"[21]

Despite Joans's other successes publishing three books between 1969 and 1971, "A Black Man's Guide" stalled because Grossman could not move on things like dispersing funds without the express written permission of both parties on the contract, which frustrated Joans to no end. By 1970, Halifax had left Africa to go back to the States, and Joans was bouncing around on his own, from Liberia to the Ivory Coast, seemingly in a new country every week, impossible to catch up with. On their end, Grossman Publishers was becoming increasingly impatient over protracted delays, and pled with Joans's agent, Gunther Stuhlmann, "to get the contract untangled."[22] In April 1971, Dick Grossman himself dashed off an irate letter to Joans—addressed "Listen, Joans"—saying that "I signed you up to write a book with your wife. You received a generous advance," and indignant that Joans had failed to hold up his "side of the bargain."[23] He concludes by admonishing Joans for "having hustled Grossman Publishers." It's not clear precisely why Joans ultimately failed to deliver the manuscript to Grossman, since he did complete a polished typescript, but the deal did fall apart irreparably. Stuhlmann was still negotiating with Grossman into the middle of 1972, but to no avail.[24]

Eventually, as he did, Joans moved on, content that, "being hip, I did get my advance money for my enjoyable adventurous work."[25]

35

Black Pow-Wow to *Afrodisia*

The difficulties with "A Black Man's Guide to Africa" notwithstanding, the later 1960s was an extraordinarily creative time for Joans, and one of his most productive in terms of actually getting work published, something that wasn't always a priority for him. In 1969, he published *Black Pow-Wow: Jazz Poems* with his first big house, Hill & Wang in New York.[1] Langston Hughes had given Joans a letter of introduction to publisher Arthur Wang, yet another act of generous support that led to Hill & Wang publishing both *Black Pow-Wow* and then, a year later, *Afrodisia: New Poems* (1970), Joans's two major poetry collections of this period.[2]

Joans said he "detest[ed]" the color scheme of *Black Pow-Wow*'s cover (Figure 35.1): "I hate psychedelic design."[3] The cover of the first US edition of *Afrodisia* was much more to his liking, boldly red, a color which for the Yoruba "signals *àshe* and potentiality," and featuring a photograph of a wooden door carved by Yoruba artists.[4] On the back was that portrait of Joans mentioned earlier that managed to be both serene and defiant: he is completely naked except for his knitted skullcap, leather cuffs on his biceps, and a necklace with a lone cowrie shell. He is posed in a totemic triangle, gazing straight ahead at the camera—and the potential reader of the book. For the UK edition of *Afrodisia*, published in 1976, Joans added several collages illustrating how the idea of Afrodisia was flowing out of his head, while also flowing through him (Figure 35.2).

Black Pow-Wow and *Afrodisia* are complementary books showcasing Joans's knowledge of and experiences in Africa, fusing his Surrealist techniques, eroticism, black humor, and a more strident hand grenade sensibility. *Black Pow-Wow* contains both older, Beat era poems, as well as more recent Black Arts era poems, while *Afrodisia* consists of new material (despite the UK edition being subtitled "Old & New Poems").[5] Like "A Black Man's Guide," a basic impulse underlying *Black Pow-Wow* is Joans's desire to promote solidarity among Black Americans and Africans. The title is borrowed from the Native American sense of a Pow-wow as "a ceremony

FIGURE 35.1 *Cover of Ted Joans,* Black Pow-Wow *(1969) with its "psychedelic design" that he hated.*

with cultural and spiritual significance," as the Oxford English Dictionary puts it, and refers to the meeting and communing of Joans with his readers—and, more abstractly, to Black Americans connecting with Africa over shared experiences, and Joans's own exploratory commitments to non-white aesthetics. In the poem "Pow-Wow," Joans writes: "Listen to me colored brothers / Hear me shout our song / we all are well aware / of how long we all been done wrong"—"Unity is our thing/to swing!"[6] The hyphen in *Black Pow-Wow* also isolates the word "wow," whose etymology Joans traced back to Africa, and associated with the energetic power of jazz: "The 'wow' word is an African word (*wolof*) brought to the USA by some of those West Africans who were sold into slavery. It is now used by millions of people all over the globe, just as jazz music healthy contaminates the world populace. The word 'wow' means 'yes,' or commenting in awe of something unusually good or bad."[7]

In the late 1960s, Joans also used the term "Pow Wow" to refer to gatherings focused on African culture or Black Power, including cultural conferences he attended in North America in 1968, as well as Africa-based

FIGURE 35.2 *Cover of the British edition of* Afrodisia *(1976). Unlike the first Hill & Wang edition, this one, published by Marion Boyars, included collages by Joans reinforcing the book's themes, desire and freedom among them.*

festivals such as the First Pan-African Cultural Festival in Algiers.[8] *Black Pow-Wow* is in fact partly a product of a trip Joans took back to the States in 1968, the first time he had traveled there since leaving in 1961. One immediate catalyst for this trip was the assassination of Martin Luther King, Jr. on April 4, 1968. Although Joans insisted he was "never a follower" of King's "Christian philosophy, nor a believer in his passive resistance movement," he appreciated King as a central animating figure of the Black liberation movement who "gave international publicity to the struggle of the black people. He was a kind of Salvador Dali of the Afroamerican revolution."[9] The day after King's murder, Joans was in Holland, and dispatched an urgent message to the Paris Surrealist group, imploring them to chip in for a ticket back to the States: "If you of the surrealist in Europe, wish to aid the black people in the United States—then help send me back to the war front. That is where the revolutionary battle is being fought."[10]

After securing funds, Joans finally did return to the States in late summer, with the intention of attending the 3rd National Black Power

Conference in Philadelphia (August–September), and the Congress of Black Writers in Montreal (October 11–14), experiences which solidified his sense of duty to lend more explicit support to Black Power.[11] At the Philadelphia conference he served as co-chairman of the Communications Workshop, whose tasks included, among other things, instilling "the desire for Black Nationalism and an undying loyalty toward the Black Nation," and attacking "relentlessly all enemies of Black Nationalism and defend[ing] vehemently all friends of the Black Nation."[12] Reflecting on the Philadelphia Black Power Conference the day after it concluded, Joans asked himself: "Why did I return [to the States]?" The answer had shifted thanks to the conference: "To see my family/read my poems/obtain supplies/and to be published. Those were my reasons for returning. Now I have changed some of my plans. Black people need me in the struggle."[13] Joans was excited by the creative and political energies he encountered back in the States—in Black communities but, pointedly, not in white ones: "There never was so much creativeness as this in all the places that I had visited in Europe or Africa. Black Art is alive and the people of the black community is digging it."[14]

———

In Montreal that October, Joans was a memorable participant in the Congress of Black Writers at McGill University, a gathering that included such luminaries as Stokely Carmichael, Walter Rodney, James Forman, C. L. R. James, and many others. Historian David Austin calls the Congress "one of the most important black international gatherings of the post-Second World War period"—and Joans was in the middle of it all.[15] He spoke and read his poetry after being introduced by the Guyanese intellectual and firebrand Walter Rodney as "Brother Ted Joans," the renowned jazz poet who was currently living "back in his own roots" in Timbuktu, "right in the heart of the old tradition of Mali."[16] If others emphasized Joans's connection to the "old tradition" in Timbuktu, he himself urged the participants to embrace their Blackness, which meant ignoring or rejecting whiteness: "I was clad in a colorful West African outfit," he recalled of the Congress, "and the news media photographers zeroed often on me."[17] Austin notes that Joans was "perhaps the most outspoken exponent of excluding whites" of anyone at the conference, although Joans himself remembered "some tough-looking West Indian students controlling who was allowed in. There were big groups of white media and students waiting to get in. But they were not allowed to enter until every Third World (actually First World) human being was seated."[18]

When it was Joans's turn to speak, he said:

I happened to go through one of them white universities in America unbrainwashed so see I don't need Shakespeare and I don't think he needed me ... And don't need that alcoholic, Dylan Thomas, I don't need him either. See, I don't buy their books and I don't need their books. I can learn, I learn everything about them, but after that you must get rid of it. See like Bird, Charlie Parker, Lester Young, Coleman Hawkins, Ornette Coleman, you see, black jazz musicians they take these European-made instruments and they do other things with them ... The brothers are getting themselves together, you get yourself together.[19]

Of course at this time and in this context especially Joans downplayed any proximity to whiteness, rejecting Shakespeare and Dylan Thomas, but not mentioning his abiding admiration for André Breton, even as *Black Pow-Wow* contains poems such as "Nadja Rendezvous," dedicated to Breton— and "Southern Landscapers," dedicated to his white "friends," Jim Haynes, Paul Bowles, and Charles Henri Ford (there are also poems dedicated to fellow participants at the Montreal Congress, including Walter Rodney ["Get It!"], Stokely Carmichael ["S.C. Threw S.C. into the Railroad Yard,"] and Harry Edwards ["The Athlete"]).

Aside from his flamboyant presence itself, Joans's main contribution to the Congress was his poetry, and he wanted to share what he called his "black pride" poems that would soon be collected in *Black Pow-Wow*.[20] He read poems including "Hallelujah, I Love Jazz So," "The .38," "My Ace of Spades," and ended with "The Nice Colored Man." He called his old Beat era poem "The .38" a "violent poem," cautioning the audience to "hold on to your seat."[21] "My Ace of Spades" was read in remembrance of Malcolm X, whom Joans called "one of the greatest black men that ever walked the face of the earth," to bursts of applause from the audience.[22] His finale was "The Nice Colored Man" (the poem that also ends *Black Pow-Wow*), "my most detonating handgrenade poem," as he said, that "was birth[ed] by my memories of all the ways I had heard White people use" that most disgusting of racial epithets.[23] "When I recited the last hip lines of that long rhythmical poem," Joans said, "the Canadian Black audience exploded with loud screams and applause an emotional jubilant approval of what that poem demystified and advised. The few whites amongst the joyful Blacks were either red faced embarrassed or snow white in fear."[24]

As attested by the page from his FBI file shown in Figure 35.3, Joans's connections to Black nationalist and other radical thinkers and political figures in the late 1960s and early 1970s were "militant" enough to warrant the US government's interest in his whereabouts and activities. He was hardly alone in his position as a Black writer who drew the attention of J. Edgar Hoover's FBI, and the various reports and memoranda in his file show concern that he was known to have "attended Black Power meetings," and that he wrote poetry on Black nationalist themes.[25] From around 1968 to 1972, agents at field offices around the country monitored his entry into and movement around the States, even going so far to

UNITED STATES DEPARTMENT OF JUSTICE

FEDERAL BUREAU OF INVESTIGATION

New York, New York
December 17, 1968

*In Reply, Please Refer to
File No.* NYfile 157-2950

Theodore Jones Also
Known As Ted Joans

A confidential source, who has furnished reliable
information in the past, advised on October 2, 1968, that an
individual by the name of Ted Joans described as Negro male,
age 36 - 38, approximately 5 feet 11 inches, who wears his
black hair in Afro style and has full beard, supposedly re-
turned to the United States from North Africa.

According to this source, Joans was in Philadelphia,
Pennsylvania, recently (August, 1968) to attend a Black Power
conference. At this conference, Joans was heard to remark
about recently having been in contact or a meeting with some
"other revolutionaries in Europe".

The source was not aware of the particular identity
of the "other revolutionaries" referred to by Joans or the time
and/or place of the meeting. The source believes that from the
general conversation Joans attended this meeting during the
early part of 1968.

The source surmised that Joans is a poet or writer
and that he had recently wrote a poem for a fund-raising activity
held by the Black Panther Party (BPP) during September, 1968
at the Renaissance Ballroom at New York City.

A characterization of the BPP
is attached.

"The Guardian" newspaper dated August 31, 1968, page
18, under the Music Section contained an article captioned "Jazz
at Randall's Island" dealing with the "Randall's Island Jazz
Festival in New York City" consisting of all Negro entertainment.

This document contains neither recommendations
nor conclusions of the FBI. It is the property
of the FBI and is loaned to your agency; it and
its contents are not to be distributed outside
your agency.

ENCLOSURE

157-10590-8

NW 5415   DocId:59161167   Page 42

FIGURE 35.3 *Excerpt from FBI memorandum pertaining to the surveillance of Ted
Joans in connection to his "Black revolutionary" activities. This report notes that he
attended the 3rd National Black Power Conference in Philadelphia and the Congress
of Black Writers in Montreal, and that he had "been in contact or a meeting with
some 'other revolutionaries in Europe.'" FBI; memorandum dated December 17,
1968. Fittingly, in "Outer Space," Joans describes how the scandal of white people
being "turned black" was "keeping the FBI and the government agencies busy" (21).*

interview his mother, Zella, in Fort Wayne, Indiana, reporting that Joans "told Mrs. McKinley [his mother] he liked living in Africa very much and never planned to come back to the United States to live."[26] The FBI took note of his attendance at the Philadelphia and Montreal conferences, that he had published provocative books such as *Black Pow-Wow* and *Afrodisia*, and summarized what they considered to be the most important part of an article Joans had written on a jazz festival in New York. In this summary, the FBI agent writes: "[Joans's] article indicated that the festival, located across the river from Harlem, had more black people than white in the audience and there weren't very many white policemen at the scene and there was no trouble."[27] The FBI even followed up on a report that a fugitive Eldridge Cleaver had been spotted in Marrakesh, but that the person had turned out to be Joans.[28]

These excerpts from Joans's FBI file give a glimpse of how charged it was for him to be so visibly involved in Black Power activities—which the Bureau characterized as "Extremist Matters"—and to publish a book like *Black Pow-Wow*. As Joans put that book together, he was thinking about many of the people in attendance at (or noticeably absent from) these various events in which he participated. Writing about the Philadelphia conference, for example, he zeroed-in on the work of LeRoi Jones, his "old buddy of Beat Generation days," who was for Joans an example of "living poetry," a "powerful African seer" whose creative works were "actually revolutionary teaching."[29] Given his stature, Jones's absence in Montreal was glaring. Earlier in 1968, in January, he had been sentenced to a prison term for illegal possession of firearms in connection to the so-called Newark race riots the previous July, and Joans speculated that he himself had been invited to Montreal as a kind of consolation because LeRoi Jones could not leave the States—a "neonazi racist obstacle," as Joans put it.[30] *Time* magazine took special delight in reporting Jones's sentence, calling him "the snarling laureate of Negro revolt," and emphasizing that his court appearance was sullied by his shouting: "You are not a righteous judge!" to the one presiding, Leon Kapp.[31]

Joans immediately wrote a rejoinder to *Time* protesting what he took to be their biased coverage, defending Jones as a "great black poet," and arguing that "instead of giving black revolutionaries prison sentences, America should be giving them awards and help ... LeRoi Jones must be free if America is a democracy."[32] *Time* declined to publish the letter, but undeterred, Joans reworked an earlier poem to speak to Jones's situation, calling it "Its Curtains," later included in *Black Pow-Wow*. The title is taken from the *Time* piece, "Curtains for LeRoi," the implication being that the prison sentence would not only subdue "snarling" Jones but also stem the rising tide of Black Power. Joans's response is darkly ominous, suggesting as it does that it could *never* be curtains for Jones or for Black Power:

All god's SPADES wear dark shades
   and some of god's SPADES
   ...
   carry l   o   n   g sharp
   protective blades[33]

In his unpublished letter to *Time*, Joans declared that "'Curtains for LeRoi'
is what many white Americans and some brainwashed black Americans
would like to believe was the 'final curtain for LeRoi.' But you know that
cannot be; for every un-brainwashed black man that dreams and carries
those dreams out into a reality, is a LeRoi Jones." In the poem "Its Curtains,"
Joans takes this same covertly-Surrealist sentiment and expresses it more
poetically, so the guns at issue in Jones's court case are transformed to
the long sharp blades that all Black people *might* carry, either literally or
metaphorically, the idea being that the spirit of resistance and revolution
can never be extinguished.[34] "Its Curtains" is thus a good example of how
the poetry in *Black Pow-Wow* could be directly "political," insofar as it
intervenes in or comments on highly charged current events.

   The specter of violence undergirding "Its Curtains" runs through many
poems in *Black Pow-Wow*, which interrogate the nature of white physical
and ideological violence. In "Lets Get Violent!," for example, Joans plays
on the popular (white) association of Black Power with physical violence to
attack a deeper sort of mental or ideological violence:

LETS GET VIOLENT!   AND ATTACK THE WHITEWASH
   ICING CAKED

ON OUR BLACK MINDS

LETS GET VIOLENT   THAT WE LEAVE that white way
   of thinking

IN THE TOILET   BENEATH OUR   BLACK BEHINDS   LETS
GET VIOLENT![35]

By late 1969, for poems like this, Joans had enough of a reputation for
militancy that he could tell *The Guardian*, "They say I'm too violent ...
I have poems that sound like a Louis Armstrong trumpet solo, but I also
have poems that sound like Albert Ayler catching you in a telephone booth.
It's as if I threw a lion in there with you. They want to pull the teeth out
of the lion."[36] But his version of getting "VIOLENT" is a kind of aesthetic
shock, and so what's urged in "Lets Get Violent!" isn't necessarily physical,
but a deliberate mental break from "that white way of thinking." By titling
the poem with the exclamatory—inflammatory—"Lets Get Violent!" Joans
teases an endorsement of physical violence, but then swerves to underscore

the imperative to cast off white knowledge regimes, which are to him—and to those in the wider Black Arts/Black Power movements—inherently violent. That said, it's also true that as "Its Curtains" implies, there were times when he wouldn't shy away from proposing physical violence to meet physical violence; he wrote in *A Black Manifesto*, "The black resistance movement must escalate beyond mere bottles and bricks. Guns! ... There will be no more lynchings / when we all got guns to cut the lynch mob down."[37]

Black Pow-Wow is dedicated to "Langston Hughes and allyall," and there are accordingly poems about Hughes, including the wonderful "Passed on Blues: Homage to a Poet" and "Promised Land." But naturally Joans extends the Teducation to poems about or dedicated to other figures. There is "Duke's Advice," in which the speaker recalls composer Billy Strayhorn's tune "Take the 'A' Train" that became one of Duke Ellington's signatures. The A Train is the one that runs to Harlem, and Joans's speaker has taken "Duke's Advice" and gone there, where he is warmed to be "surrounded by my tribe again" (35). "My Bag" is dedicated to Joans's friend, the jazz pianist and poet Cecil Taylor (48). As mentioned above, "Git It!" is dedicated to Walter Rodney, whom as we know Joans met in Montreal. Rodney's subsequent book, *How Europe Underdeveloped Africa* (1972), would become a classic of postcolonial critique—Joans thought it mandatory reading for "all young and youthful-thinking surrealists" (and for his political activism, Rodney was assassinated in Georgetown, Guyana, in 1980).[38] "S.C. Threw S.C. into the Railroad Yard" is dedicated to Stokely Carmichael, and depicts Carmichael throwing away his St. Christopher's medal (the second "S.C." in the poem's title) so that he "is no longer under the spell of false god/A white man's medal-god ... He has a gri-gri of his own" (81).

Carmichael liked this last poem so much that he and his wife Miriam Makeba wrote Joans "a fan letter from your two best admirers."[39] They found "S.C. Threw S.C. into the Railroad Yard" "very beautiful"—but more important to them was the fact that in *Black Pow-Wow* as a whole, Joans was speaking directly to (and educating) Black people:

> We were inspired because in your book you teach. For example the poem in which you speak about the Blackman not beating up his woman. Your poem to younger Poets encouraging them to seek higher levels. Your tribute to jazz, the poem to Your Mom, as we said the entire book is very beautiful. We have all-ready [*sic*] read it several times and have passed it around [in Conakry, Guinea].

Carmichael and Makeba's letter implies another way to see the value of Black literature at this time. While anything approaching didacticism was generally frowned upon by academic poets, literary critics, and other gatekeepers and tastemakers, *Black Pow-Wow*'s capacity to "teach" was precisely what seemed so powerful and uplifting to Carmichael and Makeba, who were measuring aesthetic worth by a totally different yardstick.

Perhaps due to its teacherly dimensions, *Black Pow-Wow* wasn't as widely reviewed as it should have been, although Kirkus did give it a positive notice, calling it Joans's "first big book for a major publisher," and "exciting and energetic ... definitely one of the most exhilarating collections to emerge in the last few years."[40] Echoing Carmichael and Makeba, Jamaican poet Mervyn Morris, writing in *Caribbean Quarterly*, argued that *Black Pow-Wow*'s "poems are undoubtedly *useful*: like good posters of a sound-address system, they amplify The Message (down for whites, up for blacks, we dig women and jazz)."[41] For many Black "revolutionary" readers at the time, this was the primary way *Black Pow-Wow* was received, as a poetic contribution to the struggle whose most important dimension was polemical. Morris even placed the collection as a whole in an aesthetic and political environment in which: "The author who claims to have any feeling for the underprivileged is invited to use his talents for social or political polemic, for 'revolutionary art.' In such a context the artist who chooses primarily to explore the personal consciousness is seen as self-indulgent, as irrelevant or worse; unless that journey into the self produces material which will also serve propagandist purposes."[42]

Morris's observation here about what he calls the "orthodoxy" of Black Arts thinking—that the aesthetic *must* be political—again explains Carmichael and Makeba's appreciation of *Black Pow-Wow*. It also helps explain the reaction in *Freedomways*, the left-leaning journal of Black thought, which complained that its poetry "often trails off into surrealism"— for this reviewer, Surrealism wasn't immediately legible as being "useful" in a Black radical context, though for Joans it was always revolutionary.[43]

As we know from the ideas of Aimé Césaire and others, certainly Black Surrealist poetry does something revolutionary, insofar as it showcases an avowedly, unabashedly, Black "personal consciousness" that is never solely concerned with the self alone, but rather sees this self in relation to other Black people. In this way, *Black Pow-Wow* is really about exploring what it means to have a globally-minded Black Consciousness in the tumultuous 1960s. Thus Joans is writing for other Black people, as in the poem "Pow-Wow":

Listen to me colored brothers
Hear me shout our song
we all are well aware
of how long we all been done wrong
We all know
white has to go

out of our lives
like long long time ago
  No more imperialism/paternalism/capitalism/ or forced
    communism for you!
Unity is our thing/to swing!!
Unity is what
we many colored
nations must do
to get our face
out of the white
butt And
start a life a new! THATS WHAT!!⁴⁴

This is the sort of poem that may seem to some readers too straightforward, too literal, too angry, and too earnest an appeal to unity—as one contemporary critic wrote of *Black Pow-Wow*, "Joans screams of the Third World and of its revolution, which is not only on its way, he says, but is presently advancing its columns among 'us.' ... Joans could be a rather good poet if he could raise himself over that hurdle so many black writers ... seem forever stuck behind: Anger at a world too white."⁴⁵

But the earnest, in-your-face style of this poem is precisely the point, and the most crucial work it does comes not through irony or paradox or metaphor—or any of the other features of a "well-made poem," according to 1960s-era gatekeepers—but rather with communicating a simple, urgent truth that need not be adorned. In this way, the position of the poem resonates with Walter Rodney's remarks to his audience at the Black Congress in Montreal:

> I, as a black historian, am speaking to fellow blacks. That means that, as far as the white audience is concerned, here and in the world at large, they are perfectly entitled to listen but I am not engaged in the game that they set up by which they say to me, "You prove, black, that you're a man. Prove it to me by showing that you have civilization."⁴⁶

Like Rodney, Joans is speaking to his fellow Black people (though others may listen), and like Rodney, he is utterly uninterested in "proving" his literary merit or facility with what constitutes a "good" poem according to white norms. Instead, he rejects those norms outright with a poem like "Pow-Wow"—which seems unpoetic only when viewed from certain "literary" points of view.

"Pow-Wow," as a poem, also functions like the real-life gatherings of Black writers, artists and intellectuals that Joans attended in both North America and across Africa. If "Pow-Wow" declares "Unity is our thing/to swing!!," Joans also stressed "unity" as the fundamental justification for these gatherings. When writing, for example, about the first Pan African Cultural Festival in a dispatch titled "The Pan African Pow Wow," Joans framed it as "the big reassurement of African unity."[47] Echoing the language in the poem "Pow-Wow," in the essay Joans emphasized the fraternal feelings among Black Americans and Black Africans, noting that "Within a few days everybody was swinging in an African unity bag."

As he does in much of his work, in his account of the Pan African Cultural Festival in Algiers (held July 21 to August 21, 1969), Joans proposes a realignment of history: on July 20 the Americans had landed on the surface of the moon, an event celebrated as the zenith of Western technological achievement, and widely held as *the* contemporary instantiation of a white impulse for "exploration" (for better or worse, depending on your perspective). And yet for Joans and many other participants at the Pan African Cultural Festival, the reaction to this momentous, world-historical event was indifference, as attention was trained instead on Black concerns and Black achievement: "From July 21st to August 21st the city of Algiers was the swingingest city in the entire world. Pan-African Power was the driving force. The American moon bit was hardly noticed. The Algerian newspapers headlined the festival and not the Moon Landing."[48] In Joans's telling, then, the Pan African Cultural Festival represented a radical realignment of what ought to be considered a world-historical event, and the moon landing is bumped from the front page in order to center Blackness, a realignment in keeping with his reorienting the world map to center Timbuktu. Another way to think about this: it's a real-life version of Joans's "dream" in "Outer Space," and again provides context for a poem like "Pow-Wow," which is interested only in celebrating Black unity, without apology or compromise. While the rest of the world seemed glued to their television sets, Joans toured Algiers with poet Don Lee (later Haki Madhubuti) and *Negro Digest/Black World* editor Hoyt Fuller, delighted to encounter people "very friendly to us because we were Black Americans and NOT imperialist Negro Americans."[49]

Poems in the "Pow-Wow" vein are not the only ones in *Black Pow-Wow*, however, and the longest in the collection, "Gri-Gris," while about Black African (and diasporic) spiritual and cultural belief, is Surrealist in execution, at once playful and extremely dense, offering another perspective on Black consciousness. As its title suggests, the poem is an exploration of "gri-gri," a catch-all term for West African—and Caribbean and Creole—charms and amulets with potent protective powers. Joans once referred to gri-gri as "like U.S. type of insurance policy."[50] In the poem "Gri-Gris," completed in Niamey, Niger in January 1967, Joans attempts a feel for gri-gri through evocative images, "gri-gri between the teeth of sharpness of surrealism / gri-gri the long erected prick of jazz."[51] By 1968, he was, he said, "infested with gris-gris, black magic amulets, black powers that I spiritually believe in. Black Power is an old traditional thing in Africa."[52] In private he assured friends "I still wear my grigri (juju) amulet. A Gogon hogon (priest) laid it on me more than ten years ago. I do believe in all the traditional religions of Africa."[53]

"Gri-Gris" is a poetic affirmation of such beliefs, a performance of Black magic via accretive assemblage, a roundabout illustration of gri-gri and its power that Joans sees as purposively and potently non-white and non-Western—a Black thing that defies efforts to categorize or define it. "Gri-Gris" opens in seemingly familiar territory, invoking the switchblade image from "Its Curtains": "I carried my switchblade from Harlem tribe through the dangerous dangers of Deutschland & Britain fog thick with uncouth thugs" (117), but then goes on to show how gri-gri is a more effective weapon than knives. "I tote gri-gri tonight in Yankee Doodle den being well protected" (117); "I wore gri-gri instead of fashionable clothing & hairbrushes" (118).

The poem quickly piles up Surrealist images, puns, and idiosyncratic allusions, depicting gri-gri as locked in perpetual struggle against whiteness: "It was gri-gri that caused the death of your destructive devilmen of tall Tuetonic [sic] temple torn ideologies by cyclone barefeet" (118). The flip side to which is that "Onto Gorée island they say that godamned slave marketeer threw my ancestor gri-gri away into a sharks pit [sic], placed my griot grand grand great daddy on sugar cane peanut and awful looking water diet for twenty seven days & twenty nine nights" (119). The suggestion here, that the "cyclone barefeet"—evoking a whirlwind of wandering connected to the Earth—can kill off Teutonic (white) "ideologies," is counterpointed by an originary scene of transatlantic chattel slavery on Gorée island, just off the coast of Dakar, the symbolic "point of no return" for enslaved Africans being trafficked to the New World (in 1962, the so-called House of Slaves on Gorée island had been converted into a museum and a memorial to the victims of the slave trade). Joans imagines his griot ancestor having his all-important "gri-gri" trashed by a "slave marketeer" just as he is about to endure the horrors of the Middle Passage. In this view, "gri-gri" is essential to Blackness, a "black magic" power that threatens and is threatened by whiteness, but that will ultimately endure: "gri-gri is the black power that continues man's greatest climax just after humping along a dusty trail looking for the winkled page of prose found now and then poets whores worldly called: a muse!" (121).

As a collaged assemblage of Joans's observations and opinions gathered from his travels around the globe, "Gri-Gris" also reads like a hinge into *Afrodisia*, the collection he published in 1970, a year after *Black Pow-Wow*. Subtitled "New Poems" in its first, American edition, *Afrodisia* showcases a poetics and point of view shaped by Joans's immersion in Africa, and his methodical study of Black aesthetics and thought, illustrating the growth of the poet's mind as it expanded through contact with Africa.

Afrodisia is divided into two parts, "Africa" and "Erotica," but a through-line connecting both halves is the idea of liberation—in the senses of personal, political and sexual liberation, things Joans saw as interconnected—and offers sketches of Africa as seen through his restless, radical sensibility. In this way, the work in *Afrodisia* can be read as poetic counterparts to the more practical descriptions found in "A Black Man's Guide to Africa," which he was working on at the same time he wrote many of the poems in this collection.

Afrodisia opens with "Africa," a poem Joans had read at the Black Congress in Montreal and dedicated then to "two warriors in Newark," Brother Abu Ansar and LeRoi Jones (this dedication is not included in *Afrodisia*): "Africa / I guard your memory / Africa you are in me / My future is your future / … Africa I live and study for thee."[54] "Africa" sets the tone for *Afrodisia* as a whole, insofar as Joans wants to emphasize the fusing together of his subjective experience of the world and a greater, collective Black experience that he awakened to after returning "back home again … with my tribe BLACK."[55] As one review of *Afrodisia* thought, "Ted Joans' poetry wins over by its genuineness, its cleverness, the clarity and directness of its meaning … Joans belongs to a Black community, and this sense of belonging is powerful and stimulating."[56]

Joans uses this basic technique of linking his personal experience to a wider Black experience in other poems in *Afrodisia*, such as "The Boat Ride," an exercise of historical imagination detailing the horrors of the Middle Passage: "You brought over in chains / like a stalk of bananas ME / in your ship's stuffed hole / the rough passage of ocean."[57] As in so many accounts of his poem-life, here archival truth is subordinate to poetic truth, as the speaker vividly imagines continuity among enslaved peoples of the past and the Blackness or Afrodisia of the poem's present-day speaker, who sees a perverse echo of slavery-era objectification and commodification in those who "mop your Wall Street / banks whilst our beautiful / black women display on / TV nightclub their hot / belly rub flashing flanks" (21). As discussed earlier, Joans learned such techniques from Aimé Césaire and works like *Notebook of a Return to the Native Land*, and a poem such as "The Boat Ride" enacts a similar kind of Surrealist linkage of the contemporary subjective "I" with a visceral sense of a collective past activated by the imagination.

Despite the raw power of poems like "The Boat Ride," it's important to note that these sorts of works, the hand grenade poems that tend to index Black experience in terms of white violence or oppression, are not the predominant kind of poetry found in *Afrodisia*. Instead, Joans wanted to fill the book with affirmative poems that celebrated Blackness and Black joy, and the varieties of African experience that he had encountered in his time there. A few years after *Afrodisia* was published, Joans explained that he had come to see contemporary Black poetry as too fixated on white supremacy: "some people spend so much time writing about Him, the Almighty White Villain, that they can't write about anything else."[58] He admitted that poets writing in this vein were making a "valid statement," and a poem like "The Boat Ride" certainly does attack the "Almighty White Villain," but even at the height of his engagement with Black Power, he worried that sticking to poems *only* of this type would be limiting the potential and expansive irreducibility of Black expression (this is why, in 1973, Joans contributed to an anthology of "Black Love Poems"; in the introduction, editor Lindsay Patterson speculated that love was "perhaps the most powerful and potent tool we possess").[59]

On his trip back to the States in 1968, Joans had listened to a lot of Black "revolutionary" poetry, and told a story about paging through a notebook of poems a young Black writer had asked him to read:

> All the poems were dedicated to white villains, to white racism and white villains. So, I asked him what did he read to his Mother or his lover, like when he's sitting on the front porch with his old lady. Doesn't he have any *love* poems? Doesn't he have any poems about bears, about potatoes, or poems about the sense of smell, the sense of taste, or hearing? You understand, many people let racism stop their raison d'etre. My raison d'etre is not racism. I attack racism; I avoid cold weather. They are both my enemies. But I'll tell you—every poem in my book is not dedicated to them.[60]

Refusing to let white villainy dictate the terms of his own work, Joans populated *Afrodisia* with celebratory poems about Africa: "Ouagadougou Ouagadougou," "Palm Tree," "Souk," "The African Ocean," "Still Traveling," among others. These poems are joyful and optimistic paeans to Africa or the connections Joans perceived among Black Americans and what he took to be particularly African forms of expression or experience. "OUAGADOUGOU," he writes, delighting in the ululating sound of the word itself, Burkina Faso's capital, "THELONIUS MONK SALUTES YOU / MUSICALLY FROM AFROAMERICA ... WHO SENT SURREALIST ME / TO EXPERIENCE YOU."[61] In "The African Ocean," Joans is "proud to reveal" the true name of "that slave name Atlantic [Ocean]": "AFRICAN OCEAN!"[62] Imagine Nommo, the power of the word, making something happen in the real world, in this case another Surreal adjustment to the world map—and Joans did actually pursue projects such as renaming Lake

Victoria, from what he called the "old antique imperialist whore's name (Victoria) to Lake Satchmo or Lake Louis Armstrong."[63]

Part 2 of *Afrodisia*, "Erotica," is filled with poems Joans might have read to his lovers, notably "Cuntinent," a poem that imagines in exquisite sensorial detail the geography of a woman's body. As Joans remarked of the punning title, "It is an invented name for a female body, and I often apply it to the continent of Africa. It is not a derogatory term, it is a passionate wide open likable (lickable?) journey onward across a deserving woman's awaiting body."[64] He associated the poem with one particular lover, an Algerian woman he had met in Adrar, whom he identified only as Jemmina. For Joans, Jemmina was a living extension of Arab-African history, as he claimed a distant ancestor of hers had "designed and later built in 1623 that great Islamic mosque in the Magreb style, Ali Bitchi[n]" in Algiers.[65] Aside from being tickled by the sound of the mosque's name to an English speaker's ear, Joans further associated Jemmina with the natural beauty of the Sahara, as he would wake before dawn to watch sunrises with her, "hipped to the natural panoramic show and it didnt cost one penny, plus the show was never obvious or boring. When I wrote Cuntinent I often had Jemmina in mind, for she was sorta like a Sahara. She was beautiful, colorful, brown, dark eyes, and mysterious in her silence."[66]

"Cuntinent" is one of the lengthiest poems in *Afrodisia*, and moves in loving detail across a female body that also seems a metonym for Africa itself: "My tongue and lips shall chart your cuntinent" (72). A corrective to Joans's notion that there was a general lack of Black poems exploring and celebrating the senses of smell, taste, touch, and hearing, "Cuntinent" is awash in erotic sensory experiences, and the reader is guided on a tour of how the speaker's body slowly, deliberately, connects to and communes with his lover's body:

> my tongue sliding around the insides of that vast cave of meat (72)

> my tongue maps the contours of your outer and inner ear republic (73)

> my lips rave up and across the vast sweet smelling valley of Tit
> a bit confused as to which peak of the twin tit to climb (74)

> I stop only to investigate some part that I perhaps left untouched
> crossing the vast desert of upper stomach I blow and hum (75)

> to the tropic vagina basin
> down there is where the most sought after prize in all the world lies
> down there is why humanity has continued it is place of birth (75)

As these lines illustrate, "Cuntinent" is an erotic poem describing the sexual connection between two people. But this intimate connection is also given heft by the way the lover's body resonates with or even represents the larger continent, so the speaker displaces the long history of white exploration of Africa to become a Black explorer of a Black body.[67] Although certainly one could fault this poem for objectifying a woman's body, breaking it down into its constituent, eroticized parts, for Joans it was a celebration of Black bodies, his version of the "Black is Beautiful" ethos of the era.

Joans felt that this message was important enough that "Cuntinent" was one of the rare poems he submitted for publication. On the recommendation of his friend Shel Silverstein, a longtime cartoonist there, Joans sent "Cuntinent" to *Playboy*. An editor at *Playboy* was apparently enthused enough that he even began talking about making a poster of the poem, but—for reasons unknown to me—it never wound up being published there at all, let alone in poster form.[68]

Joans saw "Cuntinent" as doing liberatory work in the Surrealist vein, noting, "Like any surrealist worth his testicle's seven unwrinkled folds on his unshaven scrotum, I share a fixation on the erotic."[69] He elaborated on the connection between Surrealism and eroticism in the headnote to the "Erotica" section of *Afrodisia*:

> "The only cause worth serving is the emancipation of mankind," said the poet André Breton. I feel that Black people in these United States must have a total revolution to liberate themselves, not only from well-known daily oppressions, but *self-inflicted oppressions* such as acute puritanism bordering on hysteria. Sex and sensuality is a natural fact of most Black people, and only those who are hung-up on borrowed "anti-erotic" attitudes are against the nitty gritty of telling it like it damn show is and showing where it's really at [...] These poems like jazz music and jazz dance come erotically into the Black Power bag. If you can dig it, then dig it, and if not ... ass yo' mammie! (69, unbracketed ellipses in original).

With the invocation of Breton, Joans enlists his erotic poems in the Surrealist cause of the "emancipation of mankind," then playing on the racialized sense of the word "emancipation" to connect "puritanism" and "'anti-erotic' attitudes" to whiteness and white supremacy, finally proposing sensuality as a "natural fact of most Black people," hence his invention of the punning term "Afrodisia."[70] However essentialist it may be to make blanket declarations about the sexual habits of "most Black people," at the time Joans really did feel that uninhibited sexuality could be a form of politicized self-expression, which is why he places his erotica poems in the "Black Power bag," and why he ends this headnote by routing it back to Langston Hughes via a reference to his collection *Ask Your Mama: 12 Moods for Jazz*, which had been published by Hill & Wang, *Afrodisia*'s publisher, back in 1961.

Even when he was engaging in identifiably "Black poetry," Joans never really turned away from Surrealism, nor stopped being essentially Surrealist in his creative point of view. If a poem like "Cuntinent" savors the senses as the speaker lingers over his lover's body, other poems in the collection such as "Sure Really," dedicated to Breton, remind readers of Joans's Surrealist bona fides and enact a playful derangement of the senses that performs those abstract liberatory politics announced above.

> I HAVE THE SHAPE OF COTTON TYPEWRITERS
> I HAD THE SMELL OF TIMBUKTU
> BUT LOST IT IN HAMMERFEST
> I HAVE EYES IN MY HEAD AND SHOES
> MY EYES ARE NOT CLOSED ON SUNDAYS
> THEY EVEN STAY OPEN WHEN I KISS!
> THE SHOE EYES ARE NOT BLUE YET THEY HAVE THE BLUES
> FROM WALKING UP AND DOWN SEEING THE WORLD
> ...
> MY TEETH ARE AT THE TOP AND BOTTOM OF THE WORLD
> SHARP AND CLEAN! READY TO RUIN
> A RAG DOLL OF DELICIOUS ROSES
> I HAVE TOLD YOU WHAT I GOT
> NOW LET ME   SEE   HEAR   FEEL   TOUCH   AND
>   TASTE   WHAT   YOU HAVE GOT ! ! ![71]

While, like "Cuntinent," this poem is ostensibly about the poet's senses, there is a totally different orientation or understanding of those senses, and the barrage of puns enact a kind of slippage of the real. "I HAVE EYES IN MY HEAD AND SHOES" plays on different senses of the words "eyes" and the plural "Is," and on the sense of a contraction of "I is": so what is the sense of "I" in this poem? A construct of linguistic play, a collage in poem-form that presents competing and unresolvable senses of a word— and of senses—not through the juxtaposition of images, but in the punning play of language, yielding a Surreal image of the real beyond what the senses of "SEE HEAR FEEL TOUCH AND / TASTE" can apprehend. As "Sure Really" might suggest, while the affordances of Black Arts and Black Power were certainly generative for Joans, it would be a mistake to think that he had ever abandoned Surrealism as a point of view, and he would in fact intensify his Surrealist commitments in the 1970s and beyond.

36

New Doors to Surrealism

The day André Breton died, September 28, 1966, Joans was in Brussels, and composed an elegy for him, "An Exquisite Encounter," which was finished that October in Amsterdam. The poem was subsequently published in the Dutch Surrealist journal *Brumes Blondes* in 1968. "Oh André," Joans writes, "you father of everything. / You who prepared me and the others / for anything, anywhere, anytime! / You the key that made us ready."[1] Joans praises his "father of surreality" for *living* poetry rather than merely writing it, something that Joans himself was always striving to do ("Poetry was your every gesture and thought ... You knew how to find the truth / without submitting to reality's sadass reasoning"). In this poem, Breton lives despite his corporal death, in no small part through Joans himself: "But André Breton was, and is, and shall always be / Because now André Breton is in me!" As this raw and heartfelt poem attests, while his Black Arts/Black Power poetry was most visible in the later 1960s and into the 1970s, still he celebrated his "February Father" Breton and the kind of Surrealism he so tirelessly theorized and promoted. And though it may seem that a door had closed with Breton's death, Joans insisted in this poem that "keys like you are never lost" and "now that you've unlocked the doors and left them ajar / We all shall row on." A complement to this poem, Joans had also created an object-poem in tribute to Breton titled *The White Hair Revolver is Still Loaded* (1967), which features an oil portrait of him, teeth, a toothbrush, hair, a sleeve cuff with "1713" written on it, and most prominently positioned, a key for all the doors Breton would unlock.[2]

Another door to Surrealism was in fact opened that same year, introducing new opportunities for connection and collaboration that would last until Joans's own passing nearly four decades later. In December 1965, Franklin and Penelope Rosemont, self-identified "revolutionist" poets and writers in their early twenties, traveled to Paris from their native Chicago with the intention of meeting the Paris Surrealist group.[3] As Franklin Rosemont recalled, "with almost a decade of radical activism behind us, and motivated by our thoroughgoing commitment to the surrealist project and our special passion for vernacular surrealism," he and Penelope arrived in Paris eager "to meet André Breton and the younger surrealists."[4] They were introduced to most members of this group at a New Year's Eve party, then later met André and Elisa Breton themselves at the café Promenade de Vénus, the longtime haunt where Breton and his fellow Surrealists had gathered and held court for decades. During the course of the Rosemonts' five-month stay in Paris, Joans, the elusive "surrealiste Afro-Américain," came back into town from his circuits through Africa, and someone urged them to seek him out if at all possible. Given their special interest in "vernacular surrealism," what Franklin Rosemont defined as "*true* poetry surfaced in odd corners of popular culture," the Rosemonts were excited to meet Joans, who had long located a kind of Black vernacular Surrealism in blues culture, an idea encapsulated by Joans's frequent mention of his grandfather's saying, "Well shut my mouth wide open."[5] They began asking around: where could Ted Joans be found?

"You'll meet him," a friend assured them. "You'll just run into him."[6]

Sure enough, less than 48 hours later, the Rosemonts ran into Joans by chance on the rue Ancienne-Comedie—just as Joans had run into Breton himself on rue Bonaparte some six years earlier—and they struck up a conversation about their mutual interests in Surrealism and the blues. A lifelong friendship was born.[7]

With Breton's blessing, in the spring of 1966, the Rosemonts went on to found the Chicago Surrealist Group, what Ron Sakolsky calls the "first indigenous collective expression of surrealism in the United States" and a "key factor in what amounted to a worldwide renewal of surrealist revolution."[8] The Chicago Surrealist Group blossomed quickly and became the core and nexus of organized Surrealist activity in the United States, so the Rosemonts and Joans would be mutually drawn to one another in the coming years. Joans admired Franklin's industry and point of view, and by 1971 was calling Penelope Rosemont and Jayne Cortez his two favorite "femmes fatale des poésie," insisting that Rosemont was "NUMBER ONE VOICE SURREAL NATURAL IN BABYLON."[9]

Beyond their interests in Surrealism, the Rosemonts also shared with Joans an earlier connection to the Beat Generation. Franklin Rosemont was born in Chicago in 1943 into an avowedly labor union family, and came to Surrealism via both this union sensibility, and the novels of Jack Kerouac, which inspired him to hitchhike around the States, landing for a time in North Beach, San Francisco, an epicenter of Beat activity in the late 1950s.[10] Penelope, born in 1942, recalled that when she met Franklin and others who would form the core of the Chicago Surrealist Group, "we found that we had all been the 'beatniks' of our high schools ... One Old Leftist at Roosevelt [University in Chicago] called us 'the Left Wing of the Beat Generation,' and in no time that's the way the whole Chicago Left identified us."[11] In other words, early contact with Beat sensibilities informed how they thought about and developed their own senses of Surrealism. Franklin Rosemont started *Surrealist Insurrection* (1968) and *Arsenal: Surrealist Subversion* in 1970, and would go on to edit an English-language edition of Breton's selected writings called *What is Surrealism?* (1978), an enormously influential volume for anglophone readers interested in the movement.

Joans's affinities with the Rosemonts illustrate the ways in which he still very much considered himself a Surrealist, and took pains to meet and collaborate with Surrealist groups, even as he was also developing a reputation as a Black Power poet—as Penelope Rosemont recalled, "Joans became a close friend, visiting the Chicago group almost yearly."[12] For Joans as for the Rosemonts, there was no fundamental conflict between the broad goals of Black Power and those of Surrealism: while they could differ in their methods, the ultimate aim of liberation was a key point of convergence. The Rosemonts' interest in "vernacular Surrealism" led them often to explore not only the blues but also other expressions of Black vernacular, a connection illustrated in both Paul Garon's influential *Blues and the Poetic Spirit*, mentioned in Part One, and in a special "supplement" to *Living Blues* magazine, "Surrealism and the Blues," that Franklin Rosemont edited in 1976. As the preface to the supplement announced: "Surrealism is the exaltation of freedom, revolt, imagination and love. The surrealists could hardly have failed to recognize aspects of their combat in blues (and in jazz), for freedom, revolt, imagination and love are the very hallmarks of all that is greatest in the great tradition of black music."[13]

This supplement was anchored by Rosemont's essay, "A Revolutionary Poetic Tradition," which framed the American blues tradition in a radical, Surrealist light (naturally the essay was illustrated with one of Joans's collages, repurposed from *The Hipsters*).[14] In the piece, Rosemont argued the following about the blues: "Most important, blues is *black*, the autonomous creation of the descendants of slaves stolen from Africa—men and women especially qualified to speak of human freedom"; "blues is a *popular* movement" (unlike the "general development of poetry"); "Blues is poetry intended not as reading matter but as *song*"; "Blues is essentially a *collective* creation, antithetical to the anemic individualism of false poets"; and that blues has a decidedly "*muscular* character": "Its direct, aggressive, energetic and *physical* presentation distinguishes blues from all other English poetry."[15] For these reasons, Rosemont saw the blues and blues musicians as perfect examples of vernacular Surrealism, and given this position, Joans's attraction to the Rosemonts and the Chicago Surrealist Group is clear, since he had long recognized resonances among Black musical traditions and Surrealism—just as he considered the latter a "weapon," so too did he write of jazz, "they created it for a damn good reason / as a weapon to battle our blues."[16]

In their decades-long correspondence, Joans would report on Surrealist happenings around the world—particularly in the Third World—while the Rosemonts would keep him updated on what was going on back in the States. Joans would forever insist on the continuity among Black music and Surrealism, telling Franklin Rosemont that Charlie Parker "flew across the planet disguised in a nickname 'BIRD,' the truth is, that that there guy wasn't really but he be surreally, the one and the same (only change of time and name) of great fame: M A L D O R O R !!"[17] Claiming Parker as "one and the same" as Lautréamont's great antihero and favored ancestor of the Surrealists, Joans not only blurs historical distinctions among fiction and fact (one of his favorite things to do) but also emphasizes the shared attitude and eccentric posture of those otherwise disparate figures.

By such lights we can see again how Joans's Black Power period was not so much a break from or abandonment of Surrealism, but a practical application of Surrealism's primary goals by different means. As he once explained to Franklin Rosemont:

> Breton knew I wrote "hand grenade" poems for aiding the African struggle. He knew that I had to throw these toss-iable poems into the guilty laps of USA. That is why Shuster [Jean Schuster] and the entire Promenade de Vénus group showed up at the Mutualité Hall in 1968 to dig me reading "non-surrealist" poetry alongside Aimé Césaire. They dug what I was doing, and what I wouldnt do: join the Black Panthers Party (no way!), although reading Black hand grenade poems to aid their cause which was to raise money for lawyer fees for wellknown Huey Newton and at that time lesser-known Eldridge Cleaver.[18]

Joans frames his "hand grenade" poems in that broader Surrealist light: implying that Breton approved of his "non-surrealist" poems because they were *doing* something material in the struggle for liberation (helping to raise money for Newton and Cleaver), he nonetheless insists that despite his reputation as author of books like *Black Pow-Wow*, *Afrodisia*, and *Black Manifesto in Jazz Poetry and Prose*, he would refuse to officially join a political organization such as the Black Panthers, instead reasserting his fundamental commitment to Surrealist liberation that could not be codified in this way.

And other doors continued to open. In late 1967, for instance, Joans met Joyce Mansour, commemorating the occasion with a frottage-collage piece titled "the birth of a friendship."[19] He had admired Mansour as one of the finest living Surrealist poets, and once their connection was birthed, they remained friends and sometime-collaborators until her death in 1986. Joans called Mansour his "surrealist soul-sister," and lavished on her what was some of his highest praise, that beyond even her written work, she was "the poetess who lives her poems," the true goal of a Surrealist.[20] Born in England the same month and year as Joans, Mansour was raised in a Jewish Syrian family in Egypt, living her young adult life amid Cairo's cosmopolitan high society. She was twenty-five when her first book of poetry, *Cris* (1953), was published, and her work caught the attention of André Breton, who wrote her an admiring letter the following year. In the aftermath of the 1952 Egyptian Revolution, Mansour was forced to flee Egypt for France, where she was welcomed into the Surrealist group in Paris, where she participated in the infamous 1959 Exposition InteRnatiOnale du Surréalisme, or EROS exhibition, and where she would eventually meet Joans.[21]

Beyond their erotically charged Surrealist points of view, the arc of Mansour's and Joans's careers share certain similarities insofar as both were committed to collaboration in various forms, and both chose to publish their poetry in scattered small editions. Although a native English speaker, Mansour wrote almost all her work in French, and this fact, combined with the challenge of finding her original books, mean that her reputation in the anglophone world is not what it ought to be.[22] In 1991, the omnibus *Prose & Poésie* gathered Mansour's hard-to-find work, announcing that it contained her "Œuvre Complète" and listing her collaborations with visual artists, some of whom were also among Joans's favorites: Hans Bellmer, Wifredo Lam, Jorge Camacho, and Roberto Matta.[23] But what *Prose & Poésie: Œuvre Complète* does not acknowledge is that in 1978, Mansour published a joint book of poetry with another poet and visual artist, Ted Joans.[24]

Titled after the name Joans had given to Elisa Breton's nippy pet parrot, *Flying Piranha* (1978) was published a little over ten years after he and Mansour met, by fellow poet Jayne Cortez, through her Bola Press. Cortez had established Bola specifically as a counter to mainstream publishers, when "Mainstream is a metaphor for whitestream, a stream set up with standards to exclude all other streams."[25] Cortez felt there was a "real need to develop a publishing industry and distribution network which would include the cultural experiences and language of all the people in the United States." Given their rather fugitive publishing histories, Joans and Mansour were perfect writers for Bola to showcase, with the point being to showcase them *together* (and Joans would also go on to publish a joint poetry book with Cortez herself, *Merveilleux Coup de Foudre* [1982], which I'll discuss later). *Flying Piranha* features poems in English by Joans and Mansour and is illustrated throughout with Joans's collages. The cover image is by their mutual friend Heriberto Cogollo (see Figure 36.1).

Flying Piranha is divided into two sections of poetry by Mansour and Joans, each beginning with a biographical statement that insists on the parallels between them: "Joyce Mansour was born African, but not in Africa, and yet it was 1928, and she was brought up in Cairo Egypt"; "Ted Joans was born African, but not in Africa, and yet in Cairo, and the year was 1928 in Illinois."[26] Worldly, uprooted yet rooted in an essential connection

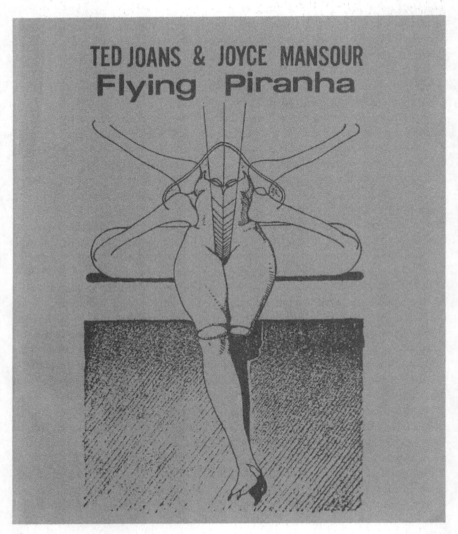

FIGURE 36.1 *Cover of* Flying Piranha *(1978), a dual poetry collection by Ted Joans and Joyce Mansour, illustrated throughout with Joans's collages. Cover image by Heriberto Cogollo.*

to Africa—this is how Mansour and Joans framed themselves and their poetry in *Flying Piranha*.

The parallels are underscored again as each section of the book opens with the same epigraph:

"The Black Sphinx Of Objective Humor can not fail to meet on the dusty road, the road of future, the White Sphinx of Objective Chance, and all ulterior human creations will be the fruit of their embrace."
André Breton
Anthologie de l'Humour Noir/1940[27]

Breton's use of "objective humor" was born, he writes, from a reading of Hegel's use of the term in connection to Romantic art, an idea which Slavoj Žižek has more recently explained as "a humor which, by way of focusing on significant symptomal details, brings out the immanent inconsistencies/ antagonisms of the existing order."[28] Identifying inherent contradictions in "the existing order" was of course one of Joans's specialties, so it isn't surprising that he and Mansour should identify the "Black Sphinx Of Objective Humor" as an animating figure of *Flying Piranha*. In the context of that book in particular, the Sphinx also indexes Mansour's Egyptian connections. Although she was born in Britain and exiled in France, Mansour was often described as Egyptian—writing about the EROS exhibition, for example, *l'Express* called her a "talentueuse poétesse égyptienne," or "talented Egyptian poet"—and Joans tended as well to associate her with Egypt: "She a dark slit of beauty," he writes in the poem "Promenade du Venus," "having escaped from a large sphinx's paws."[29] His poem "Elle Ma Dit," dedicated to Mansour, is further redolent with images of "that hour when children of / Cairo fly on kite strings" and "cool vibrations / the coloured pyramid's central stone."[30]

The Sphinx also of course routes us to Cairo, which Joans saw as "the great gateway to Africa." As he wrote in "A Black Man's Guide to Africa," "if you can start at Cairo you will be starting at the beginning of civilization ... Cairo is one of the most thrilling places in the world."[31] While physically removed from Cairo, Mansour was deeply interested in African art and thought, filling her home with various kinds of masks, fetish figures, and other objects, and making frequent use of ideas and images from Egyptian mythology in her poetry.[32] Joans picked up on this thread in his imaginative characterizations of her, as in "Promenade du Venus" and in a drawing he did the same year *Flying Piranha* appeared, which depicts a voluptuous Mansour in an ancient Egyptian headdress, arm covered in hieroglyphs, and bearing an ankh with the legend 1713.[33]

Mansour's work in *Flying Piranha* includes the lengthy "Anvil Flowers," which unwinds a series of disjunctive images, many of which approximate the strange experience of inhabiting a perennially-decaying body, as we all do (anvils turn up regularly as a motif in Joans's work—see, for example, the cover of *Our Thang* [Figure 49.2]).[34] Other poems include the sometimes-unsettling erotica that was one of her signatures. One such poem, "In the Darkness to the Left," Joans paired with a surgical textbook illustration of a womb operation, which he collaged with drawings of varieties of fish that seem to be either probing the woman's peeled-back flesh or floating in space, other kinds of flying piranha.

Joans's poetry in *Flying Piranha* is a mix of old and new, ranging from early 1950s work such as "Pygmy Stay Away from My Door" to new work such as the virtuoso "Unsurpassed U of Timbuktu," each line of which begins with U, delivering an onslaught of Surreal images that constellate around Timbuktu as both a personified U / "you" *and* the Teducating University of Timbuktu: "Urchin of everything sharp / Undaunted sister to Sahara ... Urban comb with bent teeth / Upset sworn lies of dishes / Urgency of future revolutions" (39).

One new poem worth singling out is "Common Place Bulues," dedicated to American poet and playwright Ntozake Shange. The poem is addressed to Shange, and playfully adopts and revises the Black Humor found in the blues, turning on inventive sexual innuendo:

I want to put something in your frigerator
I want to put something in your oven too
...
I want to play with your radio
I want to tickle your piano too
...
I want to screw in your light bulb
I want to turn my key in your lock. (40)

Joans was back in New York in fall 1978 when *Flying Piranha* was published, in part to promote the book, and he would perform this poem in particular at readings. Mansour remained in Paris at the time, but Joans reported to her that the "book is very handsome and has been received well here in Greenwich Village and Harlem. I go to the universities Yale and University of Connecticut tomorrow. I shall speak and read about Flying Piranha, and my favorite poet Joyce Mansour."[35] At the University of Connecticut the following day, he opened with selections from *Black Pow-Wow* and *Afrodisia*, but then turned to his new work, "Common Place Bulues," from *Flying Piranha* (available for purchase), noting again for the audience his and Mansour's mutual connection to distant Cairos.[36]

In introducing "Common Place Bulues" at the University of Connecticut, Joans praised Shange's recent poetic play, *for colored girls who have considered suicide / when the rainbow is enuf,* saying that he "loved" Shange, and explaining why his poem used the term "bulues" rather than "blues": "the reason it's not blues is that anybody that can find an electrical plug and stick it in is doing 'blues' now."[37] In other words, he was using "bulues"—with that errant U perhaps snuck over from "Unsurpassed U of Timbuktu"—to differentiate what he was doing from the tepid, whitewashed, commercialized "blues" he saw as increasingly pervasive. "Common Place Bulues" builds to a real blues climax, which is, naturally, infused with surreality:

> Then finally after heating your hallway
> Hot-hand-ling your porch and sweaty garden green
> I'll scrub your porchstairway of sponges
> > with erected umbrella
> Verifying for all times
> > that all unfunky furniture is
> Overtly OBSCENE![38]

In the context of *Flying Piranha*, it could be that in this line about "erected umbrella" we can hear an echo of Mansour's "Anvil Flowers," with its lines "sperm explodes as a lizard from its skin / As fire from a tiger / Or an oath from an umbrella" (8). And in playing with the erotic in this way—perhaps, again, Joans's "porchstairway of sponges / with erected umbrella" contains a ghostly imprint of Wolfgang Paalen's piece, *Nuage articulé* or *Articulated Cloud* (1937), an umbrella made of sponges—"Common Place Bulues" explicitly links the American blues tradition as Franklin Rosemont and Paul Garon framed it with a kind of Surrealist eroticism practiced by Mansour—or, rather, the poem shows how those links were already there, waiting to be recognized.

37

Spetrophilia and the Dutch Scene

Beyond Paris, one strong magnetic field for Joans in the 1960s and 1970s was Amsterdam, which was receptive to his unique blend of Black Power and Surrealism. In 1970, he had published excerpts from *A Black Manifesto*, translated into Dutch and titled *Mijn Zwarte Gedachten* or *My Black Thoughts*. A slim booklet of 36 pages published by a large house headquartered in Amsterdam, *Mijn Zwarte Gedachten* sold 780 copies that first year—certainly not a best-seller, but a respectable volume that suggests a general appetite for his work in the Netherlands.[1]

Joans's point man on the Amsterdam literary scene was Laurens Vancrevel, who with Her de Vries was editor of *Brumes Blondes*, the journal where Joans's tribute to Breton, "An Exquisite Encounter," had first appeared. Vancrevel was an important force in Dutch Surrealism, editing publications like *Brumes Blondes*, bringing together like-minded artists across national borders, and, with his wife Frida de Jong, amassing a world-class collection of Surrealist art. Joans had known Vancrevel since at least the late 1960s, when Vancrevel published Joans's *The Truth* in 37 languages, and by the 1970s, Vancrevel served as a kind of American Express office for Joans, as friends knew they could send mail to him care of Vancrevel, and it would eventually be forwarded on to Joans in whatever distant locale he was in that month, or else held for him to pick up on his return to Amsterdam; for these reasons, Joans called Vancrevel his "Dutch agent."[2]

In addition to the practical assistance Vancrevel and de Jong offered Joans (including the occasional check or a place to crash), they also represented, like the Rosemonts and Joyce Mansour, yet another door to Surrealism beyond Breton and the Paris group. One of Vancrevel's missions in life was in fact to champion the burgeoning Surrealist energies in his native Holland, which had often been eclipsed by those energies in France and other countries. He and de Vries had founded *Brumes Blondes* as an outlet for and demonstration of Dutch Surrealism. This is Vancrevel explaining the journal's origins:

The name was a quotation from the title of the unsigned article "Du pays des brumes blondes" in the Paris Surrealist Magazine *Bief* in 1960, which welcomed the creation of the Dutch group in 1959. The original intention behind the magazine was to give the contacts we had made with Surrealists in France, Belgium and Denmark, who regularly sent us their publications, an idea of Dutch activity. Over the years, this unpretentious little sheet, initially mimeographed, played an important role in strengthening our international contacts.[3]

"Contact" was a theme of *Brumes Blondes*, and of Joans's poem-life, so it seems another fitting operation of Objective Chance that Joans and Vancrevel should have met and become friends, with Vancrevel publishing Joans's elegy for Breton in *Brumes Blondes*. Vancrevel supported Joans and his work throughout his life, complaining on his behalf, for instance, about Joans's absence in the "Surrealist Movement in the US" section of Lawrence Ferlinghetti's *City Lights Anthology* (1974)—"Not dogmatic enough?" he wondered to Joans (referring to Joans's work).[4] Vancrevel also wrote a Foreword to Joans's collection of poetry and collage, *Spetrophilia*.

That short book was published by De Engelbewaarder Literary Café in Amsterdam, an important place for Joans at the time. Founded in 1971 by publisher Bas Lubberhuizen, De Engelbewaarder or The Guardian Angels, was (and is) meant to be a space where art, jazz, and literary readings can come together. De Engelbewaarder also printed another seven-page stapled pamphlet of Joans's work, "Black Flower Poems," which he would read to the music of Ornette Coleman, Bessie Smith, Eric Dolphy, Art Blakey, Charlie Parker and John Coltrane, and then sell copies to audience members, thus linking once more jazz and his Surrealist point of view.[5]

He made this link again after he had heard free jazz musician Idris Ackamoor, a protégé of Cecil Taylor, playing at De Engelbewaarder in 1972. Ackamoor was then working on what would be *King of Kings* (1974), a self-produced—i.e., non-commercial—album with his group The Pyramids. Connections to Egypt were reared once more, and Joans was impressed by what he heard, that the group "caused all that were fortunate to be there to swing in our OWN FREE WAY," and he agreed to write liner notes for the album. Titled "Real Free," Joans's contribution is really a declaration and endorsement of The Pyramids specifically and free jazz more broadly, associating it with the Surrealist spirit of liberation, circling back to that favored phrase of his grandfather:

"WELL SHUT MY MOUTH WIDE OPEN!" is an old surrealist term of expression that Afro-Americans created when they were emancipated, due to the fact that emancipation wasn't a reality, but a much dreamed of condition that they hoped would become a reality ... Our Black musics are not yet free of the "hang-ups" that have kept them in commercial bondage for so long ... But now the reality of a "real free" music is a much dreamed of reality that is becoming a living reality due to a new spiritual group of round-earthy-sounds called The Pyramids.[6]

In the spring of 1973, after reading and performing in Amsterdam throughout the 1960s, Joans read at De Engelbewaarder during an evening of "Jazz and Poetry," and *Spetrophilia* was published on the occasion of that event. At only about 30 pages, *Spetrophilia* is very much in the boutique chapbook tradition, featuring Joans's collages alongside love poetry, including the lengthiest poem, the elegy for André Breton first published in *Brumes Blondes*. Naturally Breton haunts the book, and its title, *Spetrophilia*, is a dual reference to him and to certain kinds of traditional spiritual practices Joans had encountered on his travels around Africa, both of which are challenges to existing order in a stridently rational sense.

In the first use, spetrophilia (or its alternative spelling, spectrophilia) is a nod to the opening of *Nadja*: "Who am I? If this once I were to rely on a proverb, then perhaps everything would amount to knowing whom I 'haunt.'"[7] If Joans is whom he haunts, then *Spetrophilia* is a paean to those whom he had loved—aside from the poem to Breton and another to Elisa Breton, the balance of the poems in the book are addressed to various of his lovers: Anna, Olivia, Christine, Joan, Sofie, Petronia, meditations on the riddles of their relationships, the agonies and ecstasies of romantic love—and on those geographies they haunted together. In this way, Joans's own love life, which so often involved white women, is figured as itself a challenge to "existing order," as in "Mixed Marriages," which uses a collage-like juxtaposition of disjunctive images to elaborate the idea of interracial coupling: "Mixed Marriage / rhinoceros is the groom to kitchen sink / bottles made of straw fornicate with / open legs of letters on their wedding day / Mixed Marriages! / French fried potatoes fiancéed to / Senegalese pineapples was announced / in the Natural News by their parents."[8]

But there is another, perhaps more literal sense of spetrophilia that Joans also had in mind when he would define the word as meaning "the act of having sexual intercourse with spirits." Just as he often questioned the value of archives and other Western repositories of knowledge, he was also quick to point out that spetrophilia, an "all important word," was not to be found in English or French dictionaries—but that such an absence should hardly lead one to conclude spetrophilia is not "real":

In certain societies on the continent of Africa there are women and men who practice spectrophilia. It is also prevalent in cults of Caribbean and South America. The sensual spirits which I have had full sexual intercourses with, were sometimes of familiar imagery and at other times strange. At dawn hours most of the familiar imagery spirits are dangerous,

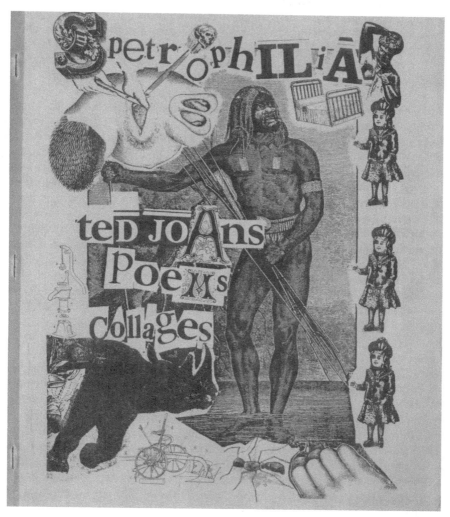

FIGURE 37.1 *Ted Joans's collaged cover of* Spetrophilia *(1973). Published by a literary café in Amsterdam, this work is rare and now difficult to find. Note the ghostly imprint of previous collage work in the use of the same girl on the right (see Figure 19.2).*

hostile or, at least, disagreeable, but they can be sexual useful to someone who knows how to conciliate or coerce them enough into bringing one to orgasm. To do this one must have the appropriate magical rites to seduce and control such spirits ... I can recall fucking-a-round with a Yoruba spirit: Aje. This female demon (or angel) spirit approached my bed in the familiar form of a whirlwind ... Aje <u>fucks</u> man, man does not fuck Aje— this spirit selects and is not selected. I was fortunate. Spectrophilia is done between wide awake and dream sleep. If you wake up or unfortunately experience coitus-interruptus during spectrophilia it can be fatal.[9]

The statements here are underwritten by Joans's recognition of some continuities among Surrealist ideas of "the real" and traditional African ideas of "the real." From a Western (white), rational or scientific perspective, a claim to have copulated with a spirit may be explained as, at best, poetic metaphor—or at worst naïve superstition, or even psychosis. But, as Joans insisted elsewhere, he was "beyond the walls of Western <u>ways</u> and means."[10] In this clinical, matter-of-fact telling, Joans seems to abjure metaphor, casting his encounter with the Yoruba spirit Aje as so real as to be a matter of potentially fatal consequence. And of course this reality is surreality, poised between states of consciousness, "done between wide awake and dream sleep."[11] This is the liminal state of the poems in *Spetrophilia*, as in "Straight Croissants," a poem to Elisa Breton: "a long silent telephone rings itself dry / a rose colored woman with voice of flan / rendezvous in red fabric of skin / Elisa again she the enchanter of Never-Grow-Old (but if so with grace)."[12]

———

By the time Joans published *Spetrophilia*, he was fond of declaring that he was no longer interested in writing hand grenade poems, but was instead turning his attention again and with full force to Surrealism. This is the case, for example, in what is still one of the more useful and wide-ranging interviews with him, conducted by Henry Louis "Skip" Gates, Jr., and published in 1975. Gates would go on to become one of the world's most renowned scholars of African American literature, publishing groundbreaking critical studies such as *The Signifying Monkey: A Theory of Afro-American Literary Criticism* (1988) and co-editing the canon-making *Norton Anthology of African American Literature* (1996).

But at the time, Gates was still in his early twenties, a recent Yale graduate who was trying to decide between law school and a literature PhD. He had worked for a time in a "desolate village" in Tanzania and then hitchhiked across equatorial Africa, only to wind up at the American Center in Paris, a hotbed of Black expatriate literary and artistic activity, where he met the likes of Beauford Delaney, the African American Modernist painter and friend of Joans's.[13] By 1973, Gates was spending the summer in England working for *Time* magazine's London Bureau. He had heard about Joans while still an undergraduate at Yale—probably, he recalled, via Amiri Baraka—and met Joans at a poetry reading in London that summer.[14] Joans and Gates got to know each other, with Joans sometimes crashing on Gates's floor when he was in London, and borrowing money here and there, when Gates could spare it. For his part, Joans introduced Gates to some of the Black intelligentsia in Europe, and it was through Joans that Gates was able to contact Eldridge and Kathleen Cleaver, who were then lying low on the Paris underground, a meeting which led in turn to another important interview.[15]

Gates's interview with Joans first appeared as the cover story in *Transition*, an African interest magazine then published out of Accra, Ghana, and edited by the Nigerian writer (and later Nobel Laureate) Wole Soyinka. The interview was clearly framed by Gates's interest in contemporary Black poetry—and by *Transition*'s general focus on Pan-Africanist issues—as he pressed Joans about "the state of black poetry today," asking him about "what subjects would you urge black poets to consider." Joans answered these questions patiently, but kept steering the conversation to Surrealism: "So, the surreal life I live, I don't advocate for everyone. I'm a living poem. It's a poem I'm living and I live it automatically. The French—or should I say, the internationalist—surrealists of the late 1920s used to *write* automatically. Well, I have gone beyond even that—I *live* automatically. So, the result is each day is a new page for me."[16]

Here again we find Joans insisting on a continuity among Black revolutionary postures and his Surrealist project of being "a living poem" insofar as both have the potential to fundamentally reorient the world and his position in it.

Consider, for example, how Franklin Rosemont explained a Surrealist notion of poetry:

> For surrealists, poetry is the *fundamental* experience, the root of all knowledge, the surest guide to action. It is not a "literary" experience, not at all a question of edification, confession or consolation, and it defies description in the reified terminology of traditional esthetics. For surrealism, poetry is rather an immeasurably intensified awareness that involves an electrifying perception, an all-encompassing sense of the wonder and magic of all things and the relationships between things. It is the revelation of the world of our deepest internal desires and their unceasing interplay with external reality.[17]

This is the sort perspective Joans had in mind when he explained to Gates that he is a "living poem"—he was referring to his poem-life, a materially different, deeper and more absolute sense of "poetry" than the overtly political, engagé Black Arts poetry that was the most visible kind of Black

FIGURE 37.2 *Ted Joans on the cover of the Ghanaian magazine* Transition *(1975),*
which includes a feature-length interview with Henry Louis Gates, Jr.

poetic expression in the latter 1960s and early 1970s. And a couple of years later, Joans told Elias Wilentz that "my new poems, which are all surrealist, and very few of my latest (I mean 'latest') poems are engagé, that is not to say there is not anymore racism, imperialism, and other anti-humanisms to stir me to write a poem against it."[18]

When Gates asked Joans if he felt "compelled to create political poems, given our particular situation in the United States," he replied:

> My poems are black poems and they say it. But I don't have to mention a white person to make them black. I do have a lot of poems that are blatant rhetoric—poems I wrote in 1967, soon after I met Stokely [Carmichael] here in Britain that year. They served their purpose, and that was all. They were hand-grenade poems: poems you pulled the pin out of, threw and BOOM that was it. But they are gone to glory. I don't live by their merits. These were not my stronger poems.[19]

This statement is not at all about turning away from "black poems," but from a particular kind of stridently political, anti-white poetry. Joans insists that his work is Black, not merely because of his own identity, but because of the sensibility and point of view that infuses this poetry. At the end of the interview, Joans once again steered Gates back to Surrealism, underscoring the idea that the aesthetic energies emanating from the Third World ought not to be understood exclusively in terms of a Black Arts/Black Power or Pan-African standpoint, but as a fulfillment of the promise of Surrealism: "Europe is one big cemetery—dead, dead, and dull, dull. People come here to collect old dates, like 1697 or 1423. Like André Breton said, if there is a continuation of surrealism, it would come out of the Third World, the dues payers."[20]

PART FOUR

Hip Ambassador to the World

38

Le Griot Surrealiste

While Surrealism remained his ever-constant point of view, Joans spent the 1970s positioning himself as by turns a knowing interpreter of Africa for Americans and Europeans (a position exemplified in works like *Afrodisia* and "A Black Man's Guide to Africa"), and, when on African soil, as the paradigmatic Black American poet, ideally situated to explain jazz and Black American history to African audiences. This was the decade when Joans emerged as a kind of itinerant teacher and—in certain circles, icon—known to many for the very fact of his constant circulation, his unrelenting movement between points in Africa, Europe, and North America, an embodiment of connections that transcend difference, of synergies among the varieties of Black experience around the world. If he had consummated a relationship with the Yoruba spirit Aje, who had taken the form of a whirlwind, Joans was a whirlwind himself, sweeping into cities, always just in from Elsewhere, a torrent of gri-gri, poetry, music, art, strong opinions about Blackness, colonialism, the ways of white folks, and of beauty, truth, and love.

In Paris Joans frequented the storied American Center for Students and Artists on Boulevard Raspail. By the early 1980s, the American Center had become "one of the leading institutions of cultural exchange" in the city, a place that Joans's old friend Jean-Jacques Lebel called "*the* experimental free space that had been lacking in Paris."[1] Introducing Joans for one of his appearances at the American Center, Art Kahn conjured the whirlwind version of the poet-artist-traveler:

> Life for Ted is a "happening." Since his annual pilgrimage takes him from Tangier to Timbuctoo with a swing across the European Continents [*sic*], he has acquired the title of "Hip Ambassador to the Western World" ...

Now when he travels he carries two bags with him. One under his arm, a canvas case marked in red "TOP SECRET U.S.A." and has his horn inside. The other is slung over his shoulder and usually flies out behind him as he strides about town. It can contain anything from an empty wine bottle which he is going to return (for the deposit) to valuable sketches.[2]

This is Joans as "le griot surrealiste," an enigmatic troubadour with bottomless magic bags, perennially circumambulating the globe. Those bags seldom contained extra cash, so still he was obliged to patch together enough to support himself through poetry readings, lectures, buying and selling art, and making his own—by the early 1980s, he had amassed a collection, as he put it, of "more than 400 pieces of ritual art [representing] major African ethnic groups."[3] Opportunities for money-making were scarce in Africa, virtually non-existent in Timbuktu, and so in summer months he would migrate up to Europe to replenish his bank account to the extent possible. As he told Gates, "I came to Africa not to live off Africa; I came to live in Africa. I came to contribute to its growth, not to take away from her—that's been done too much, for too long. Mine is to add. And as soon as I made money in Rome, or in Paris, I send it back to my bank in Africa."[4]

The flip side to this attitude was to extract as much as possible from Europe, as Europeans had for so long extracted people and resources from Africa: "you must do this to Europe; you must use it like you would have a hammer, or a pair of scissors, tractors or something like that. You must use it, other than that, there is no other reason."[5]

This commitment to contributing to, but not taking from, Africa went hand in hand with Joans's continued exploration of the vast continent's diversity. He loved to savor particular places, which would in turn make their way into his writing and artwork. In the spring of 1971, to take an especially literary example, he stopped in Harar, Ethiopia, where he was excited to locate the home French poet Arthur Rimbaud had lived in some ninety years prior. The young and restive Rimbaud, later a great hero to the Beats and other countercultural poets of the postwar period, had fled a complicated and suffocating environment in France to the remote walled city of Harar, like Timbuktu an intellectual, artistic, and religious center that had only been opened to outsiders in the mid-nineteenth century.[6] Joans was ecstatic: "At last I'm here in Harar! Ethiopia is great. Rimbaud lived here in this tiny mountainous town. I visited his pad it still stands."[7] To Franklin Rosemont, Joans explained that Rimbaud's house had become "a semi-tourist attraction now since a very hip American peacecorps cat was renting it" (today there is an Arthur Rimbaud Cultural Center in Harar), and that he stayed in the house "for eight poetic prolific terrific days."[8]

These experiences in Harar inspired "Cinque Maggio," a poem addressing Rimbaud directly, a meditation on the colonial implications of a white Frenchman traveling to Harar in the 1880s, just before the first

Italo–Ethiopian War would break out, a conflict which stemmed from Italy's (obviously disputed) claim to Ethiopia as a protectorate. Joans writes: "Rimbaud, were you a white man, instead of a poet at Harar? where dark women nursed sick strangers who were a long way from home?"[9] This poem wrestled with whether to understand Rimbaud's presence in Harar negatively, as of a piece with white European "exploration" of Africa, or generatively, as a like-minded poetic ancestor whose adopted home he was now inhabiting. Although in Harar Joans spoke to Rimbaud, another kind of spetrophilia, his "ghost never materialized, but poems were born."[10]

An acute though deep awareness of colonial histories and contemporary power imbalances of course informed Joans's poem-life in Africa, and he remained staunch in his commitment to and enthusiasm for "traditional"— Black—Africa. When he went to Nairobi in early 1971, he read at the opening of the Gallery Africa at the Kenya National Arts Gallery, an institution intended to showcase traditional art. During the opening festivities, Joans and Kenyan poet Albert Ojuka read "a chain of poems expressing the feeling that Kenya must not go on losing its traditional artistic heritage by selling its works of arts to foreigners" (see Figure 38.1).[11] In this way, Joans's interest in "traditional" African art and culture was itself an anti-colonial position, something that was not always visible to observers and critics at the time.

For example, that particular trip to Nairobi prompted a withering profile piece in Kenya's *Daily Nation* by Barbara Kimeneye, a mixed-race, British born journalist and children's book author who had been living in the capital for some twenty years. Apparently Kimeneye felt protective of her adopted home, derisively dubbing Joans "Soul Brother Ted," and noting that he had been "swanning around Africa, on and off, since 1961."[12] She goes on to explain that Joans had recently landed in East Africa in connection to "A Black Man's Guide to Africa":

> This book he describes as his own contribution towards the improvement of Africa's economy. "If I were a millionaire, I'd build bridges, or maybe a road to link every independent state so there would be freer exchange of commerce and ideas," he says. "As things are, I'm writing a book to encourage more dollar-bringing tourists." (A strange remark coming from a man who after inviting me to coffee, found he had no Kenya currency and wondered whether the management would accept a dollar. They did).[13]

Joans's statements here are in keeping with his desire to "contribute" to Africa, and the fantasy of building actual bridges and roads is a more literal, material version of his efforts to build a global imagined community through both constant travel and his writing and art. But Kimeneye remained doubtful about his "exuberant acceptance of the picturesque, the romantic, the mysterious in Africa [which] appears to blind him to the social

FIGURE 38.1 *Joans and Kenyan poet Albert Ojuka at the opening of Gallery Africa at the Kenya National Arts Gallery in Nairobi, February 1971.*

aspirations towards a better standard of living for everybody, bushman or city slicker, in developing countries."

In some sense, Kimeneye's skepticism seems fair enough, since Joans may have appeared to her an outsider purporting to explain Africa to other outsiders, or even one among a string of African Americans suddenly interested in communing with a weakly-imagined African past (hence the moniker "Soul Brother Ted"). But his commitment to Africa was as real and profound as his commitment to Surrealism, and whatever its limitations, his granular "Black Man's Guide" is hardly dilettantism, and had it seen publication, it may well have changed Kimeneye's somewhat glib dismissal.

In his capacity as Hip Ambassador to the World, Joans gave readings everywhere from Lagos to London and points in between—he often read to jazz accompaniment, and audiences were left in the thrall of his performative skills. Of a reading he did at London's Institute for Contemporary Arts in 1974, publisher Peter Hodgkiss breathlessly summarized, "the words <u>are</u> the music, the music is the words ... it was <u>JAZZ</u> all the way ... not poetry with a jazz background ... but the voice using jazz timing and inflections and really digging in with the instruments."[14] In 1979, at the First International Festival of Poets in Rome, it didn't even matter that Joans was reading in English rather than Italian, because the audience there connected with how he emoted and performed those words. "Ted Joans took that audience downtown," Rome's English-language paper reported, "all around and back again and, when he was finished, the audience called for more. What made the audience's response remarkable was that the man who calls himself 'The Jazz Poet' read only in his own language. No translations. Other poets had floundered on the translation barrier. Joans was able to fly over it."[15] Like Charlie Parker deep in a solo, Joans knew how to soar in front of audiences whatever their first language, and leveraged this to his advantage as he crisscrossed Africa and Europe delivering his truth.

39

Festac '77 to USIS

The largest cultural event in Africa in the 1970s was the Second World Black and African Festival of Arts and Culture in Lagos, more widely known as Festac '77. Of course Joans would not miss it. Because it seemed that anyone back in the States interested in Black culture was "demanding to be invited to Festac," it was not possible for Joans to be included as part of the American contingent. However, through his connections, some Black actors and poets in London—in particular the Bermudian actor Earl Cameron—Joans was able to attend Festac as a representative of Britain.[1] Festac '77 was *the* major international gathering of Black and African arts, and it attracted some 17,000 participants—and a half million spectators—over the course of its month-long programming. Among the aims of Festac were "to ensure the revival, resurgence, propagation and promotion of black and African culture and black and African cultural values and civilization," and "to present black and African culture in its highest and widest conception."[2] By all accounts, the festival was a rousing success, with a packed program of cultural productions—music, dance, sculpture, film, poetry, and more—from all over Africa and the Black world such that it would have been "physically impossible" as one attendee put it, "for a single person to have attended more than a small sampling of the events."[3]

Even amid all this excitement, Joans stood out—he was what another festival-goer, Theo Vincent, called "one of the most spectacular persons around, in Festac, particularly in the literature event."[4] Joans himself loved Festac for the opportunity to see performances from all over Africa: "I don't go to see my tribe [fellow Americans] very much. I go to see the other people. I'd rather spend the whole day listening to the Mozambicans, the Angolans and the different groups from Nigeria than see those from California, USA. Those I can see all the time."[5] He did, however, draw a connection between the dizzying scope and variety at Festac and his experiences as a Black American: because enslaved peoples had been so limited in their ability to create art and music as they wanted, Joans thought, they had to

"Africanize," and so Black American cultural expression bears the imprints of long-standing African practices and traditions—for those who know how to look. "We Africanized many things, the religion," Joans told Theo Vincent at Festac:

> Think of those people who sing about Jesus. We aren't talking about Jesus. We're talking about getting out of this: "Steal away, steal away to Jesus / Steal away, Steal away." You run away up to Canada, and that's it … And here at this Festac it is so great to see the groups on stage perhaps singing praises to Shango or something like that. But I can see, I can see my grandmother, maybe in those churches singing about Christ now. But I can see it wasn't Christ. She was just using those words; man, it was here.[6]

Here Joans is again describing the shock of recognition he had also depicted in *Afrodisia*, where he stressed the deep continuities among his personal experiences as a Black American, and a collective experience of African Blackness. One poem he read at Festac from *Afrodisia*, "The Reward," makes this connection explicit:

> Here, Africa take this gift of me
> I was born outside of you
> But you remained inside of me
> I was grown up outside of you, studied
> and learned outside of you too
> I did not know what made me so natural
> beautiful and strong
> Here Africa take me, forgive me for
> being away so long.[7]

As part of Festac itself, Joans performed several poems, including "The Nice Colored Man," which had been received so well at the Congress of Black Writers in Montreal. *The Lagos Daily Times* reported that Joans "stole the show," and that he was met with a reception more familiar to a rock star than a poet: "The thrilled audience beamed with pride and nodded and clapped with great applause as he read his poems. When he was leaving he was mobbed and not freed until he made a promise to read again."[8]

During the festival Joans also appeared with Randy Weston, an American-born jazz pianist who like Joans had eventually moved to Africa, even opening a jazz club in Tangier. Joans and Weston had known each other from back in New York in the 1950s, what Weston called the "Five Spot days in the Village."[9] Weston reconnected with Joans in the late 1960s, when the State Department had sponsored the Randy Weston Quintet on a tour of Africa, and Joans had met them at the Niamey airport, ready to show them the real sites of Niger. As Weston recalled: "He took us to places where we could get fantastic African food for something like 25 cents a bowl. I remember him taking us out to the desert to see the Tuareg people."[10] By that time Weston was celebrated for his groundbreaking album *Uhuru Afrika* (1960), which featured lyrics by Langston Hughes: "Uhuru!" the album opens over Nigerian percussionist Babatunde Olatunji's rhythmic drumming, "Freedom First! Afrika, where the great Congo flows / Afrika, where the whole jungle knows ... a young nation awaits."[11] Although it appeared in the early part of the 1960s, *Uhuru Afrika* was very much in keeping with the later Black Arts ethos, and with what Joans was doing in his Hughes-inspired poetry (at Festac, after reading his poem "The Black Repeater" to interviewer Theo Vincent, Vincent remarked, "That sounds like a train moving," and Joans corrected him: "That's a drum, brother").[12] Weston and Joans reconnected once again at Festac '77, where Weston refused to begin his set until Joans agreed to act as "Master of Ceremonies" for the performance, which they both conceived as a tribute to the late Langston Hughes.[13]

When he wasn't appearing at festivals, throughout the 1970s Joans often performed his work at libraries and cultural centers connected to the American State Department's United States Information Agency (USIA) and its wing, the United States Information Service (USIS). A diplomatic enterprise established in 1953, USIA's motto was "Telling America's Story to the World," and during the Cold War, it found great success with its programs that exported American culture in the form of music, literature, dance, and other arts, exerting a soft influence around the world that, as historian Nicholas Cull has put it, amounted to "a sustained long game of move and countermove against Moscow's propaganda machine, made for control of the contested spheres of Europe, Asia, and eventually the developing world."[14] As Penny Von Eschen further explains, soon after the establishment of the USIA, jazz in particular emerged as a "pet project of the State Department," both because it could be touted as an indigenous American art form, and because it seemed to show the Third World that America's domestic racial problems were overblown: "Government officials and supporters of the arts hoped to offset what they perceived as European and Soviet superiority in classical music and ballet, while at the same time shielding America's Achilles heel by demonstrating racial equality in action."[15] In the ensuing decades, the State Department sponsored numerous Black American jazz musicians on extended tours of Europe and Africa, including, in the 1950s, giants such as Dizzy Gillespie and Louis Armstrong—and, later, Randy Weston on that tour where he connected with Joans in Niger—with the idea of countering "Soviet superiority in classical music and ballet" and demonstrating "racial equality in action," but also of showcasing a musical form that was widely seen as exemplifying a uniquely American freedom of expression.

FIGURE 39.1 *Joans (r.) being congratulated by Alioune Sene, Senegalese Minister of Culture, on occasion of the inaugural African American History Week held at the Centre Culturel Américain in Dakar, February 1977, just after Festac '77 in Lagos. Cover of* Panorama *[Senegal] (February 25, 1977). In 1978, the Centre would publish a 12-page pamphlet of Joans's jazz poems,* Poète de Jazz.

Beyond these tours, one of the USIA's most successful projects was the Voice of America (VOA) radio broadcasts it beamed around the world, and for a long time the most popular hour on VOA was Willis Conover's *Music USA*, which focused on jazz, drawing from Conover's personal collection of some 40,000 records. While he tended to avoid overt propaganda on *Music USA*, Conover's general perspective was, as he said, that jazz was "structurally parallel to the American political system ... It's a musical reflection of the way things happen in America. We're not apt to recognize it over here, but people in other countries can feel this element of freedom. They love jazz because they love freedom."[16]

The US State Department's decades-long interest in the diplomatic potential of jazz and the circulation of Black American artists abroad is one context in which to see Joans's own circulation through Africa. If he was a Hip

Ambassador to the World, he was decidedly more nimble and independent in his travels than a figure like Gillespie, whose state funding allowed him to assemble a 22-piece band and develop a program illustrating "the history of jazz as well as the latest experimental music," to be performed in points as distant as Beirut and Dacca.[17] Joans was never officially sponsored by the State Department in this way, but he did find in USIS centers local cultural hubs in a variety of African cities that were interested in him as a jazz poet, artist, and representative of Black American culture. In the latter 1960s and 1970s, USIS-affiliated centers were increasingly established across Africa, and Joans was in turn attracted to these centers for the practical reasons that he could expect an honorarium and might perhaps sell a few books or paintings to attentive crowds, and for the deeper reason that he could through these places connect with ordinary Africans—by 1984, he said, he had "recited his poetry in more than 30 U.S.I.S. cultural centers on the African continent."[18]

On the one hand, it may seem somewhat surprising to imagine Joans appearing at USIS libraries given that his aversion to American racial and political ideology was vocal enough that the FBI had begun to track his movements. But on the other hand, beyond the obvious practical benefits to a person who was so often living hand-to-mouth, Joans saw his visits to USIS centers as opportunities to share a version of Black American art and poetry both unapologetic in its celebration of Africa, and uncompromising in its insistence on the liberation of Black people across the Third World. "We need self-criticism," Joans told Gates, "but we do not need to *academize* the cultural revolution. I'm a cultural guerilla. Check out just who is on the shelves in the USIS libraries in Africa. Sure Nikki Giovanni is there, but just try to find Sonia Sanchez. No way. Or Ted Joans."[19]

Joans had never forgiven the Black American poet Nikki Giovanni for performing in South Africa in 1974 and for refusing to sign on to boycotts in protest of Apartheid, calling her a "traitor to the cause that Malcolm X and Martin Luther King, Jr. died for."[20] For her part, Giovanni always insisted that she had merely transited through Johannesburg on the way to Swaziland, Lesotho and Botswana, but the popular perception in the Black artistic community at the time was broadly aligned with Joans's, as many people felt she had betrayed the principles of the Black Arts Movement by even traveling to South Africa at all—as Haki Madhubuti/Don Lee remarked to Joans after the incident, "As far as Nikki Giovanni is concerned, she never was serious about the liberation of black people. But she has always had a good rap and the ability to put it over."[21] This is why Joans saw Giovanni as a perversely perfect Black poet for African USIS libraries to feature, rather than Sonia Sanchez or he himself.[22]

In a sense, Joans saw his role as a "cultural guerilla" as involving infiltration of the USIS, even as he did tend to focus on performing his jazz poems rather than his more strident hand grenade poems or more esoteric

Surrealist poems, as evidenced by the pamphlets *Poète de Jazz*, published in 1978 by the Centre Culturel Américain in Dakar, a USIS center, and *A Few Poems*, published in 1981 by the USIS center in Lomé (and for his USIS readings, he would also sometimes soften his language, as for example when he replaced the phrase "the hipster will ball a bitch" with "the hipster will cook with a chick").[23] Joans's frequent appearances at USIS centers were also a likely source for the rumors that had begun to sprout up around Paris that he secretly worked for Interpol or the CIA, a strange piece of gossip to stick to him—when I mentioned this rumor once to Laura Corsiglia, she shuddered visibly and said "categorically that is untrue."[24]

A coda of sorts to Joans's connections to the USIS came in 1994, when he finally did travel to South Africa after the end of Apartheid. In February 1994—just two months before Nelson Mandela would be elected president of South Africa—Joans went to Johannesburg "under the auspices of the United States Information Service," as the local *Weekly Mail* put it, to give readings, lectures, and joint seminars with authors from the Congress of South African Writers, a leftist, anti-Apartheid group that had been formed in 1987.[25] Performing at USIS offices in Johannesburg, in theaters and on the streets, Joans felt that "to be in South Africa in this historical time is part of the dream become reality, everything that is, was once, imagined."[26] That same year in Cameroon, he also published, likely through the USIS office in Yaoundé, a fifteen-page stapled poetry pamphlet, *Poems for You: In & Out of Africa*, that carried as an epigraph a "Teducation Declaration": "Everything that IS was one day IMAGINED."[27] Given that Joans had also recently quoted this sentiment to a reporter in Johannesburg, we can see it as both a declaration of his Surrealist point of view, and a statement specific to the radically changing political landscape in South Africa, an acknowledgement of the hard-won liberation in a country long a symbol and exemplar of white supremacy.[28]

Beyond his brief appearances at USIS centers and other venues around Africa and Europe, occasionally Joans would pause for slightly longer stretches at various institutions to serve as a visiting fellow or poet-in-residence—and even visiting professor—usually in Europe or the States because they generally had more resources than their African counterparts. Even so, he always did his best to carve out a month a year to teach jazz and Black American history in Mali.[29]

In November 1973, he was invited to be the visiting Hadley Fellow in Black Music at Bennington College in Vermont.[30] It speaks volumes about the state of African American Studies at the time that the College's Literature division was utterly uninterested in inviting Black writers to campus. It was Bill Dixon, a celebrated free jazz trumpeter and composer who was then heading the Black Music division at Bennington, who fought to bring Joans in as a Hadley Fellow—and while he was in residence, apparently no faculty

FIGURE 39.2 *Cover of* A Few Poems, *a 10-page stapled pamphlet produced in Lomé, Togo in 1981, through a USIS center. Cover drawing by Alicia Fritchle; note, in addition to Joans in his skullcap, the cowrie and zigzag motif, repeated nine years later in* Old Cuntry *(Figure 31.1).*

from the Literature division even bothered to attend Joans's public talks, or express interest in his work.[31]

But still Joans was able to cobble together short appointments that gave him the chance to teach: after Bennington, he was invited to Howard University for three days with Sterling Brown and Léon Damas (who were then teaching there), as well as poet Haki Madhubuti/Don Lee.[32] As at Bennington, at the University of Connecticut, he was invited not by the literature department but the music department, where a friend, composer Hale Smith, had him out several times in the 1970s, lauding him as "one of the most important poets that 20th Century America has produced."[33] Smith arranged for Joans to receive $250 each time he came to read, lecture, and show slides of his experiences in Timbuktu and elsewhere in Africa.[34] In spring 1973, Joans was back in England serving as Poet-in-Residence at Dartington Hall College; and three years later, he was Poet-in-Residence again, this time at Loughborough University (fall 1976).[35] These sorts of positions were opportunities to Teducate, and make a little money, and are glimpses of recognition from the academy, although such recognition was far from widespread at the time.

In 1980, Joans alighted for the spring semester as a visiting professor and poet-in-residence at UC Berkeley, "an unusual adventure for me," he wrote, "because I never stay in one place long enough to mold the minds of others."[36] At the time, there was a lot of energy in Berkeley's relatively new African American Studies department, and Joans's visiting position was a result of "encouragement" by a trio of Black artistic and intellectual titans there: Ishmael Reed, David Henderson, and Barbara Christian, all of whom became decades-long friends and colleagues. Reed and Henderson were already-established writers affiliated with the Black Arts and Umbra movements, respectively. Reed's novel *Mumbo Jumbo* (1972) was a favorite of Joans's ("Many international surrealists detest the modern novel," he said. "I myself only read Amos Tutola, Ron Sukenick, Ishmael Reed, and William Burroughs").[37] *Mumbo Jumbo*, a difficult, provocative, hilarious satire of white, Western fears about and conceptions of Blackness, reimagines racialized power relations in ways broadly similar to what Joans does in "Outer Space." Reed in particular became an advocate for him and his work—and would in fact go on to publish Joans's poetry collection, *Okapi Passion* (1994), through his eponymous publishing company. In 2008, Reed, never one to dole out praise lightly, called Joans "the greatest jazz poet of the 20th century."[38]

But Joans recalled Barbara Christian as the organizing force behind his time as poet-in-residence. At Berkeley since 1971, she had been instrumental in founding the African American Studies department there, and went on to become an influential Black feminist literary critic (and, in 1978, the first Black woman tenured at Berkeley). According to Joans, Christian had long appreciated his work, and told him that on her first trip to Greenwich Village way back when, he had been "the very first poet that she had heard read his poems like a jazz musician blowing an instrument."[39] Joans had been familiar with Christian from her essay in *Black World*, "Whatever Happened to Bob Kaufman?" (1972), which had appeared immediately following his own essay in that issue, "The Langston Hughes I Knew." In her searching piece on Kaufman, Christian had placed Joans among the leading lights of the Beat Generation: "My students respond to the name of Allen Ginsberg, howling Jewish-incantation style, to the name of Ted Joans, bopping in Black rhythms, to the name of Jack Kerouac, forever on the road. But Bob Kaufman—who is he?"[40] Joans, a once and future champion of Kaufman's, shared Christian's sense that he was unjustly "forgotten," and was impressed that she was "the very first black person" to write on Kaufman.[41]

At Berkeley Joans taught African American Studies 159, "Jazz and Afro-American Poetry," for which he assigned *Black Pow-Wow* and *Afrodisia*.[42]

FIGURE 39.3 *Note and drawing by Joans to Lawrence Ferlinghetti, requesting a "letter of academic (Beat G university!) nature as recommendation for my ten week installment as jazz poet at Berkeley" (ca. 1980). Joans pictures himself in a Sherlockian deerstalker cap, standing on a legend celebrating his seven totem animals; flanking him are Charlie Parker (l.) and Jack Kerouac (r.), whom Joans calls "My Men of March 12"—Parker had died on Kerouac's birthday, March 12. On letterhead from Jim Haynes's Atelier A-2. From City Lights Books Records, Additions, Bancroft, box 31, folder 10.*

He taught the class twice a week and gave what the local paper called a "free hour-long jazz-poetry concert" at Wheeler Hall.[43] It was a rare opportunity, "the very first longtime position for me," as he said, and inaugurated a connection to Berkeley that would eventually open doors to the school's Bancroft Library purchasing Joans's papers in the late 1990s. But back in the early 1980s, Berkeley was but a temporary way station, and once the term of Teducation was complete, he was on the road again, circulating back through Europe and Africa, before settling in 1983–4 in West Berlin, thanks to an arts fellowship supported by the German state.

————

Perhaps paradoxically for a man so invested in forging links of connection around the world, Joans wasn't in these years particularly connected to the children he had left in his wake. Having officially divorced Grete back in 1969, he didn't see too much of Tor and Lars—or Russell, his son with Sheila Kerr—after that time, nor did he see his kids with Joan or Joyce from the time they were quite small. Terence Blacker, a friend who with his wife, Caroline, would host Joans at their London house in the 1970s, recalled that while Joans was always convivial and entertaining when he stayed at their place, when Caroline announced she was pregnant, Joans said they wouldn't be seeing him around much more.[44] After the birth of the child, Joans disappeared from Blacker's life, a piece of a pattern that suggested to Blacker that, as he once wrote, "In spite of managing to father 10 children, he had never been a family man."[45]

From at least as far back as the summer of 1966, the Domestic Relations Division in San Bernardino County, California was receiving requests from Joans's family there for assistance in locating his whereabouts.[46] Those requests met only dead ends as Joans was hardly easy to find, but a glimmer of hope came through his books themselves: when his daughter Daline was about fifteen or sixteen, she was amazed to discover a copy of *Black Pow-Wow* in the San Bernardino County Public Library, the one with a photograph of her father on the cover staring back at her. She immediately checked the book out (never to return it), found the publisher Hill & Wang's address in New York, and wrote them to see if they could put her in touch with her father.[47] She didn't hear anything back, but a few years later, in January 1976, Daline's younger sister Teresa, now eighteen and living in Rialto, California, wrote again to Hill & Wang, explaining that she was looking for her father and could they help her contact him—a query that, like these others, encapsulates the degree to which Joans was at best a dim presence in the lives of his children, however large he may have loomed in their imaginations.[48]

Unlike the earlier attempts, Teresa's was successful, and by that June, she did catch up with her father in Paris, the first contact that any of his

FIGURE 39.4 *Ted Joans and his five children with Joyce in 1977, after they had sought him out to re-establish contact. From left to right: Daline, Ted, Teresa, Ted Joans, Jeannemarie, and Robert. Though only partially visible, Joans is wearing a favorite shirt, bearing the motto: "Jazz is my religion."*

children with Joyce had had with him since the early 1960s, when he had left the States. He seemed pleasantly surprised, as he put it, that "One of my long lost daughters arrived here and found me."[49] After the reunion, Teresa wrote again to her father that November, bubbling with excitement about a big trip she was planning to "Afrika," enclosing a detailed packing list recommended by a friend and asking for his expert advice.

This letter took on another life when Joans included it as an "Epilogue" to his short poetry collection, *Sure, Really I Is* (1982). The letter was preceded by "No Kosher Kouskous," the final poem in the collection, a wistful reflection on Joans's far-flung children: "There are ten / They remain different / Each has fingerprints / Similar and just as unique / As their mirror image / The zebra."[50] A statement of fatherly admiration, though made from a distance, and filtered, as always, through his foundational point of view: "They are all mine / The only surreal ones / I've got." Less abstract was that hopeful letter from Teresa, reprinted in full, typos and all, implying a father-daughter reunion just over the horizon: "Can you tell me when you are leaving," Teresa writes, "so I can make plans to meet you somewhere in France or Afrika? ... Please write or call me collect ... Also can you send me a list of what I will need to bring and what shots I need to get? I will be looking forward to hearing from you."[51]

They never did meet up in Africa, but in 1985, Joans traveled to Southern California to visit Teresa, Daline, Jeannemarie, Ted, Jr., and Robert, and feature them in his short film, *Family or MomWow*. This film was one of his "Silent Poems" that I will discuss in more detail later, but for now it suffices to say that these Teducation Films were shot with a Super 8 camera and meant to be played to varying kinds of musical accompaniment. *Family or MomWow* is divided into two parts, the first capturing scenes of Joans in Southern California with the kids, and then in Fort Wayne with his mother Zella. The opening intercuts shots of various photographs of Joans and his mother with photographs of Joans with his own children (including the photograph in Figure 39.4), insisting on the connections and continuities among generations, even as they might be geographically distant. The film then presents quick references to Joans's pantheon of artistic greats, Romare Bearden, Jorge Camacho, and Wifredo Lam among them, and lingers over his drawing of the African continent that birthed the Joans family in the

FIGURE 39.5 *Cover of* Sure, Really I Is *(1982). This 40-page stapled booklet was published by TRANSFORMAcTION, "a review initiated in 1976 by Jacques Brunius, ELT Mesens, and John Lyle to provide a forum in Britain for the Surrealist Movement" (40).*

first place, organized not along any political lines, but into regions labeled with his totem animals. This is the background and texture of Joans's point of view, and following these shots, Joans presents scenes with his children in Southern California, posing with them at the beaches and in their homes, capturing fleeting spots of time that make up all our everyday lives: wiping down a kitchen counter, shopping for groceries, flashing a quick smile. In the context of the film, these seemingly small moments are elevated by the attention the camera lavishes, transforming them into instances of the marvelous, the inheritance of Ted Joans, who is in turn the inheritance of Zella, who is in turn the inheritance of Africa, and so on down the line—this is the same basic theme of his book "Deeper Are Allyall's Roots," discussed in the next chapter.

The final part of the film shows Joans visiting Zella in Fort Wayne just six months before she passed, at age 80 (Figure 39.6). There are tender moments of mother-son reunion, another linking of "family"—and then, inevitably, the film ends with Joans with his back to the camera, backpack strapped on, walking alone into the Greyhound bus terminal for his next adventure elsewhere. *Family or MomWow* does showcase Joans's love for his family, his children and his mother, even as he could be quite hard for them to locate in any sort of consistent way.

FIGURE 39.6 *Ted Joans and his mother, Zella, Fort Wayne, Indiana, May 1985, about six months before she died. Still from the Joans Teducation Film,* Family or MomWow *(1985).*

Joans's various girlfriends and lovers had a similarly difficult time pinning
him down. As may be inferred from that list of lovers in *Spetrophilia*—
Anna, Olivia, Christine, Joan, Sofie, Petronia—there was a new succession
of women in 1970s, some of whom stuck with him for longer periods,
while others were more fleeting connections, briefer flashes in the life of the
whirlwind forever on the road. After Joan Halifax, there was, to name one,
Heather Maisner, a young woman Joans had spotted in an airport lounge.
He had recognized her as a fellow writer, and strolled up to introduce
himself.[52] Indeed she was an aspiring writer, and Joans charmed her, as he
so often charmed women, and they wound up traveling together around
Europe and North Africa, only to part ways in Marrakesh. His explanation
was somewhat paradigmatic:

> I ted joans am NOT the right guy for long long periods with Heather
> or anybody else. I change too often and these changes are natural as
> well as necessary. I love you that I know and feel. I miss you and that I
> witness painfully just after you left. But I'm hip to the trip. I know ted
> joans and that is why you are very lucky to be separated from him at
> this time. IF I had the bread, I'd still be with you and doing fabulous
> sensual and adventurous things, but NO bread then NO consistent Ted,
> you dig?[53]

Just as Joans had insisted to Gates, as a public announcement, that he lived
"automatically," so that "the result is each day is a new page for me," in
his private relationships it was the same story, the same commitment to
"automism": "changes are natural as well as necessary."[54] His commitment
to "natural" change and liberation, movement and flow, was total, a key
ingredient in his poëm-life, but such commitment did in turn mean that
others had to accept that or move on, despite how close they may have felt
to him: as he had told Grete back in the mid-1960s, "This will be a life in
suitcases," and it was.[55]

In 1974, Joans was doing what he often did when in Paris, his privileged
European base of operation: lingering in a café, writing, drawing, holding
court with various friends and admirers. In that particular case it was the
Select Café, and in walked a new young woman with a group of friends. This
was Marion Kalter, an Austrian-born art student with an American passport
who was then (and now) based in France. Having recently completed
studies at Mount Holyoke College in Massachusetts, Kalter was still in her
early twenties when she met Joans, who was then in his mid-forties, and she
was drawn to the way "he knew how to speak and use words" and by his
charisma; they were together "off and on," she put it, throughout 1974 and
1975.[56]

Kalter was a photographer, and when she and Joans traveled together
around North Africa, she felt that he wanted to guide her, to instruct her

in the ways of what he called his "surreal 'Teducation,'" which he hoped would help her to "live more real than dream."[57] But Kalter also had a sense that, in the back of his mind, Joans liked the idea of having a photographer around to document his adventures, and to capture for posterity meetings with figures such James Baldwin, Lawrence Durrell, Beauford Delaney, Joyce Mansour, Cecil Taylor, and Robert Rauschenberg. Joans was prescient in this regard, as Kalter did go on to become a renowned photographer, and her photographs of their time together were eventually published in a slim volume, *All Around Ted Joans* (2017), which features shots of her and Joans traveling in Europe and North Africa, and meeting Baldwin, Durrell, Mansour, and many others. For Kalter's part, she found that Joans's "generosity went beyond," by which she meant he always seemed to give more than he took, and over the course of their relationship he created countless connections for her in the art world, which helped to launch her photography career.[58]

Their relationship was not without its troughs, and sometimes Joans's public railing against white people would creep into their private lives. In *Black Manifesto*, he had declared that "Black Power shatters the integration myth ... The white power system's concept of integration (even though a myth) was assimilation like the French and Belgian colonialist tried in old Africa."[59] Joans was of course far from an assimilationist, and yet as his tendency toward white wives, girlfriends, and lovers attested, however paradoxically, his love life was quite often integrated, a fact celebrated in a poem like "No Kosher Kouskous" when he likens his kids to the zebra—"the completely integrated horse," as he had quipped in *The Hipsters*. Given this potential source of tension, blow-ups were perhaps inevitable, and Kalter recalled an inflection point in their relationship, when they were traveling through Algeria, and Joans made a vicious remark that she felt projected ideas about whiteness and white supremacy on to her, and was so insulted that she immediately packed her bags and left the country.[60]

Bereft in the desert, Joans was deeply remorseful, and after Kalter abandoned him in Algeria, he wrote her long letters apologizing for his "egocentric-winter-state-of-mind, which is at times (especially while traveling) very crabby and very very antagonistic."[61] After that incident, their romantic relationship was mainly "off," although they remained in touch—years later, in 2001, Kalter even invited Joans to her fiftieth birthday bash in France.

40

"Deeper Are Allyall's Roots"

After Kalter had broken things off with Joans, he seemed depressed, and wrote her to say that "I feel almost LOST," that he was experiencing a "bad period." In order to right himself, he concluded, "I must talk with my ancestors and consult the cowries."[1] Over the next couple of years, one way he began to commune with his ancestors was to work on a new project that explored, in a characteristically circuitous way, his own ancestral roots. This became a manuscript first called "Deeper Are My Roots"—and then the "My" was expanded out to encompass "Allyall": "Deeper Are Allyall's Roots." Building on his Surrealist take on the Black Arts Movement and its lessons, the book was Joans's answer to Alex Haley's best-selling *Roots: The Saga of an American Family* (1976), which purportedly traced Haley's own African roots all the way back to the eighteenth century and a Mandinka ancestor in The Gambia named Kunta Kinte, who was captured and sold into the slave trade. *Roots* appeared in August 1976 and was an immediate sensation, spending almost a year on the *New York Times* best-seller list, and inspiring the wildly-successful television mini-series of the same name the following year. By November 1976, Joans had already been at work on "Deeper Are My Roots," and wrote to a potential publisher that he had a "very timely" project that "could be, shall we say, a Best Sweller, that is another Black book swelling the market, yet selling good."[2] Despite the clear play on Haley's book, Joans insisted that "I haven't and I shall NOT read Haley's Roots until I have finished my 'Deeper Are My Roots,' for that would jeopardize my sub-conscious mind and perhaps influence my unwritten manuscript."

The manuscript that came to be called "Deeper Are Allyall's Roots"—a change that underscores how Joans thought of his own Blackness as connected to all Black people's roots ("allyall")—rejects the pretense to historical accuracy promised in Haley's *Roots* (that book, he said, "is not my personal African roots").[3] Instead, Joans's project explores the idea of "roots" not through historical sleuthing, but via what he calls a "literary helicopter" approach, offering a bird's eye perspective, swooping and swerving and flashing back and forth from the present to deep time, and then back again to even deeper time. Echoing Breton's *Nadja*, "Deeper Are Allyall's Roots" opens with what had become, thanks to that book, perhaps *the* quintessential Surrealist question: "Who Am I?" Throughout his own text—novel, memoir, history, or something in between, like *Nadja*—Joans insists that this question cannot be answered with archival research or even by consulting griots (as Haley had done in West Africa), but via his own imagination: "Poetry is the only banner that flies in and out of this pangolin scaled helicopter. Poetry that is created by the destruction of the barrier that separates the wish from its fulfillment, the dream from waking state life, can allyall dig it?"[4] The book then thrusts readers into a realm where Joans's roots—his very Blackness—can be best explored and expressed with a Surrealist point of view, and these two states of being, Blackness and the Surreal, are shown to be mutually constitutive: "First of all, I being a surrealist is as natural as I being Black."[5]

Given the reception of Haley's *Roots*, it makes a certain sense that "Deeper Are Allyall's Roots" opens in a way that seems, at first, realistic enough (even as it goes on to revoke that apparent realism in short order). Ted Joans, "just another human being, a male of the homosapien species [*sic*]," is camping with a girlfriend in the Olduvai Gorge in Tanzania. The book details the equipment "Ted Joans" and his girlfriend had, what it was like to sleep in a tent out in the Gorge, and so on. But then it quickly becomes clear that in a book about roots, the Olduvai Gorge holds special significance as the site where anthropologists Mary and Louis Leakey had located some of the earliest known remains of Hominina, the group that would evolve into *Homo sapiens*, the species in which Joans pointedly declares his membership. Joans notes that Mary Leakey called Olduvai Gorge "the original womb"—he calls it "the cradle." In "A Black Man's Guide to Africa," Joans had insisted that "All mankind should visit OLDUVAI GORGE in Tanzania to pay personal respects. Every year there are new discoveries and strong evidence revealing that Africa was the 'garden of Eden.'"[6] By the 1970s, the Gorge had become famed for the preserved objects made by *Homo habilis*, likely the earliest human species, the first remains of which were found there—"Deeper" explains that the girlfriend's pet name for the character "Ted Joans" is "Homo Habilis, which means 'the man with ability.' I dug that name and still use it when asked by dubious characters my name." This seemingly offhand pet name in fact connects Joans to the deepest roots imaginable, and when he says he "dug" the name, we know we are in for a demonstration of spadework, a Surreal excavation of these roots that make up the balance of his whirlwind literary helicopter.

Joans goes on to claim that his earliest ancestors settled around Lake Nyanza—*not*, he notes, Lake Victoria, for "How could it be called 'victoria' by any intelligent Black person, since that old antique bitch was one of the worst imperialists that never set foot on African soil" (around this time, he also had revived his campaign to rename Lake Victoria Lake Louis Armstrong, even putting in a motion to the Organization of African Unity).[7] In "Deeper," Joans explains that his ancestors on Lake Nyanza were "later called 'The Spades,' because they could dig things so deep, so much deeper than others." These early "Spades" had a utopic existence, for in those days "it was always summertime and thus the living was easy, fish were jumping so was the music and other arts. Food prices were not high, and everybody that was anybody, was rich." As with triumphant ending of "Outer Space" in the "Blackland of Black Magic," this description, routed as it is through George Gershwin's "Summertime" (popularized by Louis Armstrong), underscores the extent to which Joans is inventing his own historicist impulse intelligible not so much through facts in the encyclopedic sense, but as "half facts and one fourth fiction that is between dream and reality."[8]

Obviously, Joans's approach to "genealogy" in "Deeper" denies the authority of the archive as constituted in a Western imaginary, but it also reimagines time itself as something other than inexorable and defined by forward movement (the march of history). "Whenever I conjure up a magnified vision of Africa," he writes, "which is where I dwell today, that is ancient Afrika by superimposing the billions of marvelous and conventional tableaus archived in my exceptional soulful computored head (instant memory), there unfolds before my eyes unbelievable bodyscapes and landscapes. That is my Youniverse." In this view, past and present are always superimposed on one another—collaged—and so the most fertile place to look for what is "archived" is not in "official records" or institutional repositories or even in the orally transmitted, custodial memories of griots, but in his own highly idiosyncratic, often eroticized, but always promiscuous and joyous imagination.

To dig as deeply as Joans does, particular kinds of spadework are required, and the book is built on collaged scenes and "flashblacks" which fluidly move across time and space. He explains: "the language of magic, which is a different grammatical form not unlike the automatic improvisations of jazz, these forms are used because of the drums of genealogy beat natural in all Black heads ... the magic of language is there, and it has evolved on the basis of love." Unlike Haley's method in *Roots*, Joans is totally uninterested in creating a "genealogy" that takes readers backward in time through history—but still the book is steeped in historical events and people, the circulation of ideas and religions, and the centuries-long encounter between white Europe and Black Africa that led to the destruction and degradation of various African peoples and cultures. This is the texture of "Deeper," but it doesn't lead to a literal tracing back through time, but rather to a Surrealist exploration of historical truth: "There I was," Joans once told Laura Corsiglia, "minding my own business under the shade of a tree in Timbuktu, reading a book—when some guys from the coast showed up. When they realized I wasn't Muslim they grabbed me and put me in chains and dragged me to a boat and sold me off to America. That was in 1619. And I've been here ever since."[9]

"Deeper" is informed by a similar orientation toward history and historical change. In it Joans tells the story, to take just one example, of a distant uncle, a "poet" and "great story teller," who lived around 600:

> My uncle's folks were direct descendants of the Olduvai Gorge group. All their bits and pieces were handed down from one generation to another to him. So he used all the essential knowledge. One day in the crowd of listeners was Mohammed, the great founder of the Islamic religion. He dug my uncle's hip rap and kinda got strungout on his Black magic. He tried to enlist my uncle in his thang, but uncle didnt have no eyes for organization.[10]

Joans's roots run deep indeed, all the way down to the pre-history of Olduvai via his griot uncle whose "Black magic" inspired none other than Mohammed to found one of the world's great religions—such is the potency of the Jones Family thang, but naturally any ancestor of his would be far too independent to join even a fledgling organized religion.

———

As sometimes happened with his more Surrealist writing, "Deeper Are Allyall's Roots" was somewhat confounding to publishers, who could not quite see Joans's vision, even as he pitched the project as a potential money maker. "Writing a novel is NOT really my thang," Joans explained to Mary Ellen and Arthur Wang, "But I need the bread, and I hope that I can spread a creative amount of words into a Deeper Are My Roots."[11] But bread would not be forthcoming. When Arthur Wang read the manuscript, he was as sympathetic as any reader was likely to be, given that he had published both *Black Pow-Wow* and *Afrodisia*, and was eager for a hit book from Joans. But he was "nervous" about the potential salability of "Deeper" due to its resolute commitment to Surreal weirdness and uncompromising repudiation of the approach that had proven so successful in Haley's *Roots*. Echoing what a number of publishers had said about "Spadework," Wang told Joans:

> Let me say two things that may seem contradictory. For me this was a lot of fun—lively, highly imaginative, filled with marvelous wordplay, humorous (and yet serious). But I'll be damned if I think we could sell it. Perhaps my view of what can be sold is "straighter" than it ought to be, but my hunch is that if we were to publish your novel, either in hardcover or paperback, we'd have a few adoring, loving customers—but let me

emphasize the word "few." And when I think of the word "few" and relate it to sales, I get nervous, begin to twitch, break out in a cold sweat, turn furtive, and generally begin to lose any semblance of my normal self.[12]

While causing a reader "to lose any semblance of my normal self" is precisely what any good Surrealist text might hope to achieve, marketing and salability were different stories, and like "Spadework" before it, "Deeper Are Allyall's Roots" was never published at all.[13]

41

In Residence in West Berlin

Despite his difficulty placing "Deeper," in the late 1970s and early 1980s, Joans did publish a string of work with a range of small publishers, from TRANSFORMAcTION in Devon, England, Handshake in Paris, and Loose Blätter Presse, out of Hamburg, West Germany. During his European forays, Joans had often circulated from Holland and France through to Germany, and returned with some frequency there, finding the arts community generally receptive to him and his work. In the Western side of divided Germany, he published not only with independent Loose Blätter—the dual language *Vergriffen; oder: Blitzlieb Poems* (1979) and its expanded edition, *Mehr Blitzliebe Poems* (1982)—but also *The Aardvark-Watcher/Der Erdferkelforscher* (1980), published in West Berlin as part of a state-funded book series showcasing esteemed world poets.[1] After these books were published, Joans scored a year-long residency in West Berlin, where he completed two other significant projects, the one-shot Surrealist journal, *Dies und Das*, and his still unpublished book, "Razzle Dazzle."

One entry point into the Berlin literary world came in June 1978, when he read at the Berliner Internationale Literaturtage, whose theme that year was "Gedichte heute" or Poetry Today. During the Berliner Internationale Literaturtage, Joans first met Michael Kellner, an energetic underground publisher in his mid-twenties who had been fascinated with the American Beat writers ever since hearing an experimental production of Allen Ginsberg's "Howl" back in 1970. The multimodal performance had actors theatrically reading the poem in the original English while German translations were projected on the wall behind dancers moving to the poem's rhythms. Seventeen-year-old Kellner was transfixed, and the next day he bought a copy of *Howl and Other Poems*, a purchase that changed the direction of his life. His interest in Ginsberg led to a deeper involvement with the underground poetry scenes in Kassel and Hamburg, and he helped to run what he called an "anti-capitalist" bookstore, Buch Handlung Welt, which specialized in German and American small press books and magazines. Eventually Kellner would go on to found a small publishing concern, Loose

Blätter Presse, as a means to print and distribute the Beat-inspired poetry he and his friends were writing. Eight years after that first encounter with "Howl," at the Berliner Internationale Literaturtage, Kellner was excited to hear Ginsberg's friend Ted Joans read alongside Anne Waldman and Kenneth Koch—and he was again transfixed. When the reading concluded, Kellner sheepishly approached Joans, and mustered the courage to suggest that if he were perhaps ever in Hamburg, a reading could be arranged at Buch Handlung Welt.

"Sure," said Joans. "How about next week?"[2]

Kellner rushed to set up the reading, and was even able to print through Loose Blätter a stapled booklet that they could sell for one mark apiece. This was the first version of two Joans editions Kellner would publish: *Vergriffen; oder: Blitzlieb Poems* (1979). Translating to "out of print," *Vergriffen* is a short collection of old and new poems, rendered into German, sometimes with the original English version on the facing page. The booklet opens with "Die Wahrheit," a translation of Joans's signature poem, "The Truth," accompanied by a photograph of a bearded, skullcapped Joans, now fifty-one, reading his poetry. *Vergriffen* also contains some new poems, including "Happy Stew Year," an excoriation of Apartheid in South Africa dedicated to the then-imprisoned dissident poet Breyten Breytenbach. The poem uses the image of a "healthy wholesome liberating continental African stew" as a metaphor for the inevitable collapse of the white supremacist, segregationist logic of Apartheid (and fans of Randy Weston's album *African Cookbook* [1969] might also hear some resonances with that work).[3] *Vergriffen* closes with "All Too Soon," a poem referencing Joans's experiences in West Berlin, watching "the movements of giraffe / tongues which reside in giraffe mouths and the / giraffes themselves resides in Berlin zoo (the / oldest zoological garden in Germany)."

That first reading Kellner had arranged at Buch Handlung Welt was well received. At the time, the bookstore tended to be a lively place, attracting devotees of American and underground poetry, and copies of *Vergriffen* continued to move after the reading: "our little booklet sells good," Kellner reported to Joans.[4] On that first trip to Hamburg, Joans had stayed with Kellner in his under-heated loft across the street from the bookstore, and the two became friends, even as Kellner remained in general awe of the elder poet. Over the next several years, Kellner would not only serve as Joans's publisher but also as an informal publicist for him, arranging readings when Joans was in the region, and promoting him and his work whenever possible.

Based on the interest in that first "little booklet," *Vergriffen*, Kellner wanted to do a new, "zweite, stark erweiterte Auflage" or second, greatly expanded edition of Joans's poetry in German translation. Kellner began thinking about what might go into this new edition very soon after *Vergriffen* was published, and planned to have it ready in time for the Frankfurt Book Fair in October 1980. That year's theme was almost too good to

FIGURE 41.1 *Cover of Ted Joans,* Vergriffen; oder: Blitzlieb Poems *(1979); the neologism "Blitzliebe" was misprinted "Blitzlieb" in this edition.*

be true: "Afrika. Ein Kontinent auf dem Weg zu sich selbst" or Africa: A Continent Asserts Its Identity.[5] Kellner thought the theme was "perfect" and proposed a broad plan for the new book: all the contents of *Vergriffen,* plus some older, Beat era poems he had heard Joans perform live, including a revised version of "Lets Play Something," one of Joans's most well-known poems from the 1950s thanks to its prominent inclusion in Elias Wilentz's anthology *The Beat Scene.*

Kellner imagined the new book as sixty-four pages, perfect bound, selling for five or six marks, with Joans to receive a royalty of 10 percent.[6] He needed a timely response to get moving on the new book if they were to have it available in Frankfurt, but Joans's unpredictable travels meant that quick replies were often sacrificed, and they missed the deadline for the fair. Still determined to promote Joans to the extent he could, Kellner did hang a broadside of "The Truth" on the back wall of his booth at the Frankfurt Book Fair, and when it caught the attention of passersby, he promised them that *Vergriffen* would be reprinted in an expanded edition soon—"so you WERE at the bookfair," he assured Joans.[7]

Owing to everything from Kellner's ever-expanding responsibilities to delays with the printer, the new book was not in fact published for almost another two years, when it finally appeared under the title *Mehr Blitzliebe Poems*. "Blitzliebe" is a neologism, what scholar Susanne Klengel describes as a "creative reversal of 'Blitzkrieg,'" something like "lightning love."[8] At the time, Kellner insisted to Joans that the word encompassed his work better than "Vergriffen": "'Blitzliebe' is a great word and it has a lot more to do with you than 'out of print,' which is funny but more or less a technical term, and bookdealers really think 'out of print' if they read 'out of print.'"[9]

True to Kellner's original plan, *Mehr Blitzliebe Poems* included the material in *Vergriffen* as well as some of those older, Beat era poems. Notable was a revised and expanded version of "Lets Play Something," which reflected Joans's global sensibility since leaving New York City. This version included new lines such as: "lets play that we are: Far Out Too Much and use the African word 'WOW' and hitch hike from Marrakesh to Katmandou and count all our travelers cheques in Hammerfest."[10] This version, revised in 1979, was the one eventually collected with only minor

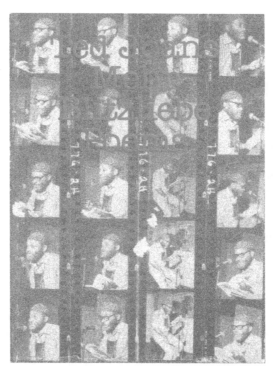

FIGURE 41.2 *Cover of* Mehr Blitzliebe Poems *(1982), an expanded edition of* Vergriffen. *Note the pouch of gri-gri around Joans's neck.*

changes in *Teducation*. In addition to these older poems, *Mehr Blitzliebe Poems* also collected more recent work drawn from *Afrodisia, Black Pow-Wow,* and *Black Manifesto* that served to showcase Joans in his guise as Black Power poet: after again opening with his signature "The Truth," the next poem, "Africa," announces: "Africa I guard your memory" (8). The volume ends by reproducing that handwritten letter from Jack Kerouac to Joans mentioned earlier, which attested to their shared sensibility: "I always loved you," writes Kerouac, "because you were so much like me, i.e., openhearted + crazy-souled + honest."[11] For Kellner, who had recently traveled to Beat-related events at the Naropa Institute in Boulder, Colorado, and who was looking forward to the upcoming Jack Kerouac Conference slated to be held in Boulder in the summer of 1982, this letter proved Joans's bona fides as an early Beat writer, "a good document about the old days and your friendship with Kerouac."[12] The association would strengthen Joans's status as one among the "original" Beats from the "old days"—as would his inclusion, the following year, in Ann Charters's groundbreaking, two-volume encyclopedia: *The Beats: Literary Bohemians in Postwar America* (1983).

And Kellner wasn't the only one in Germany interested in Joans's work: in 1980, the Literarisches Colloquium in Berlin had published a new book of his poetry, *The Aardvark-Watcher/Der Erdferkel-forscher*. This book appeared as part of the LCB-Editions, a venerable series showcasing the work of the most important contemporary world poets, from greats such as future Nobel Prize-winners Günter Grass and Elias Canetti, to Heinrich Böll, Günter Kunert, Kōbō Abe, Charles Olson and Ted Hughes. As with the many other firsts in his life, Joans was the first Black poet to be included in this series. He also thought that the book was probably the first in Germany to use the English word "motherfuckers," which had apparently confused his translator, Richard Anders, when Joans explained it could be a curse or term of endearment, depending on the context (see the poem "The Perfidious Motherfuckers"; Anders went with "Perfide Mutterficker").[13] While nearly all the poems in *Aardvark-Watcher* had been published elsewhere, their inclusion in the LCB-Editions series announced Joans's presence on the world poetry stage—at least from the point of view of German publishers—and the title paid tribute to one of Joans's totem animals, the African aardvark, whose nose, like the poet's, was always close to the ground, and whose unusual double-A spelling recalled 1714/AA/Afro-American. As recorded in the poem "All Too Soon," in Berlin Joans would frequent the zoo to see the aardvarks in particular, and though some people raised an eyebrow at the notion of an aardvark watcher, Joans would retort that bird watchers were perfectly normal, so why not an aardvark watcher?[14]

The publishers of *The Aardvark-Watcher* were associated with the Deutscher Akademischer Austauschdienst (DAAD) or German Academic Exchange Service, a program founded in Heidelberg in 1925 that has since grown to fund nearly two million scholars, writers and artists in Germany and around the world. In 1963, as part of the same Cold War cultural and political landscape that necessitated the USIA's promotion of American culture abroad, the Ford Foundation in West Berlin launched an "Artists-in-Residence" program aimed at connecting that otherwise-insulated city to the literature and culture of the West (again as a hedge against Soviet influence). In 1965, the DAAD took over this program under the name still used today, the DAAD Artists-in-Berlin Program, a prestigious, year-long residential fellowship designed to support promising and established writers and artists from around the world by housing them in Berlin and providing a livable stipend so they can focus on creative endeavors.[15]

Such a program was perfect for Joans, who otherwise had no sort of ongoing institutional support. Back in October 1980, the DAAD had paid him 400 marks to read at the Amerikhaus in Berlin, even covering his travel expenses from Paris, so he would have been familiar with the residency program from at least that time. Eventually he did submit an application for the DAAD fellowship—including four of his published books—and in a much-needed contrast to his earlier, unsuccessful attempts at landing grants or fellowships, he was named a Literature Fellow in 1983, living in residence in West Berlin with his "wife" at the time, Alicia Fritchle, for the 1983–4 program year.[16] During this residency he met numerous artists and writers in the orbit of DAAD, the Literarisches Colloquium, and Amerikhaus—the American poet and Joans's friend from New York, Robert Creeley, was also a fellow, and recalled the vibrant atmosphere, "the extraordinary spate of public readings, some 40 a week at present rate, and all with an audience of some 80 to 200 people utterly pleased to be there" (once Creeley was settled, Joans promptly turned up to show him the sights, including the beautiful beaches at Wannsee, a lake at the edge of town).[17]

As Susanne Klengel explains, while Joans was in residence in Berlin, "the Western part of the walled-in city under four-power status was defined by a thriving, highly politicized subculture that permeated daily life. Squatters, punks, alternative culture, university students, artists, intellectuals, allied troops. East German pensioners, West Berlin bureaucrats, lifelong Berliners and multicultural new Berliners shaped the image of the city and the atmosphere of communal life in West Berlin's various neighborhoods."[18]

It was in this heady mix that Joans assembled *Dies und Das: A Magazine of Contemporary Surrealist Interest*, and completed a typescript of "Razzle Dazzle," to which I'll return in the coming pages.

42

Dies und Das: A Magazine of Contemporary Surrealist Interest

True to the spirit of Surrealism in both form and content, *Dies und Das: Ein Magazin von Aktuellem Surrealistischem Interesse*—as it was titled in German—was not a typical literary or arts review. While it does present a compendium of work by people Joans admired, both living and dead, there is no table of contents, no contributors' notes, and no masthead. To experience *Dies und Das* is to experience a Surrealist disorientation; readers are plunged into a world of values alternate to what might be considered "dominant" or "high culture," both in the political and aesthetic senses: the editorial notes sprinkled throughout the magazine's pages rail against a worldview that is Western, white supremacist, and male, as well as against the "professional avant-garde" and those "French-fried-minds who have denounced the 'label' surréalisme since it is no longer lucrative for them." Joans had long dreamed of editing an "international surrealist magazine" in which "all countries should be and will be represented, from Antarctica to the Arctic."[1] *Dies und Das* was the realization of this dream.

While *Dies und Das* contains only scant artifacts explicitly attributed to Joans himself—including the poems "Jawhol Jürgen Einst" and "The Eternal Lamp of Lam," and an "Outograph by tj"—the magazine as a whole is a window into his mindset at this time, and the final page does credit him as "chefredakteur" or editor in-chief.[2] There are, however, numerous unsigned collages by Joans, as well as short editorial notes and longer statements that explain his methods and aims. Although guided by the long-standing Surrealist practice of assemblage and collage, with *Dies und Das* Joans was also exploiting a newer technology, photocopying, which allowed him to reproduce whole pages of books or newspaper and article clippings of "Surrealist interest" (that said, after the magazine appeared, Joans told J. H. Matthews that some "critics" did not "dig the photocopied presentation. But that is because we did not have enough money to pay the enormous sums demanded by Berlin printers union").[3] As one editorial note explains, much of the historical and contextual material was "Photocopied from the Surrealist Archives at Timbuktu, Mali"—the archival center of the Surrealist world. In addition to this extant material, Joans dispatched invitations around the world to his friends and acquaintances to ask for new contributions: "We sent out seven surreal animals (aardvark, echidna, pangolin, okapi, tapir, platypus and rhinoceros) to contact worthy contributors to aid and abet in the creation of this: the very first surrealist magazine to be published in Germany!"

For Joans, the materiality of *Dies und Das* was thematic, explaining in his invitation to Joyce Mansour that "the magazine will not make the mistake of being expensively done. It will be professionally laid out on the cheapest of paper."[4] Because of its deliberately ephemeral nature, *Dies und Das* is now hard to find, with a print run limited, he said, "to a mere one thousand copies."[5] *Dies und Das* lists Michael Kellner's Hamburg address as the "Redaktion Büro" or editorial office, but Kellner recalled Joans using some of his DAAD fellowship money to have the magazine printed.[6] In any case, Kellner stored about half the run for years after, selling copies when he could and forwarding them on to Joans when requested.[7] Copies did appear for brief periods in certain independent bookstores, but distribution was ad hoc. For instance, Laurens Vancrevel did what he could to move copies in Holland, but found that the magazine didn't exactly fly off the shelves, and bookstores in Amsterdam eventually returned unsold copies to his care: "Dies & Das will be very rare and expensive in the future," he lamented to Joans in 1986.[8]

In the last pages of the magazine, there is a kind of mission statement: "WHY, or Dies & Das Guarantee Against Ossification." Like the other short editorial explanations, this is unsigned but unmistakably penned by Joans (in the margin Joans had also handwritten in his winter mailing address in Timbuktu). The statement tells us that *Dies und Das* was "Collaged out of my inner necessity to service (through amalgamation) those who have been victims of benign neglect." Invoking Max Ernst ("old Max of Köln") as his inspiration, Joans explains that:

This first issue is nothing more than an exercise in collagraphics
Allowing run-away scissors to snip/snap/and cut here/there
from His/tory and mostly from Her/story

As collage and "amalgamation," *Dies und Das* is both a compendium of various "worthy" Surrealist (and some non-Surrealist) figures Joans knew and esteemed, and a reflection of his "inner necessity," a scrapbook of his own interests and point of view.

FIGURE 42.1 *Front cover of* Dies und Das *(1984).*

FIGURE 42.2 Dies und Das *back cover, featuring a portrait of Charlie Parker holding his saxophone. The photograph above Parker is (l. to r.) René Magritte, Marcel Duchamp, Max Ernst, and Man Ray (1966); in the original photograph they are holding copies of an exhibition catalogue, but Joans has altered it to read "Bird Lives," thus drawing together otherwise unconnected titans in his personal pantheon.*

This statement, "WHY, or Dies & Das Guarantee Against Ossification," is a bookend to another manifesto-like announcement that appears twenty or so pages into *Dies und Das* (the pages are of course unnumbered). This declaration, "Sure, Really We Are!" echoes the title of another recent collection *Sure, Really I Is* (1982), and explains that while *Dies und Das* is inspired by the Surrealists of the past, especially André Breton, it is also attempting to present something new insofar as it will be attuned in particular to Surrealism as expressed by Black and Third World artists, as well as by women artists: "We are not shadows of yesteryear's surrealists, although we have been nourished by 'them and those,' and their 'this and that' can be found engrained in the very marrow of our bones ... We shall bring you the contemporary facts of jazz. / We shall publish material of surrealist interest in all languages." And as he did in work such as *Spetrophilia* and *Flying Piranha*, Joans again emphasizes the importance of black humor: "Our humour," he writes:

> like our magical power, is black! Black humour is a lethal weapon in the close combat with your popular artists and writers ... Our point of view is that of contemporary surrealist interest in the active spirit of André Breton. We, the editors, wish to change "this and that" in the entire world through collective-international-action, and we are determined to succeed. We the surrealists are committed to the cause of total emancipation of humankind.

The use of the first-person plural here is not incidental, as Joans effaces somewhat his own presence by emphasizing the collective nature of his version of Surrealism, that its goal is nothing less than the "total emancipation of humankind" effected through "collective-international-action": "Jazz is *our* religion," as the back cover declares (my emphasis). Of course there is something of a tension there, since the collective liberatory sensibilities shown off in *Dies und Das* were chosen and assembled by Joans, and are therefore reflective of his particular tastes and preoccupations. In this way, we can understand *Dies und Das* as broadly in keeping with an earlier project like *Black Pow-Wow*, with its poems dedicated to Joans's pantheon of Black greats, or *Long Distance*, his exquisite corpse of some 130 contributors that, taken together, exemplify Joans's guiding point of view even as each entry is as unique as the person who contributed it.

In *Dies und Das*, there is in fact a precursor to *Long Distance*, another important exquisite corpse titled *The Seven Sons of Lautréamont* (Figure 43.1).[9] The "official" definition of an exquisite corpse is, from the *Dictionaire abrégé du surrealism*, a "game of folded paper which consists in having several people compose a phrase or a drawing collectively, none of the participants having any idea of the nature of the preceding contribution or contributions. The now classical example, which gave its name to the game, is the first phrase obtained in this manner: The exquisite—corpse—shall drink—the young—wine."[10] Breton emphasized the "uniquely collective authority" of the exquisite corpse, its "power of *drifting with the current,*" and its ability to send "the mind's critical mechanism away on vacation."[11] Joans loved the exquisite corpse as a method of Surrealist discovery, and collaborated on countless of them throughout his life, including many with Laura Corsiglia, an example of which was used on the cover of *Our Thang* (Figure 49.2).[12]

43

The Seven Sons of Lautréamont

The Seven Sons of Lautréamont originated in May 1973, and was completed, Joans said, "by chance encounter of the seven contributors."[1] As he told it, one day he was shopping for sole at a market in Paris (fitting as he had lately been dubbed "Soul Brother Ted"), and while the fish were being wrapped, a "long unstained piece of sepia wrapping paper" came loose and flitted to the ground.[2] Seeing as how the paper was now of no practical use to the fishmongers, he asked for it, and neatly folded it to a manageable size. Then, with the fish under his arm and the folded paper tucked in his shirt pocket, Joans walked over to a café on rue Jacques Callot to meet a former lover. While he was waiting, he pulled out the paper and started doodling at the top, somewhat "subconsciously." The center image, he said, represented the vagina of the former lover, and he flanked that with stylized versions of a Bauolé mask he had brought back from the Côte d'Ivoire.[3] This mask was very special to Joans, accompanied him for decades around the world, and frequently turns up as a motif in his work.[4] "He sees these pieces as alive," Corsiglia reminded me, "and maintains conversation with them"— the inclusion of the Bauolé mask drawing in what would become *The Seven Sons of Lautréamont* was one way to maintain this conversation.[5] "O great black masque," he had written in a poem with that title, "that is me / that travels with me in spirit ... O great black masque who is our / ancestors with your cave mouth / filled with sharp teeth to chew / the ropes that bind our hands and minds."[6]

In Joans's Surrealized telling, as he was completing the composition at the top of the sheet, the Afro-Colombian artist Heriberto Cogollo, whom Joans felt "the very shimmering best Black painter that I have so far encountered," just happened to be in the café.[7] Spotting Joans, Cogollo greeted him and inquired as to what he was drawing. Joans reflexively—that is, spontaneously—told him it was the beginning of an exquisite corpse, though he had not planned it that way, and Cogollo offered to continue it. Per the rules of the game, Joans folded the paper so his drawing was not visible to Cogollo, and passed it over. As the magnetic fields would have it, as Cogollo was finishing up his contribution with Joans's borrowed pen, another marvelous chance event occurred: their mutual friend, Cuban artist Agustín Cárdenas, happened by—and wanted to continue the drawing from the lines left by Cogollo. The first two contributors dutifully looked away so the discrete parts would not be prematurely revealed as Cárdenas made his drawing.

A year later, Joans was invited to a party at Cuban artist Jorge Camacho's place, and brought along the drawing with the idea that Camacho could contribute, now determined to have seven artists participate. Six months later, Joans ran into Wifredo Lam coming out of an elevator and had him continue the lines left by Camacho. When Lam asked who would contribute next, Joans said that he had to wait for another "chance encounter with one of the sons." Lam asked whose sons exactly, and Joans answered him, again "spontaneously": Lautréamont, thus giving the piece its title.

Joans realized he was now building a work with artists born "way down south in the Western hemisphere," and so when he ran into Chilean Roberto Matta in Paris in the spring of 1975, he knew he had his next contributor. Matta wanted to use color in his addition, but Joans told him that since the paper itself was colored, there could be no colors in the piece but "sepia and black." Matta agreed. Finally, six months later, he invited the final contributor, Hervé Télémaque, a French artist of Haitian origin, to complete the piece. After so many years, the bottom of the fish wrapper had been reached: "this young piece of female paper [was] seriously de-virginzed by the seven sons of Lautréamont!" When Télémaque finished his drawing, he and Joans laid the result on a table and admired it. "There she was, happy and completely surrealized. The dream was now a reality."[8]

In *Dies und Das*, this exquisite corpse appears in very poor reproduction under the title "7 Sons of Lautréamont," but without any attribution beyond the scarcely-legible signatures on the piece itself. In that context, the drawing is a testament to and embodiment of the material links Joans wanted to cultivate with the Surrealist Third World (and the work of all seven sons appear elsewhere in *Dies und Das*). In 1993, the Drawing Center in New York City was mounting a major exhibition, *The Return of the Cadavre Exquis*, and contacted Joans to see if he might be amenable to lending *The Seven Sons of Lautréamont* for the show. He explained that the "rare cadavre exquis has never been loaned before nor has it been exhibited to the public, only a small sum of surrealists have feasted their eyes upon it" (given that history, it's unclear how the Drawing Center learned about the piece in the first place).[9] But he did agree to lend it, declaring an insurance value of $47,000.[10] After being hand-carried from Paris to New York, *Seven Sons* was then an integral part of *The Return of the Cadavre Exquis*, appearing alongside exquisite corpses with contributors such as Breton, Joan Miró, Yves Tanguy, Frida Kahlo, Tristan Tzara, and Salvador Dalí.[11] The piece was again exhibited in the *Surrealism Beyond Borders* exhibit at the Metroplitain Museum of Art and Tate Modern (2021–2), then in 2023 in Paris, in a solo show put on by the Zürcher Gallery called *Surreally Ted Joans.*

Just as *The Seven Sons of Lautréamont* came to represent collaboration among Joans and Third World artists, so too can we see *Dies und Das* as fundamentally a project conceived to counter the "benign neglect" of those people Joans thought unjustly overlooked, even in Surrealist circles—he was annoyed, for instance, that the omnibus *Dictionnaire Général du Surréalisme et de ses environs* had failed to include Heriberto Cogollo, the second son of Lautréamont.[12] *Dies und Das* in fact opens with a portrait of another of the seven sons, Wifredo Lam, who had recently passed away. The ensuing pages are part memorial and part demonstration of Lam's importance: there is a timeline of his life, examples of his art, and an essay on him by Benjamin Péret. Included also is Joans's own celebratory "chant," "The Eternal Lamp of Lam" (Lam's lamp would continue to burn on as Joans used one of his drawings, *Bird / Man*, for the cover of *Teducation*).

A particular favorite of Joans's was Lam's monumental painting *La Jungla* or *The Jungle* (1943), which depicts figures in a Cuban sugar cane field. "The figures stand camouflaged," writes Karen Grimson, "amid the dense bamboo and sugarcane; their totemic forms, simultaneously voluptuous and angular, gesture provocatively in a mysterious scene evoking '*lo real maravilloso*' (the marvelous real), a term coined by the Cuban novelist Alejo Carpentier to describe the genuinely surreal nature of everyday life in the Caribbean."[13] Little wonder that Joans should have been drawn to this work, and in 1975 he sent a lengthy appreciation of *La Jungla* to Lam and his wife Lou, detailing what it was like to see and interact with the piece at the MoMA, "having myself an art orgy."[14] Noting that in the mask-like faces of his figures Lam seems to allude to (and reclaim) Picasso's famous use of African masks in *Demoiselles d'Avignon* (1907), Joans calls the figures in *La Jungla* "three AfroAsian demoiselles": "Listen to the masked poet murmur ... The three marvelous jungle Jills whom have never known clothes ... What hands have these three forest femme fatales ... What feet have these women of the wild woods / But all three are not just mere human women but also part tree." His experience of seeing *La Jungla* was the experience of "lo real maravilloso," as it induced him to exist in simultaneous realities at once: "But for now I sit listening / To this JUNGLE I sit Smelling this JUNGLE I sit / Tasting this JUNGLE I sit Feeling this JUNGLE."[15]

Joans elaborated in *Dies und Das* why it was so important to showcase work by Lam and others like him:

> Creations from the Third World, especially Africa, have often inspired surrealist ideas, and the men and women who were inspired by such black art (Oceania included) often forgot them just as quickly—or, at best, they unconsciously assimilated them, and as a result, they sincerely believed themselves as being the original!

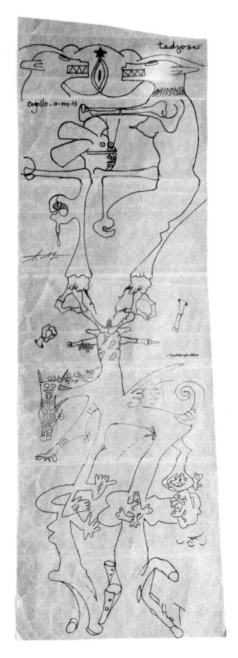

FIGURE 43.1 *Ted Joans, Heriberto Cogollo, Agustín Cárdenas, Jorge Camacho, Wifredo Lam, Roberto Matta, Hervé Télémaque,* The Seven Sons of Lautréamont *(ca. 1973–5). Ink on brown paper.*

This not only happens with traditional Third World surreality, but also in the magnetic field of jazz. Dies & Das Magazine shall combat such behaviour of cultural genocide by direct confrontation, even to the extent of utilizing "unmerciful Manhattan Mau Mau mugging" tactics. Such acts of unpopular complicity could physically undermine such financially secure "artists."

In *Dies und Das*, Joans used a variety of tactics to combat "benign neglect" and demonstrate synergies among "Third World surreality" and "the magnetic field of jazz." He created, for example, a "Jazz Inquiry" questionnaire that his industrious army of "seven surreal animals" dispatched to John Welson, Jorge Camacho, Konrad Klapheck, Maurice Henry, Louis Lehmann, Jean-Louis Bédouin, Georges Gronier, Chris Starr, and Roberto Matta—all of whom attested to their long and deep love of various forms of jazz, implying—without drawing direct lines of "influence"—how Surrealist art has been "inspired by such black art." *Dies und Das* also includes, and promotes, work by women, as Joans felt women were, generally speaking, underrepresented in the male-dominated Surrealist sphere. In the magazine's pages one finds Elisa Breton, Unica Zürn, Marie Wilson, Leonora Carrington, Mimi Parent, Dorothea Tanning, Aube Elléouët, Betye Saar, Joyce Mansour, and Penelope Rosemont.

These names are just a hint of the riches in *Dies und Das*, and such a summary cannot do justice to the experience of paging through its contents, getting lost in the multiple languages (he chose not to translate much of the non-English work because "humankind doesnt speak one language, especially the surrealists"), or the sometimes grainy photocopies.[16] Ultimately—and this is the case in many of Joans's Surrealist undertakings—precisely for the ways *Dies und Das* showcases a diversity of talents, it can somewhat counter-intuitively be taken as a kind of autobiography, if autobiography can mean assemblages of styles, tastes, ideologies, aesthetics.

44

"Razzle Dazzle"

If we can loosely read *Dies und Das* as intellectual and aesthetic autobiography, then we can do this as well with "Razzle Dazzle," a typescript Joans completed while in residence in Berlin. Despite his general refusal to accommodate the demands of the literary marketplace, he was nonetheless highly conscious of those demands, an awareness reflected in the way he framed "Razzle Dazzle." The book was, he said, conceived as a "deliberate worst seller," and he delighted in the fact that it would be impossible to categorize under those existing labels one might find at a bookstore: "If any category except 'worst seller' could be placed on it, then it would possibly be classified as a 'highly-publicized gothic surreal no-nonsense storybook,' and of course, that would be too clumsy to be used as a label" (2). It also didn't help that Joans imagined the book's "real" title to be "How I Fucked Your Daughter in Paris." Its literary ancestors are similarly unclassifiable works like Lautréamont's *Les Chants de Maldoror*, Charles Robert Maturin's *Melmoth the Wanderer*, Raymond Roussel's *Locus Solus*, and Breton's *Nadja*—as well as playful, reality-bending books like Lewis Carroll's *Alice in Wonderland*.[1] The book's "theme," Joans said, is "the nonviolent adventures of one human being which start in New York City with some real heroic figures and ends in April in Paris with some not so real people" (2). This human being is Theodor Green—the surname is borrowed from the character "Ned Green" in Cecil Brown's *Jiveass*, the lightly fictionalized version of Joans himself, thus implying the plot will at least flirt with autobiography. But in "Razzle Dazzle," things are nothing if not distorted and turned inside out, so while Green does share some biographical similarities with Joans—he was, he tells another character, "recently a resident of New York's bohemian quarters, Greenwich Village, where I attempted to contribute to the creative life there by writing poems and painting in oils" (82)—Green is a white man, a self-identified WASP from Boston, and this is just one of the many ways the book confounds expectations.

As it unfolds, "Razzle Dazzle" has one foot in the real and one foot in the "not so real," a kind of dreamscape, so that it offers both highly-realistic descriptions of New York or Paris (see those scenes at the Beat Hotel discussed in Part Two), only to then place Green in impossible situations, most memorably a garden party during which he meets in the flesh not just Lautréamont, Maturin, Roussel, and Carroll themselves but also Sigmund Freud, Edgar Allan Poe, and Ann Radcliffe—as well as fictional characters such as Sherlock Holmes.[2] Just as *Dies und Das* houses Joans's personal pantheon of largely Third World Surrealists, in "Razzle Dazzle," he dispenses with historical plausibility or even possibility to showcase "a special elite of cultural insurgents" representing his aesthetic and philosophical ancestors (152). Plot and character development are beside the point, for as Joans writes: "the form (if there is any) of this book is to 'raz' and the characters at times may 'dazzle.' The total interaction of the text and context is a toss-up, that is IF you can catch (ketch!)" (4).

In the book's final pages, Joans returns to the question of "form" to again address the reader directly: "Razzle Dazzle's component parts had to liberate themselves from the conventional object in such a way that he too could set up entirely new relationships with other elements, escaping from the reality principle and yet gaining a certain importance on the surreal plane, therefore disrupting the notion of relation" (332). This gloss is useful for understanding what Joans is up to in "Razzle Dazzle," reminding us that it unfolds on the "surreal plane" and that the relationship among its constituent parts is unexpected, but perhaps all the more revelatory for this unexpectedness. Green's adventures include trading witty banter with Lewis Carroll and his real-life girl muse Alice Liddell, dodging stampedes of rhinoceroses that have crashed through the hedgerows, and sweating through athletic sex with Gothic novelist Ann Radcliffe and "a certain female ghost that haunted Place Dauphine" (251), a key locale in Breton's *Nadja*, moments that "raz" and "dazzle" as they tease deeper kinds of "meaning" or symbolic connection to Joans's own poem-life.

For me, thinking about "Razzle Dazzle" in the context of Joans's literary career, the real story is how insistently he had framed it as a "worst seller" even before he submitted it to publishers, a statement against not merely the publishing industry but also against what was expected of him as a Black writer and artist. His most successful books to date had been *Black Pow-Wow* and *Afrodisia*, Black Power-adjacent books that, despite (or because of) their excoriations of white society, were legible to publishers as belonging to an identifiably marketable category. This was not the case with his more stridently Surrealist books, and after he turned away from the hand grenade sensibility in the early 1970s, Joans had more and more trouble placing his work with more mainstream houses such as Hill & Wang, and even with smaller independent presses such as City Lights or Grove. Instead, throughout the 1970s and 1980s, he published short books with boutique venues (*Spetrophilia*, *Flying Piranha*, and *Vergriffen*), or else pamphlets through USIS centers and the like (*A Few Poems* [1981], *Poems for You: In & Out of Africa* [1994]). Despite this market reality, he was defiant in his determination to write "true" (but saleable) books, insisting, as he wrote in "Razzle Dazzle," that he did not create characters as "puppets used to prove a point or advance a theory as most Black novelists, like some of their white American counterparts, have done, especially the Black writers stretching from Richard Wright's important all-American naturalism, to the studied consumers' literary-interest-characters of Toni Morrison" (3–4).

In this regard, there is a through-line from "Spadework: An Autobiography of a Hipster" (which he never placed due to its collage-like form and potentially libelous content), to "Razzle Dazzle," which he knew would be similarly difficult to sell. In "Spadework," Joans was often performatively self-reflexive, wondering in the text itself if that book would ever be "published and acclaimed as a good piece of literature," even as he refused to change any of it to appease gatekeepers in the publishing industry.[3] That was back in 1962, and some twenty years later, when he was completing "Razzle Dazzle," he remained determined to reject what he took to be artificial, biased, and wrong-headed notions of "good" literature altogether:

> American and English criticism is a deliberate industry, created for their highly-sought-after target: G O D O L L A R. Therefore, this godollar industry is constantly in need of new raw material. It thrives on popular conventional novels that good and bad writers excrete mechanically ... This book is a WORST SELLER, the complete opposite of those books that you read about in 'Time' and 'Newsweek' magazines. (1–2)

In this view, "good literature"—as the publishing industry defines it—is simply what will sell, a premise Joans refuses by aiming to write a "worst seller," a book paradoxically good or aesthetically honest *because* it is unclassifiable and therefore unsaleable. "I did not write this invention," he declares of "Razzle Dazzle," "according to my bank account or traditional avant-garde literary laws" (recall that even though he seemed to like it, Arthur Wang had rejected "Deeper Are Allyall's Roots" because, he said, "I'll be damned if I think we could sell it").[4]

Joans did persist in sending the manuscript of "Razzle Dazzle" out to a variety of publishers, from Calder and Boyars, the British publishers of *A Black Manifesto*, to Michael Kellner back in Hamburg, to City Lights Books in San Francisco.[5] Although Kellner expressed interest in the project, at the time Joans had queried him (fall 1986), he was focusing his attention on enterprises other than publishing, and besides, his operation simply didn't have the capacity to publish a book of that length.[6] When Kellner could not do the book, Joans approached City Lights, but was careful to send the manuscript to Nancy Peters, who had recently become a co-owner, rather than to Lawrence Ferlinghetti, because he felt Ferlinghetti's tastes were too "conventional," perhaps still stung from his response to "Spadework."[7] City Lights never published the manuscript, nor, for that matter, did any other house, and so "Razzle Dazzle" ironically became more of a "worse seller" than Joans had even imagined.

45

Teducation Films

It was in and around West Berlin that Joans also began to experiment in earnest with a new art form: short films. One day he had been strolling around the city, and spotted a used Super 8 camera in a shop window. The clerk knew enough English to explain that if Joans were truly interested in making "serious films," he should purchase a more professional 16mm camera, rather than the portable 8mm, which was generally used for home movies. The one in the window wasn't even able to record sound, but Joans was interested anyway, against the clerk's advice: "I bought the cheaper pocketsize Sony Super 8mm cassette loading used camera and the rest is teducated film history!"[1]

That Super 8 camera he named Slappy, and used it to create a series of collage-like short films. The earliest reference I have seen to a Joans film is "Lautréamont's Laundromat" (1980/1984), which was what he called an "homage to Benjamin Péret."[2] This was one of his "SILENT POEMS," a series of twelve short films he began or completed while in residence in Berlin ("Lautréamont's Laundromat" was evidently begun in 1980 and completed in 1984). As Joans explained it, the "SILENT POEMS" were "12 super 8mm films shot in various European and American locations plus The Republic of Mali, [which] feature internationally known poets, writers, artists, and jazz musicians. Backed by selected musical recordings (usually jazz) SILENT POEMS capture both the private and the public moments of its stars."[3] In other words, when Joans screened these films, he would play musical accompaniment that created all sorts of interesting and unexpected conjunctions, amounting to what he described as "an ongoing collaged-cadavre exquis ... utilizing unsync unplanned instrumental music as part of the risk, and the active chance that images with motion offer the subconscious mind."[4]

The films in the first SILENT POEMS series run anywhere from five to thirty minutes, with most being in the ten minute range, and include several shot around Germany: "Heiligengeistbrucke Bulues" (1983/1984), named for a bridge in Hamburg, where it was filmed; "Meanwhile Messing Around Majestically at Dies Messe" (1984), shot at a stadium complex in West Berlin; "Up Against Die Mauer Mutter!" (1984), a reference to the Berlin Wall and shot in the East and West sides of the city (and featuring poet Michael McClure); and "Jazz Poet Mit Surrealist Wings" (1983), shot in West Berlin and Hamburg, and featuring Robert Creeley. (In addition to starring in one of the SILENT POEMS, Creeley also enjoyed seeing them screened around West Berlin, and he recalled Joans "having a *finissage* of his surrealist and historical artifacts—including a great film of himself in Timbuktu, which the Germans loved"; this film was almost certainly "Timbuctu and Back" [1981/1982], a 10 minute piece shot there.)[5]

Beyond this first series of twelve SILENT POEMS, Joans continued to make short films for the rest of his life, and there are more than fifty extant Teducation Films shot from the early 1980s to about 1999. With titles such as "Godollar Defamed by Lodoicea Maldivica's Légitime Défense" (1984), "Colors of the Rainbow Vowels" (1989), "Ask Me Now" (1998), and "Creative Aspects of Failure" (1998–1999), these films were shot everywhere from Paris to Southern California to Mexico City to Fez to Timbuktu to

FIGURE 45.1 *Brochure for Joans's poetry and film presentation "Teducation: Poems for Eyes & Ears" (December 1, 1989). Joans used the cover of this particular brochure to write a brief note to Nancy Peters at City Lights Books, urging her and her husband, poet Philip Lamantia, to read the manuscript of "Razzle Dazzle," which he calls "this first 'novel' from me." From City Lights Books Records, Additions, Bancroft, box 31, folder 10.*

Amsterdam to Zimbabwe, and feature huge casts of Joans's family, friends, lovers, acquaintances, and even passersby.

In elaborating the theories underlying these Teducation Films, Joans wrote: "Teducation film is merely a surrealist affirmation of spirit: to revolt ... [and] is above all uncompromising in its highly personal selection of imagery and 'chance encounter of stars.'"[6] The idea was that wherever he happened to be in time and space could be a suitable "set," and precisely because he was in that moment in time and space, whoever happened to be around would make the perfect "stars." "Teducation is not all created by tedjoans," he said, "yet it is 'teducated' by those who participate, including the many camera-persons who wield the Teducation camera on the continents of Europe, Africa and North America. Those individuals were chosen by chance, just as many Teducation 'stars' are encountered by chance. Collectively we transform whoever, whatever, whenever and the where-ever that is being filmed, the teducation results is often revelatory."[7] This de-emphasis of Joans's own intentions or control—as well as his reference to his films as "collaged-cadavre exquis"—links them to one of the enduring themes of his later poem-life, the experience of collective or collaborative creation, where Joans didn't necessarily want to be a lone inspired figure in the old Romantic sense, but rather a facilitator who sparked creativity around him. "Teducation Films does not seek stars," he wrote, "it only has found them."

46

Paris, Chance-Filled Paradise

Although Joans's time in Berlin had been very generative for him creatively, when in Europe, he had always felt most at home in Paris, and the city holds a special place in his poem-life. Given the tradition of African American writers and artists fleeing the States for the relative freedom and openness of France, it's worth revisiting a line quoted earlier, at the end of Part Two, "I did not choose Paris or Europe as my <u>destination</u> when I made my strategic withdrawal from the U.S.A ... <u>No, I did not follow</u> in Wright's, Himes' and Baldwin's <u>Europebound</u> footsteps. Instead, I rode a slowboat back to ... AFRICA."[1] Here Joans isn't necessarily denigrating Paris, but emphasizing his belief that, as we have seen, Europe was there to be tapped, a fount of resources just waiting to be redistributed to the Third World and used to fund his own excursions around Africa and the rest of the globe. To say Joans was more itinerant than most other American expatriates is an understatement, and while he maintained a winter home in Timbuktu while he circulated, Paris was another of his bases of operation, where he would keep a snug "nid" or nest. He had a series of these nests in Paris. In the early 1990s, his nest was on rue d'Auteuil in the 16th arrondissement. Although located in a somewhat bourgeois neighborhood, the nest itself was anything but fancy, almost like a glorified storage closet, an echo of la cabine téléphonique from back in his early Greenwich Village days, accessible only down lots of twisting, turning hallways, and neatly packed and stacked with Joans's things.[2]

While the nest was mainly for creating and reflecting and sleeping, Joans lived much of his life out in the city, and throughout the 1980s and 1990s, was known for being a "standard fixture in Paris bookshops," and for holding court at the Café Le Rouquet on Boulevard Saint Germain, where he stationed himself at certain hours during certain times of the year ("<u>never</u> in the winter months!").[3] As he had it, Café Le Rouquet was patronized by "rare intellectuals from all over the world" and in "recent years young French men and many potential surrealist women frequent this plain no-chic-shit restauration place."[4] He would emphasize that back in their day

Breton and his friends often stopped at Café Le Rouquet on the way to or from galerie A L'Etoile Scellée, and that Roberto Matta, Octavio Paz, and Elisa Breton were known still to drop by—an ideal place for Joans to ensconce himself most afternoons when in Paris.

His poem, "Chez Café Le Rouquet," is a swinging romp dedicated to Joyce Mansour "as though she wrote it," and gives readers a portrait of Joans at Le Rouquet as if from Mansour's point of view:

> At the Café Le Rouquet
> Where he sits
> Afternoons of each
> When-In-Paris-Day
> He sits often alone
> Reading writing or
> In aristocratic composure
> ...
> He sits always
> In the left corner
> Comme un surréaliste Jacques Horner
> Poeting or pontificating
> His "Dies und Das" teducation
> Jeden Tag except closed Sundays
> Being the magnetic center
> Until winter coldness
> Sends him to Africa way
> Long long distance from
> The Café Le Rouquet[5]

From this relatively "straight" opening description, dense with allusions to Joans's work, the poem spins out into a Surrealist galaxy of imagination, so the seemingly innocuous spot in the café is revealed to be "Where he surrealizes / Parade of paranoid pangolins / En route to softer helicopters / That await such treasured scale" (21), where "Baobob [sic] holy tree of sighs" proliferate (21), and "Where her anvil flowers / Are licked by new rhinoceros tongues" (24). The poem is about being present in both the real and Surreal senses, and establishes the Café Le Rouquet as a privileged base of imaginative operations.[6] Friends and acquaintances around the world knew to seek out Joans at Café Le Rouquet, "where he picks up his mail in Paris," as a friend, novelist Herbert Gold, informed readers interested in learning about worldwide "Bohemia."[7]

As Gold suggests, it is the case that if casual readers and art enthusiasts know anything about Joans beyond his late 1950s affiliation with the Beat Generation, it is often that he was for many years associated with Paris, particularly later in his life. He was "probably the most colorful poet in

Paris," wrote friend and fellow poet James Emanuel in 1992.[8] In his guise as "the most colorful poet in Paris," Joans also became a mentor to a younger generation of writers, particularly African American expatriate writers such as Jake Lamar, who recalled that "the pivotal moment" for his writing life came in 1993, when meeting "older Black American writers—Ted Joans, James Emanuel, Hart Leroy Bibbs—who would help give me the confidence to try to make a life for myself as a writer in Paris."[9] As we will see in the coming pages, this was a pattern that repeated itself throughout his later decades, when Joans would often seem to change the trajectory of a younger writer's life through his generosity and hard-won advice.

Joans as the paradigmatic African American expatriate writer in Paris is another dimension of his legend that places him, despite the qualifiers cited above, as a latter-day example of the African American artist in Paris, a trope dating from and popularized during the days of Josephine Baker and Langston Hughes back in the 1920s. In terms of scholarly reception, this dimension of the Joans legend arose, in part, from what was for many years the best and most sustained critical treatment of his life and work, the chapter on him in Michel Fabre's *From Harlem to Paris: Black American Writers in France, 1840–1980* (1991), an expanded version of his earlier French-language book *La Rive Noire: De Harlem a la Seine* (1985). Fabre was a longtime professor of African American literature at various universities in Paris, and an authority on Richard Wright.

Fabre and Joans had met sometime in the late 1960s or early 1970s, and Fabre had invited Joans to come speak to his classes. True to his position that one should extract from Europe when possible, Joans naturally required to be paid for any appearances, partly as a practical matter, and partly on principle. As he insisted to Fabre: "if Sorbonne has a class of students interested in Afroamerican English and they are not willing to pay at least 100 NF to hear just one of its exponents in poetry and ready to answer all the intellectual questions in French or English that they wish ... then, alas, there is NO REASON AT ALL FOR THEM joveass [*sic*] students to study MY tribes poetry."[10]

To underscore his point, he quoted from Aimé Césaire's *Cahier d'un retour au pays natal*: "je veux cet égoïsme beau et qui s'aventure / et mon labour me remémore d'une implacable étrave" or "I summon this beautiful egotism that ventures forth / and my ploughing reminds me of an implacable cutwater."[11] These lines come right after Césaire's statement that he was "leaving timid Europe which collected and proudly overrates itself"; Joans refused to underrate himself, and came to collect: No Bread, No Ted. Eventually Fabre did accept his terms.

Following these early negotiations, Joans became friendly with Fabre and his wife, Geneviève, and Joans gave Fabre interviews and unpublished material that were used to enrich the chapter devoted to him in *From Harlem to Paris.*[12] In the book, Fabre placed Joans in that venerable company of African American expatriates in France stretching back to W. E. B. Du Bois, Hughes, Countee Cullen, Claude McKay, Richard Wright and James Baldwin; for these figures as for Joans, "Paris was a capital of culture, an international meeting place where the exchange rate for the dollar often made life cheaper than at home" (7). While Fabre did of course acknowledge Joans's contributions to the Beat and Black Arts/Black Power movements, he presented him primarily as "The Surrealist Griot," and consequently the book's portrait looks very different from the impressions one might get from reading *The Beat Scene* or a book like *Black Manifesto*. "By defining himself as a black surrealist," Fabre writes, "Joans emphasized the link between the open, creative weltanschauung proclaimed by the French avant-garde of the 1920s and the soul-expanding force of black power that reached its peak in the United States in the mid-1960s" (308). In Fabre's telling, Paris was for Joans a field ripe for magnetic connection: "in galleries, at vernissages, and even in the streets, Joans had many encounters in which he liked to see the hand of 'objective chance'" (315), and he describes Joans's running into the likes of André Breton and Jacques Prévert, noting also that he "attended many of the frequent surrealist meetings at the Promenade de Vénus" (314).

This was an image of Joans as late insider of the formal international Surrealist group orbiting Breton—an image that is true, so far as it goes, but its inclusion in *From Harlem to Paris* also had the effect of burnishing the Joans legend in this regard. Fabre writes: "During Breton's life he and Joans had become inseparable, and Joans's devotion to Elisa Breton continued their friendship" (321). Joans approved of Fabre's general treatment of him in *From Harlem to Paris*, but because he could be a stickler for certain kinds of truth, he was sure to correct that statement: "It is NOT true that Breton and I were 'inseparable.' But that is the way myths are made, so I forgive your mystic magic" (he did remain very close to Elisa Breton after her husband's death, would visit her at the house in Saint-Cirq-Lapopie, come for tea at 42 rue Fontaine, and see her frequently up until her own death in 2000).[13]

Joans himself made "mystic magic" in Paris, and often understood the city in those terms. Glimpses of the city as he saw it at age 62 are visible in "Aardvarkian Surreal Stroll Through Paris" (1990), part travel guide, part love letter to the city and its rich Surrealist history. The piece, only some of which has been published, adopts the pose of a travel guide, but quickly cedes the authority embedded in travel guides to chance itself, and the moods of the reader and would-be visitor. What one encounters via "Aardvarkian" is: "A Paris of your own creation—no thought-police or tourist tyrant leader talking down at you as though you are sheep to be shepherded. No schedules, No set time, Only Adventure and love—also self-discovery. Here shall be a Paris world that isn't but a Paris as it could be, and for certain V.I.P. readers who liberate their imagination—a Paris as it should be."[14]

"Aardvarkian Surreal Stroll" proceeds to offer suggestions for "spontaneous strolling" through non-tourist Paris, and the sights Joans recommends are usually palimpsests, with layers of history to them, so that he directs visitors to various cafés once "used as rendez-vous places by the yesteryore surrealists," or to Musée Gustave Moreau, an undersung museum beloved by Breton, whom Joans quotes: "My discovery, at the age of sixteen, of the Musée Gustave Moreau influenced forever my idea of love."

Love is—with Surrealism—a predominant theme of Joans's Paris, and his recommendations move from certain little parks and squares especially suitable for lovers "to embrace, kiss, fondle and have mutual pleasures" (he recommends in particular Square Récamier [now Roger Stephane]), to wider-angle concepts dear to Surrealists, as when he advises visiting the statue of Charles Fourier, whose "concept was of universal harmony, effected in this world through peaceful means, whereby the human mind and heart would be wholly in accord with the laws of nature." In "Aardvarkian," Joans's Paris comes alive as eccentric, magical, dynamic yet haunted by deeper histories: "Today is where it is at," he writes, "but one must always imagine the tomorrow, simultaneously understanding laughable yester-hysterical history."

Beyond the physical spaces—the antique shops, art galleries, bookstores, and vanishing old-fashioned passages—Paris was a "chance-filled paradise" because of its magnetic tendency to attract like-minded people together, and this is surely the most important legacy of Joans's time in Paris. "Nowhere are the mysteries of objective chance greater," he wrote, "and its revelations more astonishing, than in the supreme encounter of love."[15] From running in to André Breton way back in 1960 to meeting Laura Corsiglia, the last great love of his life, in 1991, the city was always ripe for fortuitous encounters, and for cultivating love.

47

Jim Haynes, Handshake Press, and *Duck Butter Poems*

On the literary side of Joans's poem-life, one crucial Parisian connection was Jim Haynes, a fellow expatriate American with a long history on the European arts and publishing scenes. After being discharged from the Air Force—where he had been stationed in Scotland—Haynes liked Edinburgh so much that he decided to settle there, and in 1959 opened The Paperback, a bookshop that, like City Lights in San Francisco, took advantage of the "paperback revolution" to sell inexpensive paperback books, mainly to the University of Edinburgh crowd. But The Paperback rapidly morphed into something beyond a mere bookshop; as Haynes recalled, "The bookshop was not just a bookshop, it was also a salon, it was a coffee house, it was a gallery, it was a meeting place, it very quickly became a real centre."[1] If such a magnetic place were not enough to draw Joans, The Paperback's "symbol" was a genuine stuffed rhinoceros head, a rare one-horned Indian species. Haynes had rescued the rhinoceros when he saw it was being tossed out on the curb by a swanky club on Princess Street—he mounted the head to the right of the bookshop's door, and used it to hang signs advertising readings and other events.[2]

Joans had met Haynes in Edinburgh sometime in the early 1960s, when he saw an advertisement for The Paperback featuring the rhino head (when the shop finally closed, Haynes had apparently wanted to gift the rhino head to Joans, but someone else had already snagged it).[3] At the time when they first met, in addition to running The Paperback, Haynes was also mounting major literary conferences and festivals, including one in 1962 that drew the likes of Mary McCarthy, Henry Miller, Norman Mailer, Lawrence Durrell and William Burroughs. He had also started the Traverse Theatre, and, down in London, co-founded what would become an influential "underground" newspaper, *International Times*, where Joans would intermittently publish.[4] *International Times* became a mainstay of London's countercultural scene, and was, as Haynes said, "definitely looked upon as the community's paper. Anyone could get a news story inside ... Right from the beginning we had weekly listings in which we'd publicize free any interesting or alternative events that people told us about."[5]

In 1969, Haynes moved to Paris, where lived until his death in 2021. There he continued promoting "alternative" literary and cultural ventures, and maintained his famed Atelier A-2 on the rue de la Tombe Issoire in the 14th arrondissement, where he would hold weekly gatherings for any interested artists who happened to be in town. In a 1986 profile piece for the *Los Angeles Times*, Elizabeth Venant described these gatherings as "a renowned, eclectic, infamous mix of the *paparazzi*, poseurs and authentic artists who pass through this city's English-speaking expatriate community. It is a literary salon in the roughest sense: a raunchy combo of intellectual grist, grub and amorous adventures."[6] Naturally Joans was a "fixture" at these gatherings, as he felt Haynes was "the very best unofficial diplomat that has ever 'graduated' from the U.S.A.," and the Sunday dinners were ideal opportunities for Teducated diplomacy.[7] Venant reported that at the dinner she attended, Joans was in classic form, filming a "young woman in a 8-millimeter movie and tell[ing] her to meet him at the 'Suicide Bridge' at the Buttes de Chaumont [Parc des Buttes Chaumont] for the next day's shoot." As Venant reports, a "'Beth from Berlin' has phoned Joans [at Haynes's phone] about going to Africa with him ... 'I wouldn't mind going to Africa,' one of the Texas women [at the dinner] pipes up. 'You got any oil wells, darling?' Joans rejoins."

Aside from hosting such Parisian gatherings for some fifty years, Haynes was also involved in numerous small publishing ventures throughout his life. In 1980, he launched a new imprint, Handshake Editions, partly because he wanted to help out his old friend Ted Joans, who was about to give a poetry reading at UNESCO in Paris. "I suggested we put together a book of the poems he was going to read that evening," Haynes recalled, "so that he could give them away or sell them ... I called the imprint Handshake Editions because the contract with the author is a handshake. The copyright belongs to the author and I strive to keep the book in print."[8] Haynes stressed that these were not expensively-bound editions, and were produced in short runs of fifty or 100 copies made on a high-speed Xerox machine: "The quality is quite good, the binding is terrible—usually the book falls apart after about ten readings—but at least it exists."[9]

The first booklet Handshake printed was Joans's *Old and New Duck Butter Poems*, a twenty-four-page, comb-bound collection of collages and poetry that exists in a first edition (February 29, 1980) and a second edition (March 19, 1980). Haynes's description of the somewhat ephemeral nature of those early Handshake editions helps explain why *Old and New Duck Butter Poems* is now quite difficult to find—but it did its job at the time. As Haynes told me, "Handshake came into existence for the pragmatic reason of printing some books quickly and making money from poetry and for Ted to survive."[10] Small booklets like *Old and New Duck Butter Poems*, combined with readings, the occasional fellowship or residency, and sometimes selling artwork, allowed Joans to "survive" as a poet and multidisciplinary artist without an otherwise conventional job or institutional affiliation.

Joans had defined "duck butter" as a term originating in "the ghettos where some jazz was born," the "jive gutter name" for smegma; for him, "duck butter" connoted not only jive and jazz but his own origins as well, representing as it did the circumstance that he and everyone else is a product of physical coupling.[11] Despite its fragile material state, *Old and New Duck Butter Poems* contains some strong work, including a revision of his 1950s poem "Lets Play Something"; an ode to Gregory Corso, "Along the Paris Corso"; "Flutterbye," the last words of which flutter by like a butterfly on the page; and Surreal poems such as "Silver Globular," "Get For Dont: Surreal Blues," and "In Hand Out Hand," the last of which offers imagistic flashes correlating to various Surreal animals: "Washstand filled with you my platypus ... Stamp echidna with love my darling ... Bookends here and yesteryear aardvark honey ... Worktable pangolin for divine you."[12] There is a playful elegy to Groucho Marx, "Animal? No! Cracker? No! Groucho? Yes!!!" and an excoriation of Howard Hughes, "You Cant Tell the Difference When the Sun Goes Down"—Joans had been fascinated by a report in *Time* that near the end of his life, reclusive but obscenely wealthy Hughes was known to sing "aloud and time again the lyrics of that jazz hit, Hey-Baba-Rebop," a spirited old Lionel Hampton tune.[13] In the collages accompanying these poems, images of various kinds of bird nests abound, cousins, perhaps, to Joans's own nest in the 16th arrondissement (see Figure 47.1).

Duck Butter contains "Why I Shall Sell Paris," dedicated to Joans's long-time friend Robert Benayoun and a precursor to "Aardvarkian Surreal Stroll Through Paris" in its dismissal of the touristy and inauthentic side of Paris:

> I shall sell Paris
> All its arrondissements   All its famous and infamous monuments
> All its 'theatres et spectacles'   All its 'cabarets artistiques'
> All of 'gai Paris attractions et principaux cinemas' with
> All those do-nothing jiveushers demanding money as you enter (8)

This is the Paris that has sold itself, and its soul, and therefore Joans perversely wants a piece of the action: "Dommage you are too late/ For Paris has been sold" (9). He is especially hard on "the biggest jive boulevard in the world: Champs Elyssee" (9), but, as in "Aardvarkian," he makes an exception for special Surrealist points of interest: "I shall only keep the stone pedestal of Charles Fourier at Clichy" and "the Pont des Arts and Tour St Jacques all for me" (8).

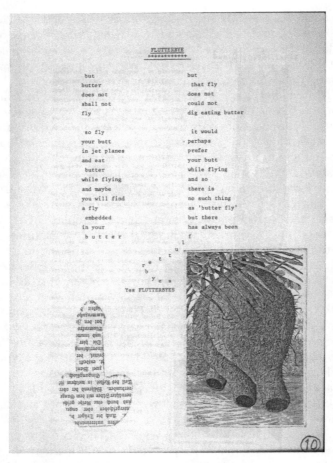

FIGURE 47.1 *"Flutterbye" as it appeared in the second edition of* Old and New Duck Butter Poems *(1980). Note the cut-out in the shape of a phallus on the left, and the bird nests on the right, perhaps another version of Joans's nid or nest in Paris, and in this case also a home for the phallus.*

Handshake did also print a third "augmented" edition of *Duck Butter Poems* in April 1982. As though to confound future bibliographers, the cover bears the title *New Duck Butter Poems*, but the title page retains "Old and New Duck Butter Poems." This third edition contains all the poems of the first editions, but then adds twelve more, including two pertaining to Jack Kerouac, whose work was experiencing a revival of interest at the time: "Holy Hijinks," a reminiscence about the Beats that had first appeared in the Kerouac fanzine *Moody Street Irregulars* in 1980, and "A 'K' Page," which marvels at the fact that his late buddy Kerouac was by then important enough to appear in the "big fat/American heritage [/] Dictionary."[14] The third edition of *Duck Butter* includes also "Women of the Western World," which laments the beauty standards to which those women are held, and "Eternal Lamp of Lam," which one would be able to find again in *Dies und Das*.

Another slim but noteworthy volume published by Handshake was *Merveilleux Coup de Foudre* (1982), a dual collection of poetry and collage by Joans and Jayne Cortez, the Black American poet whose Bola Press had published *Flying Piranha*, Joans's book with Joyce Mansour. As explained earlier, Cortez had envisioned Bola as a counter to publishers too invested in the "mainstream," when that word meant "a stream set up with standards to exclude all other streams."[15] The story of *Merveilleux Coup de Foudre* illustrates Cortez's point about the exclusionary nature or general lack of vision in mainstream publishing. Joans had long wanted to do a "joint book" with her, but had been turned down by conventional houses, even ones that had published his own work. He had in fact pitched the joint book idea to Mary Ellen Wang back in 1973: "I've got a new Afro-angle. This is it: I would like to do a 'His & Her' book of poems ... [with] a female poet. That female poet would be poetess JAYNE CORTEZ." He went on to praise Cortez as a "stronger" poet than himself, "the only jazz poetess" he had ever encountered, and "the very best Black lady poet"—second only in his estimation to Gwendolyn Brooks. He thought the "His & Her" project would make for a unique "booking" opportunity, and that it would sell: "That is if yall could understand the great potential of a joint book. It would perhaps start a trend of unselfishness, which is so badly needed in the USA, both amongst the Blks as well as Whites."[16] Hill & Wang did not in fact understand Joans's proposal, and the project languished until the early 1980s, when Jim Haynes, always open to counter-intuitive, commercially-dubious projects, finally did publish Cortez and Joans together in *Merveilleux*, in a small edition of 100.

The poems in *Merveilleux* are in French, but the title page informs readers: "Translations from the American by: Ms. Ila Errus & M. Sila Errus," those enigmatic, slippery Surrealists who are also credited with the collages and drawings. As in *Dies und Das* two years later, *Merveilleux* opens with a two-page spread dedicated to Wifredo Lam and announcing: "Ted Joans recontre Wifredo Lam à Paris en 1968," while Cortez did so in "Havanne en 1978," again emphasizing the connections among Black American artists and Black artists from the Third World, connections Joans kept stressing from the mid-1960s on.

The poetry section opens with Cortez's "Je Suis New York City," a translation of "I Am New York City." This was a favorite of Joans's, as he called it "one of the most marvelleous poems to hear her read ... a poem of urbane surreality," and included it as well in *Dies und Das*.[17] Joans's section is populated by poems such as "Croissants" (which had appeared in *Spetrophilia* as "Straight Croissants"), "Common Place Bulues," which had appeared in *Flying Piranha*, and his classic poem of the Beat era, "Why Try?" translated here as "A Quoi Bon Essayer?" which pokes fun at a white hipster trying to be Black. In their irreverent and surprising juxtapositions and images, the poems showcase both Joans's Surrealist point of view, and his commitment to a sense of ineffable natural Blackness that is the theme of "Why Try?" and that he had elaborated and theorized in the late 1960s and 1970s. In this way, the selection of Joans's work in *Merveilleux* is largely retrospective, but as in *Flying Piranha*, an important aim of the book is to dispense with the notion that single-author poetry collections are the best or only way to disseminate one's work—"unselfishness" is the watchword, "*coup de foudre*" meaning literally "lightning bolt" but idiomatically "love at first sight," and so the beauty of the collection is in the marvelous pairing of the two poets.

Haynes was always willing to publish Joans's shorter work, and one other book worth mentioning is *Honey Spoon* (1991), a prose-poem which

FIGURE 47.2 *A dual book of poetry by Ted Joans and Jayne Cortez, published by Jim Haynes's Handshake Press in Paris (1982). Cover collage by Joans, reprising his cowrie motif from other books and featuring an image of Cortez.*

circles back to Tangier in the 1960s: its title refers to the spoon needed to cook majoun, a technique Joans had learned from Ahmed Yacoubi some thirty years before. "He carried the honey spoon," Joans writes of his protagonist, "in the upper left side pocket of his safari jacket although it had long been empty of its original contents yet it was still potent permeated with majoun magic."[18] *Honey Spoon* began, as Joans explained, "in Tangiers Morocco on December 30 1990 as a birthday present for my friend the writer PAUL BOWLES. The poem developed into riffs of prose starting with HE, just as though I was blowing a trumpet."[19] The result is a seventy-four-page prose-poem in which each verse or paragraph begins with "He" and follows various kinds of imagistic associations that draw heavily on Joans's experiences in North Africa and the Sahara Desert.[20]

By the late 1990s, Joans and Haynes had developed a long and deep friendship, and Joans felt Handshake might be the most fitting place to publish a retrospective volume of Selected Poems. Haynes was interested, but try as he might, he could not make the numbers work—it was simply too expensive for his "kitchen sink" press to produce a book of that size.[21] *Teducation: Selected Poems* would eventually be published by Coffee House Press in Minneapolis. Whatever their professional relationship at any given moment in time, Joans and Haynes remained close for the rest of Joans's life.

48

Merveilleux Coup de Foudre at Shakespeare and Company

Although over the years Paris meant countless connections, cafés, art openings, and poetry performances, one other particular place bears special mention for the way it changed the trajectory of Joans's poem-life. Shakespeare and Company was (and is) a landmark English-language bookstore on the Left Bank, in view of Notre Dame. Founded in the early 1950s by another American expatriate, George Whitman, and named in homage to the famed Lost Generation-era bookshop run by Sylvia Beach, Shakespeare and Company was in the second half of the twentieth century a magnet for readers, writers, poets, bohemians, and eccentrics from all over the world. Whitman lived to be 98 years old, and over seven decades cultivated the bookshop as his domain, a place overrun with books that welcomed impecunious travelers—nicknamed Tumbleweeds—to stay in the upper floors in exchange for doing a little work around the shop. As Whitman once put it, "We're slowly reconstructing the ancient monastery that existed here centuries ago, but in the form of a wonderland of books, friends, writers, comrades, such as never before existed on land or sea, a socialist utopia masquerading as a bookstore."[1] Given such broadly socialist commitments, for Whitman the economics of bookselling tended to be secondary to his desire to oversee that "wonderland of books," a tiny republic of letters and safe haven for literary wayfarers. He liked, on his more poetic days, to compare the shop to a novel come alive: "All the characters in this bookstore are fictitious so please leave your everyday self outside the door … I created this bookstore like a man would write a novel, building each room like a chapter, and I like people to open the door the way they open a book, a book that leads into a magic world of their imaginations."[2]

It's not hard to see why such a perspective would have appealed to Joans—as it appealed to countless literary wanderers over the decades—and Shakespeare and Company became one of his favorite haunts in Paris. It was a "literary institution," he wrote in 1993, "the very first of its kind, to give a visiting writer a room to create in free of charge."[3] The bookstore figures in "Razzle Dazzle," where George Whitman has a cameo as "C.M. Spitman," a "benign bohemian," and where Theodor Green's love interest, Theodora Oregon, serves as a "housemother." Before taking up with Theodor, she had lived at Shakespeare in exchange for doing "a certain amount of chores in the bookshop."[4] In real life, Joans had met another of his femmoiselles, "Annab," there in the early 1970s—"Well, there goes my House Mother," Joans reported Whitman as saying. "She'll be off to Tangiers or Timbuktoo, or some other desert place in Africa."[5] Joans and Whitman in fact grew so close over the years that when his daughter, Sylvia, was born in the late 1970s, Joans became what she called one of her "first friends." Sylvia was more or less raised in the bookshop (and took it over after her father's passing), and Joans had watched her grow up. "I consider myself very lucky," she told me, "to have had that contact and chance to see the world through his eyes at such a young age!"[6]

Joans read at Shakespeare and Company countless times over the years, and his events were draws for those in the know, and delightful moments of serendipity for those who were not yet Teducated. Writer and theorist Manthia Diawara has described in vivid detail what it was like stumbling upon a Joans reading at Shakespeare and Company back in the early 1970s, and how the encounter then changed the course of his life. Born in Bamako, Mali, Diawara had come to Paris to be a writer, and one day wandered into Shakespeare and Company just as Joans was about to read. He was struck by the figure Joans cut: "He had a salt-and-pepper beard, a Hausa Kufi hat, a green vest over a long Indian shirt that came down to his knees, and white Indian pants to match his shirt."[7] Barely in his twenties at the time, Diawara was fascinated that Joans kicked off the reading with greetings in French, Arabic, Swahili, Mossi or Mooré, and English. And in fact, before getting to the poetry, Joans spent a long, leisurely time telling stories about the bookshop, about various writers he had known, and then explaining important concepts from Surrealism and African art. It was only then that he opened one of his books: "Joans read like the African bards who recite the Sunjata epic. That meant that he read as many words together as possible, and came to a sudden stop-time pause. In this staccato manner, his poetry was like a jazz song, and one could almost predict where the lines began and where they ended."[8] Although Diawara's English was not yet proficient enough to understand everything Joans was reading, it almost didn't matter because the words were like "music and therefore universal."

When the reading concluded, Joans pointed to Diawara through the crowd and said, "When I was reading my poems, I could feel the guy standing over there. He was with me, and I could feel it. If you are a poet, you know what I'm talking about, ya dig?"[9]

FIGURE 48.1 *Ted Joans, aged 60, at Shakespeare and Company, one of his favorite haunts in Paris (April 1989). Photo by Daline Jones. During Daline's visit to Paris, Joans held a reading at Shakespeare "dedicated to all daughters," specifying that "spiritually" the evening was dedicated to "Whitman's daughter Sylvia Beach Whitman and to my own daughter Daline, who is doing her very first Apriling in Paris" (Shakespeare and Company Archives).*

Diawara was by turns hot-faced and thrilled to be "anointed" by Joans in this way, and went along with the crowd heading over to an after-party of sorts at the Café Le Rouquet, where Joans was to hold court again. There he regaled everyone with more stories while also "pulling out of his bag the books and drawings that he autographed to sell to our group."[10] He was willing to entertain, encourage and mentor, but no bread, no Ted.

From that evening on, Diawara and Joans became friends—"more like brothers," as Diawara thought—with Joans taking the younger writer under his wing and giving him advice on how to live the creative life. Diawara, for his part, was in disbelief that Joans had taken an interest in him. "Everybody admired him," he recalled. "People romanticized him as a poet, a jazz musician, and someone who had withstood American Jim Crow racism and survived … His friendship automatically legitimized you as a sophisticated person."[11] Joans's advice to Diawara as a bright young African was to get himself to the States. He had seen countless African writers and intellectuals languishing around Paris, unable get a foothold in the culture:

They have been here twenty, thirty years without finishing school. They can't get a job here, and they can't go home, either. If you stay here, that's your future. You won't be a writer or anything else here … They like Africans better in the States than they do black Americans. That's why I am here. I can't stand it there. Go there, and you'll have a chance of succeeding.[12]

Joans gave Diawara addresses of friends he should seek out in the States: Amiri Baraka, Toni Cade Bambara, Jayne Cortez, Mel Edwards, Charles Sanders, Lois Mailou Jones, and others. "They are all very important people," Joans told him. "They can help you with school, or with your writing."[13] With such an amazing list of contacts in hand, Diawara did heed Joans's advice and went to the States, earning a PhD (coincidentally, at Indiana University in Bloomington), and going on to have a very successful career. But he always traced his move to the States to Ted Joans and that first reading at Shakespeare and Company. Ten years later, when Diawara returned to Paris as a married assistant professor, Joans took him back to Shakespeare and Company and introduced him around: "He's now a fancy professor at the University of California. And I told him to go to America. I knew it! Ha, ha, ha!"[14]

———

There are many, many stories of Joans at Shakespeare and Company that he or others told over the years. One of his favorites was the time George Whitman asked him and an ex-army colonel, Hank, to serve as "sergeants at arms" for an Anaïs Nin reading. Joans had met Nin once before, at a signing at the Gotham Book Mart back in the late 1960s, and was looking forward to seeing the literary icon once again. But he was perplexed by Whitman's request: "George," he said, "what does a sergeant at arms do?"

"Well," said Whitman. "You keep people movin. You don't let them hold up Anaïs."[15]

Joans dutifully settled in to "guard" Nin with Hank, the ex-colonel, an American who had come to Paris to try his hand at writing a best-selling novel. Whitman presided over the affair, as Joans recalled, in a "paisley oversized jacket, dark stained trousers, and tartan plaid shirt with a thick striped tie twisted into a tortured knot around his marabout stork neck."[16] He brought out some questionable-looking tea, and Nin remarked, "You are still serving tea in those little dirty glass jelly-jam jars; why don't you buy a proper tea serving set? No, George, I don't want any of your tea." While this was going on, Joans was sipping from a bottle of the just-released Nouveau Beaujolais, and offered to share some with her, even though no proper glasses were to be found. Not a problem, said Nin, and showed Joans how to tip the bottle just so, to create a "long cleanly flow" right into her mouth, without it touching lips, or spilling wine down her front. "That was the very last encounter," Joans said, "that I had in person with Anaïs Nin, the fabulous femmoiselle whose journals dare to kiss 'n' tell."[17]

Shakespeare and Company was such a home to Joans that he collected his mail there, and once in a while would even man the shop's cluttered front desk, and in this way was readied for any new operations of Objective Chance. One day when he was serving in this capacity, who should stroll in but David Gascoyne, poet and author of *A Short Survey of Surrealism*, one of the books that had introduced Joans to Surrealism way back when he was a kid, another full-circle moment for him. Gascoyne was up there in years, but had never met George Whitman, and mistook Joans for him, a serendipitous error that tickled Joans's fancy since Whitman was a white man whose pronounced goatee made him resemble Trotsky and Colonel Sanders. After the case of mistaken identity was sorted out, a new friendship was forged, and Gascoyne would ramble around the city with Joans, telling him stories about "the surrealists in the Golden Years" and pointing out various places of Surreal interest, an experience that one can partly replicate by following the suggestions in "Aardvarkian Surreal Stroll Through Paris," where Joans again transmits this sort of knowledge.[18]

———

Such wondrous run-ins notwithstanding, there is no doubt that Joans's most significant encounter at Shakespeare and Company occurred in 1991, when he met a young Canadian art student, Laura Corsiglia. Although she was then living with some relatives on the northern edge of Paris, Corsiglia had been raised in a small First Nations village in British Columbia's Nass Valley. Born to an Italian American father and French mother—a linguist who also spoke Nisga'a fluently—Corsiglia had grown up speaking both French and English. She later characterized those early years as a special kind of Surrealist education:

> In the northern First Nations village where we lived since I was three, the masks were danced and there were potlatch feasts and the first pole-raising ceremony in a hundred years. (This village, Gitlakdamiks, is near where Kurt Seligmann had traveled.) Surrounded by rainforest, the village is crisscrossed by near trails and wolves sing at night. People discussed these happenings in terms where natural and supernatural (real and surreal) were not divided. Animals communicate through mental pictures, images that are not confined by language to inexact words.[19]

At 18, she brought this interest in and awareness of Surrealism with her when she came to study at Paris's École Nationale Supérieure des Beaux-Arts.

One day she decided to check out a poetry reading at Shakespeare and Company, and there was Joans, in a pink seersucker suit and handmade plastic tie covered in crawfish designs, a memorable ensemble to say the least, and she later learned the tie had been sewn for him by a fan.[20] But it was the way Joans had read that made the real impression on her, and in the magic vulnerability of his poetry, she "recognized him in a way that startled me."[21] She didn't speak to him that day, but when the reading was over, Joans passed around a collection plate, suggesting that people could toss in coins or Métro tickets—as a poor student, Corsiglia had no money to spare, but she did contribute a Métro ticket.

A few months later, on November 11, 1991, Corsiglia once again found herself at Shakespeare and Company, sitting among the overstuffed shelves, and drawing in her notebook. As he often was, Joans happened to be there as well, spotted a fellow artist at work, and waited until she seemed finished with the drawing to approach her. She was not yet nineteen at the time, and Joans was sixty-three, but they were both struck by le merveilleux coup de foudre, and Corsiglia thought to herself: "Oh, there you are! Oh, it's you." As she told me, "Certain obvious differences that we had kind of melted away in the face of how interested in poetry and art we both were," and their connection became "obvious very quickly."[22] As they chatted that day, Joans mentioned the recent passing of American actress Gene Tierney, best known for playing the title role in the classic film Laura (1944), remarking that he had "just lost Laura and was finding a new one." Corsiglia, taking up the thread, brought up the most famous Laura in literature, Petrarch's beloved and muse.[23] Already there was a meeting of minds. Leaving Shakespeare and Company, they took a stroll around Paris, and at one point Joans turned to Corsiglia with a revelation: "I would like to see you every day."

She wanted to see him everyday, too, but there was a slight wrinkle: Joans already had tickets to fly to the States in one week. So they initially had just seven days together, during which Joans had invited Corsiglia back to the nest, and in fact had entrusted her with a key, encouraging her to read and create there while he was traveling. The place was even tinier for two, its only luxury a small sink, but it was packed with books and writing and records and African masks—from her perspective, "it was so full and so filled with thoughts ... a place of wonderful richness."[24] After those seven days, Joans flew to the States as planned, but they had vowed to write each other over the next months—it didn't matter that he would be on the move, as he gave her his friend and lawyer Hy Shore's MacDougal Street address, and the address of City Lights Books in San Francisco, covering both coasts for good measure.

Their bond only intensified as they corresponded over those months, and in a short story he wrote in 1993, Joans offered dreamy musings on letters between his alter ego, Dr. Rotapep, and Rotapep's "worthy companion-lover Laureine de Boisiglia," whose own "letters were apertures onto her subconscious that caused valid augmentations to our on-going romance."[25] This is just the merest of glimpses into what Joans must have thought of his correspondence with Corsiglia, but it does hint at the power of that particular coup de foudre. By the time he finished his "Collaged Autobiography" in the early 2000s, he announced that he was:

FIGURE 48.2 *Ted Joans and Laura Corsiglia in Paris, at Jacques Bisceglia's bookstall (1995). Laurated Archive.*

spiritually married by love to my femmoiselle Laura, who is intelligent and scandalously beautiful. Mais oui, we therefore continue adventuring our ongoing poem life twogether [*sic*] as Laurated! Our poem life is truly a greater one, a surreality unlike any other the world has known ... She is equally intelligent as I, thus we both learn from one another. She reads faster than I could ever and we both have mutual interest in contemporary world art and literature, plus the human condition. We dress often as attractive twins, especially when we be On The Roads.[26]

Once he returned to Paris they were reunited, and soon started on those Roads together. Their first adventure was a bus trip from Paris to Prague, a sort of test to see if they could travel well with each other. It went marvelously, and they were a resolved couple from then on; as he states in those lines from his "Collaged Autobiography": Laura + Ted = Laurated. "It never seemed to me," said Corsiglia, "like a choice to be in love with Ted."[27]

49

Laurated

Paris was a base of operations, and Laurated moved into a slightly larger nest near the Jardin des Plantes—a place replete with the luxuries of two hot plates, a fridge, and even a small bathroom.[1] From this nest they travelled the world, from Morocco to Zimbabwe to Oaxaca, Mexico, where they began returning annually. Corsiglia stressed to me that no matter where they were in the world, these were years of constant creation and imaginative attention to whatever was encountered: "we basically talked about art and made art all the time," she said, and cultivated the idea of life as art, as a poem-life, which meant, in part, "*seeing*, walking along and seeing and seizing upon certain things. Being aware of a network of correspondences as you move through the world."[2]

The Paris years were rich, but eventually they left the city for Seattle— partly because Corsiglia missed the towering trees and mountains of North America's Pacific Coast, partly because they had friends in Seattle and family in nearby Vancouver, and partly because Joans felt it was time to give living in the States another try after so many decades abroad. Despite all his globe-trotting, he had never made it to Asia, and he imagined Seattle as halfway between Paris and Tokyo, hoping to someday get there, though he never did. In Seattle they moved to the International District, which had once been the city's Chinatown, renamed to reflect the diversity of people who were then actually living there. But America was short-lived.

In February 2000, Laurated had been visiting New York City when they heard news that shook them both, as it did many others.[3] A year before in the city, a 23-year-old Guinean student, Amadou Diallo, was shot 41 times by plainclothes police officers—a "41 Bullet Lynch," as Joans put it in his poem about Diallo's murder.[4] While Joans and Corsiglia were visiting, those officers were acquitted after their trial had been moved up to Albany. He turned to her and said, "I don't want to live in this country anymore." They began plans to move to Vancouver, which they had talked about before—Joans had been there many times, Corsiglia was born there, it was an international city, and so it seemed a suitable place. They rented an apartment in the Kitsilano neighborhood, which Corsiglia for one found more "international" than Seattle, "more arts more literary life and more languages too."[5]

During these last eleven years of his life, Joans kept characteristically busy with his art and writing, publishing five more poetry collections: *Double Trouble* (with Hart Leroy Bibbs) (1992); *Okapi Passion* (1994); *Teducation: Selected Poems* (1999); *Wow* (1999); and *Our Thang* (with Corsiglia) (2001), as well as shorter poetry booklets such as *Poèmes* (1993); *Poems for You: In & Out of Africa* (1994); and *Select One or More: Poems* (2000). These last three are very difficult to find, and handsome objects in and of themselves. *Select One or More* in particular was beautifully produced, 7 × 12 inches, handset and printed by the Bancroft Library's Albion handpress on French paper and featuring as a frontispiece a tipped in head-on photograph of a rhinoceros by Ron O'Connor (Joans had lent it). The poems themselves do not appear elsewhere, and include a charming ode to librarians "Love Thy Librarian"; "Not on Most Maps," which compares St-Cirq-Lapopie, where the Bretons kept a house, to Timbuktu; and an elegy for his longtime friend, Hy Shore, "No Bye Bye." In those years he also wrote a major Surrealist memoir, "Collaged Autobiography" (completed in 2002), which in his dreams become reality would be printed in a run of 50,000 hardcovers, with 100 special copies including "a small plastic slip containing sand from the Sahara."[6] In our own reality, still we are waiting for the manuscript to be published at all.

   In keeping with a theme of his poem-life, much of the work he produced in those years was marked by collaboration. Published in Paris, *Double Trouble* is, as its title announces, a dual collection of Joans's work alongside that of Hart Leroy Bibbs, a fellow expat, poet and musician. Bibbs's early book, *Poly Rhythms to Freedom* (1964), was dedicated to "the Militant Young Blacks," and featured strident poetry reminiscent of Joans's hand grenade poems, including one that seemed to prefigure the title *Double Trouble*, "Double Talk," about the inherent contradiction of being a Black person in an America devoted to freedom only in the most abstract of senses.[7] Joans's work in *Double Trouble* was a mix of old and new poetry, as many of his collections were, because he wanted to resist notions of poetic "development" by instead showing a non-chronological sampling of his work. This same sensibility was on display in *Teducation*, his edition of Selected Poems. That book is divided into two parts: "Hand Grenade" and "Fertileyes & Fertilears," and despite his publisher's strong protestations, he insisted on the poems being in alphabetical rather than chronological order, all the better to frustrate neat, retrospective ideas of developmental artistic arcs.

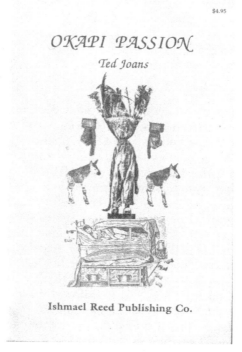

$4.95

OKAPI PASSION

Ted Joans

Ishmael Reed Publishing Co.

FIGURE 49.1 *Collaged cover of* Okapi Passion *(1994) published by Ishmael Reed.*

Just as the title *Double Trouble* emphasizes the collaborative vibe to be found within, so too does *Our Thang*, the last book Joans published in his lifetime. *Our Thang* is subtitled *Several Poems, Several Drawings* and features eighteen poems by Joans and thirty-nine drawings by Corsiglia, so the book really is an exhibit of both Joans's poetry *and* Corsiglia's drawings, rather than a poetry collection illustrated by drawings. The poetry is mainly work from the 1990s and early 2000s that revisits some of Joans's familiar themes—movement, Surrealism, liberation, his pantheon of writers and artists, and the magnetic pull of Timbuktu. Far from mimetic illustrations of the poems, the drawings are Surrealist figures that are often half-human, half-animal, recalling both the transformation masks of the Nisga'a village where Corsiglia grew up, and something like the "symbolic portrait of the two of us" André Breton includes in *Nadja*.[8] As poet and novelist John Olson put it in his dreamy, perceptive review of *Our Thang*:

Without otherness, there is no consciousness and no direction. If there were only one entity—say it is a sphere called "me"—there would be no

Universe: no otherness: no awareness: no consciousness: no direction. When one otherness complements another we have synergy: dollops of morning light bedazzling us all with hope and coral. Poet Ted Joans and artist Laura Corsiglia have pooled their respective resources to create a synergistic garden of words and illustrations, a magnetic field of surrealist energies.[9]

Despite more than a half-century of sustained creativity in writing and film and visual and performance arts, "official," institutional recognition was still scant. In fact, it would seem that only an institution such as Ishmael Reed's Before Columbus Foundation, established in 1976 to "provide recognition and a wider audience for the wealth of cultural and ethnic diversity that constitutes American literature," would be suited to recognize Joans's accomplishments—and indeed they did in 2001, with a Lifetime Achievement Award.[10] More typical of how Joans's reputation circulated was his inclusion in Ann Charters's wide-ranging *Portable Beat Reader* (1992). His poems "The Sermon," "Afrique Accidentale," and "A Few Blue Words to the Wise," were featured in the first edition, but owing to a dispute, Joans was not included at all in the subsequent paperback edition— except that Part 4, dedicated to "Other Fellow Travelers," is still titled "A Few Blue Words to the Wise," so he casts an unacknowledged shadow over the anthology, perversely fitting as he remains there but not there, a situation that mirrors his general position in American—and transnational—art and letters.[11]

Impinging on future assessments of this position were two events that occurred in the late 1990s, when Joans was just edging into his seventies: in June 1998, he sold the bulk of his papers to UC Berkeley; and in 1999 he published *Teducation: Selected Poems.* I see these two events as interconnected insofar as they inaugurate the archival phase of Joans's poem-life, ironic in that the very thing he questioned or refashioned throughout his poem-life— institutional archives—would become a condition for the persistence of this poem-life. The Ted Joans Papers are a wealth of unpublished material, notebooks, correspondence, artwork, and the like, while *Teducation* collects a sampling of work from the previous half-century, offering a taste of his forty-plus books and booklets, which are so often difficult to hunt down. As critic and radio host Jack Foley—another of Joans's friends—remarked when *Teducation* was published,

One of the best pieces of news for readers in this year 2000 is the appearance of a widely-distributed, easy-to-find, generous selection of the poems of Ted Joans ... Those of us who have had the good luck to hear Ted Joans read know what he's about: we have had to search in rare book stores, used book stores, even new book stores, just to get a shot of that wonderful, wildly imaginative oeuvre of his; people who have heard him know, and so we look for his books.[12]

FIGURE 49.2 *Cover of* Our Thang *(2001) by Ted Joans and Laura Corsiglia, featuring an exquisite corpse by Joans and Corsiglia. The couple created countless exquisite corpses between 1991 and 2003, ten of which are featured in* Surreally Ted Joans, *72–83.*

Teducation was, then, a lifeline for readers and aficionados. However narrowly construed it may seem when held against Joans's lifetime of multimodal creative achievement, the book is the closest we have (as of this writing) to an omnibus edition of his work, although a true omnibus would require many more pages to show the scope and multiplicity of just his written work, to say nothing of his considerable, and highly varied, efforts in the visual, plastic, and filmic arts.

And of course a third significant factor in how we understand Joans and his legacy is Laura Corsiglia herself—every Van Gogh needs a sister-in-law like Johanna Bonger, every Kafka a Max Brod, and Corsiglia's efforts to both preserve his writing and correspondence not yet in the Berkeley archives, and to make his visual work more well known across the landscape of the artworld, have been paramount. As was the case in those last eleven years of Joans's life, when Corsiglia was his constant companion, "muse," and collaborator, since that time she has remained his dedicated champion and sensitive interpreter. I'm conscious of how lightly I'm treading over Joans's years with Corsiglia because I really do want to leave the details of those years to her or others to share (or not) on some future project as yet unwritten.

But during one of our conversations, she did write this to me, sketching out a vision for what a book about Ted Joans might look like:

> To approach a literary biography of Ted, as you'll appreciate, a serious rendezvous with Surrealism would be required, and with the Music and its creators, colonialism at home and abroad, visual art of all time periods in North America, Africa, Europe and Oceania, and an appreciation for Ted's appreciation of the autonomy of wild animals, especially the Rhinoceros, Okapi, Tapir, Aardvark, Pangolin, Echidna and Platypus, his friendships in many directions and decades, his skepticism toward institutions that did not preclude an affectionate relationship with museums and libraries, his sincere belief in love, garlic, animism, and objective chance, Langston Hughes, André Breton, Joyce Mansour, radio and cinema, the Undercommons avant la lettre, collaborative cadavres exquis and solo hitchhiking (never in the USA), his assumed anti-nationalistic standing place that includes a love for the lifesaving high arts of creativity and pleasure as self defense invented by African Americans specifically, as well as his life in movement as a traveler who was never once slumming and did not see life as a boy gang at all—and you'd probably have to stand still at several points of the globe, probably in person ... to look at the sky and the leaves, to start with.[13]

To start with. This book, *Black Surrealist*, I realize with each passing day, each time I reread a poem or study a new artwork I had not seen, is nothing but a start, a first attempt to dig a bit into Joans's poem-life while digging him and his point of view. "They all want to know," he wrote in "Spadework," "my factual as well as fictional life before I have it exposed to the public. How would they know what was true and the real, or what was surreal and wishful imagination of ted joans"?[14] So "getting the facts straight is difficult for friendly biographers"—truer words were never written, it turns out, but maybe *Black Surrealist*, however pale an imitation it is of his life, will be a spring of sorts for others curious about the man, the facts, the legend, the multifaceted body of work. Maybe elaborations will bloom, or corrections, deepening this legend, bringing its complexity into better, convulsive focus, amplifying our sense of a true original, one of the great liberated poet-artists of the twentieth century, Ted Joans, born July 4, 1928 on a riverboat in Cairo, Illinois ...

FIGURE 49.3 *Ted Joans playing trumpet on a plinth in the Jardin du Luxembourg in Paris (1964). Evidently this was part of a Happening, but one thinks also of Joans's poem to André Breton, "The Statue of 1713."*

Coda: Atmospheric Rivers

As I was deep at work on this book, Laura Corsiglia graciously invited me out to her place in Northern California to discuss Ted Joans, and to look through some material she had carefully preserved since his passing. I had flown from New York to San Francisco, right into a major weather system, an "atmospheric river" wreaking havoc throughout the state. It was a five-hour drive from SFO to Laura's under the best conditions, and though I had once lived north of San Francisco myself, I was unaccustomed to the deluges caused by these atmospheric rivers, which had been appearing with more and more frequency, evidence of a changing planetary climate. I drove headlong into the storm nonetheless, feeling I was inside Joans's poem "Rain & Rain"—"What a torrential downpour / Wind augmenting the rain / Visibility only a few feet."[1]

That's how immersed in his work I had been at the time, pushing through as darkness fell and remembering how "Rain & Rain" concludes, with the surprising turn from the power of a rainstorm to an appreciation of a natural force that recognizes no race or national boundaries: "It is raining again / Somewhere else in / This big round universal world / Rain has no nationality."[2] But if I had been immersed in Joans and his poem-life, it was an immersion in a "Ted Joans" constructed in my own imagination, built from books and manuscripts and interviews and artworks and faded letters catalogued now in distant libraries, a banal truism that made me wonder, as I continued north through that unremitting storm, if perhaps I could be inching closer to a Ted Joans more tangible, more real. In Sonoma County, my stomping grounds of yesteryear, as he would say, I disregarded blinking portable signs pointing out the obvious: "Severe Weather." Joans did his best to be in Timbuktu when "severe winters" rolled into Europe—but I remained blithely confident in my severe weather driving abilities from seven years in brutal winter Wisconsin. But somewhere around Ukiah I discovered that the atmospheric river was indifferent enough to my needs that the 101 had been flooded and closed and I was forced to hunker down in a motel for the night.

Roads were passable in the morning, according to the gossip in the motel parking lot, and I made it up through Humboldt and its stately, fog-bound redwoods, one of the real vitalizing drives in California. Finally beyond the forests, flung out on the coast again, I arrived at Laura's, and was amazed by what she had prepared. There was a Research Room, as she called it, set up in a garage space that was then warehousing the riches she had preserved: Joans's papers, some of it first shipped by freighter from Paris to Seattle when they had made their move to the States. Over the next days, she pulled treasure after treasure from this room, the Laurated Archive, sharing manuscripts and artworks and letters that have been invaluable to the shape and scope of this book.

"Existence is elsewhere," said Joans quoting Breton, and one artifact I did not see directly in the Laurated Archive was one of Joans's crowning artistic achievements, the exquisite corpse *Long Distance*, which had recently been shown at a major retrospective, *Surrealism Beyond Borders*, mounted at the Met in New York (October 4, 2021–January 30, 2022), then at the Tate Modern in London (February 25—August 29, 2022). I had marveled at *Long Distance* when it was displayed at the Met, positioned at the end of the show and unfolded in all its thirty-foot glory on the longest vitrine I can recall seeing, its label on the wall explaining:

> Joans's equation of Surrealism, travel, and community is powerfully represented in *Long Distance*, a more than thirty-foot-long cadavre exquis ... drawing that the artist began in 1976. It would move alongside Joans to London, Lagos, Dakar, Marrakesh, New York, Rome, Berlin, Mexico City, Toronto, and beyond, growing with invited contributions. With a production span of thirty years (two beyond Joans's own life) and 132 participants, *Long Distance* extends the Surrealist idea of collaborative authorship to far-flung people the artist united through his travels.[3]

Many personalities who have animated this book contributed to *Long Distance*, including Gregory Corso, Charles Henri Ford, Joyce Mansour, Jayne Cortez, Paul Bowles, Laurens Vancrevel, Tuli Kupferberg, Jean-Jacques Lebel, David Gascoyne, Lawrence Ferlinghetti, William Burroughs, Nancy Joyce Peters, Philip Lamantia, Ishmael Reed, Alan Ansen, Michel Leiris, Amiri Baraka, Robert Benayoun, Konrad Klapheck, Roberto Matta, Robert Creeley, Franklin and Penelope Rosemont, and Robert Farris Thompson—this list is of course a mere sampling as there are a hundred other contributors, a truly mind-boggling act of assemblage and aesthetic communion across time and space. This was Joans at his best: 132 artists over thirty years, creating together the longest exquisite corpse ever made.

Long Distance was birthed in London in May 1976, when Joans asked a Surrealist artist friend, Conroy Maddox, to start an exquisite corpse. Ever interested in repurposing found material, Joans produced some dot

FIGURE 50.1 *Ted Joans et al.,* Long Distance *(1976–2005).*

matrix printer paper he had come across, cut it down to make it a bit more narrow, and Maddox did the first drawing—this would be the beginning of a project thirty years in the making. Over all that time, *Long Distance* was never mailed, but carried personally by Joans—and then Joans and Corsiglia—on many circuits around the globe, and when he would invite someone to participate, he would reverently unpack *Long Distance* from its protective coverings, various envelopes he called the work's "skins," and the person would add a drawing without knowing anything about the rest of the work, per the rules of the old "cadavre exquis" game. Only when the new addition was finished was the whole of *Long Distance* revealed. In this way Joans amassed dozens upon dozens of contributions from artists and writers all over the world, some famous and some not as well known, his own perambulations and tastes forming the tissue holding the work together.

One delight of *Long Distance* for Joans was in fact that it linked work of so many wildly different personalities, and though it was never displayed during his lifetime, he knew that were it ever exhibited, part of its power would come from the fact that no visitor to any gallery or museum would be familiar with every single contributor, and that the piece would be impossible to take in all at once. Viewers would have to move around the sheer length of *Long Distance*, interact with it in physical space as they perhaps recognize certain names while also discovering many more, so the experience of discovery and recognition would be ever-changing and unique to each person.

In 2001, Joans gifted *Long Distance* to Corsiglia, and expressed his wish that she contribute to it in the future, perhaps after he had gone on to the ancestors. The last participant during Joans's life was David Hammons, who made his addition on September 8, 2001. In 2005, two years after Joans's passing, Corsiglia felt ready to add to *Long Distance* again, and invited their old friend Ron Sakolsky, whose clear-eyed definition of Surrealism I quoted at the beginning of this book, to add a drawing. He did so on November 8, 2005, and as *Long Distance* had been opened once more, Corsiglia decided it was time for her to add a final contribution and "close" the piece. She did so on November 11, 2005, the 14th anniversary of the day she and Joans had first encountered each other at Shakespeare and Company in Paris. She repacked *Long Distance* in its skins and put it away for safe keeping.

One day years later, Penelope Rosemont mentioned to Corsiglia that a thoughtful new exhibition about international Surrealism was in the works in New York. One thing led to another, and Stephanie D'Alessandro reached out about the possibility of including *Long Distance*, along with some other work by Joans, and Corsiglia agreed to lend the pieces—with the stipulation that she could honor the work's history by hand-carrying it across the continent. When it came time for *Long Distance* to be exhibited in New York, she brought it herself from the West Coast, taking immense pride in walking it—and Ted Joans—through the front door of the Metropolitan Museum of Art.

Following the *Surrealism Beyond Borders* exhibition, the Museum of Modern Art in New York expressed interest in *Long Distance*, and eventually convinced Corsiglia that MoMA would be the right home for the work. In 2024, MoMA did acquire *Long Distance* for its permanent collection, a development that Joans had, naturally, anticipated. Way back in 1961, when he was demanding a moral revolution in the United States, he declared the time was now "for the Museum of Modern Art to show my paintings"—it had taken sixty-three years for some version of this dream to become real, but then the world is still catching up with him in many ways.[4]

So *Long Distance* was not at Laura's when I visited, but existence might be elsewhere, and another rich opportunity did present itself in that particular moment in time and space. When David Hammons contributed to *Long Distance* in 2001, he documented the process in a short film, which also captured Joans unfolding the entire piece as Hammons made his addition. This film, "Ted Joans: Exquisite Corpse," was shot in the New York City apartment of Robin D. G. Kelley and Diedra Harris-Kelley, and had only been shown publicly once, in conjunction with the sole previous exhibition of *Long Distance*, in Lisbon in 2019 (a printed facsimile of *Long Distance* had also once been shown in Dakar). But Laura had a copy, and offered to screen it for me.

The atmospheric river still had not quite exhausted itself, and it was chilly in the Research Room as Laura found a copy of Hammons's film on her laptop. The wind was whipping up, creeping around the seals of the door, straining the capabilities of the space heater humming at the wall. She got the film going and we balanced on stools.

The camera focuses mainly on Joans, who at seventy-three is spry enough to sit on the hardwood floor and unfurl *Long Distance* down a hallway in the Kelleys' apartment. With each new contribution, Joans describes the participant, the circumstances of the invitation, the person's personal quirks or artistic forbearers, moving down the hall with each additional drawing, and as the piece asserts itself in physical space, it seems more and more like a river, and I was on the stool remembering another phrase of Joans's, the "vast and endless river of surrealism," thinking suddenly of those rivers flowing through his poem-life, the Mississippi, the Niger, the Seine, which like all rivers are ever-changing means of connection—"I have traveled," he wrote once, "up rivers longer than white history."[5]

An experience of simultaneity: the atmospheric river resolving itself outside, the river of *Long Distance* washing down the hallway onscreen, Joans himself wading side-saddle in the alluvial parquetry, all the rivers winding through his life: "Dear Langston," he wrote, "The rivers: Nile, / Niger, last month the Congo / Now at last the Zambezi … Yes Sir, / I too have known rivers."[6] So what I was seeing was *Long Distance* coursing down that hallway, a repudiation in fact of time and space, an exuberance come together through Joans as he free-associates the Who, What, When,

Where, How of each contribution, animating a magnetic, magic river of connection.

But the simultaneities only multiplied from there, because just as Laura herself was onscreen in the film, so too was she sitting beside me on her stool. 2001 Laura stood near Joans as *Long Distance* proceeded down the hall, working its way to Hammons, and she would announce the name of each new contributor as he unfolded it, jogging his memories, and in the present moment, in the Research Room among the manuscripts and auras, she began, almost as an aside, to describe the little things that were happening on the day the film was shot, but not captured by the camera. Reality was bursting at the seams.

Absent from the film, she was telling me, were not only marginal conversations in the apartment, the march of current events outside in the wider world, but also what happened when the film was over and *Long Distance* was repacked away with Hammons's new addition. Remember all this was taking place in Lower Manhattan on September 8, 2001, and it must have been the next day when Joans and Corsiglia were strolling around SoHo, attuned as always to the magnetic fields, alive to connections, other kinds of meaning, and they stumbled upon an object nestled incongruously in the gutter: a horseshoe. As Laura described that horseshoe in the middle of a city, I couldn't help but think about the very first photographic plate in *Nadja*, depicting a horse and carriage standing at the ready, captioned by Breton: "My point of departure will be the Hôtel des Grands Hommes ..."[7] Ellipsis in original, suggesting what was yet to come.

A century on in New York, Joans bent and picked up the horseshoe, having a flash of interpretation, feeling a shower of sparks, struck by the realization that it symbolized a new point of departure: "Horseshoe," he said. "Iron horse. We should take the train." The operation of Objective Chance once more, and they bought Amtrak tickets out to the West Coast for the following day, narrowly avoiding the terrorist attacks, and so had by that Tuesday put a long, long distance behind them, with many more distances ahead, seventeen hundred and thirteen imaginative possibilities for freedom on the horizon, liberated poem-lives beckoning again from elsewhere.

NOTES

Preface

1 "Deeper."

2 Steve Dalachinsky, "'Jazz Is My Religion'—All of Ted Joans & No More," *Shuffle Boil* 4 (summer/fall 2003), 60.

3 Amiri Baraka, Foreword to "Collaged," n.p.

4 Author interview with Yuko Otomo (September 19, 2022).

Chapter 1

1 André Breton, *Nadja*, trans. Richard Howard (New York: Grove Press, [1928] 1960), 11.

2 "Ted Joans Speaks," in *Black, Brown, & Beige: Surrealist Writings from Africa and the Diaspora*, ed. Franklin Rosemont and Robin D. G. Kelley (Austin: University of Texas Press, 2009), 229–30; "Deeper."

3 "I, Too," 4.

4 *FP*, 27.

5 "Deeper."

6 "Last Words" in *ATJ*, 94.

7 Joans uses this phrase in his dedication to *HS*, n.p.

8 Joans to Michel Fabre (January 24, 1978), MFA, box 9, folder 37.

9 "Money Soon," n.p. Justin Desmangles states that "*femmemoiselle*" was "a neologism Ted borrowed from fellow Surrealist Jacques Hérold" (Desmangles, "Remembering Ted Joans: Black Beat Surrealist," SFMOMA's Open Space [December 5, 2017]): https://openspace.sfmoma.org/2017/12/remembering-ted-joans-black-beat-surrealist/

10 From a résumé in a "Professional Career" folder, TJP, carton 3, folder 47.

11 "I Went," 46. Note that part of this handwritten manuscript is reproduced in Joans, *PP2*, 11–16. The full manuscript in the Ted Joans Papers runs to 49 pages.

12 Yuko Otomo, "Let's Get TEDucated! Tribute to Ted Joans," *Artedolia* (June 2015): https://www.arteidolia.com/tribute-to-ted-joans-yuko-otomo/; Author interview with Michael Kellner (October 7, 2022).

13   "Jadis," 94.

14   "Deeper."

15   Joans to Michel Fabre (January 24, 1978), MFA, box 9, folder 37. See also TJP, box 19, folder 20: "my Holy Trinity: Food/Sex/and Art. This is the direct road to the marvelous."

16   Joans, résumé (ca. 1984), HBR, box 8, Joans folder.

17   Robin D. G. Kelley, "Ted Lives!" *Shuffle Boil* 4 (summer/fall 2003), 3.

18   "I See," 252.

19   "Spadework," 86.

20   Janet Malcolm, *The Silent Woman: Sylvia Plath and Ted Hughes* (New York: Vintage, 1994), 8–9.

21   For a good discussion of the historical and political conditions from which Surrealism emerged—and splintered—see Kirsten Strom, *Making History: Surrealism and the Invention of a Political Culture* (Lanham, MD: University Press of America, 2002), 13–49.

22   André Breton, *Manifestoes of Surrealism,* trans. Richard Seaver and Helen R. Lane (Ann Arbor: University of Michigan Press, 1972), 26.

23   Ron Sakolsky, "Surrealist Subversion in Chicago," *Race Traitor: Surrealism in the USA* 13–14 (summer 2001), 5.

24   Joans, "Toronto Canada Notes," TJP, box 19, folder 12.

25   Breton, *Manifestoes,* 14.

26   "I, Too," 4.

27   Breton, *Manifestoes,* 4; "Shut Mouth," 6.

28   "I, Too," Preface, n.p.

29   Joans, "Toronto Canada Notes," TJP, box 19, folder 12.

30   "Ted Joans Speaks," in *Black, Brown, & Beige,* 229. This letter was originally published, in French, as Ted Joans, "Fragments du lettres," *La Brèche 5* (October 1963), 66–7.

31   "Shut Mouth," 53.

32   René Depestre, "An Interview with Aimé Césaire," in Césaire, *Discourse on Colonialism,* trans. Joan Pinkham (New York: Monthly Review Press, 2000), 83.

33   See Aimé Césaire, *Les Armes miraculeuses* (Paris: Gallimard, 1946).

34   Robin D. G. Kelley, "A Poetics of Anticolonialism," in Césaire, *Discourse on Colonialism,* 18.

35   Robin D. G. Kelley, *Freedom Dreams: The Black Radical Imagination* (New York: Beacon, 2002), 168. This book offers an excellent discussion of the links between the Black radical tradition, European Surrealism, and examples of vernacular Surrealism such as the blues. For another valuable account of the kind of Surrealism with which Joans deeply engaged, see Jonathan P. Eburne, "Decolonial Surrealism," in *Surrealism,* ed. Natalya Lusty (New York: Cambridge University Press, 2021), 342–62.

36   "Collaged," 129.

37   Stevenson quoted in Malcolm, *Silent*, 80.

38   James A. Miller, "Ted Joans," in *The Beats: Literary Bohemians in Postwar America* (*Dictionary of Literary Biography* 16), ed. Ann Charters (Detroit, MI: Gale, 1983), 268.

39   Kurt Hemmer, "Joans, Ted," in *Beat Culture: Icons, Lifestyles, and Impact*, ed. William T. Lawlor (Santa Barbara, CA: ABC-Clio, 2005), 159; A. Robert Lee, "Ted Joans," in *Encyclopedia of Beat Literature*, ed. Kurt Hemmer (New York: Facts on File, 2007), 157.

40   See Joanna Pawlik, *Remade in America: Surrealist Art, Activism, and Politics, 1940–1978* (Oakland: University of California Press, 2021), 109.

41   Joans, résumé (ca. 1984), HBR, box 8, Joans folder.

42   Biographical Statement in "Teducation: Poems for Eyes and Ears" (1989), City Lights Books Records, Additions, box 31, folder 10, and *Okapi*, 28; Anton Mikofsky, "Joys and Moans of Ted Joans," *CORE Magazine* (fall/winter 1973), 70.

43   "Shut Mouth," 60.

44   See Mark Polizzotti, *Revolution of the Mind: The Life of André Breton* (New York: Farrar, Straus and Giroux, 1995), which opens with a reflection on why Breton changed his birthday (3–4).

45   André Breton, *Arcanum 17*, trans. Zack Rogow (Københaven and Los Angeles: Green Integer, 2004), 165. See also Patrick Lepetit, *The Esoteric Secrets of Surrealism: Origins, Magic, and Secret Societies*, trans. Joe E. Graham (Rochester, VT: Inner Traditions, 2014), which discusses Breton's interest in tarot and its connection to 1713.

46   "Spadework," 52.

47   "I See," 224.

48   "I See," 255.

49   "I See," 256.

50   Robert Farris Thompson, *Flash of the Spirit: African and Afro-American Art and Philosophy* (New York: Vintage, 1984), 74. In "Collaged," Joans describes submerging himself in a "sacred lake" outside Ibadan, Nigeria, in order to find favor with Oshun, the most powerful water goddess or orisha in the Yoruba religion; the water is "the bosom of Oshun. She, and only she shall be the judge" (65–8; quotation on 67).

51   Pawlik, *Remade*, 106.

52   Saidiya Hartman, "Venus in Two Acts," *small axe* 26 (June 2008), 2.

53   Hartman, "Venus," 7.

54   Hartman, "Venus," 11.

55   For an essay that refers to Hartman in the context of discussing the use of archives in Joans's edited magazine, *Dies und Das*, see Terri Geis, "'Snip/snap/and cut'": Ted Joans and *Dies und Das*," *Dada/Surrealism* 24 (2023), 1–20.

56 Hartman, "Venus," 9.

57 "I See," 228.

58 Justin Desmangles associates this method of Joans's with the use of the contrafact in bop: "The Be-Bop use of the contrafact, variously employed by Joans, is then also a vibrant, vigorous counternarrative that is often a damaging critique of imperialism, as the slave-system of the West is called. This Be-Bop invention of contrafacts in substance is entirely akin to the creation of the poetry of 'miraculous weapons,' as Aimé Césaire would describe them with such vivaciousness and life affirming verve" (Desmangles, "'Jazz Is My Religion': The Be-Bop Optics of Ted Joans," in Joans, *Jazz Is My Religion* Exhibition Catalogue [Paris and New York: Zürcher Gallery, 2024], 12–13).

59 "I See," 227.

60 "I See," 227.

Chapter 2

1 Joans, "Spades and Foreign Fays," TJP, box 18, folder 24.

2 "Spades and Foreign Fays," TJP, box 18, folder 24.

3 "Shut Mouth," 3; "(sic)" in original.

4 "I See," 227.

5 "Shut Mouth," 4.

6 *Our*, 10.

7 *Afrodisia*, 97. Note also in "Le Griot surréaliste" in *Jazz Hot* (1969), Joans opens by claiming he was born on a riverboat, insisting also that he heard the sounds of jazz in his mother's womb (22); see, further, the poem "Pre-Birth Memories," *Teducation*, 195–96.

8 "Shut Mouth," 4.

9 "Shut Mouth," 8.

10 Joans, "1714," TJP, box 1, folder 46. Note that box 1, folder 46 in TJP is catalogued as "America, 1961"; Joans often typed multiple poems on a single sheet of paper, something that is not currently reflected in the TJP Finding Aid. "1714" is typed on the same sheet as "America," and is totally different from "Le 1714" (box 1, folder 43).

11 "Shut Mouth," 8.

12 Thomas A. Hale, *Griots and Griottes: Masters of Words and Music* (Bloomington: Indiana University Press, 1998), 350–6.

13 Hale, *Griots*, 57.

14 Hale, *Griots*, 19.

15 "Shut Mouth," 9.

16   "Collaged," 145.

17   Joseph Conrad, *Heart of Darkness*, ed. Paul B. Armstrong, 4th edition (New York: Norton, 2006), 7–8.

18   "Collaged," 145–6.

19   1920 US Census, Arlington, Carlisle County, Kentucky, population schedule, Enumeration District: 50, p. 7A, lines 2–11, entry for Limm Pile and family; digital images, *Ancestry*, "1920 United States Federal Census," citing NARA Film: T625_564: https://www.ancestry.com/discoveryui-content/view/113784602:6061/

20   "Deeper."

21   "Spadework," 2.

22   "Spadework," 52.

23   "Shut Mouth," 88.

24   "Shut Mouth," 90.

25   W. E. B. Du Bois, from "Of Our Spiritual Strivings" in *The Souls of Black Folk* (New York: Penguin, [1903] 1996), 5. Joans once cited *The Souls of Black Folk* as one of the "five most influential books on the black man's condition" (Henry Louis "Skip" Gates, Jr., "Ted Joans: Tri-Continental Poet" *Transition* 48 [April/June 1975], 12).

26   "Shut Mouth," 90.

27   "Spadework," 2.

28   Joans, fragment, TJP, box 19, folder 29.

29   Joans, "Langston Hughes: Poet for Real," TJP, box 16, folder 39.

30   Joans, "Langston Hughes: Poet for Real," TJP, box 16, folder 39.

31   "I, Too," n.p.

32   Paul Garon, *Blues and the Poetic Spirit* (San Francisco: City Lights, [1975] 1996), 53–4.

33   "I See," 225–6; "madly" quotations from "Langston Hughes: Poet For Real," TJP, box 16, folder 39.

34   David Gascoyne, *A Short Survey of Surrealism* (San Francisco: City Lights, [1935] 1982), 61.

35   "Langston Hughes: Poet for Real," TJP, box 16, folder 39.

Chapter 3

1   Author interview with Yvette Johnson (February 21, 2022).

2   "Spadework," 4.

3   "Spadework," 4.

4   "I Went," 36–7.

5 "I See," 256.

6 "Shut Mouth," 60.

7 Joans, untitled fragment, TJP, box 19, folder 30.

8 "Spadework," 61.

9 See, for example, Dominic J. Capeci, Jr. and Martha Wilkerson, *Layered Violence: The Detroit Rioters of 1943* (Jackson: University Press of Mississippi, 1991), which analyzes the merits and shortcomings of these early reports and studies.

10 Author interview with Yvette Johnson (February 21, 2022).

11 Hartman, "Venus," 9.

12 Hartman, "Venus," 2; "I See," 256.

13 Thomas Klug, email to Author (January 26, 2023).

14 "26 Negroes Slain Before Peace Restored in Detroit," *The Chicago Bee* (June 27, 1943), 2; "Motorman Beaten," *Michigan Chronicle* (June 26, 1943), 5.

15 "Race War in Detroit," *Life* (July 5, 1943), 94, 95.

16 Hartman, "Venus," 9.

17 *ATJ*, 85.

18 Joans, "Mes Février Fathers," *Teducation*, 180.

Chapter 4

1 "I Went," 36–7; Author interview with Yvette Johnson (February 21, 2022).

2 See: https://digital.library.louisville.edu/concern/images/ulpa_cs_195859?locale=en/

3 "Spadework," 100; Kevin Johnson, "Renaissance Jazzman Ray Johnson is on a Roll," *Louisville Music News* (February 2003): http://www.louisvillemusicnews.net/webmanager/index.php?WEB_CAT_ID=49&storyid=1580/

4 Sam Clark, Letter to the Editor, *Our World* 2.9 (October 1947).

5 Brazzle Tobin, "Scouting Derbytown," *Louisville Defender* (September 22, 1955), 13.

6 Ben Sidran, *Black Talk* (New York: Da Capo, 1981), 105.

7 Sidran, *Black Talk*, 105.

8 See also Judith Wilson, "Garden of Music: The Art and Life of Bob Thompson," in Thelma Golden, ed. *Bob Thompson* (New York: Whitney Museum of American Art, 1998), which notes that Joans and Horace Bond founded an "International Bebop Society" in Louisville sometime in the late 1940s or early 1950s (36). Many years later, Joans encountered this information about himself at the Bob Thompson Whitney exhibit, and noted "Actually it was 'on and off/in and out' that I spent time in 'Loavule'

and started the Contemporary Art Society, made up of painters, writers and musicians even a disc-jockey. It was an early period of teducation before the word teducation" ("Collaged," 103).

9   Joans, "Mr. Gillespie was Also Exuberance," TJP, box 18, folder 22.

10 Mort Schillinger, "Dizzy Gillespie's Style, Its Meaning Analyzed," *Downbeat* XI (February 11, 1946), 14.

11 Brazzle Tobin, "Scouting Derbytown," *Louisville Defender* (July 2, 1953), 8.

12 See "Bebop Fashions: Weird Dizzy Gillespie Mannerisms Quickly Picked Up as Accepted Style for Bebop Devotees," *Ebony* (December 1948), 31–3.

13 Joan Locke, Letter to the Editor, *Ebony* (February 1949), 9.

14 Author interview with Yvette Johnson (February 21, 2022).

15 See the documentary film, "The Beecher Terrace Story," dir. Lavel White (2020): https://www.youtube.com/watch?v=cFVvJIWE4uM/

16 Sigmund Chandler, "That Joans Boy—Greenwich Village and Pagans," *Louisville Defender* (August 11, 1955), 13.

17 Brazzle Tobin, "Scouting Derbytown," *Louisville Defender* (October 13, 1951), 9.

18 Malcolm, *Silent*, 136.

19 "Former Musician Dunks Horn, Turns to Painting," *Louisville Defender* (July 2, 1952), 15.

20 "Spadework," 54–5.

21 "Shut Mouth," 14; there are many references to Joans's managerial positions in the *Louisville Defender* from this period, but see, for example: *Louisville Defender* (December 17, 1952), 1, which features a photograph of Joans as manager of the Palace Theater, looking respectable in a three-piece suit and spectacles; and *Louisville Defender* (January 5, 1952), 14, which features a photo of him in his capacity as Palace manager, presiding over an event which "gave a free movie and refreshments to some under-privileged children from Jefferson County during the Christmas holidays."

22 "Shut Mouth," 14.

23 "Shut Mouth," 14.

24 Author interview with Yvette Johnson (February 21, 2022).

25 Brazzle Tobin, "Scouting Derbytown," *Louisville Defender* (March 26, 1953), 8.

26 "Contemporary Art Club," *Louisville Defender* (March 17, 1951), 18; Brazzle Tobin, "Scouting Derbytown," *Louisville Defender* (August 4, 1951), 17.

27 Georgetta Chambers, "The Younger Generation," *Louisville Defender* (July 23, 1952), 10.

28 See, for example, "Parties and Picnics," *Louisville Defender* (June 25, 1953), 11.

29 "Former Musician Dunks Horn, Turns to Painting," *Louisville Defender* (July 2, 1952), 15.

30 Brazzle Tobin, "Scouting Derbytown," *Louisville Defender* (June 9, 1951), 17.

31 "Former Musician Dunks Horn, Turns to Painting," *Louisville Defender* (July 2, 1952), 15.

32 Brazzle Tobin, "Scouting Derbytown," *Louisville Defender* (January 5, 1952), 12.

33 "Tobe Howard to Celebrate His Tenth Year in Radio August 30," *Louisville Defender* (August 22, 1957), 13; Brazzle Tobin, "Scouting Derbytown," *Louisville Defender* (March 29, 1952), 15.

34 Anita, "Scribbling Socially," *Louisville Defender* (May 21, 1953), 11; "hung up" quotation from Joans to Franklin Rosemont (July 28, 1970), RP, box 80, folder 3; for the poem, see *ATJ*, 38–9.

35 "Ex-City Artist, Ted Jones, Clicks in N.Y.," *Louisville Defender* (September 9, 1954), 8.

36 Joans painted a whole series of portraits from the Lincoln statue in the park outside the Louisville Public Library, which at the time did not serve Black people.

37 "Spadework," 70.

38 "Artist to Continue Exhibit at Bar," *The Louisville Times* (July 11, 1952), 4.

39 Kay Flemming, "Louisville's Salvador Dali," *Glare* (May 1952), 22–3; quotation on 22.

40 Flemming, "Louisville's," 22.

41 "Greenwich Village in Derbytown Apt.," *Louisville Defender* (April 23, 1952), 9.

42 "Greenwich Village in Derbytown Apt.," *Louisville Defender* (April 23, 1952), 9.

43 Georgetta Chambers, "The Younger Generation," *Louisville Defender* (May 28, 1952), 9.

44 Georgetta Chambers, "The Younger Generation," *Louisville Defender* (June 11, 1952), 9.

45 Brazzle Tobin, "Scouting Derbytown," *Louisville Defender* (August 13, 1953), 8.

46 See "Professional Career," TJP, carton 3, folder 47.

47 Joans, résumé (ca. 1984), HBR, box 8, Joans folder.

48 Miller, "Ted Joans," 268.

49 "Former Musician Dunks Horn, Turns to Painting," *Louisville Defender* (July 2, 1952), 15.

50 "Greenwich Village in Derbytown Apt.," *Louisville Defender* (April 23, 1952), 9.

51 Dina Kellams, email to Author (April 27, 2022). Kellams also searched through Indiana University's student directories from 1945–46 to 1951–52, and there was no mention of Ted Jones, nor does he appear in any Bloomington city directories in 1945, 1946, 1948, 1950, or 1952.

52 Dina Kellams, email to Author (July 2, 2022).

53 Dina Kellams, email to Author (July 7, 2022).

54 "I, Too," 1.

55 "Spadework," 55, ellipses in original.

56 "Spadework," 52. The full passage is: "I was studying for a BA in painting, fine arts was my major. But not to teach, just to learn the fundamentals of painting and the history of art. I worked hard and under men like Alton Pickens, Edward Melcarth, Boris Margo, Bradley W. Tomlin, Ulfert Wilkie, Justis Beir [Justus Bier], and countless others who were either artists in

residence or was added to the faculty" (52). At the time, some of these people, such as Surrealist Alton Pickens, did teach at Indiana University, but most were connected to the University of Louisville, including, in addition to Bier, Edward Melcarth, a Louisville native, and German-born painter Ulfert Wilkie.

57 Justus Bier, "Surrealist Exhibition in Chicago Proves Exciting," *The Courier-Journal* (December 7, 1947), section 3, page 5.

58 "The Current Art Calendar," *The Courier-Journal* (September 28, 1952), section 5, page 18.

59 "Former Musician Dunks Horn, Turns to Painting," *Louisville Defender* (July 2, 1952), 15.

60 Justus Bier, "Junior Gallery to Exhibit Animal Prints," *The Courier-Journal* (June 3, 1951), section 5, page 4.

61 "First Negro Gets U.L. Art Degree," *Louisville Defender* (August 18, 1955), 1.

62 Joans, "Dont Fucketh With Me," TJP, box 16, folder 45. This date 1949 is typed on the typescript itself, but at the end of the typescript, there is Joans's signature, in blue ink, and the date "Oct 14, 1962," which could have been the date he made the few scattered blue ink corrections on the typescript.

63 Joans, "Dont Fucketh With Me," TJP, box 16, folder 45.

64 Breton, *Manifestoes*, 14.

65 "Spadework," 39.

66 "Sanctified Rhino," *ATJ*, 21.

67 Joans to Franklin and Penelope Rosemont (December 1991), RP, box 80, folder 3.

68 "Spadework," 42.

69 Brazzle Tobin, "Scouting Derbytown," *Louisville Defender* (December 10, 1959), 13. Probably "'39" is a typo for "'49" as Joans would have been only 11 in 1939.

70 Brazzle Tobin, "Scouting Derbytown," *Louisville Defender* (September 16, 1954), 12.

71 Author interview with Yvette Johnson (February 21, 2022).

72 "I, Too," 14; "I See," 224.

Chapter 5

1 "I, Too," 52.

2 Gerald Nicosia, "Sharing the Poem of Life: An Interview with Ted Joans," *Beat Angels*, ed. Arthur and Kit Knight (California, PA, 1982), 139.

3 "Shut Mouth," 78–9; "I, Too," 52; 114.

4 "Spadework," 47.

5 Joans later recalled that Elizabeth Taylor had "bought one of my chapbooks," and pronounced her "A beautiful woman, a real person. Nothing phony about

her at all" (Gerald Williams, "Ted's Dead: Hushing the Fuzz," *Massachusetts Review* [2005], 246). In "I, Too," however, Joans writes that "No one bought any of my paintings, although I did give them copies of my book of poems" (52).

6　"I, Too," 50.

7　"I, Too," 51.

8　"I, Too," 51. Joans also mentioned this incident in a poem dedicated to Kerouac, "Holy Hijinks": "Yep, it is best to piss / in Cedar bar sink than / forest green cord pants / charcoal grey flannel baggy / trousers" (Joans, "Holy Hijinks," *Moody Street Irregulars* 6/7 [winter/spring] 1980), 15; this poem appears also in *NDB*, n.p.

9　"Spadework," 50.

10　*Hipsters*, n.p.

11　Margaret Randall, *I Never Left Home: Poet, Feminist, Revolutionary* (Durham, NC: Duke University Press, 2020), 84. Randall knew Joans, describing him as "brilliant and very human." She remembered Joans, Chayefsky and Krim as "regulars" at the Cedar, telling me that though it "may well have been Ted who brought" Taylor and Fisher to the Cedar, she just didn't remember that detail, only the fact of the famous couple turning up at the bar. Margaret Randall email to Author (April 26, 2022).

12　"I, Too," 52–3.

13　Joans, "Je Suis Un Homme," *ATJ*, 4.

14　Robert Reisner, "Intro," in *FJP*, n.p.

Chapter 6

1　Gerald Nicosia, "A Lifelong Commitment to Change: The Literary Non-Career of Ted Joans," in *Teducation*, iii.

2　Franklin and Penelope Rosemont, "Poet of Marvelous Liaisons," in "Collaged," n.p.

3　Penelope Rosemont, "Surrealism, Encounters, Ted Joans," in Rosemont, *Surrealist Experiences: 1001 Dawns, 221 Midnights* (Chicago: Black Swan Press, 2000), 83. For André Breton's influential, foundational exploration of *le hasard objectif*, see Breton, *Communicating Vessels*, trans. Mary Ann Caws and Geoffrey T. Harris (Lincoln: University of Nebraska Press, 1990); this work was originally published in 1932. Mary Ann Caws's introduction to the English translation, "Introduction: Linkings and Reflections," offers a useful gloss on Breton's ideas about *le hasard objectif*, which were in turn important to Joans.

4　Rosemont, "Surrealism," 85–6.

5　"Collaged," 47; Laura Corsiglia on "Cover to Cover" radio program with Jack Foley (November 26, 2003).

6　"Ted Joans, Poet Talking to Dave Kennard," *Other Scenes* (April 1, 1968), 4.

7   Joans, "An Abbreviated Autobiography of AfroAmerican Artists Over Yonder," TJP, box 16, folder 30.

8   Michel Carrouges, *André Breton and the Basic Concepts of Surrealism*, trans. Maura Prendergast (Tuscaloosa: University of Alabama Press, 1974), 180.

Chapter 7

1   Although in "Spadework," Joans says "breezy spring of 1951" (55), and in "Collaged," he insists that the bus came from Fort Wayne, not Louisville (135).

2   "I, Too," 7.

3   "I, Too," 6.

4   "I, Too," 6.

5   John Donald Gustav-Wrathall, *Take the Young Stranger by the Hand: Same-Sex Relations and the YMCA* (Chicago: University of Chicago Press, 1998), 181.

6   "I, Too," 8.

7   "I, Too," 9.

8   "I, Too," 9.

9   "Mad Genius," *Hue* 2.3 (January 1955), 36.

10 Nicosia, "Sharing," 131–2.

11 "Spadework," 5.

12 See Nicosia, "Sharing," 132–3.

13 "Collaged," 113.

14 "IBS," 46.

15 Ralph Ellison, "Harlem is Nowhere," in *Collected Essays*, ed. John F. Callahan (New York: Modern Library, 2003), 321–2.

16 Ellison, "Harlem," 321–2.

Chapter 8

1   "I, Too," 13.

2   "I See," 228.

3   "I, Too," 14; see Jeff Gold, *Sittin' In: Jazz Clubs of the 1940s and 1950s* (New York: Harper Design, 2020).

4   See C. Gerald Fraser, "Lewis Michaux, 92, Dies; Ran Bookstore in Harlem," *New York Times* (August 27, 1976), 34.

5   "I, Too," 32.

6   "I, Too," 14; 23.

7   Langston Hughes, *The Weary Blues* (Garden City, NY: Dover, [1926] 2022), 3; *BPW*, 2. Joans capitalized "In the Dark" to emphasize the reference to a Count Basie song of the same name.

8   Arthur P. Davis, "Jesse B. Semple: Negro American," *Phylon* 15.1 (1954), 21.

9   "I, Too," 14–15.

10 Joans to Langston Hughes (January 1963), LHP, box 89, folder 1689.

11 Joans, "The Langston Hughes I Knew," *Black World* (September 1972), 14–18; quotation on 15.

12 Joans interviewed by Jack Foley (Berkeley, CA: Pro Verse, 1989). Cassette tape in Bancroft Library, UC Berkeley, Phonotape 2262 C. In this interview Joans also referred to his "Hand Grenade poems" as "influenced by my first mentor and guide, Langston Hughes."

13 *BM,* 72.

14 "Ted Joans on Langston Hughes" [interview with St. Clair Bourne], *The Langston Hughes Review* 15.2 (winter 1997), 72.

15 Langston Hughes, *The Collected Works of Langston Hughes,* vol. 2: *The Poems, 1941–1950,* ed. Arnold Rampersad (Columbia: University of Missouri Press, 2001), 53.

16 *ATJ,* 26. The poem was also published in *FJP* (n.p.) and *BPW* (17). There's an extant draft of "Uh Huh" dated 1954 which is very close to the published version in *ATJ*, except that it is labeled "Paducah, Ky 1954" ("Uh Huh," TJP, box 1, folder 12). When the poem was reprinted in *Teducation*, it was labeled "Pulaski, TN 1949" (107); that version is also somewhat altered from earlier printings (it is rendered in all capital letters, for example). The shifting times and places attached to the poem mean that the exact Southern location that inspired it remains uncertain—but of course underscore the widespread reach of Jim Crow.

17 "Ted Joans on Langston Hughes," 71; Joans, "Once Upon a Time There Was a Poet of Harlem," TJP, box 16, folder 41.

18 "I See," 230.

19 Joans to Langston Hughes (January 1963) LHP, box 89, folder 1689; Joans to Langston Hughes (February 10, 1963), LHP, box 89, folder 1689.

20 Hughes, *Weary Blues,* 77.

21 "I See," 228.

22 "Ted Joans on Langston Hughes," 72.

23 Arnold Rampersad, *The Life of Langston Hughes*, vol. 2: *1941–1967* (New York: Oxford University Press, 2002), 408. Joans mentions this evening in "Langston Hughes I Knew," and "Ted Joans on Langston Hughes," 75. A week after the Shakespeare and Company reading, Joans wrote a poem, "Promised Land," dedicated to Langston Hughes: "a poet full of blues": "Langston Hughes / paid his dues / in the Harlems / of the U.S.A."; see Joans, "Promised Land," TJP, box 2, folder 23, and the published version in *Teducation*, 69.

Chapter 9

1   *ATJ*, 74–6. This poem was first printed in *ATJ*, then again in *BPW*, and in *Teducation*. An early draft from 1953 survives and is quite close to the version in these books, the most notable difference is the final line, which reads "I hear it speak as the voice of death saying 'This is IT' the 38!" (TJP, box 1, folder 9).

2   "I, Too," 27.

3   "Collaged," 73; Bob Sylvester, blurb in Babs Gonzales, *I Paid My Dues* (New York: Lancer Books, 1967), n.p.

4   Gonzales, *I Paid*, 57; all these incidents are discussed in *I Paid*.

5   Kerouac, "Beatific," in *Portable Jack Kerouac*, ed. Ann Charters (New York: Viking, 1995), 569.

6   Maurice Kulas, "Some Notes on the Author," in Babs Gonzales, *Movin' on Down the Line* (Newark, NJ: Expubidence Publishing, 1975), n.p.

7   Gonzales, *I Paid*, 48–9.

8   "I See," 223.

9   "I, Too," 28; in "I, Too," Joans recalls this apartment as being a 139th Street Brownstone "across from the famous blond brick block of apartments, Strivers Row" (28), but in "Shut Mouth," he recalls it being "the top floor of a tenement on 118th at 8th Avenue" (18).

10 "Shut Mouth," 18.

11 *ATJ*, 74.

12 Joans tells the story of Mrs. Johnson in "Shut Mouth," 18–20, and I'm summarizing and quoting from that account.

13 "Shut Mouth," 20.

14 "Shut Mouth," 20. In 1964, "The .38" was reprinted in *Underdog*, a literary review out of Liverpool edited by poet Brian Patten, of future *The Mersey Sound* (1967) fame, suggesting Joans's growing reputation across the Atlantic (see Joans, "The .38," *Underdog* 5 [1964], n.p.). Two years later, in his somewhat arch and often dismissive overview of Black American writing, *Black on White: A Critical Survey of Writing by American Negroes* (New York: Grossman, 1966), David Littlejohn only mentioned Joans in passing, but did call "The .38" "a stunning existential happening poem" (95).

Chapter 10

1   Joans, "Worthy Beat Women," in *Women of the Beat Generation*, ed. Brenda Knight (Berkeley, CA: Conari Press, 1996), 332; Joans, "I Went," 5.

2   "I, Too," 36–7. This conversation is reproduced from the specifics Joans recalled in "I, Too"; he recounts the particular language of the conversation somewhat differently in "I See," 220–1, but the substance is the same.

3   "I, Too," 44; "I Went," 29.

4   "I Went," 28; "I, Too," 114.

5   "I Went," 28.

6   Gregory Corso to Don Allen (September 7, 1957), in *An Accidental Autobiography: The Selected Letters of Gregory Corso*, ed. Bill Morgan (New York: New Directions, 2003), 54.

7   "Spadework," 77.

8   Ronald Sukenick, *Down and In: Life in the Underground* (Middletown, CT: Invisible Starfall Books, [1987] 2022), 15. This book is a great account of the New York bohemian underground in the 1950s and early 1960s, and features Joans prominently throughout.

9   "I, Too," 74.

10   "I, Too," 74.

11   "I, Too," 83.

12   "Spadework," 77.

13   "I, Too," 77.

14   "I, Too," 35.

15   "Collaged," 157.

16   *Afrodisia*, 32.

17   See J. Olumide Lucas, *The Religion of the Yorubas* (Lagos: C.M.S. Bookshop, 1948), 156; *Afrodisia*, 65.

18   Joans, "On Dada in Nigeria" [typed-up excerpts from work on Africa; 1952], TJP, box 19, folder 5. This page is labeled 1952 in the archives because Joans has written this date in under "Reggin Nam, Sudanese Rituals," but Miner's *The Primitive City of Timbuctoo* appeared in 1953, so the page was likely typed up then.

19   Joans, "The Air Conditioned Oasis" (1967), TJP, box 17, folder 29.

20   Horace Miner, *The Primitive City of Timbuctoo* (Princeton, NJ: Princeton University Press, 1953), 161.

21   "Collaged," 157.

22   "Collaged," 157–8.

23   Breton, *Nadja*, 60.

24   Michel Fabre, *From Harlem to Paris: Black American Writers in France, 1840–1980* (Urbana: University of Illinois Press, 1991), 310.

25   Joans quoted in Mort Rosenblum, "Black American Foreigners in Africa," *St. Louis Post-Dispatch* (September 9, 1970), 74; "African official" quotation from Fabre, *From Harlem*, 310.

26   Edward O. Ako, "The African Inspiration of the Black Arts Movement,"
      Diogenes 34.135 (1986), 94.

Chapter 11

1   Joans, "Last Words" in *ATJ*, 94.

2   Joans, "Happy Hip Happenings" (1965), TJP, box 17, folder 28.

3   Joans, "Happy Hip," TJP, box 17, folder 28.

4   "Spadework," 96. A website devoted to Le Gip notes that "Weegee captured
      him drumming at rent parties, perhaps organized with his friend Ted Joans":
      https://www.legip.org/timelinepreview/

5   "Greenwich Village Open House," *Our World* (January 1955), 72.

6   "Greenwich Village Open House," 72.

7   "Village Frenzy," *Our World* (September 1955), 73.

8   Joel Foreman, "Mau Mau's American Career, 1952–57," in *The Other Fifties:
      Interrogating Midcentury American Icons*, ed. Foreman (Urbana: University
      of Illinois Press, 1997), 79.

9   "Collaged," 181.

10   "'Mau Mau' Queen," *Jet* (March 8, 1956), 62. This short notice includes a
      photo of Joans dressed in his Mau Mau regalia helping to bestow the crown
      on Sheppard.

11   Brian Priestley, *Chasin' the Bird: The Life and Legacy of Charlie Parker* (New
      York: Oxford University Press, 2006), 103. This photograph may be found in
      Weegee, *The Village* (New York: Da Capo, 1989).

12   "New Gallery Opens with 'Save Works of Art' Call," *Daily Nation*
      (Kenya) (February 12, 1971), 12; "BMG," 24; "No Mo Space For Toms"
      memorializes: "Dedan Kimathi / drove a Mau Mau train to victory / there out
      there in 'British' East" (*Afrodisia*, 35).

13   "Shut Mouth," 53; *ATJ*, 93.

14   Joans, "Mau Mau Manifesto," TJP, box 18, folder 20. See also the poem
      "MAU MAU MESSAGE TO LIBERALS," which is addressed to white people
      who "LOOK LIKE THE ENEMY" (*BM*, 67); and an untitled 1956 drawing
      in which Mau Mau seems collapsed with Surrealism (reproduced in Pawlik,
      Remade, 105).

15   "All Quiet on MacDougal," *Village Voice* (October 14, 1959), 1.

16   "Cops on the Beatnik," *The Evening Herald* (Pottsville, PA) (October 9,
      1959), 1.

17   This piece is reproduced in Lisa Phillips, *Beat Culture and the New America:
      1950–1965* (New York: Whitney Museum, 1995), 158.

Chapter 12

1 "Mad Genius," *Hue* 2.3 (January 1955), 36.

2 "Mad Genius," 38–9; Brazzle Tobin, "Scouting Derbytown," *Louisville Defender* (September 16, 1954), 12.

3 Ian Gibson, *The Shameful Life of Salvador Dalí* (New York: Norton, 1997), 533.

4 *Dies und Das*, n.p.

5 Joans to Franklin and Penelope Rosemont (ca. 1992), RP, box 80, folder 3.

Chapter 13

1 "I, Too," 88.

2 Café Rienzi menu, ca. 1962; "I, Too," 115.

3 Amiri Baraka, *The Autobiography of LeRoi Jones* (Chicago: Lawrence Hill Books, 1997), 184.

4 "I, Too," 114–15.

5 Joans, "Yeah, Your Mother #1" (1985), TJP, box 18, folder 4.

6 This account of Joans's first meeting Joyce Wrobleski (now Hollinger) is based on his recollections, as described in "Yeah, Your Mother #1" (1985), TJP, box 18, folder 4. Hollinger remembers the details slightly differently, but certainly it did occur in March or April, 1955 at Café Rienzi.

7 Author interview with Joyce (Wrobleski) Hollinger (April 29, 2022).

8 Author interview with Joyce (Wrobleski) Hollinger (April 29, 2022).

9 Bill Morgan, *The Beat Generation in New York: A Walking Tour of Jack Kerouac's City* (San Francisco: City Lights, 1997), 130; "I, Too," 156.

10 "Collaged," 133.

11 Joans, "Qui Suis-Je?" TJP, box 24, folder 13.

12 "Collaged," 134.

13 *Land of the Rhinoceri* was purchased by the Virginia Museum of Fine Arts in 2021. The painting lent its title to an exhibition at the VMFA, *Ted Joans: Land of the Rhinoceri*, curated by Valerie Cassel Oliver (June 1 to November 17, 2024). This exhibition also included 30 Joans pieces from a collection titled "Drawings from Africa," dated 1956. The works in "Drawings from Africa" are watercolor, crayon, pen and pencil drawings on paper. Some are more lifelike portraits of Black figures in various kinds of African dress, while others are slightly more abstracted, but they all have a certain charm.

14   "I Went," 22.

15   "I Went," 22.

16   "I, Too," 95.

17   "Spadework," 47.

18   "Spadework," 47. For a photograph of Joans and Kline together, see Fred W. McDarrah, *The Artist's World in Pictures* (New York: E.P. Dutton, 1961), 65. This book is an invaluable visual record of the New York art scene in the 1950s.

19   "I Went," 22.

20   "Ted Joans," *Arts* 33.4 (January 1959), 63. This review also singles out one of Joans's now well-known paintings of Charlie Parker, *Bird Lives!* (1958), erroneously described as *C. Porter* (it may have been titled *C. Parker* at the time): "a hunched-over silhouette in black, like a single note of music, on a white ground" (this work is visible behind Joans in Figure 19.3).

21   "I Went," 22.

22   Joans, "drawing advertising the opening of Galerie Fantastique," reproduced in Pawlik, *Remade*, 111.

23   Author interview with Joyce (Wrobleski) Hollinger (April 29, 2022).

24   John Wilcock, "How to Get by on $40 per Week," in *The Village Voice Reader*, ed. Daniel Wolf and Edwin Fancher (New York: Grove, 1963), 114.

25   Baraka, *Autobiography*, 185. See also Juliette Harris, "The Struggles Away or Towards This Peace: Amiri Baraka's Life in Visual Art": http://iraaa.museum.hamptonu.edu/page/The-Struggles-Away-or-Towards-This-Peace/

26   Author interview with Joyce (Wrobleski) Hollinger (April 29, 2022).

Chapter 14

1   Ralph Ellison, "On Bird, Bird-Watching, and Jazz," *Collected Essays*, 262. Ellison is referring to Joans's poem "I Love a Big Bird," which appeared in Robert Reisner, *Bird: The Legend of Charlie Parker* (New York: Bonanza Books, 1962), 117–18.

2   Joans, "Bird and Beats," 15.

3   Reisner, *Bird*, 241.

4   Scott DeVeaux, *The Birth of Bebop: A Social and Musical History* (Berkeley: University of California Press, 1997), 18.

5   See DeVeaux, *Birth*.

6   Thelonius Monk quoted in LeRoi Jones, *Blues People: Negro Music in White America* (New York: Morrow Quill, 1963), 198.

7   Hughes, *Collected Poems*, 387.

8   Langston Hughes, *The Best of Simple* (New York: Hill and Wang, 1961), 118–19.

9   "Shut Mouth," 80–1.

10 Sidran, *Black Talk*, 108–9.

11 Sidran, *Black Talk*, 109.

12 "I See," 248.

13 "Bird and Beats," 14; "I, Too," 102.

14 "I See," 221.

15 "I See," 222.

16 "I See," 222.

17 Robert Reisner, "I Remember Bird," in *Bird*, 26.

18 "Jadis," 93.

19 Joans in Reisner, *Bird*, 116.

20 "Bird and Beats," 15.

21 Ahmad Basheer in Reisner, *Bird*, 39.

22 Nicosia, "Sharing," 132.

23 Joans in Reisner, *Bird*, 116.

24 "I, Too," 102; Joans, "*Bird Lives* Review 2," *Coda Magazine* (December 1973), 8.

25 Nicosia, "Sharing," 132.

26 Ross Russell, *Bird Lives! The High Life and Hard Times of Charlie (Yardbird) Parker* (New York: Da Capo, [1973] 1996), 341.

27 Joans, "*Bird Lives* Review 2," 8.

28 "Bird and Beats," 15.

29 "I, Too" 142.

30 "I, Too," 141.

31 "I, Too," 141.

32 "I, Too," 142.

33 Louis van Gasteren, dir. *Jazz and Poetry* (1964). This film is available in two parts on YouTube: Part I: https://www.youtube.com/watch?v=uc9yodZ29UE&t=303s; Part II: https://www.youtube.com/watch?v=hLH3ofveJEo/

34 Tuli Kupferberg, "Greenwich Village of My Dreams," *The Beat Scene*, ed. Elias Wilentz (1960), 67.

35 *BPW*, 105.

36 *BPW*, 30; an early version of this poem is dated March 15, 1962, Timbuktu (TJP, box 1, folder 24). The poem appears in *Teducation* as "They Forget Too Fast," so the "to" in title in *BPW* is likely a typo (98).

37 Harry Pincus recalled that Joans "wanted to build a statue of Charlie Parker, 10 stories tall, straddling the Sheridan Square subway entrance, blowing that genius sax," Pincus, "Now More Than Ever, the Republic of the Village," *AMNY* (January 5, 2017): https://www.amny.com/news/now-more-than-ever-the-republic-of-the-village/

38   Joans, *Dear Bird* (1999; marker and crayon on wood), an image of which is in *Jazz Is My Religion*, 117. Joans echoed this language in a letter to the Rosemonts around this same time (Joans to Rosemonts [ca. 1999], RP, box 80, folder 3).

39   "I, Too," 103; Joans to Harry Nudel (April 24, 1984); collection of Harry Nudel.

40   Quoted in Reisner, *Bird*, 131.

41   Baroness Pannonica de Koenigswarter in Reisner, *Bird*, 134.

42   "Shut Mouth," 77.

43   "Shut Mouth," 77–8.

44   To my mind, one of the most beautiful of Joans's poems about Parker is "Poem for the Dull Brainers," which like "Birdeath" connects Parker back to previous "classical" art forms, this time John Keats's poem "Ode on a Nightingale." This poem is found in *Heads I Win Tails You Lose*.

45   "Ted Joans, 74, Jazzy Beat Poet Known for 'Bird Lives' Graffiti," *New York Times* (May 18, 2003), N43.

46   "Jadis," 93.

47   Reisner, "I Remember Bird," in *Bird*, 26.

48   Joans, "*Bird Lives* Review 2," 9.

49   "Jadis," 93; Joans, "*Bird Lives* Review 2," 9.

50   Joans, "*Bird Lives* Review 2," 9.

51   Amor Kohli, "Sounding across the City: Ted Joans's *Bird Lives!* As Jazz Performance," in *Beat Drama: Playwrights and Performances of the "Howl" Generation*, ed. Deborah R. Geis (London: Bloomsbury Methuen Drama, 2016), 104, 105.

52   "I See," 252; Kohli, "Sounding," 105.

53   See *Wow! Ted Joans Lives!*, dir. Kurt Hemmer and Tom Knoff (Harper College), 2010.

Chapter 15

1   Allen Ginsberg, *The Book of Martyrdom and Artifice: First Journals and Poems, 1937–1952*, ed. Juanita Liebermann-Plimpton and Bill Morgan (Cambridge, MA: Da Capo Press, 2006), 48.

2   Jack Kerouac, "About the Beat Generation" (1957), *Portable Kerouac*, 559–60.

3   Allen Ginsberg, *Howl and Other Poems* (San Francisco: City Lights, 1956), 9, 12.

4   Jack Kerouac, *On the Road* (New York: Penguin, [1957] 1991), 113.

5   Joans, "Bird and Beats," 14.

6   Jack Kerouac, *The Subterraneans* (New York: Grove, 1958), 13.

7   Jack Kerouac, "Essentials of Spontaneous Prose," *Portable Kerouac*, 484.

8   "Spadework," 86.

9   "I Went," 17–18.

10 "Bird and Beats," 14.

11 Jack Kerouac, "From *Mexico City Blues*," *Measure* 2 (winter 1958), 18.

12 "I, Too," 71–2.

13 Joans, "I, Too, at the Beginning" [poem], in Joans, "I See," 226.

Chapter 16

1   "I Went," 23.

2   Ginsberg, "Howl," 21.

3   Charles Kuralt, "William Morris at the Gaslight Café," CBS News (June 9, 1959): http://gvh.aphdigital.org/items/show/227/

4   "I, Too," 107.

5   "Telling It Like It Damn Show Is !!" TJP, box 18, folder 25.

6   "I, Too," 55.

7   *BFP*, n.p.

8   "I See," 233.

9   "I, Too," 101.

10 "I, Too," 106.

11 "A Pad Fad: Beatniks for Rent," *Des Moines Tribune* (November 16, 1960), 52.

12 See *Village Sunday*, dir. Stewart Wilensky (1960): https://archive.org/details/Greenwic1960/

Chapter 17

1   Liner Notes, *Café Bizarre Presents Assorted Madness* (LP: Musitron-102, 1959).

2   Rick Allmen, *Stanley: The Don Juan of Second Avenue* (New York: Harper & Row, 1974), n.p.

3   "I See," 233; Liner Notes, *Assorted Madness*.

4   "City Presses Campaign to Enforce New Zoning Rule," *New York Times* (March 25, 1964), 43.

5   John Strausbaugh, *The Village: 400 Years of Beats and Bohemians, Radicals and Rogues* (New York: HarperCollins, 2013), 379.

6   "I, Too," 53.

7   "I, Too," 106.

8   "I, Too," 177.

9   Danny Land and Mike Charnee, "Loud Noises for a Manufacturer of Poetry," *The Village Voice* (September 15, 1960), 4.

10   In addition to later collections, "The Sermon" is included in *FJP*, *ATJ*, and *Poetry of the Beat Generation,* an anthology of poetry read at the Gaslight Café.

11   "Shut Mouth," 14.

12   "Preface," *ATJ*, n.p.

13   Joans, "Worthy Beat Women," 331.

14   "I See," 233.

15   I'm quoting from the version of "The Sermon" in the revised edition of *ATJ*, 32. In *Teducation*, the poem is dated 1955, but it was heavily revised after its composition; an extant early draft retains the spirit of the advice in the version published in *ATJ*, but details and language are different. For example, the Beat works recommended in the later version are absent from the draft, suggesting the way in which Joans wanted the poem to be understood (or consumed) as a "Beat Generation" poem. That draft does draw a distinction between Beats and Beatnik wannabes: "beware of bearded beatniks, that may be a creepnik" ("The Sermon," TJP, box 1, folder 27.) In *The Hipsters*, Joans defines "Creepnik" as "always on the scene, digging lonely young chicks, pets that are left alone, and other valuables he can steal" (n.p.).

16   See Joans, "In Homage to Heavy Loaded Trane, J.C.," *BPW*, 111–12.

17   Gregory Corso, "Marriage," in *The Happy Birthday of Death* (New York: New Directions, 1960), 29.

Chapter 18

1   "I, Too," 64–5. Joans also recalled Ginsberg inviting him to the Seven Arts Coffee Gallery, so this reading could have taken place there ("I Went," 2).

2   Sam Moskowitz, "The First College-Level Course in Science Fiction," *Science Fiction Studies* 23.3 (November 1996), 417.

3   "Spadework," 36.

4   "I, Too," 86.

5   "Spadework," 36; Joans, "Veröffentlichte Arbeiten" [Published Works], TJP, carton 3, folder 48.

6   Note that although it was actually published in 1958, *Funky Jazz Poems* carries a publication date of 1959.

7   See Jack Kerouac, "The Roaming Beatniks," *Holiday* (October 1959), 82.

8   "Spadework," 37.

9   "I, Too," 66.

10   Reisner, "Intro," *FJP*, n.p.

Chapter 19

1   John Wilcock, "The Revolving Reader," *The Village Voice* (September 7, 1961).

2   "I See," 234.

3   "I See," 234.

4   In a later book, Joans would satirize the way white American politicians were prone to fetishizing "EXACT COPIES OF AN OLD PYGMY IN THE CONGO FROM A BELGIUM SCHOOL BOOK" ("Outer," 18).

5   "Pygmy Stay Away From My Door" is included also in *AW*, where it is dated 1952 (10).

6   Joans to John Simon Guggenheim Memorial Foundation (September 13, 1985), TJP, box 22, folder 15. See also Jean-Jacques Lebel, "Le 'Jazz Poetry'" (Interview with Joans), *La Quinzaine Littéraire* 330 (1980), 30–1.

Chapter 20

1   Laura Corsiglia to Author (June 30, 2024).

2   *ATJ*, 30; forward slashes and underlining handwritten in; the forward slashes likely indicate alternative line breaks.

3   When Ginsberg passed in 1997, Joans wistfully told Michel Fabre that "The Truth" was "dedicated to him [Ginsberg] when it was first published[.] He lived in the Croton Apartments building at the time. He encouraged me" (Joans to Michel Fabre [July 1997]), MFA, box 9, folder 37). In an early typescript of "Voice in the Crowd," Joans had also specified that it was "dedicated to Allen Ginsberg" (TJP, box 1, folder 46).

4   Bill Morgan, *Beat Generation in New York*, 120–1.

5   Albert Saijo, "A Recollection," in Jack Kerouac, Albert Saijo, and Lew Welch, *Trip Trap* (Bolinas, CA: Grey Fox Press, 1973), 7.

6   "I Went," 21; see also "I, Too," 88.

7   See Joans, *The Truth* (Amsterdam: Surrealistisch Kabinet, 1968). Joans once explained that when he was traveling and "ran into someone who spoke a different language," he would ask them to translate "The Truth" into that language (Ted Joans Lecture, University of Connecticut [October 12, 1971]: https://collections.ctdigitalarchive.org/islandora/object/20002%3A860679982).

8   *NDB*, n.p.

9   *ONDB*, 23. This poem also appears in *Teducation*, 68.

10 Joans also associated the poet in "The Truth" with Bob Kaufman; see "Bird Lives & Bob Still GIVES" (*Beatitude* 29 [1979], 57); "Kaufman is a Bird Called Bob," TJP, box 16, folder 18; and "Laughter You've Gone And … " which is dedicated to Kaufman, in *FP*, 34–5.

11 "I Went," 21.

12 "I See," 243.

13 "I, Too," 154–55. Although Kerouac admired Hughes's work, I'm unaware of any evidence to suggest he had read Hughes's story "On the Road"; for more on the Kerouac-Hughes connection, see: http://www.americanlegends.com/Interviews/david-amram.html/

14 "I, Too," 109.

15 "I, Too," 109.

16 "I, Too," 85.

17 "I, Too," 85.

18 "Bird and Beats," 1.

19 "I, Too," 111; Joans even said Kerouac knew "more about the old jazz haunts than I did" ("I See," 242).

20 Joans, "Tape Recording at The Five Spot," in *The Beats*, ed. Seymour Krim (Greenwich, CT: Gold Medal Books, 1960), 212.

21 "I, Too," 110.

22 "I, Too," 132.

23 "I, Too," 133.

24 "I, Too," 9; 133.

25 Jack Kerouac, poem fragment, TJP, box 24, folder 19.

26 "I, Too," 133. Elsewhere Joans recalled a slightly different version of this poem: "I know man who writes in white and black / And his name is Jack the Kerouac" ("I Went," 9).

27 "I, Too," 134–5; "Beatnik going-ons" line from "I Went," 8.

28 "I Went," 6.

29 Joans offered a slightly different account of this anecdote in "Spadework," 50–1, adding a detailed story about picking up some young women with Kerouac and taking them back to his Astor Place studio.

30 Jack Kerouac to Joans (February 13, 1963), in *MBP*, 58–60. Joans eventually sold this letter for $500 to Roger Richards, the owner of the Rare Book Room on Greenwich Avenue in New York; see Joans to Joy Walsh (May 11, 1980), Moody Street Irregulars Collection (PCMS-0096), University of Buffalo, box 72, folder 27; see also Joans's poem "What ever happened ..." which mentions an "aerogram" Kerouac had sent to him in Tangier, and that Joans subsequently sold to Richards (*Moody Street Irregulars* 18/19 [fall 1987], 44).

Chapter 21

1 "For Hip Hosts," *Time* (February 15, 1960), 69.

2 Gilbert Millstein, "Rent a Beatnik and Swing," *New York Times* (April 17, 1960), SM26, SM28.

3 "I Went," 19.

4   Fred McDarrah and Gloria McDarrah, *Beat Generation: Glory Days in Greenwich Village* (New York: Schirmer Books, 1996), 211. McDarrah's brief account here contradicts slightly the contemporaneous account given by Gilbert Millstein.

5   "A Pad Fad," 42.

6   "Spadework," 47.

7   Joans quoted in Millstein, "Rent a Beatnik and Swing," SM29.

8   Leonard Lyons, "The Lyons Den: Village News Preferred," *The News and Observer* (Raleigh, NC) (June 3, 1961), 8. The Lyons Den was syndicated in many newspapers; this citation from the *News and Observer* is thus one of many possible sources.

9   "I, Too," 174; "lost souls" quotation from "I Went," 20.

10 "For Hip Hosts," *Time*, 69.

11 Val Duncan, "The Beats Make the Suburban Scene," *Newsday* (Nassau Edition) (March 27, 1961), 65.

12 Laura Corsiglia to Author (June 30, 2024).

13 "I Went," 18.

14 Elias Wilentz, ed. *The Beat Scene* (1960), 111, 112. These and other photographs appear also in Fred McDarrah and Gloria McDarrah, *Beat Generation*, as part of the chapter "Ted Joans's Birthday Party" (91–101).

15 "I Went," 18.

16 Fred and Gloria McDarrah, *Beat Generation*, 211.

17 *The Beat Scene*, 101.

18 "I Went," 18.

19 "Spadework," 48. See also the account of Rent-a-Beatnik Joans gave to Ronald Sukenick, in which he stressed its missionary dimensions, and noted "It was successful till the Internal Revenue stepped in, and that was the end of it" (Sukenick, *Down and In*, 126–27; quotation on 127).

20 "I, Too," 157.

21 "I, Too," 157–8.

Chapter 22

1   Joans, "Black-Flower (or The Negro and The Hippies)," TJP, box 16, folder 33.

2   Joan Wilentz quoted in Kevin Howell, "Consummate Bookseller Ted Wilentz Dies at 86," *Publisher's Weekly* (May 17, 2001): https://www.publishersweekly.com/pw/print/20010514/37928-consummate-bookseller-ted-wilentz-dies-at-86.html/

3   Ted Wilentz and Bill Zavatsky, "Behind the Writer, Ahead of the Reader: A Short History of Corinth Books," *TriQuarterly* 43 (1978), 596.

4   "Memorandum of Agreement," TJP, carton 4, folder 2.

5   Gascoyne, *Short Survey*, 55.

6   "I Went," 11.

7   See Pawlik, *Remade*, 137.

8   There are no page numbers in *Hipsters*, so they will not be cited throughout.

9   Ira Henry Freeman, "Bohemian Flair Fades in the Village: New Projects Will Change the Face—and Character—of the Washington Square Area," *New York Times* (December 8, 1957), W1.

10   Bob Dylan, *Chronicles, Volume One* (New York: Simon & Schuster, 2004), 47.

11   "City Acts to Silence Minstrels' Playing in Washington Sq," *New York Times* (March 28, 1961), 37.

12   Paul Hofman, "Folk Singers Riot in Washington Sq.," *New York Times* (April 10, 1961), 1.

13   The source images are "Burton's March Towards Central Africa" and "A Wild Rush into the Lake" in James W. Buel, *Heroes of the Dark Continent* (Guelph: J.W. Lyon, 1890), 123, 522. As mentioned earlier, the same collage sourced from "Burton's March Towards Central Africa" was used for a stand-alone piece titled "The Ronnie Manhattan Mau Mau Return from Mexico" and is dated 1959, demonstrating both that Joans was working with the images that would comprise *The Hipsters* for at least two years, and that he was thinking about the images from *Heroes of the Dark Continent* in the context of his appropriation of the term "Mau Mau."

14   See Samuel White Baker, *Ismailïa: A Narrative of the Expedition to Central Africa for the Suppression of the Slave Trade*, 2 vols. (London: Macmillan, 1874). The engraving appears in Buel, *Heroes of the Dark Continent*, 171.

15   Norman Mailer, "The White Negro," in *Advertisements for Myself* (Cambridge, MA: Harvard University Press, [1959] 2005), 340–1.

16   Joans, "Black-Flower (or The Negro and The Hippies)," TJP, box 16, folder 33.

17   This language was again echoed three years after *Hipsters* was published, when Joans wrote a brief treatment for a film or play about "a Hipster in his environment," in which he noted that "it was in New York and the black ghettos of the USA that produced the HIPSTER. Because it is the HIPSTER that uses the big cities of America to survive" (Joans, "A Movie Written by and for Ted Joans" [1964], TJP, box 17, folder 13).

18   See James Baldwin, "The Black Boy Looks at the White Boy," in *Collected Essays* (New York: Library of America, 1998), 277–8.

19   Henry Morton Stanley, *In Darkest Africa*, vol. 2 (Frankfurt: Outlook Verlag, [1890] 2020), 318.

20   Langston Hughes on *Hipsters*, TJP, box 24, folder 16.

21   The quoted language is from Joans paraphrasing Breton in a letter to Langston Hughes (July 4, 1963), LHP, box 89, folder 1689.

22 "I Went," 11–12.

23 See Grégory Pierrot, *Decolonize Hipsters* (New York: OR Books, 2021).

24 Joans, Autobiographical Fragment, TJP, box 19, folder 20.

25 Sean Wilentz, *Bob Dylan in America* (New York: Anchor Books, 2011), 65.

26 David Leeming, *James Baldwin: A Biography* (New York: Arcade, [1994] 2015), 183.

27 Desmangles, "Remembering."

Chapter 23

1 "I, Too," 187.

2 Author interview with Joyce (Wrobleski) Hollinger (April 29, 2022).

3 "I, Too," 162.

4 Joans, "1530 A.D.," TJP, box 1, folder 29; see also "Il Etait une Beau fois," an eleven-page prose-poem about various women he knew in Greenwich Village in the 1950s (TJP, box 17, folder 19).

5 Dylan Foley interview with Gloria McDarrah (November 8, 2019): https://lastbohemians.blogspot.com/search?q=joans/

6 "Spadework," 93–4.

7 "I, Too," 188. The poem "Is Your Fuzz Against My Junk?" dated November 4, 1960, is set on the "Staten Island-Manhattan subway J-train," reflecting Joans's experiences commuting between the Village and the family home on Staten Island (*ATJ*, 17–18).

8 FBI; memorandum dated December 17, 1968.

9 Brazzle Tobin, "Scouting Derbytown," *Louisville Defender* (June 30, 1960), 13.

10 Joans, "Yes Today" (June 8, 1960), Laurated Archive.

11 André Breton, "The Object-Poem," in Breton, *Surrealism and Painting*, trans. Simon Taylor Watson (New York: Harper & Row, 1972), 284.

12 *Teducation*, 220; for an analysis of this poem, see Pawlik, *Remade*, 144–7.

13 André Breton, *Earthlight*, trans. Bill Zavatsky and Zack Rogow (Los Angeles: Sun and Moon Press, 1993), 128. This poem originally appeared in Breton's collection *The Pistol with White Hair* (Zavatsky and Rogow's translation), also often translated, as in "The Statue of 1713," as *The White-Haired Revolver*.

14 "I See," 253.

15 "I See," 254. See also Joans, "Le Maison d'André Breton," *Homnesies* 3 (March 1985), 27–9.

16 See Joans, "Fragments du lettres," *La Brèche* 5 (October 1963), 66–7; and Joans, "Black Flower," *L'Archibras* 3 (March 1968), 8–11.

17   This letter was reprinted, translated from French into English, as "Ted Joans Speaks," *Black, Brown, and Beige*, 229–30.

18   "I See," 254.

19   *Dictionnaire Général du Surréalisme et de ses environs*, ed. Adam Biro and René Passeron (Fribourg: Presses Universitaires de France, 1982), 226.

20   Joans to J. H. Matthews (August 7, 1978), JHMP, box 2, folder 7.

21   *Spetrophilia*, n.p. Underlining handwritten in.

22   Author interview with Joyce (Wrobleski) Hollinger (April 29, 2022).

23   Joans to Seymour Krim (September 7, 1960), Seymour Krim Papers, University of Iowa, Series 1, Box 1, folder v.

24   Fabre, *From Harlem*, 311. The real-life Nadja was artist Léona Delcourt.

25   See *ATJ*, 66–71.

26   See also two short pieces Joans wrote about the Beat Hotel: "The Rain Came As I Signed," TJP, box 1, folder 35; and the poem "Ye Olde Historic Replay," in which he writes about visiting 9 Git-le-Coeur twenty years later, in the summer of 1980 (*Our*, 83–4).

27   "Spadework," 77.

28   Ted Morgan, *Literary Outlaw: The Life and Times of William S. Burroughs* (New York: Norton, 2012), 293.

29   Bill Morgan, *The Beat Hotel: Ginsberg, Burroughs, and Corso in Paris, 1958-1963* (New York: Grove, 2000), 143.

30   William Burroughs, "Foreword," in Harold Chapman, *The Beat Hotel* (Montpellier/Geneva: Gris Banal, 1984), n.p.

31   Harold Chapman to Lars Movin (June 10, 2003); email courtesy of Lars Movin.

32   "Razzle," 213–14.

33   Quoted in Morgan, *Literary*, 293.

34   Gregory Corso to Allen Ginsberg (ca. August 2, 1960), in Corso, *Accidental Autobiography*, 255.

35   Joans to Langston Hughes (September 1, 1962), LHP, box 89, folder 1689; Joans to Tuli Kupferberg (1962), Tuli Kupferberg and Sylvia Topp Papers, Fales Library and Special Collections, New York University Libraries, box 42, folder 52.

36   *ONDB*, 6.

37   Laura Corsiglia to Author (June 30, 2024).

38   A version of "Travelin'" was also published in Tuli Kupferberg's *Birth* in 1960; this version includes 30 lines that do not appear in *ATJ*; for example: "In the hip section of New York there's / a bar called the Cedar Street Tavern where / some of the best American painters and / broads meet, I was there one night sipping / a 15 cent beer, and started doing some / serious thinking about the true poets" (Joans, "Travelin'," *Birth* 3, Book 1 [Autumn 1960]), 6.

39   *ATJ*, 67, 69, 67.

40   Fabre, *From Harlem*, 312.
41   "Spadework," 22.
42   "Spadework," 22.
43   "Spadework," 23.
44   FBI; memorandum dated December 17, 1968.
45   Author interview with Joyce (Wrobleski) Hollinger (April 29, 2022).
46   Joans to Christine [Gondre] (undated; ca. 1960–1), TJP, box 20, folder 3.
47   Author interview with Daline Jones (May 5, 2024).
48   Author interview with Daline Jones (January 27, 2022).
49   Author interview with Robert Jones (April 28, 2024).
50   "Spadework," 34.
51   *Afrodisia*, 149.
52   *BPW*, 48.
53   "I, Too," Preface, n.p.
54   Joans quoted in "Beatnik Poet-Artist 'Exiles,'" *Jet* (January 4, 1962), 60–1.

Chapter 24

1   "Spadework," 4.
2   Joans to Langston Hughes (January 1962), LHP, box 89, folder 1689.
3   "I, Too," Preface, n.p.; "BMG," 1.
4   "Spadework," 22.
5   Harold Norse, *Memoirs of a Bastard Angel* (New York: William Morrow, 1989), 393.
6   Mailer, *Advertisements for Myself*, 468.
7   John Hopkins, *Tangier Diaries* (London: Tauris Parke, 2015), 53.
8   Michelle Green, *The Dream at the End of the World: Paul Bowles and the Literary Renegades in Tangier* (New York: HarperCollins, 1991), xi.
9   Green, *Dream*, 14.
10   "Money Soon" (1995), TJP, box 14, folders 14–18.
11   William Burroughs, "Tangier," *Esquire* (September 1964), 118.
12   Paul Bowles to Allen Ginsberg (January 17, 1962), in Bowles, *In Touch: The Letters of Paul Bowles*, ed. Jeffrey Miller (New York: Farrar, Straus and Giroux, 1994), 336.
13   "Collaged," 45.
14   William Burroughs, "Comments on the Night before Thinking," *Evergreen Review* 5.20 (September–October 1961), 31.
15   "I See," 247; *HS*, n.p.

16   *Tanger*, 140; "I See," 247. See also Joans, "Wölfi K.O.'s Dalí," in *Free Spirits: Annals of the Insurgent Imagination*, ed. Paul Buhle et al. (San Francisco: City Lights, 1982), 151–52.

17   "Collaged," 45.

18   "I See," 247.

19   "I See," 247.

20   "Spadework," 66.

Chapter 25

1   "I See," 239.

2   Joans, "The Rhinoceros Story," TJP, box 15, folders 11–12; quotation on 105. The item in the Ted Joans Papers is a copy of the original manuscript, which is housed at the Fales Library at NYU, originally in connection to William Burroughs. The manuscript is not numbered, but here I provide page numbers, by my count, for ease of reference.

3   William Burroughs, "The Cut-Up Method of Brion Gysin," in *A Casebook on the Beat*, ed. Thomas Parkinson (New York: Thomas Y. Crowell, 1961), 105.

4   "I See," 238.

5   "I, Too," 63. Joans wrote a caption to this drawing in "dialect," which also appears on the cover of *Yeah* #1. For more on *Yeah*, see Steven Belletto, "Tuli Kupferberg's *Yeah*: A Satyric Excursion," *Princeton University Library Chronicle* 79.1 (spring–summer 2022), 102–30.

6   Tuli Kupferberg, "The Function of Bohemia," Tuli Kupferberg and Sylvia Topp Papers, Fales Library and Special Collections, New York University Libraries, box 8, folder 10.

7   "Big Step Ahead on the High Road," *Life* (December 8, 1961), 32.

8   "I See," 238.

9   "I See," 239.

10   "The Rhinoceros Story" is catalogued as Ted Joans, "Rhinoceros Book," Fales Manuscript Collection, Fales Library, New York University, box 97, folder 17.

11   Pages from "The Rhinoceros Story" (on loan from the Fales Library) were included as part of the exhibition "Notable Notes: Drawings by Writers and Composers" at the Joseph Helman Gallery in New York (December 3, 1997 – January 17, 1998). Curator Diane Waldman evidently had Joans's blessing to exhibit the pages, as in the catalogue she thanks him for reminding her that "to be an artist in Greenwich Village in the late 1950s and early 1960s was to have it all"; see Diane Waldman, *Notable Notes: Drawings by Writers and Composers* (New York: Joseph Helman Gallery, 1997), 5.

Chapter 26

1   Joans, "The Book of the Best Travels to and Back from Timbuktu," TJP, box 17, folder 24.

2   Laura C. Boulton, "Timbuktu and Beyond," *The National Geographic Magazine* 79, no. 5 (May 1941), 641.

3   Boulton, "Timbuktu," 631.

4   Joans, "Book of the Best Travels," TJP, box 17, folder 24.

5   *BPW*, 82.

6   Joans, "A Letter from Timbuktu," *Negro Digest* (September 1967), 98.

7   John Oliver Killens, "The Black Writer Vis-à-vis His Country" (1965), in *The Black Aesthetic*, ed. Addison Gayle (Garden City, NY: Doubleday, 1971), 390. Killens himself had visited Timbuktu in 1962, in the course of traveling some 12,000 miles around Africa by Land Rover; see Killens, *Black Man's Burden* (New York: Trident, 1965). In the British version of *BPW*, titled *A Black Pow-Wow of Jazz Poems* (1973), Joans dedicated the poem "Watermelon" to Killens: "its one of / them foods from Africa ... its soul food thing" (40).

8   Stephanie D'Alessandro and Matthew Gale, "The World in the Time of the Surrealists," in *Surrealism Beyond Borders*, ed. D'Alessandro and Gale (New York: Metropolitan Museum of Art, 2021), 9; Joans to Charles Henri Ford (October 1964), CHFP, box 14, folder 1.

9   "Community Notice," Bennington College (November 1973): https://crossettlibrary.dspacedirect.org/bitstream/handle/11209/9679/1973NovTed.pdf?sequence=1&isAllowed=y/

10 Joans to Mary Ellen Wang (ca. spring 1975), FSG, box 450, Joans folder.

11 "Collaged," 180.

12 Joans, "A Letter from Timbuktu," 99.

13 "BMG," 46.

14 "Collaged," 173.

15 "BMG," 48.

16 "BMG," 47.

17 Joans to unknown publisher (January 1, 1979), TJP, box 19, folder 21.

18 Joans to unknown publisher (January 1, 1979), TJP, box 19, folder 21.

19 Joans, Letter to *Village Voice* (March 29, 1962), 4; "Spadework," 73; "Collaged," 173.

20 "Collaged," 172–3.

21 "Spadework," 73.

22 Joans, "Book of the Best Travels," TJP, box 17, folder 24.

23 Author interview with Marion Kalter (September 30, 2022).

24   "Book of Best Travels," n.p.; Joans, "A Letter from Timbuktu," 99. In 2015, Joans's friend, poet Bob Holman, traveled to Timbuktu and there searched for Joans's house. People in Timbuktu recalled Joans fondly, and Holman met locals he described as Joans's "guide" and "landlord," and was taken to Joans's last residence. This is all captured in "The Griots of West Africa," an episode of Holman's remarkable web series "On the Road with Bob Holman," which can be viewed on YouTube: https://www.youtube.com/watch?v=9nqD8XWybpQ/

25   "Shut Mouth," 11.

26   "I Went," 24.

27   *HS*, 63.

28   "I Went," 24.

29   Joans, inscription in *Afrodisia*; collection of Lafayette College. On the first hardcover edition of *Afrodisia*, there is a different, tamer author photo: Joans posing with a pair of knocking bones, naked still, but with only his torso visible in the shot.

30   John Woodford, "A Black Man Who Went Home to Timbuktu—and Stayed," *Muhammad Speaks* (August 23, 1968), 21, 32; quotation on 32.

31   "BMG," 49.

Chapter 27

1   "BMG," 63.

2   Joans, "Qui Suis-Je?" TJP, box 24, folder 13.

3   Joans, "Yeah, Your Mother #2," (1985), TJP, box 18, folder 4.

4   *Tanger*, 106.

5   *Tanger*, 107.

6   Joans, "Yeah, Your Mother #2."

7   Tor Jones, email to Author (November 14, 2021).

8   *Tanger*, 107.

9   "Spadework," 74.

10   *Tanger*, 107.

11   *Tanger*, 118.

12   *Tanger*, 120.

13   *Tanger*, 123.

14   Joans to Langston Hughes (September 1, 1962), LHP, box 89, folder 1689.

15   *Afrodisia*, 102.

16   *Tanger*, 128.

17   *Tanger*, 127–8.

Chapter 28

1   Joans to John Wilcock (February 21, 1963), printed in *Other Scenes* (April 1, 1968), 4.

2   Miller, "Ted Joans," 270.

3   "Strange Taste," *Newsweek* (November 26, 1962), 94.

4   Gerald Williams, "Ted's Dead," 245.

5   Gerald Williams, "Ted's Dead," 247.

6   Gerald Williams, "Ted's Dead," 246.

7   Gerald Williams to Joans (September 16, 1963), TJP, carton 3, folder 8. Joans anticipated such a reaction, admitting to Langston Hughes that "Spadework" "may be banned because of the deliberate obscenity, provocative profanity, and iconoclasm," calling his "surrealist autobiography" a "mixture of Burroughs, Wright and Langston Hughes," Joans to Langston Hughes (January 1963), LHP, box 89, folder 1689.

8   "Spadework," 21.

9   Joans, "Afrique Accidentale," *City Lights Journal* 1 (1963), 77.

10 Lawrence Ferlinghetti to Joans (February 16, 1963), TJP, box 22, folder 2.

11 Joans to Lawrence Ferlinghetti (February 22, 1963), City Lights Records, box 6, folder 34.

12 An excerpt from "Afrique Accidentale" was also published alongside the work of Derek Walcott, Aimé Césaire, Langston Hughes, and others in *Negro Verse*, ed. Anselm Hollo (London: Vista Books, 1964), 28–9.

13 Guy Pierre Buchholtzer recalled Joans calling West Africa "Afrique Accidentelle Française": https://www.emptymirrorbooks.com/beat/tedjoanslives-5/

14 Robert Benayoun, *Le Rire des Surréalistes* (Paris: La Bougie du sapeur, 1988), 105. Benayoun writes: "Ted Joans écrit de la poésie *orale*, ou le scat se mêle à l'invention verbale, et si André [Breton] le hante comme un père totem de toutes lès clés, il sait que le relais lui en a été implicitement consenti dès 1963 par celui dont l'idole de granit, la Statue 1713, comme il l'appelle, sculptée par les féticheurs dogons du haut Mali, se dresse, dit-il, au croisement des pistes du desert à Tanezrouft, et l'inspire désormais" (105).

15 Images of Joans's "Trader Joes Bags Series" (2002), four of which feature drawings inspired by the "ted joans en route to Timbuktu" photograph, may be found in *Jazz Is My Religion* Exhibition Catalogue, 98–111.

16 Joans, "Afrique Accidentale," *City Lights Journal*, 75. The version of the poem in *Afrodisia* has a slightly different ending (8), and adds a dedication to Hoyt Fuller, one-time editor of *Ebony* magazine and then *Black World* who would publish his autobiography, *Journey to Africa*, in 1971, a year after *Afrodisia* appeared.

17 *Tanger*, 143.

18   Joans to Lawrence Ferlinghetti (February 4, 1965), City Lights Records, box 6, folder 34.

19   Lawrence Ferlinghetti to Joans (September 14, 1965), TJP, box 22, folder 2.

20   Joans to Lawrence Ferlinghetti (September 22, 1965), City Lights Records, box 6, folder 34.

21   Lawrence Ferlinghetti to Joans (November 10, 1965), TJP, box 22, folder 2.

22   "I See," 227.

23   "I See," 227.

24   "I See," 227.

25   "Deeper."

26   Joans to Langston Hughes (ca. January–February 1966), LHP, box 89, folder 1689.

27   Joans to Mary Ellen Wang (ca. December 1972), FSG, box 450, Joans folder.

28   Lawrence Hill to Joans (December 1, 1982), TJP, box 22, folder 11. Back in 1973, Hill had told Joans's agent, Gunther Stuhlmann, that "the autobio mss." is "material rather than a finished product and also it seems there is too much lecturing on surrealism and not really enough of you" (Gunther Stuhlmann to Joans [November 1, 1973], TJP, box 23, folder 20; the quoted language is Stuhlmann paraphrasing Hill for Joans).

Chapter 29

1   *Tanger*, 137.

2   Joans to Langston Hughes (February 10, 1963), LHP, box 89, folder 1689; "Spadework," 63.

3   Joans to John Wilcock (February 21, 1963), in *Other Scenes* (April 1, 1968), 4.

4   *Tanger*, 137.

5   *Tanger*, 139.

6   Joans to Langston Hughes (ca. June–July 1963), LHP, box 89, folder 1689.

7   *Tanger*, 139; "human-encyclopedia" quotation from "Collaged," 44.

8   Exhibition Flier, TJP, carton 3, folder 49.

9   Langston Hughes to Joans (June 10, 1963), Laurated Archive.

10   Joans to Langston Hughes (ca. June–July 1963), LHP, box 89, folder 1689.

11   Joans to Langston Hughes (January 1963), LHP, box 89, folder 1689.

12   Joans to Robert Benayoun (June 26, 1963), Robert Benayoun Papers Relating to Ted Joans (JWJ MSS 40), Beinecke Library, Yale University, box 1, folder 1.

13   *BPW*, 33 (unbracketed forward slashes in original).

14   "I See," 246.

15   *Tanger*, 143.

16 One viewable collage piece from 1963 is titled "Tombouctou: Force et fragilié"; the source material was a comic book evidently involving Eskimos— as he wrote in "Spadework": "comic books into avant garde collages tomorrow" (81). The piece was featured in Paul Renaud, *Surréalisme: de londres a prague et ailleurs* (Paris: Paul Renaud, 1985), 14. Some other artwork on paper from this period is housed in the Ted Joans Papers.

17 *Tanger*, 143.

18 Joans to John Wilcock (February 21, 1963), in *Other Scenes* (April 1, 1968), 4.

19 Leonidas Christakis quoted in Eftychia Mikelli, "The Greek Beat and Underground Scene of the 1960s and 1970s," *CLCWeb: Comparative Literature and Culture* 18.5 (2016), 2.

20 *Tanger*, 139.

21 Joans, "Athens Greece: The Nothing HAPPENING," CHFP, box 16, folder 1.

22 Joans, "Athens Greece: The Nothing HAPPENING," CHFP, box 16, folder 1.

23 This is according to a (likely) unsent letter from Joans to Lawrence Ferlinghetti (ca. late 1963), Laurated Archive.

24 Charles Henri Ford's *Poem Poster* of Joans (1964–5) is reproduced in Pawlik, *Remade*, 31.

25 Joans to Langston Hughes [handwritten in after "Friend" in form letter] (December 31, 1963), LHP, box 89, folder 1689.

26 "New York Beat," *Jet* (February 27, 1964), 62.

27 This story was told by Mimi Burns McCartney as a tribute to Joans posted here: https://www.emptymirrorbooks.com/beat/tedjoanslives-12/

28 *BPW*, 122–3.

29 Joans, "Athens Greece: The Nothing HAPPENING," CHFP, box 16, folder 1.

30 Tor Jones, email to Author (January 23, 2021).

31 Joans, "Yeah, Your Mother #4" (1985), TJP, box 18, folder 4.

32 Author interview with Russell Kerr (April 11, 2024).

33 Joans to Charles Henri Ford (March 1, 1964), CHFP, box 14, folder 1.

34 "BMG," 61.

35 Joans to Charles Henri Ford (December 1964), CHFP, box 14, folder 1.

36 Author interview with Russell Kerr (April 11, 2024).

37 *Our*, 88.

Chapter 30

1 Michael McEachrane, "The Midnight Sun Never Sets: An Email Conversation About Jazz, Race and National Identity in Denmark, Norway and Sweden," in *Afro-Nordic Landscapes: Equality and Race in Northern Europe*, ed. Michael McEachrane (New York: Routledge, 2014), 69.

2   Cecil Brown, "Midnight Sun," in *Afro-Nordic Landscapes*, 74–5.

3   Brown quoted in Martyn Bone, "Transnational and Intertextual Geographies of Race, Sex, and Masculinity: Cecil Brown's *The Life and Loves of Mr. Jiveass Nigger*," *African American Review* 52.4 (winter 2019), 365.

4   Joans, "Andaconda" (1964), TJP, box 16, folder 1. "Andaconda" [*sic*] is a short story set in Copenhagen, and describes places Joans frequented in the early 1960s.

5   Allan Kaprow, "A Statement," in *Happenings: An Illustrated Anthology*, ed. Michael Kirby (New York: E.P. Dutton, 1965), 47.

6   Allan Kaprow, *Assemblage, Environments & Happenings* (New York: Harry N. Abrams, 1966), 198, 202.

7   Kaprow, "Preface," in *Assemblage*, 202.

8   For a discussion of the relationship between Dada, Surrealism, and Happenings, see Michael Kirby, "Introduction," in *Happenings: An Illustrated Anthology* (New York: E.P. Dutton, 1965), 29–9.

9   Joans, "Happy Hip Happenings" (1965), TJP, box 17, folder 28.

10   "Spadework," 38; Mildred Glimcher, *Happenings: New York, 1958–1963* (New York: Monacelli Press, 2012), 37.

11   Joans, "Ted Joans' Happy Hip Happening" (1964), CHFP, box 14, folder 1.

12   Jean-Jacques Lebel, "Theory and Practice," trans. G. Livingstone-Learmouth, in *New Writers IV: Plays and Happenings*, ed. Lebel et al. (London: Calder and Boyars, 1967), 28.

13   Kaprow, "Preface," in *Assemblage*, 169.

14   Erik Andersen, "Danske Trommer": https://dansketrommer.dk/?p=2597. This website, an accompaniment to Andersen's book *Danske Trommer* (2012), also contains several photographs of Joans performing at Vingården, as well as a copy of *All of Ted Joans and No More* he warmly inscribed to Andersen.

15   Jean-Jacques Lebel, "Theory and Practice," 45. The moniker "French high priest of Happenings" comes from "Censor Hits at Happenings," *The Sunday Telegraph* (March 13, 1965), 1.

16   Lars Movin, *Beat: på sporet af den amerikanske beatgeneration* (Denmark: Informations Forlag, 2008), 336. For those who read Danish, Movin's book has a great chapter on Joans.

17   Joans, "A Message from Timbuctu: a happy hip happening," TJP, box 17, folder 28.

18   Allan Kaprow, *Assemblage*, 234.

19   Joans, "Happy Hip Happenings" (1965), TJP, box 17, folder 28. For a description of Joans's participation in the 2nd "Festival de la libre expression" (May 1965) organized by Jean-Jacques Lebel, see Jean-Jacques Lebel and Androula Michaël, *Happenings, ou l'insoumission radicale* (Paris: Hazan, 2009), 143–71. As part of this event, Joans read from his poem "Nice Colored Man"; note also that *Happenings, ou l'insoumission radicale* contains a

photograph of Joans and Lawrence Ferlinghetti, who also participated in this Happening (162).

20 Allan Kaprow, "Preface," in *Assemblage*, 163.

21 Fabre, *From Harlem*, 314.

22 "Deeper."

23 "Deeper."

24 "Deeper."

25 Lebel, "Theory and Practice," 38.

26 *ATJ*, 88-9.

27 In Paris in May 1965, Joans also wrote a synopsis for a "surrealist film" called "Negative Cowboy" that shares some of the broad characteristics of his Happenings, except it was conceived as being more expansive, collaging scenes from eighteenth-century Mali with an American Western "boomtown" and a "Gold Coast Slavery Supermarket," where "Arab families are pushing cart loads of young Negroes in chain around from neon lighted booths" ("Negative Cowboy," TJP, box 17, folder 14).

28 Joans, "A Happy Hip Happening" (1965), TJP, box 17, folder 28.

29 Joans, "A Happy Hip Happening" (1965), TJP, box 17, folder 28.

30 Joans, "The Nice Coloured Man" (1965), TJP, box 2, folder 6.

31 Joans, "A Happy Hip Happening" (1965), TJP, box 17, folder 28.

32 Josephine Rydeng, email to Author (August 5, 2024). Two of these watercolors were purchased at the time by Danish art dealer Jørgen Immanuel Madsen, who later sold them to Hans Rydeng, owner of the club Jazz 64. These two pieces (watercolor on paper embellished with crayon and chalk, 9 × 6.5 in. and 7 × 8 in.), are undated but ca. 1964 (Collection of Author). Madsen told the story of how these pieces originated to Hans Rydeng, a close friend, whose daughter Josephine then told the story to me; these particular pieces may or may not have been part of an official Happening, but are examples of art Joans performatively created at the Vingården and then sold.

33 Joans, "A Happy Hip Happening" (1965), TJP, box 17, folder 28.

34 Cecil Brown, *The Life and Loves of Mr. Jiveass Nigger* (Hopewell, NJ: Ecco Press, [1969] 1991), 49.

35 Joans to Geneviève Fabre (February 19, 1973), MFA, box 9, folder 37.

36 See Cecil Brown's endorsement on the back cover of Joans, *Okapi*.

37 On Joans and the performing arts scene in Amsterdam at this time, see Grégory Pierrot, "Ted Joans, the Other Jones: Jazz Poet, Black Power Missionary, and Surrealist Interpreter," in *Radical Dreams, Surrealism, Counterculture, Resistance*, ed. Elliott King and Abigail Susik (State College: Penn State University Press, 2022), 43-60.

38 Joans, "Third Son" (December 27, 1965), TJP, box 19, folder 30.

39 Joans to Langston Hughes (January 1, 1966), LHP, box 89, folder 1689.

40   Tor Jones, email to Author (November 14, 2021).

41   Joans to Charles Henri Ford (October 1964), CHFP, box 14, folder 1.

42   Joans to Charles Henri Ford (ca. end of 1964), CHFP, box 14, folder 1.

43   *Afrodisia*, 138.

44   Joans, "God Blame America!!," in *BM*, 79.

45   For another lengthy send-up of consumerism, see Joans, "Toymaker," in *10 Poets 10 Poems*, collected by O. G. Bradbury (London: Graphix Press, 1971).

46   Joans to Langston Hughes (January 1, 1966), LHP, box 89, folder 1689.

47   Joans to Langston Hughes (ca. January–February 1966), LHP, box 89, folder 1689.

48   Joans to Langston Hughes (ca. January–February 1966), LHP, box 89, folder 1689. There are two Joans poems in *Beyond the Blues*, "Think Twice and Be Nice," and "Why Try"; see Rosey E. Pool, ed. *Beyond the Blues: New Poems by American Negroes* (Hythe, Kent, UK: The Hand and Flower Press, 1962), 131–2.

Chapter 31

1   LeRoi Jones, "The Revolutionary Theatre" (1965), in *Home: Social Essays* (New York: Ecco Press, 1998), 213, 214.

2   Larry Neal, "The Black Arts Movement," in *The Black Aesthetic*, ed. Addison Gayle (Garden City, NY: Doubleday, 1971), 272.

3   Knight quoted in Neal, "Black Arts," 273–4.

4   Neal, "Black Arts," 274.

5   Stokely Carmichael and Charles V. Hamilton, *Black Power: The Politics of Liberation in America* (New York: Vintage, 1967), 44.

6   Joans, "Letter to *Time* Editor," TJP, carton 1, folder 31.

7   Neal, "Black Arts," 290.

8   Clayton Eshleman and Annette Smith, "Notes," in Césaire, *Notebook*, 60. See also Souleymane Bachir Diagne, "Négritude," *The Stanford Encyclopedia of Philosophy* (summer 2018 edition), Edward N. Zalta (ed.): https://plato. stanford.edu/archives/sum2018/entries/negritude/

9   "I, Too," n.p. For a discussion of Césaire's influence on Joans, see Kathryne V. Lindberg, "Mister Joans, to You: Readerly Surreality and Writerly Affiliation in Ted Joans, Tri-Continental Ex-Beatnik," *Discourse* 20.1/2 (winter/spring 1998), 198–227.

10   *Afrodisia*, 71. Note that in the poem, the word "ITS" is inconsistently punctuated.

11   Césaire, *Notebook*, 25.

12   André Breton, "A Great Black Poet," in Césaire, *Notebook*, xvi.

13   Gates, "Tri-Continental," 6.

14 Joans, "First Papers on Ancestral Creations," *Black World* (August 1970), 67.

15 Joans, "Natural Africa," *Black World* (May 1971), 4–7.

16 This is something Joans had noted from at least the early 1960s: "African sculptures were not created to be works of art by the western standard of 'works of art,' they were made because they function as part of the religious and magical ceremonies which form the very basis of African social organization" ("Spadework," 58).

17 Author interview with Laura Corsiglia (May 4, 2022).

18 Joans, "Splinter Tongue (or woodyn you)," TJP, box 17, folder 42.

19 Joans's exhibition of "Jazz Drawings" on wood was opened at the Jazz Museum in New York on September 24, 1977. This exhibition included over 150 line portraits of jazz musicians, a complete list of which is found in the exhibition catalogue: Joans, *Jazz Drawings* (New York: The Jazz Museum, 1977). Five pieces from this series are featured in the *Jazz Is My Religion* catalogue, *Jazz Must Be a Woman, Bird in Blue Striped Suit, Bird and Bud a Dynamite Duo, Bluesman of K.C. Jay McShann and Bird*, and *Langston Hughes backed by Henry Red Allen and Charles Mingus* (all 1977) (128–9).

20 Pawlik, *Remade*, 147; Pawlik is relying here on an interview with Laura Corsiglia. In my own conversations with Corsiglia, she elaborated on this idea, pointing out that people have long had "a relationship with the singularity of hair and its connection to someone's distinct individuality," noting other contemporary Black artists who have productively and provocatively used hair in their work, such as David Hammons. "And also," she reminded me, "it's beautiful, as a substance, a cloud—so as an aesthetic part of a collage, it is beautiful" (Interview with Author [May 4, 2022]).

21 "Aardvarkian," n.p.

22 Breton, "The Object-Poem," 284.

23 Joans, "Toronto Canada Notes," TJP, box 19, folder 12.

24 Janheinz Jahn, *Muntu: African Culture and the Western World*, trans. Marjorie Grene (New York: Grove Press, [1961] 1989), 132. This book was titled *Muntu: The New African Culture*, when it first appeared in English translation in 1961.

25 Césaire quoted in *Muntu*, 135.

26 Jahn, *Muntu*, 135.

27 Jahn, *Muntu*, 135.

28 *BPW*, 92.

29 Jahn, *Muntu*, 136.

30 Joans, "Poem Why," *BM*, 92.

31 Léopold Sédar Senghor, "Preface Letter," in *The Surreptitious Speech: Présence Africaine and the Politics of Otherness, 1947–1987*, ed. V. Y. Mudimbe (Chicago: University of Chicago Press, 1992), xi.

32 Diop quoted in Jacques Howlett, "*Présence Africaine* 1947–1958," *The Journal of Negro History* 43.2 (April 1958), 140.

33   Monica Popescu, *At Penpoint: African Literatures, Postcolonial Studies, and the Cold War* (Durham, NC: Duke University Press, 2020), 56. For an elaboration of how the politics and aesthetics of *Présence Africaine* intersected with those of Négritude, see Christopher L. Miller, "Alioune Diop and the Unfinished Temple of Knowledge," in *Surreptitious Speech*, 427–34.

34   "BMG," 8.

35   Joans to Elias Wilentz (February 28, 1972), Elias Wilentz Collection, University of Buffalo, box 3, folder 32. In suggesting to Wilentz that he put a similar fetish in his 8th Street Bookshop in New York, Joans did note that they would also want to hedge their bets: "Of course we will have to put up notices explaining its black power and warning the potential thieves of its black magic which would 'do-them-in' if they stole a book."

36   "Collaged," 80.

Chapter 32

1   Ruth Porter, "Paris Meeting Hears Malcolm X," *The Militant* (December 7, 1964), 1.

2   *ATJ*, 36.

3   Joans, "Info on Powerful Black Postcard," MFA, box 9, folder 37.

4   Porter, "Paris Meeting," 1.

5   Joans, "Angry Apostle," *Lookout on Costa del Sol* (May 1967), TJP, carton 4, folder 1. That said, as mentioned in Chapter 26, in 1968, Joans did agree to be profiled by *Muhammad Speaks*, the Nation of Islam's newspaper, emphasizing in that context Timbuktu's Islamic history.

6   *BPW*, 117; "I See," 250.

7   Joans, "Info on Powerful Black Postcard," MFA, box 9, folder 37; Black Power Postcard, Laurated Archive. Joans had planned to invite Jayne Cortez to sign the postcard, but that never happened (Laura Corsiglia to Author [June 30, 2024]).

8   Joans, "True Blues for a Dues Payer," *For Malcolm: Poems on the Life and the Death of Malcolm X*, ed. Dudley Randall and Margaret G. Burroughs (Detroit, MI: Broadside Press, [1967] 1969), 25.

9   *BPW*, 124. In the version of the poem included in *For Malcolm*, Joans had also wondered why other Black leaders he considered complicit in the maintenance of white power structures were never assassinated, naming in particular "that sad Uncle Ralph Bunch" ("Uncle" being a reference to Uncle Tom) or "one of those black blue bloods who attend the White House policy lunch" (25). In the version in *BPW*, Joans omitted these lines, perhaps in the name of underscoring a more widespread Black unity, as the audience for *For Malcolm* was a comparatively narrow circle of like-minded people than was the audience for the more widely-distributed *BPW*. Joans also changed "quiet Maghreb bright night sky" to "quiet & bright African sky," revising out some

specificity for the sake of linking his experience to the more universal, though generalized, image of "Africa." *For Malcolm* also includes Joans's poem "My Ace of Spades" (5).

10   Joans, "Black February Blood," *Présence Africaine* 60 (4 trimestre) (1966), 126. This poem was published in a slightly different form under the title "Black February Blood Letting" in *BPW*; in that version, the layout on the page is more compressed and the line "or even a CUBAN RED" was changed to "OR ANY OTHER KINDA RED" (65). For other work in *Présence Africaine*, see also "It Is Time" and "The .38" *Présence Africaine* 57 (1966), 357–9.

11   See Popescu, *Penpoint,* 72–8.

12   Malcolm X, *The Autobiography of Malcolm X*, with the assistance of Alex Haley (New York: Ballantine Books, 1965), 347.

13   "I, Too," 5.

14   *Afrodisia*, 69.

15   Apollinaire quotation in Joans to Franklin Rosemont (July 28, 1970), RP, box 80, folder 3; Joans, "I, Too," 5.

16   "Outer," 44.

17   "BMG," 1.

Chapter 33

1   "Shut Mouth," 69; "I, Too," 7. See also a postcard to Hoyt Fuller (ca. 1973) in which Joans identifies himself as "that international Black cultural guerilla" (Hoyt Fuller Collection, Atlanta University Center, Robert W. Woodruff Library, box 1, folder 47).

2   "Shut Mouth," 70.

3   "Shut Mouth," 69.

4   "Shut Mouth," 70.

5   "Shut Mouth," 72.

6   LeRoi Jones, "state/meant," in *Home: Social Essays*, 252; "Shut Mouth," 74.

7   Joans to Charles Henri Ford (December 1964), CHFP, box 14, folder 1.

8   "Outer," 26.

9   William L. Van Deburg, *New Day in Babylon: The Black Power Movement in American Culture, 1965–1975* (Chicago: University of Chicago Press, 1992), 286.

10   Césaire quoted in Kelley, *Freedom Dreams*, 159.

11   Porter, "Paris Meeting," 1.

12   Stokely Carmichael, "Stokely Carmichael on Black Power," in *The Afro-Americans: Selected Documents*, ed. John H. Bracey et al. (Boston: Allyn and Bacon, 1972), 741.

13   "Collaged," 76.

14   Joans to Arthur Wang (ca. January 1977), FSG, box 450, Joans folder.

15   Hy Shore to Joans (March 3, 1969), TJP, carton 3, folder 16.

Chapter 34

1   Tor Jones, email to Author (January 23, 2021).

2   *Afrodisia*, 64.

3   Joans, "First Papers," 71–2.

4   Joans, "Ted Joans" [autobiographical career statement], HBR, box 8, Joans folder.

5   Joans, "Africa Is the Richest Continent," TJP, box 17, folder 37.

6   Joans, "Natural Africa," *Black World*, 7.

7   Joans to Langston Hughes (January 1963), LHP, box 89, folder 1689.

8   See Michel Leiris, *Phantom Africa*, trans. Brent Hayes Edwards (Calcutta: Seagull Books, 2019). The phrase "anthropological expedition" is from the jacket copy of this excellent English translation.

9   On this point, see Van Deburg, *New Day*, 216–20; quotation on 220.

10   Joans to Hoyt Fuller (ca. 1970), Hoyt Fuller Collection, Atlanta University Center, Robert W. Woodruff Library, box 9, folder 10.

11   "BMG," 1; see also "Demystify" in *BPW*, 42.

12   "BMG," 20; Author interview with Laura Corsiglia (May 4, 2022).

13   Gates, "Tri-Continental," 7.

14   In the Ted Joans Papers, the typescript is catalogued as "A Black Man Guides All Yall to Africa" (box 12, folders 10–16), although elsewhere in the Finding Aid the work is referred to as "A Black Man's Guide to Africa." It's not clear that there was a definitive, finalized title for the guidebook, but in official documents such as a February 11, 1970 credit voucher recording an installment payment from Grossman Publishers to Joans for his work on the project, the title is given as "Black Man's Guide to Africa" (TJP, box 23, folder 20).

15   Michael Loeb to Joans (March 24, 1971), TJP, carton 2, folder 32.

16   Michael Loeb to Joans (January 26, 1971), TJP, carton 2, folder 32.

17   "Aardvarkian," 4; Joan Halifax, email to Author (January 13, 2023).

18   Identifying her only by her first name, Michel Fabre describes Joan Halifax as "a southern white anthropologist and SNCC militant, Joan: Ted 'married' her at a luncheon with [Michel] Leiris, who inscribed his *Afrique fantôme* for them in the shadow of the Eiffel Tower" (*From Harlem*, 320).

19   Joan Halifax to Joans (January 22, 1970), TJP, carton 2, folder 34.

20   Joans to Arthur Wang (October 8, 1970), TJP, carton 2, folder 37; Marion Boyars to Joans (April 3, 1970), TJP, carton 2, folder 19.

21   *Afrodisia,* 142.

22 Gunther Stuhlmann to Joans (June 21, 1971), TJP, box 23, folder 20.

23 Dick Grossman to Joans (April 6, 1971), TJP, carton 2, folder 32.

24 Gunther Stuhlmann to Joans (May 8, 1972), TJP, box 23, folder 20.

25 "I Went," 14.

Chapter 35

1 In 1973, Calder and Boyars in London published *A Black Pow-Wow of Jazz Poems.* While the title is similar to *Black Pow-Wow: Jazz Poems,* and it does contain almost all the same poems, it is a different book. Unlike *Black Pow-Wow: Jazz Poems, A Black Pow-Wow of Jazz Poems* is organized into three sections "like a Jazz Orchestra": "Reed Section," "Brass Section," and "Rhythm Section," and the poems that appear in the American edition of *Black Pow-Wow: Jazz Poems* are re-ordered to fit these sections. Joans also omitted a few poems from *Black Pow-Wow: Jazz Poems,* and added eleven new ones, notably "Your Role of My Soul Theatre" (13), which opens *A Black Pow-Wow of Jazz Poems,* "Horny Harrar House Blues" (26), and "Surreal-Eyes-For-You" (58).

2 "I See," 255.

3 Joans, inscription in *BPW* (1992); collection of Harry Nudel.

4 Thompson, *Flash of the Spirit,* 6.

5 An exception is the poem "125 Ways to Sex or Sexplosion," one of his signatures, a version of which appeared in *ATJ.*

6 *BPW,* 98.

7 *Wow,* n.p.

8 See Joans, "Pan African Pow Wow," *Other Scenes* 3.16 (November 1, 1969), n.p.; this piece was reprinted in *Journal of Black Poetry* 1.13 (winter–spring, 1970), 4–5.

9 Joans to Les Surréaliste (April 5, 1968), in *Surreally Ted Joans* Exhibition Catalogue (Paris and New York: Zürcher Gallery, 2023), 110. When King won the Nobel Peace Prize in 1964, Joans said on a Norwegian radio interview that it should have been awarded to Malcolm X (Joans, "Jeg er vred også når jeg smiler" ["I'm Even Angry When I Smile"], *Ekstra Bladet* [December 27, 1966], 10).

10 Joans to Les Surréaliste (April 5, 1968).

11 Joans had tried to publish his report on the Philadelphia Black Power Conference with *The Village Voice,* but according to him, his piece was "returned after being torn almost in half." This experience made him "more convinced than ever that there is need for a Black news media" (Joans, "A Black Writer Comes Home to Black Power," *Other Scenes* 1.7 [October 1968], n.p.). See also the poem "The Village Voice" in *BPW*: "allyall my enemies! !" (63).

12 "3rd Annual Black Power Conference" (agenda), TJP, carton 4, folder 5.

13 Joans, "A Black Writer Comes Home to Black Power," n.p.

14 Joans, "A Black Writer Comes Home to Black Power," n.p.

15 David Austin, "Introduction: The Dialect of Liberation," in *Moving Against the System: The 1968 Congress of Black Writers and the Making of Global Consciousness*, ed. and intro by Austin (London: Pluto Press, 2018), 2. This volume is the definitive account of the Congress, and includes a comprehensive introduction, as well as material by the participants themselves; the introduction includes also a photo of Joans at the conference, up on the stage, listening as Stokely Carmichael speaks (35), and another of him posing with Walter Rodney and Rocky Jones (55).

16 Rodney quoted in Austin, "Introduction: The Dialect of Liberation," 56.

17 "Collaged," 96.

18 "Collaged," 97.

19 Austin, "Introduction: The Dialect of Liberation," 53; Joans quoted on 54.

20 "Collaged," 97.

21 Joans quoted in Austin, "Introduction," 55.

22 Joans quoted in Austin, "Introduction," 55.

23 "Collaged," 97.

24 "Collaged," 98; see also: "Black Militants Walk Out of Writer's Congress," *The Globe and Mail* (October 14, 1968), 13.

25 See William J. Maxwell, *F.B. Eyes: How J. Edgar Hoover's Ghostreaders Framed African American Literature* (Princeton, NJ: Princeton University Press, 2015); FBI; memorandum dated 24 July 1971.

26 FBI; memorandum dated November 27, 1971.

27 FBI; memorandum dated December 17, 1969.

28 FBI; memorandum dated April 2, 1969. It's also likely that Joans was for a time during this period under surveillance by the British security service; his son Russell recalled conversations in Scotland in the 1960s and 1970s about mail from Joans to his mother, Sheila Kerr, being opened and read (Author interview with Russell Kerr [April 11, 2024]).

29 Joans, "A Black Writer Comes Home to Black Power," n.p.

30 "Collaged," 95.

31 "Races: Curtains for LeRoi," *Time* (January 12, 1968), 14.

32 Joans to *Time* magazine (January 22, 1968), TJP, carton 1, folder 31. This letter is also reproduced in *PP1*, 42.

33 *BPW*, 78. This poem appeared, in a slightly different form, under the title "Think Twice and Be Nice"—addressed to "white bigots only"—in *Beyond the Blues*, 131.

34 Thulani Davis sees a droll edge to this poem, citing it as an example of 1960s Black poets with a sense of humor, "who could play with those scary-looking, jive talking, cross-the-street-when-you-see-us images of African-Americans that define us now more and more" (Davis, "Harlem Sings America: The

Legacy of the Harlem Renaissance Endures in Lyrical Novels and Prescient Poetry," *Los Angeles Times* [February 26, 1995], 1).

35   *BPW*, 12.

36   "Bitter Lion," *The Guardian* (September 11, 1969), 11. In another essay praising Albert Ayler, Joans recounted the shock of first hearing Ayler and his group play live: "Their sound was so different, so rare and raw, like screaming the word 'FUCK' in Saint Patrick's Cathedral on crowded Easter Sunday … It was like a giant tidal wave of frightening music. It completely overwhelmed everybody … Pure black power of sounds" (Joans, "Spiritual Unity Albert Ayler: Mister AA of Grade Double A Sounds," *Coda* [August 1971], 2–4; quotation on 2).

37   *BM*, 27. Compare these sentiments in *Black Manifesto* to the poem "Dead Serious," discussed on page 35.

38   *Dies*, n.p.

39   Stokely Carmichael and Miriam Makeba to Joans (November 25, 1969), TJP, box 21, folder 14. This letter is also reproduced in *PP1*, 43–4.

40   Review of Ted Joans, *Black Pow-Wow*, *Kirkus Reviews* (September 1, 1969).

41   Mervyn Morris, "Review of *Black Pow-Wow*," *Caribbean Quarterly* 15.4 (December 1969), 59.

42   Morris, "Review of *Black Pow-Wow*," 58.

43   Brief notice on *Black Pow-Wow*, *Freedomways* (Second Quarter, 1970), 190. For other reviews, see "Tomato," "Black Pow-Wow," *Berkeley Tribe* (September 26–October 3, 1969), 17; and "Black Poetry Growing," *Milwaukee Star* (January 20, 1972), 3.

44   *BPW*, 98.

45   L. T. Brown, "Jazz Poet Joans Pow-Pows Reader," *The Indianapolis News* (October 4, 1969), 36.

46   Walter Rodney, "African History in the Service of Black Liberation," in *Moving Against the System*, 128.

47   Joans, "The Pan African Pow Wow," n.p.

48   Joans, "The Pan African Pow Wow," n.p.

49   "BMG," 62.

50   "BMG," 49.

51   "Gri-Gris," *BPW*, 121.

52   Joans, "A Black Writer Comes Home to Black Power," n.p.

53   Joans to Allen Ginsberg (December 27, 1970), Allen Ginsberg Papers, Stanford University, Department of Special Collections and University Archives, box 126, folder 22.

54   Austin, "Introduction: The Dialect of Liberation," 56; Joans, "Africa," *Afrodisia*, 3. Abu Ansar, editor of *Black Newark*, was then serving a prison sentence for "refusal to serve racist America in Vietnam"; see *Black Dialogue* (spring 1969), 45. Ansar had been chair of the Communication Workshop at the National Black Power Conference in Philadelphia, for which Joans served

as co-chair (he was listed in the spring 1969 issue of *Black Dialogue* as a member of the editorial board, under Africa: "Ted Joans—West").

55   *Afrodisia*, 20.

56   Review of Joans, *Afrodisia*, *Africa* (December 1976), 52.

57   Joans, *Afrodisia*, 21.

58   Gates, "Tri-Continental," 4.

59   Lindsay Patterson, "Introduction," in *A Rock against the Wind: Black Love Poems* (New York: Dodd, Mead & Company, 1973), xvi. Joans's contribution is "LOVE TIGHT" (9).

60   Gates, "Tri-Continental," 4.

61   *Afrodisia*, 9.

62   *Afrodisia*, 31.

63   Joans to Franklin Rosemont (June 10, 1975), RP, box 80, folder 3.

64   "I See," 244.

65   "Shut Mouth," 34.

66   "Shut Mouth," 34.

67   See also "Salute to the Sahara," which describes the Sahara Desert as "a big brown woman with legs spread wide / waiting for the masculine and brave to come inside" (*BPW*, 49).

68   "I See," 244.

69   "I See," 244.

70   In this way, Joans's eroticism shared several affinities with other French Surrealists in the 1960s who "recognized," as Alyce Mahon has shown, "the potential of Eros as one of man's primary means of unsettling and interrogating reality, of recovering collective psychic forces, and of launching socio-political revolt" (Mahon, *Surrealism and the Politics of Eros, 1938–1968* [London: Thames & Hudson, 2005], 16). This book's history of Surrealist Eros in the two decades after the Second World War offers another radical context outside of Black Power specifically that helps one see what Joans is doing in *Afrodisia* and related work. That said, Mahon does also briefly point to Joans's presence in *L'Archibras* (March 1968) to show the Surrealists' "support of [Revolutionary] Cuba and Black Power" (209).

71   *Afrodisia*, 104.

Chapter 36

1   Joans, "An Exquisite Encounter," *Brumes Blondes* Nouvelle Série 1 (Primtemps 1968), n.p. This poem was later reprinted in Joans, *Spetrophilia*.

2   *The White Hair Revolver is Still Loaded* is pictured in Pawlik, *Remade*, 146, and there is a good analysis of the piece on 145–7.

3   Ron Sakolsky, "Surrealist Subversion in Chicago," 19.

4   Franklin Rosemont, "Surrealism, Poetry, and Politics," *Race Traitor: Surrealism in the USA* 13–14 (summer 2001), 61.

5   Rosemont, "Surrealism, Poetry, and Politics," 60.

6   Franklin and Penelope Rosemont, "Poet of Marvelous Liaisons," in "Collaged," n.p.

7   Franklin and Penelope Rosemont, "Poet of Marvelous Liaisons, " in "Collaged," n.p.

8   Sakolsky, "Surrealist," 3, 22.

9   Joans to Franklin Rosemont (June 20, 1971), RP, box 80, folder 3.

10 Sakolsky, "Surrealist," 7–8.

11 Penelope Rosemont quoted in Sakolsky, "Surrealist," 11.

12 Penelope Rosemont, "Surrealism in Chicago," in *The Routledge Companion to Surrealism*, ed. Kirsten Strom (New York: Routledge, 2023), 201.

13 The Surrealist Movement, "Surrealism & Blues," *Living Blues* (January–February 1976), 19.

14 Joans's collage is on page 21; in *Hipsters*, this collage is captioned: "Three hipsters, all cool, seek a pleasant pad but run into drunken racial discrimination from an old lush-head superintendent."

15 Franklin Rosemont, "A Revolutionary Poetic Tradition," *Living Blues* (January-February 1976), 20–3; quotations on 22–3.

16 *AJT*, 48.

17 Joans to Franklin Rosemont (June 10, 1975) RP, box 80, folder 3.

18 Joans to Franklin Rosemont (June 10, 1975) RP, box 80, folder 3.

19 See Joans, "the birth of a friendship" (December 8, 1967), in *Surreally Ted Joans*, 100–1.

20 Joans to Joyce Mansour (n.d.), *Surreally Ted Joans*, 107.

21 A thumbnail sketch of Mansour's life is available in Emilie Moorhouse, "Translating Desire: The Erotic-Macabre Poetry of Joyce Mansour," in Mansour, *Emerald Wounds: Selected Poems*, trans. Moorhouse (San Francisco: City Lights, 2023), 1–12. Fuller biographical accounts in French include Marie-Laure Missir, *Joyce Mansour: Une étrange demoiselle* (Paris: Éditions Jean-Michel Place, 2005) and Marie-Francine Mansour, *Une vie Surréaliste: Joyce Mansour complice d'André Breton* (Chaintreaux: Éditions France-Empire Monde, 2014). Missir's *Joyce Mansour: Une étrange demoiselle* contains discussions of Mansour and Joans, and features a photograph of Mansour and Joans with poets John Digby and Bill Wolock, both of whom appeared with Joans in *Free-For-All* in 1978 (214).

22 Two recent editions are starting to correct this situation: *Emerald Wounds* and *In the Glittering Maw*, trans. C. Francis Fisher (New York: World Poetry Books, 2024); an earlier volume of interest to anglophone readers is *Essential Poems and Writings of Joyce Mansour*, ed. and trans. Serge Gavronsky (Boston: Black Widow Press, 2008).

23 Joyce Mansour, *Prose & Poésie: Œuvre Complète*, ed. Hubert Nyssen (Arles: Actes Sud, 1991). *Joyce Mansour: Une étrange demoiselle* has a very

useful section on "Joyce Mansour et la peinture," which discusses these collaborations as well as things like Mansour's own sculptures made from nails and other ordinary objects which resemble certain African fetish figures by which Joans was also inspired (200).

24 In *Joyce Mansour: Une étrange demoiselle*, Missir also discusses another collaboration between Joans and Mansour from this period: *Caniculaire* (1977), a portfolio of Heriberto Cogollo's lithographs that includes poems by Joans and Mansour about these lithographs. Missir emphasizes that *Caniculaire* was an expensive volume and was displayed in September 1978—around the time *Flying Piranha* was published—at the Art et Culture bookstore on the rue de Rennes in Paris (213–14). Due to its rarity, I have not personally seen *Caniculaire*, but Laura Corsiglia remembered it as being very handsomely produced.

25 Jayne Cortez, "Mainstream Statement," in *Surrealist Subversions: Rants, Writings & Images by the Surrealist Movement in the United States*, ed. Ron Sakolsky (Brooklyn, NY: Autonomedia, 2002), 278.

26 *FP*, 6, 27. These biographical statements were evidently written by Joans, as there is an extant draft of them in his hand (see "Joyce Mansour," TJP, box 19, folder 24).

27 *FP*, 5, 25; for the source of this phrase, translated slightly differently, see André Breton, "Lightning Rod" [preface to *Anthology of Black Humor*], in Breton, *What Is Surrealism? Selected Writings*, ed. Franklin Rosemont (New York: Pathfinder, 1978), 188.

28 Slavoj Žižek, "Hegel on Donald Trump's 'Objective Humor,'" *The Philosophical Salon* (January 15, 2018): https://thephilosophicalsalon.com/hegel-on-donal-trumps-objective-humor/. For an elaboration on how Breton is reading Hegel, see Daniel Barbiero, "Oedipus and the Other Two Sphinxes," *The Decadent Review*, which quotes also from the Žižek essay: https://thedecadentreview.com/corpus/oedipus-and-the-other-two-sphinxes/

29 *Afrodisia*, 98.

30 An image of a typescript of "Elle Ma Dit," complete with Joans's drawings, collages, and other embellishments, is reproduced in Missir, *Joyce Mansour* (215–16; quotation on 215).

31 Quoted in Marie-Francine Mansour, *Une vie Surréaliste*, 192; *BMG*, 138.

32 Missir, *Joyce Mansour*, passim.

33 Joans's drawing of Mansour is imaged in *Surreally Ted Joans*, 117; on Surrealist interest in the Sphinx, see also Marie-Francine Mansour, *Une vie Surréaliste*, 238.

34 See also "Anvil Am She," *Wow*, n.p.

35 Joans to Joyce Mansour (October 2, 1978), *Surreally Ted Joans*, 108.

36 Joans, Reading at University of Connecticut (October 3, 1978). A recording of this reading may be heard here: https://collections.ctdigitalarchive.org/node/1220402/

37 Joans, Reading at University of Connecticut (October 3, 1978). Justin Desmangles sees a connection between Shange's technique in *for colored girls*

and Joans's poem-life: "It was his day-to-day that invited the marvelous with each waking moment, always open to the possibilities of learning and new discoveries. (This philosophy is illustrated in Ntozake Shange's theatrical concept of the 'choreopoem' [which she uses in *for colored girls*] wherein breath line, physical movement, dance, speech, and music are all melded into a single unified gesture.)" ("Remembering").

38   *FP*, 41.

Chapter 37

1   C. Mulder to Joans (April 1, 1971), TJP, carton 3, folder 22. See Ted Joans, *Mijn Zwarte Gedachten* (Amsterdam: Van Gennep, 1970).

2   Joans to Michel Fabre (September 18, 1972), MFA, box 9, folder 37.

3   Laurens Vancrevel, "Laurens Vancrevel and Frida de Jong's Collection of Surrealist Art," in Saskia van Kampen-Prein and Vancrevel, *Creative Chance: Surrealist Art and Literature from the Laurens Vancrevel and Frida de Jong Collection* (Rotterdam: Museum Boijmans Van Beuningen, 2021), 45.

4   Laurens Vancrevel to Joans (March 9, 1975), TJP, box 24, folder 1. Vancrevel found the "Surrealist Movement in the US" section of *City Lights Anthology* "rather interesting" but "very very orthodox."

5   Mikofsky, "Joys and Moans," 70; see also *BFP*.

6   Joans, "Real Free" (1972), in The Pyramids, *King of Kings* (Pyramid Records, 1974).

7   Breton, *Nadja*, 11.

8   "Mixed Marriages," in *Spetrophilia*, n.p.

9   Joans, "Spectrophilia" fragment (November 23, 1984), TJP, box 19, folder 30.

10   Joans, "Black Nailed Fetish Prayer," in *BM*, 57.

11   Note that in "Deeper Are Allyall's Roots," a novel-memoir also poised between "wide awake and dream sleep," Joans describes similar scenes: "Moshongokuba … was guarding a sacred tree where a woman had climbed to submit to spectrophilia. The Bakuba has its natural ancestral worshipping and animism. There is no cult of a 'supreme being' (GOD)" ("Deeper").

12   "Straight Croissants," *Spetrophilia*, n.p.

13   Henry Louis Gates, Jr., "Going to Meet the Man," in *Beauford Delaney: From New York to Paris*, ed. Patricia Sue Canterbury (Minneapolis: Minneapolis Institute of Arts, 2004), 10.

14   Henry Louis Gates, Jr., email to Author (March 15, 2023).

15   Later, when *The Norton Anthology of African American Literature* appeared, Joans was upset that he had not been included (Joans to Michel Fabre [July 1997], MFA, box 9, folder 37). See also "Skip the Byuppie" (1997), a poem included in *Teducation* (76–7).

16   Gates, "Tri-Continental," 5.

17   Franklin Rosemont, "Surrealism, Poetry, and Politics," 55.

18   Joans to Elias Wilentz (November 12, 1977), Elias Wilentz Papers, University of Buffalo, box 3, folder 35.

19   Gates, "Tri-Continental," 8.

20   Gates, "Tri-Continental," 12.

Chapter 38

1   Jason Weiss, "The American Center Breathes New Life," *Passion: The Magazine of Paris* (December 10–23, 1981), 6.

2   Art Kahn, "Ted Joans Hip Poet," TJP, carton 3, folder 71. For a brief but useful meditation on Joans's relationship to figurations of "hip," see Aldon Lynn Nielsen, "Ted Talk," *Journal of Beat Studies* 8 (2020), 41–7.

3   Joans, résumé (ca. 1984), HBR, box 8, Joans folder.

4   Gates, "Tri-Continental," 6.

5   "Ted Joans in Interview with Theo Vincent," in *Festac '77: 2nd World Black and African Festival of Arts and Culture*, decomposed, an-arranged and reproduced by Chimurenga (Cape Town: Afterall Books, 2019), 313. *Festac '77* is an extremely useful assemblage of materials—media articles, interviews, photographs, and the like—pertaining to the festival; a blurry photograph of Joans reading at a microphone appears next to his interview on 313.

6   See Charles Nicholl, *Somebody Else: Arthur Rimbaud in Africa, 1880–91* (London: Jonathan Cape, 1997). Although the Rimbaud house that Joans visited still stands in Harar today, Nicholl shows that this was almost certainly not the actual house in which Rimbaud lived.

7   Joans to Allen Ginsberg (April 16, 1971), Allen Ginsberg Papers, box 126, folder 22.

8   Joans to Franklin Rosemont (June 20, 1971), RP, box 80, folder 3.

9   *Afrodisia*, 16.

10   Joans, "Qui Suis-Je," TJP, box 24, folder 13. For a helpful, detailed reading of "Cinque Maggio," see Grégory Pierrot, "Ted Joans, the Other Jones," 55–7.

11   "New Gallery Opens with 'Save Works of Art' Call," *Daily Nation* (Kenya) (February 12, 1971), 12.

12   Barbara Kimeneye, "Soul Brother Ted—A Misguided Guide to Africa?" *Daily Nation* (Kenya) (February 23, 1971), 15.

13   Kimeneye, "Soul Brother Ted," 15.

14   Peter Hodgkiss, "Ted Joans at the ICA," *Poetry Information* 11 (Autumn 1974), 21.

15   Timothy Hoey, "'Jazz Poet' Ted Joans Takes His Flights on Surrealist Airlines," *Daily American* (Rome) (July 6, 1979), n.p.

Chapter 39

1   "Collaged," 110–11.

2   Ife Enohoro, "The Second World Black and African Festival of Arts and Culture: Lagos, Nigeria," *The Black Scholar* (September 1977), 21.

3   Iris Kay, "Festac 77," *African Arts* 11. 1 (October 1977), 51.

4   "Ted Joans in Interview with Theo Vincent," 312.

5   "Ted Joans in Interview with Theo Vincent," 312.

6   "Ted Joans in Interview with Theo Vincent," 312.

7   This layout is from "Ted Joans in Interview with Theo Vincent," 312; but the poem, "The Reward," also appears differently arranged in *Afrodisia*, 24.

8   Caroline Nwankwo, "Literary Shows and the Missing 'Giants,'" *Lagos Daily Times* (1977), reproduced in *Festac '77*, 304; see also "Il est poete, américain il revient du FESTAC et parle l'afroanglais," *Togo Presse* (1977), 5.

9   Randy Weston, *The Autobiography of Randy Weston*, arranged by Willard Jenkins (Durham, NC: Duke University Press, 2010), 119.

10 Weston, *Autobiography*, 120.

11 Randy Weston (music) and Langston Hughes (lyrics), *Uhuru Afrika* (Roulette, 1960).

12 "Ted Joans in Interview with Theo Vincent," 313.

13 "Ted Joans in Interview with Theo Vincent," 312.

14 Nicholas J. Cull, *The Cold War and the United States Information Agency: American Propaganda and Public Diplomacy, 1945–1989* (New York: Cambridge University Press, 2008), xvii.

15 Penny Von Eschen, *Satchmo Blows Up the World: Jazz Ambassadors Play the Cold War* (Cambridge, MA: Harvard University Press, 2004), 6.

16 Willis Conover quoted in Von Eschen, *Satchmo*, 16–17.

17 Von Eschen, *Satchmo*, 32.

18 Joans, résumé (ca. 1984), HBR, box 8, Joans folder.

19 Gates, "Tri-Continental," 6.

20 Joans to Franklin Rosemont (ca. December 1984), RP, box 80, folder 3.

21 Haki Madhubuti to Joans (May 30, 1974), TJP, box 23, folder 4; see also William Raspberry, "Black Poet on a Blacklist," *Washington Post* (December 10, 1984).

22 See, for example, Joans to Mary Ellen Wang (November 27, 1973), FSG, box 450, Joans folder.

23 Note that Joans listed *Poète de Jazz* as being published by "USIA (Dakar, Senegal)" ("I See," 257); see also his handwritten corrections on a copy of the poem "The Hipster is …, " which notes language to "substitute for U.S.I.S." (TJP, box 1, folder 82).

24   For a discussion of rumors of Joans as an Interpol or CIA agent, see Williams, "Ted's Dead," 244; Author interview with Laura Corsiglia (January 5, 2023).

25   Gwen Ansell, "Ted Joans and the Poetry of Jazz," *Weekly Mail* (Johannesburg) (February 11, 1994), n.p.

26   Joans quoted in Maureen Isaacson, "Swing is What Counts for Joans," *Saturday Star* (Johannesburg) (February 19, 1994).

27   Joans, *Poems for You: In & Out of Africa* (no publisher stated: Yaoundé, Cameroon, 1994), 2. In 1994, the USIS had a special project going to promote American literature in Yaoundé, so it seems likely to me that *Poems for You* was printed through the USIS; see Steven H. Gale, "The Emperor Jones," *African Affairs* 95.381 (October 1996), which recounts Gale's time as a USIS "Academic Specialist" at Yaoundé University in 1994 (606).

28   There is a photo of Joans at an "anti-apartheid protest" in 1986, with Franklin and Penelope Rosemont; this photograph is reproduced in Penelope Rosemont, "Surrealism in Chicago," *Routledge Companion to Surrealism*, 204.

29   Joans, résumé (ca. 1985), TJP, carton 3, folder 47.

30   "Jazz Poet Ted Joans is Fellow in Black Music at Bennington," *Bennington Banner* (November 9, 1973), 7.

31   Bill Dixon to Reinhard Mayer (May 30, 1978), Bennington College Digital Repository: http://hdl.handle.net/11209/13852/

32   Joans to Michel Fabre (November 23, 1973), MFA, box 9, folder 37.

33   Hale Smith introducing Ted Joans, University of Connecticut (September 11, 1979).

34   Joans read at the University of Connecticut seven times between 1971 and 1982. High-quality recordings of those appearances are available here: https://archivessearch.lib.uconn.edu/repositories/2/digital_objects/2813/

35   This list is according to a detailed résumé (ca. 1985), TJP, carton 3, folder 47.

36   Joans, untitled fragment, City Lights Books Records, Additions, box 31, folder 10.

37   "I, Too," n.p. Joans's favorite Tutola novel was *The Palm-Wine Drinkard* (1952). For an example of a poem that seems to play with the sort of Pidgin English Tutola adopts in *The Palm-Wine Drinkard*, see "No Mad Talk": "AT TIMES ME FEEL LIKE ME JES BACK FROM / ANOTHER MOTHER PLANET" (*BPW*, 20). Joans frequently performed "No Mad Talk" at readings.

38   Dwight Garner, "Stray Questions for: Ishmael Reed," *ArtsBeat: New York Times Blog* (March 21, 2008): https://archive.nytimes.com/artsbeat.blogs.nytimes.com/2008/03/21/stray-questions-for-ishmael-reed/. See also Reed's poem for Joans, "Ted Joans Said 'Jazz is My Religion,'" *Shuffle Boil* 4 (summer/fall 2003), 2–3.

39   Joans, untitled fragment, City Lights Books Records, Additions, box 31, folder 10.

40   Barbara Christian, "Whatever Happened to Bob Kaufman?" *Black World* 21.11 (1972), 21–9; quotation on 21.

41   Joans, untitled fragment, City Lights Books Records, Additions, box 31, folder 10.

42 Joans to Arthur Wang (April 1, 1980), FSG, box 450, Joans folder.

43 "Jazz-poetry Concert," *North East Bay Independent and Gazette* (May 30, 1980), 5.

44 Author interview with Terence Blacker (May 20, 2022).

45 Terence Blacker, "An American Surrealist Who Made His Life His Art," *The Independent* (May 30, 2003), 8.

46 FBI; memorandum dated December 17, 1968.

47 Author interview with Daline Jones (May 5, 2024).

48 Teresa Jones to Arthur Wang (January 17, 1976), FSG, box 450, Joans folder.

49 Joans to Franklin and Penelope Rosemont (June 28, 1976), RP, box 80, folder 3.

50 *Sure*, 36.

51 *Sure*, 38. Joans used a similar technique on the last page of *Honey Spoon*, which features a photograph of one of his sons: "Who is HE, where is HE now? You can see, HE did not write Honey Spoon but poet Ted Joans did" (76).

52 Author interview with Heather Maisner (July 1, 2022).

53 Joans to Heather Maisner (February 1972); collection of Heather Maisner.

54 Gates, "Tri-Continental," 5.

55 *Tanger*, 143.

56 Author interview with Marion Kalter (September 20, 2022).

57 Joans to Marion Kalter (January 1, 1975), in Kalter, *All Around Ted Joans* (Karlsruhe: Center for Art and Media Karlsruhe, 2017), 13.

58 Author interview with Marion Kalter (September 20, 2022).

59 *BM*, 24.

60 Author interview with Marion Kalter (September 20, 2022).

61 Joans to Marion Kalter (January 1, 1975), in Kalter, *All Around Ted Joans*, 12.

Chapter 40

1 Joans to Marion Kalter (January 9, 1975), in Kalter, *All Around Ted Joans*, 18.

2 Joans to Mary Ellen and Arthur Wang (November 10, 1976), FSG, box 450, Joans folder.

3 "I, Too," n.p.

4 "Deeper."

5 "Deeper."

6 "BMG," 1.

7 See, for example, the various news clippings in TJP, carton 3, folder 71.

8 Joans to Mary Ellen and Arthur Wang (November 10, 1976), FSG, box 450, Joans folder.

9 Laura Corsiglia to Author (June 30, 2024).

10   "Deeper."

11   Joans to Mary Ellen and Arthur Wang (November 10, 1976), FSG, box 450, Joans folder.

12   Arthur Wang to Joans (February 23, 1977), FSG, box 450, Joans folder.

13   Eventually, New Directions also rejected "Deeper" (see Joans to Lawrence Ferlinghetti [November 12, 1984]), City Lights Books Records, Additions, box 31, folder 10.

Chapter 41

1   For some context on why an American "jazz poet" might have found a welcome reception in West Germany at this time, see Uta Poiger, *Jazz, Rock, and Rebels: Cold War Politics and American Culture in a Divided Germany* (Berkeley: University of California Press, 2000).

2   Author interview with Michael Kellner (October 7, 2022).

3   *Vergriffen*, n.p.

4   Michael Kellner to Joans (October 18, 1979), TJP, carton 2, folder 45.

5   See Hans M. Zell, "Frankfurt Book Fair 1980," *The African Book Publishing Record* (1981), 5.

6   Michael Kellner to Joans (May 1, 1980), TJP, carton 2, folder 45.

7   Michael Kellner to Joans (October 23, 1980), TJP, carton 2, folder 45.

8   Susanne Klengel, *"Dies und Das": Black Surrealism from Berlin in 1984* (Hamburg: Edition Michael Kellner, 2023), 14. This edition is an expansion and English translation of Klengel's essay "Black Surrealism in Ted Joans' Zeitschrift *Dies und Das* (Berlin 1984)," which was published earlier in 2023, and is the best source of information about *Dies and Das* and Joans's literary activities in Germany in the early 1980s.

9   Michael Kellner to Joans (June 10, 1981), TJP, box 22, folder 18.

10   *MBP*, 23–4. This version of "Lets Play Something" had also been published in *ONDB*, 20–1.

11   Kerouac to Joans (February 13, 1963), in *MBP*, 58.

12   Michael Kellner to Joans (June 6, 1980), TJP, box 22, folder 18.

13   "Collaged," 130.

14   Author interview with Laura Corsiglia (January 6, 2023).

15   I'm paraphrasing here from the history of DAAD given on their current website: https://www.berliner-kuenstlerprogramm.de/en/digital-archive/program-history-preview/

16   Barbara Richter to Joans (October 22, 1980), TJP, carton 2, folder 26.

17   Robert Creeley, "Letter from Berlin," *The Washington Post* (December 18, 1983), BW15.

18   Klengel, *"Dies und Das,"* 15.

Chapter 42

1   Joans, "Excerpts from a Letter," *Arsenal: Surrealist Subversion* 1 (1970), 57. As far back as 1962, Joans had been planning a review out of Tangier with Paul Bowles that they were going to call "Tangerine," and in 1965, he told Lawrence Ferlinghetti he was gathering material for a new magazine to be titled "Fuck Who (For United Cool Kind Who)—dig food sex and art" (Joans to Rosey Pool [February 6, 1962], Rosey Pool Papers, Howard University, box 82-2, folder 80; Joans to Lawrence Ferlinghetti [September 22, 1965], City Lights Records, box 6, folder 34). Eventually Joans used a version of this latter title for a thirty-six-page booklet he published in 1988: *For United Cool Kind Marvelously Evolved*, featuring his poetry and collages.

2   Despite Joans using the title chefredakteur, in a letter to Joyce Mansour, he wrote of *Dies und Das*: "Richard Anders and Christian Boerschamm are my worthy co-editors," but it is not clear the extent to which these three collaborated on the magazine; from my perspective, as a whole *Dies und Das* very strongly reflects Joans's idiosyncratic sensibilities, so it could have been that Anders and Boerschamm mainly assisted him with the German-language contributions since, by his own admission, Joans did "not yet speak or read German as well as I do French which is lacking also!!!" (Joans to unspecified addressee [Joyce Mansour] (ca. early 1984), TJP, box 15, folder 6). Richard Anders was a Berlin-based poet, born the same year as Joans, who had translated Joans's English poems into German for *The Aardvark-Watcher* and gave readings with him in the city; after *Dies und Das* came out, Boerschamm contacted Michael Kellner to request a discount on copies of the magazine because, he explained, he was "one of the editors" (Kellner to Joans [November 23, 1984], TJP, carton 2, folder 48).

3   Joans to J. H. Matthews (June 1, 1984), JHMP, box 2, folder 7.

4   Joans to unspecified addressee [Joyce Mansour] (ca. early 1984), TJP, box 15, folder 6.

5   Joans, "Dies & Das Is Sold Here," City Lights Books Records, Additions, box 31, folder 10.

6   Author interview with Michael Kellner (October 7, 2022).

7   Michael Kellner to Joans (October 27, 1986), TJP, carton 2, folder 48.

8   Laurens Vancrevel to Joans (January 26, 1986), TJP, box 21, folder 1.

9   Sometimes when the title of this piece is given, as for example in *Surrealism Beyond Borders* (306) and *Surreally Ted Joans* (70), it is represented as *The Seven Sons of Lautréamont (and His Dutiful Beautiful Daughter)*. The parenthetical phrase "*and His Dutiful Beautiful Daughter*" refers to Joyce Mansour, who wrote poems for each of the sections/artists; these poems are not on the piece itself, and are unpublished.

10   Quoted in André Breton, "The Exquisite Corpse, Its Exaltation," in Breton, *Surrealism and Painting*, trans. Simon Taylor Watson (New York: Harper & Row, 1972), 289. See also J. H. Matthews, *Languages of Surrealism* (Columbia: University of Missouri Press, 1986), especially the chapter "Language and Play: *le cadavre exquis*," 119–38.

11 Breton, "Exquisite," 290.

12 See *Surreally Ted Joans* for high-quality reproductions of many such exquisite corpses (71–85).

Chapter 43

1 Joans to J. H. Matthews (September 7, 1984), JHMP, box 2, folder 7.

2 Joans, "The Unpremeditated Birth of an Immaculate Cadavre Exquis," TJP, box 16, folder 25.

3 A mask like Joans's can be seen in the following link: https://www. metmuseum.org/art/collection/search/321329. The Met describes the mask as "composed of elements from different animals and represents a 'bush spirit,' emphasizing that it has no counterpart on earth ... The long horns, open jaws and teeth are supposed to inspire fear."

4 See, for example, his painting *Tribute to Magritte* (1962), which also features the stylized Bauolé mask; the painting is reproduced in *Surreally Ted Joans*, 26–7.

5 Laura Corsiglia to Author (June 30, 2024).

6 *BWP*, 5.

7 Joans to Franklin Rosemont (June 10, 1975), RP, box 80, folder 13.

8 These quotations, and the general account of how *The Seven Sons of Lautréamont* came together, are taken from Joans's own recounting of the piece's origins, "Unpremeditated Birth." The extent to which the particular circumstances hew to reality is, of course, an open question. In a letter to Franklin Rosemont, dated June 1975, Joans mentions his "collective cadavre exquis Les Septs Fils De Lautréamont," and that he had "to work nearly three years" to get the contributions from the other six artists, suggesting that the piece was complete by mid-1975 (Joans to Franklin Rosemont [June 10, 1975], RP, box 80, folder 3). In "On Rue Jacques Callot," an ode to that street published in 1969, Joans plays up its Surrealist associations, as it is where "a black flower first saw a Man Ray" and "where exquisite corpses drink no wines / the moon is pregnant with loud poems" (*BPW*, 47), so the detail of birthing *The Seven Sons of Lautréamont* at a café on rue Jacques Callot could perhaps reflect a poetic truth—or not.

9 Joans to Ingrid Schaffner (July 22, 1993), TJP, box 21, folder 22.

10 "Loan Agreement," TJP, box 21, folder 22.

11 See the exhibition catalogue, *The Return of the Cadavre Exquis* (New York: Drawing Center, 1993). An image of *Seven Sons of Lautréamont* appears on page 22, where the dates given are 1973–80.

12 Joans to J. H. Matthews (January 22, 1984), JHMP, box 2, folder 7.

13 Karen Grimson, "Wifredo Lam," in *Among Others: Blackness At MoMA*, ed. Darby English and Charlotte Barat (New York: Museum of Modern Art, 2019), 264.

14 Joans to Lou and Wifredo Lam (September 12, 1975), in *Surreally Ted Joans*, 97.

15 Joans to Lou and Wifredo Lam (September 12, 1975), in *Surreally Ted Joans*, 96–7.

16 Joans to J. H. Matthews (June 1, 1984), JHMP, box 2, folder 7.

Chapter 44

1 For a discussion of Surrealist precursors that includes many figures on this list, see Strom, *Making*, 57–101.

2 Note that with the exception of Sherlock Holmes, all these figures (as well as many others) are found in Franklin Rosemont's "Surrealist Glossary" appended to his edition of Breton's *What is Surrealism?*, which appeared a few years before Joans drafted "Razzle Dazzle." Rosemont's glosses are instructive for understanding why Joans may have chosen these particular figures.

3 "Spadework," 42.

4 Arthur Wang to Joans (February 23, 1977), FSG, box 450, Joans folder.

5 Joans, "Journal Jottings" (1985), TJP, box 18, folder 3. Despite Calder and Boyars not publishing "Razzle Dazzle," in John Calder's obituary for Joans, he singled out "Razzle Dazzle" as "outstanding" (John Calder, "Ted Joans," *The Guardian* [May 27, 2003]: https://www.theguardian.com/news/2003/may/27/guardianobituaries.booksobituaries).

6 Michael Kellner to Joans (October 27, 1986), TJP, carton 2, folder 45; Kellner, email to Author (September 27, 2023).

7 Joans to Philip Lamantia (ca. April 1990), Lamantia Papers, Bancroft Library, UC Berkeley, carton 1, folder 20.

Chapter 45

1 "Collaged," 167.

2 Joans, résumé (ca. 1984), HBR, box 8, Joans folder.

3 Joans, résumé (ca. 1984), HBR, box 8, Joans folder.

4 "Collaged," 175–6. For a useful history of sound in Surrealist film, see J. H. Matthews, "Sound in Surrealist Cinema," *Languages*, 217–37.

5 Creeley, "Letter from Berlin," BW15.

6   Joans, "Teducation Films," MFA, box 9, folder 37.

7   Joans, "Toronto Canada Notes," TJP, box 19, folder 12.

Chapter 46

1   "I, Too," Preface, n.p.

2   Author interview with Laura Corsiglia (January 5, 2023).

3   Contributor Note, in *Fire Readings*, ed. David Applefield, Richard Hallward, and T. Wignesan (Vincennes: Frank Books, 1991), 195; Joans, inscription in *Dies und Das;* collection of Author.

4   "Aardvarkian," n.p.

5   *Double*, 16–17.

6   For Steve Dalachinsky's poetic tribute to his friend Joans, set at Café Le Rouquet, see https://www.emptymirrorbooks.com/poems/poems-by-steve-dalachinsky?

7   Herbert Gold, *Bohemia: Digging the Roots of Cool* (New York: Touchstone, 1994), 142.

8   James Emanuel, "Preface: An Appreciation," in *Double*, n.p.

9   Lindsey Tramuta, "Leaving America Questionnaire #1: Jack Lamar," *The New Paris Dispatch* (November 16, 2024): https://bonjour.lindseytramuta.com/p/leaving-america-questionnaire-1/

10 Joans to Michel Fabre (November 20, 1972), MFA, box 9, folder 37.

11 Joans quoted these lines, in the original French, to Michel Fabre (November 28, 1972), MFA, box 9, folder 37; the quoted English translation is taken from *The Complete Poetry of Aimé Césaire: Bilingual Edition*, trans. A. James Arnold and Clayton Eshleman (Middletown, CT: Wesleyan University Press, 2017), 31.

12 Because Fabre relied on Joans himself for biographical information, some details repeated in *From Harlem to Paris* are true in the sense that Joans's poem-life was true, and so should be approached accordingly.

13 Joans to Michel Fabre (February 14, 1992), MFA, box 9, folder 37; Laura Corsiglia to Author (June 30, 2024). For poems about Saint-Cirq-Lapopie, see "The First Saint-Cirq-Lapopie Poem" (*FP*, 30), its translation, "Premier Poème de Saint-Cirq-Lapopie" (*Poèmes*, n.p.), and "Not on Most Maps" (*Take One or More*, n.p.).

14 "Aardvarkian Surreal Stroll Through Paris," TJP, box 14, folder 7. A short excerpt from this piece appears in *PP2*, 43–56; although "Aardvarkian" is dated 1992 in *PP2*, the typescript in TJP is signed "ted joans, age 22,730 Days Old," making Joans sixty-two at the time of composition, which is why I use the date of 1990 for this piece. Joans had wanted the Rosemonts to publish "Aardvarkian Surreal" and when they did not, he wrote to Penelope Rosemont that they had erred in passing on his "black humorous guide to

Paris ... a hysterical moment and monumental Maldoroic printing" (Joans to Penelope Rosemont [February 1994], RP, Box 80, folder 3).

15 Joans, "Toronto Canada Notes," TJP, box 19, folder 12.

Chapter 47

1 Jim Haynes, *Thanks for Coming! An Autobiography* (London: Faber and Faber, 1984), 41.

2 John Krueger, "A Rhinoceros Head and a Pile of Books," *Stars and Stripes* (October 9, 1960), in Haynes, *Thanks*, n.p.

3 "Collaged," 124.

4 See, for instance, Joans, "AA! AA? Yeah, AA!," *International Times* (December 12–25, 1966), 7, on Albert Ayler; and Joans, "Hommage to Bosch," *International Times* (October 5–20, 1967), 15, a review of a major Bosch exhibit in Holland.

5 Haynes, *Thanks*, 144.

6 Elizabeth Venant, "The Third Wave: Paris' Expatriate Scene," *Los Angeles Times* (September 21, 1986).

7 Joans, "Teducated Points of Views of Paris" (1993), TJP, box 16, folder 31.

8 Haynes, *Thanks*, 264.

9 Haynes, *Thanks*, 264.

10 Jim Haynes, email to Author (July 14, 2020).

11 "Shut Mouth," 3.

12 *ONDB*, 11.

13 *ONDB*, 4.

14 *NDB*, n.p. (unbracketed forward slash in original). This poem was written for Carolyn Cassady, widow of Neal Cassady, the model for Dean Moriarty in Kerouac's *On the Road*.

15 Jayne Cortez, "Mainstream Statement," in *Surrealist Subversions*, 278.

16 Joans to Mary Ellen Wang (November 27, 1973), FSG, box 450, Joans folder.

17 Joans, review of Jayne Cortez, *Coagulations: New and Collected Poems* (1984), *Présence Africaine* 136 (4e Trimestre 1985), 184.

18 *HS*, 71.

19 *HS*, n.p. There is a 1993 reprint edition of *Honey Spoon* published by Gediminas Butkus in Vilnius, Lithuania.

20 Note that housed in TJP is a 70-page typescript titled "Money Soon," which Joans called a "sister prose" to *Honey Spoon*. This piece was completed in 1995 and was to be published by Handshake—and may have been, in a very small run—but I have only seen the typescript.

21 Jim Haynes to Joans (February 8, 1998), TJP, carton 2, folder 35.

Chapter 48

1 George Whitman quoted in Krista Halverson, "Introduction," *Shakespeare and Company, Paris: A History of the Rag & Bone Shop of the Heart*, ed. Halverson (Paris: Shakespeare and Co., 2016), 231. This book is the best available history of Shakespeare and Company, and my brief summary is borrowed from it.

2 Whitman quoted in *Shakespeare and Company, Paris*, 255, 30.

3 Joans, "Teducated Points of Views of Paris" (1993), TJP, box 16, folder 31.

4 "Razzle," 199.

5 "Collaged," 199.

6 Sylvia Whitman email to Author (July 11, 2024). Joans material in the Shakespeare and Company archives includes a poem he wrote to Sylvia on her tenth birthday, "An April Golden Rule," which promises her "A portable satchel box / From / Far-a-way T I M B U K T U," and a line drawing of him and young Sylvia under the legend "Sylvia & Company Bookshop."

7 Manthia Diawara, *We Won't Budge: A Malaria Memoir* (New York: Basic Books, 2003), 210.

8 Diawara, *We Won't Budge*, 211.

9 Diawara, *We Won't Budge*, 212.

10 Diawara, *We Won't Budge*, 214.

11 Diawara, *We Won't Budge*, 224; 215–16.

12 Diawara, *We Won't Budge*, 220–1.

13 Diawara, *We Won't Budge*, 221.

14 Diawara, *We Won't Budge*, 221.

15 Joans, "Anaïs Nin was a delicious woman," *Shakespeare*, 203.

16 Joans to Karl Orend (January 18, 1995), in *Anaïs Nin: A Book of Mirrors*, ed. Paul Herron (Huntington Woods, MI: Sky Blue Press, 1996), 126.

17 Joans to Karl Orend (January 18, 1995), *Anaïs Nin*, 127. *Anaïs Nin: A Book of Mirrors* also includes "Lovescience," Joans's playful, affectionate poem about Nin—the title is a pun on Louveciennes, a town in the Western suburbs of Paris where Nin had a house from 1930 to 1935 (18–19).

18 "I See," 225.

19 Laura Corsiglia, "Surrounding Area," *Surrealist Subversions*, 530.

20 Laura Corsiglia on "Cover to Cover" radio program with Jack Foley (November 26, 2003).

21 Author interview with Laura Corsiglia (February 26, 2024).

22 Author interview with Laura Corsiglia (May 4, 2022).

23 Laura Corsiglia on "Cover to Cover."

24 Author interview with Laura Corsiglia (February 26, 2024).

25 Joans, "The Case of the Four Rhino Horns," TJP, box 18, folder 11.

26   "Collaged," 116.

27   Laura Corsiglia on "Cover to Cover."

Chapter 49

1   Author interview with Laura Corsiglia (January 5, 2023).

2   Author interview with Laura Corsiglia (May 4, 2022).

3   See, for example, Diawara, *We Won't Budge*, which opens: "The idea for this book came from a deep frustration I felt on the death of Amadou Diallo, who was violently killed by New York City police. He was on his way back to his apartment, after a long day's labor, when they gunned him down. I was saddened and angry because I felt that his short life in America mirrored my own beginning here, and that his American dream was betrayed by a violent and senseless killing" (vii).

4   *Our*, 93–4; this poem is the last one in *Our Thang*, emphasizing its importance.

5   Joans and Corsiglia to Jim Haynes (August 3, 2000), TJP, carton 2, folder 35.

6   "Collaged," 176. During this period, Joans also dabbled in writing Sherlockian mysteries in which the lead investigator is none other than Dr. Rotapep; see Joans, "The Case of the Four Rhino Horns," TJP, box 18, folder 11, a story that amounts to 81 notebook pages handwritten between March and April 1993.

7   Hart Leroy Bibbs, *Poly Rhythms to Freedom* (New York: MacNair, 1964), 14–15.

8   See Breton, *Nadja*, 118.

9   John Olson, review of *Our Thang*, *Rain Taxi* (fall 2022): https://raintaxi.com/our-thang/

10   Before Columbus Foundation, "Our Story": https://www.beforecolumbusfoundation.com/our-story/

11   See *The Portable Beat Reader*, ed. Ann Charters (New York: Viking, 1992), 385–92. Joans's friend Yuko Otomo told me that he had pulled his poems from the paperback version of the *Portable Beat Reader* because he felt that "The Sermon" had been changed without his permission (Author interview with Yuko Otomo [September 19, 2022]). In her correspondence with Joans from the early 1990s, Charters details her sources for "The Sermon," writing: "As you can see, I have not added or changed a word of this printed poem, and to accuse me of bowdlerizing 'The Sermon' because of its sexual content, as Tuli [Kupferberg] says you told him, is ridiculous" (Ann Charters to Joans [February 26, 1992], Ann Charters Papers, University of Connecticut, box 2011-0121.6).

12   Jack Foley, Review of *Teducation* and *Wow*, *Konch* (2000): https://web.archive.org/web/20130317052944/http://www.ishmaelreedpub.com/articles/foley2.html

13   Laura Corsiglia email to Author (July 4, 2020).

14   "Spadework," 47.

Coda: Atmospheric Rivers

1   *Teducation*, 200.

2   *Teducation*, 201.

3   Object label for Joans et al., *Long Distance*. In exhibition *Surrealism Beyond Borders* at the Museum of Modern Art, New York (October 4, 2021 – January 30, 2022). The full list of contributors to *Long Distance* is available in the excellent exhibition catalogue, *Surrealism Beyond Borders*, ed. Stephanie D'Alessandro and Matthew Gale (New York: Metropolitan Museum of Art, 2021), 314.

4   *AJT*, 55.

5   "Aardvarkian," 26; *Afrodisia*, 65.

6   Joans, *A Few Poems* (Lomé: No Publisher Stated, 1981), n.p.

7   Breton, *Nadja*, 21.

BIBLIOGRAPHY

Works by Ted Joans

Note: this bibliography is a (likely partial) list of Ted Joans's published written work; a list of principal unpublished work is given after the published list. Joans often chose to publish smaller books and booklets in various places around the world and in very limited editions, and the rarer works are accordingly difficult to find; because there tend to be errors in existing bibliographies, I have only listed work which I have personally seen. So readers may have a better sense of the type of publication, I have listed the page count and, if known, the edition size. Further information about these works is in the text.

Books and Booklets

Funky Jazz Poems. New York: Rhino Review, 1959. 19 pp.

All of Ted Joans and No More. New York: Excelsior, July, 1961. 1st ed. 80 pp. Edition of 500.

All of Ted Joans and No More. New York: Excelsior, September, 1961. New Revised ed. 95 pp. (with collages by Joans). Edition of 2000.

The Hipsters. New York: Corinth Books, 1961. 91 pp. (with collages by Joans).

The Truth: A Poem. Amsterdam: Surrealistisch Kabinet, 1968. 37 pp.

Black Pow-Wow: Jazz Poems. New York: Hill and Wang, 1969. 130 pp.

Proposition pour un Manifeste Black Power Pouvoir Noir, trans. Jeannine Ciment and Robert Benayoun. Paris: Eric Losfeld, 1969. 75 pp.

Afrodisia: New Poems. New York: Hill and Wang, 1970. 150 pp.

Mijn zwarte gedachten: een manifest. Amsterdam: Van Gennep, 1970. 36 pp.

A Black Manifesto in Jazz Poetry and Prose. London: Calder and Boyars, 1971. 92 pp.

Black Flower Poems: Readings Jazz & Poetry. Amsterdam: Amsterdamsch Litterair Café, no date stated, but ca. 1972. 7 pp.

Spetrophilia. Amsterdam: Amsterdamsch Litterair Café, 1973. 30 pp. (with collages by Joans).

Jazz is Our Religion: Jazz Poemes, trans. Pollar et Carles. Nancy, France: Imprimerie des Celestins, 1973. 8 pp.

A Black Pow-Wow of Jazz Poems. London: Calder and Boyars, 1973. 159 pp.

Afrodisia: Old & New Poems. London: Marion Boyars, 1976. 150 pp. (with collages by Joans).

Jazz Drawings. Exhibition Catalogue. New York: The Jazz Museum, 1977. 8 pp.

Flying Piranha (with Joyce Mansour). New York: Bola Press, 1978. 45 pp. (with collages by Joans).

Free-For-All (with John Digby, Valery Oisteanu and Bill Wolak). Fort Lee, NJ: Somniloquist's Press, 1978. 16 pp. (with collages by Digby).

Poète de Jazz. Dakar, Senegal: Centre Culturel Américain, 1978. 13 pp.

Vergriffen; oder: Blitzlieb Poems. Kassel and Hamburg: Loose Blätter Presse, 1979. 27 pp.

The Aardvark-Watcher/Der Erdferkel-forscher. Berlin: Literarisches Colloquium, 1980. 57 pp.

Heads I Win, Tails You Lose. Amsterdam: Surreal Kasteel, 1980. 30 pp. (with collages by Joans). Edition of 100.

Old and New Duck Butter Poems. Paris: Handshake, 1980. 24 pp. (with collages by Joans).

A Few Poems. Lomé, Togo: No Publisher Stated [USIS], 1981. 10 pp.

Merveilleux Coup de Foudre (with Jayne Cortez). Paris: Handshake, 1982. 14 pp. (with collages by Joans). Edition of 100.

New Duck Butter Poems. Paris: Handshake, 1982. 48 pp. (with collages by Joans).

Mehr Blitzliebe Poems. Hamburg: Verlag Michael Kellner, 1982. 63 pp.

Sure, Really I Is. Harpford, Sidmouth, Devon: TRANSFORMAcTION, 1982. 38 pp. Edition of 350.

Dies und Das: Ein Magazin von Aktuellem Surrealistischem Interesse (editor). Berlin: 1984. 200 pp. (with collages by Joans and others). Edition of 1000.

Some Sum of Surrealist Poems. Toronto: Privately Printed by Letters Bookshop, 1987. 27 pp. Edition of 20.

For United Cool Kind Marvelously Evolved. Berlin: No Publisher Stated, 1988. 36 pp. (with collages by Joans). Edition of 60.

Poems of Ted Joans (A 1989 Homage to Langston Hughes). Marrakesh, Morocco: DAR America, 1989. 14 pp. Edition of 100.

Honey Spoon. Paris: Handshake, 1991. 76 pp.

Double Trouble (with Hart Leroy Bibbs). Paris: Revue Noire Editions Bleu Outremer, 1992. 125 pp. (with collages by Joans).

Okapi Passion. Oakland: Ishmael Reed Publishing, 1994. 28 pp.

Poèmes. Lonpré-Épinal, France: Éditions du Rewidiage, 1993. 14 pp. Edition of 200.

Poems for You: In & Out of Africa. Yaoundé, Cameroon: No Publisher Stated, 1994. 15 pp.

Teducation: Selected Poems. Minneapolis: Coffee House Press, 1999. 228 pp.

Wow. Mukilteo, Washington: Quartermoon Press, 1999. 56 pp. Edition of 350. (with drawings by Laura Corsiglia).

Select One or More: Poems. Berkeley, CA: Bancroft Library Press, 2000. 11 pp.

In Thursday Sane, ed. Sandra McPherson. Davis, CA: Swan Scythe Press, 2001. 9 pp. (with drawings by Joans).

Our Thang (with Laura Corsiglia). Victoria, BC: Ekstasis Editions, 2001. 96 pp. (with drawings by Corsiglia).

Poet Painter / Former Villager Now / World Traveller, Parts I and II, ed. Wendy Tronrud and Ammiel Alcalay. New York: CUNY Center for the Humanities, 2016. 58 pp. [Part I]; 60 pp. [Part II].

Surreally Ted Joans. Exhibition Catalogue. Paris and New York: Zürcher Gallery, 2023. 134 pp. (with numerous artworks by Joans).
Jazz Is My Religion. Exhibition Catalogue. Paris and New York: Zürcher Gallery, 2024. 136 pp. (with numerous artworks by Joans).

Essays and Other Short Prose

Note: book reviews and individual poems are cited in the text.

"Fragments du lettres." *La Brèche* 5 (October 1963), 66–7. (with collage by Joans).
"AA! AA? Yeah, AA!" *International Times* (December 12–25, 1966), 7.
"Jeg er vred også når jeg smiler" ["I'm Even Angry When I Smile"]. *Ekstra Bladet* (December 27, 1966), 10.
"Letter from Timbuktu." *Negro Digest* (September 1967), 97–8.
"Hommage to Bosch." *International Times* (October 5–20, 1967), 15.
"Black Flower." *L'Archibras* 3 (March 1968), 8–11.
"Ted Joans, poet talking to Dave Kennard." *Other Scenes* (April 1, 1968), 4.
"Jazz at Randall's Island." *The Guardian* (August 31, 1968), 18.
"A Black Writer Comes Home to Black Power." *Other Scenes* (October 1968), n.p.
"Niggers from Outer Space." *Other Scenes* (December 1968), n.p.
"I Am That Way." *Black Culture Weekly* 1.2 (December 21, 1968), n.p.
"Le Griot surréaliste." *Jazz Hot* 252 (July-August 1969), 21–5.
"The Pan-African Pow Wow." *Other Scenes* (November 1, 1969), n.p.
"Excerpts from a Letter." *Arsenal: Surrealist Subversion* 1 (1970), 57.
"First Papers on Ancestral Creations." *Black World* 19 (August 1970), 66–72.
"The Pan African Pow Wow." *Journal of Black Poetry* 1.13 (winter–spring 1970), 4–5.
"Freedom Now." *Jazz Forum* 7 (1970), 76–7.
"Hommage from Africa." *Jazz Magazine* 189 (May 1971), 36.
"Natural Africa." *Black World* (May 1971), 4–7.
"Spiritual Unity Albert Ayler: Mister AA of Grade Double A Sounds." *Coda* (August 1971), 2–4.
"International Jazz Festival Loosdrecht, Holland." *Coda* (November/December 1972), 31–2.
"The Langston Hughes I Knew." *Black World* 21 (September 1972), 14–18.
"A Few Fact Filled Fiction of African Reality," in *We Be Word Sorcerers*, ed. Sonia Sanchez. New York: Bantam, 1973. 125–7.
"Musiques noires en Holland." *Jazz Magazine* (November 1973), 34–5.
"Real Free." Liner Notes in The Pyramids, *King of Kings* (Pyramid Records, 1974).
"An Afro-Arduous Apropos Apologue," in Rudolph Kizerman, *I'm Here*. London: Blackbird Books, 1975. 97.
"Ted Joans: Tri-Continental Poet" [Interview with Henry Louis "Skip" Gates, Jr.]. *Transition* 48 (April/June 1975), 4–12.
"Betty Carter." *Coda* (March 1976), 10–11.
"Archie Shepp." *Jazz Magazine* (March 1976), 6.
"Votez Carter (Betty)." *Jazz Magazine* 249 (November 1976), 8–9.
"Bill Dixon." *Coda* (December 1976), 10–11.

"New York: Paroles et Musique" *Jazz Magazine* (December 1976), 9.
"Le 'Jazz Poetry.'" [Interview with Jean-Jacques Lebel]. *La Quinzaine Littéraire*
    330 (1980), 30–1.
"Bird and the Beats." *Coda* (December 1981), 14–15.
"Sharing the Poem of Life: An Interview with Ted Joans" by Gerald Nicosia. *Beat
    Angels*, ed. Arthur and Kit Knight (California, PA: unspeakable visions of the
    individual, 1982), 128–40.
"The Funeral of Thelonius Monk." *Coda* (April 1982), 33–4.
"Wölfi K.O.'s Dali," in *Free Spirits: Annals of the Insurgent Imagination*, ed. Paul
    Buhle et al. San Francisco: City Lights, 1982. 151–2.
"I, Black Surrealist." *Muzzled Ox* 10 (special issue: Blues) (1989), 46–8.
"The Beat Generation and Afro-American Culture." *Beat Scene Magazine* 13
    (December 1991), 22–3.
"An Abbreviated Autobiography of AfroAmerican Artists Over Yonder," in *Paris
    Connections: African American Artists in Paris*, ed. Asake Bomani and Belvie
    Rooks. San Francisco: Q.E.D. Press, 1992. 38–40.
"Je Me Vois (I See Myself)." *Contemporary Authors Autobiography* 25 (1996),
    219–58.
"Worthy Beat Women: A Recollection," in *Women of the Beat Generation*, ed.
    Brenda Knight. Berkeley, CA: Conari Press, 1996. 331–3.
"Ed Clark and I," in *Edward Clark: For the Sake of the Search*, ed. Barbara Cavaliere
    and George R. N'Namdi. Belleville Lake: Belleville Lake Press, 1997. 33–4.
"Ted Joans on Langston Hughes" [Interview with St. Clair Bourne, October 21,
    1985]. *Langston Hughes Review* 15.2 (winter 1997), 71–7.
"Jadis si je me souviens bien." *Black Renaissance* (June 22, 2002), 91–4.
"Teducation Films," in *Surrealist Subversions: Rants, Writings & Images by the
    Surrealist Movement in the United States*, ed. Ron Sakolsky. Brooklyn, NY:
    Autonomedia, 2002. 571–2 [*Surrealist Subversions* also collects seven other
    short Joans pieces previously published elsewhere].

Principal Unpublished Work

"Aardvarkian Surreal Stroll Through Paris." (1990). 47 typescript pages. TJP.
"A Black Man's Guide to Africa." (1971). Approx. 200 typescript pages. TJP.
"Collaged Autobiography." (2002). 200+ typescript pages. Laurated Archive.
"Deeper Are Allyall's Roots." (ca. 1976). On continuous dot matrix printer paper,
    approximately 106 typescript pages. Laurated Archive.
"Money Soon." (1995). 70 typescript pages. TJP.
"Niggers from Outer Space." (1968). 44 typescript pages. TJP.
"And I Went As Usual to the Desert." (after 1974). 49 handwritten pages. TJP.
"I, Too, at the Beginning." (1986). 221 typescript pages. TJP.
"Razzle Dazzle." (ca. 1983). 333 typescript pages. TJP.
"Well Shut My Mouth Wide Open." (ca. 1970s) 95 typescript pages. TJP.
"Spadework: The Autobiography of a Hipster." (1962). 105 typescript pages.
    Laurated Archive.

Secondary Bibliography

"26 Negroes Slain before Peace Restored in Detroit." *The Chicago Bee* (June 27, 1943): 2.

Ako, Edward O. "The African Inspiration of the Black Arts Movement." *Diogenes* 34, no. 135 (1986): 93–104.

"All Quiet on MacDougal." *Village Voice* (October 14, 1959): 1.

Allmen, Rick. *Stanley: The Don Juan of Second Avenue.* New York: Harper & Row, 1974.

Andersen, Erik. "Danske Trommer": https://dansketrommer.dk/?p=2597/

Anita. "Scribbling Socially." *Louisville Defender* (May 21, 1953): 11.

Ansell, Gwen. "Ted Joans and the Poetry of Jazz." *Weekly Mail* (Johannesburg) (February 11, 1994).

"Artist to Continue Exhibit at Bar." *The Louisville Times* (July 11, 1952): 4.

Austin, David, ed. *Moving Against the System: The 1968 Congress of Black Writers and the Making of Global Consciousness.* London: Pluto Press, 2018.

Baker, Samuel White. *Ismailïa: A Narrative of the Expedition to Central Africa for the Suppression of the Slave Trade,* 2 vols. London: Macmillan, 1874.

Baldwin, James. *Collected Essays.* New York: Library of America, 1998.

Baraka, Amiri. *The Autobiography of LeRoi Jones.* Chicago: Lawrence Hill Books, 1997.

Barbato, John. "The Teducated Mouth: John Barbato interviews Ted Joans": https://www.emptymirrorbooks.com/beat/teducatedmouth

Barbiero, Daniel. "Oedipus and the Other Two Sphinxes." *The Decadent Review* (2023): https://thedecadentreview.com/corpus/oedipus-and-the-other-two-sphinxes/

"Beatnik Poet-Artist 'Exiles.'" *Jet* (January 4, 1962): 40–1.

"Bebop Fashions: Weird Dizzy Gillespie Mannerisms Quickly Picked Up as Accepted Style for Bebop Devotees." *Ebony* (December 1948): 31–3.

"The Beecher Terrace Story," dir. Lavel White (2020): https://www.youtube.com/watch?v=cFVvJIWE4uM/

Before Columbus Foundation. "Our Story": https://www.beforecolumbusfoundation.com/our-story/

Belletto, Steven. "Tuli Kupferberg's *Yeah*: A Satyric Excursion." *Princeton University Library Chronicle* 79, no. 1 (spring–summer 2022): 102–30.

Benayoun, Robert. *Le Rire des Surréalistes.* Paris: La Bougie du sapeur, 1988.

Bibbs, Hart Leroy. *Poly Rhythms to Freedom.* New York: MacNair, 1964.

Bier, Justus. "Junior Gallery to Exhibit Animal Prints." *The Courier-Journal* (June 3, 1951): section 5, page 4.

Bier, Justus. "Surrealist Exhibition in Chicago Proves Exciting." *The Courier-Journal* (December 7, 1947): section 3, page 5.

"Big Step Ahead on a High Road." *Life* (December 8, 1961): 32–9.

Biro, Adam and René Passeron, ed. *Dictionnaire Général du Surréalisme et de ses environs.* Fribourg: Presses Universitaires de France, 1982.

"Bitter Lion." *The Guardian* (September 11, 1969): 11.

"Black Militants Walk Out of Writer's Congress." *The Globe and Mail* (October 14, 1968): 13.

"Black Poetry Growing." *Milwaukee Star* (January 20, 1972): 3.

Blacker, Terence. "An American Surrealist Who Made His Life His Art." *The Independent* (May 30, 2003): 8.

Bone, Martyn. "Transnational and Intertextual Geographies of Race, Sex, and Masculinity: Cecil Brown's *The Life and Loves of Mr. Jiveass Nigger.*" *African American Review* 52, no. 4 (winter 2019): 357–72.

Boulton, Laura C. "Timbuktu and Beyond." *The National Geographic Magazine* 79, no. 5 (May 1941): 631–70.

Bowles, Paul. *In Touch: The Letters of Paul Bowles*, edited by Jeffrey Miller. New York: Farrar, Straus and Giroux, 1994.

Breton, André. *Arcanum 17*, trans. Zack Rogow. Københaven and Los Angeles: Green Integer, 2004.

Breton, André. "A Great Black Poet." In Aimé Césaire, *Notebook of a Return to the Native Land*, trans. Clayton Eshleman and Annette Smith. Middletown, CT: Wesleyan University Press, 2001: ix–xviii.

Breton, André. *Communicating Vessels*, trans. Mary Ann Caws and Geoffrey T. Harris. Lincoln: University of Nebraska Press, 1990.

Breton, André. *Earthlight*, trans. Bill Zavatsky and Zack Rogow. Los Angeles: Sun and Moon Press, 1993.

Breton, André. *Manifestoes of Surrealism*, trans. Richard Seaver and Helen R. Lane. Ann Arbor: University of Michigan Press, 1972.

Breton, André. *Nadja*, trans. Richard Howard. New York: Grove Press, 1960.

Breton, André. *Surrealism and Painting*, trans. Simon Taylor Watson. New York: Harper & Row, 1972.

Breton, André. *What is Surrealism? Selected Writings*, edited by Franklin Rosemont. New York: Pathfinder, 1978.

Brief notice on *Black Pow-Wow*, *Freedomways* (Second Quarter, 1970): 190.

Brown, Cecil. *The Life and Loves of Mr. Jiveass Nigger*. Hopewell: Ecco Press, (1969) 1991.

Brown, Cecil. "The Midnight Sun Never Sets: An Email Conversation about Jazz, Race and National Identity in Denmark, Norway and Sweden." In *Afro-Nordic Landscapes: Equality and Race in Northern Europe*, edited by Michael McEachrane. New York: Routledge, 2014: 57–83.

Brown, L. T. "Jazz Poet Joans Pow-Pows Reader." *The Indianapolis News* (October 4, 1969): 36.

Buel, James W. *Heroes of the Dark Continent*. Guelph: J.W. Lyon, 1890.

Burroughs, William. "Comments on the Night before Thinking." *Evergreen Review* 5, no. 20 (September–October 1961): 31–6.

Burroughs, William. "The Cut-Up Method of Brion Gysin." In *A Casebook on the Beat*, edited by Thomas Parkinson. New York: Thomas Y. Crowell, 1961.

Burroughs, William. "Foreword." In *The Beat Hotel*, by Harold Chapman. Montpellier/Geneva: Gris Banal, 1984.

Burroughs, William. "Tangier." *Esquire* (September 1964): 114–19.

Calder, John. "Ted Joans." *The Guardian* (May 27, 2003): https://www.theguardian.com/news/2003/may/27/guardianobituaries.booksobituaries/

Capeci, Jr., Dominic J. and Martha Wilkerson. *Layered Violence: The Detroit Rioters of 1943*. Jackson: University Press of Mississippi, 1991.

Carmichael, Stokely. "Stokely Carmichael on Black Power." In *The Afro-Americans: Selected Documents*, edited by John H. Bracey et al. Boston: Allyn and Bacon, 1972.

Carmichael, Stokely and Charles V. Hamilton. *Black Power: The Politics of Liberation in America*. New York: Vintage, 1967.

Carrouges, Michel. *André Breton and the Basic Concepts of Surrealism*, trans. Maura Prendergast. Tuscaloosa: University of Alabama Press, 1974.

"Censor Hits at Happenings." *The Sunday Telegraph* (March 13, 1965): 1.

Césaire, Aimé. *The Complete Poetry of Aimé Césaire: Bilingual Edition*, trans. A. James Arnold and Clayton Eshleman. Middletown, CT: Wesleyan University Press, 2017.

Césaire, Aimé. *Discourse on Colonialism*, trans. Joan Pinkham. New York: Monthly Review Press, 2000.

Césaire, Aimé. *Les Armes miraculeuses*. Paris: Gallimard, 1946.

Césaire, Aimé. *Notebook of a Return to the Native Land*, trans. Clayton Eshleman and Annette Smith. Middletown, CT: Wesleyan University Press, 2001.

Chambers, Georgetta. "The Younger Generation." *Louisville Defender* (July 23, 1952): 10.

Chandler, Sigmund. "That Joans Boy—Greenwich Village and Pagans." *Louisville Defender* (August 11, 1955): 13.

Charters, Ann, ed. *The Portable Beat Reader*. New York: Viking, 1992.

Chimurenga, ed. *Festac '77: 2nd World Black and African Festival of Arts and Culture*. Cape Town: Afterall Books, 2019.

Christian, Barbara, "Whatever Happened to Bob Kaufman?" *Black World* 21, no. 11 (1972): 20–9.

"City Acts to Silence Minstrels' Playing in Washington Sq." *New York Times* (March 28, 1961): 37.

"City Presses Campaign to Enforce New Zoning Rule." *New York Times* (March 25, 1964): 43.

Clark, Sam. "Letter to the Editor." *Our World* 2, no. 9 (October 1947).

Conrad, Joseph. *Heart of Darkness*, 4th edition, edited by Paul B. Armstrong. New York: Norton, 2006.

"Contemporary Art Club." *Louisville Defender* (March 17, 1951): 18.

"Cops on the Beatnik." *The Evening Herald* (Pottsville, PA) (October 9, 1959): 1.

Corsiglia, Laura. "Cover to Cover." Radio program with Jack Foley (November 26, 2003).

Corsiglia, Laura. "Surrounding Area." In *Surrealist Subversions: Rants, Writings & Images by the Surrealist Movement in the United States*, edited by Ron Sakolsky. Brooklyn, NY: Autonomedia, 2002: 530–31.

Corso, Gregory. *An Accidental Autobiography: The Selected Letters of Gregory Corso*, edited by Bill Morgan. New York: New Directions, 2003.

Corso, Gregory. *The Happy Birthday of Death*. New York: New Directions, 1960.

Cortez, Jayne. "Mainstream Statement." In *Surrealist Subversions: Rants, Writings & Images by the Surrealist Movement in the United States*, edited by Ron Sakolsky. Brooklyn, NY: Autonomedia, 2002: 278.

Coryell, Schofield. "Between Myth and Reality: Black American Life in Paris." *Passion: The Magazine of Paris* 44 (January 1986): 13–15.

Creeley, Robert. "Letter from Berlin." *The Washington Post* (December 18, 1983): BW15.

Cull, Nicholas J. *The Cold War and the United States Information Agency: American Propaganda and Public Diplomacy, 1945–1989*. New York: Cambridge University Press, 2008.

"The Current Art Calendar." *The Courier-Journal* (September 28, 1952): section 5, page 18.

Dalachinsky, Steve. "'Jazz is My Religion'—All of Ted Joans & No More." *Shuffle Boil* 4 (summer/fall 2003): 60.

D'Alessandro, Stephanie and Matthew Gale, "The World in the Time of the Surrealists." In *Surrealism Beyond Borders*, edited by Stephanie D'Alessandro and Matthew Gale. New York: Metropolitan Museum of Art, 2021: 8–41.

Davis, Arthur P. "Jesse B. Semple: Negro American." *Phylon* 15, no. 1 (1954): 21–8.

Davis, Thulani. "Harlem Sings America: The Legacy of the Harlem Renaissance Endures in Lyrical Novels and Prescient Poetry." *Los Angeles Times* (February 26, 1995): 1.

Depestre, René. "An Interview with Aimé Césaire." In Aimé Césaire, *Discourse on Colonialism*, trans. Joan Pinkham. New York: Monthly Review Press, 2000: 81–94.

Desmangles, Justin. "'Jazz is My Religion': The Be-Bop Optics of Ted Joans." In *Jazz is My Religion*. Exhibition Catalogue. Paris and New York: Zürcher Gallery, 2024: 9–14.

Desmangles, Justin. "Remembering Ted Joans: Black Beat Surrealist." SFMOMA's Open Space (December 5, 2017): https://openspace.sfmoma.org/2017/12/remembering-ted-joans-black-beat-surrealist/

DeVeaux, Scott. *The Birth of Bebop: A Social and Musical History*. Berkeley: University of California Press, 1997.

Diagne, Souleymane Bachir. "Négritude." *The Stanford Encyclopedia of Philosophy*, edited by Edward N. Zalta (summer 2018 edition): https://plato.stanford.edu/archives/sum2018/entries/negritude/

Diawara, Manthia. *We Won't Budge: A Malaria Memoir*. New York: Basic Books, 2003.

Du Bois, W. E. B. *The Souls of Black Folk*. New York: Penguin, (1903) 1996.

Duncan, Val. "The Beats Make the Suburban Scene." *Newsday* (Nassau Edition) (March 27, 1961): 65.

Dylan, Bob. *Chronicles, Volume One*. New York: Simon & Schuster, 2004.

Eburne, Jonathan P. "Decolonial Surrealism." In *Surrealism*, edited by Natalya Lusty. New York: Cambridge University Press, 2021: 342–62.

Ellison, Ralph. *Collected Essays*, edited by John F. Callahan. New York: Modern Library, 2003.

Enohoro, Ife. "The Second World Black and African Festival of Arts and Culture: Lagos, Nigeria." *The Black Scholar* 9, no. 1 (September 1977): 26–33.

"Ex-City Artist, Ted Jones, Clicks in N.Y." *Louisville Defender* (September 9, 1954): 8.

Fabre, Michel. *From Harlem to Paris: Black American Writers in France, 1840–1980*. Urbana: University of Illinois Press, 1991.

"First Negro Gets U.L. Art Degree." *Louisville Defender* (August 18, 1955): 1.

Flemming, Kay. "Louisville's Salvador Dali." *Glare* (May 1952): 22–3.

Foley, Dylan. Interview with Gloria McDarrah (November 8, 2019): https://lastbohemians.blogspot.com/search?q=joans/

Foley, Jack. Review of *Teducation* and *Wow*. *Konch* (2000): https://web.archive.org/web/20130317052944/http://www.ishmaelreedpub.com/articles/foley2.html

"For Hip Hosts." *Time* (February 15, 1960): 69.

Foreman, Joel. "Mau Mau's American Career, 1952–57." In *The Other Fifties: Interrogating Midcentury American Icons*, edited by Joel Foreman. Urbana: University of Illinois Press, 1997: 78–100.

"Former Musician Dunks Horn, Turns to Painting." *Louisville Defender* (July 2, 1952): 15.

Fraser, C. Gerald. "Lewis Michaux, 92, Dies; Ran Bookstore in Harlem." *New York Times* (August 27, 1976): 34.

Freeman, Ira Henry. "Bohemian Flair Fades in the Village: New Projects Will Change the Face—and Character—of the Washington Square Area." *New York Times* (December 8, 1957): W1.

Gale, Steven H. "The Emperor Jones." *African Affairs* 95, no. 381 (October 1996): 606–7.

Garner, Dwight. "Stray Questions for: Ishmael Reed." *ArtsBeat: New York Times Blog* (March 21, 2008): https://archive.nytimes.com/artsbeat.blogs.nytimes.com/2008/03/21/stray-questions-for-ishmael-reed/

Garon, Paul. *Blues and the Poetic Spirit*. San Francisco: City Lights, (1975) 1996.

Gascoyne, David. *A Short Survey of Surrealism*. San Francisco: City Lights, (1935) 1982.

Gates, Jr., Henry Louis. "Going to Meet the Man." In *Beauford Delaney: From New York to Paris*, edited by Patricia Sue Canterbury. Minneapolis: Minneapolis Institute of Arts, 2004: 10–11.

Geis, Terri. "'Snip/Snap/and Cut': Ted Joans and *Dies und Das*." *Dada/Surrealism* 24 (2023): 1–20.

Gibson, Ian. *The Shameful Life of Salvador Dalí*. New York: Norton, 1997.

Ginsberg, Allen. *The Book of Martyrdom and Artifice: First Journals and Poems, 1937–1952*. Cambridge, MA: Da Capo Press, 2006.

Ginsberg, Allen. *Howl and Other Poems*. San Francisco: City Lights, 1956.

Glimcher, Mildred. *Happenings: New York, 1958–1963*. New York: Monacelli Press, 2012.

Gold, Herbert. *Bohemia: Digging the Roots of Cool*. New York: Touchstone, 1994.

Gold, Jeff. *Sittin' In: Jazz Clubs of the 1940s and 1950s*. New York: Harper Design, 2020.

Gonzales, Babs. *I Paid My Dues*. New York: Lancer Books, 1967.

Gonzales, Babs. *Movin' on Down the Line*. Newark, NJ: Expubidence Publishing, 1975.

Green, Michelle. *The Dream at the End of the World: Paul Bowles and the Literary Renegades in Tangier*. New York: HarperCollins, 1991.

"Greenwich Village in Derbytown Apt." *Louisville Defender* (April 23, 1952): 9.

"Greenwich Village Open House." *Our World* (January 1955): 72.

Grimson, Karen. "Wifredo Lam." In *Among Others: Blackness at MoMA*, edited by Darby English and Charlotte Barat. New York: Museum of Modern Art, 2019: 264.

Gustav-Wrathall, John Donald. *Take the Young Stranger by the Hand: Same-Sex Relations and the YMCA*. Chicago: University of Chicago Press, 1998.

Hale, Thomas A. *Griots and Griottes: Masters of Words and Music*. Bloomington: Indiana University Press, 1998.

Halverson, Krista, ed. *Shakespeare and Company, Paris: A History of the Rag & Bone Shop of the Heart*. Paris: Shakespeare and Co., 2016.

Harris, Juliette. "The Struggles away or towards This Peace: Amiri Baraka's Life in Visual Art": http://iraaa.museum.hamptonu.edu/page/The-Struggles-Away-or-Towards-This-Peace/

Hartman, Saidiya. "Venus in Two Acts." *small axe* 26 (June 2008): 1–14.

Haynes, Jim. *Thanks for Coming! An Autobiography*. London: Faber and Faber, 1984.

Hemmer, Kurt. "Joans, Ted." In *Beat Culture: Icons, Lifestyles, and Impact*, edited by William T. Lawlor. Santa Barbara, CA: ABC-Clio, 2005: 159–60.

Hemmer, Kurt and Tom Knoff, dir. *Wow! Ted Joans Lives!* (2010).

Herron, Paul, ed. *Anaïs Nin: A Book of Mirrors*. Huntington Woods, MI: Sky Blue Press, 1996.

Hodgkiss, Peter. "Ted Joans at the ICA." *Poetry Information* 11 (Autumn 1974): 21.

Hoey, Timothy. "'Jazz Poet' Ted Joans Takes His Flights on Surrealist Airlines." *Daily American* (Rome) (July 6, 1979).

Hofman, Paul. "Folk Singers Riot in Washington Sq." *New York Times* (April 10, 1961): 1.

Hollo, Anselm, ed. *Negro Verse*. London: Vista Books, 1964.

Holman, Bob. "On the Road with Bob Holman": https://www.youtube.com/watch?v=9nqD8XWybpQ/

Hopkins, John. *Tangier Diaries*. London: Tauris Parke, 2015.

Howell, Kevin. "Consummate Bookseller Ted Wilentz Dies at 86." *Publisher's Weekly* (May 17, 2001).

Howlett, Jacques. "*Présence Africaine* 1947–1958." *The Journal of Negro History* 43, no. 2 (April 1958): 140–50.

Hughes, Langston. *The Best of Simple*. New York: Hill and Wang, 1961.

Hughes, Langston. *The Collected Works of Langston Hughes,* vol. 2: *The Poems, 1941–1950*, edited by Arnold Rampersad. Columbia: University of Missouri Press, 2001.

Hughes, Langston. *The Weary Blues*. Garden City, NY: Dover, (1926) 2022.

"Il est poete, américain il revient du FESTAC et parle l'afroanglais." *Togo Presse* (1977): 5.

Isaacson, Maureen. "Swing is What Counts for Joans." *Saturday Star* (Johannesburg) (February 19, 1994).

Jahn, Janheinz. *Muntu: African Culture and the Western World*, trans. Marjorie Grene. New York: Grove Press, (1961) 1989.

"Jazz Poet Ted Joans is Fellow in Black Music at Bennington." *Bennington Banner* (November 9, 1973): 7.

"Jazz-poetry Concert." *North East Bay Independent and Gazette* (May 30, 1980): 5.

Johnson, Kevin. "Renaissance Jazzman Ray Johnson is on a Roll." *Louisville Music News* (February 2003): http://www.louisvillemusicnews.net/webmanager/index.php?WEB_CAT_ID=49&storyid=1580/

Jones, LeRoi. *Blues People: Negro Music in White America*. New York: Morrow Quill, 1963.

Jones, LeRoi. *Home: Social Essays*. New York: Ecco Press, 1998.

Kalter, Marion. *All Around Ted Joans*. Karlsruhe: Center for Art and Media Karlsruhe, 2017.

Kaprow, Allan. *Assemblage, Environments & Happenings*. New York: Harry N. Abrams, 1966.

Kaprow, Allan. "A Statement." In *Happenings: An Illustrated Anthology*, edited by Michael Kirby. New York: E.P. Dutton, 1965: 44–52.

Kay, Iris. "Festac 77." *African Arts* 11, no. 1 (October 1977): 50–1.

Kelley, Robin D. G. *Freedom Dreams: The Black Radical Imagination*. New York: Beacon, 2002.

Kelley, Robin D. G. "A Poetics of Anticolonialism." In Aimé Césaire, *Discourse on Colonialism*, trans. Joan Pinkham. New York: Monthly Review Press, 2000: 7–28.

Kelley, Robin D. G. "Ted Lives!" *Shuffle Boil* 4 (summer/fall 2003): 3–5.

Kerouac, Jack. "From *Mexico City Blues*." *Measure* 2 (winter 1958): 18.

Kerouac, Jack. *On the Road*. New York: Penguin, (1957) 1991.

Kerouac, Jack. *Portable Jack Kerouac*, edited by Ann Charters. New York: Viking, 1995.

Kerouac, Jack. "The Roaming Beatniks." *Holiday* 26, no. 4 (October 1959): 82, 84, 86.

Kerouac, Jack. *The Subterraneans*. New York: Grove, 1958.

Killens, John Oliver. *Black Man's Burden*. New York: Trident, 1965.

Killens, John Oliver. "The Black Writer Vis-à-vis His Country." In *The Black Aesthetic*, edited by Addison Gayle. Garden City, NY: Doubleday, 1971: 379–96.

Kimeneye, Barbara. "Soul Brother Ted—A Misguided Guide to Africa?" *Daily Nation* (Kenya) (February 23, 1971): 15.

Kirby, Michael. *Happenings: An Illustrated Anthology*. New York: E.P. Dutton, 1965.

Klengel, Susanne. *"Dies und Das": Black Surrealism from Berlin in 1984*. Hamburg: Edition Michael Kellner, 2023.

Kohli, Amor. "Sounding across the City: Ted Joans's *Bird Lives!* As Jazz Performance." In *Beat Drama: Playwrights and Performances of the "Howl" Generation*, edited by Deborah R. Geis. London: Bloomsbury Methuen Drama, 2016: 97–107.

Kulas, Maurice. "Some Notes on the Author." In Babs Gonzales, *Movin' on Down the Line*. Newark, NJ: Expubidence Publishing, 1975.

Kuralt, Charles. "William Morris at the Gaslight Café." CBS News (June 9, 1959): http://gvh.aphdigital.org/items/show/227/

Land, Danny and Mike Charnee. "Loud Noises for a Manufacturer of Poetry." *The Village Voice* (September 15, 1960): 4.

Lebel, Jean-Jacques. "Theory and Practice." In *New Writers IV: Plays and Happenings*, edited by Jean-Jacques Lebel et al. London: Calder and Boyars, 1967.

Lebel, Jean-Jacques and Androula Michaël. *Happenings, ou l'insoumission radicale*. Paris: Hazan, 2009.

Lee, A. Robert. *Designs of Blackness: Mappings in the Literature and Culture of Afro-America*. London: Pluto Press, 1998.

Lee, A. Robert. "Ted Joans." In *Encyclopedia of Beat Literature*, edited by Kurt Hemmer. New York: Facts on File, 2007: 157–58.

Leeming, David, *James Baldwin: A Biography*. New York: Arcade, (1994) 2015.

Leiris, Michel. *Phantom Africa*, trans. Brent Hayes Edwards. Calcutta: Seagull Books, 2019.

Lepetit, Patrick. *The Esoteric Secrets of Surrealism: Origins, Magic, and Secret Societies*. Rochester, VT: Inner Traditions, 2014.

Lindberg, Kathryne V. "Mister Joans, to You: Readerly Surreality and Writerly Affiliation in Ted Joans, Tri-Continental Ex-Beatnik." *Discourse* 20, no. 1/2 (winter/spring 1998): 198–227.

Liner Notes, *Café Bizarre Presents Assorted Madness* (LP: Musitron-102, 1959).

Littlejohn, David. *Black on White: A Critical Survey of Writing by American Negroes*. New York: Grossman, 1966.

Locke, Joan. Letter to the Editor. *Ebony* (February 1949): 9.

Lucas, J. Olumide. *The Religion of the Yorubas*. Lagos: C.M.S. Bookshop, 1948.

Lyons, Leonard. "The Lyons Den: Village News Preferred." *The News and Observer* (Raleigh, NC) (June 3, 1961): 8.

"Mad Genius." *Hue* 2, no. 3 (January 1955): 36–9.

Mahon, Alyce. *Surrealism and the Politics of Eros, 1938–1968*. London: Thames & Hudson, 2005.

Mailer, Norman. *Advertisements for Myself*. Cambridge, MA: Harvard University Press, (1959) 2005.

Malcolm, Janet. *The Silent Woman: Sylvia Plath and Ted Hughes*. New York: Vintage, 1994.

Mansour, Joyce. *Emerald Wounds: Selected Poems*, trans. Emilie Moorhouse. San Francisco: City Lights, 2023.

Mansour, Joyce. *Essential Poems and Writings of Joyce Mansour*, edited and trans. by Serge Gavronsky. Boston: Black Widow Press, 2008.

Mansour, Joyce. *In the Glittering Maw*. New York: World Poetry Books, 2024.

Mansour, Joyce. *Prose & Poésie: Œuvre Complète*, edited by Hubert Nyssen. Arles: Actes Sud, 1991.

Mansour, Marie-Francine. *Une vie Surréaliste: Joyce Mansour complice d'André Breton*. Chaintreaux: Éditions France-Empire Monde, 2014.

Matthews, J. H. *Languages of Surrealism*. Columbia: University of Missouri Press, 1986.

"'Mau Mau' Queen." *Jet* (March 8, 1956): 62.

Maxwell, William J. *F.B. Eyes: How J. Edgar Hoover's Ghostreaders Framed African American Literature*. Princeton, NJ: Princeton University Press, 2015.

McDarrah, Fred. *The Artist's World in Pictures*. New York: E.P. Dutton, 1961.

McDarrah, Fred and Gloria McDarrah. *Beat Generation: Glory Days in Greenwich Village*. New York: Schirmer Books, 1996.

McEachrane, Michael. "The Midnight Sun Never Sets: An Email Conversation about Jazz, Race and National Identity in Denmark, Norway and Sweden." In *Afro-Nordic Landscapes: Equality and Race in Northern Europe*, edited by Michael McEachrane. New York: Routledge, 2014: 57–83.

Mikelli, Eftychia, "The Greek Beat and Underground Scene of the 1960s and 1970s." *CLCWeb: Comparative Literature and Culture* 18, no. 5 (2016): https://docs.lib.purdue.edu/cgi/viewcontent.cgi?article=2964&context=clcweb/

Mikofsky, Anton. "Joys and Moans of Ted Joans." *CORE Magazine* (fall/winter 1973): 70–1.

Miller, Christopher L. "Alioune Diop and the Unfinished Temple of Knowledge." In *Surreptitious Speech: Présence Africaine and the Politics of Otherness, 1947–1987*, edited by V. Y. Mudimbe. Chicago: University of Chicago Press, 1992: 427–34.

Miller, James A. "Ted Joans." In *The Beats: Literary Bohemians in Postwar America* (*Dictionary of Literary Biography* 16), edited by Ann Charters. Detroit, MI: Gale, 1983: 268–70.

Millstein, Gilbert. "Rent a Beatnik and Swing." *New York Times* (April 17, 1960): SM26, SM28.

Miner, Horace. *The Primitive City of Timbuctoo*. Princeton, NJ: Princeton University Press, 1953.

Missir, Marie-Laure. *Joyce Mansour: Une étrange demoiselle*. Paris: Éditions Jean-Michel Place, 2005.

Moljord, Grete. *Paris Tanger*. Larvik: Forlagshuset i Vestfold, 2014.

Moorhouse, Emilie. "Translating Desire: The Erotic-Macabre Poetry of Joyce Mansour." In Joyce Mansour, *Emerald Wounds: Selected Poems*. San Francisco: City Lights, 2023: 1–12.

Morgan, Bill. *The Beat Generation in New York: A Walking Tour of Jack Kerouac's City*. San Francisco: City Lights, 1997.

Morgan, Bill. *The Beat Hotel: Ginsberg, Burroughs, and Corso in Paris, 1958–1963*. New York: Grove, 2000.

Morgan, Ted. *Literary Outlaw: The Life and Times of William S. Burroughs*. New York: Norton, 2012.

Morris, Mervyn. "Review of *Black Pow-Wow*." *Caribbean Quarterly* 15, no. 4 (December 1969): 58–61.

Moskowitz, Sam. "The First College-Level Course in Science Fiction." *Science Fiction Studies* 23, no. 3 (November 1996): 411–22.

"Motorman Beaten." *Michigan Chronicle* (June 26, 1943): 5.

Movin, Lars. *Beat: på sporet af den amerikanske beatgeneration*. Copenhagen: Informations Forlag, 2008.

Mudimbe, V. Y., ed. *The Surreptitious Speech*: Présence Africaine and the Politics of Otherness, 1947–1987. Chicago: University of Chicago Press, 1992.

Neal, Larry. "The Black Arts Movement." In *The Black Aesthetic*, edited by Addison Gayle. Garden City, NY: Doubleday, 1971: 272–90.

"New Gallery Opens with 'Save Works of Art' Call." *Daily Nation* (Kenya) (February 12, 1971): 12.

Nicholl, Charles. *Somebody Else: Arthur Rimbaud in Africa, 1880–91*. London: Jonathan Cape, 1997.

Nicosia, Gerald. "A Lifelong Commitment to Change: The Literary Non-Career of Ted Joans." In Ted Joans, *Teducation*. Minneapolis: Coffee House Press: i–vii.

Nielsen, Aldon Lynn. "Ted Talk." *Journal of Beat Studies* 8 (2020): 41–7.

Norse, Harold. *Memoirs of a Bastard Angel*. New York: William Morrow, 1989.

Olson, John. Review of *Our Thang*. *Rain Taxi* (fall 2022): https://raintaxi.com/our-thang/

Otomo, Yuko. "Let's Get TEDucated! Tribute to Ted Joans." *Artedolia* (June 2015): https://www.arteidolia.com/tribute-to-ted-joans-yuko-otomo/

"A Pad Fad: Beatniks for Rent." *Des Moines Tribune* (November 16, 1960): 52.

"Parties and Picnics." *Louisville Defender* (June 25, 1953): 11.

Patterson, Lindsay. "Introduction." In *A Rock against the Wind: Black Love Poems*, edited by Lindsay Patterson. New York: Dodd, Mead & Company, 1973.

Pawlik, Joanna. *Remade in America: Surrealist Art, Activism, and Politics, 1940–1978*. Oakland: University of California Press, 2021.

Phillips, Lisa. *Beat Culture and the New America: 1950–1965*. New York: Whitney Museum, 1995.

Pierrot, Grégory. *Decolonize Hipsters*. New York: OR Books, 2021.

Pierrot, Grégory. "Ted Joans, the Other Jones: Jazz Poet, Black Power Missionary, and Surrealist Interpreter." In *Radical Dreams, Surrealism, Counterculture, Resistance*, edited by Elliott King and Abigail Susik. University Park: Penn State University Press, 2022: 43–60.

Poiger, Uta. *Jazz, Rock, and Rebels: Cold War Politics and American Culture in a Divided Germany*. Berkeley: University of California Press, 2000.

Polizzotti, Mark. *Revolution of the Mind: The Life of André Breton*. New York: Farrar, Straus and Giroux, 1995.

Popescu, Monica. *At Penpoint: African Literatures, Postcolonial Studies, and the Cold War*. Durham, NC: Duke University Press, 2020.

Porter, Ruth. "Paris Meeting Hears Malcolm X." *The Militant* (December 7, 1964): 1, 4.

Priestley, Brian. *Chasin' the Bird: The Life and Legacy of Charlie Parker*. New York: Oxford University Press, 2006.

"Race War in Detroit." *Life* 15, no. 1 (July 5, 1943): 93–102.

"Races: Curtains for LeRoi." *Time* (January 12, 1968): 14.

Rampersad, Arnold. *The Life of Langston Hughes*, vol. 2: *1941–1967*. New York: Oxford University Press, 2002.

Randall, Margaret. *I Never Left Home: Poet, Feminist, Revolutionary*. Durham, NC: Duke University Press, 2020.

Raspberry, William. "Black Poet on a Blacklist." *Washington Post* (December 10, 1984): https://www.washingtonpost.com/archive/politics/1984/12/10/black-poet-on-a-blacklist/f0ffba5b-ea44-4916-955f-bec2a8dfdcbb/

Reed, Ishmael. "Ted Joans Said 'Jazz is My Religion,'" *Shuffle Boil* 4 (summer/fall 2003): 2.

Reisner, Robert, ed. *Bird: The Legend of Charlie Parker*. New York: Bonanza Books, 1962.

Renaud, Paul. *Surréalisme: de londres a prague et ailleurs*. Paris: Paul Renaud, 1985.

The Return of the Cadavre Exquis. New York: Drawing Center, 1993.

Review of Ted Joans, *Black Pow-Wow*. *Kirkus Reviews* (September 1, 1969).

Rodney, Walter. "African History in the Service of Black Liberation." In *Moving Against the System: The 1968 Congress of Black Writers and the Making of Global Consciousness*, edited by David Austin. London: Pluto Press, 2018.

Rosemont, Franklin. "A Revolutionary Poetic Tradition." *Living Blues* (January–February 1976): 20–3.

Rosemont, Franklin. "Surrealism, Poetry, and Politics." *Race Traitor: Surrealism in the USA* 13–14 (summer 2001): 55–63.

Rosemont, Penelope. "Surrealism, Encounters, Ted Joans." In Penelope Rosemont, *Surrealist Experiences: 1001 Dawns, 221 Midnights*. Chicago: Black Swan Press, 2000: 82–95.

Rosemont, Penelope. "Surrealism in Chicago." In *The Routledge Companion to Surrealism*, edited by Kirsten Strom. New York: Routledge, 2023.

Rosenblum, Mort. "Black Americans Foreigners in Africa." *St. Louis Post-Dispatch* (September 9, 1970): 74.

Russell, Ross. *Bird Lives! The High Life and Hard Times of Charlie (Yardbird) Parker*. New York: Da Capo, (1973) 1996.

Saijo, Albert. "A Recollection." In Jack Kerouac, Albert Saijo, and Lew Welch, *Trip Trap*. Bolinas, CA: Grey Fox Press, 1973: 1–13.

Sakolsky, Ron. "Surrealist Subversion in Chicago." *Race Traitor: Surrealism in the USA* 13–14 (summer 2001): 3–54.

Sakolsky, Ron, ed. *Surrealist Subversions: Rants, Writings & Images by the Surrealist Movement in the United States*. Brooklyn, NY: Autonomedia, 2002.

Schillinger, Mort. "Dizzy Gillespie's Style, its Meaning Analyzed." *Downbeat* XI (February 11, 1946): 14.

Senghor, Léopold Sédar. "Preface Letter." In *Surreptitious Speech: Présence Africaine and the Politics of Otherness, 1947–1987*, edited by V. Y. Mudimbe. Chicago: University of Chicago Press, 1992: xi–xii.

Sidran, Ben. *Black Talk*. New York: Da Capo, 1981.

Stanley, Henry Morton. *In Darkest Africa*, vol. 2. Frankfurt: Outlook Verlag, (1890) 2020.

"Strange Taste." *Newsweek* (November 26, 1962): 94.

Strausbaugh, John. *The Village: 400 Years of Beats and Bohemians, Radicals and Rogues*. New York: HarperCollins, 2013.

Strom, Kirsten. *Making History: Surrealism and the Invention of a Political Culture*. Lanham, MD: University Press of America, 2002.

Sukenick, Ronald. *Down and In: Life in the Underground*. Middletown, CT: Invisible Starfall Books, (1987) 2022.

The Surrealist Movement, "Surrealism & Blues." *Living Blues* 25 (January–February 1976): 19.

"Ted Joans." *Arts* 33, no. 4 (January 1959): 63.

"Ted Joans, 74, Jazzy Beat Poet Known for 'Bird Lives' Graffiti." *New York Times* (May 18, 2003): N43.

Thompson, Robert Farris. *Flash of the Spirit: African and Afro-American Art and Philosophy*. New York: Vintage, 1984.

"Tobe Howard to Celebrate His Tenth Year in Radio August 30." *Louisville Defender* (August 22, 1957): 13

Tobin, Brazzle. "Scouting Derbytown." *Louisville Defender*. Various columns from 1951 to 1960.

"Tomato." "Black Pow-Wow." *Berkeley Tribe* (September 26–October 3, 1969): 17.

Tramuta, Lindsey. "Leaving America Questionnaire #1: Jack Lamar." *The New Paris Dispatch* (November 16, 2024): https://bonjour.lindseytramuta.com/p/leaving-america-questionnaire-1/

Vancrevel, Laurens. "Laurens Vancrevel and Frida de Jong's Collection of Surrealist Art." In *Creative Chance: Surrealist Art and Literature from the Laurens Vancrevel and Frida de Jong Collection*, edited by Saskia van Kampen-Prein and Laurens Vancrevel. Rotterdam: Museum Boijmans Van Beuningen, 2021.

Van Deburg, William L. *New Day in Babylon: The Black Power Movement in American Culture, 1965–1975*. Chicago: University of Chicago Press, 1992.

van Gasteren, Louis, dir. *Jazz and Poetry* (1964).

Venant, Elizabeth, "The Third Wave: Paris' Expatriate Scene." *Los Angeles Times* (September 21, 1986): https://www.latimes.com/archives/la-xpm-1986-09-21-ca-8684-story.html/

"Village Frenzy." *Our World* 10, no. 9 (September 1955): 73.

Von Eschen, Penny. *Satchmo Blows Up the World: Jazz Ambassadors Play the Cold War*. Cambridge, MA: Harvard University Press, 2004.

Waldman, Diane. *Notable Notes: Drawings by Writers and Composers*. New York: Joseph Helman Gallery, 1997.

Weegee. *The Village*. New York: Da Capo, 1989.

Wilensky, Stewart, dir. *Village Sunday* (1960): https://archive.org/details/Greenwic1960/

Weiss, Jason. "The American Center Breathes New Life." *Passion: The Magazine of Paris* (December 10–23, 1981).

Weston, Randy. *The Autobiography of Randy Weston*, arranged by Willard Jenkins. Durham, NC: Duke University Press, 2010.

Wilcock, John. "How to Get by on $40 per Week." In *The Village Voice Reader*, edited by Daniel Wolf and Edwin Fancher. New York: Grove, 1963: 110–14.

Wilcock, John. "The Revolving Reader." *The Village Voice* (September 7, 1961): https://www.villagevoice.com/girl-watching-at-the-paperback-bookstore/

Wilentz, Elias, ed. *The Beat Scene*. New York: Corinth, 1960.

Wilentz, Sean. *Bob Dylan in America*. New York: Anchor Books, 2011.

Wilentz, Ted and Bill Zavatsky. "Behind the Writer, Ahead of the Reader: A Short History of Corinth Books." *TriQuarterly* 43 (1978): 595–613.

Williams, Gerald. "Ted's Dead: Hushing the Fuzz." *Massachusetts Review* (2005): 244–8.

Wilson, Judith. "Garden of Music: The Art and Life of Bob Thompson." In *Bob Thompson*, edited by Thelma Golden. New York: Whitney Museum of American Art, 1998: 27–80.

Woodford, John. "A Black Man Who Went Home to Timbuktu—and Stayed." *Muhammad Speaks* (August 23, 1968): 21, 32.

X, Malcolm. *The Autobiography of Malcolm X*, with the assistance of Alex Haley. New York: Ballantine Books, 1965.

Zell, Hans M. "Frankfurt Book Fair 1980." *The African Book Publishing Record* 7, no. 4 (1981): 5.

Žižek, Slavoj. "Hegel on Donald Trump's 'Objective Humor." *The Philosophical Salon* (January 15, 2018): https://thephilosophicalsalon.com/hegel-on-donal-trumps-objective-humor/

INDEX